A
Concise Dictionary
of Law

A
Concise
Dictionary
of Law

OXFORD UNIVERSITY PRESS
1983

Oxford University Press, Walton Street, Oxford OX2 6DP

London Glasgow New York Toronto
Delhi Bombay Calcutta Madras Karachi
Kuala Lumpur Singapore Hong Kong Tokyo
Nairobi Dar es Salaam Cape Town
Melbourne Auckland

and associated companies in
Beirut Berlin Ibadan Mexico City Nicosia

Oxford is a trade mark of Oxford University Press

Published in the United States
by Oxford University Press, New York

British Library Cataloguing in Publication Data

A Concise dictionary of law
1. Law—England—Dictionaries
344.208'6   K313
ISBN 0-19-825399-0

Library of Congress Cataloging in Publication Data

A Concise dictionary of law
1. Law—Great Britain—Dictionaries. 2. Law—
Great Britain—Terms and phrases. I. Oxford University Press
KD313.C66 1983   349.41'03   83-17323
ISBN 0-19-825399-0   344.1003

Printed in Great Britain
at the University Press, Oxford

Editor

Elizabeth A. Martin MA (Oxon)

Contributors

Martin R. Banham-Hall LLB *Solicitor*

Bernard Berkovits LLB *Lecturer in Law, University of Buckingham*

P. J. Clarke BCL, MA *Barrister; Fellow and Tutor in Law, Jesus College, Oxford*

Letitia Crabb LLB (Wales), LLM (London) *Solicitor; Lecturer in Law, University College of Wales, Aberystwyth*

J. W. Davies LLB, MA, BCL *Fellow of Brasenose College, Oxford*

B. Russell Davis MA, LLB *Barrister*

J. D. Feltham BA (Melb.), MA (Oxon) *Fellow of Magdalen College, Oxford*

Judith Lewis LLB *Solicitor*

Keith Uff MA, BCL (Oxon) *Lecturer in Law, University of Birmingham*

Preface

This dictionary, which is an entirely new compilation, has been written by a distinguished team of academic and practising lawyers. It is intended primarily for those without a qualification in law, who nevertheless require some legal knowledge in the course of their work; chartered surveyors and accountants, civil servants and local-government officers, social workers and probation officers, as well as businessmen and legal secretaries are typical examples of those whose work often calls for a knowledge of the precise meaning (and spelling) of a legal term.

Each article, therefore, begins with a clear definition of the entry word (or words) and, in most cases, is followed by a more detailed explanation or description of the concepts involved.

Written in concise English, uncluttered with technical jargon, the book will also be of considerable value to members of the public who come into contact with the law and lawyers—house buyers, motorists, and hire purchasers are among those who cannot escape the effects of legislation or the unique prose style in which it is usually expressed.

This dictionary reflects many recent changes in the law, notably the impact of the law of the EEC and changes in UK legislation up to and including the effects of the Criminal Justice Act 1982. However, since many provisions of this Act (and of certain other new Acts) were not in force at the time of publication, the entries to which they apply can only indicate the direction of the proposed changes.

To simplify the use of this dictionary no abbreviations are used in the text. An asterisk (*) placed before a word in a definition indicates that additional relevant information will be found under this article. Some entries simply refer the reader to another entry, indicating either that they are synonyms or that they are most conveniently explained, together with related terms, in one of the dictionary's longer articles.

Finally, I would like to thank all the contributors to this dictionary for their scholarship, industry, and patience, which has greatly simplified the task of editing their work. I am particularly grateful to Mr. Bernard Berkovits for his assistance in compiling the entry list.

E.A.M.
1983

A

abandonment *n.* **1.** The act of giving up a legal right, particularly a right of ownership of property. Property that has been abandoned is *res nullius* (a thing belonging to no one), and a person taking possession of it therefore acquires a lawful title. In marine insurance, abandonment is the surrender of all rights to a ship or cargo in a case of *constructive total loss. The insured person must do this by giving the insurer a *notice of abandonment*, by which he relinquishes all his rights to the ship or cargo to the insurer and can treat the loss as if it were an actual total loss. **2.** In civil litigation, the relinquishing of the whole or part of the claim made in an action or of an appeal. In the High Court a claim is abandoned by serving a *notice of discontinuance. In the county courts, a plaintiff may abandon part of his claim at the start of the proceedings in order to bring the case within the limits of the court's jurisdiction. If he does so, however, any judgment obtained is a full discharge of all demands in respect of his cause of action. **3.** The offence of a parent or guardian leaving a child under the age of 16 to its fate. A child is not regarded as abandoned if the parent knows and approves steps someone else is taking to look after it. The court may allow a child to be adopted without the consent of its parents if they are guilty of abandonment.

abatement *n.* **1.** (of debts) The proportionate reduction in the payment of debts that takes place if a person's assets are insufficient to settle with his creditors in full. **2.** (of legacies) The reduction or cancellation of legacies when the estate is insufficient to cover both the deceased's debts and all the legacies provided for in the will or on intestacy. The Administration of Estates Act 1925 provides that general legacies, unless given to satisfy a debt or for other con-

sideration, abate in proportion to the amounts of those legacies; specific and demonstrative legacies abate if the estate is insufficient to pay all debts, and a demonstrative legacy also abates if the specified fund is insufficient to cover it. For example, A's estate may comprise a painting, £300 in his savings account, and £700 in other money; there are debts of £100 but his will leaves the painting to B, £500 from the savings account to C, £800 to D, and £200 to E. B will receive the painting, C's demonstrative legacy abates to £300, and after the debts are paid from the remaining £700, D's and E's general legacies abate proportionately, to £480 and £120 respectively. **3.** (in land law) Any reduction or cancellation of money payable. For example a lease may provide for an abatement of rent in certain circumstances, e.g. if the building is destroyed by fire, and a purchaser of land may claim an abatement of the price if the seller can prove his ownership of only part of the land he contracted to sell. **4.** (of nuisances) The termination, removal, or destruction of a nuisance. A person injured by a nuisance has a right to abate it. In doing so, he must not do more damage than is necessary and, if removal of the nuisance requires entry on to the property from which it emanates, he may have to give notice to the wrongdoer. **5.** (of proceedings) The termination of civil proceedings by operation of law, caused by a change of interest or status (e.g. bankruptcy or death) of one of the parties after the start but before the completion of the proceedings. An abatement did not prevent either of the parties from bringing fresh proceedings in respect of the same cause of action. Pleas in abatement have been abolished; in modern practice any change of interest or status of the parties does not affect the validity of the proceedings, provided that the cause of action survives.

abduction *n.* The offence of taking an unmarried girl under the age of 16 from the possession of her parents or guardian against her will. It is no defence that the girl looked and acted as if she was over 16. It is also an offence to abduct an unmarried girl under the age of 18 or a mentally defective woman (married or unmarried) for the purpose of unlawful sexual intercourse. In this case a defendant can plead that he had reasonable grounds for believing that the girl was over 18, or that he did not know the woman was mentally defective, respectively. It is also an offence to abduct any woman with the intention that she should marry or have unlawful sexual intercourse with someone, if it is done by force or for the sake of her property. *See also* child stealing; kidnapping.

abet *vb. See* aid and abet.

abortion *n.* The termination of a pregnancy at a stage when the fetus is incapable of independent survival (i.e. any time between conception and the 28th week of pregnancy). It is an offence to induce or attempt to induce an abortion unless the terms of the Abortion Act 1967 are complied with. Under this Act the pregnancy can only be terminated by a registered medical practitioner, and two registered medical practitioners must agree that it is necessary. Grounds for agreeing to an abortion are either (1) that continuation of the pregnancy would involve a risk to the life or physical or mental health of the pregnant woman (or of other children of hers) that is greater than the risk of terminating the pregnancy, or (2) that there is a substantial risk that the child will be born with a serious physical or mental handicap. Doctors are not obliged to perform abortions, however, if they can prove that they have a conscientious objection to so doing. A husband cannot prevent his wife having a legal abortion if she so wishes. *Compare* child destruction.

absconding *n.* The failure of someone charged with a criminal offence, who has been released on bail, to *surrender to custody. Absconding is an offence punishable summarily by up to three months' imprisonment and a fine of up to £400 or upon indictment by up to 12 months' imprisonment and an unlimited fine. It may result in the issue of a warrant for arrest.

absence *n.* (in court procedure) The nonappearance of a party to litigation or a person summoned or subpoenaed to attend as a witness. *See also* beyond the seas.

absolute assignment *See* assignment.

absolute discharge *See* discharge.

absolute liability *See* strict liability.

absolute privilege The defence that a statement cannot be made the subject of an action for *defamation because it was made in Parliament, in papers ordered to be published by either House of Parliament, in judicial proceedings or a fair and accurate newspaper or broadcast report of judicial proceedings, or in an official communication between certain officers of state. *Compare* qualified privilege.

absolute title Ownership of a *legal estate in registered land with a guarantee by the state that no one has a better right to that estate. The title may, however, be subject to minor or overriding interests or to other encumbrances noted in the register. Absolute title to leasehold property guarantees that the lease was validly granted but not that the landlord's title is free from defect. *Compare* good leasehold title; possessory title; qualified title. *See also* land registration.

abstraction of water The taking of water from a river or other source of supply. It normally requires a water authority licence but there are exceptions; for example when less than 1000 gallons are taken, when the water is for domestic or agricultural use (excluding spray irrigation), or when it is removed in the course of fire-fighting or land drainage.

abstract of title Written details of the *title deeds and documents that prove an owner's right to dispose of his land. An owner usually supplies an abstract of title to an intending purchaser or mortgagee, who compares it with the original title deeds when these are produced or handed over on completion of the transaction. An abstract of title to registered land consists of a copy of the entries in the register and details of any other documents necessary to prove the owner's title, such as a marriage certificate proving a woman's change of surname. For unregistered land, the abstract of title must usually trace the history of the land's ownership from a document at least 15 years old (the *root of title) and give details of any document creating encumbrances to which the land is subject. An abstract of title may comprise extracts, often in abbreviated note form, or an *epitome* (i.e. duplicate copies) of the relevant documents.

abuse of process A tort involving the abuse of a legal process. It is a tort to prosecute someone (*see* malicious prosecution) or to institute some legal process less than prosecution, such as obtaining a warrant for the plaintiff's arrest, if this is done maliciously and without reasonable and probable cause. Other actions that are obviously frivolous, vexatious, or in bad faith can be stayed or dismissed by the court as an abuse of process.

ACAS Advisory Conciliation and Arbitration Service: a statutory body established under the Employment Protection Act 1975 to promote the improvement of industrial relations and the development of *collective bargain-

ing. In its conciliation function it may intervene, with or without the parties' consent, in a *trade dispute to offer facilities and assistance in negotiating a settlement. It employs conciliation officers who may assist parties to an application to an industrial tribunal to reach a settlement. Generally, an employee's right to complain to an industrial tribunal of unfair dismissal cannot be excluded except by an agreement recorded by ACAS after the intervention of a conciliation officer.

ACAS does not itself arbitrate in trade disputes, but with the consent of both parties it may refer a dispute to the *Central Arbitration Committee or to an independent arbitrator. ACAS may give free advice to employers, employees, and their respective representatives on matters of employment or industrial relations. It issues *codes of practice giving guidance on such matters as disciplinary procedures and *disclosure of information to trade unions. It may also conduct inquiries into industrial relations problems, either generally or in relation to particular businesses, and publish the results after considering the views of parties directly affected.

acceleration *n.* The coming into possession of a *future interest in any property at an earlier stage than that directed by the transaction or settlement that created the interest. For example, a landlord's interest in *reversion is accelerated if the tenant surrenders the lease before it has expired. When a will bequeaths an interest for life that lapses (e.g. because the legatee dies before the testator), the interest of the person entitled in *remainder is accelerated and takes effect immediately the testator dies.

acceptance *n.* Agreement to the terms of an *offer that, provided certain other requirements are fulfilled, converts the offer into a legally binding contract. If the method by which acceptance is to

3

be signified is indicated by the offeror, that method alone will be effective. If it is not, acceptance may be either express (by word of mouth or in writing) or inferred from the offeree's conduct; for example, if he receives goods on approval and starts to make use of them. The acceptance must always, however, involve some action on the part of the person to whom the offer was made: the offeror cannot assert that his offer will be treated as accepted unless the offeree rejects it. The validity of an acceptance is governed by four principal rules. (1) It must take place while the offer is still in force, i.e. before it has lapsed (*see* lapse of offer) or been revoked (*see* revocation of offer). (2) It must be on the same terms as the offer. An acceptance made subject to any variation is treated as a counteroffer. (3) It must be unconditional, thus an acceptance *subject to contract* is not a valid acceptance. (4) It must be communicated to the offeror. Acceptance by letter is treated as communicated when the letter is posted, but telex is equated with the telephone, so that communication takes place only on receipt. However, when the offer consists of a promise to confer a benefit on whoever may perform a specified act, the offeror waives the requirement of communication as a separate act. If, for example, he offers a reward for information, a person able to supply the information is not expected to accept the offer formally. The act of giving the information itself constitutes the acceptance, the communication of the acceptance, and the performance of the contract.

acceptance of a bill The written agreement by the person on whom a *bill of exchange is drawn (the *drawee*) that he will accept the order of the person who draws it upon him (the *drawer*). The acceptance must be written on the bill and signed. The signature of the drawee without additional words is sufficient, although generally the word "accepted" is used as well. Upon acceptance the drawee becomes the acceptor and the party primarily liable upon the bill. *See also* qualified acceptance.

acceptance of charge A police procedure empowering a senior officer to accept the facts reported to him by a constable and to press criminal charges against a suspect.

acceptance of service An endorsement on a writ by a defendant's solicitor that he accepts service of the writ on behalf of the defendant. The writ is then deemed to have been duly served on the defendant on the date of the endorsement.

acceptance *supra protest* (acceptance for honour) A form of *acceptance of a bill of exchange to save the good name of the drawer or an endorser. If a bill of exchange has been either the subject of a *protest for dishonour by nonacceptance or protested for better security, and it is not overdue, any person who is not already liable on the bill may, with the consent of the holder, accept the bill *supra protest*. Such an acceptance must be written on the bill to indicate that it is an acceptance for honour and be signed. The acceptor for honour engages that he will pay the bill on due presentment if it is not paid by the drawee, provided he has received notice that it has been presented for payment and protested for nonpayment. He is liable to the holder and to all parties to the bill subsequent to the party for whose honour he accepted.

accepted accounting standards Statements of standard accounting practice that define the principles upon which a company's assets and liabilities should be valued and its profits and losses computed. They are published by the Accounting Standards Committee and are not (with the exception of those that have become incorporated into the Companies Acts) legally binding. However, professional accounting bodies expect members to observe them. *See also* accounts.

access *n.* **1.** The opportunity to visit a child for a short period (*visiting access*) or for a longer period (*staying access*) that may be granted to its parent (and sometimes grandparents) when the other parent has the *care and control of the child after divorce or when a *custodianship order is in force. The granting of access and the terms of access are within the discretion of the court. Access is usually considered a parental right, but in recent years it has come to be seen as a right of the child. **2.** The opportunity for sexual intercourse between husband and wife. If it can be demonstrated that there was no such opportunity, and a child has been born to the wife, this may be evidence that the child is not legitimate.

accessory *n.* One who is a party to a crime that is actually committed by someone else (the *perpetrator*). An accessory is one who either successfully incites someone to commit a crime (*counsels or procures*) or helps him to do so (*aids and abets*). The accessory is normally subject to the same maximum penalty as the perpetrator, with the following differences: (1) strict liability does not apply to accessories: criminal intention (*mens rea*) on the part of the accessory must be proved even in crimes normally described as strict-liability crimes; (2) one cannot be an accessory to an attempted crime, although the perpetrator may be guilty of attempt; (3) duress is a defence to an accessory in murder, but not to a perpetrator.

Before 1967 an accessory was defined as one who incited a felony (*accessory before the fact*) or assisted someone who had committed a felony (*accessory after the fact*), but these definitions have now been abolished. The term "accessory" is now not a specific legal term. *See also* impeding apprehension or prosecution.

accommodation bill A bill of exchange accepted by an *accommodation party*, i.e. a person who signs without receiving value and for the purpose of lending his name (i.e. his credit) to someone else. An accommodation party is liable on the bill to a *holder for value.

accomplice *n.* One who is a party to a crime, either as a perpetrator or as an *accessory. The evidence of an accomplice must be corroborated.

accord and satisfaction The purchase by one party to a contract of a release from his obligations under it when the other party has already performed his side of the bargain. A release of this one-sided nature constitutes a *unilateral discharge* of the contract; unless granted by deed, it can at common law be effected only by purchase, i.e. by a fresh agreement (accord) for which new consideration (satisfaction) is given. If, for example, A is due to pay £1000 on a particular date to B for contractual services rendered, B might agree to accept £900 paid on an earlier date, the earlier payment constituting satisfaction. *Compare* bilateral discharge. *See also* (promissory) estoppel.

account *n.* A right at common law and later (more importantly) in equity, calling one party to a relationship (e.g. a partnership) to account to the other for moneys received or due.

account of profits A remedy that a plaintiff can claim as an alternative to damages in certain circumstances, e.g. in an action for breach of *copyright. A successful plaintiff is entitled to a sum equal to the monetary gain the defendant has made through wronging the plaintiff.

accounts *pl. n.* A statement of a company's financial position. All registered companies must present accounts annually to company members at a *general meeting. Accounts consist of a *balance sheet and a *profit-and-loss account with *group accounts (if appropriate) attached. They are accompanied by a directors' report and an auditor's report. All limited companies must deliver copies of their accounts to the *Companies Registry, where they are open to public inspection.

accumulation n. The continual addition of the interest of a fund to the capital, so that the fund grows indefinitely. Before the Accumulation Act 1800 accumulation was permitted for the length of the perpetuity period (i.e. lives in being plus 21 years: see rule against perpetuities). The periods for which accumulation is now permitted are shorter; they are listed in the Law of Property Act 1925 and the Perpetuities and Accumulations Act 1964 and include a period of 21 years from the date of the disposition, the period of the life of the settlor, and the duration of the minority of any person mentioned in the disposition.

accusatorial procedure (adversary procedure) A system of criminal justice in which the truth is revealed by the process of prosecution and defence. It is the primary duty of the prosecutor and defence to press their respective viewpoints while the judge acts as an impartial umpire, who allows the facts to emerge from this procedure. Common-law systems, as in England, adopt an accusatorial procedure. *Compare* inquisitorial procedure.

acknowledgment n. **1.** The admission that a debt is due or a claim exists. Under the Limitation Act 1939, a written acknowledgment by a debtor or his agent causes the debt to be treated as if it had accrued on the date of the acknowledgment. The result is that the limitation period of six years for bringing an action to recover the debt runs from the date of acknowledgment, rather than the date on which the debt in fact arose. *See also* limitation of actions. **2.** Confirmation by a testator in the presence of two witnesses that the

signature on his will is his own. The Wills Act 1837 requires that the testator's signature be made or acknowledged in the presence of two witnesses.

acknowledgment and undertaking Confirmation in a *title deed that a person may see and have copies of relevant deeds not in his possession, with a promise from the holder of them to keep them safely. Thus when part of an owner's land is sold, he keeps his deeds to the whole but in the conveyance gives this acknowledgment and undertaking to the purchaser, who can then prcve his title to the part from copies of the earlier deeds and by calling for production of the originals.

acknowledgment of service A stage in proceedings begun by *writ of summons or *originating summons in the High Court in which the defendant states that the writ or originating summons has been served upon him. The appropriate form must be served upon the defendant with the originating process; it includes a section giving the defendant the opportunity to give *notice of intention to defend. This procedure was introduced to replace the entering of an *appearance, which was abolished in 1979. Unlike appearance, acknowledgment of service does not constitute a submission to the jurisdiction of the court or a waiver of any irregularity in the originating process.

acquittal n. A decision by a court that a defendant accused of a crime is innocent. A court must acquit a defendant following a verdict of *not guilty or a successful plea of *autrefois acquit or *autrefois convict. Once acquitted, a defendant cannot be tried again for the same crime on fresh evidence, but an acquittal in a criminal court does not bind civil courts (for example, in relation to a libel charge against someone alleging the defendant's guilt).

action n. **1.** A proceeding in which a party pursues a legal right in a civil court. *See also in personam*; *in rem*. **2.** In the High Court, a civil proceeding initiated by writ. In this sense, actions are distinguished from *matters*, which are proceedings initiated by other means.

active trust (special trust) A trust in which the trustee has duties other than handing over the trust property to the person entitled to it (*compare* bare trust). Obligations (for example to sell the property or to maintain it) may have been imposed on the trustee or discretions may be given to him. Alternatively the beneficiary may be a minor or under a disability and therefore not immediately entitled to the property.

act of God An event due to natural causes (storms, earthquakes, floods, etc.) so exceptionally severe that no one could reasonably be expected to anticipate or guard against it.

Act of Parliament (statute) A document that sets out legal rules and has (normally) been passed by both Houses of *Parliament in the form of a *Bill and agreed to by the Crown (*see* royal assent). Under the Parliament Acts 1911 and 1949, however, passing of public Bills by the House of Lords can be dispensed with, except in the case of Bills to extend the duration of Parliament or to confirm provisional orders. Subject to these exceptions, the Lords can delay Bills passed by the House of Commons; it cannot block them completely. If the Commons pass a money Bill (for example, one giving effect to the Budget) and the Lords do not pass it unaltered within one month, it may be submitted direct for the royal assent. Any other Bill may receive the royal assent without being passed by the Lords if the Commons pass it in two consecutive sessions and at least one year elapses between its second reading in the first session and its third reading in the second.

Every modern Act of Parliament begins with a *long title*, which summarizes its aims, and ends with a *short title*, by which it may be cited in any other document. The short title includes the calendar year in which the Act receives the royal assent (e.g. The Unfair Contract Terms Act 1977). An alternative method of citation is by the calendar year together with the Chapter number allotted to the Act on receiving the assent or, in the case of an Act earlier than 1963, by its regnal year or years and Chapter number. Regnal years are numbered from the date of a sovereign's accession to the throne, and an Act is attributed to the year or years covering the session in which it receives the royal assent. (*See also* enacting words.) An Act comes into force on the date of royal assent unless it specifies a different date or provides for the date to be fixed by ministerial order.

Acts of Parliament are classified by the Queen's Printer as public general Acts, local Acts, and personal Acts. *Public general Acts* include all Acts (except those confirming provisional orders) introduced into Parliament as public Bills. *Local Acts* comprise all Acts introduced as private Bills and confined in operation to a particular area, together with Acts confirming provisional orders. *Personal Acts* are Acts introduced as private Bills and applying to private individuals or estates. Acts are alternatively classified as public or private according to their status in courts of law. A *public Act* is judicially noticed (i.e. accepted by the courts as a matter of general knowledge). A *private Act* is not, and must be expressly pleaded by the person relying on it. All Acts since 1850 are public unless they specifically provide otherwise.

act of state An act committed by an agent of a sovereign power with its prior approval or subsequent ratification that affects adversely a person who does not owe allegiance to that power. The courts have power to decide whether or not particular conduct constitutes such an act, but if it does, they have no jurisdiction to award any remedy.

actual military service *See* privileged will.

actual total loss (in marine insurance) A loss of a ship or cargo in which the subject matter is destroyed or damaged to such an extent that it can no longer be used for its purpose. If the ship or cargo is the subject of a *valued policy, the measure of indemnity is the sum fixed by the policy; if the policy is unvalued, the measure of indemnity is the insurable value of the subject insured. *Compare* constructive total loss.

actus reus [Latin: a guilty act] The essential element of a crime that must be proved to secure a conviction, as opposed to the mental state of the accused (*see* mens rea). In most cases the *actus reus* will simply be an act (e.g. appropriation of property is the act of theft) accompanied by specified circumstances (e.g. that the property belongs to another). Sometimes, however, it may be an *omission to act (e.g. failure to prevent death may be the *actus reus* of manslaughter) or it may include a specified consequence (death resulting within a year and a day being the consequence required for the *actus reus* of manslaughter or murder). In certain cases the *actus reus* may simply be a state of affairs rather than an act (e.g. being unfit to drive through drink or drugs when in charge of a motor vehicle on a road). *See also* automatism.

ad colligenda bona [Latin] To collect the goods. The court may grant *letters of administration *ad colligenda bona* to any person to deal with specified property in an estate when that property might be endangered by delay. For example, if part of the estate consists of perishable goods the court may grant administration *ad colligenda bona* to any suitable person to allow him to sell or otherwise deal with those goods for

the benefit of the estate, pending a full grant of representation to the persons entitled to deal with the whole estate.

address for service The address, which a party to court proceedings gives to the court and/or the other party, to which all the formal documents relating to the proceedings should be delivered. Notices delivered at that address (which may be, for example, the address of his solicitors) are binding on the party concerned.

ademption *n.* The cancellation or reduction of a legacy by an act of the testator during his lifetime other than revocation of his will. For example, if the will bequeaths a particular house that the testator sold during his lifetime, or if after making a will giving a legacy to his child the testator gives the child property constituting a *portion, the legacy is in each case adeemed. The gift of the house is cancelled and the child's legacy is reduced by the amount of the portion.

***ad hoc* settlement** A special form of settlement that, under the Settled Land Act 1925, enables the owner in possession of a legal estate in land to *overreach, on sale, certain equitable interests. The owner executes a deed declaring that he holds the land on trust to give effect to the equitable interests and appointing trustees (who must be two individuals approved by the court or a *trust corporation) to receive the sale proceeds. *Ad hoc* settlements are extremely rare: the relevant equitable interests normally arise only where the land is already settled (and they can be overreached in any event) or under an *ad hoc* trust for sale.

***ad hoc* trust for sale** Any *trust for sale of land under which the trustees are two individuals approved by the court, their successors in office, or a trust corporation. Under the Law of Property Act 1925 a sale of land subject to such a trust *overreaches equitable interests that would not be overreached if the trustees were not thus qualified.

ad idem [Latin: towards the same] Indicates that the parties to a transaction are in agreement. See *consensus ad idem*.

adjective law The part of the law that deals with practice and procedure in the courts. Compare substantive law.

adjournment *n.* (in court procedure) The postponement or suspension of the hearing of a case until a future date. The hearing may be adjourned to a fixed date or *sine die* (without day), i.e. for an indefinite period. If an adjournment is granted at the request of a party the court may attach conditions, e.g. relating to the payment of any *costs thrown away.

adjudication *n.* 1. The formal judgment or decision of a court or tribunal. 2. A decision by the Commissioners of Inland Revenue as to the amount (if any) of *stamp duty payable on a written document.

adjudication order A court order that makes a debtor bankrupt. When the order is made, ownership of all the debtor's property is transferred either to a court officer known as the *official receiver or to a trustee appointed by the creditors. See also bankruptcy.

adjustment *n.* 1. The determination of the amount due under a policy of insurance. 2. The working out by an average adjuster of the rights and liabilities arising in a case of general *average.

ad litem [Latin] For the suit. A guardian *ad litem* is one that may be appointed by the court to protect a minor's interests in proceedings affecting his interests (such as adoption or wardship proceedings). A grant *ad litem* is the appointment by a court of a person to act on behalf of an estate in court proceedings, when the estate's proper representatives are unable or unwilling to act.

administration *n.* 1. The collection of assets, payment of debts, and distribution to the beneficiaries of property in the estate of a deceased person. See also grant of representation. 2. The granting of *letters of administration to the estate of a deceased person to an *administrator, when there is no executor under the will. 3. The process of carrying out duties imposed by a trust in connection with the property of a person of unsound mind or a bankrupt.

administration action Proceedings instituted in court by a personal representative or any other person interested in the estate of a deceased person to obtain a *grant of representation.

administration bond A guarantee by a third party, often an insurance company, to make good any loss arising if a person to whom letters of administration are granted fails to deal properly with the estate. The court usually requires an administration bond as a condition of granting letters of administration only when the beneficiaries are considered to need special protection, e.g. when the administrator lives abroad or when there has been a dispute as to who should administer the estate.

administration order An order made in a county court for the administration of the estate of a judgment debtor. The order normally requires the debtor to pay his debts by instalments: so long as he does so, the creditors referred to in the order cannot enforce their individual claims by other methods without the leave of the court. Administration orders are issued when the debtor has multiple debts but it is thought that his bankruptcy can be avoided.

administrative powers Discretionary powers of an executive nature that are conferred by legislation on government ministers, public and local authorities, and other bodies and persons for the purpose of giving detailed effect to broadly defined policy. Examples include powers to acquire land compulsorily, to grant or refuse licences or consents, and to determine the precise nature and extent of services to be provided. Administrative powers are found in every sphere of public administration, including town and country planning, the regulation of public health and other environmental matters, the functioning of the welfare services, and the control of many professions, trades, and other activities. Their exercise is subject to judicial control by means of the doctrine of *ultra vires*.

administrative tribunal A body established by or under Act of Parliament to decide claims and disputes arising in connection with the administration of legislative schemes, normally of a welfare or regulatory nature. Examples are *supplementary benefit appeal tribunals, *industrial tribunals, and *rent assessment committees. They exist outside the ordinary courts of law, but their decisions are subject to judicial control by means of the doctrine of *ultra vires* and in cases of *error of law on the face of the record. *Compare* domestic tribunal. *See also* Council on Tribunals.

administrator *n.* A person appointed by the court to collect and distribute a deceased person's estate when he died intestate, his will did not appoint an executor, or the executor refuses to act. An administrator's authority to deal with the estate does not begin until the court has granted *letters of administration. *Compare* executor.

Admiralty Court A court forming part of the *Queen's Bench Division of the High Court whose jurisdiction embraces civil actions relating to ships and the sea. The court's work includes cases about collisions, damage to cargo, prizes (*see* prize court), and salvage, and in some cases *assessors may be called in to sit with the judge. The distinctive feature of the court's procedure is the action *in rem*, under which the property that has given rise to the cause of action (usually a ship) may be "arrested" and held by the court to satisfy the plaintiff's claim. In practice, it is usual for the owners of the property to give security for its release while the action is proceeding. If the claim is successful, the property held or the sum given by way of security is available to satisfy the judgment. Until 1971 the Admiralty Court was part of the *Probate, Divorce and Admiralty Division of the High Court.

admissibility of evidence The principles determining whether or not particular items of evidence may be received by the court. The central principle of admissibility is *relevance. All irrelevant evidence is inadmissible, but evidence that is relevant may also be inadmissible if it falls within the scope of one of the *exclusionary rules. *See also* conditional admissibility; multiple admissibility.

admissibility of records In civil cases documents containing information (records) are admissible as evidence of the facts stated in them under the Civil Evidence Act 1968. The person who compiled the record must have been acting under a duty to do so, but this does not necessarily apply to the person who supplied the information to him. In criminal cases certain business records are admissible as evidence of the facts stated in them under the Criminal Evidence Act 1965 if the person supplying the information had personal knowledge of the matters recorded and either cannot be called to testify or would be unlikely to remember the facts in question.

admission *n.* **1.** In civil proceedings, a statement by a party to litigation or by his duly authorized agent that is adverse to the party's case. Admissions may be *informal* (i.e. in a document or by word of mouth) or *formal* (i.e. made in a pleading or in reply to an interrogatory). An admission may be related to the court by someone other than the person who made it under an exception to the rule against *hearsay evidence. **2.** In criminal proceedings, a statement admitting an offence or a fact that constitutes legally acceptable evidence of the offence or fact. All admissions must be made voluntarily: if they are not, they are inadmissible as evidence. Admissions may be informal or formal. An informal admission made to a person in authority over the prosecution (e.g. a police officer) is called a *confession. Informal admissions should be viewed with caution by the judge, who has discretion whether or not to allow them. If made to a person in authority, the defence may challenge the prosecution to prove that they were made voluntarily. A formal admission may be made either before or at the court proceedings, but if not made in court, it must be in writing and signed by the defendant or his legal adviser. An admission may be made in respect of any fact about which *oral evidence could be given in court proceedings and is *conclusive evidence of the fact admitted at all criminal proceedings relating to the matter, although it may be withdrawn at any stage with the permission of the court. A plea of guilty to a charge read out in court is a formal admission. *See also* Judges' Rules.

adoption *n.* **1.** The process by which a parent's legal rights and duties in respect of an unmarried minor are transferred to another person or persons. Adoption can only take place by means of an *adoption order* made by a magistrates' court, county court, or the High Court (Family Division). Adoption differs from fostering, custody, and *custodianship in that it affects *all* the parent's rights and duties and it is a permanent change. After adoption the natural parents are (except for the rules relating to *affinity and *incest) no longer considered in law to be the parents of the child, who is henceforth re-

garded as the legal child of the adoptive parents (*see also* adoptive relationship).

The first (but not the only) consideration in deciding whether or not a child should be adopted is whether the adoption would safeguard and promote the welfare of the child. The court must, if possible, try to ascertain the child's wishes and in addition take account of all the circumstances. This may involve consulting expert opinion (e.g. of psychiatrists or social workers). The court may also appoint a guardian *ad litem* to act in the child's interests. There are many statutory provisions (in the Children Act 1975 and Adoption Act 1976) designed to make sure that an adoption would be in the child's best interests (although not all of these provisions are in force yet). Every local authority must set up an *adoption service, and *adoption societies are carefully controlled. There are rules as to who may adopt and who may be adopted and provisions for a probationary period, during which the child lives with the would-be adopter(s) and the court assesses whether he gets on well with them.

Normally a child cannot be adopted without the consent of each of its parents or guardians, but in some cases the court may make an adoption order without the parents' consent (e.g. if they cannot be found or have ill-treated the child). If the court thinks that the parents are refusing unreasonably to agree to an adoption that would be in the child's best interests, it may make an adoption order against the parents' wishes. A parent may consent either to a specific adoption or to an order *freeing for adoption by whomever the court eventually decides is best suited to adopt the child.

The Registrar General must keep a register containing details of all adoption orders, which any member of the public may consult. An adopted child over the age of 18 has a right to see a copy of his original birth certificate in order to find out who his natural parents are.

2. Reliance by a court on a rule of international law that has not been expressly made part of the law of the land but is not inconsistent with it.

3. (in constitutional law) The decision of a local authority or similar body to bring into force in their area an Act of Parliament conferring powers on them at their option.

adoption agency A local authority or an approved *adoption society. Usually only adoption agencies may make arrangements for adoption.

adoption order *See* adoption.

adoption service Under the 1975 Children Act, the different services, collectively, that local authorities must provide within their area in order to meet the needs of *adoption. These services include provision of accommodation for pregnant women and mothers, making arrangements for placing children with prospective adopters, and advising people with adoption problems.

adoption society A group of people organized to make arrangements for the *adoption of children. Adoption societies must be approved by the Secretary of State before acting as such.

adoptive relationship A legal relationship created as a result of an adoption order (*see* adoption). A male adopter is known as the *adoptive father*, a female adopter as the *adoptive mother*, and other relatives as *adoptive relatives*. The laws of *affinity are, however, not altered by the new adoptive relationship.

adulteration *n.* The mixing of other substances with food. It is an offence of *strict liability to sell any food containing a substance that would endanger health. It is also an offence to mix dangerous substances into food with the intention of selling the mixture.

adultery *n* An act of sexual intercourse between a male and a female not married to each other, when at least one of them is married to someone else and the intercourse is not by force. Intercourse for this purpose means penetration of the vagina by the penis. Adultery may be evidence of *breakdown of marriage and under certain circumstances entitles a spouse to *divorce the adulterer.

advance corporation tax (ACT) A form of *corporation tax payable by a company on its qualifying distributions (*see* imputation system).

advancement *n.* **1.** The power, in a trust, to provide capital sums for the benefit of a person who is an infant or who may (but is not certain to) receive the property under a settlement. The term is a shortened form of *advancement in the world* and has the connotation of providing a single sum for a specific purpose of a permanent nature; examples include sums payable on marriage, to buy a house for the beneficiary, or to establish the beneficiary in a trade or profession. Before 1926, a power of advancement had to be specifically included in any settlement; since 1925 a statutory power exists, subject to contrary intention. No person may receive by way of advancement more than half that to which he could ever become entitled.

2. A presumption, arising in certain circumstances, that if one person purchases property in the name of another, the property will be held beneficially by that other person and not on *resulting trust for the person who purchases it. The presumption of advancement arises when a father or other person in the position of a parent purchases property for a child. The presumption does not automatically arise in the case of a mother because until 1882 a married woman could not, during marriage, own property; her automatic exclusion from the presumption now seems nonsensical, although she will in many cases be found to be "in the position of a parent". A similar presumption has been held to exist when a husband purchases for his wife (though not *vice versa*), and occasionally a man for his mistress, but the strength (perhaps even the existence) of this presumption is doubtful.

adversary procedure *See* accusatorial procedure.

adverse occupation Occupation of premises by a trespasser to the exclusion of the owner or lawful occupier. *Trespass in itself is not usually a criminal offence, but if the premises are residential and were being occupied, the trespasser (whether or not he used force in order to enter) is guilty of an offence under the Criminal Law Act 1977 if he refuses to leave when asked to do so by the displaced *residential occupier or a protected intending occupier (or by someone acting on behalf of them). A protected intending occupier is a purchaser, someone let in by the local authority, Housing Corporation, or a housing association with written evidence of his claim to the premises, or someone granted a lease for at least 21 years.

adverse possession Occupation of land in a manner inconsistent with the rights of the person entitled to it and without his permission. A trespasser who remains in adverse possession for over 12 years may acquire a *squatter's title*, which is valid in law against the person who had been lawfully entitled to possession. If the squatter gives a written acknowledgment of the true owner's title, time for the acquisition of a squatter's title begins to run against the true owner from the date of the acknowledgment, not the date when adverse possession began.

adverse witness A witness who gives evidence unfavourable to the party who called him. If the witness's evidence is merely unfavourable he may not be impeached (i.e. his credibility may not be attacked) by the party calling him, but contradictory evidence may be called. If, however, the witness is *hostile he may be impeached.

advice on evidence The written opinion of counsel, usually prepared after *close of pleadings or *discovery and inspection of documents, identifying the issues raised on the pleadings and advising counsel's instructing solicitor what evidence it will be necessary to call in respect of them at the trial. It may also contain advice on the orders to be sought on the *summons for directions and on the prospects of success at trial.

advocate *n.* **1.** One who argues a case for a client in court. In magistrates' courts and the county courts both *barristers and *solicitors have the right to appear as advocates. In most Crown Court centres, the High Court, the Court of Appeal, and the House of Lords barristers have exclusive *rights of audience. In many tribunals there are no formal rules concerning the representation of parties, and laymen may appear as advocates. **2.** In Scotland, a member of the Faculty of Advocates, the professional organization of the Scots Bar.

Advocate General A member of the *Court of Justice of the European Communities whose function is to assist the court by presenting opinions upon every case brought before it. The Advocate General acts in some ways like an *amicus curiae* in putting forward arguments based upon his own view of the interests of the European Communities and the development of their law, rather than advocating the cause of a party to the litigation.

aequitas est quasi aequalitas See equality is equity.

affidavit *n.* A sworn written statement used mainly to support certain applications and, in some circumstances, as evidence in court proceedings. The person who makes the affidavit must swear or *affirm that the contents are true before a person authorized to take oaths in respect of the particular kind of affidavit. *See also* argumentative affidavit.

affiliation order An order of a magistrates' court against a man alleged to be the father of an illegitimate child, obliging him to make payments towards the upkeep of the child. Such payments may be weekly or monthly and may include lump sums of up to £500. Failure to comply with the terms of the order may be punished by committal to prison.

affinity *n.* The relationship created by marriage between a husband and his wife's blood relatives or between a wife and her husband's blood relatives. Some categories of people related by affinity are forbidden to marry each other (*see* prohibited degrees of relationships). The relationship of blood relatives is known as *consanguinity. *See also* incest.

affirm *vb.* **1.** To confirm a legal decision, particularly (of an appeal court) to confirm a judgment made in a lower court. **2.** To promise in solemn form to tell the truth while giving evidence or when making an *affidavit. Any person who objects to being sworn on *oath, or in respect of whom it is not reasonably practicable to administer an oath, may instead affirm. Affirmation has the same legal effects as the taking of an oath. **3.** To treat a contract as continuing in existence, instead of exercising a right to rescind it for *misrepresentation or other cause (*see* voidable contract) or to treat it as discharged by reason of repudiation or fundamental breach (*see* breach of contract). Affirmation is effective only if it takes place with full knowledge of the facts. It may take the form of an express declaration of intention to proceed with the contract, or that intention may be inferred from conduct (if, for example, the party attempts to sell goods that have been

delivered under a contract voidable for misrepresentation). Lapse of time without seeking a remedy may be treated as evidence of affirmation.

affirmative pregnant An allegation in a pleading implying or not denying some negative. *Compare* negative pregnant.

affirmative resolution *See* delegated legislation.

affray *n.* An offence at common law constituting an act of violence calculated to terrify the reasonable bystander. The act is normally fighting (and covers such acts as fights between rival football fans), but a display of force by brandishing a weapon may be sufficient. The act must be likely to terrify, not merely to frighten, but it is not necessary to prove that anyone was actually terrified. Affray must be tried on indictment and is subject to punishment at the court's discretion. *See also* assault.

affreightment *n.* A contract for the carriage of goods by sea (the consideration being called *freight*). It can be either a *charterparty or a contract whose terms are set out in the *bill of lading.

AG *See* Attorney General.

agency *n.* **1.** The relationship between an *agent and his principal. **2.** The business carried on by an agent.

agent *n.* **1.** A person appointed by another (the *principal*) to act on his behalf, often to negotiate a contract between the principal and a third party. If an agent discloses his principal's name (or at least the existence of a principal) to the third party with whom he is dealing, the agent himself is not normally liable on the contract. An *undisclosed principal* is one whose existence is not revealed by the agent to a third party; he may still be liable on the contract, but in such cases the agent is also liable. However, an undisclosed principal may not be entitled to the benefit of a contract if the agency is inconsistent with the terms of the contract or if the third party shows that he wished to contract with the agent personally.

Agents are either *general agents* or *special agents*. A general agent is one who has authority to act for his principal in all business of a particular kind, or who acts for the principal in the course of his (the agent's) usual business or profession. A special agent is authorized to act only for a special purpose that is not in the ordinary course of the agent's business or profession. The principal of a general agent is bound by acts of the agent that are incidental to the ordinary conduct of the agent's business or the effective performance of his duties, even if the principal has imposed limitations on the agent's authority. But in the case of a special agent, the principal is not bound by acts that are not within the authority conferred. In either case, the principal may ratify an unauthorized contract. An agent for the sale of goods sometimes agrees to protect his principal against the risk of the buyer's insolvency. He does this by undertaking liability for the unjustifiable failure of the third-party buyer to pay the price of the goods. Such an agent is called a *del credere agent*. *See also* mercantile agent. **2.** *See* buggery.

age of consent The age at which a girl can legally consent to sexual intercourse, or to an act that would otherwise constitute an indecent assault. This age is now 16. This age limit does not apply to girls married under a foreign law that is recognized in English law.

aggravated assault *See* assault.

aggravated burglary *See* burglary.

aggravated damages *Damages awarded when the conduct of the defendant or the surrounding circumstances increase the injury to the plain-

tiff by subjecting him to humiliation, distress, or embarrassment, particularly in such torts as assault, false imprisonment, and defamation.

aggression *n.* (in international law) According to the General Assembly Resolution (3314) on the Definition of Aggression 1974, the use of armed force by one state against the sovereignty, territorial integrity, or political independence of another state or in any way inconsistent with the Charter of the United Nations. The Resolution lists examples of aggression, which include the following. (1) Invasion, attack, military occupation, or annexation of the territory of any state by the armed forces of another state. (2) Bombardment or the use of any weapons by a state against another state's territory. (3) Armed blockade by a state of another state's ports or coasts. (4) The use of a state's armed forces in another state in breach of the terms of the agreement on which they were allowed into that state. (5) Allowing one's territory to be placed at the disposal of another state, to be used by that state for committing an act of aggression against a third state. (6) Sending armed bands or guerrillas to carry out armed raids on another state that are grave enough to amount to any of the above acts.

The first use of armed force by a state in contravention of the UN Charter is prima facie evidence of aggression, although the final decision in such cases is left to the Security Council, who may also classify other acts as aggression. The Resolution declares that no consideration whatsoever can justify aggression, that territory cannot be acquired by acts of aggression, and that wars of aggression constitute a crime against international peace. *See also* offences against international law and order; war; war crimes.

agreement for a lease A contract to enter into a *lease. The courts will only enforce it when *part performance applies or when there is a certain kind of written agreement. In the case of part performance, the person who wishes to enforce the contract has done something indicating that he intends to be bound, such as taking possession or carrying out repairs and alterations to the property. An enforceable written agreement must be signed by the person against whom the enforcement action is taken and must contain details of the parties, the rent, the property, and the period of the lease.

agricultural dwelling-house advisory committee (ADHAC) A committee that advises the local authority in its area on the agricultural need for *tied cottages. An owner of a tied cottage can apply to a local authority to rehouse a former worker who is occupying the cottage. The local authority has a duty to do this if the committee advises that possession is needed in the interests of efficient agriculture.

agricultural holding A tenancy of agricultural land. Tenants have special statutory protection and there is a procedure to fix rent by arbitration if the parties cannot agree. The landlord normally has to give at least one year's notice to quit. The tenant can usually appeal to the *agricultural land tribunal to decide whether the notice to quit should operate. The landlord is entitled to compensation at the end of the tenancy if the holding has deteriorated and the tenant is at fault; the tenant can claim compensation at the end of the tenancy for disturbance and for improvements he has made. On the tenant's death his spouse or other close relative whose livelihood depends on working on the holding can apply to the agricultural land tribunal to have the tenancy transferred to him. The application must be made within three months of the tenant's death.

agricultural land tribunal A tribunal having statutory functions in relation to tenancies of agricultural holdings. No-

tice to quit a holding is in certain circumstances inoperative without a tribunal's consent, and on the death of a tenant the tribunal has power to direct that a member of his family is entitled to a new tenancy.

aid and abet To assist in the performance of a crime either before or during (but not after) its commission. Aiding usually refers to material assistance (e.g. providing the tools or necessary information for the crime), and abetting to lesser assistance (e.g. acting as a look-out or driving a car to the scene of the crime). Aiders and abettors are liable to be tried as *accessories. Mere presence at the scene of a crime or assistance of a trivial nature are not usually regarded as aiding and abetting. It is not necessary to have a criminal motive to be guilty of aiding and abetting: knowledge that one is assisting the criminal is sufficient.

air-force law *See* service law.

air pollution *See* pollution.

airspace *n.* In English law and international law, the ownership of land includes ownership of the airspace above it (outer space is not considered to be subject to ownership). In English law an owner has rights in as much of the airspace above his land as is necessary for the ordinary use of his land and the structures on it. Within these limits a projection over one's land (such as a signboard) can be a trespass and pollution of air by one's neighbour can be a nuisance. Pollution of air is also controlled by various statutes. There is no natural right to the free flow of air from neighbouring land, but *easements for the flow of air through a defined opening (such as a window or a ventilator) can be acquired. Civil aircraft flying at a reasonable height over land do not commit trespass, but damages can be obtained if material loss or damage is caused to people or property.

alderman *n.* A senior member of a local authority, elected by its directly elected members. Active aldermanic rank now exists only in the *City of London, having been phased out elsewhere by the Local Government Act 1972. County, district,and London borough councils and the Greater London Council can, however, appoint past members to honorary rank in recognition of eminent service.

alibi [from Latin: elsewhere] *n.* A defence to a criminal charge alleging that the defendant was not at the place at which the crime was committed and so could not have been responsible for it. If the defendant claims to have been at a particular place at the time of the crime, evidence in support of an alibi may only be given if the defendant has supplied particulars of it to the prosecution not later than seven days after committal, unless the Crown Court considers that there was a valid reason for not supplying them.

alien *n.* A person who, under the law of a particular state, is not a citizen of that state. He is normally subject to certain civil disabilities, such as being ineligible to vote. For the purposes of UK statute law an alien is defined by the British Nationality Act 1981 (which came into force on 1 January 1983) as a person who is neither a Commonwealth citizen, nor a British protected person, nor a citizen of the Republic of Ireland. At common law, a distinction is drawn between friendly and *enemy aliens*. The latter comprise not only citizens of hostile states but also all others voluntarily living in enemy territory or carrying on business there; they are subject to additional disabilities. *See also* allegiance.

alienable *adj.* Capable of being transferred: used particularly in relation to real property. *See also* rule against inalienability.

alienation *n.* The transfer of property (particularly real property) from one person to another. *See also* restraint on alienation.

alieni juris [Latin: of another's right] Describing the status of a person who is not of full age and capacity. *Compare sui juris.*

alimentary trust *See* protective trust.

alimony *n.* Formerly, financial provision made by a husband to his wife when they are living apart. Alimony is now known as *maintenance or *financial provision.

allegation *n.* Any statement of fact in a *pleading, *affidavit, or *indictment. It is the duty of the party who makes an allegation to adduce evidence in support of it at trial.

allegiance *n.* The duty of obedience owed to a head of state in return for his protection. It is due from all citizens of that state and its dependencies and also from any *alien present in the state (including enemy aliens under licence; for example, internees). A person who is declared by the British Nationality Act 1981 not to be an alien but who has a primary citizenship conferred by a state other than the UK is probably governed by the same principles as aliens so far as allegiance is concerned.

allotment *n.* A contract between a public company and an applicant for shares offered for sale when a company is floated or when it makes a new issue; it confers upon the applicant the unconditional right to purchase a specified number of shares. The contract is complete when a *letter of allotment* is dispatched by the company to the applicant, stating how many shares he has been allotted. If he has been allotted fewer shares than he has applied for, he receives a cheque to the value of the unallotted balance (an application must usually be accompanied by a cheque for the full value of the shares applied for). *See also* return.

alteration *n.* A change that, when made in a legal document, may affect its validity. An alteration in a will is presumed to have been made after execution and will therefore be invalid. However, it will be valid if it is proved to have been made before execution or if it was executed in the same way as the will itself. If it completely obliterates the original words, it is treated as a blank space. If the original words can still be read, they remain effective. Alterations in deeds are presumed to have been made before execution. However, if it is shown that a material alteration was made after execution, the whole deed may be void. *See also* amendment.

alteration of share capital An increase, reduction *(see* reduction of capital), or any other change in the *authorized capital of a company. If permitted by the *articles of association, a limited company can increase its authorized capital as appropriate. It can also rearrange its existing authorized capital (e.g. by consolidating 100 shares of £1 into 25 shares of £4 or by subdividing 100 shares of £1 into 200 of 50p) and cancel unissued shares. These are reserved powers *(see* general meeting), passed – unless the articles of association provide otherwise – by an ordinary resolution.

alternative verdict A verdict of not guilty of the offence actually charged but guilty of some lesser offence not charged. Such a verdict is only permitted when there is insufficient evidence to establish the more serious offence but the evidence given is sufficient to prove the lesser offence. If, for example, in a murder case there is evidence that the defendant inflicted a wound, but no evidence that the wound caused the death, an alternative verdict of wounding or causing grievous bodily harm may be returned.

ambiguity *n.* Uncertainty in meaning. In legal documents ambiguity may be patent or latent. A *patent ambiguity* is obvious to anyone looking at the document; for example, when a blank space is left for a name. A *latent ambiguity* at first appears to be an unambiguous statement, but the ambiguity becomes apparent in the light of knowledge gained other than from the document. An example is "I give my gold watch to X", when the testator has two gold watches. In general, *extrinsic evidence can be used to clarify latent ambiguities, but not patent ambiguities. Extrinsic evidence cannot be used to give a different meaning to words capable of ordinary interpretation.

ambulatory *adj.* (of a will) Taking effect not from when it was made but from the death of the testator. Thus descriptions of property bequeathed or of beneficiaries are taken to refer to property or persons existing at that time and the will is revocable until death.

ameliorating waste Alterations made by a tenant that improve the land he leases. *See* waste.

amendment *n.* The alteration of a writ, pleading, indictment, or other document, either to correct some error or defect in the original or to raise a new claim or allegation. In the High Court a writ or pleading may be amended once before *close of pleadings without leave of the court. After that leave is required and, although frequently granted, is usually subject to the party seeking leave paying any *costs thrown away. An indictment may be amended with leave of the court or, in some circumstances, by the court of its own motion.

a mensa et thoro [Latin] From board and bed. A decree of divorce *a mensa et thoro* was the forerunner of the modern decree of judicial separation. *See also a vinculo matrimonii.*

amicus curiae [Latin: friend of the court] A counsel who assists the court by putting arguments in support of an interest that might not be adequately represented by the parties to the proceedings (such as the public interest) or by arguing on behalf of a party who is otherwise unrepresented. In modern practice, when a court requires the assistance of an *amicus curiae* it is customary to invite the *Attorney General to attend, either in person or by counsel instructed on his behalf, to represent the public interest, but counsel have been permitted to act as *amicus curiae* on behalf of professional bodies (e.g. the Law Society).

amnesty *n.* An act erasing from legal memory some aspect of criminal conduct by an offender. It is most frequently granted to groups of people in respect of political offences and is wider than a *pardon, which merely relieves an offender of punishment.

ancient lights An easement acquired by lapse of time (*see* prescription) resulting from 20 years' continuous enjoyment of the access of light to the claimant's land without any written consent from the owner of the land over which the easement is claimed.

ancillary credit business A business involved in credit brokerage, debt adjusting, debt counselling, debt collecting, or the operation of a credit-reference agency. *Credit brokerage* includes the effecting of introductions of individuals wishing to obtain credit to persons carrying on a *consumer-credit business. *Debt adjusting* is the process by which a third party negotiates terms for the discharge of a debt due under *consumer-credit agreements or *consumer-hire agreements with the creditor or owner on behalf of the debtor or hirer. The latter may also pay a third party to take over his obligation to discharge a debt or to undertake any similar activity concerned with its liquidation. *Debt counselling* is the giving of advice (other than by the original creditor and certain others) to debtors or hirers about the liquidation of debts due under consumer-credit agreements or consumer-hire agreements. In *debt*

collecting, someone other than the creditor takes steps to procure the payment of debts owing to him. A creditor may engage a debt collector for this purpose. A *credit-reference agency* collects information concerning the financial standing of individuals and supplies this information to those seeking it. The Consumer Credit Act 1974 provides for the licensing of ancillary credit businesses and regulates their activities.

ancillary probate A grant of probate to an executor appointed under a foreign jurisdiction to enable him to deal with assets of the deceased in the UK.

ancillary relief A court order incidental to another order or application. It usually refers to a *financial provision order or a *property adjustment order made in the course of proceedings for divorce or judicial separation.

animals *pl. n. See* classification of animals.

animus [Latin] *n.* Intention. The term is often used in combination; for example, *animus furandi* – the intention to steal; *animus manendi* – the intention to remain in one place (for the purposes of the law relating to *domicile).

annexation *n.* (in international law) The acquisition of legal sovereignty by one state over the territory of another. Annexation is now generally considered illegal in international law, even when it results from a legitimate use of force (for example, in self-defence). It may subsequently become legal, however, by means of *recognition by other states.

annual general meeting (AGM) A meeting of company members required by the Companies Acts 1948–81 to be held each year. Not more than 15 months should elapse between meetings, and 21 days' written notice (specifying the meeting as the annual general meeting) must be given. AGMs are concerned with the accounts, directors' and auditor's reports, dividends, the election of directors, and the appointment and remuneration of the auditor. Other matters are treated as *special business. *See also* general meeting.

Annual Practice, The *See* Supreme Court Practice, The.

annual return A document that registered companies are required by law to send to the *Companies Registry, usually each year. It contains information concerning the registered office, directors, company members, certain company debts, and various other matters. It is open to public inspection.

annual value of land The annual rent that might reasonably be expected from letting land or buildings, if the tenant pays all usual rates and taxes while other expenses (including repairs) are borne by the landlord. It is used in assessing *income tax and *rates. The Inland Revenue carry out the valuation.

annuity *n.* A sum of money payable annually for as long as the beneficiary lives, or for some other specified period provided it is terminated by the beneficiary's death. An annuity charged on land will bind third parties only if it is registered under the Land Charges Act 1925, but if the annuity arises under a settlement of land it can be *overreached and is therefore not registrable. A *joint annuity*, in which money is payable to more than one beneficiary, terminates on the death of the last survivor.

annulment *n.* **1.** A declaration by the court that a marriage was never legally valid. In all cases of nullity except nonconsummation, a decree of annulment will only be granted within three years after the celebration of the marriage. *See also* nullity of marriage. **2.** The cancellation by a court of an *adjudication order, which occurs when it considers that the debtor was wrongly made bankrupt, when all the debts have been paid in full, or when the court approves a *composition or *scheme of arrange-

ment. The power of annulment is discretionary. Annulment does not affect the validity of any sale of property or other action that has already taken place as a result of the adjudication order. **3.** The cancellation of *delegated legislation by resolution of either House of Parliament. **4.** The setting aside of legislation or other action by the *Court of Justice of the European Communities.

annus et dies [Latin] A year and a day. At common law, the Crown was entitled to take possession of the lands of a person convicted of felony and to exploit them without reserve for a year and a day. This was known as the *right of year, day, and waste*.

answer *n.* **1.** A reply to an *interrogatory. **2.** A pleading served by the respondent to a petition, e.g. an answer to a divorce petition. It is equivalent to the *defence served by the defendant to an action begun by writ.

antecedents *pl. n.* An accused or convicted person's previous criminal record or bad character. Generally, the prosecution may not give evidence at the trial of the accused's bad character, as it might unduly prejudice the jury. But this rule is relaxed if previous conduct or a *previous conviction is in issue (for instance, when the crime is such that it could only have been committed by someone who had already been convicted of an offence or had misconducted himself in a particular way) or if the accused himself raises the matter by denying that he has a bad character or a criminal record. In such circumstances the prosecution may also use *similarfact evidence. In cross-examination, the accused must not be asked questions tending to show that he has committed any previous offence or has a bad character unless proof of such matters is in issue or the accused has sought to establish his own good character, has cast aspersions on the character of the prosecution or their witnesses, or has given evidence against someone else charged with the same offence.

After conviction, however, a police officer may give the court an *antecedents report* to assist in passing sentence. It should normally give details of the accused's age, education, employment, home circumstances, and previous convictions. It may contain statements that can be supported by first-hand evidence about the accused's reputation, although it may not contain general allegations. A copy of it is normally given to the accused.

antenuptial settlement *See* marriage settlement.

anticipatory breach *See* breach of contract.

Anton Piller order [from the case *Anton Piller KG* v *Manufacturing Processes* (1976)] An order made by the High Court (usually the Chancery Division) requiring a defendant to permit a plaintiff or his representatives to enter the defendant's premises to inspect or take away material evidence that the defendant might wish to remove or destroy in order to frustrate the plaintiff's claim, or to force a defendant to answer certain questions. The order is commonly used in cases where the copyright of video films or tapes is alleged to have been infringed. By statute the *privilege against self-incrimination does not apply.

apology *n.* A defence to an action for *defamation in cases of unintentional defamation, in which the defendant unintentionally and without negligence defamed the plaintiff, or in cases where a libel is published in a newspaper or periodical without malice or gross negligence. In addition to providing a defence in these cases, the fact that the defendant has made or offered to make an apology may always be taken into account in mitigation of damages.

a posteriori [Latin: from the later (i.e. from effect to cause)] Describing or re-

lating to reasoning based on deductions from observation or known facts. *Compare a priori.*

appeal *n.* An application for the judicial examination by a higher court of the decision of any inferior court. In modern English practice most appeals are dealt with by way of *rehearing, in which the appellate court notionally rehears the case tried before the inferior court, usually using a transcript or note of the evidence before the lower court instead of hearing the witnesses in person. It may in general make any order that the lower court could have made, but there are some statutory restrictions upon this power; for example, in criminal cases the Court of Appeal may not impose a more severe sentence than the trial court. Appellate courts are usually reluctant to overrule the decisions of trial courts on questions of fact even when they have the power to do so, and consequently most of the argument on appeals tends to be directed towards legal errors allegedly committed at the trial. In some cases (e.g. appeals by *case stated from magistrates' courts) the appeal may by law be confined to questions of law. Appeal may be contrasted with *review*, in which the higher court is confined to an examination of the *record of the inferior court's proceedings. *See also* appellate jurisdiction.

appearance *n.* Formerly, a stage in proceedings begun by *writ of summons and in some cases by *originating summons in the High Court in which the defendant submitted himself to the jurisdiction of the court and waived any irregularity in the originating process or its service. If the defendant failed to enter an appearance when the originating process had been properly served upon him, the plaintiff could obtain judgment in default. Appearance was abolished in 1979 and replaced by *acknowledgment of service and *notice of intention to defend.

21

appellant *n.* A person who makes an
*appeal to a court.

Appellate Committee *See* House of
Lords.

appellate jurisdiction The power of a
higher court to hear *appeals from inferior courts. In English law the following courts have appellate jurisdiction.
The *Crown Court hears appeals from
magistrates' courts; the *High Court
hears appeals by *case stated from
magistrates' courts and appeals from a
wide variety of tribunals on questions
of law only; the *Court of Appeal
(Criminal Division) hears appeals from
the Crown Court; the Court of Appeal
(Civil Division) hears appeals from the
county courts and from the High Court
in civil cases; and the.*House of Lords
hears appeals from the Court of Appeal
and from the High Court in criminal
cases. The House of Lords is also the
highest appellate court for Scotland
and Northern Ireland.

applying the proviso *See* proviso.

appointed day The date specified in an
Act of Parliament (or in a commencement order) for its coming into force.

appointee *n.* A person in whose favour
a *power of appointment is exercised.

appointment *n. See* power of appointment.

appointor *n.* A person given a *power
of appointment to exercise.

approbate and reprobate To accept
and reject. A person is not allowed to
accept the benefit of a document (e.g. a
deed of gift) but reject any conditions
attached to it.

appropriation *n.* The allocation of a
sum of money to a particular purpose.
The annual Appropriation Act authorizes the issue from the Consolidated
Fund of money required to meet government expenditure and allocates it
between departments and by reference
to itemized heads of expenditure.

appropriation of payments The allocation of one or more payments to one
particular debt out of several owed by a
debtor to the same creditor. The power
of allocation belongs in the first instance to the debtor, but if he does not
make an appropriation at the time of
payment, then the creditor may do so.
In the case of running accounts, in the
absence of an express appropriation,
payments are normally appropriated to
the oldest outstanding debt.

appropriations in aid Day-to-day revenue received by government departments and retained to meet expenditure
instead of being paid into the Consolidated Fund.

approvement *n.* The enclosure by the
lord of a manor for his own benefit of
waste land in his manor, thereby extinguishing other persons' rights (for example, of grazing cattle on the land enclosed). The lord's common-law right of
approvement can now only be exercised
with the consent of the Secretary of
State for the Environment after a local
inquiry.

approximation of laws The process
by which member states of the EEC
change their national laws to enable the
Common Market to function properly.
It is required by the Treaty of Rome.
Compare harmonization of laws.

appurtenant *adj.* Attached or annexed
to land and enhancing the land or its
use. An *easement must be appurtenant to a *dominant tenement but a
profit *à prendre* need not. Thus a right
of way over land in Yorkshire granted
to a Sussex landowner does not benefit
his Sussex property and is not an easement, but a right to shoot game over
the Yorkshire land could give a man in
Sussex (whether landowner or not) a
valid profit *à prendre*.

a priori [Latin: from the previous (i.e.
from cause to effect)] Describing or relating to reasoning that is based on abstract ideas, anticipates the effects of

particular causes, or (more loosely) makes a presumption that is true as far as is known. *Compare a posteriori.*

arbitration *n.* The determination of a dispute by one or more independent third parties (the *arbitrators*) rather than by a court. Arbitrators are appointed by the parties in accordance with the terms of the *arbitration agreement or in default by a court. An arbitrator is bound to apply the law accurately but may in general adopt whatever procedure he chooses and is not bound by the *exclusionary rules of the law of evidence; he must, however, conform to the rules of *natural justice. In English law, arbitrators are subject to extensive control by the courts, with respect to both the manner in which the arbitration is conducted and the correctness of the law that the arbitrators have applied. The judgment of an arbitrator is called his *award*, which can be the subject of an *appeal to the High Court on a question of law under the provisions of the Arbitration Act 1979. This Act abolished the old *special case procedure. In some types of arbitration it is the practice for both parties to appoint an arbitrator. If the arbitrators fail to agree about the matter in dispute, they will appoint an *umpire*, who has the casting vote in making the award.

English courts attach great importance to arbitration and will normally stay an action brought in the courts in breach of a binding arbitration agreement.

arbitration agreement A contract to refer a dispute to *arbitration. Such agreements are of two kinds: those referring an existing dispute to arbitration and those relating to disputes that may arise in the future. The second type is much more common. No particular form is necessary, but the agreement should name the place of arbitration and either appoint the arbitrator or arbitrators or (more usually) define the

manner in which they are to be appointed in the absence of agreement between the parties. The agreement should also set out the procedure for appointing an umpire if two arbitrators are involved and they fail to agree.

arbitration clause An express term of a contract in writing (usually of a commercial nature) constituting an agreement to refer disputes arising out of the contract to *arbitration.

Area Health Authorities *See* National Health Service.

argumentative affidavit An *affidavit containing not only allegations of fact but also arguments as to the bearing of those facts on the matter in dispute.

armchair principle A rule applied in the *interpretation of wills, enabling circumstances existing when the will was made to be used to prove the meaning of words appearing in the will. For example, such evidence may establish the identity of a beneficiary referred to in the will only by a nickname.

arraign *vb.* To begin a criminal *trial on indictment by calling the defendant to the bar of the court by name, reading the indictment to him, and asking him whether he is guilty or not. The defendant then pleads to the indictment, and this completes the arraignment.

arrangement *n. See* deed of arrangement; scheme of arrangement.

array *n. See* challenge to jury.

arrest *n.* The apprehension and detention of a person suspected of criminal activities. Most arrests are made by police officers, although anybody may, under prescribed conditions, effect a *citizen's arrest. In most cases the police officer must have a *warrant of arrest* signed by a magistrate, which must be shown to the accused. A warrant is not required for *arrestable offences or in certain situations authorized by statute or common law. For example, the

arrestable offence

Street Offences Act 1959 gives powers to arrest a prostitute soliciting in public, and the Road Traffic Act 1972 gives powers to arrest a motorist with an excessive blood alcohol level as ascertained by a *breathalyser test. When an arrest is made without a warrant, the accused must be told that he is being arrested and given the true reason for his arrest. A policeman has power to search the person he is arresting for any property that may be used in evidence against him. An arrested person must be taken to a police station and brought before a magistrates' court as soon as practicable – usually within 24 hours – or released on *bail. Anyone making or assisting in an arrest may use as much force as reasonable in the circumstances. A person who believes he is wrongfully arrested may petition for *habeas corpus and may sue the person who arrested him for *false imprisonment. *See also* Judges' Rules; remand.

arrestable offence An offence for which there is a fixed mandatory penalty (at the moment this applies only to murder and treason) or for which a sentence of imprisonment for a first offender is declared by statute to be at least five years (e.g. theft). However, a crime that carries a sentence of more than five years at common law, as opposed to statute (e.g. an attempt to pervert justice), is not an arrestable offence. There are also some crimes that are declared by statute to be arrestable offences even though they do not fulfil the usual conditions. For example, taking someone else's motor car for temporary use is arrestable even though it carries a maximum of only three years' imprisonment. An attempt to commit an arrestable offence and a conspiracy relating to such an offence are themselves arrestable offences. All other crimes are termed *nonarrestable offences*. Anyone may arrest, without warrant, a person who is in the act of committing an arrestable offence or whom he suspects to be in the act of committing it. If an arrestable offence has been committed, anyone may subsequently arrest a person who is, or whom he reasonably believes is, guilty of the offence. A police officer, in addition, may arrest someone who is about to commit (or whom he reasonably suspects is about to commit) such an offence. A police officer may also enter and search any place he suspects is harbouring a person who may be arrested for an arrestable offence.

There are also special offences of assisting a person guilty of an arrestable offence or concealing (for gain) information relating to such offences.

arrested development For the purposes of the Mental Health Act 1959, a form of *mental disorder comprising subnormality and severe subnormality. *Subnormality* implies a lack of intelligence that does not amount to severe subnormality but nevertheless requires or will respond to medical treatment. *Severe subnormality* is a lack of intelligence such that the person affected is incapable of living an independent life or of protecting himself against serious exploitation.

arrest of judgment A motion by a defendant in criminal proceedings on indictment, between the conviction and the sentence, that judgment should not be given on the ground of some objection arising on the face of the *record, such as a defect in the indictment itself. Such motions are extremely rare in modern practice.

arrived ship *See* lay days.

arson *n.* The intentional or reckless destruction or damaging of property by fire without a lawful excuse. There are two forms of arson corresponding to the two forms of *criminal damage in the Criminal Damage Act 1971. Damage by smoke is not arson. Arson carries a maximum sentence of life imprisonment.

articles of association Regulations for the management of registered companies (*see* Tables A; C; D; E). Under the Companies Act 1948 they constitute, together with the provisions of the *memorandum of association, a contract between company members and the company.

artificial person *See* juristic person.

ascertained goods *See* unascertained goods.

assault *n.* An intentional or reckless act that causes someone to expect to be subjected to immediate physical harm. Actual physical contact is not necessary to constitute an assault (for example, pointing a gun at someone is an assault), but the word is often loosely used to include both threatening acts and physical violence (*see* battery). Words alone cannot constitute an assault. Assault is a form of *trespass to the person and a crime as well as a tort: an *ordinary* (or *common*) *assault*, as described above, is punishable on indictment by up to one year's imprisonment. Certain kinds of more serious assault are known as *aggravated assaults* and carry stricter penalties. Examples of these are assault with intent to resist lawful arrest (two years), assault causing actual bodily harm (five years), and assault with intent to rob (life imprisonment). *See also* indecent assault.

Assembly of the European Communities (European Parliament) An institution of the EEC and other European Communities with purely deliberative, advisory, and supervisory functions. Its members are drawn from member states of the Communities but group themselves politically rather than nationally. In the case of the UK, the members are elected under the European Assembly Act 1978 for constituencies comprising two or more UK parliamentary constituencies. The Parliament is consulted by the *Council of Ministers on legislative proposals put to the Council by the *Commission of the European Communities; it gives opinions on these after debating reports from specialist committees, but these opinions are not binding. It may also put questions to the Council and the Commission and, by a motion of censure requiring a special majority, can force the resignation of the whole Commission (but not of individual Commissioners).

The Assembly meets in Strasbourg or Luxembourg about 12 times a year.

assent *n.* A document by which personal representatives transfer property to a beneficiary under a will or on intestacy. Under the Administration of Estates Act 1925 they may transfer land to beneficiaries by an assent in writing, which must be signed by the personal representatives but need not be sealed as a deed (*compare* conveyance). A beneficiary's title to the property is not complete until the assent has been effected.

assessor *n.* A person called in to assist a court in trying a case requiring specialized technical knowledge. The High Court and the Court of Appeal have wide powers to appoint assessors to assist them in any action, but this power is rarely exercised except in Admiralty cases. In cases involving questions of navigation and seamanship, it is the invariable practice to appoint assessors who are Elder Brethren of Trinity House; in proceedings to review a *taxation of costs a practising solicitor and a taxing master are usually appointed to assist the judge.

assets *pl. n.* The total property of a *juristic person. *See also* family assets; wasting assets.

assignee *n. See* assignment.

assignment *n.* **1.** The transfer of a *chose in action by one person (the *assignor*) to another (the *assignee*). By the rules of the common law, this was not permissible. If, for example, A was owed a contract debt by B, he could not transfer his right to C so as to enable C to sue B for the money owed. The assignment of certain choses in action is now authorized and governed by particular statutes. For example, the Companies Act 1948 allows shares in a company to be transferred in the manner prescribed by the company's articles of association. These, however, are special cases; in general, choses in action, whether legal (e.g. the benefit of a contract) or equitable (e.g. a right under a trust), can be transferred either by equitable assignment or, under the Law of Property Act 1925, by statutory assignment. For an *equitable assignment*, no formality is required. It is sufficient that the assignor shows a clear intention to transfer ownership of his right to the assignee. If, however, it is a legal chose that is assigned, the assignor must be made a party to any proceedings by the assignee to enforce the right. In the above example, C can sue B for the debt, but he must join A as co-plaintiff or (if A refuses to lend his name to the action in this way) as co-defendant. A *statutory assignment* under the Law of Property Act 1925 is sometimes referred to as a *legal assignment*, but since it may relate to an equitable chose in action as well as a legal one this is not wholly accurate. It enables the assignee to enforce the right assigned in his own name and without joining the assignor to the proceedings even if it is a legal chose. There are three requirements for its validity: it must be absolute; it must be in writing; and written notice of it must be given to the person against whom the right is enforceable. For these purposes, an *absolute assignment* is one that transfers the assignor's entire interest to the assignee unconditionally. If less than his entire interest (e.g. part of a debt) is transferred, or if any condition is attached to the transfer (e.g. that the consent of a third party be obtained), the assignment is not absolute. An assignment need not, however,

be permanent to be absolute, and this is exemplified by the mortgage of a chose in action. If A, who owes money to C, assigns to C as security for that debt a debt due to him from B, with the proviso that C will reassign the debt if A settles what is due to him, the assignment is absolute despite the proviso for reassignment.

The assignment of contractual rights (which must be distinguished from *novation) is subject to certain restrictions. For reasons of public policy, the holder of a public office must not assign his salary nor a wife her right to maintenance payments awarded in matrimonial proceedings. Rights to the performance of personal services, as under contracts of employment, are also incapable of being assigned.
2. The transfer of the whole of the remainder of the term of a lease. A tenant may assign his lease unless there is a covenant against it: there is often a covenant against assignment without the landlord's consent. The landlord cannot charge a fee for giving his consent unless there is express provision for this in the lease and he may not withhold his consent unreasonably. Less commonly, a lease may contain a covenant that prohibits any assignment at all.

assignor *n.* *See* assignment.

assisting an offender Doing anything intended to help a criminal or prevent his arrest or prosecution. Under the Criminal Law Act 1967 it is a statutory crime to assist someone who has committed an arrestable offence, knowing or believing that he has committed that offence or some other arrestable offence (for example, if X assists Y, whom he believes committed a murder when in fact Y committed a theft). Any act of assistance (e.g. providing food or a car, hiding someone, destroying evidence) will suffice. The statutory crime replaced the old common-law offence of being an *accessory after the fact.

assize *n.* Originally, a sitting of a court or council or an enactment made at such a sitting. In modern times assizes were sittings of High Court judges travelling on circuits around the country with commissions from the Crown to hear cases. These commissions were either of oyer, terminer, and general gaol delivery, empowering the judges to try the most serious criminal cases, or of *nisi prius*, empowering them to try civil actions. These assizes were abolished by the Courts Act 1971, and the criminal jurisdiction of assizes was transferred to the Crown Court. At the same time, the High Court was empowered to hear civil cases anywhere in England and Wales without the need for a special commission.

associated companies Under the Finance Act 1930, companies one of which is beneficial owner of 90% or more of the issued share capital (*see* authorized capital) of the other or in which 90% or more of the issued share capital of each is in the beneficial ownership of a third company. Transfers of property between such companies may be exempt from *stamp duty.

assurance *n. See* insurance.

assured tenancy A tenancy of a new house that has similar statutory protection to a *business tenancy. It only applies in the case of houses erected since 8 August 1980 and where the landlord is approved by the Secretary of State. Otherwise the usual *protected tenancy provisions apply.

at sea *See* privileged will.

attachment *n.* A court order for the detention of a person and/or his property. Attachment can be used by the courts for the punishment of *contempt of court. However, the most common form of attachment is *attachment of earnings*, by which a court orders the payment of judgment debts and other sums due under court orders (e.g. maintenance) by direct deduction from the

debtor's earnings. Payment is usually in instalments, and the debtor's employer is responsible for paying these to the court. *See also* garnishee proceedings.

attempt *n.* (in criminal law) Any act that is carried out with the intention of committing a crime and that constitutes partial or unsuccessful performance of the crime. For example, both drawing a revolver from one's pocket with the intention of shooting someone and shooting at someone but missing could be attempts, but merely buying a revolver would not. Attempt was formerly a crime at common law but under the Criminal Attempts Act 1981 is now a statutory crime.

attendance *n.* The provision of personal services by a landlord to a tenant, such as providing clean linen or cleaning services. If a substantial proportion of a tenant's rent is payment for attendance, the tenant merely has a *restricted contract rather than a *protected tenancy.

attendance centre A nonresidential institution run by a local authority at which offenders between the ages of 17 and 21 may be ordered by a juvenile court to attend if they have not previously been sentenced to prison, borstal, or detention in a detention centre or approved school. Attendance, which is outside normal school or working hours, is for periods of up to 3 hours each, to a maximum of 24 hours. Such orders are made when it is felt that a custodial order is not required but a fine or other order would be too lenient. Various changes in the law relating to attendance centres will come into effect when the relevant provisions of the Criminal Justice Act 1982 are brought into force.

attestation *n.* The signature of witnesses to the making of a will or deed. A will is not sealed as a deed but under the Wills Act 1837 must be signed or acknowledged (*see* acknowledgment) by the testator in the presence of two witnesses. The signature of each party to a deed is usually attested by one witness.

attorney *n.* A person who has authority to act on behalf of another. *See also* power of attorney.

Attorney General (AG) The principal law officer of the Crown. The Attorney General is usually a Member of Parliament of the ruling party and holds ministerial office, although he is not normally a member of the Cabinet. He is the chief legal adviser of the government and answers questions relating to legal matters in the House of Commons. He is the leader of the English Bar and presides at its general meetings. The consent of the Attorney General is required for bringing certain criminal actions, principally ones relating to offences against the state and public order and corruption. The Attorney General sometimes appears in court as an *advocate in cases of exceptional public interest, but he is not now allowed to engage in private practice. He has the right to terminate any criminal proceedings by entering a *nolle prosequi*. *See also* Director of Public Prosecutions; Solicitor General.

attornment *n.* **1.** An act by a bailee (*see* bailment) in possession of goods on behalf of one person acknowledging that he will hold the goods on behalf of someone else. The attornment notionally transfers possession to the other person (constructive possession) and can thus be a delivery of goods sold. **2.** A person's agreement to hold land as the tenant of someone else. Some mortgages provide that the owner of the land attorns tenant of the mortgagee for a period of years that will be terminated when the debt is repaid.

auction *n.* A method of sale in which parties are invited to make competing offers (*bids*) to purchase an item. The auctioneer, who acts as the agent of the

seller, announces completion of the sale in favour of the highest bidder by striking his desk with a hammer (or in any other customary manner). Until then any bidder may retract his bid and the auctioneer may withdraw the goods. The seller may not bid unless the sale is stated to be subject to the seller's right to bid. Merely to advertise an auction does not bind the auctioneer to hold one. However, if he advertises an auction without reserve and accepts bids, he will be liable if he fails to knock the item down to the highest outside bidder. An auctioneer who discloses his agency promises to a buyer that he has authority to sell and that he knows of no defect to the seller's title; he does not promise that the buyer of a specific chattel will get a good title. An auctioneer to whom a chattel is delivered undertakes to give possession to the buyer on receipt of payment and that possession will not be disturbed by either the seller or himself.

audi alteram partem See natural justice.

auditor *n.* A person appointed to examine the *books of account and the *accounts of a registered company and to report upon them to company members. An *auditor's report* must state whether or not, in the auditor's opinion, the accounts have been properly prepared and give a true and fair view of the company's financial position. The Companies Acts 1948–81 set out the qualifications an auditor must possess and also certain rights to enable him to fulfil his duty effectively.

authority *n.* **1.** Power delegated to a person or body to act in a particular way. **2.** A governing body, such as a *local authority. **3.** A judicial decision or other source of law used as a ground for a legal proposition. *See also* persuasive authority.

authorized capital (nominal capital) The total value of the shares that a registered company is authorized to issue in order to raise capital. The authorized capital of a company limited by shares (*see* limited company) must be stated in the memorandum of association, together with the number and nominal value of the shares. For example, an authorized capital of £20,000 may be divided into 20 000 shares of £1 (the *nominal value*) each or 40 000 shares of 50p each. If the company has issued 10 000 shares of £1, it is said to have an *issued capital* of £10,000 and retains the ability, wihout an increase in capital (*see* alteration of share capital), to issue further shares in future. If the company has received the full nominal value of the shares issued, its *paid-up capital* equals its issued capital. Where a company has not yet called for payment (*see* call) of the full nominal value, it has *uncalled capital*. *Reserve capital* is that part of the uncalled capital that the company has determined (by *special resolution) shall not be called up except upon a winding-up.

authorized investments Investments in which a trustee is permitted to invest trust property. Under the Trustee Investments Act 1961 (replacing earlier legislation, which did not give wide enough powers) trustees may invest not more than half the trust fund in shares in certain companies; the other half must be invested in *authorized securities*, certain debentures, local authority loans, etc. The settlor may, however, widen or narrow the choice of the trustees. Proper professional advice is desirable, except for placing money in such investments as National Savings Certificates and ordinary deposits in Trustee Savings Banks.

authorized securities *See* authorized investments.

automatic directions Directions of the court, relating to the preparations for trial of an action for personal injuries, that take effect automatically when the pleadings in the action are closed. They include such matters as the form of and time for *discovery and inspection of documents, exchange of the reports of expert witnesses, and the time for *setting down for trial. This procedure makes it unnecessary in most personal injury cases to take out a *summons for directions, unless some special order is sought.

automatism *n.* A state of mind in which someone is unable to control his actions. A person is not criminally liable for acts carried out in a state of automatism, since there is no *mens rea*. Automatism can be a defence even to crimes of *strict liability, since the act is involuntary and there is therefore no *actus reus*. Examples of such acts are those carried out while sleepwalking or in a state of concussion, a spasm or reflex action, and acts carried out by a diabetic who suffers a hypoglycaemic incident. Automatism is not a defence, however, if it is self-induced (for example, by taking drink or drugs). When automatism is caused by a disease of the mind, the defence is treated as one of *insanity.

autopsy *n. See* post-mortem.

autrefois acquit [French: previously acquitted] A *special plea in bar of arraignment claiming that the defendant has previously been acquitted by a court of competent jurisdiction of the same (or substantially the same) offence as that with which he is now charged or that he could have been convicted on an earlier indictment of the same (or substantially the same) offence. When this plea is entered a jury is empanelled to determine the issue. If the plea is successful it bars further proceedings on the indictment. The plea may be combined with one of *not guilty. *See also nemo debet bis vexari*.

autrefois convict [French: previously convicted] A *special plea in bar of arraignment claiming that the defendant has previously been convicted by a court of competent jurisdiction of the same (or substantially the same) offence as that with which he is now charged or that he could have been convicted on an earlier indictment of the same (or substantially the same) offence. When this plea is entered a jury is empanelled to determine the issue. If the plea is successful it bars further proceedings on the indictment. The plea may be combined with one of *not guilty. *See also nemo debet bis vexari.*

autre vie *See* estate *pur autre vie.*

auxiliary jurisdiction The jurisdiction exercised by the *Court of Chancery to aid a plaintiff at common law; for example, by forcing a defendant to reveal documents and thus provide necessary evidence for his case. Auxiliary jurisdiction was rendered obsolete by the Judicature Acts 1873–75.

average *n.* **1.** (in marine insurance) A loss or damage arising from an event at sea. **2.** A reduction in the amount payable under an insurance policy in respect of a partial loss of property. All marine insurance policies are subject to average under the Marine Insurance Act 1906; other policies may be subject to average if they contain express provision to that effect (an *average clause*).

In maritime law, the expression *general average* is used in relation to certain acts, to the losses they cause, and to the rights of contribution to which they give rise. A *general-average act* consists of any sacrifice or expenditure made intentionally and reasonably to preserve property involved in a sea voyage. For example, the jettisoning of some of a ship's cargo to keep it afloat during a storm is a general-average act. The loss directly resulting from a general-average act is called *general-average loss* and is borne proportionately by all whose property has been saved. The owner of jettisoned cargo, for example, is entitled to a contribution from other cargo owners as well as the shipowners; such a contribution is called a *general-*

average contribution. The principle of general average is common to the laws of all maritime nations, but the detailed rules are not uniform. To overcome conflict of law, a standard set of rules was agreed in the 19th century at international conferences of shipowners and others held at York and Antwerp. These, known as the *York–Antwerp rules,* do not have the force of law, but it is common practice to incorporate them (as subsequently amended) in contracts of *affreightment, thereby displacing national laws. The basic principle is that an insured who has suffered a general-average loss may recover the whole of it from his underwriters without enforcing his rights to contribution; these become enforceable by the underwriters instead.

By contrast, *particular average* relates purely to marine insurance. It consists of any partial loss that is not a general-average loss (for example, the damage of cargo by seawater). It is therefore borne purely by the person suffering it and is frequently covered by a policy only in limited circumstances.

a vinculo matrimonii [Latin] From the bond of marriage. A decree of divorce *a vinculo matrimonii* allowed a spouse to remarry and was the forerunner of the modern divorce decree. *See also a mensa et thoro.*

avoid *vb.* To set aside a *voidable contract.

avoidance of disposition order An order by the High Court preventing or setting aside a transaction by a husband or wife that was made to defeat his (or her) spouse's claim to financial provision. A transaction, such as a gift, made within three years before the application is presumed to have been made in order to defeat the spouse's claim if its effect would be to defeat her claim. But a sale of property to a purchaser in good faith will not be set aside.

award *n. See* arbitration.

B

backed for bail Describing a warrant for arrest issued by a magistrate or by the Crown Court to a police officer, directing him to release the accused, upon arrest, on bail under specified conditions. The police officer is bound to release the arrested person if his sureties are approved.

bail *n.* The release by the police, magistrates' court, or Crown Court of a person held in legal custody while awaiting trial or appealing against a criminal conviction. A person granted bail undertakes to pay a specified sum to the court if he fails to appear on the date set by the court (*see also* justifying bail). This is known as *bail in one's own recognizance*. Often the court also requires guarantors (known as *sureties*) to undertake to produce the accused or to forfeit the sum fixed by the court if they fail to do so. In these circumstances the bailed person is, in theory, released into the custody of the sureties. Judges have wide discretionary powers as to whether or not bail should be granted, and for what sum. Normally an accused is granted bail unless it is likely that he will abscond, or interfere with witnesses, or unless he is accused of a serious crime (such as rape) and is likely to repeat it if released. The accused has the right to appeal to the High Court against a refusal to grant him bail. The conditions governing bail are now contained in the Bail Act 1976.

bailee *n. See* bailment.

bail hostel Accommodation for persons of no fixed address who have been released on bail.

bailiff *n.* An officer of a court (usually a county court) concerned with the serv-ice of the court's processes and the enforcement of its orders, especially warrants of *execution authorizing the seizure of the goods of a debtor. The term is often loosely applied to a sheriff's officer.

bailiwick *n.* The area within which a *bailiff or *sheriff exercises jurisdiction.

bailment *n.* The transfer of the possession of goods by the owner (the *bailor*) to another (the *bailee*) for a particular purpose. Examples of bailments are the hiring of goods, the loan of goods, the pledge of goods, and the delivery of goods for carriage, safe custody, or repair. Ownership of the goods remains in the bailor, who has the right to demand their return or direct their disposal at the end of the period (if any) fixed for the bailment or (if no period is fixed) at will. This right will, however, be qualified by any *lien the bailee may have over the goods. Bailment exists independently of contract. But if the bailor receives payment for the bailment (a *bailment for reward*) there is often an express contract setting out the rights and obligations of the parties. A bailment for which the bailor receives no reward (e.g. the loan of a book to a friend) is called a *gratuitous bailment*.

bailor *n. See* bailment.

balance sheet A document presenting in summary form a true and fair view of a company's financial position at a particular time (e.g. at the end of its financial year). It must show the items listed in either of the two formats set out in the Companies Act 1981. Its purpose is to disclose the amount that would be available for the benefit of members if the company were immediately wound up and liabilities were discharged out of the proceeds of selling its assets. *See* accounts; accepted accountancy standards.

bank holidays Days that are declared holidays for the clearing banks and are kept as public holidays under the Banking and Financial Dealing Act 1971 or by royal proclamation under this Act. In England and Wales there are currently eight bank holidays a year: New Year's Day (or, if that is a Saturday or Sunday, the following Monday), Good Friday, Easter Monday, May Day (the first Monday in May), Spring Bank Holiday (the last Monday in May), Summer Bank Holiday (the last Monday in August), and Christmas Day and the following day (or, if Christmas Day is a Saturday or Sunday, the following Monday and Tuesday).

bankruptcy *n.* The state of a person who has been adjudged by a court to be insolvent (*compare* winding-up). The court orders the compulsory administration of a bankrupt's affairs so that his assets can be fairly distributed among his creditors. To declare a debtor to be bankrupt a creditor or the debtor himself must make an application (known as a *bankruptcy petition*) either to the High Court or to a county court. If a creditor petitions, he must show that the debtor owes him at least £200. The petition must usually show that the debtor has committed an *act of bankruptcy*, by which he has demonstrated his insolvency. Such acts include failing to comply with the requirements of a *bankruptcy notice, giving notice to his creditors that he has suspended, or is about to suspend, payment of his debts, *fraudulent preference, and *keeping house. If the petition is accepted, the court makes a *receiving order. This is followed by a preliminary examination by a court officer known as the *official receiver. The debtor then prepares a *statement of affairs. The creditors receive a copy of this statement and can question the debtor at a *public examination and at a meeting of creditors. At this meeting they may agree a *scheme of arrangement with the debtor. If no agreement is reached, the court subsequently makes an *adjudication order. The official receiver, or a *trustee in bank-

ruptcy approved by the creditors, then takes possession of all of the debtor's property and, subject to certain rules, distributes it among the creditors.

A bankrupt is subject to certain disabilities (*see* undischarged bankrupt). Bankruptcy is terminated when the court makes an order of *discharge.

bankruptcy notice A document issued by a court, on a creditor's request, that requires a debtor to pay the debt due to the creditor. The debt must be one in respect of which a court judgment or order has been made against the debtor. If the debtor fails to comply with the notice he commits an act of bankruptcy and the creditor is entitled to petition for the debtor's *bankruptcy.

bankruptcy petition An application to the High Court or a county court for a *receiving order to be made against an insolvent debtor. *See* bankruptcy.

banns *pl. n.* The public announcement in church of an intended marriage. Banns must be published for three successive Sundays if a marriage is to take place in the Church of England other than by religious licence or a superintendent registrar's certificate. *See also* marriage by certificate; marriage by religious licence.

bar *n.* **1.** A legal impediment. **2.** An imaginary barrier in a court of law. Only Queen's Counsel, officers of the court, and litigants in person are allowed between the bar and the *bench when the court is in session. *See also* Bar. **3.** A rail near the entrance to each House of Parliament beyond which nonmembers may not pass but to which they may be summoned (e.g. for reprimand).

Bar *n.* *Barristers, collectively. To be *called to the Bar* is to be admitted to the profession by one of the Inns of Court.

Bar Council (General Council of the Bar) A representative organization for furthering the interests of barristers. Since 1974 it has formed part of the

*Senate of the Inns of Court and the Bar, but continues to hold a separate annual general meeting.

bare licensee A person who occupies or has rights in land by permission of the owner but has no legal or equitable interest in the land. His rights are personal to him; thus he cannot transfer them without the landowner's consent. He cannot enforce them against a third party who acquires the land from the owner. His rights can be brought to an end, in the absence of agreement, on reasonable notice. The protection of tenants under the Rent Acts does not extend to bare licensees. *See also* licence.

bare trust (naked trust, simple trust) A trust in which the trustee has no obligation except to hand over the trust property to a person entitled to it, at the latter's request. This will occur when the beneficiary is of full age and under no disability and the trustee has no duties in respect of the property. *Compare* active trust.

barratry *n.* **1.** Any act committed wilfully by the master or crew of a ship to the detriment of its owner or charterer. Examples include scuttling the ship and embezzling the cargo. Barratry is one of the risks covered by policies of marine insurance. **2.** The former common-law offence (abolished by the Criminal Law Act 1967) of habitually raising or inciting disputes in the courts.

barring of entailed interest *See* entailed interest.

barrister *n.* A legal practitioner admitted to plead at the Bar. A barrister must be a member of one of the four *Inns of Court, by whom he is *called to the Bar* when admitted to the profession. The primary function of barristers is to act as *advocates for parties in courts or tribunals, but they also undertake the writing of opinions and some of the work preparatory to a trial. With rare exceptions a barrister may only act

upon the instructions of a *solicitor, who is also responsible for the payment of the barrister's fee. Barristers have the exclusive right of audience in courts of the level of the *High Court and above and in most cases in the *Crown Court. Barristers are either *Queen's Counsel (often referred to as *leaders* or *leading counsel*) or *junior barristers.

basic award *See* compensation.

bastard *n.* An illegitimate child, born either to a woman who was unmarried at the time of its conception and birth, or as a result of adultery, or (in some cases) to a woman whose marriage is legally void. A bastard may become legitimate by the process of *legitimation. *See also* illegitimacy; legitimacy.

battered child A child subjected to physical violence or abuse by a parent, step-parent, or any other person with whom he is living. A battered child may be protected if the other parent (or person who is looking after him) applies for an injunction under the 1976 Domestic Violence and Matrimonial Proceedings Act, but only if the child is living with the applicant. The Act does not set any age limit. Alternatively, but only if the parties are married and the child is their child or is treated by them as a *child of the family, an application may be made to the magistrates' courts under the 1978 Domestic Proceedings and Magistrates' Courts Act (for the terms of both Acts, *see* battered wife). When a child is being or is likely to be ill-treated, a juvenile court may also make a supervision order or care order. *See also* care proceedings.

battered wife A woman subjected to physical violence by her husband. A battered wife (or one afraid of future violence) may now seek protection in a number of ways. She can apply to the court for a *nonmolestation order*, directing her husband not to molest, annoy, or use violence against her, or for an *exclusion order*, excluding her husband from the matrimonial home for a limited time (even if he is the sole legal owner). She can, however, only apply for these orders if she is also applying for some other matrimonial relief (e.g. a divorce petition). The court also has power, under the Matrimonial Homes Act 1967, to grant an order prohibiting, suspending, or restricting the husband's right to occupy the house. Under the 1976 Domestic Violence and Matrimonial Proceedings Act a battered wife can apply to the county court for a nonmolestation order or exclusion order, even if no other matrimonial relief is sought and no action brought in tort or criminal law. When an exclusion order or a nonmolestation order is made, and when the husband has previously caused his wife physical harm, the judge may, under the 1976 Act, also attach a power of arrest without warrant on reasonable suspicion that the husband is in breach of the injunction. In cases of emergency an *ex parte* injunction may be granted. Finally, the wife may apply to the magistrates' courts for a *personal protection order* (for protection against violence by her husband) if violence has already been used or threatened. Under more restrictive conditions of the 1978 Domestic Proceedings and Magistrates' Courts Act, magistrates may grant an exclusion order or attach a power of arrest to it.

The powers of the county courts and magistrates' courts also apply to "battered husbands" and, in the case of the county courts under the 1976 Act, to unmarried cohabitees ("battered mistresses").

battery *n.* The intentional or negligent application of physical force to someone without his consent. Battery is a form of *trespass to the person and is a crime as well as a tort, even if no actual harm results. If actual harm does result, however, the consent of the victim may not prevent the act from being criminal, except when the injury is inflicted in the course of properly conducted sports or

games (e.g. rugby or boxing) or as a result of reasonable surgical intervention. *Compare* assault; grievous bodily harm.

bearer *n.* The person in possession of a bill of exchange or promissory note that is payable to the bearer.

Beddoe order [from the case *re Beddoe* (1892)] An order made by the court granting trustees permission to bring or defend an action. The order protects the trustees against claims by the beneficiaries that the action should not have been brought and enables them to recover their costs from the trust property. If an order has not been obtained, these consequences may not follow.

bench *n.* **1.** Literally, the seat of a judge in court. The bench is usually in an elevated position at one side of the court room facing the seats of counsel and solicitors. **2.** A group of judges or magistrates sitting together in a court, or all judges, collectively. Thus a barrister who has been appointed a judge is said to have been *raised to the bench*.

Benchers (Masters of the Bench) *pl. n.* Judges and senior practitioners who form a governing body for each of the Inns of Court. They are recruited by co-option and elect one of their number annually to be the Treasurer. Benchers exercise disciplinary powers over the members of the Inn.

bench warrant A warrant for the arrest of a person who has failed to attend court when summoned or subpoenaed to do so or against whom an order of committal for contempt of court has been made and who cannot be found. The warrant is issued during a sitting of the court.

beneficial interest The rights of a beneficiary in respect of the property held in trust for him. *See also* equitable interests.

beneficial owner An owner who is entitled to the use of land or its income for his own benefit. Under the Law of

Property Act 1925 a person who for valuable *consideration conveys land as beneficial owner gives implied covenants (1) that he has the right to convey it; (2) for quiet enjoyment (i.e. that the transferee takes possession free from adverse claims to the land); (3) that the land is free from encumbrances other than any specified in the conveyance; (4) for further assurance (i.e. that the transferor will do anything necessary to cure any defect in the conveyance); and (5) when the land is leasehold (a) that the lease is valid and (b) that the convenants in the lease have been performed and the rent paid. When the owner of a legal estate is not the beneficial owner (e.g. a mortgagee, trustee, or personal representative) his only implied covenant in a conveyance of the land is that he has not himself created any encumbrance.

beneficiary *n.* **1.** A person entitled to benefit from a *trust. A beneficiary was formerly known as the *cestui que trust*. **2.** One who benefits from a will.

benevolent purposes Purposes that are for the public good but not necessarily charitable. They are wider than *philanthropic purposes. *See* charitable trust.

Benjamin order [from the case *re Benjamin* (1902)] An order made by the court for the distribution of assets on death when it is uncertain whether or not a beneficiary is alive. The order authorizes the personal representatives of the deceased (who will be administering the estate) to distribute the property on the basis that the beneficiary is dead (or on some other basis); the personal representatives are thus protected from being sued if the beneficiary is in fact alive and entitled. The beneficiary may, however, trace the trust property (*see* tracing trust property).

bequeath *vb.* To dispose by will of property other than land. *Compare* devise.

bequest *n.* A gift by will of property other than land. *Compare* devise. *See* legacy.

best-evidence rule A rule requiring that a party must call the best evidence that the nature of the case will allow. Formerly of central importance, in modern law it is largely confined to the requirement that the original of a private document must be produced in order to prove its contents; if it cannot be produced its absence must be explained.

bestiality *n.* Anal or vaginal intercourse by a man or a woman with an animal. Bestiality is a crime if penetration is proved. *See also* buggery.

beyond the seas Outside the UK, Channel Islands, and Isle of Man. When a party seeks to introduce *hearsay evidence under the provisions of the Civil Evidence Acts 1968–72, he cannot be required to call the maker of the hearsay statement as a witness if that person is absent beyond the seas.

bias *n.* *See* natural justice.

bid *n.* *See* auction.

bigamy *n.* The act of going through a marriage ceremony with someone when one is already lawfully married to someone else. Bigamy is a crime, punishable by up to seven years' imprisonment; however, there is a defence if the accused honestly and reasonably believed that his or her first spouse was dead or that their previous marriage had been dissolved or annulled or was void. There is also a special defence if the accused's spouse has been absent for at least seven years, and is therefore presumed by the accused to be dead, even if he does not have positive proof of the death. Even though a person is found not guilty of the crime of bigamy, the bigamous marriage will still be void if that person had a spouse living at the time that the second marriage was celebrated.

bilateral discharge The ending of a contract by agreement, when neither party has yet performed his obligations under it (an *executory contract*). Each party supplies consideration for the agreement to discharge by releasing the other from his existing obligations. *Compare* unilateral discharge (*see* accord and satisfaction).

bill *n.* **1.** Any of various written instruments; for example, a *bill of exchange, a *bill of indictment, or a *bill of lading. **2.** A written account of money owed; for example, a *bill of costs.

Bill *n.* A draft of a proposed *Act of Parliament, which must (normally) be passed by both Houses before becoming an Act. Bills are either public or private, and the procedure governing their passing by Parliament depends basically on this distinction. In general, a *public Bill* is one relating to matters of general concern; it is introduced by the government or by a private member (*private member's Bill*). In the House of Commons the government sets aside certain Fridays for debate on private member's Bills, and a ballot at the beginning of each session of Parliament determines the members whose Bills are to have priority on those days. A public Bill, unless predominantly financial, can be introduced in either House. It is presented by the minister or other member in charge, passed by being read three times, and then sent to the other House. Its first reading is a formality, but it is debated on second and third readings, between which it goes through a Committee stage and a Report stage during which amendments may be made. A Bill that has not become an Act by the end of the session lapses; if reintroduced in a subsequent session, it must go through all stages again.

A *private Bill* is one designed to benefit a particular person, local authority, or other body, by whom it is presented. It is introduced on a petition by the promoter, which is preceded by public advertisement and by notice to those directly affected. Its Committee stage in the first House is conducted before a small group of members, and evidence for and against it is heard. Thereafter, it follows the procedure for public Bills.

A *hybrid Bill* is a government bill that is purely local or personal in character and affects only one of a number of interests in the same class. For example, a government Bill to nationalize one only of several private-sector airlines would be hybrid. A hybrid Bill proceeds as a public Bill until after second reading in the first House, after which it is treated similarly to a private Bill.

bill of costs An account of *costs prepared by a solicitor in respect of legal services he has rendered his client. In general a solicitor may be required to furnish his client with a bill unless they have made an agreement in writing to the contrary. If no such agreement has been made the solicitor may not, without the leave of the High Court, sue for *recovery of costs* until one month after the bill of costs has been delivered. In contentious (i.e. litigious) matters the bill is subject to *taxation by the court. *See also* costs draftsman.

bill of exchange An unconditional order in writing, addressed by one person (the *drawer*) to another (the *drawee*) and signed by the person giving it, requiring the drawee to pay on demand or at a future time a specified sum of money to or to the order of a specified person (the *payee*) or to the bearer. If the bill is payable at a future time the drawee signifies his *acceptance, which makes him the party primarily liable upon the bill; the drawer and endorsers may also be liable upon a bill. The use of bills of exchange enables one person to transfer to another an enforceable right to a sum of money. A bill of exchange is not only transferable but also negotiable, since if a person without an enforceable right to the money transfers a bill to a *holder in due course, the latter obtains a good title to it. Much of the law on bills of exchange is codified by the Bills of Exchange Act 1882.

bill of indictment A formal written accusation charging someone with an *indictable offence. The usual method of preferring a bill of indictment (i.e. bringing it before the appropriate court) is by committal proceedings before a magistrates' court (*see* committal for trial). *See also* indictment.

bill of lading A document acknowledging the shipment of a consignor's goods for carriage by sea. It is used primarily when the ship is carrying goods belonging to a number of consignors (a general ship). In this case, each consignor receives a bill issued (normally by the master of the ship) on behalf of either the shipowner or a charterer under a *charterparty. The bill serves three functions: it is a receipt for the goods; it summarizes the terms of the contract of carriage; and it acts as a document of title to the goods. A bill of lading is also issued by a shipowner to a charterer who is using the ship for the carriage of his own goods. In this case, the terms of the contract of carriage are in the charterparty and the bill serves only as a receipt and a document of title. During transit, ownership of the goods may be transferred by delivering the bill to another if it is drawn to bearer or by endorsing it if it is drawn to order. The responsibilities, liabilities, rights, and immunities attaching to carriers under bills of lading are stated in the *Hague Rules*. These were drawn up by the International Law Association meeting at The Hague in 1921 and adopted by an International Conference on Maritime Law held at Brussels in 1922. They were given effect in the UK by the Carriage of Goods by Sea Act 1924 and so became known in the UK as the Hague Rules of 1924. They were amended at Brussels in 1968. The Rules, which are set out in a schedule to the Act, apply to carriage under a bill

of lading from any port in Great Britain or Northern Ireland to any other port and also to carriage between any of the states by which they have been adopted. Every bill issued in Great Britain or Northern Ireland to which the Rules apply must state that fact expressly (the clause giving effect to this requirement is customarily referred to as the *paramount clause*).

bill of sale A document by which a person transfers the ownership of goods to another. Commonly the goods are transferred conditionally, as security for a debt, and a *conditional bill of sale* is thus a mortgage of goods. The mortgagor has a right to redeem the goods on repayment of the debt and usually remains in possession of them; he may thus obtain false credit by appearing to own them. An *absolute bill of sale* transfers ownership of the goods absolutely and the grantor of the bill cannot retake possession of them. The Bills of Sale Acts 1878 and 1882 regulate the registration and form of bills of sale.

bind over To order a person to provide a bond or *recognizance by means of which he guarantees to carry out some act (e.g. to appear in court at the proper time if he has been granted bail) or not to commit some offence (such as causing a breach of the peace).

birth *n. See* proof of birth; registration of birth.

blackmail *n.* The crime of making an unwarranted demand with menaces for the purpose of financial gain for oneself or someone else or financial loss to the person threatened. The menaces may include a threat of violence or of detrimental action, e.g. exposure of past immorality or misconduct. Blackmail is punishable by up to 14 years' imprisonment. As long as the demand is made with menaces, it will be presumed to be unwarranted, unless the accused can show both that he thought he was reasonable in making the demand and that he thought it was reasonable to use the menaces as a means of pressure. Under the Administration of Justice Act 1970, there is also a special statutory crime of *harassment of debtors.

Black Rod, Gentleman Usher of the An official of the House of Lords whose title derives from his staff of office – an ebony rod surmounted with a gold lion. The office originated as usher of the Order of the Garter in the 14th century; the parliamentary appointment dates from 1522. Black Rod is responsible for maintaining order in the House and summons members of the Commons to the Lords to hear a speech from the throne.

blasphemy *n.* Statements or writings that deny – in an offensive or insulting manner – the truth of the Christian religion, the Bible, the Book of Common Prayer, or the existence of God. Blasphemy is a crime at common law, and if it is published there is no need to show an intention to shock or insult or an awareness that the publication is blasphemous. Prosecutions for blasphemy are now rare and it has been suggested that the crime be abolished.

blight notice A statutory notice by which an owner-occupier can require a public authority to purchase land that is potentially liable to compulsory acquisition by them and therefore cannot be sold at full value on the open market. The land may, for example, be shown in a development plan to be prospectively required for the authority's purposes or it may be designated in published proposals as the site of a future highway.

blood relationship *See* consanguinity.

blood specimen *See* specimen of blood.

blood test 1. An analysis of blood designed to show that a particular man could not be the father of a specified child (it cannot establish that the per-

son *is* the father). The court may order blood tests in disputes about paternity, but a man cannot be compelled to undergo the test against his will. His refusal may, however, lead the court to draw adverse conclusions. **2.** *See* specimen of blood.

blue book A form of government publication, such as a report of a committee, inquiry, or royal commission, published in blue covers.

body corporate *See* corporation.

bomb hoax A deception in which one or more people are led to believe that an explosion is likely to occur that will cause physical injury or damage to property. A bomb hoax may constitute *blackmail (if accompanied by a demand), public nuisance, threats to damage property (an offence under the Criminal Damage Act 1971), or wasting the time of the police (under the Criminal Law Act 1967). Under the Criminal Law Act 1977 it is now a special statutory offence, punishable by a fine of up to £1000 or imprisonment for up to five years, to place or send an object anywhere with the intention of leading someone to believe that it is likely to explode and cause harm. It is also an offence falsely to tell anyone that a bomb has been placed in a certain place or that some other object is liable to explode.

bona vacantia [Latin: empty goods] Property not disposed of by a deceased's will and to which there is no relation entitled on intestacy. Under the Administration of Estates Act 1925, such property passes to the Crown or to the Duchies of Lancaster or Cornwall. In practice it is usually used to provide for dependants of the deceased and anyone else for whom he might reasonably have been expected to provide.

bond *n.* **1.** A deed by which one person (the *obligor*) commits himself to another (the *obligee*) to do something or refrain from doing something. If it secures the payment of money, it is called a *common money bond*; a bond giving security for the carrying out of a contract is called a *performance bond*. **2.** A document issued by a government, local authority, or other public body undertaking to repay long-term debt with interest.

bonus issue (capitalization issue) A method of increasing a company's issued capital (*see* authorized capital) by issuing further shares to existing company members. These shares are paid for not by the shareholders but out of undistributed profits of the company or the *share premium account. The bonus issue is made to shareholders in proportion to their existing shareholding (e.g. a 1 for 2 bonus issue means that shareholders receive an extra free share for every two shares they hold).

books of account Records that disclose and explain a company's financial position at any time and enable its directors to prepare its *accounts. The books (which registered companies are required to keep by the Companies Acts) should reveal, on a day-to-day basis, sums received and expended together with details of the transaction, assets and liabilities, and (where appropriate) goods sold and purchased. Public companies must preserve their books for six years, private companies for three years. Company members have no statutory right to inspect the books; the *articles of association could confer such a right but rarely do.

borough *n.* An area of local government, abolished as such (except in *Greater London) by the Local Government Act 1972. A *district may, however, be styled a borough by royal charter.

borough court The *court of record for a borough. All remaining borough courts were abolished by the Local Government Act 1972.

borstal *n.* An institution to which

young offenders (aged 15 to 20 inclusive) may be sent instead of prison. Borstals are custodial institutions, not as strict as adult prisons, that are designed to train offenders for some activity after release. A young offender may be sentenced to borstal when convicted in a Crown Court, or when committed to the Crown Court for sentence after conviction in a magistrates' court. Borstal training is for a minimum period of six months and a maximum of two years; the sentence must include supervision after release for two years, subject to specified conditions (breach of which may result in immediate recall to borstal).

Borstals and borstal orders will be phased out when provisions of the Criminal Justice Act 1982 are brought into force and will be replaced by detention centre orders and youth custody orders. *See* juvenile offender.

bottomry *n. See* hypothecation.

boundary commissions Independent bodies established under the House of Commons (Redistribution of Seats) Acts 1949 and 1958 to carry out periodic reviews of parliamentary constituencies for the purpose of recommending boundary changes to take account of shifts in population. There are separate commissions for England, Wales, Scotland, and Northern Ireland. *Compare* local government boundary commissions.

breach of close Entry on another's land without permission: a form of *trespass to land. A close is a piece of land separated off from land owned by others or from common land.

breach of confidence 1. The disclosure of confidential information. **2.** Failure to observe an injunction granted by the court to prevent this. The injunction is most commonly granted to protect trade information (except patents, registered designs, and copyrights, which are protected under statute), but may also be granted, for example, to protect the secrecy of communications made between husband and wife during marriage.

breach of contract An actual failure by a party to a contract to perform his obligations under that contract or an indication of his intention not to do so. An indication that a contract will be breached in the future is called *repudiation* or an *anticipatory breach*, and may be either expressed in words or implied from conduct. Such an implication arises when the only reasonable inference from a person's acts is that he does not intend to fulfil his part of the bargain. For example, an anticipatory breach occurs if a person contracts to sell his car to A, but sells and delivers it to B before the delivery date agreed with A. The repudiation of a contract entitles the injured party to treat the contract as discharged and to sue immediately for *damages for the loss sustained. The same procedure only applies to an actual breach if it constitutes a *fundamental breach*, i.e. a breach of a major term (*see* condition) of the contract. In either an anticipatory or an actual breach, the injured party may, however, decide to *affirm the contract instead. When an actual breach relates only to a minor term of the contract (a warranty) the injured party may sue for damages but has no right to treat the contract as discharged. The process of treating a contract as discharged by reason of repudiation or actual breach is sometimes referred to as *rescission or repudiation, but this latter term is clearly confusing. Other remedies available under certain circumstances for breach of contract are an *injunction and *specific performance. *See also* procuring breach of contract.

breach of privilege *See* parliamentary privilege.

breach of statutory duty Breach of a duty imposed on some person or body by a statute. The person or body in

breach of the statutory duty is liable to the criminal penalty imposed by the statute, but may also be liable to pay damages to the person injured by the breach if he belongs to the class for whose protection the statute was passed. Not all statutory duties give rise to civil actions for breach. If the statute does not deal with the matter expressly, the courts must decide whether or not Parliament intended to confer civil remedies. Most actions for breach of statutory duty arise out of statutes dealing with *safety at work.

breach of the peace A riot, affray, assault, battery, or any other act in which people's safety is put at risk. It is an offence, punishable by up to six months' imprisonment or a maximum fine of £1000 (or both), to use threatening, abusive, or insulting words or behaviour in a public place that are intended or likely to provoke a breach of the peace. A police officer may arrest without warrant someone committing a breach of the peace, and it is an offence for anyone to refuse to go to his assistance when asked to do so. He may also arrest members of an *unlawful assembly if he reasonably suspects that there will be a breach of the peace. It is an offence to assault or wilfully obstruct a police officer who is attempting to prevent a breach of the peace.

breach of trust Any improper act or omission, contrary to his duty, by a trustee or other person in a fiduciary position. A breach need not be deliberate or dishonest. In all cases the trustee is personally responsible to the beneficiaries and is liable for any loss caused to the trust. Any profit made by a trustee by virtue of his position must be handed to the trust, even when the trust has suffered no loss.

break clause A clause often contained in *fixed-term tenancy agreements that provides for an option to terminate the tenancy at a particular time or when a particular event occurs.

breakdown of marriage The deterioration of a marriage to such an extent that the court will grant a decree of *divorce. The breakdown must be *irretrievable*, which can be shown only by proof of one of the following facts: (1) that the other spouse has committed *adultery *and* that the petitioner finds it intolerable (either because of the adultery or for some other reason) to live with him (or her); (2) that the other spouse has behaved in such a way that the petitioner (taking into account his (or her) particular characteristics and circumstances) cannot reasonably be expected to live with her (or him) (*see* unreasonable conduct); (3) that the other spouse has deserted the petitioner for at least two years (*see* desertion); (4) that the spouses have lived apart for at least two years (if the other spouse agrees to the divorce petition) of for five years (even if the other spouse does not agree to the petition). The spouses may live together for up to six months during the period of separation without breaking the period of living apart, but the time spent together cannot itself count towards the period of living apart.

breathalyser *n.* A device, approved by the Secretary of State, that is used in the preliminary *breath test to measure the amount of alcohol in a driver's breath. The devices currently approved are the "Alcotest R 80", "Alcotest R 80 A", "Alcolyser", "Alcolmeter", and "Alert" appliances. They each consist basically of a tube that contains potassium dichromate crystals and is attached to a balloon. The suspected driver is asked to blow through the tube to inflate the balloon in one breath, but the device should not be used within 20 minutes after consuming alcohol or on a suspect who has just been smoking. The crystals change colour if there is alcohol in the breath; if the colour change extends beyond a line marked on the tube the suspect is considered to have a blood alcohol level over the legal limit.

breath specimen *See* specimen of breath.

breath test A preliminary test applied by a uniformed police officer by means of a *breathalyser to a driver whom he suspects has alcohol in his body in excess of the legal limit, has committed a traffic offence while the car was moving, or has driven a motor vehicle involved in an accident. The test may be administered on the spot to someone either actually driving, attempting to drive, or in charge of a motor vehicle on a road or public place or suspected by the police officer of having done so in the above circumstances. If the test proves positive (*see* drunken driving), the police officer may arrest the suspect without a warrant and take him to a police station, where further investigations may take place (*see* specimen of breath). It is an offence to refuse to submit to a breath test unless there is some reasonable excuse (usually a medical reason), and a police officer may arrest without warrant anyone who refuses the test. The offence is punishable by a fine, endorsement (carrying 4 points under the *totting-up system), and discretionary disqualification. A police officer has the power to enter any place in order to apply the breath test to someone he suspects of having been involved in an accident in which someone else was injured or to arrest someone who refused the test or whose test was positive.

brewster sessions The annual meetings of justices to deal with the grant, renewal, and transfer of licences to sell intoxicating liquor. *See* licensing of premises.

bribery and corruption Offences relating to the improper influencing of people in certain positions of trust. The offences commonly grouped under this expression are now statutory. Under the Public Bodies Corrupt Practices Act 1889 (amended by the Prevention of Corruption Act 1916) it is an offence, if done corruptly (i.e. deliberately and with an improper motive), to give or offer to a member, officer, or servant of a public body any reward or advantage to do anything in relation to any matter with which that body is concerned; it is also an offence for a public servant or officer to corruptly receive or solicit such a reward. The Prevention of Corruption Act 1906 (amended by the 1916 Act) is wider in scope. It relates to agents, which include not only those involved in the business of agency but also all employees, including anyone serving under the Crown or any public body. Under this Act it is an offence to corruptly give or offer any valuable consideration to an agent to do any act or show any favour in relation to his principal's affairs; like the 1889 Act, it also creates a converse offence of receiving or soliciting by agents.

bridle way Under the Highways Act 1959, a *highway over which the public has a right of way on foot and a right of way on horseback or leading a horse, with or without a right to drive animals along the highway.

brief *n.* A document by which a solicitor instructs a barrister to appear as an advocate in court. Unless the client is receiving legal aid, the brief must be marked with a fee that is paid to counsel whether he is successful or not. A brief usually comprises a *backsheet*, typed on large brief-size paper giving the title of the case and including the solicitor's instructions, which is wrapped around the other papers relevant to the case. The whole bundle is tied up with red tape in the case of a private client and white tape if the brief is from the Crown.

Bristol Tolzey Court An ancient court of the City of Bristol that had unlimited civil jurisdiction over matters arising within the city. It was abolished by the Courts Act 1971.

British citizenship One of three new forms of citizenship introduced by the British Nationality Act 1981 to replace citizenship of the UK and Colonies. The others are *British Dependent Territories citizenship and *British Overseas citizenship.

On the date on which it came into force (1 January 1983), the Act conferred British citizenship automatically on every existing citizen of the UK and Colonies who was entitled to the right of abode in the UK under the Immigration Act 1971 (*see* immigration). As from that date, there have been four principal ways of acquiring the citizenship – by birth, by descent, by registration, and by naturalization. A person acquires it by birth only if he is born in the UK and his father or mother is either a British citizen or settled in the UK (i.e. resident there, and not restricted by the immigration laws as to length of stay). If born outside the UK, he acquires it by descent if one of his parents has British citizenship (but not, normally, if that citizenship was itself acquired by descent). Registration may be applied for by a minor, but adults are eligible only if they have particular links with the UK. In some cases (e.g. British Dependent Territories citizens, British Overseas citizens, British protected persons, and British subjects with certain residential qualifications), it is a right; in others, it is at the discretion of the Secretary of State. Any adult may apply for naturalization but there are residential and other requirements (e.g. proof of good character), and its grant is always discretionary.

A registered or naturalized citizen may be deprived of his citizenship if he obtained it improperly, behaves disloyally, or is sentenced during the first five years to imprisonment exceeding one year.

British Commonwealth *See* Commonwealth.

British Dependent Territories citizenship One of three new forms of citizenship introduced by the British Nationality Act 1981 to replace citizenship of the UK and Colonies. The others are *British citizenship and *British Overseas citizenship. The dependent territories for the purposes of this form of citizenship are listed in a schedule to the Act; they include Hong Kong and Gibraltar, among others.

On the date on which it came into force (1 January 1983), the Act conferred the citizenship automatically on a large number of existing citizens of the UK and Colonies on the grounds of birth, registration, or naturalization in a dependent territory or descent from a parent or grandparent who had that citizenship on one of those grounds. As from that date, acquisition (and deprivation in the case of registered or naturalized citizens) have been governed by principles similar to those applying to British citizenship, except that acquisition by registration relates almost exclusively to minors. A British Dependent Territories citizen can become entitled to registration as a British citizen by virtue of UK residence.

British Overseas citizenship One of three new forms of citizenship introduced by the British Nationality Act 1981 to replace citizenship of the UK and Colonies. On the date on which it came into force (1 January 1983), the Act conferred the citizenship automatically on every existing citizen of the UK and Colonies who did not qualify for either of the other new forms (*British citizenship and *British Dependent Territories citizenship). Acquisition as from that date has been by registration only, and this is confined almost completely to minors. A British Overseas citizen may become entitled to registration as a British citizen by virtue of UK residence.

British protected person One of a class of people defined as such by an order under the British Nationality Act 1981 or the Solomon Islands Act 1978 because of their connection with former protectorates, protected states, and trust territories. A British protected person may become entitled to registration as a British citizen by reason of UK residence.

British subject Under the British Nationality Act 1948, a secondary status that was common to all who were primarily citizens either of the UK and Colonies or of one of the independent Commonwealth countries. This status was also shared by a limited number of people who did not have any such primary citizenship, including former British subjects who were also citizens of Eire (as it then was) or who could have acquired one of the primary citizenships but did not in fact do so.

Under the British Nationality Act 1981 (which replaced the 1948 Act as from 1 January 1983), the status of British subject was confined to those who had enjoyed it under the former Act without having one of the primary citizenships; the expression *commonwealth citizen was redefined as a secondary status of more universal application. The Act provided for minors to be able to apply for registration as British subjects and for British subjects to become entitled to registration as British citizens by virtue of UK residence.

Broadmoor A *special hospital for the criminally insane at Crowthorne, near Camberley, in Berkshire.

brothel *n.* A place used for the purpose of female or male *prostitution. A contract for the hiring or letting of a brothel is void (as being contrary to public policy) and it is an offence for a landlord to let premises knowing that they are to be used as a brothel. It is also an offence for someone to help or manage a brothel or for a tenant or occupier of any premises to permit the premises to be used as a brothel.

buggery (sodomy) *n.* Anal intercourse by a man with another man or a

building lease

woman or *bestiality by a man or a woman. Except between consenting adult males (*see* homosexual conduct), buggery is a crime if penetration is proved (it is not necessary for there to be ejaculation). The person effecting the intercourse is guilty as the *agent*, and the other party is called (and is guilty as) the *patient*. However, criminal proceedings are not brought without the consent of the Director of Public Prosecutions against anyone under 21 for participating in buggery. It is also an offence (punishable by up to 10 years' imprisonment) to assault anyone with the intention of committing buggery. *See also* indecency; gross indecency; indecent assault.

building lease A lease, usually for 99 years, under which the tenant covenants to erect specified buildings on the land. At the end of the lease the buildings become the property of the landlord. The tenant may, however, acquire a statutory right to purchase the freehold under the Leasehold Reform Act 1967. *See also* ground rent.

building preservation notice A notice by a local planning authority (*see* town and country planning) that places a building regarded as suitable for listing and in danger of demolition or alteration under temporary control as a *listed building, pending a decision on its listing by the Secretary of State.

building scheme A defined area of land sold by a single vendor in plots for (or following) development, each plot being sold subject to similar *restrictive covenants that are clearly intended to benefit the whole. For example, restrictive covenants prohibiting trade or excessive noise are frequently imposed on the sale of plots on a housing estate, to maintain the character of the estate as a whole. The law allows the owner of any plot in a building scheme to enforce such covenants against any other plot owner, even though neither was a party

to the document that imposed the covenants.

building society A corporation established under the Building Societies Acts 1874 and 1962 for the purpose of making loans to its members on the security of mortgages on their homes, out of funds invested by its members. Generally a building society's security must be a first legal mortgage on the borrower's home.

Bullock order [from the case *Bullock* v *London General Omnibus Co.* (1907)] A form of order for the payment of costs in civil cases sometimes made when the plaintiff has, in the court's opinion, reasonably sued two defendants but has succeeded against only one of them. The order requires the plaintiff to pay the successful defendant's costs but allows him to include these costs in those payable to him by the unsuccessful defendant. It should be distinguished from a *Sanderson order* (from the case *Sanderson* v *Blyth Theatre Co.* (1903)), in which the unsuccessful defendant is ordered to pay the costs of the successful defendant directly. A Sanderson order is generally more advantageous to the plaintiff, but will not be ordered if, for example, the unsuccessful defendant is insolvent, because the successful defendant would thereby be deprived of his costs.

burden of proof The duty of a party to litigation to prove a fact or facts in issue. Generally the burden of proof falls upon the party who substantially asserts the truth of a particular fact (the prosecution or the plaintiff). A distinction is drawn between the *persuasive* (or *legal*) *burden*, which is carried by the party who as a matter of law will lose the case if he fails to prove the fact in issue; and the *evidential burden* (*burden of adducing evidence* or *burden of going forward*), which is the duty of showing that there is sufficient evidence to raise an issue fit for the consideration of the *trier of fact as to the existence or non-existence of a fact in issue.

The normal rule is that a defendant is presumed to be innocent until he is proved guilty; it is therefore the duty of the prosecution to prove its case by establishing both the *actus reus* of the crime and the *mens rea*. It must first satisfy the evidential burden to show that its allegations have something to support them. If it cannot satisfy this burden, the defence may submit or the judge may direct that there is *no case to answer, and the judge must direct the jury to acquit. The prosecution may sometimes rely on presumptions of fact to satisfy the evidential burden of proof (e.g. the fact that a woman was subjected to violence during sexual intercourse will normally raise a presumption to support a charge of rape and prove that she did not consent). If, however, the prosecution has established a basis for its case, it must then continue to satisfy the persuasive burden by proving its case beyond reasonable doubt (*see* proof beyond reasonable doubt). It is the duty of the judge to tell the jury clearly that the prosecution must prove its case and that it must prove it beyond reasonable doubt; if he does not give this clear direction, the defendant is entitled to be acquitted.

There are some exceptions to the normal rule that the burden of proof is upon the prosecution. The main exceptions are as follows. (1) When the defendant admits the elements of the crime (the *actus reus* and *mens rea*) but pleads a special defence, the evidential burden is upon him to prove his defence. This may occur, for example, in a prosecution for murder in which the defendant raises a defence of self-defence. (2) When the defendant pleads *automatism, the evidential burden is upon him. (3) When the defendant pleads *insanity, both the evidential and persuasive burden rest upon him. In this case, however, it is sufficient if he proves his case on a balance of probabilities (i.e. he must persuade the jury that it is more likely that he is telling the truth than not). (4) In some cases statute expressly places a persuasive burden on the defendant; for example, a person who carries an *offensive weapon in public is guilty of an offence unless he proves that he had lawful authority or a reasonable excuse for carrying it.

burglary *n.* The offence of either entering a building, ship, or inhabited vehicle (e.g. a caravan) as a trespasser with the intention of committing one of four specified crimes in it (*burglary with intent*) or entering it as a trespasser only but subsequently committing one of two specified crimes in it (*burglary without intent*). The four specified crimes for burglary with intent are (1) stealing; (2) inflicting *grievous bodily harm; (3) causing *criminal damage; and (4) raping any woman in the building. The two specified offences for burglary without intent are (1) stealing or attempting to steal; and (2) inflicting or attempting to inflict grievous bodily harm. Burglary is punishable by up to 14 years' imprisonment. *Aggravated burglary*, in which the trespasser is carrying a weapon of offence, explosive, or firearm, may be punished by a maximum sentence of life imprisonment.

business liability Liability (contractual or tortious) for a breach of obligations or duties arising in the course of a business (which can include the activities of a government department or local or public authority) or from the occupation of business premises. The Unfair Contract Terms Act 1977 limits the extent to which a person may rely on terms in his contracts that attempt to exclude or restrict his business liability (*see* exclusion and restriction of negligence liability).

business name The name, other than its own, under which a sole trader, partnership, or company carries on business. The choice of a business name is restricted by the Companies Act 1981 and by the common law of *passing off. The true names and addresses of the individuals concerned must be disclosed in documents issuing from the business and upon business premises. Contravention of the Act may lead to a fine and to inability to enforce contracts. *See also* company name.

business tenancy A *tenancy of premises that are occupied for the purposes of a trade, profession, or employment. Business tenants have special statutory protection. If the landlord serves a notice to quit, the tenant can usually apply to the courts for a new tenancy. If the landlord wishes to oppose the grant of a new tenancy he must show that he has statutory grounds, such as breaches of the tenant's obligations under the tenancy agreement or the provision of suitable alternative accommodation by the landlord. Otherwise the court will grant a new tenancy on whatever terms the parties agree or, if they cannot agree, on whatever terms the court considers reasonable. When the tenancy ends, the tenant may claim compensation for any improvements he has made.

buyer *n.* The party to a contract for the sale of goods who agrees to acquire ownership of the goods and to pay the price. *See also* purchaser.

byelaw *n.* A form of *delegated legislation, made principally by local authorities. District and London borough councils have general powers to make byelaws for the good rule and government of their areas, and all local authorities have powers to make them on a wide range of specific matters (e.g. public health). Certain public corporations (e.g. the British Airports Authority) also make byelaws for the regulation of their undertakings. By contrast with most other forms of delegated legislation, byelaws are not subject to any form of parliamentary control but take effect if confirmed by a government minister. They are, however, subject to judicial control by means of the doctrine of *ultra vires.*

C

C *See* Command Papers.

Cabinet *n.* A body of ministers whose function under the UK constitution is to formulate government policy and to carry it into effect (particularly by the initiation of legislation). It owes its existence to *constitutional convention, not law, and consists of the Prime Minister and senior ministers chosen by the Prime Minister.

The Cabinet is bound by the convention of *collective responsibility*, i.e. all members should fully support Cabinet decisions; a member who disagrees with a decision must resign. If the government loses a vote of confidence or suffers any other major defeat in the House of Commons, the whole Cabinet must resign.

call *n.* **1.** A ceremony at which students of the Inns of Court become barristers. The name of the student is read out and he is "called to the Bar" by the Treasurer of his Inn. Call ceremonies take place four times a year, once in each dining term. **2.** A demand by a company under the terms of the articles of association or an ordinary resolution requiring company members to pay up fully or in part the nominal value of their shares. Unless the articles provide otherwise, calls must be made equally upon all shareholders of the same class. Calls should be distinguished from *instalments*, which become due upon a date predetermined at the time the shares were issued.

calling the jury Announcing the names of those selected to serve on a jury as a result of a ballot of the jury panel.

cancellation *n.* (in equity) An order by the court that specified documents should no longer have effect. This may occur when a document has fulfilled its purpose but its continued existence could lead to improper claims against its maker.

cannabis *n.* A *controlled drug (Class B) obtained from the crushed leaves and flowers of the hemp plant (*Cannabis sativa*). In addition to the offences applying to all controlled drugs, there is a specific offence applying only to cannabis and cannabis resin (and also to prepared opium): it is an offence for an occupier, landlord, or property manager to allow these substances to be smoked on the premises he occupies or manages.

canonical disability *See* impotence.

capacity of a child in criminal law *See doli capax*.

capacity to contract Competence to enter into a legally binding agreement. The main categories of persons lacking this capacity in full are minors, the mentally disordered, the drunk, and corporations other than those created by royal charter.

A minor is capable of making valid contracts for *necessaries and is also bound by any beneficial contract of service into which he enters (i.e. any contract of employment or training that is advantageous to him taken as a whole). Certain contracts of a proprietary nature (e.g. tenancy agreements, agreements to buy company shares, and partnership agreements) are voidable in that a minor may repudiate them either before he comes of age or within a reasonable time thereafter. If he fails to repudiate, he becomes fully bound. All other contracts made by a minor are void.

A contract made by a person who is mentally disordered or drunk is voidable if the other party knows that his disorder or drunkenness will prevent him from understanding what he is doing. This means that, subject to certain limitations, he can set the contract aside by *rescission.

A corporation incorporated by royal charter has full contractual capacity, but a statutory corporation has power to contract only for purposes connected with the objects for which it was incorporated. Other contracts are *ultra vires* and void.

capias n. [Latin: that you take] One of a group of writs of assistance conferring certain supplemental powers upon the sheriff in respect of the enforcement of judgment. The only such writ to survive is the *capias ad satisfaciendum*. It may only be issued with leave of the court and is virtually obsolete.

capital *n.* **1. (share capital)** A fund representing the nominal value (*see* authorized capital) of shares issued by a registered company. In the case of a limited company, this fund is subject to rules intended to protect creditors. Thus, subject to some important exceptions, a company cannot issue shares at less than their nominal value, acquire its own shares (*but see* capital redemption reserve), or provide *financial assistance for others to acquire them. Furthermore, dividends may not be paid out of capital. *See also* reduction of capital. **2.** *See* loan capital.

capital allowance A tax allowance for businesses on capital expenditure on particular items. These include *machinery and plant, industrial buildings, agricultural buildings, mines and oil wells, and scientific equipment. For other types of expenditure neither the capital cost nor the depreciation is allowable against tax. The percentage of the expenditure allowed varies (up to 100%) according to the type of expenditure. If a business's capital allowances exceed its profit, it may carry forward the balance for setting against future profits.

capital gains tax A tax charged on gains arising from the disposal of assets. The tax due is a proportion of the *chargeable gain*, which in general terms is the amount by which the proceeds of the disposal exceed the original cost of acquiring the asset. If the disposal results in a loss, this may be offset against other chargeable gains in the same year or subsequent years. Assets that may be taxed in this way include stocks, shares, unit trusts, land, buildings, machinery, jewellery, and works of art. There are, however, a number of exemptions, including private motor vehicles, an individual's *main residence, National Savings Certificates, and most personal chattels with an expected life of less than 50 years. Marketable government securities held for longer than 12 months are also exempt. Gains arising from the disposal of business assets may be offset against the cost of acquiring replacement assets. This is known as *roll-over relief*. Capital gains tax applies only to gains accruing since 6 April 1965. If the asset was held before this date, the tax is charged on a proportion of the gain. In calculating a chargeable gain, the cost of the asset may be increased to take account of inflation. This is done by reference to the retail prices index, on a monthly basis. It applies only to increases in the index since March 1982 and only after the asset has been held for 12 months. At present (1983–84), the rate of tax is 30% and under 1983 Budget proposals the first £5300 of annual gains will be exempt.

capitalization issue *See* bonus issue.

capital money Money arising from certain transactions relating to *settled land or land held on *trust for sale. It may arise from sale, the granting of certain leases and similar transactions, borrowing on the security of a mortgage, and other circumstances in which the money should be treated as capital of the settlement; for example, the proceeds of a fire insurance claim relating to the land. Generally capital money must be received by the trustees of the settlement, not the beneficiary. When the money is raised or paid for a specific purpose (e.g. for improvements authorized by the Settled Land Act 1925) it must be applied for that purpose. Otherwise, it is invested and held by the trustees on the same trusts as the land itself was held.

capital punishment Death (usually by hanging) imposed as a punishment for crime. Capital punishment for murder was abolished in the UK in 1965, but it still exists (and is mandatory) for treason, although subject to the royal prerogative of mercy.

capital redemption reserve A fund established to ensure the maintenance of share capital when a company redeems or purchases its own shares under the Companies Act 1981. Such shares are treated as cancelled and thus the share capital is reduced by their nominal value. To counteract this, an amount representing the reduction must be transferred to the reserve. The reserve can only be used to pay up *bonus issues or in accordance with the rules relating to *reduction of capital.

capital transfer tax (CTT) A tax introduced by the Finance Act 1975 to replace estate duty. It is charged on: (1) transfers of wealth made during a person's lifetime, calculated on the loss to the donor's estate; (2) the value of a person's *estate at death; (3) certain settlements. There are two different kinds of rate of tax. Under 1983 Budget proposals, for transfers on death and three years before death the rate will progress from 30% on transfers from £60,000 to £75,000 up to 75% on transfers over £2½ million. For other lifetime transfers the rate on these amounts progresses from 15% to 50%. In both cases transfers up to £60,000 will be exempt.

When assessing the tax payable on a particular transfer, all nonexempt transfers by the transferor in the previous ten years are cumulated. The main exemptions are: (1) transfers between husband and wife; (2) outright lifetime gifts of £250 or less in any year; (3) the first £3000 of all other lifetime gifts in any year; (4) transfers to charities and political parties; (5) transfers forming part of normal expenditure; (6) transfers for national purposes or for the public benefit; and (7) certain gifts on marriage.

care and control The right to the physical possession and control of the day-to-day activities of a minor. This is also known as *actual custody*, as opposed to legal custody (*see* custody of child). In divorce proceedings, one parent may be given care and control and the other parent rights of *access or legal custody (*see* split order). *Compare* care or control.

careless driving The offence of driving a motor vehicle on a road without due care and attention. The maximum punishment is a £500 fine on a first conviction and a £500 fine and/or three months' imprisonment for subsequent convictions. Driving may be careless if it is due to an error of judgment rather than negligence. Failure to observe the Highway Code may be evidence of carelessness but is not in itself conclusive proof. This offence is subject to the requirement of a *notice of intended prosecution.

careless statement *See* negligent misstatement.

care or control Protection and guidance of a minor or the discipline of such a child. A court has authority to make orders in *care proceedings only if it is satisfied that (in addition to other specified conditions) the child is in need of care or control. In this context it is not necessary to show that all his day-to-day needs are being neglected. *Compare* care and control.

care order A court order committing the care of a child to a local authority. Such orders may be made by all courts empowered to make *supervision orders in respect of a child. Sometimes care orders must be made when a court revokes a *custodianship order. The age limits differ from those applicable to supervision orders. Orders made in wardship proceedings and upon revocation of custodianship may be made until the child is 18 (and cease when he becomes 18). Orders made in all other cases except for those in *care proceedings may only be made in respect of a child under the age of 17 and cease when he becomes 18. Orders may be made in care proceedings in respect of a child under the age of 18. If these orders were made when the child was under 16 they will cease when he becomes 18; and if made when the child was over 18 they will cease when he becomes 19.

A care order entitles a local authority to keep the child in its care despite any claims by a parent or guardian. The authority has the same powers and duties as a parent or guardian, although it cannot alter the child's religion or give consent to his adoption. A care order also entitles the local authority, under specified conditions, to assume full parental rights and duties by a special resolution.

care proceedings Proceedings taken by a juvenile court in respect of minors in need of protection. Care proceedings may be taken if the child is being (or likely to be) ill-treated, if the child's development or health is (or is in danger of) being neglected or jeopardized, if he is exposed to moral danger (e.g. drugs or sexual promiscuity), is beyond the control of his parents, is not receiving proper education, or has committed any criminal offence (except for *homicide). In addition, the court in each case must be satisfied that he is in need of *care or control. The court has wide powers to make a *supervision order, hospital order, or *guardianship order and may also make a *care order, as well as an order binding the child's parents to take proper care of him.

Care proceedings were intended to replace criminal proceedings in respect of minors, but at present both kinds of proceedings are used concurrently.

cargo *n.* Goods, other than the personal luggage of passengers, carried by a ship or aircraft. Under a ship's charterparty, the freight payable to the shipowner is normally calculated at a rate per tonne of cargo. Unless otherwise agreed, the duty of the charterer is to provide a full and complete cargo: if he fails to do this, he is liable for damages known as *dead freight*.

carriage of goods by air The act of carrying goods by air, which is normally under a contract between the consignor and a *carrier. International carriage has been the subject of several international conventions: Warsaw (1929), The Hague (1955), Guadalajara (1961), Guatemala (1971), and Montreal (1975). The UK is party to a number of these Conventions, which have been given effect by the Carriage by Air Acts 1932, 1961, and 1962 and the Carriage by Air and Road Act 1979. They deal with such matters as the nature and limit of the carrier's liability, who can sue and be sued, the right to stop in transit, the documentation of air carriage, and time limits for complaint.

carrier *n.* One who transports persons or goods from one place to another. Carriage is normally under a contract that may affect or limit the duties otherwise imposed by law, but such contracts may be subject to statutory control. Carriers of goods are bailees of the goods consigned. A *common carrier* is one who undertakes to carry any goods or persons for payment on the routes he covers. A common carrier is subject to

three common-law duties: (1) he must, if he has space, accept any goods of the type he carries or any person; (2) he must charge only a reasonable rate; and (3) he is strictly liable for all loss or damage to goods in the course of transit (*but see* inherent vice). All other carriers are *private carriers*, and they owe only a duty of reasonable care.

carrier's lien The right of a common *carrier to retain possession of goods he has carried until he has been paid his freight or charge.

cartel *n.* **1.** An agreement between belligerent states for certain types of nonhostile transactions, especially the exchange of prisoners. **2.** A national or international association of independent enterprises formed to create a *monopoly in a given industry.

case *n.* **1.** A court *action. **2.** A legal dispute. **3.** The arguments, collectively, put forward by either side in a court action.

case law The body of law set out in judicial decisions, as distinct from *statute law. *See also* precedent.

case stated A written statement of the facts found by a magistrates' court (or by the Crown Court in respect of an appeal from a magistrates' court) submitted for the opinion of the High Court on any question of law or jurisdiction involved. Any person who was a party to the proceedings or is aggrieved by the decision can request the court to state a case; if it wrongly refuses, it can be compelled to do so by order of *mandamus.

casus belli [Latin: occasion for war] An event giving rise to war or used to justify war. The only legitimate *casus belli* now is an unprovoked attack necessitating self-defence on the part of the victim.

casus omissus [Latin: an omitted case] A case inadvertently not provided for in a defective statute.

catching bargain (unconscionable bargain) A contract on very unfair terms. An example is the sale of a future interest in property at a gross undervalue, made by someone with expectations to succeed to the property who is in immediate need of money. Such a contract may be set aside or modified by a court of equitable jurisdiction.

cattle trespass An early form of strict liability for damage done by trespassing cattle, replaced in England by the Animals Act 1971. Under the 1971 Act, the owner of livestock that strays on another's land and does damage to the land or any property on it is liable for the damage and any expenses incurred in keeping the livestock or ascertaining to whom it belongs.

causa causans [Latin] The effective cause. *See* causation.

causation *n.* The relationship between an act and the consequences it produces. It is one of the elements that must be proved before an accused can be convicted of a crime in which the effect of the act is part of the definition of the crime (e.g. murder). Usually it is sufficient to prove that the accused had **mens rea* (intention, recklessness, or negligence) in relation to the consequences; the *burden of proof is on the prosecution. In tort it must be established that the defendant's tortious conduct caused the damage to the plaintiff before the defendant can be found liable for that damage. Sometimes a distinction is made between the effective cause (*causa causans*) of the damage and any other cause in the sequence of events leading up to it (*causa sine qua non*). Simple causation problems are solved by the "but for" test (would the damage have occurred but for the defendant's tort?), but this test is inadequate for cases of concurrent or cumulative causes (e.g. if the acts of two independent tortfeasors would each have been sufficient to produce the damage).

Sometimes a new act or event (*novus actus* (or *nova causa*) *interveniens*) may break the legal chain of causation and relieve the defendant of responsibility. Thus if a house, which was empty because of a nuisance committed by the local authority, is occupied by squatters and damaged, the local authority is not responsible for the damage caused by the squatters. Similarly, if X stabs Y, who almost recovers from the wound but dies because of faulty medical treatment, X will not have "caused" the murder. It has recently been held, however, that if a patient is dying from a wound and doctors switch off a life-support machine because he is clinically dead, the attacker, and not the doctors, "caused" the death. If death results because the victim has some unusual characteristic (e.g. a thin skull) or particular belief (e.g. he refuses a blood transfusion on religious grounds) there is no break in causation and the attacker is still guilty.

cause *n.* **1.** A court *action. **2.** *See* causation.

Cause Book The book recording the issue of writs in the *Central Office of the Supreme Court and certain later stages of the court proceedings.

Cause List A list of cases to be heard, displayed in the precincts of a court. The *Daily Cause List* lists all cases for trial in the Royal Courts of Justice and its outlying buildings. It also contains the *warned list* of cases about to be listed for hearing.

cause of action The grounds that entitle a person to sue. The cause of action may be a wrongful act, such as *trespass; or harm resulting from a wrongful act, as in the case of *negligence.

causing death by reckless driving An offence committed by someone who is guilty of *reckless driving that results in death (even if he did not foresee any risk of death). The offence is punishable by imprisonment of up to five years and/or a fine and by compulsory *disqualification for not less than 12 months.

caution *n.* **1.** (in criminal law) **a.** A warning given by a police officer, in accordance with the *Judges' Rules, when interrogating a suspect. **b.** A warning by a police officer, on releasing a suspect when it has been decided not to bring a prosecution against him, that if he is subsequently reported for any other offence, the circumstances relating to his first alleged offence may be taken into account. It is common practice for the police to give this type of caution, although the procedure has no statutory basis and there are no legal consequences if it is not followed. **2.** (in land law) A document lodged at the Land Registry by a person having an interest in land, recording his objection to any dealing with that land. No disposal of the land can then be registered until the cautioner has been notified, so that his objection can be investigated. For example, a caution might be lodged by someone who was induced by fraud to convey his land, to prevent the transferee from registering his title. If a caution is lodged unreasonably the cautioner may be ordered to compensate anyone to whom it causes loss.

caveat [from Latin: let him beware] *n.* A notice, usually in the form of an entry in a register, to the effect that no action of a certain kind may be taken without first informing the person who gave the notice (the *caveator*). For example, a caveat may be filed in the Probate Registry by someone claiming an interest in a deceased person's estate. The caveat prevents anyone else from obtaining a *grant of representation without reference to the caveator, who may thus ensure that his claim is dealt with in the distribution of the estate.

caveat actor [Latin] Let the doer be on his guard.

caveat emptor [Latin: let the buyer be-

ware] A common-law maxim warning a purchaser that he could not claim that his purchases were defective unless he protected himself by obtaining express guarantees from the vendor. The maxim has been modified by statute: under the Sale of Goods Act 1979 (a consolidating statute), contracts for the sale of goods have implied terms requiring the goods to correspond with their description and any sample and, if they are sold in the course of a business, to be of merchantable quality and fit for any purpose made known to the seller. Each of these implied terms is a condition of the contract. These statutory conditions do not apply to sales of land, to which the maxim *caveat emptor* still applies as far as the condition of the property is concerned. However, a term is normally implied that the vendor must convey a good *title to the land, free from encumbrances that were not disclosed to the purchaser before the contract was made.

caveat subscriptor [Latin] Let the person signing (e.g. a contract) be on his guard.

caveat venditor [Latin] Let the seller be on his guard.

Cd *See* Command Papers.

Central Arbitration Committee A statutory body, established under the Employment Protection Act 1975, consisting of a chairman and members appointed by the Secretary of State for Employment from persons nominated by *ACAS. The Committee determines disputes relating to: (1) arbitration in *trade disputes referred by ACAS with the consent of both parties; (2) *disclosure of information to trade unions; (3) the Fair Wages Resolution 1946, which requires businesses and their subcontractors undertaking work for government departments to give employees pay and conditions at least as favourable as those applying generally in private industry; (4) the application of the Equal Pay Act 1970 (*see* equal pay) to collective agreements (*see* collective bargaining); and (5) statutory requirements concerning pay and conditions of employment in the road transport, film, and independent broadcasting industries.

When the Committee makes an award of pay and/or conditions of employment these generally become incorporated in individual employees' contracts of employment and are enforceable in the courts. Its decisions concerning the Fair Wages Resolution are not enforceable, but an employer in breach may lose his government business.

Central Criminal Court The principal *Crown Court for Central London, usually known from its address as the *Old Bailey*. At least one High Court judge usually sits to try the most serious cases and there is also a large complement of judges of *circuit judge rank. *See also* Common Serjeant.

Central Office The administrative organization of the *Supreme Court in London, from which writs and summonses are issued. Its business is superintended by the Queen's Bench Masters (*see* Masters of the Supreme Court), one of whom sits each day as *practice master* to give any directions that may be required on questions of practice and procedure.

certificate of incorporation A document issued by the Registrar of Companies after *registration of a company, certifying that the company is incorporated (*see* incorporation). For a *limited company, the certificate also certifies that the company members have limited liability, and for a *public company the fact that it is a public company. The validity of the incorporation cannot thereafter be challenged.

Certification Officer An official appointed by the Secretary of State for Employment under the Trade Union and Labour Relations Act 1974, whose main duties concern the supervision of trade unions' and employers' associations' obligations as bodies corporate to keep accounting records and submit audited reports and accounts to him. He is also responsible for the certification of trade unions as independent in appropriate cases (*see* independent trade union).

certiorari [Latin: to be informed] *n.* A remedy in which the High Court orders decisions of inferior courts, tribunals, and administrative authorities to be brought before it and quashes them if they are *ultra vires* or show an *error of law on the face of the record. Since the remedy exists for the public good the applicant need not show a direct personal interest (*compare* declaration), but he must apply for it within six months and it is always discretionary (thus it may be refused if alternative remedies exist). Originally a prerogative writ, it is now obtained by an application for *judicial review.

certum est quod certum reddi potest [Latin] If something is capable of being made certain, it should be treated as certain. For example, a landlord can only distrain for rent (*see* distress) if the amount of rent is certain. However, if the amount of the rent is capable of being ascertained, it is treated as certain.

cessate grant A grant (e.g. of a lease) renewing a previous grant that has lapsed.

cesser *n.* The premature termination of some right or interest. For example, if land is held in trust for A for life so long as he does not marry and then for B, there is a cesser of A's life interest if he marries. A mortgage under which the mortgagor attorns tenant of the mortgagee (*see* attornment) provides for cesser on redemption: thus the tenancy ends whenever the debt is repaid.

cesser clause A clause inserted in a charterparty when the charterer intends to transfer to a shipper his right to have

goods carried. It provides that the shipowner is to have a lien over the shipper's goods for the freight payable
under the charterparty, and that the
charterer's liability for that freight will
cease accordingly on shipment of a full
cargo.

cestui que trust [Norman French, from
cestui à que trust, he for whom is the
trust] Formerly, a beneficiary under a
trust.

cestui que use [Norman French, from
cestui à que use, he to whose use] A person to whose use (i.e. for whose benefit)
property was held by another. *See* use.

cestui que vie [Norman French, from
cestui à que vie, he for whose life] A person for whose life an interest in property is held by another person. *See* estate *pur autre vie*.

chain of representation A rule under
the Administration of Estates Act 1925
by which the executor of someone who
was himself a sole executor stands on
the latter's death in his place as executor of the testator who appointed him.
Thus if A appoints B as his only executor and B in turn appoints C as his own
executor, on the death of A and B, C
becomes the executor of both. The rule
does not apply on intestacy or to an administrator, and the chain is broken by
a failure to obtain probate.

challenge to jury A procedure by
which the parties may object to the
composition of a jury before it is sworn.
A challenge may be *peremptory* (i.e.
with no reason for the challenge being
given) or *for cause*. In criminal cases
each defendant may challenge not more
than three jurors without cause. The
prosecution has no right of peremptory
challenge but may ask that a juror
should "stand by", in which case he re-
joins the jury panel and may be challenged for cause when the rest of the
panel has been gone through. Either
party may challenge for cause. This
may be *to the array*, in which the whole

panel is challenged by alleging some irregularity in the summoning of the jury
(e.g. bias or partiality on the part of the
jury summoning officer); or *to the polls*,
in which individual jurors may be challenged. Any challenge to jurors for
cause is tried by the judge before whom
the accused is to be tried.

chambers *pl. n.* **1.** The offices occupied
by a barrister or group of barristers.
(The term is also used for the group of
barristers practising from a set of chambers.) **2.** The private office of a judge,
master, or registrar. Most *interlocutory proceedings are held in chambers
and the public is not admitted, although judgment may be given in open
court if the matter is one of public interest.

Chancellor of the Exchequer The
minister responsible for raising national
revenue (particularly through taxation)
and controlling public expenditure in
the UK. Each year (usually in April) he
presents to Parliament a Budget pre-
dicting government expenditure and
proposing changes in taxation to meet
it.

Chancery Division The division of the
*High Court of Justice created by the
Judicature Acts 1873–75 to replace the
*Court of Chancery. The work of the
Division is principally concerned with
matters relating to real property, trusts,
and the administration of estates but
also includes cases concerned with
company law and patents. The effective
head of the Division is the *Vice Chancellor, although the *Lord Chancellor is
nominally its president. *See also* Companies Court.

Chancery Masters *See* Masters of the
Supreme Court.

change of name A person may change
his *surname simply by using a different name with sufficient consistency to
become generally known by that name.
A change is normally given formal publicity (e.g. by means of a statutory dec-

laration, deed poll, or newspaper advertisement), but this is not legally necessary. A young child, however, has no power to change his surname, nor does one parent have such a power without the consent of the other, even if that parent has sole custody of the child. (An injunction may be sought to prevent a parent from attempting to change a child's name unilaterally.) When a mother has remarried after divorce or is living with another person, and wishes to change the name of the child to that of her new partner, a court order must be obtained and the welfare of the child will be the first and paramount consideration.

A person's Christian name (i.e. a name given to him at baptism) can, under ecclesiastical law, be changed only on his subsequent confirmation.

character *n.* (in the law of evidence) **1.** The reputation of a party or witness. In civil cases the reputation of a party is not admissible unless it is directly in issue, as it may be in an action for *defamation. In criminal cases the accused may call evidence of his good character. If he does so, the prosecution may call evidence in rebuttal, but any such evidence must be limited to evidence of reputation and not include opinions about the accused's *disposition. Evidence of the reputation for truthfulness of a witness may be given in both civil and criminal cases. **2.** Loosely, the disposition of a party.

charge *n.* **1.** A formal accusation of a crime, usually made by the police after *interrogation. *See also* indictment. **2.** Instructions given by a judge to a jury. **3.** A legal or equitable interest in land, securing the payment of money. It gives the creditor in whose favour the charge is created (the *chargee*) the right to payment from the income or proceeds of sale of the land charged, in priority to claims against the debtor by unsecured creditors. Under the Law of Property Act 1925 the only valid legal charges

are: (1) a *rentcharge payable immediately and for a fixed period or in perpetuity; (2) a charge by way of legal *mortgage; and (3) certain charges arising under statute. All others take effect as equitable interests. Equitable charges, and second or subsequent legal mortgages, will be enforceable against third parties only if they are registered (*see* registration of encumbrances). *See also* equitable charge. **4.** An interest in company property created in favour of a creditor (e.g. as a *debenture holder) to secure the amount owing. Most charges must be registered at the Companies Registry. A *fixed charge* is attached to a specific item of property (e.g. land); a *floating charge* is created in respect of circulating assets (e.g. cash, stock in trade), to which it will not attach until *crystallization*, i.e. until some event (e.g. winding-up) causes it to become fixed. Before crystallization unsecured debts can be paid out of the assets charged. After, the charge is treated as a fixed charge and therefore unsecured debts (except those given preference under the Companies Acts) rank after those secured by the charge (*see also* fraudulent preference). A charge can also be created upon shares. For example, the articles of association usually give the company a *lien in respect of unpaid *calls, and company members may, in order to secure a debt owed to a third party, charge their shares, either by a full *transfer of shares coupled with an agreement to retransfer upon repayment of the debt or by a deposit of the *share certificate.

chargeable gain A profit made on the disposal of an asset, which may attract *capital gains tax.

charge by way of legal mortgage *See* mortgage.

charge certificate A certificate issued by the Land Registry to a mortgagee of registered land as evidence of his title. It will only be issued if the *land certificate is deposited at the Land Registry for the duration of the mortgage.

charge sheet A document in which an officer at a police station records an accusation against a suspect. It normally also gives details of his name and those of his accusers, who should sign the sheet.

charges register *See* land registration.

charging clause A clause in a trust entitling a trustee to charge for his services. When a solicitor or other professional person is appointed trustee, he is usually authorized to charge for his services. In the absence of such a clause neither he nor his firm is entitled to charge for his professional services, although he may recover expenses incurred during the course of his trusteeship.

charging order A court order obtained by a judgment creditor by which the judgment debtor's property (including money, land, and shares) becomes security for the payment of the debt and interest.

charitable trust A trust for purposes that the law regards as charitable. In this sense, a purpose is charitable only if it is for the furtherance of religion, for the advancement of education, for the relief of poverty, or for other purposes beneficial to the community. In every case the purpose must be for the benefit of the public or a section of it (though in cases of relief of poverty this is very easily satisfied); the precise meaning depends on the class of charity in question. The last class is taken to include every object of general utility to the public; it includes, for example, trusts for the protection of animals generally and for the provision of fire brigades. On the other hand, trusts supporting antivivisection and for the benefit of inmates of a local authority home for deprived and delinquent children are not charitable. A trust cannot be charitable unless it is solely and ex-

clusively for charitable purposes: *benevolent* and *philanthropic purposes* are not necessarily charitable. A charitable trust has many advantages over a private noncharitable trust: its objects do not have to be certain; charitable trusts are not subject to the *rules against perpetuities or against perpetual trusts; if the objects are or have become impossible or impracticable, the trust may be saved by the *cy-près doctrine; and the trustees may act by a majority. The greatest benefit to a charitable trust is that it has fiscal advantages: a charity is either wholly or partially exempt from income tax, capital gains tax, capital transfer tax, development land tax, and rates.

charity *n.* A body established for one of the charitable purposes specified by statute (*see* charitable trust). With certain exceptions, all charities are required to be registered with the *Charity Commissioners.

Charity Commissioners A body, now governed by the Charities Act 1960, generally responsible for the administration of *charities. The Commissioners are responsible for promoting the effective use of charitable resources, for encouraging the development of better methods of administration, for giving charity trustees information and advice on matters affecting charity, and for investigating and checking abuses. The Commissioners maintain a register of charities and decide whether or not a body should be registered; an appeal from their decision may be made to the High Court.

charter *n.* A document evidencing something done between one party and another. The term is normally used in relation to a grant of rights or privileges by the Crown; for example, the grant of a royal charter to a university.

charterparty *n.* A written contract by which a person (the *charterer*) hires from a shipowner, in return for the payment of freight, the use of his ship or part of it for the carriage of goods by sea. The hiring may be either for a specified period (a *time charter*) or for a specified voyage or voyages (a *voyage charter*), and the charterer may hire the ship for carrying either his own goods alone or the goods of a number of shippers, who may or may not include himself. A special but now rare type of charterparty is the *charter by demise*. It is analogous to a lease of land and gives the charterer full possession and control of the ship. The normal charterparty is a *simple charter*, under which the shipowner retains possession and control and the primary rights of the charterer are confined to placing goods on board and choosing the ports of call. A number of standard forms (known by codenames such as Austwheat and Shelltime) have been developed for use in particular trades. *See also* bill of lading; cesser clause.

chastisement *n.* Physical punishment as a form of discipline. A parent or guardian has the right to inflict reasonable and moderate punishment on his children. A husband does not, however, have the right to chastise his wife. Illegal chastisement may amount to one of the *offences against the person.

chattel *n.* Any property other than freehold land (*compare* real property). Leasehold interests in land are called *chattels real*, because they bear characteristics of both real and personal property. Tangible goods are called *chattels personal*.

cheat *n.* A common-law offence, now restricted to defrauding the public revenue (e.g. the tax authorities). Such offences are usually also covered under the Theft Act 1968 or the Theft Act 1978 (*see also* deception). It is also a statutory offence, punishable by up to three years' imprisonment, for someone who is not at his place of abode to have with him any article for use in connection with a cheat (e.g. false documents).

cheque *n.* A *bill of exchange drawn on a banker payable on demand. Since a cheque is payable on demand it need not be presented to the drawee bank for acceptance. A cheque operates as a mandate or order to the drawee bank to pay and debit the account of its customer, the drawer.

cheque card A card issued by a bank to one of its customers containing an undertaking that any cheque signed by the customer and not exceeding a stated sum will be honoured by the bank. This is normally subject to certain conditions; for example, the cheque must be signed in the presence of the payee, the signature must correspond with a specimen on the card, and the payee must write the card number on the reverse of the cheque. The bank thus undertakes to the payee of the cheque that the cheque will be honoured regardless of the state of the customer's account with the bank.

chief rent *See* rentcharge.

child *n.* **1.** A young person. There is no definitive definition of a child: the term has been used for persons under the age of 14, under the age of 16, and sometimes under the age of 18 (an *infant). Each case depends on its context and the wording of the statute governing it. **2.** An offspring of parents. Sometimes the word includes a *bastard and sometimes it also includes an adoptive child (*see* adoptive relationship). In wills, the scope of the word "child" depends on the testator's intentions.

child abuse Molestation of children, by parents or others (*see* battered child). If the molestation is of a sexual nature, the offender may be guilty of *gross indecency with children. Under the Protection of Children Act 1978, it is now a special statutory offence to take or allow the taking of indecent photographs of a child under the age of 16 or to distribute or show such photographs or to advertise that one intends to distribute or show them.

child destruction An act causing a viable unborn child to die during the course of pregnancy or birth. (A fetus is considered to be viable, i.e. capable of being born alive, if the pregnancy has lasted at least 28 weeks.) If carried out with the intention of causing death, the offence is subject to a maximum punishment of life imprisonment. There is a defence, however, if the act can be proved to have been carried out in good faith in order to preserve the mother's life (or, possibly, to prevent serious injury to her health); it is sufficient if the defendant thought that his act was necessary for that purpose, even if he was mistaken. *Compare* abortion.

child employee A child of compulsory school age (i.e. between 5 and 16 years) who undertakes paid work. It is illegal to employ a child under 13 at all, or any child during school hours, at night, or for more than two hours on a Sunday. It is also illegal to employ children in certain mining, construction, and transport industries. Other regulations restricting the employment of children are made by local authorities and remain in force until the Secretary of State exercises his power to make regulations under the Employment of Children Act 1973.

child of the family A minor considered in law to be the child of a couple, although not born to or adopted by them, on the grounds that he has been treated by them as their own child. Courts have powers to make orders in favour of children of the family in divorce cases, disputes over custody during the marriage, and to protect *battered children.

child protection in divorce The legal rules designed to safeguard the position of children of prospective divorcees. No divorce or nullity decree may be made absolute, and no decree of judicial sep-aration may be made, unless the court expressly declares that the children of the family are named in the decree and it is satisfied that the arrangements for their welfare are the best possible in the circumstances. In exceptional cases the court may accept an undertaking by the spouses to refer the arrangements for the children to the court within a specified time. A decree made in contravention of the above rules is void.

Divorce courts also have wide powers to make financial provision and property adjustment orders in favour of children of the family, as well as orders for their custody and education and (if necessary) supervision orders or care orders. The children's interests must also be considered in deciding whether to allow a divorce petition to be made in the first three years of a marriage; the children's interests are also relevant in deciding whether or not to grant a divorce petition based on a five-year separation when the petition is opposed by the respondent.

child stealing The act of taking away, enticing, or detaining a child under the age of 14 by using force or fraud against the child or its parent, or harbouring such a child knowing that it has been taken in this way. There must be an intention either to deprive the parent of possession of the child or to steal anything the child has with him. The offence is punishable by up to seven years' imprisonment. There is a defence when the stealer is a parent. *See also* abduction; kidnapping.

Chiltern Hundreds, stewardship of the An appointment that, as a nominal office of profit under the Crown, disqualifies its holder from membership of the House of Commons. Although the appointment has been a sinecure since the 18th century, it has been retained as a disqualifying office to enable members to give up their seats during the lifetime of a parliament (a member cannot by law resign his seat). After obtaining the stewardship (an application for which is never refused), the member resigns the office so as to make it available for re-use.

A second office used for the same purpose is the stewardship of the *Manor of Northstead*. The law relating to both these offices is now contained in the House of Commons Disqualification Act 1975.

chose *n.* A thing. Choses are divided into two classes. A *chose in possession* is a tangible item capable of being actually possessed and enjoyed, e.g. a book or a piece of furniture. A *chose in action* is a right (e.g. a right to recover a debt) that can be enforced by legal action.

Church of England The established Church in England, of which the sovereign is the supreme head. Structurally, the Church consists of the two provinces of Canterbury and York, which are divided into dioceses, and these into parishes. For each province there is an archbishop (that of Canterbury being Primate of all England, and that of York Primate of England), and for each diocese a bishop. A suffragan bishop has no diocese of his own but assists an archbishop or a diocesan bishop. The archbishops and other senior bishops are members of the House of Lords.

The governing body of the Church is the General Synod (formerly the Church Assembly, but renamed and reconstituted by the Synodical Government Measure 1969). It consists of a House of Bishops, a House of Clergy, and a House of Laity and has legislative functions. A *Measure* passed by each House and granted the royal assent following a resolution of each House of Parliament has the force of an Act of Parliament. There are also diocesan synods, and certain matters require the approval of a majority of these before they can be finally approved by the General Synod. The Dioceses Measure 1978 authorizes the reorganization of diocesan structure and the creation of

area synods, to which diocesan synods may delegate functions. *See also* ecclesiastical courts.

c.i.f. (cost, insurance, freight) contract A type of contract for the international sale of goods by which the seller agrees not only to supply the goods but also to make a contract of carriage with a sea carrier, under which the goods will be delivered at the contract port of destination, and a contract of insurance with an insurer, to cover them while they are in transit. The seller performs his contract by delivering the relevant documents to the buyer: an invoice specifying the goods and their price, a *bill of lading evidencing the contract of carriage, a policy of insurance, and any other documents specified in the contract. The contract will normally provide for payment against documents. The risk of accidental loss or damage normally passes to the buyer on or as from shipment.

circuit administrator A civil servant having responsibility for the administration of the courts within a circuit (*see* circuit system). He liaises closely with the *presiding judge of the circuit in the allocation of resources and particularly the sittings of judges and recorders.

circuit judge Any of the judges appointed under the provisions of the Courts Act 1971 from among barristers of not less than 10 years' standing and solicitors who have been *recorders for at least three years. They sit in the *county courts and the *Crown Court and may, by invitation of the Lord Chancellor, sit as High Court judges. All judges of county courts and other judges of comparable status were made circuit judges in 1971.

circuit system The system of dividing England and Wales into regional *circuits* for the purpose of court administration. It is based upon the traditional regional groupings adopted by the Bar and consists of the South-Eastern,

circumstantial evidence

Western, Midland and Oxford, Welsh, Northern, and North-Eastern circuits. Each circuit is administered by a *circuit administrator and supervised by two *presiding judges. *See also* circuit judge.

circumstantial evidence (indirect evidence) Evidence from which the judge or jury may infer the existence of a fact in issue but which does not prove the existence of the fact directly. *Compare* direct evidence.

citation *n.* **1.** A summons to a person to appear before a court. **2.** A notice, issued in the Probate Registry by an executor proving a will in solemn form (*see* probate), calling upon persons to come forward if they object to the grant of probate to him. **3.** The quoting of a legal case or authority.

citizen's arrest (private arrest) An arrest by a private person. This is permitted (1) if someone either is or is suspected of being in the process of committing an *arrestable offence; (2) if someone is suspected of having committed an arrestable offence; (3) to prevent a breach of the peace; (4) if an *indictable offence is being committed in the night; and (5) when statute expressly gives a private person the power to arrest. A person who makes a citizen's arrest must take the arrested person to the police or a magistrate as soon as is practicable. Shop "detectives" are, for these purposes, private citizens; if they arrest or detain someone in breach of these conditions they may be guilty of false imprisonment.

citizenship of the UK and Colonies A form of citizenship created by the British Nationality Act 1948. By the British Nationality Act 1981, it was replaced as from 1 January 1983 by *British citizenship, *British Dependent Territories citizenship, and *British Overseas citizenship.

City Code on takeovers and mergers A body of rules regulating those engaged in the conduct of *takeovers and *mergers of public companies. It is administered by a Panel representing the major City financial institutions, e.g. the *Stock Exchange and the Issuing Houses Association. The principal aim is to ensure that company members (rather than the directors) decide upon the merits of accepting a bid, that they are fully informed about what is going on, and that shareholders of the same class are treated equally in the event of a takeover or merger. The rules are not legally binding, but if they are contravened the Stock Exchange may impose sanctions on the company.

City of London That part of *Greater London which, for local government purposes, is administered (in conjunction with the Greater London Council) by the City of London Corporation. In addition to special powers under ancient royal charters, the Corporation has all the functions of a London borough council, which it exercises principally through a Court of Common Council consisting of the Lord Mayor, aldermen elected for life, and common council men elected annually. Limited governmental functions are exercised through a separate Court of Aldermen, and formal functions through a Court of Common Hall.

civil court A court exercising jurisdiction over civil rather than criminal cases. In England the principal civil *courts of first instance are the *county courts and the *High Court. *Magistrates' courts have limited civil jurisdiction, mainly confined to matrimonial proceedings.

civil law 1. The law of any particular state, now usually called *municipal law. **2.** Roman law. **3.** A legal system based on Roman law, as distinct from the English system of *common law. **4.** *Private law, as opposed to criminal law, administrative law, military law, and ecclesiastical law.

civil liability contribution The right of a person who is liable for damage to recover from any other person who is liable for the same damage a contribution to represent his share of responsibility for the damage. When two or more people are liable for causing the same damage, the injured person is entitled to recover full compensation for his losses from any one of them. The wrongdoer who is sued may then ask for contribution from the other wrongdoers. Since the Civil Liability (Contribution) Act 1978, the right to contribution is available in all forms of civil liability, whether tort, breach of contract, breach of trust, or otherwise. The court assesses the amount of contribution on the basis of what would be just and equitable, taking into account the parties' responsibility for the damage.

Civil List The sum authorized by statute to be paid annually out of the *Consolidated Fund for meeting the expenses of the royal household and for making allowances to certain members of the royal family. It may be increased in amount by Treasury order, but this is liable to annulment by the House of Commons.

civil remedy *See* remedy.

Civil Service The body of *Crown servants that are employed to put government policies into action and are paid wholly out of money voted annually by Parliament. Civil servants include the administrative and executive staff of government departments (e.g. the Home Office and Treasury) and the industrial staff of government dockyards and factories. The police (not being Crown servants), the armed forces, government ministers, and those (e.g. judges) whose salaries are charged on the Consolidated Fund are not civil servants.

civil wrong An infringement of a person's rights, for which the person wronged may sue for damages or some other civil remedy. Examples are *torts and *breaches of contract.

claim *n.* A demand for a remedy or assertion of a right. The term is used in certain court pleadings, such as *statement of claim.

claim of privilege *See* privilege.

class gift A gift to people of a certain specified category (e.g. "to my daughters"), rather than to people named individually, (e.g. "to my daughters A and B").

classification of animals At common law animals were formerly classified as wild by nature (*ferae naturae*) or tame by nature (*mansuetae naturae*), referring to the species in general rather than the individual animal. The owner of a wild animal was strictly liable for any damage it caused. The owner of a tame animal was liable for damage it caused if he knew that it had a vicious tendency abnormal in the species (the *scienter rule*). Special rules applied to damage done by cattle (*see* cattle trespass; distress damage feasant) and dogs. The common law classifications have been largely replaced by modern statutes.

For purposes of civil liability in England, animals are now classified as belonging to a dangerous or a nondangerous species (Animals Act 1971). A dangerous species is one not commonly domesticated in the British Isles, fully grown members of which are likely to cause severe damage. The keeper of an animal of a dangerous species is strictly liable for any damage it causes. Liability for damage done by other animals arises either under the Animals Act, if the animal was known by its owner to be likely to cause damage because of its unusual characteristics or the particular circumstances, or under ordinary rules of tort liability. For example, allowing a dog to stray on the highway can give rise to liability in negligence if it causes an accident, and excessive smell from a pig farm can be an actionable nuisance. Dangerous wild animals are separately classified for licencing requirements under the Dangerous Wild Animals Act 1976 (*see* dangerous animals). The Animals Act imposes *strict liability for damage done by trespassing livestock, which includes cattle, horses, sheep, pigs, goats, and poultry. The keeper of a dog that kills or injures livestock is liable for the damage caused, except when the livestock strays on the keeper's land. If livestock is worried by a dog, the owner of the livestock (or the owner of the land on which the livestock lives) may kill or injure the dog to protect the livestock.

Other statutes protect various species, control importation of animals, and deal with animal diseases.

class meeting A meeting of a special class of company members (e.g. holders of preference shares), usually convened to consider a proposed alteration in *class rights.

class rights Any rights attached to a special class of share. For example, dividend, capital, and voting rights are class rights when attached to preference shares but not when attached to ordinary shares. Class rights can only be altered with the consent of the class; shareholders who do not agree to the change can apply to have the alteration cancelled (Companies Acts 1948 and 1980).

clean break The principle that, upon divorce, spouses should try to settle their financial affairs in a final manner, either by means of a *property adjustment order or a lump-sum order rather than a continuous periodical payments order. The courts have recently emphasized the desirability of achieving a clean break wherever possible.

clean hands A phrase from a *maxim of equity: he who comes to equity must come with clean hands, i.e. a person

who makes a claim in equity must be free from any taint of fraud with respect to that claim. For example, a person seeking to enforce an agreement must not himself be in breach of it.

clearance *n.* **1.** A certificate acknowledging a ship's compliance with customs requirements. **2.** An indication from a taxing authority that a certain provision does not apply to a particular transaction. The procedure is laid down by statute in some cases.

clearance area An area declared as such by a housing authority (usually a district or London borough council) on the ground that the houses in it are unfit for human habitation or otherwise dangerous or injurious to health and are best demolished. The authority, which must also be satisfied that alternative accommodation exists and that its resources are sufficient, then acquires the area and carries out the demolition. *See also* rehabilitation order. *Compare* housing action area.

Clerk of the House The principal permanent officer of the House of Commons.

Clerk of the Parliaments The principal permanent officer of the House of Lords.

clerk to the justices (justices' clerk, magistrates' clerk) A barrister or solicitor of not less than five years' standing, appointed to assist magistrates in court, particularly by giving advice about law, practice, or procedure on questions arising in connection with the discharge of their or his functions. The clerk or one of his staff will sit in court with the justices in order to advise them, but should not retire with them when they consider their verdict. He may, however, advise them in private during their retirement, at their request, but should return to the court when his advice has been given. *See also* magistrates' court.

client *n.* A person who employs a solicitor to carry out legal business on behalf of himself or someone else. The relationship between a solicitor and his client is a *fiduciary one and any other transactions between them may be affected by *undue influence. A solicitor's client cannot consult a barrister directly but only through his solicitor: the solicitor is therefore the barrister's client.

clog on the equity of redemption Any provision in a *mortgage deed to prevent redemption on payment of the debt or performance of the obligation for which the security was given. Such provisions are void. An example is an option contained in the mortgage deed for the mortgagee to purchase the mortgaged property before or after the mortgage has been redeemed. *Unconscionable* provisions in a mortgage (for example, one to prevent redemption for 100 years) are also void. However, a company may issue irredeemable *debentures. A provision that would otherwise be unconscionable may be valid if the transaction containing it is a commercial arrangement rather than a mortgage. Thus, such provisions in mortgages of public houses or garages by their tenants or owners to breweries or oil companies will be upheld, provided that they do not infringe the contractual rules against *restraint of trade.

close *n.* **1.** Land that is enclosed. **2.** *See* close of pleadings.

close company A company under the control of its directors or five or fewer *participators*. The participators have or are entitled to acquire a share or interest in the capital or income of the company and can include *loan creditors. Special tax provisions apply to such companies.

closed-shop agreement A collective agreement requiring members of a particular group of employees to be or become members of a specified trade union. A *pre-entry agreement* is one that prohibits an employer from engaging a relevant employee unless he is already a member of the union concerned. The more common *post-entry agreement* requires employees to join the specified union within a certain time after the employment commences.

Under the Employment Protection (Consolidation) Act 1978 as amended by the Employment Acts 1980 and 1982, the dismissal of an employee for joining or participating in an independent trade union, for failing to be a member of any union, or for failing to join a specified union is ordinarily treated as unfair (*see* unfair dismissal). However, subject to certain exceptions a dismissal is treated as fair if a *union membership* (i.e. closed-shop) *agreement* required the employee to join a specified union, the employee was dismissed for failing to comply with the agreement, and the agreement was approved within five years before the dismissal. An approved agreement is one in which all the employees affected have been ballotted on the application of the agreement to them; agreements coming into force after 14 August 1980 must be approved by 80% of those entitled to vote. Agreements after 1 November 1984 must be approved in secret ballot by 80% of those entitled to vote or 85% of those actually voting.

The exceptions to this principle cover (1) persons genuinely objecting on grounds of conscience or deeply held personal conviction to joining a union; (2) persons employed before the agreement took effect and who have not joined the union since; (3) employees who have or are seeking a declaration under the 1980 Act from an industrial tribunal that they have been unreasonably excluded or expelled from union membership; and (4) those bound by their qualifications to observe a written code that would conflict with an obligation of union membership to participate in industrial action.

The 1982 Act also established a scheme for compensating employees dismissed for not joining trade unions between 16 September 1974 and 15 August 1980 (when the statutory requirements for exemption from closed-shop agreements were much stricter). Application must be made to the Department of Employment by 1 November 1983. The Department's assessor awards the sum that an industrial tribunal would have awarded had it not been precluded by legislation then in force from finding that the employee was unfairly dismissed. Interest is awarded in addition.

close of pleadings A stage in the course of pleading in an action in the High Court that occurs 14 days after service of the *reply or, if there is no reply but only a defence to counterclaim, 14 days after service of the defence to counterclaim. If neither a reply nor a defence to counterclaim is served, it occurs 14 days after service of the defence. The significance of this stage is that (1) it creates an implied joinder of issue on the pleading last served; (2) it fixes the date by reference to which the *summons for directions in the action must be issued; (3) it fixes the date by reference to which *automatic directions in personal injury actions take effect.

closing order An order made by a local authority under the Housing Act 1957 prohibiting the use of a house that it considers unfit for human habitation.

closure *n.* The curtailing of debate on a question, particularly in the House of Commons, by carrying a motion (which cannot itself be debated) "that the question be now put". The result is that a vote on the question under debate must be taken immediately. *Compare* guillotine.

club *n.* An association regulated by rules that bind its members according to the law of contract. Club property is either vested in trustees for the members (*members' club*) or owned by a proprietor (often a limited company) who operates the club as a business for profit (*proprietary club*). The committee is usually liable for club debts in the case of a members' club; the proprietor in the case of a proprietary club.

Cmd *See* Command Papers.

Cmnd *See* Command Papers.

coastal waters The sea adjoining the coast of any country. In the case of the UK, the Channel Islands, and the Isle of Man, the extent of the coastal waters is the same as that of their fishery limits (at present 12 nautical miles).

code *n.* A complete written formulation of a body of law, (e.g. the *Code Napoléon* in France). A code of English law does not exist, but a few specialized topics have been dealt with in this way by means of a *codifying statute (e.g. the Sale of Goods Act 1893, re-enacted with modifications by the Sale of Goods Act 1979).

code of practice A body of rules for practical guidance only and not having the force of law, e.g. the *Judges' Rules and the Highway Code. Under the provisions of the Fair Trading Act 1973 the *Director General of Fair Trading has the duty of encouraging trade associations to prepare and distribute to their members codes of practice for guidance in safeguarding and promoting the interests of UK consumers. Several such codes have been approved by the Director General. Codes of practice have also been published by *ACAS, the Health and Safety, Equal Opportunities, and Racial Equality Commissions, and the Secretary of State of Employment, providing guidance to employers, employees, and their representatives on the fulfilment of their statutory obligations in relevant fields.

Generally, failure to comply with a code of practice does not automatically expose the party in breach to prosecution or any civil remedy. It may, however, be relied on as evidence tending to show that he has not fulfilled some relevant statutory requirement.

codicil *n.* A document supplementary to a will, which is executed with the same formalities under the Wills Act 1837 (*see* execution of will) and adds to, varies, or revokes provisions in the will. A codicil normally republishes a will (*see* republication of will) and may revive a will that has been revoked if that is the testator's clear intention.

codifying statute A statute that sets out the whole of the existing law (i.e. both statute law and case law) on a particular subject. Such statutes are extremely rare. *Compare* consolidating statute. *See also* interpretation of statutes.

coercion *n.* A common-law defence available only to married women who have committed a crime in the presence of, and under pressure from, their husbands. Its scope is usually taken to be wider than that of *duress in that it covers moral as well as physical pressure, but its exact limitations are uncertain. The Law Commission in 1977 recommended its abolition.

cognates *pl. n.* Persons descended from a common ancestor.

cohabitation *n.* Living together as husband and wife. Married persons generally have a right to expect their spouses to live with them. To resume cohabitation for more than six months after separation may bar a decree of *divorce based on adultery, desertion, or separation (*see also* breakdown of marriage). When the divorce is based on unreasonable behaviour, however, the bar is discretionary.

Unmarried people living together as husband and wife do not usually have the status of a married couple (*see also* common-law marriage). But under the *cohabitation rule* the resources and requirements of an unmarried couple living together are aggregated for the purposes of claiming social security benefits under the Supplementary Benefits Act 1976.

collateral 1. *adj.* Describing the relationship between people who share a common ancestor but are descended from him through different lines of descent. *See also* consanguinity. **2.** *adj.* Ancillary; subordinate but connected to the main subject, etc. **3.** *n.* Security that is additional to the main security for a debt. For example, a lender may require as collateral the assignment of an insurance policy in addition to the principal security of a mortgage on the borrower's home.

collateral contract A subsidiary contract that induces a person to enter into a main contract. For example, if X agrees to buy from Y goods made by Z, and does so on the strength of Z's assurance as to the high quality of the goods, X and Z may be held to have made a collateral contract consisting of Z's promise as to quality given in consideration of X's promise to enter into the main contract with Y.

collective agreement *See* collective bargaining.

collective bargaining Negotiations between trade unions (acting for their members) and employers about terms and conditions of employment. Under the Trade Union and Labour Relations Act 1974, a *collective agreement* (an agreement between trade union and employer resulting from collective bargaining) is not legally binding unless it is in writing and specifically states the parties' intention to be bound. Unenforceable collective agreements frequently include terms (relating to pay, discipline, etc.) that will become incorporated in individual employees' binding contracts of employment. In these respects the written particulars of employees' contracts, which the employer must give under the Employment Protection (Consolidation) Act 1978, must refer the employee to the collective agreement, which must be readily accessible to him. When a collective agreement provides that individual employees' contracts will circumscribe their right to strike, the employees will only be bound if their contracts contain that provision and the collective agreement was negotiated by an *independent trade union, is in writing, and is readily accessible to employees during working hours. The parties to a collective agreement containing procedures for determining complaints of unfair dismissal may apply to the Secretary of State for an order that those procedures be substituted for the statutory jurisdiction of industrial tribunals. An order will only be made if the agreement was negotiated by an independent trade union, sufficiently identifies the employees affected, and gives them remedies as beneficial as the statutory scheme and a right to independent arbitration or adjudication.

collective responsibility *See* Cabinet.

collision clause (running-down clause) A clause in a marine insurance policy binding the underwriters to indemnify the insured in respect of any damages in tort he may be liable for as a result of his ship colliding with another. At common law, such a policy covers only the insured's physical losses. The clause is customarily restricted to three quarters of the damages in question.

collusion *n.* An improper agreement or bargain between parties that one of them should bring proceedings against the other. Collusion is no longer a bar to divorce or nullity proceedings, but it may affect the validity of a declaration of legitimacy.

colony *n.* A territory that forms part of the Crown's dominions outside the UK. Although it may enjoy internal self-government, its external affairs are controlled by the UK government.

colourable *adj.* Describing that which is one thing in appearance but another in substance; for example, a symbolic residence in a parish for the purpose of qualifying for marriage there.

Command Papers Documents that the government, by royal command, presents to Parliament for consideration. They include *white papers* and *green papers*. The former contain statements of policy or explanations of proposed legislation; the latter are essentially discussion documents. For reference purposes they have serial numbers, with (since 1869) prefixes. The prefixes are *C* (1870–99), *Cd* (1900–18), *Cmd* (1919–56), and *Cmnd* (1957–).

Commercial Court A court forming part of the *Queen's Bench Division of the High Court and specializing in the trial of commercial cases, mostly relating to shipping and commodity trading. Many of the court's cases arise from the awards of arbitrators (*see* arbitration). The judges of the court are nominated by the Lord Chancellor from among the Queen's Bench *puisne judges who have special experience of commercial matters.

commission *n.* **1.** Authority to exercise a power or a direction to perform a duty; for example, a commission of a *justice of the peace. **2.** A body directed to perform a particular duty. Examples are the *Charity Commissioners and the *Law Commission. **3.** A sum payable to an *agent in return for his performing a particular service. This may, for example, be a percentage of the sum for which he has secured a contract of sale of his principal's property. The circumstances in which a commission is payable depend on the terms of the contract between principal and agent. **4.** Authorization by a court or a judge for a witness to be examined on oath by a court, judge, or other authorized person, to provide evidence for use in court proceedings. The procedure is used when the witness is unlikely to be able to attend the hearing (e.g. because of illness). If the witness is still unable to attend when the court hearing takes place the written evidence is read by the court.

commissioner for oaths A person appointed by the Lord Chancellor to administer oaths or take affidavits. By statute, every solicitor who holds a *practising certificate has the powers of a commissioner for oaths, but he may not exercise these powers in a proceeding in which he is acting for any of the parties or in which he is interested.

Commission for Racial Equality A body appointed by the Home Secretary under the Race Relations Act 1976 with the general function of working towards the elimination of *racial discrimination by promoting equality of opportunity and good relations between different racial groups. It keeps the working of the Act under review, investigates alleged contraventions and, when necessary, issues and applies for injunctions to enforce nondiscrimination notices.

Commission of the European Communities An organ of the EEC and other European Communities having both executive and legislative functions. Its members are appointed by member states by mutual agreement (at least one and not more than two by each), and each Commissioner assumes responsibility for a particular field of activity. The Commission's executive functions include administration of the Communities' budgets and ensuring that Community law is enforced (*see* Court of Justice of the European Communities). Its legislative functions consist primarily of submitting proposals for legislation to the *Council of Ministers, in some cases on the orders of the Council and in others on its own initia-

tive (*see also* Assembly of the European Communities). It also has legislative powers of its own, partly under the Treaty of Rome and partly by virtue of delegation by the Council, but only on a limited range of subjects (*see* Community legislation).

Commissions for Local Administration Two commissions, one each for England and Wales, established by the Local Government Act 1974 to investigate complaints by the public of injustice suffered through maladministration by a local authority, police authority, or water authority. The *Parliamentary Commissioner for Administration is a member of both commissions and there are three Local Commissioners for England and one for Wales. Certain matters (e.g. decisions affecting the public generally and the conduct of criminal investigations) are outside their competence. Complaints to a Commissioner must normally be made in writing through a member of the authority concerned, but if a complaint is not duly passed on it can be accepted directly by the Commissioner. Commissioners' reports are sent to the person complaining and the authority concerned and are also made public.

committal for sentence The referring of a case from a magistrates' court to the Crown Court, which occurs when the magistrates have found the accused guilty and consider that their powers of sentencing are insufficient for the case in question.

committal for trial The referring of a case from a magistrates' court for trial at the Crown Court following a *preliminary investigation by the magistrates. The committal proceedings may consist of taking *depositions from all the witnesses in the form of oral evidence. Alternatively the committal may take a short form under section 1 of the Criminal Justice Act 1967 (*section 1 committal*). This occurs when the accused agrees that the prosecution should put all its evidence in writing; the justices may then commit for trial without considering the evidence. The accused does not have to disclose any defence that he intends to put forward at the trial, but must give notice of any intended alibi and details of the witnesses he is going to call in support of it. Section 1 committal may only take place if the accused is legally represented.

The press may normally only report certain limited facts about committal proceedings, such as the name of the accused and the charges. However the accused may, if he wishes, ask that reporting restrictions be lifted and the magistrates may then make an order allowing publication of full details of the proceedings. No restrictions apply when the magistrates decide not to commit the accused for trial.

committal in civil proceedings A method of enforcing judgment by obtaining an order that a person be committed to prison. It is most commonly sought when the person has committed a *contempt of the court (e.g. by disobedience of an order of the court). In modern practice it is very occasionally available to enforce an order for the payment of a debt.

committee of inspection 1. A committee of creditors and contributories that may be appointed to supervise the *liquidator when a company is wound up. It is established by the court for a *compulsory winding-up by the court and by the creditors in the case of a creditors' *voluntary winding-up. **2.** A committee that may be appointed by creditors to supervise the trustee appointed to handle the affairs of a bankrupt. A committee consists of between three and five creditors and their duty is to see that the distribution of the bankrupt's assets is carried out as quickly and economically as possible. *See also* bankruptcy.

Committee of the whole House A committee of which all members of the House of Commons or the House of Lords are members. In the Lords it sits for the committee stage of all public Bills. In the Commons the committee stage is normally taken by a standing committee, but major Bills (particularly if controversial) are sometimes referred instead to a whole House committee. Certain matters concerning expenditure and taxation were formerly considered by the whole House sitting as the *Committee of Supply* or the *Committee of Ways and Means*, but since 1967 they have been dealt with by the House sitting as such.

common *n.* A *profit *à prendre* enjoyed by a number of landowners over *common land. A right of common may be *appurtenant, in gross (i.e. without restriction), or *pur cause de vicinage* (the right to allow animals grazing common land to stray onto adjoining common land). They generally comprise rights of pasture (grazing), piscary (fishing), turbary (a right to take turf), or *estovers, and unless they exist in gross are usually limited to the reasonable needs of the *dominant tenements.

common assault *See* assault.

common carrier *See* carrier.

common duty of care The duty of an occupier of land or premises to take reasonable care to see that visitors will be reasonably safe in using the premises for the purposes for which they are invited or permitted to be there. *See* occupier's liability.

common fund basis The basis of *taxation of costs under which a reasonable amount is allowed in respect of all costs reasonably incurred. The common fund basis is more generous than the party and party basis and is used in all taxations under the *legal aid scheme.

common land Land subject to rights of *common. The Commons Registration Act 1965 provides for the registration with local authorities of all common land in England and Wales, its owners, and claims to rights of common over it. Subject to the investigation by Commons Commissioners of disputed cases, and to exceptions for land becoming or ceasing to be common land, registration provides conclusive evidence that land is common land and also of the rights of common over it.

common law The part of English law based on rules developed by the royal courts during the first three centuries after the Norman Conquest (1066) as a system applicable to the whole country, as opposed to local customs. The Normans did not attempt to make new law for the country or to impose French law on it; they were mainly concerned with establishing a strong central administration and safeguarding the royal revenues, and it was through machinery devised for these purposes that the common law developed. Royal representatives were sent on tours of the shires to check on the conduct of local affairs generally, and this involved their participating in the work of local courts. At the same time there split off from the body of advisers surrounding the king (the *curia regis*) the first permanent royal court – the *Court of Exchequer, sitting at Westminster to hear disputes concerning the revenues. Under Henry II (reigned 1154–89), to whom the development of the common law is principally due, the royal representatives were sent out on a regular basis (their tours being known as *circuits*) and their functions began to be exclusively judicial. Known as *justiciae errantes* (wandering justices), they took over the work of the local courts. In the same period there appeared at Westminster a second permanent royal court, the *Court of Common Pleas. These two steps mark the real origins of the common law. The judges of the Court of Common Pleas so successfully superimposed a single system on the multiplicity of local customs that, as

early as the end of the 12th century, reference is found in court records to the custom of the kingdom. In this process they were joined by the judges of the Court of Exchequer, which began to exercise jurisdiction in many cases involving disputes between subjects rather than the royal revenues, and by those of a third royal court that gradually emerged – the Court of King's Bench (*see* Court of Queen's Bench). The common law was subsequently supplemented by *equity, but it remained separately administered by the three courts of common law until they and the Court of Chancery (all of them sitting in Westminster Hall until rehoused in the Strand in 1872) were replaced by the *High Court under the Judicature Acts 1873–75.

common-law marriage 1. A marriage recognized as valid at common law although not complying with the usual requirements for marriage. Such marriages are only recognized today if (1) they are celebrated outside England and there is no local form of marriage reasonably available to the parties or (2) they are celebrated by military chaplains in a foreign territory (or on a ship in foreign waters), and one of the parties to the marriage is serving in the Forces in that territory. The form of marriage is a declaration that the parties take each other as husband and wife. **2.** Loosely, the situation of two unmarried people living together as husband and wife. In law such people are treated as unmarried, although recently they have been recognized as equivalent to married persons for purposes of protection against battering and for some provisions of the Rent Acts (such as succession to *statutory tenancies).

Common Market *See* EEC.

common mistake *See* mistake.

common money bond *See* bond.

Common Serjeant The title held by one of the *circuit judges at the *Central Criminal Court. It was formerly an ancient office of the City of London, first mentioned in its records in 1291. Serjeants-at-law were the highest order at the English Bar from the 13th or 14th centuries until the King's Counsel took priority in the 17th century. Until 1873 the judges of the common law courts were appointed from the serjeants; although the order of serjeants was dissolved in 1877, the title remains in the Common Serjeant.

Commonwealth (British Commonwealth) *n.* A voluntary association consisting of the UK and many of its former colonies or dependencies (e.g. protectorates) that have attained full independence and are recognized by international law as separate countries. The earliest to obtain independence (e.g. Canada and Australia) did so by virtue of the Statute of Westminster 1931, but the majority have been granted it individually by subsequent Independence Acts. Some (such as Canada and Australia) are still technically part of the Crown's dominions; others (e.g. India) have become republics. All accept the Crown as the symbol of their free association and the head of the Commonwealth.

commonwealth citizen Under the British Nationality Act 1948, a status synonymous with that of *British subject. By the British Nationality Act 1981 (which replaced the 1948 Act as from 1 January 1983 and gave the expression British subject a very limited meaning), it was redefined as a wide secondary status. It now includes every person who is either a British citizen, a British Dependent Territories citizen, a British Overseas citizen, a British subject (in its new sense), or a citizen of one of the independent Commonwealth countries listed in a schedule to the 1981 Act.

commorientes [Latin] *pl. n.* Persons who die at the same time. Under the Law of Property Act 1925, when the order of death is uncertain commorientes are presumed (so far as the devolution of their property is concerned) to have died in order of seniority. Thus a bequest by the younger to the elder is treated as having lapsed. However, under the Intestates' Estates Act 1952 the rule does not apply when intestate spouses die at the same time: an intestate husband's property passes as though his wife had not survived him, even though she was the younger.

community *n.* A *local government area in Wales consisting of a division of a *district. All communities have meetings and many have an elected community council, which is a *local authority with a number of minor functions (e.g. the provision of allotments, bus shelters, and recreation grounds). A community council may by resolution call its area a town, itself a town council, and its chairman the town mayor.

community home An institution for the accommodation and maintenance of children and young persons in care. Community homes are provided by local authorities and voluntary organizations according to plans prepared by children's regional planning committees and approved by the Home Secretary.

community land *See* development land.

Community law (EEC law) The law of the European Communities (as opposed to the national laws of the member states). It consists of the treaties establishing the Communities (together with subsequent amending treaties), *Community legislation, and decisions of the *Court of Justice of the European Communities. Any provision of the treaties or of Community legislation that is directly applicable in a member state forms part of the law of that state and prevails over its national law in the event of any inconsistency between the two.

Community legislation Laws made by the *Council of Ministers or *Commission of the European Communities. Each body has power to make regulations, issue directives, and take decisions. *Regulations* are of general application, binding in their entirety, and directly applicable in all member states (*see* Community law). *Directives* are addressed to one or more member states and require them to achieve (by amending national law if necessary) specified results. *Decisions* may be addressed either to states or to persons and are binding on them in their entirety. Like regulations, some directives and decisions have been held to be directly applicable in member states. Both the Council and the Commission may also make *recommendations*, but these are not legally binding.

community of assets (community of property) The sharing of ownership of matrimonial property, such as the home and furniture, as an automatic consequence of marriage. *See* family assets.

community service order An order that requires an offender (who must be aged at least 17) to perform unpaid work for between 40 and 240 hours under the supervision of a probation officer. Such an order replaces any other form of punishment (e.g. imprisonment); it is usually based on a probation officer's report, must be with the consent of the offender, and is carried out within 12 months (unless extended). Breach of the order may be dealt with by fine or by revocation of the order and the imposition of any punishment that could originally have been imposed for the offence. Various changes in the law relating to community service will come into effect when the relevant provisions of the Criminal Justice Act 1982 are brought into force.

commutative contract *See* contract of exchange.

Companies Court A court forming part of the *Chancery Division of the High Court and dealing with matters arising out of the Companies Acts 1948–81, principally the formation, management, and winding-up of limited liability companies (*see* limited company).

companies register The official list of companies registered at the Companies Registry (*see* registration of a company).

Companies Registry The office of the Registrar of Companies (*see* registration of a company). Companies with a registered office in England or Wales are served by the registry at Cardiff; those in Scotland by the registry in Edinburgh. Certain documents lodged there are open to inspection. These include the accounts of limited companies, the annual return, any prospectus, the *memorandum and *articles of association, and particulars of the directors, the secretary, the registered office, and some types of company charge.

company *n.* An association of people (*company members) formed to conduct business or other activities in the name of the association. Most companies are incorporated (*see* incorporation) and therefore have a legal personality distinct from those of their members. Incorporation is usually by *registration under the Companies Acts 1948–81 but may be by private Act of Parliament (*see* statutory company) or by royal charter (*chartered company*). *See* foreign company; limited company; private company; public company; unlimited company; Welsh company.

company meeting *See* class meeting; general meeting.

company member A person who holds *shares in a company or, in the case of a company that does not issue shares (such as a company limited by guarantee), any of those who have signed the *memorandum of association or have been admitted to membership by the directors.

company name The title of a registered company, as stated in its *memorandum of association and in the companies register. The names with which companies can be registered are restricted (*see also* business name). The name must appear clearly in full outside the *registered office and other business premises, upon the company seal, and upon certain documents issuing from the company. Noncompliance may be a criminal offence and render the person responsible personally liable for company debts.

company secretary An officer of a company who has authority in administrative rather than management matters. The secretary thus acts as an agent of the company; he may be a *director (but not the sole director) of the company.

compellable witness A person who may lawfully be required to give evidence. In principle every person who is competent to be a witness is compellable (*see* competence), but in some criminal prosecutions the spouse of the accused may be competent but not compellable; for example, a wife is not a compellable witness against her husband when he has been charged with violence against her.

compensation *n.* Monetary payment to compensate for loss or damage. When someone has committed a criminal offence that caused personal injury, loss, or damage, and he has been convicted for this offence or it was taken into account when sentencing for another offence, the court may make a *compensation order* requiring the offender to pay compensation to the person suffering the loss (with interest, if

need be). Magistrates' courts may not make an order for more than £1000. The court must take into account the offender's means and should avoid making excessively high orders or orders to be paid in long-term instalments. If the offender cannot afford to pay both a fine and compensation, priority should be given to payment of compensation. A compensation order cannot cover loss caused to dependants by the death of their breadwinner (although they may apply for compensation to the *Criminal Injuries Compensation Board) or loss in cases of road accidents. Under the Theft Act 1968, a *restitution order in monetary terms may be made when the stolen goods are no longer in existence; this kind of order is equivalent to a compensation order. Compensation orders may be made in addition to, or instead of, other sentences.

A person who has been wrongfully convicted of or charged with a criminal offence may apply to the Home Secretary for *ex gratia* compensation, to be awarded upon the assessment of an independent assessor. A court must order a parent or guardian of an offender under the age of 17 to pay a compensation order on behalf of the offender unless the parent or guardian cannot be found or it would be unreasonable to order him to pay it.

An *industrial tribunal may order an employer to pay compensation to an employee who has been unfairly dismissed (*see* unfair dismissal). The compensation comprises a *basic award* of a sum equivalent to the *redundancy payment to which a redundant employee would be entitled (with a minimum of £2000 when dismissal is for trade union activity), and a *compensatory award* representing the loss that the employee suffers because of the dismissal. This will include compensation for the loss of his earnings and other benefits of the former employment, and for the loss of his statutory rights in respect of unfair dismissal and redundancy in the initial period of any new employment he obtains (*see* continuous employment). Additional compensation and/or a special award may be made in certain circumstances. Limits on the amount of weekly pay that can be used in these calculations, and on the total amount of compensation that can be awarded, are set by regulations made by the Secretary of State for Employment and reviewed annually. The tribunal may reduce any compensation by an appropriate proportion when the employee's conduct has contributed to his dismissal. The employee is under the same duty to mitigate his loss as someone claiming damages in the courts. Thus if he unreasonably refuses an offer of a new job he will not be compensated for his continued unemployment thereafter.

competence *n.* (of witnesses) The legal capacity of a person to be a *witness. Since the abolition in the 19th century of certain ancient grounds of incompetence, every person of sound mind and sufficient understanding has been competent, subject to certain exceptions. For example, a child may be sworn as a witness only if he understands the solemnity of the occasion and that the taking of an oath involves an obligation to tell the truth over and above the ordinary duty of doing so. In criminal cases, however, a child may be permitted to give *unsworn evidence. The spouse of an accused person is generally not a competent witness for the prosecution but in some circumstances (e.g. where the charge is one of violence against the spouse) may be competent but not *compellable.

complainant *n.* A person who alleges that a crime has been committed. A complainant alleging rape, attempted rape, incitement to rape, or being an accessory to rape is allowed by statute to remain anonymous; evidence relating to her previous sexual experience can-

not be given (unless the court especially rules otherwise).

complaint *n.* **1.** The initiating step in civil proceedings in the *magistrates' court, consisting of a statement of the complainant's allegations. The complaint is made before a *justice of the peace or, if the complaint is not required to be on oath, before a *clerk to the justices, who may then issue a *summons directed to the defendant. **2.** An allegation of a crime. A complaint made by the victim of a sexual offence directly after the commission of the offence is admissible as evidence of the consistency of the complainant's story.

completely constituted trust *See* executed trust.

completion *n.* (in land law) The point at which ownership of land that is the subject of a contract for its sale changes hands. The purchaser hands over any unpaid balance of the price in exchange for the title deeds and a valid conveyance of the land to him.

composition *n.* An agreement between a debtor and his creditors discharging the debts in exchange for payment of a proportion of what is due. The debtor may have to register the agreement as a *deed of arrangement. *See also* scheme of arrangement.

compound *vb.* **1.** To make a *composition with creditors. **2.** *See* compounding an offence.

compounding an offence The offence of accepting or agreeing to accept consideration for not disclosing information that might assist in convicting or prosecuting someone who has committed an arrestable offence (consideration here does not include reasonable compensation for loss or injury caused by the offence). There is also a special statutory offence of advertising a reward for stolen goods on the basis that "no questions will be asked" or that the person producing the goods "will be safe from inquiry".

compound settlement A settlement of land arising from a series of trust instruments, e.g. a resettlement following the barring of an *entailed interest. Under the Settled Land Act 1925 the trustees of the original settlement (or if there are none, those of the resettlement) are treated as the trustees of the compound settlement. Thus the tenant for life is always able to overreach the interests of all other beneficiaries (*see* overreaching).

compromise *n.* The settlement of a disputed claim by agreement between the parties. Any court proceedings already started are terminated. The terms of the settlement can be incorporated in a judgment by the court (called a *consent judgment*) or the terms can form a contract between the parties.

compulsory purchase The enforced acquisition of land for public purposes, by statutory authority and on payment of compensation. Authority may be given for a specific acquisition, but public and local authorities have wide powers to acquire any land required for particular functions, such as education. These powers are normally exercised under the Acquisition of Land (Authorisation Procedure) Act 1946, and compensation is assessed under the Land Compensation Acts 1961 and 1973. A compulsory purchase order is submitted for confirmation to the appropriate government minister, whose decision is preceded by an inquiry into public objections. Any dispute about compensation is decided by the *Lands Tribunal. *See also* special procedure orders.

compulsory winding-up by the court A procedure for winding up a company that is initiated when a *petition for winding-up* is presented to the court, usually by a creditor or qualified *contributory. The petition must be based upon one of seven grounds specified in the Companies Act 1948 (*see also* just and equitable winding-up). The usual ground is that the company is unable to pay its debts. The *liquidator is supervised by the court, the *committee of inspection, and the Department of Trade. A statement of the company's affairs must be submitted to the liquidator by company officers and he must report on these to the court. *See also* winding-up.

computer documents (in the law of evidence) In civil cases a document produced by a computer is admissible under the Civil Evidence Act 1968 as evidence of any fact recorded in it of which direct oral evidence would be admissible, provided that the computer had been operating properly throughout the material time and had been supplied with information of the kind contained in the document. It is uncertain whether or not at common law documents produced by a computer are inadmissible on the ground that they are *hearsay.

concealed fraud A deliberate fraud in relation to land, by which the true owner's rights are concealed to enable fraudulent entry or occupation. Fraud of this sort may amount to the offence of obtaining by *deception or *suppression of documents. Examples are the destruction of title deeds and the concealment of one's illegitimate status. Time does not begin to run against the true owner for purposes of the statute of limitation until he discovers the fraud.

concealment *n. See* nondisclosure.

concealment of securities The offence (punishable by up to seven years' imprisonment) of dishonestly concealing, destroying, or defacing any *valuable security*, will, or any document issuing from a court or government department for the purpose of gain for oneself or causing loss to another. Valuable securities include any documents concerning rights over property, authorizing payment of money or the delivery of property, or evidencing such rights or the satisfying of any obligation.

concert party (consortium) An agreement (which may or may not be legally binding) between a number of people to acquire shares in a company in order to accumulate a significant holding of its voting shares to facilitate a *takeover bid or to influence company policy. This procedure is colloquially known as *warehousing*. Under the Companies Act 1981 anyone becoming interested in 5% or more of the voting shares of a public company must disclose this to the company; a member of a concert party is deemed to be interested not only in his own shares but also in those of any other members. *Compare* dawn raid.

conclusive evidence Evidence that must, as a matter of law, be taken to establish some fact in issue and that cannot be disputed. For example, the certificate of incorporation of a company is conclusive evidence of its incorporation.

concurrent interests Ownership of land by two or more persons at the same time; for example, *joint tenancy and *tenancy in common.

concurrent jurisdiction That part of the jurisdiction of the *Court of Chancery before the Judicature Acts 1873–75 that was enforced equally in the common law courts; equity usually took jurisdiction because the common law remedies were inadequate. Since the Judicature Acts the jurisdiction of all divisions of the High Court has been concurrent in name, but certain remedies (for example, specific performance and injunction) are more commonly sought in the Chancery Division. *Compare* exclusive jurisdiction.

concurrent lease A lease granted by a landlord to run at the same time as another lease of the same premises. The effect is that the lessee of the concurrent lease acquires the rights and duties of the landlord in relation to the other lease.

concurrent sentence A *sentence to be served at the same time as one or more other sentences, when the accused has been convicted of more than one offence. Concurrent sentences are usually terms of imprisonment, and in effect the accused serves the term of the longest sentence. Alternatively the court may impose *consecutive sentences*, which follow on from each other.

concurrent tortfeasors *See* joint tortfeasors.

concurrent writ A duplicate of an original *writ of summons. Concurrent writs may be issued when the original writ is issued or at any time after that but before the original writ ceases to be valid. They are issued, for example, when the original writ is lost before service or when one of the defendants is resident out of the jurisdiction.

condition *n*. **1.** A major term of a contract. It is frequently described as a term that goes to the root of a contract or is of the *essence of a contract* (*see also* time provisions in contracts); it is contrasted with a *warranty*, which is a term of minor importance. Breach of a condition constitutes a fundamental breach of the contract and entitles the injured party to treat it as discharged, whereas breach of warranty is remediable only by an action for damages (*see* breach of contract). A condition or a warranty may be either an *express term or an *implied term. In the case of an express term, the fact that the contract labels it a condition or a warranty is not regarded by the courts as conclusive of its status. **2.** A provision that does not form part of a contractual obligation but operates either to suspend the contract until a specified event has happened (a *condition precedent*) or to bring it to an end in specified circumstances (a *condition subsequent*). When X agrees to buy Y's car if it passes its MOT test, this is a condition precedent; a condition in a contract for the sale of goods that entitles the purchaser to return the goods if dissatisfied with them is a condition subsequent.

conditional admissibility The *admissibility of evidence whose *relevance is conditional upon the existence of some fact that has not yet been proved. The courts permit such evidence to be given conditionally, upon proof of that fact at a later stage of the trial. Such evidence is sometimes said to have been received *de bene esse.

conditional agreement An agreement that will take effect, if at all, upon the happening of some uncertain event.

conditional discharge *See* discharge.

conditional interest An interest that is liable to be forfeited, on the occurrence of a specified event, at the instance of the person who created it; for example, when A conveys land to B in fee simple subject to a rentcharge and reserves a right of forfeiture for nonpayment. Under the Law of Property (Amendment) Act 1926 a conditional interest in land qualifies as a *fee simple absolute in possession and can therefore exist as a legal estate. *Compare* contingent interest; determinable interest.

conditional sale agreement A contract of sale under which the price is payable by instalments and ownership does not pass to the buyer (although he is in possession of the goods) until specified conditions relating to the payment of the price or other matters are fulfilled. The seller retains ownership of the goods as security until he is paid. A conditional sale agreement is a *consumer-credit agreement; it is regulated by the Consumer Credit Act 1974 if the buyer is an individual, the credit does not exceed £5000, and the agreement is not otherwise exempt.

condition precedent *See* condition.

condition subsequent *See* condition.

condominium *n.* **1.** Joint sovereignty over a territory by two or more states (the word is also used for the territory subject to joint sovereignty). For example, the New Hebrides Islands in the South Pacific were a Franco-British condominium until 1980. **2.** Individual ownership of part of a building (e.g. a flat in a block of flats) combined with common ownership of the parts of the building used in common.

condonation *n.* Forgiving a matrimonial offence or turning a blind eye to it. A spouse petitioning for divorce on the basis of the other party's adultery or unreasonable behaviour may be deemed to have forgiven it, and therefore to have lost the right to rely on it in the petition, if he (or she) has continued living with the other party for more than six months.

conference *n.* **1.** A meeting of members of the House of Lords and the House of Commons appointed to attempt to reach agreement when one House objects to amendments made to one of its Bills by the other. **2.** A meeting between counsel and a solicitor to discuss a case in which they are engaged. Conferences usually take place at counsel's chambers. If the barrister involved is a QC, the meeting is called a *consultation*.

confession *n.* An *admission by an accused person of his guilt made to a person in authority over the prosecution (e.g. a police officer). No distinction is drawn in practice between a complete and partial admission of guilt for this purpose. Confessions are admissible in evidence only if they are voluntary, i.e. have not been obtained as a result of some threat or *inducement held out by a person in authority. A confession is generally admissible only against the party who made it. *See also* Judges' Rules.

confession and avoidance A pleading in the *defence that, while admitting or assuming the truth of the material facts alleged in the statement of claim (the *confession*), seeks to avoid or destroy the legal consequences of those facts by alleging further facts constituting some defence to the claim (the *avoidance*). An example is a plea of self-defence to an action for assault.

confidential communication (in the law of evidence) The mere fact that a communication is confidential does not in itself make it inadmissible; it will only be so if it is within the scope of an evidentiary *privilege, such as legal professional privilege or public-interest privilege.

conflict of laws *See* private international law.

confusion of goods The mixing of goods of two or more owners in such a way that their original shares can no longer be distinguished. The owners hold the goods in common, in proportion to their shares.

conjugal rights The rights of either spouse of a marriage, which include the right to the other's consortium (company), cohabitation (sexual intercourse), and maintenance during the marriage. There is, however, no longer any legal procedure for enforcing these rights. The old action for restitution of conjugal rights was abolished in 1971.

connivance *n.* Behaviour of a person designed to cause his or her spouse to commit a matrimonial offence. A person who persuaded his or her spouse to commit adultery, for example, or who agreed to it in advance, could not rely on it in a divorce petition. Connivance is no longer an absolute bar to divorce, but may still be evidence that there is no real *breakdown of marriage.

consanguinity (blood relationship) *n.* Relationship by blood, i.e. by descent from a common ancestor. People descended from two common ancestors are said to be of the *whole blood*. If they share only one ancestor, they are of the *half blood*. *Compare* affinity.

consecutive sentences *See* concurrent sentence.

consensus ad idem [Latin: agreement on the same thing] The agreement by contracting parties to identical terms that is necessary for the formation of a legally binding contract. *See* acceptance; mistake; offer.

consent *n.* Acquiescence. Consent is essential in a number of circumstances. For example, contracts and marriages are invalid unless both parties give their consent. Consent is a defence to *rape. Consent must be given freely, without duress or deception, and with legal competence and sufficient mental capacity to give it. *See also* age of consent.

conservation area An area designated as such by a local planning authority (*see* town and country planning) because it is of special architectural or historic interest the character of which ought to be preserved or enhanced. Each building in the area becomes protected as if it were a *listed building, and trees not protected by a *tree preservation order may only be lopped, felled, etc., after notice to the authority.

consideration *n.* An act, forbearance, or promise by one party to a contract that constitutes the price for which he buys the promise of the other. Consideration is essential to the validity of any contract other than one made by deed. Without consideration an agreement not made by deed is not binding; it is a *nudum pactum* (naked agreement), governed by the maxim *ex nudo pacto non oritur actio* (a right of action does not arise out of a naked agreement).

The doctrine of consideration is governed by four major principles. (1) A *valuable consideration* is required, i.e. the act, forbearance, or promise must have some economic value. *Good consideration* (natural love and affection or a moral duty) is not enough to render a promise enforceable. (2) Consideration need not be adequate but it must be sufficient. Not to be adequate in this context means that it need not constitute a realistic price for the promise it buys, as long as it has some economic value. If X promises to sell his £50,000 house to Y for £5000, Y is giving valuable consideration despite its inadequacy. That it must be sufficient means sufficient in law. A person's performance of, or promise to perform, an existing duty cannot in law constitute consideration. (3) Consideration must move from the promisee. Thus if X promises to give Y £1000 in return for Y's promise to give employment to Z, Z cannot enforce Y's promise, for he has not supplied the consideration for it. (4) Consideration may be executory or executed but must not be past. A promise in return for a promise (as in a contract of sale) is *executory consideration*; an act or forbearance in return for a promise (as in giving information to obtain a reward) is *executed consideration*. However, a completed act or forbearance is *past consideration* in relation to any subsequent promise. For example, if X gives information to Y gratuitously and Y then promises to reward him this is past consideration, which does not constitute consideration.

Consolidated Fund The central account with the Bank of England maintained by the government for receiving public revenue and meeting public expenditure. Most payments from it are authorized annually by Consolidated Fund Acts, but some (e.g. judicial salaries) are permanent statutory charges on it.

consolidating statute A statute that repeals and re-enacts existing statutes relating to a particular subject. Its purpose is to state their combined effect and so simplify the presentation of the law. It does not aim to alter the law unless it is stated in its long title to be a consolidation with amendments. *Compare* codifying statute. *See also* interpretation of statutes.

consolidation of actions A procedure in civil cases by which two or more cases that are pending (i.e. in which the originating process has been served) may be amalgamated. It is generally necessary to show that some common question of law or fact will arise in all the cases. The purpose of consolidation is to save costs and time.

consolidation of mortgages The right of a mortgagee who has taken mortgages on two or more properties from the same mortagor to require the mortgagor to redeem all of the mortgages or none, provided that the contractual date of redemption (*see* power of sale) for all of them has passed. The right arose because it was considered unfair to a mortgagee to have one security redeemed when another, given by the same mortgagor, might be inadequate. Since 1881 at least one of the mortgage deeds must show an intent to allow consolidation for the mortgagee to exercise the right. *Compare* tacking.

consortium *n.* **1.** The right of one spouse to the company, assistance, and affection of the other. Formerly, a husband could bring an action in tort (*per quod consortium amisit*) against anyone who, by a tortious act against his wife, deprived him of consortium. A wife had no corresponding action. The action for loss of consortium was abolished by the Administration of Justice Act 1982. **2.** *See* concert party.

conspiracy *n.* An agreement between two or more people to behave in a manner that will automatically constitute an offence by at least one of them (e.g. two people agree that one of them shall steal while the other waits in a getaway car). The agreement is itself a statutory crime, usually punishable in the same way as the offence agreed on, even if it is not carried out. *Mens rea*, in the sense of knowledge of the facts that make the action criminal, is required by at least two of the conspirators, even if the crime is one of *strict liability. One may be guilty of conspiracy even if it is impossible to commit the offence (for example, when two or more people conspire to take money from a safe but, unknown to them, there is no money in it). A person is, however, not guilty of conspiracy if the only other party to the agreement is his (or her) spouse. Nor is there liability when the acts are to be carried out in furtherance of a trade dispute and involve only a summary and nonimprisonable offence. Incitement and attempt to conspire are no longer crimes.

Some forms of criminal conspiracy still exist at common law. These are now limited to: (1) conspiracy to *defraud (e.g. to commit fraud, theft, obtain property by deception, or infringe a copyright) or to cause an official to act contrary to his public duty; (2) conspiracy to corrupt public morals (*see* corruption of public morals); and (3) conspiracy to outrage *public decency (this might include an agreement to mount an indecent exhibition). In the latter two cases, however, the conduct agreed upon must not be such that it would be an offence if carried out by only one person.

A conspiracy to injure a third party is a tort if it causes damage to the person against whom the conspiracy is aimed. If unlawful means are used, the motive of the conspirators is irrelevant. If unlawful means have not been used, conspiracy is not actionable if the predominant purpose of the conspirators was legitimate. Protection of one's own financial or trade interests is thus a legitimate purpose; retaliation for an insult to one's dignity is not. The operation of the tort in *trade disputes is limited by statute.

constable *n. See* police officer.

constituency *n.* An area of the UK for which a representative is elected to membership of the *House of Commons or the *Assembly of the EEC. *See also* boundary commissions.

constitution *n.* The rules and practices that determine the composition and functions of the organs of central and local government in a state and regulate the relationship between the individual and the state. Most states have a written constitution, one of the fundamental provisions of which is that it can itself be amended only in accordance with a special procedure. The constitution of the UK is largely unwritten. It consists partly of statutes, for the amendment of which by subsequent statutes no special procedure is required (*see* Act of Parliament), but also, to a very significant extent, of *common law rules and *constitutional conventions.

constitutional conventions Practices relating to the exercise of their functions by the Crown, the government, Parliament, and the judiciary that are not legally enforceable but are commonly followed as if they were. One of the most important is that the Crown must exercise its constitutional powers only in accordance with the advice of ministers who collectively command the support of a majority of the House of Commons. There is no single reason why conventions are observed. For example, it is a very old convention that Parliament must be summoned at least once a year. If that were not to happen, there would be no annual Finance Act and the government would be able to function only by raising illegal taxation. By contrast, if the Crown broke the convention that the royal assent must not be refused to a Bill duly passed by Parliament, illegal conduct would not necessarily follow (although the future of the monarchy could well be at risk). The basic reason for obeying conventions is to ensure that the machinery of government should function smoothly; they have not been codified into law so that they may be modified informally to meet changing circumstances.

construction *n. See* interpretation.

constructive *adj.* Describing anything that is deemed by law to exist or to have happened, even though that is not in fact the case.

constructive desertion Behaviour by one spouse causing the other to leave the matrimonial home. If the behaviour is so bad that the party who leaves is forced to do so, it is the spouse who stays behind who is considered, in law, to have deserted, and not the spouse who actually left. A petition for divorce may therefore be brought, after two years, on the ground of *desertion by the spouse who remained behind.

constructive dismissal Termination of a contract of employment by an employee because his employer has shown that he does not intend to be bound by some essential term of the contract. Although the employee has resigned, he has the same right to apply to an industrial tribunal as one who has been unfairly dismissed by his employer. *See also* unfair dismissal.

constructive fraud (legal fraud) Any of certain forms of unintentional deception or misrepresentation (*compare* fraud). The concept is applied by equity to those cases in which the courts will not enforce or will set aside certain transactions (e.g. contracts) because it is considered unfair for a person to insist on the transaction being completed. This unfairness may be inferred from the terms of the transaction (when these are such that no person with proper advice would have entered the transaction) or from the relationship of the parties (for example, that of solicitor and client).

constructive malice The intention to commit an offence that is ascribed to a person charged with that offence although he did not actually have this intention. The main example of this now is in relation to manslaughter, which can be committed by a person carrying out an unlawful and dangerous act incidentally causes death but is intended to have some other effect (e.g. to frighten). Constructive murder, however, has now been abolished.

constructive notice Knowledge that the law presumes a person to have even if he is actually ignorant of the facts. A purchaser of land has constructive notice of all matters that a prudent purchaser would discover on a proper investigation of the title: those that are registered and those that are revealed to his solicitor. He is bound by all matters of which he has constructive, as well as actual, notice. Those dealing with registered companies have constructive notice of the contents of documents open to public inspection at the *Companies Registry.

constructive total loss A loss of a ship or cargo that is only partial but is treated for the purposes of a marine insurance policy as if it were an *actual total loss. This may occur when an actual total loss either appears unavoidable (e.g. when a perishable cargo becomes stranded indefinitely) or can only be prevented by incurring expenditure greater than the value of the ship or cargo. The insured must serve a notice of *abandonment of the ship or cargo on the underwriters. This must be unconditional and served within a reasonable time of his learning of the loss; once accepted by the underwriters, it is irrevocable. The underwriters become liable to indemnify him as for a total loss and in return are entitled to all his rights in the ship or cargo.

constructive trust A *trust imposed by equity to protect the interests of the beneficiaries when a trustee or some other person in a fiduciary relationship gains an advantage through his position. It differs from an *implied trust in that no reference is made to the expressed or presumed intention of the parties. The constructive trust is sometimes regarded as a flexible device to prevent an injustice; for example, when a person who has acquired by fraud the property of another seeks to retain it.

consumer-credit agreement A *personal-credit agreement in which an individual (the debtor) is provided with credit not exceeding £5000. Unless exempted, consumer-credit agreements are regulated by the Consumer Credit Act 1974, which contains provisions (many of which are not yet in force) regarding the seeking of business, entry into agreements, matters arising during the currency of agreements, default and termination, security, and judicial control. A loan to an individual businessman for business purposes can be a consumer-credit agreement.

consumer-credit business Any business that comprises or relates to the provision of credit under *consumer-credit agreements regulated by the Consumer Credit Act 1974. With certain exceptions, e.g. local authorities, a licence is required to carry on a consumer-credit business.

consumer-credit register The register kept by the Director General of Fair Trading, as required by the Consumer Credit Act 1974, relating to the licensing or carrying on of *consumer-credit businesses or *consumer-hire businesses. The register contains particulars of undetermined applications, licences that are in force or have at any time been suspended or revoked, and decisions given by the Director under the Act and any appeal from them. The public is entitled to inspect the register on payment of a fee.

consumer goods Goods normally supplied for private use or consumption. The Unfair Contract Terms Act 1977 provides that if consumer goods prove defective when used otherwise than exclusively for business purposes as a result of negligence of a manufacturer or distributor, that person's *business liability cannot be excluded or restricted by any guarantee under which the goods are sold.

consumer-hire agreement An agreement made by a person with an individual, partnership, or other unincorporated body (the *hirer*) for the *bailment of goods to the hirer. Such an agreement must not be a *hire-purchase agreement, must be capable of subsisting for more than three months, and must not require the hirer to make payments exceeding £5000. The concept thus does not include a hiring by a company. Consumer-hire agreements, unless exempted, are regulated by the Consumer Credit Act 1974. *Compare* consumer-credit agreement.

consumer-hire business Any business that comprises or relates to the bailment of goods under *consumer-hire agreements regulated by the Consumer Credit Act 1974. With certain exceptions, e.g. local authorities, a licence is required to carry on a consumer-hire business.

consumer protection The protection, especially by legal means, of consumers. It is the policy of current legislation to protect consumers against unfair contract terms. In particular they are protected against terms that attempt to restrict the seller's implied undertakings that he has a right to sell the goods, that the goods conform with either description or sample, and that they are of merchantable quality and fit for their particular purpose (Unfair Contract Terms Act 1977). There is also provision for the banning of unfair *consumer trade practices (Fair Trading Act 1973). Consumers (including individual businessmen) are also protected against obtaining credit (Consumer Credit Act 1974) and there is provision for the imposition of standards relating to the safety of goods under the Consumer Safety Act 1978.

consumer trade practice Any practice carried on in connection with the supply of goods (by sale or otherwise) or services to consumers. These practices include the terms or conditions of supply and the manner in which they are communicated to the consumers, the promotion of the supply of goods or services, the methods of salesmanship employed in dealing with consumers, the way in which goods are packed, or the methods of demanding or securing payment for goods or services. Under the Fair Trading Act 1973, consumer trade practices are controlled by the Minister, the *Director General of Fair Trading, and the Consumer Protection Advisory Committee, who may ban any practice that adversely affects the economic interests of consumers in the UK.

consummation of a marriage The "completion" of a marriage by an act of sexual intercourse. It is defined for these purposes as complete penetration of the vagina by the penis (although ejaculation is not necessary). A marriage may be consummated despite the use of a contraceptive sheath. If a spouse is incapable of consummation or refuses without good reason to consummate the marriage, these may be grounds for *annulment of the marriage. If one of the partners refuses to arrange an additional marriage ceremony (e.g. in a church) without which he knows his spouse will not agree to have intercourse, this may be a good reason for the spouse's refusal to have intercourse. In this case it is the partner who refused to arrange the ceremony who is regarded as not having consummated the marriage, even though he himself is willing to have intercourse.

contemporanea expositio [Latin: contemporaneous interpretation] The interpretation of a document in the sense in which it would have been interpreted at the time of its making. This principle is applied particularly to the interpretation of ancient documents.

contempt of court 1. (civil contempt) Disobedience to a court judgment or process, e.g. breach of an injunction or improper use of discovered documents. **2. (criminal contempt)** Conduct that obstructs or tends to obstruct the proper administration of justice. At common law criminal contempt includes the following categories. (1) Deliberately interfering with the outcome of particular legal proceedings (e.g. attempting improperly to pressurize a party to settle legal proceedings) or bribing or intimidating witnesses, the jury, or a judge. (2) *Contempt in the face of the court*, e.g. using threatening language or creating a disturbance in court. (3) Scandalizing the court by "scurrilous abuse" of a judge going beyond reasonable criticism or attacking the integrity of the administration of justice. (4) Interfering with the general process of administration of justice (e.g. by disclosing the deliberations of a jury), even though no particular proceedings are pending.

Under the Contempt of Court Act 1981 it is a statutory contempt to publish to the public, by any means, any communication that creates a substantial risk that the course of justice in particular legal proceedings will be seriously impeded or prejudiced, if the proceedings are active. Such publications constitute *strict-liability contempt*, in which the intention to interfere with the course of justice is not required, but there are various special defences. It is also contempt under the Act to obtain or disclose any particulars of jury discussions and to bring into court or use a tape recorder without permission. The Act also protects (subject to certain exceptions) sources of information against disclosure in court.

contempt of Parliament *See* parliamentary privilege.

contemptuous damages A very small sum of *damages awarded when, although the plaintiff is technically entitled to succeed, the court thinks that the action should not have been brought. Contemptuous damages are often awarded in "gold-digging" actions for defamation.

contentious business Business of a solicitor when there is a contest between the parties involved, especially litigation. It is important in relation to *costs, since different rules govern contentious and noncontentious costs.

contentious probate business Disputed applications to the court relating to the validity of wills and the administration of estates.

continental shelf The sea bed and the soil beneath it that is adjacent to the coast of a maritime state and outside the limits of the state's territorial waters. The 1958 Geneva Convention on the Continental Shelf limits the extent of the shelf to waters less than 200 metres deep or, beyond that limit, to waters that are of such a depth that exploitation of the natural resources of the sea bed is possible. The coastal state is granted exclusive sovereign rights of exploitation over mineral resources and nonmoving species in its continental shelf, provided that this causes no unreasonable interference to navigation, fishing, or scientific research. The 1982 Conference on the Law of the Sea extends the continental shelf, in some cases, to a distance of 200 nautical miles from the baselines around the coast from which the breadth of the territorial sea is measured. It also makes special provisions for delimiting the continental shelf between states with adjacent or opposite coastlines, but does not lay down rules of law for such delimitation. Rocks that cannot sustain human habitation do not have a continental shelf.

contingent interest (contingent remainder) An interest that can only come into being upon the occurrence of a specified event; for example, when A conveys land to B provided he marries. As a contingent interest can only come into being in the future, if at all, it cannot exist as a legal estate in land. Such a transaction creates a settlement to which the Settled Land Act 1925 applies, and contingent interests are consequently *equitable interests only. *Compare* conditional interest; determinable interest.

contingent legacy A bequest that only takes effect if a particular condition is fulfilled, e.g. a bequest "to A if he shall marry within five years".

contingent remainder *See* contingent interest.

continuous bail Bail granted by a magistrates' court directing the accused to appear at every time and place to which the proceedings may from time to time be adjourned, as opposed to a direction to appear at the end of a fixed period of remand.

continuous employment The period for which a person's employment in the same business has subsisted. Under the Employment Protection (Consolidation) Act 1978, employees have the right to claim certain statutory remedies only if they have been continuously employed for certain minimum periods. Full-time employees (i.e. those with a normal working week of 16 hours or more) may only appeal to an industrial tribunal against *unfair dismissal after 52 weeks (104 weeks if the employment began after 1 October 1980 and the employer has at no time within the two years preceding the dismissal employed more than 20 persons). Their right to statutory redundancy payments and to *guarantee payments arises after 104 weeks' and 4 weeks' continuous employment, respectively. The minimum period of *notice to terminate an employee's contract also depends on his period of continuous employment in the business. When a business changes ownership as a going concern, the employee's period of continuous employment under both the old and the new employer counts in calculating the total. When an employee is dismissed without notice, the minimum notice to which he was entitled is added to the actual period of employment in calculating whether or not he has served the minimum continuous period. Part-time employees (i.e. those whose normal working week is less than 16 hours) have few statutory rights until they have completed five years' continuous employment in the business.

Periods during which an employee was on strike do not break the continuity, but are excluded from his total period of continuous employment. Continuity is not broken when a woman resigns or is dismissed because of pregnancy or confinement, provided she takes up her right to return to work within 29 weeks after the baby's birth (*see also* maternity rights).

contraband *n.* **1.** Goods whose import or export is forbidden. **2. (contraband of war)** Goods (such as munitions) carried by a neutral vessel during wartime and destined for the use of one belligerent power against the other. The latter belligerent is entitled to seize and confiscate such goods (*see also* search of ship).

contra bonos mores [Latin] Against good morals. It is a matter of controversy to what extent the criminal law should, or does, prohibit immoral conduct merely on the grounds of its immorality. The tendency in recent years has been to limit legal intervention in matters of morals to acts that cause harm to others. However, there are still certain offences regarded as essentially immoral (e.g. *incest and *buggery).

There are also offences of conspiring to corrupt public morals (although *corruption of public morals is not in itself criminal) and of outraging (or conspiring to outrage) *public decency, although the scope of these offences is uncertain. *See also* obscene publications.

contract *n.* A legally binding agreement. Agreement arises as a result of *offer and *acceptance, but a number of other requirements must be satisfied for an agreement to be legally binding. (1) There must be *consideration (unless the contract is by deed). (2) The parties must have an intention to create legal relations. This requirement usually operates to prevent a purely domestic or social agreement from constituting a contract (*see also* honour clause). (3) The parties must have *capacity to contract. (4) The agreement must comply with any formal legal requirements. In general, no particular formality is required for the creation of a valid contract. It may be oral, written, partly oral and partly written, or even implied from conduct. Certain transactions are, however, valid only if effected by deed (e.g. transfers of shares in British ships) or in writing (e.g. promissory notes), and certain others, though valid, can at law only be enforced if evidenced in writing (*see* unenforceable contract). (5) The agreement must be legal (*see* illegal contract). (6) The agreement must not be rendered void either by some common-law or statutory rule or by some inherent defect, such as operative mistake (*see* void contract). Certain contracts, though valid, may be liable to be set aside by one of the parties on such grounds as misrepresentation or the exercise of undue influence (*see* voidable contract).

contract of employment (contract of service) A contract by which a person agrees to undertake certain duties under the direction and control of the employer in return for a specified wage or salary. The contract need not be in writing, but under the Employment Protection (Consolidation) Act 1978 the employee must be given a written statement giving particulars of certain basic terms. Implied in every contract of employment are a duty of mutual confidence and trust, the employer's duty to protect the employee from danger and risks to his health, and the employee's duty to do the work to the best of his ability. Employees who have been continuously employed in the same business for certain minimum periods (*see* continuous employment) have statutory rights, relating for example to *unfair dismissal and *redundancy, that do not apply to the self-employed. A self-employed person is engaged under a contract for services and owes his employer or customer no other duty than to complete the specified work in accordance with the terms of the individual contract; he is not otherwise under the direction or control of the employer as to how or when he works.

contract of exchange (commutative contract) A barter contract in which property is transferred from one party to the other in return for other property. No money passes from one party to the other. A contract of exchange of goods is not governed by the Sale of Goods Act 1979. *Compare* sale of goods.

contract of record A judgment or recognizance enrolled in the record of the proceedings of a *court of record, implying a debt that arises from the entry on the record and not from any agreement between the parties.

contract of sale *See* sale; sale of goods.

contract of service *See* contract of employment.

contract under seal *See* deed.

contribution *n.* The payment made by each of two or more people in respect of damage or a loss for which they are jointly liable. In tort, when two or more people are jointly liable for the same damage and the person injured has recovered his losses from one of them, that person may seek contributions from the other tortfeasors (*see* civil liability contribution; joint tortfeasors). In the case of a general-average loss (*see* average), the person who has sustained the loss is entitled to contributions from others with an interest in the property.

contributory *n.* Any of the past or present members of a company, who are potentially liable to contribute to the company's assets in the event of a *winding-up. Members whose liability to contribute is limited or has been previously discharged or who have been exempted from contributing (for example, because they ceased to be members) at least one year before the winding-up may still present a petition for winding-up (*see* compulsory winding-up by the court).

contributory negligence A person's carelessness for his own safety or interests, which contributes materially to damage suffered by him as a result partly of his own fault and partly of the fault of another person or persons. Thus careless driving, knowingly travelling with a drunken driver, and failure to wear a seat belt are common forms of contributory negligence in highway accidents. The effect of contributory negligence is to reduce the plaintiff's damages to an amount that the court thinks just and equitable. The defence is most common in actions for negligence, but can be pleaded in some other torts: *nuisance, *Rylands* v *Fletcher*, *breach of statutory duty, or under the Animals Act 1971 (*see* classification of animals). Contributory negligence may also be a defence to some actions for breach of contract. It is not a defence to conversion or intentional trespass to goods.

controlled drugs Dangerous drugs that are subject to criminal regulation. In the Misuse of Drugs Act 1971 these are grouped in three classes: A, B, and C. Class A is the most dangerous and includes opium and its natural and synthetic derivatives (e.g. morphine and heroin) and cocaine. Class B includes *cannabis and amphetamine, and C – the least dangerous class – includes the stimulant pemoline. It is an offence to possess a controlled drug or to supply or offer it to another. In the case of an occupier or someone concerned in the management of premises, it is an offence (1) to allow the smoking of cannabis, cannabis resin, or prepared opium on the premises (but it is not an offence to allow the premises to be used for injecting heroin or consuming any other controlled drug); (2) to prepare opium for smoking; and (3) to produce or supply a controlled drug on the premises. The defendant is liable on a charge of possession for the minutest quantity of the drug and without proof of *mens rea*, unless he can prove that he did not believe or suspect that it was a controlled drug.

controlled mortgage A mortgage to which the Rent and Mortgage Interest (Restrictions) Act 1920 would have applied had neither of the Rent Acts 1968 and 1977 been passed. The rate of interest chargeable by the mortgagee and his powers of enforcement are restricted by provisions in the Rent Act 1977.

controlled tenancy A type of *protected tenancy that sometimes occurred with tenancies created before 6 July 1957. Since 28 November 1980 all controlled tenancies have been converted into *regulated tenancies.

controlled trust A trust of which one or more solicitors or their employees are sole trustees. Such trusts are subject to special accounts rules made under the Solicitors Act 1974; breaches of these rules may be reported to the Solicitors' Disciplinary Tribunal.

controller *n.* (in company law) Strictly, one who holds shares conferring a majority of the *voting power that can be exercised at a general meeting. In practice, effective control can often be exercised by a director with no voting power or a minority of it if he is able to manipulate *proxy voting.

convention *n.* **1.** A *treaty, usually of a multilateral nature. The International Law Commission prepares draft conventions on various issues for the progressive development of international law. **2.** *See* constitutional conventions.

conversion *n.* **1.** (in tort) The tort of wrongfully dealing with a person's goods in a way that constitutes a denial of the owner's rights or an assertion of rights inconsistent with the owner's. Wrongfully taking possession of goods, disposing of them, destroying them, or refusing to give them back are acts of conversion. Mere negligence in allowing goods to be lost or destroyed was not conversion at common law, but is a ground of liability under the Torts (Interference with Goods) Act 1977. The plaintiff in conversion must prove that he had ownership, possession, or the right to immediate possession of the goods at the time of the defendant's wrongful act (*see also jus tertii*). Subject to such exceptions as sale in *market overt, it is no defence that the defendant acted innocently. **2.** (in equity) The changing (either actually or fictionally) of one kind of property into another. For example, if land is sold the interest of those entitled to the property changes from an interest in the land to an interest in the money that represents it. Before 1926 (and to a lesser extent thereafter) it was important to know whether a person entitled to property had interests in land or in the proceeds of its sale: to leave the determination of these rights to be decided by the precise moment of a sale could have led to uncertainty and injustice. The doctrine of conversion stated that if there was a *duty to convert* the property, equity would assume the property to have been converted forthwith: "equity looks on that as done which ought to have been done" (*see* maxims of equity). There may be an express order by the settlor to convert property or the duty may be imposed by statute, under a partnership or a contract. Conversion occurs, for example, when land is held on a *trust for sale: those entitled to the property have interests in the proceeds of its sale (personalty), not in the land itself (realty). In some recent cases, however, the doctrine has been considered to be an unnecessary and complicated fiction, and the interests have been regarded as continuing in or over land until the property is actually sold.

converted tenancy A tenancy that has been converted from a *controlled tenancy into a *regulated tenancy. Since 28 November 1980 all controlled tenancies have been converted into regulated tenancies.

conveyance *n.* **1. a.** A document (other than a will) that transfers an interest in land. It is usually a deed. **b.** Transfer of an interest in land by means of this document. *See also* conveyancing. **2.** Any vehicle, vessel, or aircraft manufactured or subsequently adapted to carry one or more people. It is a statutory offence (and also an *arrestable offence), punishable by up to three years' imprisonment, for anyone to take a conveyance for his own or someone else's use without permission or to drive or be transported in a conveyance knowing that it has been taken without authority, even if the necessary element of theft cannot be proved.

conveyancing *n.* The procedures involved in validly creating, extinguishing, and transferring ownership of interests in land. Only a practising solicitor may charge a fee for undertaking the most essential parts of such transactions. Apart from preparing the deeds or other documents by which the

transaction is effected, certain investigative steps are usually required. For example, the sale and purchase of a residential house in England or Wales will generally involve the following.

(1) Preparation of a contract by the vendor's solicitor defining the terms of the transaction, describing the property concerned, and disclosing *land charges and other interests in it that will affect the purchaser.

(2) Written inquiries by the purchaser's solicitor seeking assurances from the vendor that matters which may not be apparent from inspection of the site will not impose any unforeseen liability on the purchaser. These questions generally cover such potential problems as disputes over boundaries, the construction or treatment of buildings, compliance with planning and rating authorities' requirements, and liability for maintenance of shared facilities (such as boundary walls).

(3) *Official search by the purchaser's solicitor in the local land charges register to ensure there are no undisclosed legal charges that could bind the purchaser. The local authority is also asked to disclose other information, such as proposals for building new roads near the property.

(4) If the purchaser is raising a *mortgage loan towards the price, his solicitor will ensure that the funds will be available at the appropriate time and that any conditions imposed by the mortgagees can be satisfied.

(5) The purchaser's solicitor may then negotiate alterations to the draft contract with the vendor's solicitor, to ensure its compliance with the purchaser's requirements and to cover points arising from the earlier inquiries and search. For example, if an unforeseen local land charge has been discovered, a term may be inserted requiring the vendor to clear it before the transaction is completed.

(6) When there is a chain of sales and purchases dependent on one another,

the solicitors for the parties involved liaise with one another through all steps of the transactions, particularly in arranging a date for completion, to ensure that the various completions coincide.

(7) The parties become legally committed to buy and sell respectively upon *exchange of contracts. It is then usual for the purchaser to pay 10% of the price to the vendor's solicitor as stakeholder.

(8) The vendor's solicitor next prepares and delivers an *abstract of title to the purchaser's solicitor, who studies it to ensure that the vendor's title is proved in accordance with the contract. As final checks on the vendor's title, he conducts an official search in the *Land Charges Department (for unregistered land) or HM *Land Registry as appropriate, and raises *requisitions on title requiring the vendor to clear any defects or adverse interests revealed by the abstract or search.

(9) The purchaser's solicitor prepares the deed (usually a conveyance, transfer, or assignment) by which the property is to be transferred to his client, and has its terms approved by the vendor's solicitor. He also ensures that the purchaser's mortgage deed (if any) is in order.

(10) In preparation for completion, the purchaser's solicitor arranges with the necessary parties for the funds to be available on the completion date and ensures that the necessary deeds will be executed by the time completion takes place.

(11) On completion, the purchaser's solicitor checks the vendor's original *title deeds against the abstract of title, and takes possession of them together with the deed of transfer. He hands over the price, and the transaction is then legally completed.

(12) After completion, the transfer deed is produced to the Inland Revenue, and any stamp duty paid, by the purchaser's solicitor on his client's behalf. He also gives formal notice of the transaction when appropriate; for example, when a leasehold interest is purchased, the lessor must usually be notified. In the case of registered land, the purchaser's solicitor lodges the relevant deeds with HM Land Registry for registration of his client's title.

These basic steps in respect of the sale and purchase of a house are common to many other conveyancing transactions, although the complexity of the particular requirements varies according to the nature of the transaction.

conviction *n.* **1.** (for the purposes of the Bail Act 1976) In criminal proceedings, a finding of *guilty or an acquittal on the grounds of insanity. In a magistrates' court, a finding that the accused carried out the act for which he was charged (*see* summary conviction). **2.** (for the purposes of the Rehabilitation of Offenders Act 1974) Any finding (except one of insanity), either in criminal proceedings or in care proceedings, that a person has committed an offence or carried out the act for which he was charged. *See also* spent conviction.

copyhold *n.* Ownership of land enforceable only in the court of the lord of the manor and not protected by the sovereign's courts (*see* feudal system). The owner's title comprised a copy of an entry in the rolls of the lord's court. By the Law of Property Act 1922 copyhold tenure was abolished and existing copyholds were converted into freeholds.

copyright *n.* The exclusive right to reproduce or authorize others to reproduce artistic, dramatic, literary, or musical works. It is conferred by the Copyright Act 1956, which also extends to sound broadcasting, cinematograph films, and television broadcasts. Copyright lasts for the holder's lifetime plus 50 years from the end of the year in which he died; it can be assigned or transmitted on death. The principal remedies for breach of copyright (known as *piracy*) are an action for *damages and *account of profits or an *injunction.

co-respondent *n.* The party with whom a married person is alleged to have committed adultery. A co-respondent must normally be made a party to divorce proceedings and may be required to give evidence relating to the alleged adultery.

coroner *n.* An officer of the Crown whose principal function is to investigate deaths either by ordering a post-mortem examination or conducting an *inquest. The coroner also holds inquests on *treasure trove. Coroners are appointed by the Crown from among barristers, solicitors, and qualified medical practitioners of not less than five years' standing.

corporate personality *See* incorporation.

corporation (body corporate) *n.* An entity that has legal personality, i.e. it is capable of enjoying and being subject to legal rights and duties (*see* juristic person). It may be either a corporation aggregate or a corporation sole. A *corporation aggregate* (e.g. a *company registered under the Companies Acts) consists of a number of members who fluctuate from time to time. A *corporation sole* (e.g. the *Crown) consists of one member only and his or her successors. *See also* incorporation.

corporation tax A tax on the worldwide profits of limited companies and certain other bodies resident or trading in the UK. Corporation tax started on 6 April 1966 (before this date companies paid income tax and profits tax). It applies to all bodies corporate and unincorporated associations, including limited companies, building societies, cooperative societies, unit trusts, and investment trusts, but excluding local authorities.

The tax is based on the profits shown in the company's audited accounts after adding back certain nonallowable deductions, which include depreciation of *machinery and plant, provisions for doubtful debts, and political contributions. However, *capital allowances and *stock relief are deductible for corporation tax purposes, as are losses carried forward from earlier years. Any *advance corporation tax that the company has paid on its distributed profits is offset against corporation tax liability. Although *chargeable gains count as profits for corporation tax purposes, only a fraction of the gain is chargeable to tax. The effect of this is to bring the tax paid by companies on such gains into line with *capital gains tax paid by individuals, and similar rules apply for offsetting losses and adjusting for inflation. The rates of corporation tax are announced in arrears, usually as part of the Chancellor's Budget speech. The 1983 Budget has proposed that the rates will be 52% for companies with profits exceeding £500,000 and 38% for those with profits below £100,000. A sliding scale will operate between these two thresholds.

corporeal hereditament *See* hereditament.

corpus delicti [Latin: body of an offence] The former term for **actus reus*.

corroboration *n.* Evidence that confirms the accuracy of other evidence *in a material particular*. In general, English law does not require corroboration and any fact may be proved by a single item of credible evidence. But in some cases (e.g. in relation to the evidence of *accomplices or that of the complainant in sexual offences) a *corroboration warning* must be given: the jury must be warned of the danger of acting on uncorroborated evidence. In some other cases the existence of corroboration is mandatory (e.g. in cases of *perjury and in respect of the *unsworn evidence of children).

corrupt and illegal practices Offences defined by the Representation of the People Act 1949 in connection with conduct at parliamentary or local elections. Corrupt practices, which include bribery and intimidation, are the more serious of the two. The most frequent illegal practice is spending by a candidate in excess of the amount authorized for the management of his campaign.

corruption *n. See* bribery and corruption.

corruption of public morals Conduct "destructive of the [moral] fabric of society". It is uncertain whether such acts are crimes or not, although those who published "directories" with details of prostitutes or magazine advertisements encouraging readers to meet the advertisers for homosexual purposes have been found guilty of conspiring to corrupt public morals. *See also* conspiracy; *contra bonos mores.*

cost, insurance, freight *See* c.i.f. contract.

costs *pl. n.* Sums payable for legal services. A distinction is drawn between *contentious* and *noncontentious costs* (broadly, the distinction between costs relating to litigious and nonlitigious matters). Solicitors' costs are normally divided into *profit costs* (representing the solicitor's profit and overheads) and *disbursements* (any out-of-pocket expenses he may have incurred in the conduct of the case).

In civil litigation the court has a wide discretion to make an award in respect of the costs of the case, but the general principle applied is that the *costs follow the event*, i.e. the loser of the case must pay the costs of the winner. The court will order what *basis of taxation* is to be applied, i.e. on what basis the costs will be assessed. In normal adversary litigation this is *party and party costs*, in which the loser pays all costs reasonably and necessarily incurred by the winning party, but other bases of taxation

may be ordered in particular cases (*see* common fund basis; indemnity basis; solicitor and own client basis of costs). If the parties cannot agree upon the sum payable there will be a *taxation of costs. See also* costs in any event; costs in the cause; costs reserved.

costs draftsman A person (usually a legal executive rather than a qualified solicitor) who specializes in drawing up *bills of costs. Some work in solicitors' firms and some in independent firms of costs specialists.

costs follow the event *See* costs.

costs in any event An order for costs made in *interlocutory proceedings by which the winner of the interlocutory hearing in question (e.g. a summons before the master) shall be paid the costs of that stage in the proceedings whatever the outcome of the trial. *Compare* costs in the cause.

costs in the cause An order for costs made in *interlocutory proceedings by which the costs of the interlocutory hearing in question are payable in accordance with the order for costs to be made at the trial. This will usually have the effect that they are paid by the overall loser of the litigation. *Compare* costs in any event.

costs reserved An order for costs made in *interlocutory proceedings by which the costs of the interlocutory hearing in question are reserved for the decision of the trial judge rather than decided by the master or district registrar at the interlocutory hearing itself.

costs thrown away Costs either unnecessarily incurred by a party as a result of some procedural error committed by the other party or properly incurred but wasted as a result of a subsequent act of the other party (e.g. by amending the writ or pleadings).

Council for the Securities Industry A voluntary supervisory body established to coordinate the activities of

City institutions involved in the securities industry, e.g. the *Stock Exchange, the Panel on Takeovers and Mergers (*see* City Code). It consists of the representatives of these institutions.

council housing Residential accommodation provided for renting by local authorities (primarily by district and London borough councils, who, as housing authorities, have a general statutory duty to meet housing needs in their areas). Authorities may build new properties and acquire existing ones for the purpose. The allocation and management of housing stock is in general within their sole discretion, but statute does impose certain priorities (e.g. towards homeless persons) and the Housing Act 1980 gives their tenants a measure of security of tenure.

Council of Legal Education A body established by the four *Inns of Court to supervise the education and examination of students for the Bar of England and Wales. It administers the Inns of Court School of Law in Gray's Inn.

Council of Ministers of the European Communities The organ of the EEC and the other European Communities that is primarily concerned with the formulation of policy and (in conjunction with the *Commission and *Assembly of the Communities) the adoption of Community legislation. The Council consists of one member of government of each of the member states of the Communities (normally its foreign minister, but other ministers may attend instead for the consideration of specialized topics), and its presidency is held by each state in turn for periods of six months. The Council is serviced by a Committee of Permanent Representatives (COREPER). This consists of senior civil servants of each state and its primary function is to clarify national attitudes for the assistance of the Council in reaching its decisions. It also disposes on behalf of the Council of matters that are not controversial. *Compare* European Council.

Council on Tribunals A body appointed under the Tribunals and Inquiries Act 1971 to report on the functioning and advise on the procedure of the more important administrative tribunals. Appointment is by the Lord Chancellor and Lord Advocate, who may refer any matter concerning any tribunal for a special Council report.

counsel *n.* A barrister or barristers collectively.

Counsellors of State Persons appointed under the Regency Acts 1937 to 1953 to exercise royal functions while the sovereign is ill (but not totally incapacitated, in which case the functions pass to a *regent) or temporarily absent from the UK. They are appointed by the sovereign by letters patent, which must specify the functions delegated to them. These must not include the function of dissolving Parliament, except on the sovereign's express instructions, or that of creating new peers. The persons to be appointed are the sovereign's spouse, the four next in line to the throne (omitting anyone not qualified to be Regent or intending to be abroad during the period of delegation), and Queen Elizabeth, the Queen Mother.

count *n. See* indictment.

counterclaim *n.* A cross-claim brought by a defendant in civil proceedings that asserts an independent cause of action but is not also a defence to the claim made in the action by the plaintiff. *See also* set-off.

county *n.* A first-tier *local government area in England (outside Greater London) or Wales. The Local Government Act 1972 created 45 counties for England and 8 for Wales, dividing the former into 6 metropolitan and 39 nonmetropolitan counties. The metropolitan counties are Greater

county council

Manchester, Merseyside, South Yorkshire, Tyne and Wear, West Midlands, and West Yorkshire. *See also* county council; local government boundary commissions.

county council A *local authority whose area is a *county. A county council has certain exclusive responsibilities (e.g. fire services, highways, and police) and shares others (e.g. food and drugs, town and country planning) with the councils of the districts in its area. In England some responsibilities (e.g. education and the personal social services) belong to the county council if the county is nonmetropolitan but to the district councils if it is metropolitan. In Wales the functions of a county council are, with minor variations, the same as those of a nonmetropolitan county council in England.

county court Any of the civil courts forming a system covering all of England and Wales, originally set up in 1846. The area covered by each court does not invariably correspond to the local government county boundary. The jurisdiction of the county court is purely statutory and now derives from the County Courts Act 1959. It has jurisdiction over actions in contract and tort in which the amount claimed is not more that £5000 and extensive jurisdiction over disputes concerning land, especially disputes between landlord and tenant, in addition to jurisdiction derived from a wide variety of statutes. All divorce cases also must be started in the county court. Each court has a *circuit judge and a *registrar.

course of employment The scope of the work a person is employed to do. An employer may be held responsible under the principle of *vicarious liability for his employee's wrongful acts that are necessarily incidental to his work or authorized (expressly or by implication) by the employer.

court *n.* **1.** A body established by law for the administration of justice by *judges or *magistrates. **2.** A hall or building in which a court is held. **3. a.** The residence of a sovereign. **b.** The sovereign and her (or his) family and attendants or officials of state.

Court for Consideration of Crown Cases Reserved A court created by the Crown Cases Act 1848 for considering questions of law arising out of the conviction of a person for treason, felony, or misdemeanour and reserved by the trial judge or justices for the consideration of the court. Its jurisdiction was exercised by the judges of the *High Court, at least five of whom had to sit together. The Court was abolished in 1907 and its jurisdiction transferred to the *Court of Criminal Appeal, which had wider powers.

court martial A court convened within the armed forces to try offences against *service law. It consists of from three to five serving officers, who sit without a jury and are advised on points of law by a legally qualified *judge advocate. Their findings of guilty, and their sentences, are subject to confirmation by higher military authority. Since 1951 there has been a Courts-Martial Appeal Court, which consists of the Lord Chief Justice and other members of the Supreme Court. After first petitioning the Defence Council for the quashing of his conviction, a convicted person may appeal to the Court against the conviction but not against sentence. Either he or the Defence Council may then appeal to the House of Lords.

When a member of the armed forces is charged in the UK with conduct that is an offence under both service law and the ordinary criminal law the trial must in certain serious cases (e.g. treason, murder, manslaughter, and rape) be held by the ordinary criminal courts (and is in practice frequently held by them in other cases). Provision exists to ensure that a person cannot be tried twice for the same offence. *See also* standing civilian court.

Court of Appeal A court created by the Judicature Acts 1873–75, forming part of the *Supreme Court of Judicature. The Court exercises *appellate jurisdiction over all judgments and orders of the High Court and most determinations of judges of the county courts. In some cases the Court of Appeal is the *court of last resort, but in most cases its decisions can be appealed to the *House of Lords, with *leave of the Court of Appeal or the House of Lords. The Court is divided into a *Civil Division* (presided over by the *Master of the Rolls) and a *Criminal Division* (presided over by the *Lord Chief Justice). The ordinary judges of the Court are the *Lords Justices of Appeal, but *puisne judges may also sit by invitation and frequently do so, especially in the Criminal Division.

Court of Arches The ecclesiastical court of appeal of the Archbishop of Canterbury. The judge of the court, the *Dean of Arches*, hears appeals from bishops or their chancellors, deans and chapters, and archdeacons. The court's name is derived from its original location, the church of St Mary-le-Bow, whose steeple was erected upon arches.

Court of Chancery The original court of *equity, presided over by the *Lord Chancellor. By the Judicature Acts 1873–75 its jurisdiction was merged into that of the High Court, of which it became the *Chancery Division.

Court of Chivalry An ancient court having jurisdiction over questions relating to armorial bearings and questions of precedence. It is not a *court of record.

Court of Common Pleas One of the three courts of *common law (the others being the *Court of Queen's Bench and the *Court of Exchequer) whose jurisdiction was merged into that of the High Court by the Judicature Acts 1873–75. It became the *Common Pleas Division*, which in 1880 was merged into the *Queen's Bench Division.

Court of Criminal Appeal A court created by the Criminal Appeal Act 1907 to take over the jurisdiction formerly exercised by the *Court for Consideration of Crown Cases Reserved. Its powers were greatly extended, particularly in considering questions of fact as well as law, but it was abolished by the Criminal Appeal Act 1968 and its jurisdiction transferred to that of the *Court of Appeal (Criminal Division).

Court of Ecclesiastical Causes Reserved A court created by the Ecclesiastical Jurisdiction Measure 1963 and having both original and appellate jurisdiction covering the provinces of Canterbury and York. Its original jurisdiction is to hear and determine proceedings in which a person in Holy Orders is charged with an offence against ecclesiastical law involving matters of doctrine, ritual, or ceremonial and all suits of *duplex querela*. Its appellate jurisdiction is in respect of appeals from decisions of consistory courts involving matters of doctrine, ritual, or ceremonial. The court comprises five judges and three diocesan or ex-diocesan bishops. *See also* ecclesiastical courts.

Court of Exchequer One of the three courts of *common law (the others being the *Court of Queen's Bench and the *Court of Common Pleas) whose jurisdiction was merged into that of the High Court by the Judicature Acts 1873–75. It became the *Exchequer Division*, which in 1880 merged into the *Queen's Bench Division. The judges of the Exchequer were known as *Barons*.

court of first instance 1. A court in which any proceedings are initiated. **2.** Loosely, a court in which a case is tried, as opposed to any court in which it may be heard on appeal.

court of inquiry A body convened by naval, army, or air force authorities to investigate and report upon the facts of any happening (e.g. the loss or destruction of service property), particularly for the purpose of determining whether or not disciplinary proceedings should be instituted.

Court of Justice of the European Communities (European Court) An institution of the EEC and the other European Communities that has three primary judicial responsibilities. It interprets the treaties establishing the Communities; it decides upon the validity and the meaning of *Community legislation; and it determines whether any act or omission by the Commission of the Communities, the Council of Ministers, or any member state constitutes a breach of *Community law.

The Court sits at Luxembourg. It consists of judges appointed by the member states by mutual agreement and assisted by *Advocates General. Proceedings before the Court involve both written and oral submissions by the parties concerned. Proceedings against the Commission or the Council may be brought by the other of these two bodies, by any member state, or by individual persons; proceedings to challenge the validity of legislative or other action by either Commission or Council are known as proceedings for *annulment*. Proceedings against a member state may be brought by the Commission, the Council, or any other member state. The decisions of the Court are binding and there is no appeal against them.

The Court also has power, at the request of a court of any member state, to give a preliminary ruling on any point of Community law on which that court requires clarification.

court of last resort A court from which no appeal (or no further appeal) lies. In English law the *House of Lords is usually the court of last resort (although some cases may be referred to the *Court of Justice of the European Communities). However, in some cases the *Court of Appeal is by statute the court of last resort.

Court of Probate A court created in 1857 to take over the jurisdiction formerly exercised by the ecclesiastical courts in relation to the granting of probate and letters of administration. By the Judicature Acts 1873–75 the jurisdiction of the court was transferred to the *Probate, Divorce and Admiralty Division of the High Court.

Court of Protection A court that administers the property and affairs of persons of unsound mind. The head of the court is called the *Master*.

Court of Queen's Bench Until 1875, one of the three courts of *common law (the others being the *Court of Common Pleas and the *Court of Exchequer). Its principal functions were the trial of civil actions in contract and tort and the exercise of supervisory powers over inferior courts. By the Judicature Acts 1873–75 its jurisdiction was transferred to the *Queen's Bench Division of the High Court. When the sovereign was a king, it was known as the *Court of King's Bench*.

court of record A court whose acts and judicial proceedings are permanently maintained and recorded. In modern practice the principal significance of such courts is that they have the power to punish for *contempt of court. *See also* contract of record.

Court of Session A Scottish court corresponding to the *Supreme Court of Judicature in England and Wales. It consists of an Outer House (corresponding to the *High Court) and an Inner House (corresponding to the *Court of Appeal).

court of summary jurisdiction *See* magistrates' court.

court order *See* order.

covenant *n. See* deed.

covenant running with the land 1. A *restrictive covenant affecting freehold land and binding third parties who acquire the land. A restrictive covenant created after 1925 will bind such third parties if it is registered (*see* registration of encumbrances); an earlier one binds those who have notice of it. A positive covenant (i.e. an obligation to perform an act) does not run with the land. **2.** In a lease, a covenant that affects the nature, value, or enjoyment of the land. Such a covenant will bind successors in title of the landlord and the tenant provided there is *privity of estate between them.

covenant to repair A clause contained in most *leases that sets out each party's obligations to carry out repairs. The standard of repair depends on the terms of the covenant and the kind of property. The general rule is that the property must be maintained in the condition that a reasonable tenant of that property would expect. The person carrying out the repairs must, so far as possible, restore the property to the condition it was in before the damage occurred. In the case of a block of flats or offices, the landlord is often responsible for external, and the tenant for internal, repairs. When one party alone is responsible for repairs, this is more likely to be the landlord in the case of a short lease and the tenant in the case of a longer lease.

If the tenant does not fulfil his repairing obligations the landlord's remedies are *forfeiture or suing the tenant for damages. If the landlord is in breach of covenant, the tenant's remedies are as follows: he can sue for damages equal to the difference between the value of the property as it is and the value it should have if repaired; he can sue for *specific performance, a court order to compel the landlord to carry out his obligations; or, if he is sure that the land-lord is in breach of covenant and he has told the landlord about the breach, he can carry out the repairs himself and recover the cost from future rent.

coverture *n.* The status of a woman during, and arising out of, marriage. At common law a wife "lost" her own personality, which became incorporated into that of her husband, and could only act under his protection and "cover". Married women no longer suffer disabilities as a result of coverture. *See also* unity of personality.

credit *n.* **1.** The agreed deferment of payment of a debt. Under the Consumer Credit Act 1974, credit also includes any other form of financial accommodation, including a cash loan. It does not include the charge for credit but does include the total price of goods hired to an individual under a *hire-purchase agreement less the aggregate of the deposit and the total charge for credit. **2.** (in the law of evidence) The credibility of a witness. It must be inferred by the *trier of fact from the witness's demeanour and the evidence in the case. A witness may be cross-examined as to credit (i.e. *impeached*) by reference to his *previous convictions, bias, or any physical or mental incapacity affecting the credibility of his evidence.

credit limit 1. The maximum credit allowed to a debtor. **2.** (under the Consumer Credit Act 1974) The maximum debit balance allowed on a running-account credit agreement during any period.

creditor *n.* **1.** One to whom a debt is owed. *See also* judgment creditor; loan creditor; secured creditor; unsecured creditor. **2.** (under the Consumer Credit Act 1974) The person providing credit under a *consumer-credit agreement or the person to whom his rights and duties under the agreement have passed by assignment or operation of law.

credit sale agreement A contract for the sale of goods under which the price is payable by instalments but the contract is not a *conditional sale agreement, i.e. ownership passes to the buyer. A credit sale agreement is a *consumer-credit agreement; it is regulated by the Consumer Credit Act 1974 if the buyer is an individual, the credit does not exceed £5000, and the agreement is not otherwise exempt.

crime *n.* An act (or sometimes a failure to act) that is deemed by statute or by the common law to be a public wrong and is therefore punishable by the state in criminal proceedings. Every crime consists of an *actus reus* accompanied by a specified *mens rea* (unless it is a crime of *strict liability), and the prosecution must prove these elements of the crime beyond reasonable doubt (*see* burden of proof). Some crimes are serious wrongs of a moral nature (e.g. murder or rape); others interfere with the smooth running of society (e.g. parking offences). Most *prosecutions for crime are brought by the police (although they can also be initiated by private people); some require the consent of the Director of Public Prosecutions. Crimes are customarily divided into *indictable offences (for trial by judge and jury) and *summary offences (for trial by magistrates); some are hybrid (*see* offences triable either way). Crimes are also divided into *arrestable offences and nonarrestable offences. The *punishments for a crime include death (for treason), life imprisonment (e.g. for murder), imprisonment for a specified period, suspended sentences of imprisonment, conditional discharges, probation, binding over, and fines; in most cases judges have discretion in deciding on the punishment (*see* sentence). Some crimes may also be civil wrongs (*see* tort); for example, theft and criminal damage are crimes punishable by imprisonment as well as torts for which the victim may sue for damages.

crimen falsi [Latin: the crime of falsity] The common-law offence of *forgery.

criminal bankruptcy order An order made by the Crown Court against a person convicted of an offence that has caused loss or damage to someone (otherwise than through personal injury) exceeding a certain sum (currently £15,000). The result of such an order, which is administered by the Director of Public Prosecutions in his role as *Official Petitioner, is that the offender is deemed to have committed an act of *bankruptcy on the date on which the order was made. No appeal may be made against a criminal bankruptcy order, but it must be discharged if the appellant successfully appeals against his conviction for the offence.

criminal court A court exercising jurisdiction over criminal rather than civil cases. In England all criminal cases must be initiated in the *magistrates' courts. *Summary offences and some *indictable offences are also tried by magistrates' courts; the more serious indictable offences are committed to the *Crown Court for trial.

criminal damage The offence of intentionally or recklessly destroying or damaging any property belonging to another without a lawful excuse. It is punishable by up to ten years' imprisonment. There is also an aggravated offence, punishable by a maximum sentence of life imprisonment, of damaging property (even one's own) in such a way as to endanger someone's life, either intentionally or recklessly. Related offences are those of threatening to destroy or damage property and of possessing anything with the intention of destroying or damaging property with it.

Criminal Injuries Compensation Board A board under the direction of the Home Office for awarding *ex gratia* payments from public funds to victims who have suffered personal injury from *criminal violence, on the same basis as civil damages would be awarded (*see also* compensation). Damage to property is not included in the scheme, but compensation may be claimed from public funds for damage resulting from a riot.

criminal libel *See* libel.

criminal violence For purposes of the *Criminal Injuries Compensation Board, any crime involving the use of violence against another person. Such crimes include rape and sexual assaults, arson, poisoning, and criminal damage to property involving a risk of danger to life; traffic offences other than a deliberate attempt to run the victim down are not included.

cross-appeals *pl. n.* Appeals by both parties to court proceedings when neither party is satisfied with the judgment of the lower court. For example, a defendant may appeal against a judgment finding him liable for damages, while the plaintiff may appeal in the same case on the ground that the amount of damages awarded is too low.

cross-examination *n.* The questioning of a *witness by a party other than the one who called him to testify. It may be *to the issue*, i.e. designed to elicit information favourable to the party on whose behalf it is conducted and to cast doubt on the accuracy of evidence given against that party; or *to credit*, i.e. designed to cast doubt upon the credibility of the witness. *Leading questions may be asked in cross-examination. *See also* credit.

Crown *n.* The office (a *corporation sole) in which supreme power in the UK is legally vested. The person filling it at any given time is referred to as the *sovereign* (a *king* or *queen*: *see also* Queen). The title to the Crown is hereditary and its descent is governed by the Act of Settlement 1701 as amended by His Majesty's Declaration of Abdication Act 1936 (which excluded Edward VIII and his descendants from the line of succession). The majority of governmental powers in the UK are now conferred by statute directly on ministers, the judiciary, and other persons and bodies, but the sovereign retains a limited number of common-law functions that, except in exceptional circumstances, can be exercised only in accordance with ministerial advice (*see* royal prerogative).

At common law the Crown could not be sued in tort, but the Crown Proceedings Act 1947 enabled civil actions to be taken against the Crown (*see* Crown proceedings). It is still not possible to sue the sovereign personally.

Crown Agents for Overseas Governments and Administrations A body operating under the Crown Agents Act 1979 to provide commercial, financial, and professional services to overseas governments, international bodies, and public authorities. After the discovery of heavy financial losses between 1968 and 1974, the body was restructured by the 1979 Act and a tribunal of inquiry was set up to investigate its activities during those years.

Crown Court A court created by the Courts Act 1971 to take over the jurisdiction formerly exercised by *assizes and *quarter sessions, which were abolished by the same Act. It is part of the *Supreme Court of Judicature. The Crown Court has an unlimited jurisdiction over all criminal cases tried on *indictment and also acts as a court for the hearing of appeals from *magistrates' courts. Unlike the courts it replaced, the Crown Court is one court that can sit at any centre in England and Wales designated by the Lord Chancellor. *See also* three-tier system.

Crown Court rules Rules regulating the practice and procedure of the *Crown Court. The rules are made by the Crown Court Rule Committee under a power conferred by the Courts Act 1971.

Crown privilege The right of the Crown to withhold documentary evidence in any legal proceedings on the grounds that its disclosure would injure the public interest. It was expressly preserved by the Crown Proceedings Act 1947 (see Crown proceedings). In certain limited cases, however, the courts have demanded to inspect documents for which *privilege is claimed and rejected the claim as unwarranted.

Crown proceedings Actions against the Crown brought under the Crown Proceedings Act 1947. The prerogative of perfection (the King can do no wrong; see royal prerogative) originally resulted in immunity from legal proceedings, not only of the sovereign personally but also of the Crown itself (including government departments and all other public bodies that were agencies of the Crown). It gradually became possible, however, to take proceedings against the Crown for damages for breach of contract or for the recovery of property. The form of the proceedings was a *petition of right* (not an ordinary action), and the procedure governing them was eventually regulated by the Petition of Right Act 1860. The Crown Proceedings Act 1947 replaced petitions of right by ordinary actions. It also made the Crown liable to action for the tort of any servant or agent committed in the course of his employment, for breach of its duties as an employer and as an occupier of property, and for breach of any statutory duty that is binding on the Crown. It does not affect the presumption of interpretation (see interpretation of statutes) that statutes do not bind the Crown, nor does it affect *Crown privilege.

Crown servant Any person in the employment of the Crown (this does not include police officers). It is an implied term of every contract of employment with the Crown that the Crown can dismiss the servant at will. Since 1971, however, statute has given civil servants the right to bring proceedings for *unfair dismissal before industrial tribunals. A civil servant can bring proceedings against the Crown for arrears of pay but a member of the armed forces cannot.

cruelty *n.* Formerly, behaviour serious enough to injure a spouse's physical or mental health. Technically cruelty is no longer a basis in itself for a divorce petition or for orders in magistrates' courts, but will usually support a petition or order on the basis of *unreasonable conduct (see also breakdown of marriage). There is no need to prove intention to be cruel; for example, a mentally ill spouse may be cruel without realizing it. The test is whether the petitioner should be called upon to put up with the behaviour.

cum testamento annexo See letters of administration.

cur. adv. vult (c.a.v.) [Latin *curia advisari vult*, the court wishes to consider the matter] An abbreviation in law reports indicating that the judgment of the court was delivered not extempore at the end of the hearing but at a later date.

curtain provisions Provisions in the Settled Land Act 1925 enabling the title of the *tenant for life of settled land to be proved by the deed that vests the fee simple in him. The trust instrument that declares the beneficial interests in the land is not revealed to a purchaser: as those interests are *overreached by the sale, they do not concern him.

custodianship order An order, made by the courts under the Children Act 1975, granting the applicant limited rights over a child. The applicant, known as a *custodian*, will have legal custody of the child (see custody of child). Custodianship orders are an alternative to fostering on the one hand and *adoption on the other. A custodian has greater powers than a *foster parent but is not in the position of an adopter.

custodian trustee A trustee who has care and custody of trust property; other trustees (the *managing trustees*) are responsible for its management.

custody *n.* **1.** Imprisonment or confinement. *See* remand; surrender to custody. **2.** Legal possession, guardianship, or control. *See* custody of child.

custody disputes Arguments over the *custody of a child. Such arguments are settled by court proceedings, in which the court has wide discretionary powers, subject to the overriding condition that the child's welfare is the first and paramount consideration. Children may even exceptionally be removed from the custody of their natural parents in favour of nonrelations, if this is in their best interests.

Proceedings in custody disputes may be brought before different courts and under different Acts. In divorce, nullity, or judicial separation proceedings the issue of custody will be decided by the High Court or county court, under the Matrimonial Causes Act 1973. When parents disagree about custody but no divorce proceedings are pending, the issue may be decided by the High Court, county court, or magistrates' court under the Guardianship of Minors Act 1973. Spouses may also apply to the magistrates' courts during the continuation of the marriage, under the Domestic Proceedings and Magistrates' Courts Act 1978 (especially on the grounds of nonmaintenance or unreasonable behaviour). Application may also be made by anyone to the High Court to have a child made a *ward of court and to obtain custody of the child. This power may be used, for example, by foster parents or potential adopters in dispute with natural parents. Local authorities may also obtain custody of a child under the Children and Young Persons Act 1969.

custody of child Control exercised by an adult (usually a parent) over a minor, or the right to exercise such control. In its wider sense custody includes all parental rights (*see* parent), but sometimes it is used in a narrower sense to refer to control over long-term decisions (such as the manner of education), as opposed to *care and control. The Children Act 1975 distinguishes between *legal custody* (the rights over a child affecting his person, including how he spends his time), and *actual custody* (physical possession of the child). Persons other than the natural or adoptive parents may be given custody of a child. Such persons may be other relatives, guardians, a local authority (e.g. in *care proceedings), or the court itself (e.g. in *wardship proceedings). *See also* custody disputes.

custom *n.* A practice that has been followed in a particular locality in such circumstances that it is to be accepted as part of the law of that locality. It must be reasonable in nature and it must have been followed continuously, and as if it were a right, since the beginning of legal memory. Legal memory began in 1189, but proof that a practice has been followed within living memory raises a presumption that it began before that date.

customs duty A charge or toll payable on certain goods exported from or imported into the UK. Customs duties are charged either in the form of an *ad valorem* duty, i.e. a percentage of the value of the goods, or as a specific duty charged according to the volume of the goods. All goods are classified in the Customs Tariff but not all goods are subject to duty. The Commissioners of Customs and Excise administer and collect customs duties. Membership of the EEC has required the abolition of import duties between member states and the establishment of a common external tariff. *Compare* excise duty.

cy-près doctrine [French: *cy*, here;

près, near] A doctrine that in some circumstances enables a gift to charity that would otherwise fail to be diverted to another related charitable purpose. If, for example, the purpose for which a charitable gift is made cannot, either initially or subsequently, be achieved in exactly the way intended, or if the funds available are more than sufficient to achieve the purpose, the court or the Charity Commissioners may make a scheme for the funds to be applied to a charitable purpose as close as possible to the original one.

D

Daily Cause List *See* Cause List.

damage *n.* Loss or harm. Not all forms of damage give rise to a right of action; for example, an occupier of land must put up with a reasonable amount of noise from his neighbours (*see* nuisance), and in the case of bereavement there is no right to compensation for grief or sorrow, except in the limited statutory form of damages for bereavement (*see* fatal accidents). Damage for which there is no remedy in law is known as *damnum sine injuria*. Conversely, a legal wrong may not cause actual damage (*injuria sine damno*). If the wrong is actionable without proof of damage (such as trespass to land) and no damage has occurred, the plaintiff is entitled to nominal damages. For the torts of *slander and public *nuisance, an action may not be brought unless the plaintiff has suffered actual damage (known as *special damage*).

damages *pl. n.* A sum of money awarded by a court as compensation for a tort or a breach of contract. Damages are awarded as a *lump sum. The general principle is that the plaintiff is entitled to full compensation (*restitutio in integrum*) for his losses. *Substantial

damages are given when actual damage has been caused, but *nominal damages* may be given for breach of contract and for some torts (such as trespass) in which no damage has been caused, in order to vindicate the plaintiff's rights. Damages may be *aggravated by the circumstances of the wrong. In exceptional cases in tort (but never in contract) *exemplary damages may be given to punish the defendant's wrongdoing. Damages may be classified as unliquidated or liquidated. *Liquidated damages* are a sum fixed in advance by the parties to a contract as the amount to be paid in the event of a breach. They are recoverable provided that the sum fixed was a fair pre-estimate of the likely consequences of a breach, but not if they were imposed as a penalty. *Unliquidated damages* are damages the amount of which is fixed by the court. Damages may also be classified as *general and special damages.

The purpose of damages in tort is to put the plaintiff in the position he would have been in if the tort had not been committed. Recovery is limited by the rules of *remoteness of damage. The plaintiff must take reasonable steps to mitigate his losses and so may be expected to undergo medical treatment for his injuries or to seek alternative employment if his injuries prevent him from doing his former job. Damages may also be reduced for the plaintiff's *contributory negligence. The purpose of damages in contract is to put the plaintiff in the position he would have been in if the contract had been performed, but, as in the case of damages in tort, recovery is limited by rules relating to remoteness of damage. Again as in the case of torts, the plaintiff is also under a duty to take all reasonable steps to mitigate his losses and cannot claim compensation for any loss caused by his failure to do this. If, for example, a hotel reservation is cancelled, the hotelier must make all reasonable attempts to relet the room for the period in question or as much of it as possible.

dangerous animals Animals the keeping or use of which is regulated by statute because of their propensity to cause damage. Under the Dangerous Wild Animals Act 1976, the keeping of apes, bears, crocodiles, tigers, venomous snakes, and other potentially dangerous animals requires a local-authority licence. The use of *guard dogs is strictly controlled by the Guard Dogs Act 1975. *See also* classification of animals.

dangerous driving Driving a motor vehicle in a dangerous manner or causing death through such driving. Both these offences have been abolished by the Criminal Law Act 1977, but such conduct is still governed by the law relating to *reckless driving.

dangerous intoxication A new offence proposed by the Butler Committee (1975) but not yet in force. When a person is charged with a *dangerous offence* (i.e. one involving injury to the person, death, aggravated *criminal damage, or a sexual attack on another), and the jury is not satisfied that he had the necessary *mens rea*, it is proposed that the accused may be convicted instead of dangerous intoxication, if the jury is satisfied that he carried out the act charged and was voluntarily drunk at the time. *See also* intoxication.

dangerous machinery An employer is under a duty to safeguard employees from dangerous machinery. By the Factories Act 1961, all dangerous parts of machinery must be securely fenced, unless they are in such a position or of such construction that they are as safe as if they were securely fenced. The Mines and Quarries Act 1954 deals with the safety of machinery in mines and quarries.

dangerous things *See Rylands* v *Fletcher*, rule in.

dawn raid An offer to buy a substan-

tial quantity of shares in a public company at above the market value, the offer remaining open for a very short period (usually hours). Because of the speed required smaller shareholders may have little opportunity to avail themselves of the offer.

days of grace The three days that were added to the time of payment fixed by a *bill of exchange not payable on demand before the Banking and Financial Dealings Act 1971 came into force. A bill drawn on or after 16 January 1972 is due and payable in all cases on the last day of the time of payment fixed by the bill or, if that is a nonbusiness day, on the succeeding business day.

day-training centre A place that provides social education and intensive probation supervision. A court may order a person subject to a *probation order to attend such a centre.

death *n. See* registration of death.

death duties Taxes charged on a person's property on his death. These formerly consisted of *estate duty, legacy duty, and succession duty but have now been replaced by *capital transfer tax.

death penalty *See* capital punishment.

de bene esse [Latin: of well-being] Denoting a course of action that is the best that can be done in the present circumstances or in anticipation of a future event. An example is obtaining a *deposition from a witness when there is a likelihood that he will be unable to attend the court hearing.

debenture *n.* A document that states the terms of a loan, usually to a company, including the date of repayment and the rate of interest. The debt, which is usually long-term, may be secured by a *charge on company property; a *naked debenture* is simply an undertaking to repay. A debenture may be issued to an individual creditor (a *debenture holder*) or a debenture trust deed may be drawn up in favour of trustees for a large group of creditors (*debenture stock holders*). Capital derived from the issue of debentures is termed *loan capital*. *Compare* share.

de bonis asportatis [Latin: of goods carried away] One form of trespass to goods (*see* trespass), not distinguished in modern law from other direct interferences with the possession of goods.

de bonis non administratis [Latin: of unadministered goods] A grant of *letters of administration of the estate of a deceased person when administration has previously been granted to someone who has himself died before completing the distribution of the estate.

debt *n.* **1.** A sum of money owed by one person or group to another. **2.** The obligation to pay a sum of money owed.

debt adjusting *See* ancillary credit business.

debt collecting *See* ancillary credit business.

debtor *n.* **1.** One who owes a debt. *See also* judgment debtor. **2.** (under the Consumer Credit Act 1974) The individual receiving credit under a *consumer-credit agreement or the person to whom his rights and duties under the agreement have passed by assignment or operation of law.

debtor-creditor agreement A *consumer-credit agreement regulated by the Consumer Credit Act 1974. It may be (1) a *restricted-use credit agreement to finance a transaction between the debtor and a supplier in which there are no arrangements between the creditor and the supplier (e.g. when a loan is paid by the creditor direct to a dealer who is to supply the debtor); (2) a restricted-use credit agreement to refinance any existing indebtedness of the debtor's to the creditor or any other person; or (3) an unrestricted-use credit agreement (e.g. a straight loan of money) that is not made by the creditor under arrangements with a supplier in

the knowledge that the credit is to be used to finance a transaction between the debtor and the supplier.

debtor-creditor-supplier agreement A *consumer-credit agreement regulated by the Consumer Credit Act 1974. It may be (1) a *restricted-use credit agreement to finance a transaction between the debtor and the creditor, which may or may not form part of that agreement (e.g. a purchase of goods on credit); (2) a restricted-use credit agreement to finance a transaction between the debtor and a supplier, made by the creditor and involving arrangements between himself and the supplier; or (3) an unrestricted-use credit agreement that is made by the creditor under preexisting arrangements between himself and a supplier in the knowledge that the credit is to be used to finance a transaction between the debtor and the supplier.

deceit *n.* A tort that is committed when someone knowingly or recklessly makes a false statement of fact intending that it should be acted on by someone else and that person does act on the false statement and thereby suffers damage. *See* fraud.

deception *n.* A false representation, by words or conduct, of a matter of fact (including the existence of an intention) or law that is made deliberately or recklessly. Deception itself is not a crime, but there are three crimes in which deception is involved. (1) Obtaining property, an overdraft, an insurance policy, an annuity contract, or the opportunity to earn money in a job or to win money by betting by means of a deception. These offences are punishable by up to ten years' imprisonment. (2) Obtaining any services on the understanding that they will be paid for (e.g. the services of a driver or typist or the hiring of a car) by means of a deception. (3) Bringing about the following as a result of a deception: (a) causing someone to forego a debt owing to him; (b) obtaining an exemption from liability to pay for something (e.g. obtaining free travel by falsely pretending to be a senior citizen); (c) persuading a creditor to wait for payment if one never intends to pay. These offences are punishable by up to five years' imprisonment. It is not an offence, however, to deceive someone in any other circumstances, provided there is no element of *forgery or *false accounting.

declaration *n.* **1.** (in the law of evidence) An oral or written statement not made on oath. The term is often applied to certain types of out-of-court statement that are admissible as an exception to the rule against *hearsay; for example, *declaration against interest, *declaration concerning pedigree, *declaration concerning public and general rights, and *declaration in course of duty. *See also* statutory declaration. **2.** A discretionary remedy involving a bare finding by the High Court as to a person's legal status, rights, or obligations. A declaration cannot be directly enforced, but is frequently sought both in private law (e.g. to answer a question as to nationality or rights under a will) and in public law (e.g. to test a claim that delegated legislation or the decision of some inferior court, tribunal, or administrative authority is *ultra vires*). In both public and private law the applicant must show standing, i.e. that the issue affects him directly. *Compare certiorari. See also* judicial review.

declaration against interest A *declaration by a person who has subsequently died which he knew, when he made it, would be against his pecuniary or proprietary interest. It may be related to the court as an exception to the rule against *hearsay. It is disputed whether or not it can be extended to include declarations that might have exposed the deceased to criminal liability.

declaration concerning pedigree A *declaration made by a person who has subsequently died, or to be inferred from family conduct, concerning a disputed pedigree of a blood relation or the spouse of a blood relation. The declaration must have been made before the dispute in which it is tendered as evidence had arisen. It may be related to the court as an exception to the rule against *hearsay. This exception to the hearsay rule is preserved for civil cases by the Civil Evidence Act 1968 so far as it relates to evidence of reputation. Most statements of fact concerning pedigree would also be admissible under the same Act.

declaration concerning public or general rights A *declaration made by a person who has subsequently died concerning the reputed existence of a public or general right. *Public rights* affect everyone (e.g. a public *right of way) while *general rights* affect a class of people (e.g. a right of *common). Such a declaration is admissible as an exception to the rule against *hearsay, provided that it was made before the dispute in which it is tendered as evidence had arisen and, in the case of a general right, that the declarant had competent knowledge.

declaration in course of duty A *declaration by a person who has subsequently died made while pursuing a duty to record or report his acts. It is admissible as evidence of the truth of its contents under an exception to the rule against *hearsay, provided that the record or report was roughly contemporaneous with the event related and that the declarant had no motive to misrepresent the facts.

declaration of intention *See* offer.

declaration of trust A statement indicating that property is to be held on trust. No specific words are necessary, as long as the intention to declare a trust is made clear. A declaration of trust is made when the person intended to be trustee has the property but is not entitled to hold it for his own benefit.

declaratory judgment A judgment that merely states the court's opinion on a question of law or declares the rights of the parties, without normally including any provision for enforcement. A claim for declaration may, however, be combined with one for some substantive relief, such as damages.

decree *n.* A court order. *See also* decree absolute; decree nisi.

decree absolute A decree of divorce, nullity, or presumption of death that brings a marriage to a legal end, enabling the parties to remarry. It is usually issued six weeks after the *decree nisi (unless there are exceptional reasons why it should be given sooner). A list of decrees absolute is kept at the Divorce Registry and access to it is open to the public.

decree nisi A conditional decree of divorce, nullity, or presumption of death. For most purposes the parties to the marriage are still married until the decree is made absolute (although not for all purposes; for example, a husband may be guilty of raping his wife after a decree nisi). During the period between decree nisi and decree absolute the Queen's Proctor or any member of the public may intervene to prevent the decree being made absolute and the decree may be rescinded if obtained by fraud. If the parties effect a reconciliation, they may have the decree nisi rescinded.

deed *n.* A written document that is signed, sealed, and delivered. If it is a contractual document, it is referred to as a *contract under seal* (or a *specialty*). A promise contained in a deed is called a *covenant* and is binding even if not supported by *consideration. Covenants may be either express or implied. A deed normally takes effect on delivery; actual delivery constitutes handing it to the other party; constructive delivery involves (in strict theory) touching the seal with the finger, and saying words such as "I deliver this as my act and deed". If a deed is delivered but is not to become operative until a future date or until some condition has been fulfilled, it is called an *escrow. The *recitals* of a deed are those parts that merely declare facts and do not effect any of the substance of the transaction. They are usually inserted to explain the reason for the transaction. The *operative part* of a deed is the part that actually effects the objects of the deed, as by transferring land. The *testatum* (or *witnessing part*) constitutes the opening words of the operative part, i.e. "Now this deed witnesseth as follows". The *premises* are the words in the operative part that describe the parties and the transaction involved. The *parcels* are the words in the premises that describe the property involved. The *testimonium* is the concluding part, beginning "In witness whereof", and containing the signatures of the parties and witnesses. The *locus sigilli* is the position indicated for placing the seal. When a deed refers to itself as "these presents", "presents" means present statements. *See also* deed poll.

deed of arrangement A written agreement between a debtor and his creditors, when no *receiving order has been made, arranging the debtor's affairs either for the benefit of the creditors generally or, when the debtor is insolvent, for the benefit of at least three of the creditors. A deed of arrangement is regulated by statute and must be registered with the Department of Trade within seven days. It may take a number of different forms: it may be a *composition, an *assignment of the debtor's property to a trustee for the benefit of his creditors, or an agreement to wind up the debtor's business in such a way as to pay his debts. The debtor usually agrees to such an arrangement in order to avoid bankruptcy. A similar arrangement can be agreed after a receiving order is made, but this is regulated in a different way (*see* scheme of arrangement).

deed of covenant A *deed containing an undertaking to pay an agreed amount over an agreed period. Certain tax advantages can be obtained through the use of covenants, particularly in the case of four-year covenants in favour of charities.

deed of gift A deed conveying property from one person (the *donor*) to another (the *donee*) when the donee gives no *consideration in return. The donee can enforce a deed of gift against the donor. Gifts made other than by deed are not generally enforceable.

deed poll A *deed to which there is only one party; for example, one declaring a *change of name.

deemed *adj.* Treated as being something. Many documents (particularly statutes) rely upon the device of deeming. They state that a certain thing is to be deemed to fall within a certain expression or description used in them, either to remove any doubt on the point or (it being clear that, in ordinary language, this proposition is not true) as a convenient form of drafting shorthand, implying that, for purposes of the statute, the deemed thing should be treated as if it were the thing it is deemed to be.

de facto [Latin: in fact] Existing as a matter of fact rather than of right. The government may, for example, recognize a foreign government *de facto* if it is actually in control of a country even though it has no legal right to rule (*see* recognition). *Compare de jure.*

defamation *n.* The *publication of a statement about a person that tends to lower his reputation in the opinion of right-thinking members of the community or to make them shun or avoid him. Defamation is usually in words, but pictures, gestures, and other acts can be defamatory. In English law, a distinction is made between defamation in permanent form (*see* libel) and defamation not in permanent form (*see* slander). This distinction is not made in Scotland. The remedies in tort for defamation are damages and injunction.

In English law, the basis of the tort is injury to reputation, so it must be proved that the statement was communicated to someone other than the person defamed. In Scottish law, defamation includes injury to the feelings of the person defamed as well as injury to reputation, so an action can be brought when a statement is communicated only to the person defamed. If the statement is not obviously defamatory, the plaintiff must show that it would be understood in a defamatory sense (*see* innuendo). It is not necessary to prove that the defendant intended to refer to the plaintiff. The test is whether reasonable people would think the statement referred to him, but the defendant may escape liability for *unintentional defamation* by making an offer of amends (*see* apology). Other defences are *justification, *fair comment, *absolute privilege, and *qualified privilege.

All those involved in the publication of a defamatory statement, such as printers, publishers, and broadcasting companies, are liable and every repetition of a defamatory statement is a fresh publication, giving rise to a new cause of action. A mere distributor of a book, newspaper, etc., is not liable if he did not know and had no reason to know of its defamatory contents.

default *n.* Failure to do something required by law, usually failure to comply with mandatory rules of procedure. If a defendant in civil proceedings is in default (e.g. by failing to give notice of intention to defend), the plaintiff may obtain *judgment in default*. If the plaintiff is in default, the defendant may apply to the court to dismiss the action.

default notice A notice that must be served on a contract breaker before taking action in consequence of his breach.

default summons

Under the Consumer Credit Act 1974 a default notice must be served on a debtor or hirer before the creditor or owner is entitled to terminate the agreement; to demand earlier payment of any sum; to recover possession of any goods or land; to treat any right conferred on the debtor or hirer by the agreement as terminated, restricted, or deferred; or to enforce any security. The notice must specify the nature of the breach, what action (if any) is required to remedy it, and the date before which that action is to be taken. If the breach is not capable of remedy, the notice must specify the sum (if any) required in compensation and the date before which it is to be paid.

default summons A summons used to initiate all proceedings in the county courts when the only relief claimed is the payment of money. The summons requires the defendant, within 14 days after service of the summons, to meet the plaintiff's claim or file a form of *admission, *defence, or *counterclaim; if he fails to do so, the plaintiff may obtain judgment in *default.

defect *n.* A fault or failing in a thing. The defect may be obvious (a *patent defect*) or it may not be apparent at first (a *latent defect*). In a sale of goods, the buyer usually has a legal remedy against a professional seller if the goods have a latent defect. If there is a patent defect he usually has no such remedy if he had an opportunity to inspect the goods before purchase. *See also* merchantable quality.

defective equipment An employer's duty to provide his employees with a safe system of work, so far as is reasonably practicable, includes the provision and maintenance of safe tools and equipment for the job. The employer is liable to an employee injured by a defect in the equipment he provides, even if the defect was due to the fault of some third party, such as the manufac-turer of the equipment. *See also* safety at work.

defective premises Liability for defective premises can arise at common law or by statute. Builders, architects, surveyors, etc., are liable in tort on ordinary principles for *negligence but may also be subject to statutory duties; for example, under the Defective Premises Act 1972, in respect of work connected with the provision of a dwelling. A local authority may be liable for negligence in exercising its statutory powers to inspect building operations. A landlord who is responsible for repairs, or who has reserved the right to enter and carry out repairs, may be liable for defects in the premises that are due to the absence of repair. For the liability of occupiers of premises, *see* occupier's liability.

defective products *See* products liability.

defence *n.* **1.** A pleading served by the defendant in answer to the plaintiff's *statement of claim. In the High Court the defence must be served within 14 days after the time for *acknowledging service of the writ or of the service of the statement of claim, whichever is the later. If the defendant fails to serve a defence within the prescribed time, the plaintiff may obtain judgment in default. **2.** In civil and criminal proceedings, an issue of law or fact that, if determined in favour of the defendant, will relieve him of liability wholly or in part.

defendant *n.* A person against whom court proceedings are brought. *Compare* plaintiff.

deferred debt In bankruptcy proceedings, a debt that by statute is not paid until all other debts have been paid in full.

deferred sentence A *sentence imposed by a magistrates' court or the Crown Court after a period of up to six months from conviction for the offence.

The court may postpone sentencing, if the convicted person agrees, when it wishes to assess any change in the offender's conduct or circumstances during that time.

defrauding *n.* Any act that deprives someone of something that is his or to which he might be entitled or that injures someone in relation to any proprietary right. It is a crime (a form of *conspiracy at common law) to conspire to defraud someone. There are also various statutory offences in which defrauding is an element, including deception, blackmail, cheat, forgery, and false accounting.

de jure [Latin] As a matter of legal right. *See* recognition. *Compare de facto.*

del credere **agent** [Italian: of trust] *See* agent.

delegated legislation (subordinate legislation) Legislation made under powers conferred by an Act of Parliament (an enabling statute, often called the parent Act). The bulk of delegated legislation is governmental: it consists mainly of *Orders in Council and instruments of various names (e.g. orders, regulations, rules, directions, and schemes) made by ministers (*see also* government circulars). Its primary use is to supplement Acts of Parliament by prescribing the detailed and technical rules required for their operation; unlike an Act, it has the advantage that it can be made (and later amended if necessary) without taking up parliamentary time. Delegated legislation is also made by a variety of bodies outside central government, examples being *byelaws, the *Rules of the Supreme Court, and the codes of conduct of certain professional bodies (*see also* Orders of Council).

Most delegated legislation (byelaws are the main exception) is subject to some degree of parliamentary control, which may take any of three principal forms: (1) a simple requirement that it be laid before Parliament after being made (thus ensuring that members become aware of its existence but affording them no special method or opportunity of questioning its substance); (2) a provision that it be laid and, for a specified period, liable to annulment by a resolution of either House (*negative resolution* procedure); or (3) a provision that it be laid and either shall not take effect until approved by resolutions of both Houses or shall cease to have effect unless approved within a specified period (*affirmative resolution* procedure). In the case of purely financial instruments, any provision for a negative or affirmative resolution refers to the House of Commons alone. (*See also* statutory instrument; special procedure orders.)

All delegated legislation is subject to judicial control under the doctrine of *ultra vires.* Delegated legislation is interpreted in the light of the parent Act, so particular words are presumed to be used in the same sense as in that Act. This rule apart, it is governed by the same principles as those governing the *interpretation of statutes.

See also subdelegated legislation.

delegation *n.* **1.** The grant of authority to a person to act on behalf of one or more others, for agreed purposes. **2.** A doctrine under the law of *vicarious liability postulating that someone who has handed over all his authority to a manager, or is absent from premises leaving another person in charge, may be guilty of an offence despite his ignorance that it was being committed. The doctrine usually applies to licensing offences. Thus a publican will be guilty of selling intoxicating liquor to a drunken person on his premises if the barmaid sells it without his knowledge.

delegatus non potest delegare [Latin] A person to whom something has been delegated cannot delegate further, i.e. one to whom powers and duties have been entrusted cannot entrust them to another. The rule does not apply if there is express or implied authority to delegate. Trustees, for example, have always been entitled to employ agents when this was necessary (for example, they can employ solicitors to do legal work). Since 1925, a trustee may delegate any business of the trust to an agent provided that he does so in good faith. Further, since 1971, any trustee may delegate, for a period not exceeding one year, any trusts, powers, or discretions he has; this delegation may be repeated.

de lege ferenda [Latin: of (or concerning) the law that is to come into force] A phrase used to indicate that a proposition relates to what the law ought to be or may in the future be.

de lege lata [Latin: of (or concerning) the law that is in force] A phrase used to indicate that a proposition relates to the law as it is.

delivery *n.* The transfer of possession of property from one person to another. Under the Sale of Goods Act 1979, a seller delivers goods to a buyer if he delivers them physically, if he makes *symbolic delivery* by delivering the document of title to them (e.g. a bill of lading) or other means of control over them (e.g. the keys of a warehouse in which they are stored), or if a third party who is holding them acknowledges that he now holds them for the buyer. In *constructive delivery*, the seller agrees that he holds the goods on behalf of the buyer or the buyer has possession under a hire-purchase agreement and becomes owner on making the final payment.

demanding with menaces *See* blackmail.

de minimis non curat lex [Latin] The law does not take account of trifles. It will not, for example, award damages for a trifling nuisance.

demise (in land law) **1.** *vb.* To grant a lease. **2.** *n.* The lease itself.

demise of the Crown The death of the sovereign. The Crown, in fact, never dies: the accession of the new sovereign takes place at the moment of the demise, and there is no interregnum.

demonstrative legacy *See* legacy.

demurrage *n.* Liquidated *damages payable under a charterparty at a specified daily rate for any days (*demurrage days*) required for completing the loading or discharging of cargo after the *lay days have expired. The word is also used to denote the unliquidated damages to which the shipowner is entitled if, when no lay days are specified, the ship is detained for loading or unloading beyond a reasonable time.

departure *n.* The *pleading of a new allegation of fact or the raising of a new ground or claim inconsistent with the party's earlier pleading. Departure is not permitted by the rules of pleading, but does not prevent the *amendment of pleadings provided that the amended pleadings do not contain any departure. The principal effect of the rule is to prevent a plaintiff from setting up in his *reply a new claim that is inconsistent with the cause of action alleged in the statement of claim.

dependant *n.* A person who relies on someone else for maintenance or financial support. On the death of the latter, the courts now have wide discretionary powers to award financial provision to dependants out of the estate of the deceased. The list of dependants includes not only spouses, former spouses, children, and children of the family, but anyone (e.g. a mistress, housekeeper, or servant) who was being maintained to some extent by the deceased immediately before his death. *See also* reasonable financial provision.

dependent relative revocation Revocation of a will by a testator who intends to replace it by another, effective will. The law disregards the revocation if the intended will is invalid or is never made. For example, when a testator removes his signature from his will, intending to make another but dying before doing so, the original will remains valid.

dependent territory A territory (e.g. a colony) the government of which is to some extent the legal responsibility of the government of another territory.

deportation *n.* The expulsion of a person from the UK. This is authorized by the Immigration Act 1971 in the case of any person who does not have the right of abode there (*see* immigration). He may be ordered to leave the country in four circumstances: if he has overstayed or broken a condition attached to his permission to stay; if another person to whose family he belongs is deported; if (he being 17 or over) a court recommends deportation on his conviction of an offence punishable with imprisonment; or if the Secretary of State thinks his deportation to be for the public good. The Act enables appeals to be made against deportation orders. Normally, they are either direct to the *Immigration Appeal Tribunal or to that tribunal after a preliminary appeal to an adjudicator.

depose *vb.* To make a *deposition or other written statement on oath.

deposit *n.* **1.** A sum paid by one party to a contract to the other party as a guarantee that the first party will carry out the terms of the contract. The first party will forfeit the sum in question if he does not carry out the terms, even if the sum is in excess of the other party's loss. If the contract is completed without dispute the deposit becomes part payment. In land law a deposit is usually made by a purchaser when exchanging contracts (*see* exchange of contracts) for the purchase of land. The contract stipulates whether the recipi-

ent (usually the vendor's solicitor or estate agent) holds the deposit as agent for the vendor, in which case the vendor can use the money pending *completion of the transaction, or as stakeholder, in which case the funds must remain in the stakeholder's account until completion or (in the case of a dispute) a court has decided who should have it. If the contract is rescinded the purchaser is entitled to the return of his deposit. **2.** The placing of title deeds with a mortgagee of land as security for the debt. A mortgagee not protected by deposit (such as a second mortgagee of unregistered land) registers his mortgage (*see* registration of encumbrances) and is then entitled to receive the title deeds from prior mortgagees whose security is redeemed.

deposition *n.* A statement made on oath before a magistrate or court official by a witness and usually recorded in writing. In criminal cases depositions are taken during committal proceedings before the magistrates' court (*see* committal for trial). The usual procedure is that the prosecution witnesses give their evidence on oath and may be cross-examined by the accused or his legal advisers. The statement is then written down by the magistrates' clerk, read out to the witness in the presence of the accused, signed by the witness, and certified by the examining magistrate. The accused must be present throughout and be allowed to cross-examine. If these conditions are not fulfilled, both the committal proceedings and the subsequent trial will be null and void. There are special arrangements for depositions to be written down out of court if a witness is dangerously ill and cannot come to court, and also for depositions by children. Depositions made in committal proceedings are accepted as evidence at the trial if the witness is dead or insane, unfit to travel because of illness, is being kept out of the way by the accused, or was given a conditional *witness order (requiring him to attend only if given notice to do so); they are also accepted to show a discrepancy between the deposition evidence and evidence given later on orally at the trial.

In civil cases the court may order an examiner of the court to take depositions from any witnesses who are (for example) ill or likely to be abroad at the time of the hearing. At the taking of the deposition the witness is examined and cross-examined in the usual way, and the examiner notes any objection to admissibility that may be raised. The deposition is not admissible at the trial without the consent of the party against whom it is given, unless the witness is still unavailable. *See also* letter of request.

deprave *vb.* To make morally bad. The term is used particularly in relation to the effect of *obscene publications. A person is considered to have been depraved if his mind is influenced in an immoral way, even though this does not necessarily result in any act of depravity.

derivative action Civil proceedings brought by a minority of company members in their own names seeking a remedy for the company in respect of a wrong done to it. Such proceedings are exceptional; usually an action should be brought by the company (the injured party) in its own name. A derivative action will only be permitted when a serious wrong to the company is involved, which cannot be ratified by an ordinary resolution of company members (e.g. an *ultra vires* or illegal act or a case of *fraud on the minority) and the majority of members will not sanction an action in the company's name. *Compare* representative action.

derivative deed A deed that is supplemental to another, whose scope it alters, confirms, or extends. An example is a deed admitting a new partner to a firm on terms set out in a principal deed executed by the original partners.

derivative trust *See* subtrust.

desertion *n.* **1.** The failure by a husband or wife to cohabit with his or her spouse. Desertion usually takes the form of physically leaving the home, but this is not essential: there may be desertion although both parties live under the same roof, if all elements of a shared life (e.g. sexual intercourse, eating of meals together) have ceased. Desertion must be a unilateral act carried out against the wishes of the other spouse, with the intention of bringing married life to an end. If it continues for more than two years, it may be evidence of *breakdown of marriage and entitle the deserted spouse to a decree of divorce. *See also* constructive desertion. **2.** An offence against service law committed by a member of the armed forces who leaves or fails to attend at his unit, ship, or place of duty. He must either intend at the time to remain permanently absent from duty without lawful authority or subsequently form that intention. One who absents himself without leave to avoid service overseas or before the enemy is also guilty of desertion.

de son tort *See* executor *de son tort*; trustee *de son tort*.

detain *vb.* To deprive a person of his liberty against his will. The police have no general power to detain simply for questioning or while investigations are carried out, and even a person detained under lawful arrest must normally be brought before a court as soon as is reasonably practicable. A person arrested under the Prevention of Terrorism (Temporary Provisions) Act 1976 may, however, be detained for 48 hours without any charge being preferred, and the Home Secretary may extend that period by up to a further five days.

detention centre A place to which a person aged over 14 and under 21 may be sent for a short term of suitable disciplinary treatment if he has been convicted of an offence that, in the case of an adult, would be punishable by imprisonment. *See* juvenile offender.

determinable interest An interest that will automatically come to an end on the occurrence of some specified event (which, however, may never happen). For example, if A conveys land to B until he marries, B has a determinable interest that would pass back to A upon his marriage. But if B dies a bachelor the *possibility of a reverter to A is destroyed and B's heirs acquire an absolute interest. An interest that must end at some future point (e.g. a *life interest) is not classified as a determinable interest. A determinable legal estate in land prior to 1925 was known as a *determinable fee*, but under the Law of Property Act 1925 it can now exist only as an equitable interest. *Compare* conditional interest; contingent interest.

deterrence *n*. *See* punishment.

detinue *n*. An action to recover goods, based on a wrongful refusal by the possessor of the goods to restore them to the owner. The medieval form of action was abolished by the Judicature Acts 1873–75 and detinue was abolished altogether by the Torts (Interference with Goods) Act 1977. Recovery of goods is now governed by the provisions of the 1977 Act.

devastavit [Latin: he has wasted] *n*. The failure of a personal representative to administer a deceased person's estate promptly and in a proper manner. For example, if he pays in full a legacy that should abate he is personally liable for the loss suffered by other beneficiaries and caused by his *devastavit*.

development *n*. (in *town and country planning) Generally, the carrying out of any building or other operation affecting land and the making of any material change in the use of any buildings or land. Development does not include alterations to buildings not materially affecting their external appearance or changes of use that fall within certain *use classes* prescribed by statutory instrument. For example, office use is a use class and a mere change in the type of office business is not development. All development requires planning permission.

development land (community land) Under the Community Land Act 1975, land classified by a local authority as needed for commercial development and required to be brought first into public ownership, thus effectively nationalizing its development value. This Act was repealed by the Local Government, Planning and Land Act 1980.

development land tax A tax charged on the *realized development value of land. Tax is charged at the time of the disposal of the interest in the land. The commencement of a material development project is deemed to be a disposal. The rate of tax (in 1983–84) is 60%. There is an exemption for the first £50,000 of realized development value; the other main exemption is for an individual's main residence and up to one acre of attached land.

development plan *See* town and country planning.

deviation *n*. (in marine insurance) The departure of a ship from an agreed course. A ship must follow the course specified in a voyage or mixed insurance policy (*see* time policy); if no course is specified, the ship must follow the usual course for the voyage. Deviation discharges the underwriters from all liability for subsequent loss unless it is caused by circumstances beyond control or is justified on certain very limited grounds (e.g. to ensure the safety of the ship or to save human life, but not merely to save property). Between the parties to a voyage charter, the possibility of deviation is normally the subject of an express deviation clause in the *charterparty. For goods carried under a *bill of lading, permitted deviation is dealt with by the Hague Rules.

devil 1. *n.* A junior member of the Bar who does work (usually settling pleadings or writing opinions) for a more senior barrister under an informal arrangement between them and without reference to the senior's instructing solicitor. The Junior Counsel to the Treasury is sometimes referred to as the *Attorney General's devil.* **2.** *vb.* To act as a devil.

devise 1. *n.* A gift by will of *real property (*compare* legacy); the beneficiary is called the *devisee.* A devise may be *specific* (e.g. "my house, Blackacre, to A"), *general* (e.g. "all my real property to B"), or *residuary* (e.g. after a specific devise "...and the rest of my real property to C"). **2.** *vb.* To dispose of real property by will.

devolution *n.* **1.** The delegation by the central government to a regional authority of legislative or executive functions (or both) relating to domestic issues within the region. **2.** The passing of property from one owner to another, which may occur on death or sale, as a gift, or in any other way.

dictum [Latin: a saying] *n.* An observation by a judge with respect to a point of law arising in a case before him. *See also obiter dictum.*

dilapidation *n.* A state of disrepair. The term is usually used in relation to repairs required at the end of a lease or tenancy.

diminished responsibility An abnormal state of mind that does not constitute *insanity but is a special defence to a charge of murder. The abnormality of mind (which need not be a brain disease) must substantially impair the mental responsibility of the accused for his acts, i.e. reduce his powers of control, judgment, or reasoning to a condition that would be considered abnormal by the ordinary man. It may be

caused by disease, injury, or mental subnormality, and is liberally interpreted to cover such conditions as depression or *irresistible impulse. If the defendant proves the defence, the charge is reduced from murder to manslaughter.

diplomatic immunity The freedom from legal proceedings in the UK that is granted to members of diplomatic missions of foreign states by the Diplomatic Privileges Act 1964. This Act incorporates some of the provisions of the Vienna Convention on Diplomatic Relations (1961), which governs diplomatic immunity in international law. The extent of the immunity depends upon the status of the member in question, as certified by the Secretary of State. If he is a member of the mission's diplomatic staff, he is entitled to complete criminal immunity and to civil immunity except for actions relating to certain private activities. A member of the administrative or technical staff has full criminal immunity, but his civil immunity relates only to acts performed in the course of his official duties. For domestic staff, both criminal and civil immunity are restricted to official duties.

Similar immunities are granted to members of Commonwealth missions by the Diplomatic and other Privileges Act 1971, and to members of certain international bodies under the International Organisations Act 1968.

direct evidence (original evidence) **1.** A statement made by a witness in court offered as proof of the truth of any fact stated by him. *Compare* hearsay evidence. **2.** A statement of a witness that he perceived a fact in issue with one of his five senses or that he was in a particular physical or mental state. *Compare* circumstantial evidence.

direct examination *See* examination-in-chief.

direction to jury *See* jury.

directly applicable law Any provision of the law of the European Communities that forms part of the national law of a member state. *See* Community law; Community legislation.

director *n.* An officer of a company appointed by or under the provisions of the *articles of association. Directors may have a contract of employment with the company (*service directors* and *managing directors) or merely attend board meetings (*nonexecutive directors*). (*See also* shadow director.) Contracts of employment can be inspected by company members; long-term contracts may require approval by ordinary resolution. Usually, general management powers are vested in the directors acting collectively, although they may delegate some or all of these powers to the managing director. Directors act as agents of their company, to which they owe *fiduciary duties (in the performance of which they must consider the interests of both company members and employees) and a *duty of care. Transactions involving a conflict between their duty and their personal interests are regulated by the Companies Acts. Directors can be dismissed by ordinary resolution despite the terms of the articles or any contract of employment, but dismissal in these circumstances is subject to the payment of damages for breach of contract.

Remuneration of directors for their services may be due under a contract of employment or determined by the general meeting. Under the Companies Act 1948 and 1967 the aggregate amount of directors' remuneration must be shown in the accounts. If it exceeds £40,000, more details must be shown, e.g. the salary of the chairman and the number of directors whose salaries fall within the categories £0–£5000 p.a., £5000–£10,000 p.a., etc.

Director General of Fair Trading The head of the Office of Fair Trading, who has responsibility for administer-ing the Fair Trading Act 1973, the Consumer Credit Act 1974, and the Restrictive Trade Practices Act 1976. His principal concerns are consumer affairs (e.g. the eradication of unfair *consumer trade practices), consumer credit (particularly the licensing of *consumer-credit and *consumer-hire businesses), the review of commercial activities so as to identify *monopoly situations and draw them to the attention of the Secretary of State, and the registration of *restrictive trade practices, which he may refer to the *Restrictive Practices Court.

Director of Public Prosecutions (DPP) The official responsible for the prosecution of certain important criminal offences. It is the duty of the DPP to institute, undertake, or carry on such criminal proceedings and to give such advice and assistance to chief officers of police, justices' clerks, and others concerned in these proceedings as the *Attorney General may direct. In practice the DPP prosecutes all cases of murder and crimes amounting to an interference with justice, such as perjury. Some offences must be prosecuted by the DPP, in other cases his consent to prosecution is required. The DPP is appointed by the Home Secretary and must be a barrister or solicitor of not less than ten years' standing. *See also* Official Petitioner.

disabled person A person who is substantially handicapped by injury, disease, or congenital deformity from obtaining or keeping work suitable for his age, experience, and qualifications. Under the Disabled Persons (Employment) Act 1944 every employer of 20 or more persons (excluding those working less than 10 hours per week and counting those working between 10 and 30 hours as half a unit) is obliged to employ a quota of disabled persons registered as such with the Department of Employment. When this quota results in a fraction, less than one half is ignored and a half or more counts as one unit. An employer who does not fulfil his quota may only employ a nondisabled person to fill a vacancy if he first obtains a permit from the Department. An employer in breach of these requirements commits a criminal offence.

disablement benefit *See* industrial disablement benefit.

disabling statute A statute that disqualifies a person or persons of a specified class from exercising a legal right or freedom that he or they would otherwise enjoy.

disbar *vb.* To expel a barrister from his Inn of Court. The sentence of disbarment is pronounced by the *Benchers of the barrister's Inn, subject to a right of appeal to the judges who act as visitors of all the Inns of Court.

discharge *n.* Release from an obligation, debt, or liability, particularly the following. **1.** *Discharge of contract. **2.** The release of a debtor from all *provable debts (with minor exceptions) at the end of *bankruptcy proceedings. In certain circumstances discharge is automatic. In other cases, the debtor or the official receiver may apply to the court for an *order of discharge*. This may be subject to conditions, such as further payments by the debtor to his creditors out of his future income, or it may be suspended until the creditors receive a higher proportion of the amount due to them. After discharge the debtor is freed from most of the disabilities to which he was subject as an *undischarged bankrupt. **3.** The release of a convicted defendant without imposing a punishment on him. A discharge may be absolute or conditional. In an *absolute discharge* (common in crimes of *strict liability) the defendant is completely free of any criminal liability in respect of the offence and may not subsequently be punished for it. His conviction may, however, be accompanied by a *compensation order or by *en-

dorsement of his driving licence or *disqualification from driving. A *conditional discharge* releases the defendant without punishment, on condition that he is not convicted of any other offence within a specified period (usually three years). If he is convicted within that time, the court may sentence him for the original offence as well. Three conditions are required for the court to order a discharge: (1) that a probation order is not appropriate; (2) that the punishment for the offence must not be fixed by law; and (3) that the court thinks it inadvisable to punish the defendant in the circumstances.

discharge of contract The termination of a contractual obligation. Discharge may take place by: (1) *performance of contract; (2) express agreement, which may involve either *bilateral discharge or unilateral discharge (*see* accord and satisfaction); (3) *breach of contract; or (4) *frustration of contract.

disclaimer *n.* The refusal or renunciation of a right, claim, or property. A beneficiary under a will that leaves him both a burdensome and a beneficial gift (e.g. a racehorse that never wins and £50) may disclaim the former and take the latter. A company's liquidator may disclaim the company's lease, to avoid liability for the rent. A trustee may disclaim a trust if he has not yet accepted it; once he has accepted his trusteeship he may no longer disclaim it but he may resign (*see* retirement of trustees). Trusts and powers are normally disclaimed by deed.

disclosure *n.* **1.** (in contract law) *See* nondisclosure; *uberrimae fidei*. **2.** (in company law) **a.** A method of protecting investors that relies on the company disclosing and publishing information, which is then evaluated by the investors, their advisers, and the press. *See also* Stock Exchange. **b.** A method of regulating the conduct of directors and promoters by requiring them, on *fiduciary principles or by statutory provisions, to disclose to the company any relevant information, e.g. an interest in a contract with the company.

disclosure of documents (in court proceedings) *See* discovery and inspection of documents.

disclosure of information (in employment law) Communication by an employer to employees and their trade-union representatives of information relevant to *collective bargaining, proposed *redundancies, and the preservation of employees' health and *safety at work. Under the Employment Protection Act 1975, employers must disclose the following to the representatives of a recognized *independent trade union. (1) Information that is essential for the maintenance of good industrial relations or for the formulation of wage and related demands. When disclosure would damage national security or harm the business (apart from its effect on collective bargaining), or the information is *sub judice* or relevant only to particular individuals, disclosure need not be given. Guidelines on disclosure are published by *ACAS (*see also* code of practice). When an employer refuses to disclose essential information, the *Central Arbitration Committee is empowered on the application of the trade union to make awards of wages and conditions that are ultimately enforceable in the courts. (2) Details of any redundancies proposed by the employer. He must give the union 90 days' notice when 100 or more employees are to be made redundant over a period of 90 days or less, and 30 days' notice when there are to be 10 or more redundancies over 30 days or less. He must also give similar notice to the Department of Employment, otherwise he will forfeit up to 10% of the rebate on *redundancy payments to which he is entitled. The employer's notice must specify the reason for his proposals, the numbers and job descriptions of employees involved,

the way in which employees have been selected for redundancy, and the procedures for their dismissal. He must consider any representations made by the union, but need not comply with its demands. If the employer fails to give the required notice, the union can apply to an industrial tribunal, which may make a protective award to the redundant employees.

Under the Health and Safety at Work Act 1974, an employer must give his employees at large such information, instruction, and supervision as will ensure their health and safety so far as is reasonably practicable. He must also give copies of any relevant documents to safety representatives appointed by a recognized trade union.

disclosure of interest The duty of local authority members to disclose (at the time or by prior notice to the authority) any pecuniary interest they or their spouses have in any matter discussed at a local authority meeting. They must also abstain from speaking and voting on it. Breach of the duty is a criminal offence.

discontinuance of action *See* notice of discontinuance.

discovery and inspection of documents Disclosure by a party to civil litigation of the *documents in his possession, custody, or power relating to matters in question in the action (*discovery*) and their subsequent *inspection* by the opposing party. In the High Court discovery is *automatic and mutual* in actions begun by *writ, i.e. all parties must make discovery without an order of the court by serving a *list of documents* on the other parties. In other proceedings in the High Court, and in the county court and certain tribunals, discovery may only take place by order of the court or tribunal. At inspection, copies of the documents included in the list of documents may be taken, but a party need not produce for inspection any document in respect of which he claims a *privilege. *See also* failure to make discovery; nondisclosure.

discretion *n.* *See* judicial discretion.

discretionary trust A trust under which the trustees are given discretion as to who, within a class chosen by the settlor, should receive trust property and how much each should receive. A settlor must give some indication as to the limits of the class of people he intends to benefit, but the trustees do not need to have an exhaustive list. A beneficiary under a discretionary trust has no enforceable right to any part of the property or its income, although the trustees must consider his claims together with those of the other beneficiaries. Discretionary trusts have been invaluable in planning to mitigate liability to tax, but recent fiscal legislation has reduced their advantages.

discrimination *n.* Treating one or more members of a specified group unfairly as compared with other people. Discrimination may be illegal on the grounds of sex, race, or nationality, but it is not illegal to discriminate on grounds of religion. Under the European Convention on Human Rights, however, all the rights guaranteed by the Convention must be guaranteed to everyone, without discrimination on the grounds of religion. *See* racial discrimination; sex discrimination.

disentailing deed *See* entailed interest.

disentailment *n.* The barring of an *entailed interest.

dishonour *n.* (in commercial law) Failure to honour a bill of exchange. This may be by nonacceptance, when a bill of exchange is presented for *acceptance and this is refused or cannot be obtained (or when *presentment for acceptance is excused and the bill is not accepted); or by nonpayment, when the bill is presented for payment and payment is refused or cannot be obtained (or when presentment is excused and

the bill is overdue and unpaid). In both cases the holder has an immediate right of recourse against the drawer and endorsers, but foreign bills that have been dishonoured must first be protested (*see* protest). *See also* notice of dishonour.

dismissal *n.* (in employment law) The termination of an employee's contract of employment by the employer. An employer usually dismisses the employee by giving him the required period of *notice, but dismissal without notice may be justified in certain circumstances (e.g. for gross misconduct). An employer's failure to renew a fixed-term employment contract also counts as dismissal. An employee having the required length of service in the business (*see* continuous employment) can apply to an industrial tribunal if he is unfairly dismissed (*see* unfair dismissal); the tribunal can order his *reinstatement or *re-engagement or can award him *compensation. An employee dismissed for *redundancy after two years' continuous employment in the business is entitled to a *redundancy payment under the Employment Protection (Consolidation) Act 1978. An employee dismissed without due notice or before his fixed-term contract expires can also claim damages in the courts for *wrongful dismissal. *See also* statement for reasons of dismissal.

An employee dismissed because of her pregnancy or some reason connected with it retains her *maternity rights irrespective of the *effective date of termination of her employment, provided that she would have been in continuous employment for at least two years by the end of the 12th week before the expected date of her confinement. However, she must have informed her employer of her intention to return to work as soon as reasonably practicable after the effective date of termination.

dismissal of action The termination of a civil action in favour of the defendant. An order for dismissal of action may be made at the conclusion of the trial, but is usually made during the *interlocutory proceedings; for example, for breach of some rule of procedure. Dismissal for *want of prosecution* occurs if the plaintiff has been guilty of inordinate and inexcusable delay in circumstances in which there is a risk that a fair trial is no longer possible or in which there has been prejudice to the defendant.

dismissal procedures agreement A collective agreement containing provisions relating to the dismissal of employees and intended to replace the statutory provisions concerning *unfair dismissal. *See also* collective bargaining.

dismissal statement *See* statement of reasons for dismissal.

disorderly house A *brothel or a place staging performances or exhibitions that tend to corrupt or deprave and outrage common decency. It is a misdemeanour at common law to keep a disorderly house.

disparagement of goods *See* slander of goods.

disposal of uncollected goods The sale by a bailee of goods in his possession or under his control when the bailor is in breach of an obligation to collect them (*see* bailment). When the original contract does not require the bailor to collect the goods, the bailee may, by giving notice, impose such an obligation. The relevant statutory provisions in the Torts (Interference with Goods) Act 1977 lay down conditions relating to the giving of notice of the bailee's intention to sell, allowing the bailor a reasonable opportunity to collect. The bailee should adopt the best method of sale available and must account to the bailor for the proceeds of sale less any sum due before he gave notice of intention to sell. There is pro-

vision for a bailee to have a sale authorized by a court.

disposition *n.* **1.** (in land law) The transfer of property by some act of its owner, e.g. by sale, gift, will, or exchange. **2.** (in the law of evidence) The tendency of a party (especially the accused) to act or think in a particular way. Evidence of the accused's disposition may generally not be given unless it is based upon admissible evidence of character or admissible *similar-fact evidence. Evidence of *previous convictions, other than those admitted as similar-fact evidence or under the Criminal Evidence Act 1898, may tend to suggest to the *trier of fact that the accused has a particular disposition, but is technically admissible only on the question of his credibility. *See also* character.

disqualification *n.* Depriving someone of a right because he has committed a criminal offence or failed to comply with specified conditions. Disqualification is usually imposed in relation to activities requiring a licence, and in particular for traffic offences. In the case of many traffic offences, the court has discretion to disqualify drivers for a stated period. There are also seven traffic offences for which disqualification for at least 12 months is compulsory (unless the offender can show special reasons relating to the circumstances of the offence, not to his personal circumstances). These offences are: (1) manslaughter; (2) *causing death by reckless driving; (3) a conviction for *reckless driving for the second time within three years or within three years of a conviction for causing death by reckless driving; (4) driving or attempting to drive while unfit; (5) driving or attempting to drive with an excess blood-alcohol level (*see* drunken driving); (6) failure (in certain cases) to provide a *specimen of breath, blood, or urine; (7) racing or speed trials on the highway.

If a person is convicted for a second

time within ten years of a driving offence involving drink or drugs, he must be disqualified for at least three years. The courts may also disqualify anyone who commits an indictable offence of any kind involving the use of a car. There is also a *totting-up system of endorsements, which can result in disqualification. When someone is disqualified from driving, his licence will usually also be endorsed with details of the offence (but not with any penalty points for the purpose of totting up). The court may also make a *driving-test order. A person who has been disqualified from driving may apply to have the disqualification removed after two years or half the period of disqualification (whichever is longer) or, when he has been disqualified for ten years or more, after five years. *See also* driving while disqualified.

dissolution *n.* **1.** The legal termination of a marriage; for example, by a decree of divorce or nullity or presumption of death. **2.** The dissolving of a company. If this is achieved by *winding-up, the dissolution can be declared void within two years. In the case of defunct companies, which are struck off the register of companies because the Registrar has reasonable cause to believe that they are no longer carrying on business, the dissolution can be declared void within 20 years. **3.** *See* Parliament.

distinguishing a case The process of providing reasons for deciding a case under consideration differently from a similar case referred to as a *precedent.

distortion of competition *See* EEC.

distrain *vb.* To seize goods by way of *distress.

distress *n.* The seizure of goods as security for the performance of an obligation. The two principal situations covered by the remedy of distress are (1) between landlord and tenant when the rent is in arrears (*see* distress for rent); and (2) when goods are unlawfully on

an occupier's land and have done or are doing damage (*see also* distress damage feasant). In the latter case the occupier may detain the chattel until compensation is paid for the damage.

distress damage feasant A right to detain animals found doing damage on one's land as security for compensation. This right was abolished in England by the Animals Act 1971 and replaced by a statutory power to detain and ultimately to sell the animals. The statutory power is subject to detailed requirements of giving notice of detention and taking care of the animals.

distress for rent The seizing of a tenant's goods by the landlord to secure payment of rent arrears. If the tenant fails to pay the rent arrears after distress has been levied, the landlord may sell the goods and keep the amount due. In the case of a *protected or *statutory tenancy the landlord must obtain a court's permission before levying distress.

distribution *n.* **1.** The process of handing over to the beneficiaries their entitlements under a deceased person's will or on his intestacy. **2.** Any payment made by a company to a shareholder out of its distributable profits in cash or kind. It does not include payments made in the course of a winding-up or repayments of the capital originally subscribed or subsequently received by the company. *See also* qualifying distribution.

district *n.* A *local government area in England (outside Greater London) or Wales consisting of a division of a *county. The Local Government Act 1972 divided the 6 metropolitan and 39 nonmetropolitan counties in England into 36 metropolitan and 296 nonmetropolitan districts, respectively, and the 8 counties in Wales into 37 districts. A district may be styled a borough by royal charter granted on the petition of the *district council. *See also* local government boundary commissions.

district auditors Civil servants who audit the accounts of all local authorities except those who choose audit by approved commercial accountants. If any transaction involved unlawful expenditure, they may obtain a court order for repayment by the persons responsible.

district council A *local authority whose area is a *district. A district council has certain exclusive responsibilities (e.g. housing and rating) and shares others (e.g. food and drugs, town and country planning) with the council of the county to which the district belongs. In England some responsibilities (e.g. education and the personal social services) belong to the district council if the district is metropolitan, but to the county council if it is not. If a district has the style of borough, its council is called a borough council and its chairman the mayor.

district registrars *See* Masters of the Supreme Court.

district registry An office of the High Court outside London, corresponding in function to the *Central Office; however, only a limited number of district registries exercise full powers in relation to proceedings in the *Chancery Division. There are district registries in all major towns and cities in England and Wales.

distringas [Latin: that you distrain] *n.* A writ, now obsolete, commanding the sheriff to distrain on a person for a certain purpose. In modern practice it has been replaced by a *stop notice, sometimes called a *notice in lieu of distringas*, which prevents dealings in securities that are subject to a *charging order.

disturbance *n.* **1.** The infringement of a right, e.g. the obstruction of a right of way. **2.** The removal of a person's rights under a statutory power. For example,

compensation for disturbance may be payable to a landowner if his land is compulsorily acquired by a local authority.

dividend *n.* The payment made by a company to its shareholders out of its distributable profits. It is calculated as a percentage of the nominal value of their *shares, which is fixed for holders of preference shares and fluctuating for holders of ordinary shares. Dividends are payable in a financial year only if they are *declared* by the *annual general meeting on the recommendation of the directors (*final*) or by the directors themselves between such meetings (*interim*).

divisible contract *See* performance of contract.

division *n.* The taking of a vote on any matter in either House of Parliament.

Divisional Court A court consisting of not less than two judges of one of the Divisions of the High Court. There are Divisional Courts of each of the Divisions. Their function is to hear appeals in various matters prescribed by statute; they also exercise the supervisory jurisdiction of the High Court over inferior courts. Most of this jurisdiction is exercised by the Queen's Bench Division, which also hears applications for *judicial review and appeals by *case stated from magistrates' courts. The Chancery Division hears appeals in *bankruptcy matters and the Family Division hears appeals from magistrates' courts in matters of family law.

Divisions of the High Court *See* Chancery Division; Family Division; Queen's Bench Division.

divorce *n.* The legal termination of a marriage and the obligations created by marriage, other than by a decree of nullity or presumption of death. Proceedings are initiated by either spouse filing a *petition for divorce*, stating the facts that have led to the breakdown of the

divorce by mutual consent

marriage. Normally a divorce will not be given within the first three years after celebration of the marriage (except in cases of *exceptional hardship or depravity). A divorce may only be given upon proof that the marriage has broken down completely (*irretrievable breakdown*), which may be evidenced by a number of facts (*see* breakdown of marriage). Divorce decrees are issued by specially designated divorce county courts in two stages, a *decree nisi followed by a *decree absolute, and there is now a *special procedure* available, which enables the proceedings to be conducted by post, without either party appearing in court. If either spouse contests the divorce petition, however, the case must be heard in the High Court (*see also* undefended cause). Divorce courts have wide discretionary powers to make orders in respect of the children and to adjust financial and property rights (*see* child protection in divorce; financial provision order; maintenance; property adjustment order).

divorce by mutual consent Divorce based on the agreement of the parties, without proof of a marital offence (such as adultery or desertion). English law does not recognize mutual consent to divorce as a sufficient basis for a divorce decree, unless the parties have lived apart for at least two years.

Divorce Registry The section of the Family Division of the High Court with jurisdiction over divorce proceedings.

dock brief The procedure, now obsolete, by which a defendant to a criminal charge could, on indictment, select any barrister robed and present in the court who was not otherwise engaged to represent him, on payment of a nominal fee.

doctrine of incorporation The doctrine that rules of international law automatically form part of municipal law. It is opposed to the *doctrine of transfor-*

mation, which states that international law only forms a part of municipal law if accepted as such by statute or judicial decisions. It is not altogether clear which view English law takes with respect to rules of customary *international law. As far as international treaties are concerned, the sovereign has the power to make or ratify treaties so as to bind England under international law, but these treaties have no effect in municipal law (with the exception of treaties governing the conduct of war) until enacted by Parliament. However, judges will sometimes consider provisions of international treaties (e.g. those relating to *human rights) in applying municipal law.

document *n.* Something that records or transmits information, typically in writing on paper. For the purposes of providing evidence to a court, documents include books, maps, plans, drawings, photographs, graphs, discs, tapes, soundtracks, and films (*see also* computer documents). Some legal documents are only valid if they meet certain requirements (*see* deed; will). Documents that are to be used in court proceedings must be disclosed to the other party in a procedure known as *discovery and inspection of documents. In court, the original of a document must be produced in most cases. In the case of a public document a particular kind of copy must be produced; for example, a copy of a statute must be a government printer's copy, and a copy of a byelaw must be certified by the clerk to the local authority concerned. The authenticity of private documents must be proved by the evidence of a witness. In practice this procedure is often avoided or simplified by each party admitting the authenticity of particular documents prior to the court hearing. *See also duces tecum*; parol evidence rule; production of documents.

documentary evidence Evidence in written rather than oral form. The admissibility of a document depends upon (1) proof of the authenticity of the document and (2) the purpose for which it is being offered in evidence. If it is being offered to prove the truth of some matter stated in the document itself it will be necessary to consider the application of the rule against hearsay (*see* hearsay evidence) and its many exceptions.

dogs *pl. n. See* classification of animals; guard dog.

doli capax [Latin] Capable of wrongful intention. A child under the age of 10 is deemed incapable of committing any crime. Between the ages of 10 and 14 he may be convicted if the prosecution can prove that he knew that what he was doing was morally or legally wrong. A boy under the age of 14 cannot, however, be convicted of rape or attempted rape (although if he in fact rapes a woman he can be convicted of indecent assault). Above the age of 14 children are *doli capax* and are treated as adults, although they will usually be tried in special juvenile courts (with the exception of homicide and certain other grave offences) and subject to special punishments. *See* juvenile offender.

domestic agreements Agreements made between spouses about such matters as housekeeping money. These are not normally legally enforceable, unless they are clearly business arrangements or the parties have separated or are about to separate.

domestic premises A private residence, together with its garden, yard, and attached buildings (such as garages and outhouses).

domestic tribunal A body that exercises jurisdiction over the internal affairs of a particular profession or association under powers conferred either by statute (e.g. the disciplinary committee of the Law Society) or by contract between the members (e.g. the disciplinary committee of a trade union). The

decisions of these tribunals are subject to judicial control under the doctrine of *ultra vires* and, if they are statutory, when there is an *error of law on the face of the record. *Compare* administrative tribunal.

domestic violence *See* battered wife.

domicile *n.* The country that a person treats as his permanent home and to which he has the closest legal attachment. A person cannot be without a domicile and cannot have two domiciles at once. He acquires at birth a *domicile of origin*. Normally, if his father is then alive, he takes his father's domicile; if not, his mother's. He retains his domicile of origin until (if ever) he acquires a *domicile of choice* in its place. A domicile of choice is acquired by making a home in a country with the intention that it should be a permanent base. It may be acquired at any time after a person becomes 16 and can be replaced at will by a new domicile of choice. *See lex domicilii.*

dominant tenement Land the ownership of which entitles the owner to rights comprising a legal or equitable interest (such as an easement or profit *à prendre*) in other land, called the *servient tenement*.

Dominions *pl. n.* Formerly, the group of UK colonies that, by virtue of the Statute of Westminster 1931, were the first to become fully independent. Certain of these (but not, for example, South Africa), together with many other former colonies, are now collectively known as the *Commonwealth.

donatio mortis causa [Latin: a gift on account of death] A gift of personal property made in anticipation of the donor's imminent death and intended to be effective upon his death. The property must be delivered to the donee at the time of the gift and must be of a kind that can legally be transferred by delivery.

double portions

double portions *pl. n. See* rule against double portions.

DPP *See* Director of Public Prosecutions.

driver *n.* For purposes of the Road Traffic Acts, anyone who uses the ordinary controls of a vehicle (i.e. steering and brakes) to direct its movement. This includes anyone steering a car when the engine is off or when being towed by another vehicle, whether or not he knows how to drive himself.

driving licence An official authority to drive a motor vehicle, granted upon passing a driving test. A renewable provisional driving licence, valid for 12 months, may be granted to learner drivers, but the holder of a provisional licence may not drive a motor car on a public road unless accompanied by a qualified driver and unless he displays 'L' plates on the front and rear of the vehicle.

A full licence may be obtained by anyone who has passed the Department of the Environment driving test, or held a full licence issued in Great Britain, Northern Ireland, the Isle of Man, or the Channel Islands within ten years before the date on which the licence is to come into force. It is normally granted until the applicant's 70th birthday. After the age of 70, licences are granted for three-year periods. The applicant must disclose any disability and may be asked to produce his medical records or have a medical examination.

An applicant will not normally be granted a licence if he is suffering from certain types of disability, including epilepsy, sudden attacks of disabling giddiness or fainting, or a severe mental illness or defect. In the case of epilepsy, however, he may still be granted a licence if he can show that he has been free of all attacks for at least two years or that he has only had attacks during sleep for more than three years. If an applicant for a licence has diabetes or a heart condition, is fitted with a heart pacemaker, has been treated within the previous three years for drug addiction, or is suffering from any other disability (e.g. loss or weakness of a limb) that would affect his driving, the grant of a licence is usually discretionary.

It is an offence to knowingly make a false statement in order to obtain a driving licence, not to disclose any current *endorsements, or not to sign one's name in ink on the licence. A police officer may require a driver to show his driving licence or produce it personally at a specified police station within five days. He may also ask to see the licence of someone whom he believes was either driving a vehicle involved in an accident or had committed a motoring offence. Failure to produce one's licence in these circumstances carries a fine of £50. *See also* driving without a licence.

driving-test order An order by the court that a person who has been convicted of an offence that is subject to *disqualification should be disqualified from driving until he passes a test showing that he is fit to drive. The order should only be made where there is reason to suspect that the person is not fit to drive; for example, because he is very old or unwell, and has shown evidence of incompetence in his driving. It is not meant as a punishment but to protect the public.

driving while unfit *See* drunken driving.

driving while disqualified An offence committed by someone who drives a motor vehicle on a public road when he is disqualified from driving (*see* disqualification). This is an endorsable offence (carrying 6 points under the *totting-up system) and the courts have discretion to impose a further period of disqualification.

driving without a licence An offence committed by someone who drives a motor vehicle on a public road without a *driving licence or provisional driving licence valid for the vehicle he is driving. If the circumstances are such that he would in fact have been refused a licence had he applied for one, or if he fails to comply with the conditions applicable to a provisional licence, his licence (if he subsequently obtains one) will usually be endorsed (the endorsement carries 2 points under the *totting-up system) and the court has discretion to order disqualification from driving (if he applies for a licence during the disqualification period). Otherwise this is not an endorsable offence.

driving without insurance An offence committed by someone who uses or allows someone else to use a motor vehicle on a public road without valid *third-party insurance. The offence is one of *strict liability (except when an employee is using his employer's vehicle) and applies even if, for example, the insurance company who issued the insurance suddenly goes into liquidation. The offence is punishable by a fine, endorsement (it carries 4–8 points under the *totting-up system), and disqualification at the discretion of the court.

drugs *pl. n. See* controlled drugs.

drunken driving Driving while affected by alcohol. Drunken driving covers two separate legal offences.

(1) *Driving while unfit.* It is an offence to drive or attempt to drive a motor vehicle on a road or public place when one's ability to drive properly is impaired by alcohol or drugs. Drugs include medicines (such as insulin for diabetics), and the offence appears to be one of *strict liability. It is also an offence to be in charge of a motor vehicle on a road or in a public place while unfit to drive because of drink or drugs, but the defendant will be acquitted if he can show that there was no likelihood of his driving the vehicle in this condition (for example, if he arranged for someone else to drive him if he became drunk). A police officer can arrest without a warrant anyone whom he reasonably suspects is committing or has been committing either of these offences; he may also (except in Scotland) enter any place where he believes the suspect to be, using force if necessary.

(2) *Driving over the prescribed limit.* It is an offence to drive or attempt to drive a motor vehicle on a road or in a public place if the level of alcohol in one's breath, blood, or urine is above the specified prescribed limit (35 micrograms of alcohol in 100 millilitres (ml) of breath; 80 milligrams (mg) of alcohol in 100 ml of blood; 107 mg of alcohol in 100 ml of urine – roughly equivalent to 2½ pints of beer, or 5 glasses of wine, or 5 single whiskys). It is also an offence to be in charge of a motor vehicle on a road or in a public place when the proportion of alcohol is more than the prescribed limit, subject to the same defence as in being in charge while unfit. Both these offences are offences of strict liability: it is therefore not a defence to show that one did not know that the drink was alcoholic or that it exceeded the prescribed limit. The normal way in which offences involving excess alcohol levels are proved is by taking a *specimen of breath for laboratory analysis, but this is not necessary if the offence can be proved in some other way (for example, by evidence of how much a person drank before driving). There is no power to arrest a person on suspicion of committing or having committed an offence of this sort before administering a preliminary *breath test.

Most charges involving drinking and driving are brought under the offence of driving over the prescribed limit rather than driving while unfit, but the powers to administer a breath test or to take a specimen of breath for analysis apply to both offences. The penalties for either of these offences are a fine and/or imprisonment, *endorsement, and obligatory *disqualification (in cases of driving or attempting to drive) or discretionary disqualification (in cases of being in charge). Under the *totting-up system, the discretionary disqualification offences carry 10 points and the compulsory disqualification offences carry 4 points (which are only imposed if there are special reasons preventing disqualification).

drunkenness *n. See* intoxication.

dualism *n. See* monism.

dubitante [Latin] *adj.* Doubting. The term is used in law reports in relation to a judge who is doubtful about a legal proposition but does not wish to declare it wrong.

duces tecum [Latin: you shall bring with you] A *subpoena ordering a person to appear before a court and bring with him a document or other evidence that the court wishes him to produce.

dum casta vixerit [Latin] As long as she lives chastely. A clause sometimes inserted in a separation agreement, freeing the husband from the terms of the agreement (e.g. maintenance obligations) if his wife commits adultery.

dum sola [Latin] While single: the status of a single woman or widow.

duplex querela [Latin: double complaint] The procedure in ecclesiastical law for challenging a bishop's refusal to admit a presentee to a benefice.

durante absentia [Latin: during the absence of] Describing a grant of *letters of administration of a deceased's estate to some appropriate person while the executor is abroad.

duress *n.* Pressure, especially actual or threatened physical force, put on a person to act in a particular way. Acts carried out under duress usually have no legal effect; for example, a contract obtained by duress is voidable (*see also* undue influence). In criminal law, when the pressure is such that the defendant's power to resist is destroyed (e.g. by a threat of death or personal injury), he will have a defence to a criminal charge,

although he has the *mens rea* for the crime and knows that what he is doing is wrong. As a result of the recent decision of the Court of Appeal in *R.* v *Graham* [1982] it is uncertain whether or not duress is a defence to a charge of murder as a principal in the first degree (i.e. to someone who actually carries out the murder himself) and if so, what sort of threat is required to establish duress, although it is still a defence to someone charged with aiding and abetting murder. The threat need not be immediate; it is sufficient that it is effective; for example a threat in court to kill a witness may constitute duress and thus be a defence to a charge of perjury, even though it cannot be carried out in the courtroom.

during Her (*or* His) Majesty's pleasure A phrase colloquially used to describe the period of detention imposed upon a defendant who is found not guilty by reason of *insanity. Such a person was consequently known as a *pleasure patient.* The defendant must still be admitted to a hospital specified by the Home Secretary (either a local psychiatric hospital or a *special hospital) and remain there until otherwise directed, but the phrase "during Her Majesty's pleasure" is no longer used in the statute.

duty *n.* **1.** A legal requirement to carry out or refrain from carrying out any act. *Compare* power. **2.** A payment levied by the state, particularly on certain goods and transactions. Examples are *customs duty, *excise duty, and *stamp duty.

duty of care The legal obligation to take reasonable care to avoid causing damage. There is no liability in tort for *negligence unless the act or omission that causes damage is a breach of a duty of care owed to the plaintiff. There is a duty to take care in most situations in which one can reasonably foresee that one's actions may cause damage to the person or property of others. The duty is owed to those people likely to be affected by the conduct in question. Thus doctors have a duty of care to their patients and users of the highway have a duty of care to all other road users. But there is no general duty to rescue persons or property in danger, liability for careless words is more limited than liability for careless acts, and there is no general duty not to cause economic loss. In these and some other situations, the scope of the duty of care is limited for reasons of policy. Most duties of care are the result of judicial decisions, but some are contained in statutes, such as the Occupiers' Liability Act 1957 (*see* occupier's liability).

duty solicitors *Solicitors who attend voluntarily by rota at magistrates' courts in order to assist defendants who are otherwise unrepresented.

duty to convert (in equity) *See* conversion.

dying declaration An oral or written statement by a person on the point of death concerning the cause of his death. A dying declaration is admissible at a trial for the murder or manslaughter of the declarant as an exception to the rule against *hearsay, provided that he would have been a competent witness had he survived (*see* competence).

E

earned income For *income tax purposes, a person's earnings, including wages, salary, fees, or other income from an office or employment; profits from a trade or profession; and pension. There is an income-tax allowance for a wife's earned income. Income other than earned income is *investment income and taxed accordingly.

easement *n.* A right enjoyed by the owner of land (the *dominant tenement*) to a benefit from other land (the *servient tenement*). An easement benefits and binds the land itself and therefore continues despite any change of ownership of either dominant or servient tenement, although it will be extinguished if the two tenements come into common ownership. It may be expressly granted (e.g. by *deed giving a right of way), arise by implication (e.g. an easement of support from an adjoining building), or be acquired by *prescription. (*See also* profit *à prendre*.) An easement can exist as either a legal or an equitable interest in land. Only easements created by statute, deed, or prescription and held on terms equivalent to a *fee simple absolute in possession or *term of years absolute qualify as *legal easements* and are binding on all who acquire the servient tenement or any interest in it. All others, such as easements subsisting for life or created by contract not made under seal, are *equitable easements* and must generally be registered to be enforceable against a third party who acquires the servient tenement. *See* registration of encumbrances.

easement of light An easement giving the owner of a *dominant tenement the right to the access across the servient tenement of a sufficient quantity of light for the ordinary purposes to which the dominant tenement may be put. No easement can be acquired for a greater amount of light than is necessary for such purposes.

ecclesiastical courts Courts responsible for the administration of the ecclesiastical law of the Church of England. They comprise *consistory courts* (the courts of each diocese); the *Court of Arches and the *Chancery Court of York*, which hear appeals from consistory courts in their respective provinces; the *Judicial Committee of the Privy Council, which hears appeals from the provincial courts in matters not involving doctrine, ritual, or ceremonial; and the

*Court of Ecclesiastical Causes Reserved.

education authorities The authorities responsible for the statutory system of education introduced by the Education Act 1944, i.e. the Secretary of State for Education and Science and local education authorities. The latter are county councils (or district councils if metropolitan) and, within *Greater London, the outer London borough councils and the Inner London Education Authority.

EEC (European Economic Community) One of the three *European Communities. It was created by the Treaty of Rome in 1957 with the broad object of furthering economic development within the Community by the establishment of a *Common Market* and the approximation of the economic policies of member states. Its more detailed aims include eliminating customs duties internally and adopting a common customs tariff externally, the following by member states of common policies on agriculture and transport, promoting the free movement of labour and capital between member states, and outlawing within the Community all practices leading to the *distortion of competition.*

The original members of the EEC were Belgium, France, Germany, Italy, Luxembourg, and the Netherlands. The UK, the Republic of Ireland, and Denmark joined in 1972, and Greece in 1981. The changes in UK law necessary as a result of her joining were made by the European Communities Act 1972.

EEC law *See* Community law.

effective date of termination The date on which a contract of employment comes to an end, i.e. the date of expiry of any *notice given or of a fixed-term contract or the date of the employee's dismissal or resignation if no notice is given. However, an employee dismissed without the statutory minimum notice is treated as having worked for that period after his dismis-

sal for the purpose of calculating whether or not his length of service (*see* continuous employment) qualifies him to apply to an industrial tribunal in respect of redundancy, unfair dismissal, etc.

ei qui affirmat non ei qui negat incumbit probatio [Latin: the burden of proof lies upon the person who affirms, not upon the person who denies] A general principle for the allocation of the *burden of proof. It is, however, subject to some exceptions; for example, if the accused raises a defence of insanity, the burden of proving insanity falls on him.

ejusdem generis **rule** *See* interpretation of statutes.

Elder Brethren *See* assessors.

election *n.* **1.** The process of choosing by vote a member of a representative body, such as the House of Commons or a local authority. For the House of Commons, a *general election* involving all UK constituencies is held when the sovereign dissolves Parliament and summons a new one; a *by-election* is held if a particular constituency becomes vacant (e.g. on the death of the sitting member) during the life of a Parliament. Local government elections (apart from those to fill casual vacancies) are held at statutory intervals (*see* local authority). The conduct of elections is regulated by the Representation of the People Acts 1949 to 1977. Voting is secret and normally in person, but postal voting is available to the armed services and certain others (e.g. the physically handicapped). Any dispute as to the validity of a particular election is raised on an election petition, which is decided by an Election Court consisting of two High Court judges.

2. A doctrine of equity, commonly applied to wills, based on the principle that a person must accept both benefits and burdens under one document, or reject both. It arises when there are two gifts in one document, one of A's (the creator's) property to B and one of B's property to C. B must choose whether to accept the gift of A's property to him and transfer his own property to C, or to reject both gifts.

elector *n.* **1.** A person entitled to vote at an *election. For parliamentary and local government elections, a *register of electors* is maintained. A new register comes into force on 16 February each year and governs elections held during the following 12 months. It records electors by reference to their residence on the preceding 10 October (the qualifying date) and includes people who will become 18 (and so entitled to vote) in the year following its publication. Inclusion on the register is a requirement for voting. A person on it cannot be prevented from voting but incurs penalties if he votes without in fact being entitled to do so. *See* franchise. **2.** (in equity) One who makes an election.

electronic surveillance The use of *telephone tapping, hidden microphones or cameras, or similar means to obtain evidence. Evidence obtained by electronic surveillance can usually be used in court proceedings: it has been compared with the evidence of an eavesdropper.

eleemosynary corporation [from Latin: *eleemosyna*, alms] Originally, a lay (rather than an ecclesiastical) charity. An eleemosynary corporation is now a charity directed to the relief of individual distress.

embezzlement *n.* The dishonest appropriation by an employee of any money or property given to him on behalf of his employer. Before 1968 there was a special offence of embezzlement; it is now, however, classified as a form of *theft.

emblements *pl. n.* Cultivated crops that are normally harvested annually. A tenant for life of settled land may continue to harvest crops he has sown if his interest in the land ceases for any rea-son other than by his own act. For example, he may continue to harvest his crops if his interest ends on the death of another person but not if his interest was for life until remarriage and he remarries. When he dies, his personal representatives are entitled to reap for the benefit of his estate any crops sown by him before his death.

emergency powers Powers conferred by government regulations during a *state of emergency*. The existence of such a state is declared by royal proclamation under the Emergency Powers Acts 1920 and 1964. A proclamation, which lasts for one month but is renewable, may be issued whenever there is a threat (e.g. a major strike or natural disaster) to the country's essentials of life. The regulations made may confer on government departments, the armed forces, and others all powers necessary to secure the supply and distribution of necessities and the maintenance of public peace and safety.

eminent domain *See* expropriation.

emoluments *pl. n.* A person's earnings, including salaries, fees, wages, and profits. They are subject to *income tax under Schedules D and E in the Income and Corporation Taxes Act 1970.

empanel *vb.* To swear a jury to try an issue.

employee *n.* A person who works under the direction and control of another (the *employer) in return for a wage or salary. *See also* contract of employment; employer and employee.

employees' inventions Products, equipment, or techniques invented by an employee in the course of his employment. Under the Patents Act 1977 these belong to the employer if the invention was made in the course of the employee's normal duties and these were likely to lead to an invention or in the course of any duties involving a special obligation to further the employer's business. The employee may, however, be awarded compensation by the Comptroller General of Patents, Designs and Trademarks if the invention is of outstanding benefit to the employer. Generally, copyright works also belong to the employer if the employee is paid to produce such works.

employees' share scheme A method of sharing company profits with employees either by distributing shares already paid up by the company, either to the employees themselves or to trustees for them, or by conferring upon them options to acquire shares on favourable terms. Certain schemes carry tax concessions.

employer *n.* A person who engages another (the *employee) to work under his direction and control in return for a wage or salary (*see also* contract of employment). Companies are *associated employers* if one of them controls the other or others or if they are themselves controlled by the same company.

employer and employee The relationship between the parties to a *contract of employment. (It was formerly known as *master and servant*.) The relationship is governed by the express and implied terms of the contract and by statutory rules that the contract cannot exclude. These relate, for example, to *unfair dismissal, *redundancy, *maternity rights, *trade union membership and activity, and health and *safety at work. On the principle of *vicarious liability, third parties may hold an employer responsible for certain wrongs committed by his employee in the course of his employment.

employers' association An organization whose members are wholly or mainly employers and whose principal purposes include the regulation of relations between employers and workers or trade unions. Under the Trade Union and Labour Relations Act 1974, employers' associations have similar le-

gal status to *trade unions, being immune from certain civil legal proceedings in tort relating to interference with contracts and restraint of trade.

Employment Appeal Tribunal (EAT) A statutory body established to hear appeals from *industrial tribunals. The EAT consists of a High Court judge as chairman and two or four lay members who have special knowledge or experience as employers' or employees' representatives. They can only hear appeals on questions of law, issues of fact being in the exclusive jurisdiction of industrial tribunals. The EAT may allow or dismiss an appeal or, in certain circumstances, remit the case to the industrial tribunal for further hearing. It does not generally order either party to pay the other's costs, except when the appeal is frivolous, vexatious, or improperly conducted. The parties may be represented at the hearing by anyone they choose, who need not have legal qualifications. The EAT cannot enforce its own decisions; thus, for example, when an employer fails to comply with an order for compensation that the EAT upholds, separate application must be made to the court to enforce the order. A party may appeal to the Court of Appeal from a decision of the EAT, but only with the leave of the EAT or the Court of Appeal.

enabling statute A statute that confers rights or powers upon any body or person.

enacting words The introductory words in an *Act of Parliament that give it the force of law. They follow immediately after the long title and date of royal assent, unless preceded by a preamble, and normally run: "Be It Enacted by the Queen's most Excellent Majesty, by and with the advice and consent of the Lords Spiritual and Temporal, and Commons, in this present Parliament assembled, and by the authority of the same, as follows ... ". A special formula is used in cases when the Parliament Acts 1911 and 1949 apply.

enactment *n.* An Act of Parliament, a Measure of the General Synod (*see* Church of England), an order, or any other piece of subordinate legislation, or any particular provision contained in any of these (e.g. a particular section or article).

encroachment *n.* The act of extending one's own rights at the expense of others, particularly by taking in adjoining land to make it appear part of one's own. If the encroachment is acquiesced in for 12 years, the land taken is considered to be annexed to the land of the person who made the encroachment.

encumbrance (incumbrance) *n.* A right or interest in land owned by someone other than the owner of the land itself; examples include easements, leases, mortgages, and restrictive covenants. When title to the land is registered (*see* land registration), encumbrances other than minor and overriding interests are recorded in the Charges Register. Certain encumbrances affecting unregistered land will only be enforceable against third parties if registered at the Land Charges Registry. *See also* registration of encumbrances.

endorsement (indorsement) *n.* **1.** The procedure in which the particulars of a driving offence are noted on one's driving licence. When the court orders endorsement for an offence carrying obligatory or discretionary *disqualification but the driver is not disqualified, the endorsement also contains particulars of the number of penalty points imposed for the purposes of *totting up. When the court orders disqualification, only the particulars of the offence are noted. The courts can order endorsement upon a conviction for most traffic offences (the main exceptions being parking offences and causing an obstruction) and in many cases they must

order an endorsement, unless there are special reasons (e.g. a sudden emergency) why they should not. A person whose licence is to be endorsed must produce it for the court; if he does not do so, his licence may be suspended. A driver whose licence has been endorsed may apply to have a new "clean" licence after a certain number of years has elapsed (usually 4 years, but 11 in the case of offences involving *drunken driving). **2.** The signature of the holder on a bill of exchange, which is an essential step in negotiating or transfering a bill payable to order. The endorsement must be completed by delivering the bill to the transferee. An *endorsement in blank* is the bare signature of the holder and makes the bill payable to bearer. A *special endorsement* specifies the person to whom (or to whose order) the bill is payable (e.g. "Pay X or order").

endorsement of service A statement by a solicitor acting on behalf of a defendant to an *action in the High Court confirming that he accepts service of the writ on behalf of the defendant. This statement is endorsed on the writ (i.e. written on the back of it). The writ is then deemed to have been duly served on the defendant.

endorsement of writ A writ of summons must be endorsed with (1) the plaintiff's address and (when appropriate) his solicitor's name and address and (2) either a *statement of claim (formerly known as a *special endorsement*) or a concise statement of the nature of the claim or the remedy required (formerly known as a *general endorsement*). When the action is for a debt or a liquidated demand the writ must also be endorsed with a claim for an amount of costs fixed by rules of court.

endowment *n.* **1.** The provision of a fixed income for the support of a charity. **2.** Any property belonging permanently to a charity.

enforcement notice A notice by a local planning authority (*see* town and country planning) that requires certain steps to be taken within a specified time to remedy an alleged breach of planning control. An example of such a breach would occur if development was carried out without planning permission or contrary to conditions attached to planning permission. Appeal against the notice may be made to the Secretary of State. *See also* stop notice.

enforcement of judgment The processes by which the orders of a court may be enforced. Orders for the payment of money may be enforced by a variety of methods, including a writ of *fieri facias* (in the county courts, a warrant of execution), *garnishee proceedings, *charging orders, the appointment of a *receiver, a writ of *sequestration, and (rarely) an order of committal (*see* committal in civil proceedings). In the county courts (and in the High Court in certain matrimonial proceedings only) *attachment of the debtor's earnings is also available.

Judgments for possession of land may be enforced by *writ of possession (in the county courts, a warrant of possession). Judgments for delivery of goods may be enforced by *writ of delivery (in the county court, a warrant of delivery). Judgments relating to performance of or abstention from some act (e.g. an *injunction) may be enforced by order of committal or writ of sequestration.

enfranchise *vb.* **1.** To give to a person or class of people the right to vote at elections. **2.** To give to an area or a class of people the right to be represented on an elected body.

enfranchisement of tenancy A method for acquiring the freehold or an extended lease of a leasehold house. A tenant has a statutory right of enfranchisement when he has a long lease (exceeding 21 years) at a low rent (less than two-thirds of the rateable value) of a house within certain rateable value limits and the house has been his *main residence for at least three years. The valuation of the freehold, or rent of an extended lease, is based on the value of the land without the buildings on it.

engagement to marry An agreement, verbal or in writing, to marry at a future date. Such agreements are no longer treated as enforceable legal contracts, and no action can be brought for breach of such an agreement or to recover expenses incurred as a result of the agreement. Engagement rings are deemed to be absolute gifts and cannot be recovered when an engagement is broken. There is a special statutory provision that property rights between engaged parties (for example, in respect of a house purchased with a view to marriage) are to be decided in accordance with the rules governing property rights of married couples.

engross *vb.* To prepare a fair copy of a deed or other legal document ready for execution by the parties.

enlarge *vb.* (in land law) To acquire further rights in land, thereby increasing one's interest to some greater estate or interest. For example, a *tenant in tail may enlarge his interest into a fee simple by executing a disentailing deed (*see* entailed interest). A mortgagee in possession for 12 years may, by executing a deed, enlarge his interest into a fee simple free from the mortgage.

enrolment *n.* The official registration of a document. It used to be obligatory to enrol many documents in the Enrolment Office, a department of the Chancery Division. Nearly all such obligations were abolished by the Judicature Acts 1873–75.

entailed interest An *equitable interest in land under which ownership is limited to a person and the heirs of his body (either generally or those of a specified class). Such heirs are still those who would inherit under the law of intestacy as it applied before the Administration of Estate Act 1925. Thus when land is settled on "A and the heirs of his body", the principle of primogeniture applies, and a daughter will inherit only in the absence of male heirs. Descent to females can, however, be provided for, e.g. by a settlement on "A and the female heirs of his body", and the class of potential heirs can be limited to those born of a specified spouse, e.g. by settlement on "A and the heirs of his body begotten on Mary". An entailed interest subsists so long as there are members of the specified class of heirs, but when they die out ownership of the land passes to any remainderman nominated in the settlement (*see* remainder), or to the person who created the entailed interest (the reversioner), or whoever is entitled in succession to them.

The restriction on succession to an entailed interest (which formerly prevented the beneficial owner from selling the land) can now be avoided by *barring the entail*. Under the Fines and Recoveries Act 1833 a person of full age entitled in possession may, by executing a *disentailing deed*, enlarge his entailed interest into a legal fee simple. This terminates all the future interests of his descendants and of any remainderman or reversioner. However, if his interest is not in possession (e.g. if it arises after a subsisting life interest) a disentailing deed will bar only his descendants unless the *protector of the settlement consents to the disentailment. The interest created in such circumstances (an equitable base fee) will therefore end — even if it has been sold to a third party — when his heirs die out.

Under the Law of Property Act 1925, entailed interests may now be created in property other than land.

enter *vb.* **1.** (in the law of *burglary) To make "an effective and substantial" entry as a trespasser. This does not necessarily require entry of the whole of the

defendant's body, but it is not settled whether or not entry of a small part of the body (such as fingers inserted through a window) is enough to constitute an entry. Sometimes inserting an instrument (e.g. a jemmy) may be considered an entry. **2.** (in land law) *See* entry into possession.

entering judgment A procedure in civil courts in which a judgment is formally recorded by the court after it has been given. In the Queen's Bench Division it is necessary for the party seeking to have judgment entered to draw up the judgment and present it to an officer of the court for entry together with the certificate of the associate (clerk of the court) and the *pleadings. In the county courts, the court itself draws up and enters the judgment.

entire contract *See* performance of contract.

entrapment *n.* Deliberately trapping a person into committing a crime in order to secure his conviction, as by offering to buy drugs or obscene publications. English courts do not recognize a defence of entrapment as such, since the defendant is still considered to have a free choice in his acts. However, the courts sometimes exclude evidence obtained by unfair entrapment; if an informer has been used in such a way that his actions affect the quality of the offence this must be disclosed at the trial. Entrapment may also be used as a reason for mitigating a sentence.

entry into possession The act of going upon land to assert some right over it. For example, a lease usually gives the landlord the right to enter and take possession if the tenant fails to pay the rent or commits a breach of covenant. A mortgagee has the right to recover possession from a defaulting mortgagor who is in possession. In general, such rights of entry cannot be enforced unless the court orders the defaulter to give up possession.

entry without warrant Entry by a police officer onto private premises without the authority of a warrant. This is in general unlawful except with the occupier's consent (which is revocable), but it is permitted by statute for the purpose of arresting for certain offences (*see* arrestable offence) and in certain circumstances to search premises (*see* power of search); it is also allowed at common law to stop an actual or apprehended breach of the peace.

epitome of title *See* abstract of title.

equality clause A clause in a contract of employment for a woman stipulating that if she is employed on similar work to a man in the same employment, or on work rated as equivalent to his, the terms of her contract must place her in no less favourable a position than the man. A contract not containing such a clause (either directly or as a result of some collective agreement) is deemed to include one by virtue of the Equal Pay Act 1970 as amended by the Sex Discrimination Act 1975. However, the clause does not affect certain statutory requirements concerning the employment of women (e.g. under the Factories Act 1961), their *maternity rights, or provisions relating to their death or retirement. *See also* equal pay; sex discrimination.

equality is equity [from Latin: *aequitas est quasi aequalitas*] A *maxim of equity stating that if there are no reasons for any other basis of division of property, those entitled to it shall share it equally.

Equal Opportunities Commission A body established by the Sex Discrimination Act 1975 to work towards the elimination of discrimination, to promote equality of opportunity between the sexes, and to keep the working of the Act, and of the Equal Pay Act 1970, under review. It consists of 8–15 Commissioners. *See* sex discrimination.

equal pay The requirement of the Equal Pay Act 1970 that men and women in the same employment must be paid at the same rate for like work or work rated as equivalent. They are in the same employment if they work at the same establishment (or if one works at an establishment that includes the other's) and they work for the same or an associated *employer. The establishments must also be those at which the terms and conditions of employment are observed generally or for employees of the relevant description. "Like work" is work that is broadly similar, where any differences between the man's work and the woman's are not of practical importance. Work is rated as equivalent when the employer has undertaken a study to evaluate his employees' jobs in terms of the skill, effort, and responsibility demanded of them and the woman's job is given the same grade as the man's. Thus when the employer's job-grading system recognizes that the woman's job is as demanding as the man's, they are entitled to equal pay even though the nature of the work they do is very different. *See also* equality clause.

equitable *adj.* **1.** Recognized by or in accordance with the rules of equity: applied to distinguish certain concepts used in both common or statute law and in equity. For example, assignments and mortgages can be either legal or equitable. **2.** Describing a right or concept recognized by the Court of Chancery. **3.** Just, fair, and reasonable. For example, a document may have two meanings, one strict and the other (the equitable construction) more benevolent.

equitable assignment *See* assignment.

equitable charge 1. *See* equitable mortgage. **2.** A *charge created by designating specific property for the discharge of some debt or other obligation. No special form of words is necessary to create an equitable charge, manifested intention being sufficient. *See* general equitable charge.

equitable easement *See* easement.

equitable estate A right in property recognized by the Court of Chancery, as distinct from a *legal estate recognized in common law courts (*see* estate). Equitable estates reflected legal interests but could be more flexible (*compare* shifting use; springing use). Before 1926, most types of estate could exist either at law or in equity; since 1925 only a limited number of legal estates can exist; all other interests in land are called *equitable interests. The term equitable estate is now technically incorrect.

equitable estoppel *See* estoppel.

equitable execution Means of enforcing the judgment of a court when the judgment creditor cannot obtain satisfaction from the normal methods of *execution. For example, the creditor may appoint a receiver to manage the defendant's property or he may obtain an injunction to prevent the defendant from dealing with the property. These remedies are often regarded as relief granted by the court, rather than as execution.

equitable interests Interests in property originally recognized by the Court of Chancery, as distinct from legal interests recognized in the common-law courts. They arose in cases when it was against the principles of *equity for a person to enforce a legal right. Originally equitable rights (e.g. a trust or the equity of redemption under a mortgage) were enforceable against the person with a legal right over property in question. Later, however, those who were given the property by the holder of the legal interests took it subject to equitable interests; later still, anyone who bought property knowing of the equitable interests was bound by them. In the developed law, everyone took property subject to equitable interests

except those who bought it and neither knew nor ought to have known of the equitable interests. Since 1925, equitable interests may be protected either by the doctrine of *overreaching or under the system of *land charges.

equitable lease An agreement for the grant of an interest in land on terms that correspond to a *legal lease but do not comply with the necessary formal requirements of a legal lease. For example, if L purports to grant T a lease for seven years but the transaction is effected by simple written contract rather than by deed, the court will enforce the contract between the parties. Further, T's rights under the contract could be registered as an *estate contract and thus bind any third party acquiring L's interest in the land.

equitable lien *See* lien.

equitable mortgage (equitable charge) A *mortgage under which the mortgagee does not obtain a *legal estate. Mortgages are equitable when the subject matter of the mortgage is an interest under a trust and when there is a written agreement to make a mortgage or an informal mortgage by deposit of deeds or documents.

equitable presumptions *Presumptions assumed by equity in certain cases. The main examples are the presumption of *resulting trust, the presumption of *advancement, and the presumption of equality (*see* equality is equity).

equitable remedies Means granted by *equity to redress a wrong. Since the range of legal remedies was originally very limited, equity showed great flexibility in granting remedies, which were discretionary: the conduct of the parties, particularly that of the plaintiff, was taken into account (*see* clean hands). The main equitable remedies are now *specific performance, *rescission, *cancellation, *rectification, *account, *injunction, and the appointment of a *receiver. These remedies may be sought in any division of the High Court or, in some instances, in the county courts; they are still discretionary in nature, although the discretion is often exercised on established lines.

equitable rights Rights recognized by *equity. *See* equitable interests; equitable remedies.

equitable waste Alterations made by a tenant that cause serious damage to the leased property. *See* waste.

equity *n.* **1.** That part of English law originally administered by the *Lord Chancellor and later by the *Court of Chancery, as distinct from that administered by the courts of *common law. The common law did not recognize certain concepts (e.g. uses and trusts) and its remedies were limited in scope and flexibility, since it relied primarily on the remedy of damages. In the Middle Ages litigants were entitled to petition the king, who relied on the advice of his Chancellor, commonly an ecclesiastic ("the keeper of the king's conscience"), to do justice in each case. By the 15th century, petitions were referred directly to the Chancellor, who dealt with cases on a flexible basis: he was more concerned with the fair result than with rigid principles of law (hence the jurist John Selden's jibe that "equity varied with the length of the Chancellor's foot"). Moreover, if a defendant refused to comply with the Chancellor's order, he would be imprisoned for contempt of the order until he chose to comply (*see in personam*). In the 17th century conflict arose between the common-law judges and the Chancellor as to who should prevail; James I resolved the dispute in favour of the Chancellor. General principles began to emerge, and by the early 19th century the Court of Chancery was more organized and its jurisdiction, once flexible, had ossified into a body of precedent with fixed principles. The Court of Chancery had varying types of jurisdiction (*see* auxil-

iary jurisdiction; concurrent jurisdiction; exclusive jurisdiction) and many of its general principles were stated in the form of *maxims of equity; equity had (and still has) certain doctrines (*see* election; conversion; reconversion; performance of contract; satisfaction). Under the Judicature Acts 1873–75, with the establishment of the High Court of Justice to administer both common law and equity, the Court of Chancery was abolished (though much of its work is still carried out by the *Chancery Division). The Judicature Acts also provided that in cases in which there was a conflict between the rules of law and equity, the rules of equity should prevail. The main areas of equitable jurisdiction now include *trusts, *equitable interests over property, relief against *forfeiture and penalties, and *equitable remedies. Equity is thus a regulated scheme of legal principles, but new developments are still possible ("equity is not past the age of child-bearing"): recent examples of its creativity include the *Mareva injunction and the *Anton Piller order.
2. An equitable right or claim, especially an *equitable interest, or *equity of redemption, or *mere equity.
3. A share in a limited company.

equity of redemption The rights of a mortgagor over his mortgaged property, particularly the right to redeem the property. This right of redemption allows a mortgagor to redeem the mortgaged property at any time on payment of principal, interest, and costs, even after the contractual date of redemption, as stated in the mortgage deed, has passed. Any *clogs on the equity of redemption are void, but the mortgagor's rights may be terminated under certain circumstances (*see* mortgage).

Before 1926 a mortgage was commonly effected by the transfer of the mortgagor's interest in the property to the mortgagee, but the mortgagor's rights as described above were recognized by equity. Since 1925 the mortgagor retains legal ownership of the property in all cases: the term equity of redemption is still used, however, although the right to redeem is no longer strictly an equitable interest.

error *n.* A mistake of law in a judgment or order of a court or in some procedural step in legal proceedings. A *writ of error* was formerly used to instruct an inferior court to send records of its proceedings for review by a superior court. It was abolished in civil cases by the Judicature Acts 1873–75 and in criminal cases by the Criminal Appeal Act 1907 and replaced by the modern system of *appeal.

error of law on the face of the record A mistake of law that is made by an inferior court or tribunal in reaching a decision and is apparent from the record of its proceedings. The decision can be quashed by the High Court by the remedy of *certiorari* except in the case of a *domestic tribunal with purely contractual powers. *See also ultra vires.*

escape *n.* The common-law offence of escaping from lawful custody. The custody may be in prison or a police station, or even in the open air. The escaper need not have been charged with any offence, provided his detention is lawful (e.g. he may be detained to provide a *specimen of breath). Nor is it necessary for him to commit any act of breaking out. It is also an offence to help the escape of a prisoner and to permit a prisoner who is detained in relation to a criminal matter to escape. If someone actually breaks out of a building in which he is lawfully confined he commits a separate offence of *prison breaking.*

escrow *n.* *See* deed.

espionage *n.* *See* spying.

essence of a contract *See* condition.

estate *n.* **1.** (in land law) The character and duration of a person's ownership of land. For example, an estate in fee sim-

ple confers effectively absolute ownership; an estate for a term of years (called *leasehold*) or for life are lesser estates. Under the Law of Property Act 1925 only a *fee simple absolute in possession (called *freehold*) and a *term of years absolute can exist as legal estates in land. All other forms of ownership, e.g. an estate for life or an estate in fee simple coming into effect only on someone's death, are equitable only. **2.** (in revenue law) The aggregate of all the property to which a person is beneficially entitled. *Excluded property*, which includes most reversionary interests and certain foreign matters, is not taken into account for the death charge (*see* capital transfer tax).

estate contract A contract in which the owner of land agrees to create or convey a legal estate in the land; for example, he may contract to grant a lease or to sell or he may grant a valid option to purchase. The contract confers on the purchaser an equitable interest that is enforceable against third parties if registered. *See* registration of encumbrances.

estate duty An obsolete tax formerly levied on the value of property passing on death. It has been replaced by *capital transfer tax.

estate for years Ownership of land subsisting by reference to a period of time. *See* term of years.

estate owner The owner of a *legal estate in land.

estate *pur* (or *per*) *autre vie [from Norman French: *autre vie*, other life] An interest in property for the lifetime of someone else. If A is given property for B's life, A is the tenant *pur autre vie* and will hold the property during the lifetime of B (the *cestui que vie*). If A dies before B, the persons entitled under A's will or on his intestacy will take the interest for the remainder of B's life; if B dies before A, A's interest thereupon terminates. The interest is a kind of *life interest and an estate of freehold, i.e. it could be inherited; since 1925 it has been an *equitable interest only.

estate rentcharge *See* rentcharge.

estate subsisting at law *See* legal estate.

estoppel [from Norman French *estouper*, to stop up] *n.* A rule of evidence or a rule of law that prevents a person from denying the truth of a statement he has made or from denying facts that he has alleged to exist. The denial must have been acted upon (probably to his disadvantage) by the person who wishes to take advantage of the estoppel or his position must have been altered as a result. There are several varieties of estoppel. *Estoppel by conduct* (or *in pais*) arises when the party estopped has made a statement or has led the other party to believe in a certain fact. *Estoppel by deed* prevents a person who has executed a deed from saying that the facts stated in the deed are not true. *Estoppel by record* (or *per rem judicatam*) prevents a person from reopening questions that are *res judicata* (i.e. that have been determined against him in a previous legal proceeding). *See also* issue estoppel.

There are two forms of *equitable estoppel* – promissory and proprietary. The doctrine of *promissory estoppel* applies when one party to a contract promises the other (by words or conduct) that he will not enforce his rights under the contract in whole or in part. Provided that the other party has acted in reliance on that promise, it will, though unsupported by consideration, bind the person making it: he will not be allowed subsequently to sue on the contract. When applicable, the doctrine thus modifies the common-law rules relating to *accord and satisfaction. Under the doctrine of *proprietary estoppel*, the court will not permit a landowner to deny that another has acquired rights in his land when the owner has acquiesced and the other has

incurred expenditure. For example, if A, with B's consent, builds himself a house on B's land, B and his successors in title will not be allowed to dispossess A.

estovers *pl. n.* The right to cut timber for certain purposes from land not in one's own absolute ownership. The right arises in favour of a lessee or *tenant for life under a settlement of the land and it can exist as a *profit *à prendre*. Estovers comprise the right to take timber as: (1) *house bote*, for repairing a dwelling or for use as firewood in it; (2) *plough bote*, for repairing farm implements; and (3) *hay bote*, for repairing fences. In each case the lessee or tenant may take only sufficient timber for present needs.

estreat [from Old French *estrait*, an extract from a record] *vb.* To forfeit a *recognizance, especially one given by the surety of someone admitted to bail.

European Communities The European Economic Community (*see* EEC), established in 1957; the European Atomic Energy Community (Euratom), also established in that year; and the European Coal and Steel Community, established in 1951. The UK joined the Communities in 1972.

European company A proposed type of company to be incorporated under European *Community law rather than under the national law of a member state. European companies would be recognized by all member states and would facilitate mergers between two or more limited companies each incorporated under the national law of a member state.

European Convention on Human Rights A convention, originally formulated in 1950, aimed at protecting the *human rights of all people in the member states of the Council of Europe. Part 1 of the Convention, together with a number of subsequent protocols, define the freedoms that each member state must guarantee to all within its jurisdiction. The Convention established a *Commission on Human Rights* and a *Court of Human Rights* in Strasbourg. The Commission may hear complaints (known as *petitions*) by one state against another. It may also hear complaints by an individual, group, or nongovernmental organization claiming to be a victim of a breach of the Convention, provided that the state against which the complaint has been made declares that it recognizes the authority of the Commission to receive such petitions. The Commission cannot deal with any complaint, however, unless the applicant has first tried all possible remedies in the national courts (in England he must usually first appeal to the House of Lords). All complaints must be made not later than six months from the date on which the final decision against the applicant was made in the national courts. The Commission will only investigate a complaint if it is judged to fulfil various conditions that make it admissible. If the Commission thinks there has been a breach of the Convention, it places itself at the disposal of the parties in an attempt to achieve a friendly settlement. If this fails, the Commission sends a report on the case to the Committee of Ministers of the Council of Europe. The case may then be brought before the Court within three months by either the Commission or one of the states concerned (an individual victim cannot take the matter to the Court himself). No case can be brought before the Court, however, unless the state against which the complaint is made has accepted the Court's jurisdiction. The Court then has power to make a final ruling, which is binding on the parties, and in some cases to award compensation. If the matter is not taken to the Court, a decision is made instead by the Committee of Ministers.

The Convention has established a considerable body of jurisprudence. Although it is not directly binding in British courts, the British authorities invariably respect the decision of the Court made in cases of alleged breach of human rights.

European Council A body consisting of the heads of government of the member states of the European Communities. It is not a formal organ of the Communities (*compare* Council of Ministers), but meets occasionally to consider major developments of policy. It inspired, for example, the European Monetary System.

European Court *See* Court of Justice of the European Communities.

European Court of Human Rights *See* European Convention on Human Rights.

European Economic Community *See* EEC.

European Parliament *See* Assembly of the European Communities.

eviction *n.* The removal of a tenant or any other *residential occupier from occupation. Under the Protection from Eviction Act 1977 the eviction of a residential occupier, other than by proceedings in the court, is a criminal offence. It is also an offence to harass a residential occupier to try to persuade him to leave (*see* harassment of occupier). Many tenants have statutory protection and the landlord must prove to a court that he has appropriate grounds for possession. *See* agricultural holding; assured tenancy; business tenancy; long tenancy; protected shorthold tenancy; protected tenancy; secure tenancy; restricted contract.

evidence *n.* That which tends to prove the existence or nonexistence of some fact. It may consist of *testimony, *documentary evidence, *real evidence, and, when admissible, *hearsay evidence. The law of evidence comprises all the rules governing the presentation of facts and proof in proceedings before a court, including in particular the rules governing the *admissibility of evidence and the *exclusionary rules. *See also* circumstantial evidence; conclusive evidence; direct evidence; extrinsic evidence; primary evidence; secondary evidence.

evidenced in writing *See* unenforceable contract.

evidence in rebuttal Evidence offered to counteract (*rebut*) other evidence in a case. There are some restrictions on the admissibility of evidence in rebuttal, for example if it relates to a collateral question, such as the *credit of a witness.

evidence obtained illegally Evidence obtained by some means contrary to law. If *real evidence is obtained illegally (e.g. as a result of a search of premises without a search warrant) it is not inadmissible but the court may exclude it as a matter of discretion. An illegally obtained *confession is likely to be involuntary and is therefore inadmissible.

evidence of character *See* character.

evidence of disposition *See* disposition.

evidence of identity That which tends to prove the identity of a person. A person's identity may be proved by *direct evidence (even though it may involve an expression of *opinion) or by *circumstantial evidence. *Secondary evidence of an out-of-court identification by a witness (e.g. that he picked the accused out of an identification parade) may also be given to confirm the witness's testimony. In criminal cases, if the evidence of identity is wholly or mainly based on visual identification the jury must be specially warned of the danger of accepting the evidence; any *corroboration must be pointed out to them by the judge.

evidence of opinion *See* opinion evidence.

evidence of user Evidence of the manner in which the parties to a contract have acted. In a limited number of circumstances, evidence of user is admissible to assist the court in resolving a dispute between the parties as to their precise obligations. It may, for example, help to clarify an ambiguity in the wording of the contract or an allegation that written terms have been varied by oral agreement.

ex aequo et bono [Latin] As a result of fair dealing and good conscience, i.e. on the basis of *equity.

examination *n.* The questioning of a witness on oath or affirmation. In court, a witness is subject to *examination-in-chief, *cross-examination, and *re-examination. In some circumstances a witness may be examined prior to the court hearing (*see* commission).

examination-in-chief (direct examination) The questioning of a witness by the party who called him to give evidence. *Leading questions may not be asked, except on matters that are introductory to the witness's evidence or are not in dispute or (with leave of the judge) when the witness is *hostile. The purpose of examination-in-chief is to elicit facts favourable to the case of the party conducting the examination. It is followed by a *cross-examination by the opposing party.

examining justices Justices of the peace sitting upon a preliminary inquiry into whether or not there is sufficient evidence to commit an accused person from the magistrates' court to the Crown Court for trial on indictment.

excepted perils Risks expressly excluded from the cover given by an insurance policy.

exception *n.* Formerly, a formal objection to the sufficiency of an *affidavit or *answer to interrogatories in the Court of Chancery. The filing of exceptions no longer exists.

exceptional hardship or depravity Unusually difficult circumstances suffered by a spouse or unusually bad conduct by a spouse. A divorce petition may not normally be presented within three years after the celebration of a marriage unless the petitioner alleges circumstances of exceptional hardship or depravity. (In Scotland, however, there is no such bar.) The court hearing such a petition has wide discretion (used only rarely) to admit the case; if it does, it is then dealt with by a divorce court in the ordinary manner.

exchange of contracts The point at which a purchaser of land exchanges a copy of the sale contract signed by him for an identical copy signed by the vendor. At that point the contract becomes legally binding on both parties.

exchange of medical reports The exchange of medical reports in personal injury actions in the hope that they can be agreed before the hearing of the case, thus saving time and expense. Since 1980, the exchange of reports that are intended to be relied on at the hearing is compulsory, unless the court's permission not to disclose is obtained.

Exchequer *n.* *See* Chancellor of the Exchequer; Court of Exchequer.

excise duty A charge or toll payable on certain goods produced and consumed within the UK. Payments for licences, e.g. for the sale of spirits or dog licences, are also classed as excise duty. *Compare* customs duty.

exclusion and restriction of contractual liability *See* exemption clause.

exclusion and restriction of negligence liability The Unfair Contract Terms Act 1977 provides that a person cannot exclude or restrict his *business liability for death or injury resulting from negligence. Nor can he exclude or restrict his liability for other loss or damage arising from negligence, unless any contract term or notice by which he seeks to do so satisfies the requirement of reasonableness (as defined in detail in the Act). For the purposes of this provision, negligence means the breach of any contractual or common-law duty to take reasonable care or exercise reasonable skill or of the *common duty of care imposed by the Occupiers' Liability Act 1957.

exclusionary rules Rules in the law of evidence prohibiting the proof of certain facts or the proof of facts in particular ways. Although all irrelevant evidence must be excluded, the rules are usually restricted to relevant evidence, e.g. the rule against *hearsay. Exclusionary rules may be justified in various ways; for example, by the desirability of excluding material that is of little evidentiary weight or may be unfairly prejudicial to an accused person.

exclusion order 1. An order of the Secretary of State under the Prevention of Terrorism (Temporary Provisions) Act 1976 excluding a named person from Great Britain, Northern Ireland, or the UK in order to prevent terrorist acts aimed at influencing policy or opinion concerning Northern Ireland. **2.** *See* battered wife.

exclusive jurisdiction That part of the jurisdiction of the *Court of Chancery that belonged to the Chancery alone. The jurisdiction ceased after the Judicature Acts 1873–75, but the matters under exclusive jurisdiction (e.g. trusts, administration of estates) are now dealt with in the Chancery Division. *Compare* concurrent jurisdiction.

excusable homicide The killing of a human being that results in no criminal liability, either because it took place in lawful *self-defence or by misadventure (an accident not involving gross negligence).

ex debito justitiae [Latin] As a matter of right. The phrase is applied to remedies that the court is bound to give when they are claimed, as distinct from those that it has discretion to grant.

executed *adj.* Completed. A contract that has been carried out by both parties is said to have been executed, and *consideration that has been actually given for a contract is described as *executed consideration*. *See also* executed trust. *Compare* executory.

executed trust (completely constituted trust, perfect trust) A trust that is complete and enforceable by the beneficiaries without further acts by the settlor. *Compare* executory trust.

execution *n.* **1.** The process of carrying out a sentence of death imposed by a court. *See also* capital punishment. **2.** The enforcement of the rights of a judgment creditor (*see also* enforcement of judgment). The term is often used to mean the recovery of a debt only, especially by seizure of goods belonging to the debtor under a writ of **fieri facias* or a warrant of execution. In the case of property not subject to ordinary forms of execution, e.g. an interest under a trust, judgment is enforced by means of *equitable execution. **3.** The signing of a *deed or any other document (such as a will) that only becomes valid after it has been signed. *See also* execution of will.

execution of will The process by which a testator's will is made legally valid. Under the Wills Act 1837 the will must be signed at the end by the testator or by someone authorized by him, and the signature must be made (*see* acknowledgment) by the testator in the presence of at least two witnesses, present at the same time, who must themselves sign the will in the testator's presence. A will witnessed by a beneficiary is not void, but the gift to that beneficiary is void.

executor *n.* A person appointed by a will to administer the testator's estate. A deceased person's property is vested

in his executors, who are empowered to deal with it as directed by the will from the time of the testator's death. They must, however, usually obtain a grant of *probate from the court in order to prove the will and their right to deal with the estate. Appointment as an executor confers only the power to deal with the deceased's property in accordance with his will, and not beneficial ownership, although an executor may also be a beneficiary under the will. *Compare* administrator.

executor *de son tort* [French: by his own wrongdoing] A person who, although he has no right to a deceased person's estate, deals with the deceased's property to the detriment of the beneficiaries or creditors of the estate. He may be sued by any beneficiary or creditor who has suffered loss or by the deceased's personal representatives.

executor's year The period of a year, starting from the death of the deceased, within which his personal representatives should complete the administration of his estate. Under the Administration of Estates Act 1925, personal representatives are not generally bound to distribute the estate within that period.

executory *adj.* Remaining to be done. A contract that has yet to be carried out is said to be an *executory contract*, and *consideration that has still to be given for a contract is described as *executory consideration*. *See also* executory interest; executory trust. *Compare* executed.

executory interest An interest in property that arises or passes to a particular person on the occurrence of a specified event. For example, when property is settled in trust "for A, but for B if he marries Mary", then B has an executory interest. Under the Law of Property Act 1925 executory interests in land can only exist as equitable interests. *Compare* remainder; reversion.

executory trust (imperfect trust, incompletely constituted trust) A trust that is incomplete, i.e. one that the beneficiaries are unable to enforce until some further act is done by the settlor or a third party. *Compare* executed trust.

exemplary damages (punitive damages, vindictive damages) Damages given to punish the defendant rather than (or as well as) to compensate the plaintiff for harm done. Such damages are exceptional in tort, since the general rule is that damages are given only to compensate for loss caused. They can be awarded in three cases: (1) when expressly authorized by statute; (2) to punish oppressive, arbitrary, or unconstitutional acts by government servants; (3) when the defendant has deliberately calculated that the profits to be made out of committing a tort (e.g. by publishing a defamatory book) may exceed the damages at risk. In such cases, exemplary damages are given to prove that "tort does not pay". Exemplary damages cannot be given for breach of contract.

exemption clause A term in a contract purporting to exclude or restrict the liability of one of the parties in specified circumstances. The courts do not regard exemption clauses with favour. If such a clause is ambiguous, they will interpret it narrowly rather than widely. If an exclusion or restriction is not recited in a formal contract but is specified or referred to in an informal document, such as a ticket or a notice displayed in a hotel, it will not even be treated as a term of the contract (unless reasonable steps were taken to bring it to the notice of the person affected at the time of contracting). The Unfair Contract Terms Act 1977 contains complex provisions limiting the extent to which a person can exclude or restrict his *business liability towards consumers. *See also* exclusion and restriction of negligence liability; international supply contract.

exempt supply A supply that is outside the scope of *value-added tax. Examples include sales of land, the supply of certain financial and insurance services, and the services performed in the course of employment. *See also* zero-rated supply.

ex gratia [Latin] Done as a matter of favour. An *ex gratia* payment is one not required to be made by a legal duty.

exhibit 1. *n.* A physical object or document produced in a court, shown to a witness who is giving evidence, or referred to in an *affidavit. Exhibits are marked with an identifying number, and in jury trials the jury is normally permitted to take exhibits with them when they retire to consider their verdict. **2.** *vb.* To refer to an object or document in an *affidavit.

ex nudo pacto non oritur actio See consideration.

ex officio [Latin] By virtue of holding an office. Thus, the Lord Chief Justice is *ex officio* a member of the Court of Appeal.

ex officio **information** A criminal information laid by the Attorney General on behalf of the Crown. It was abolished in 1967. *See* laying an information.

ex officio **magistrate** A magistrate by virtue of holding some other office, usually that of mayor of a city or borough. Most *ex officio* magistrateships were abolished by the Justices of the Peace Act 1968 and the Administration of Justice Act 1973, but High Court judges are justices of the peace *ex officio* for the whole of England and Wales and the Lord Mayor and aldermen are justices *ex officio* for the City of London.

ex parte [Latin] **1.** On the part of one side only. For example, an *ex parte* injunction is one granted after hearing only the party making the application. *See also ex parte* inspection order. **2.** On behalf of. This term is used in the headings of law reports together with the name of the person making the application to the court in the case in question.

ex parte **inspection order** A court order that allows documents to be inspected without warning being given to the holder of the documents. Such an order is granted when the applicant shows that the holder of the documents may otherwise prevent their disclosure, by destruction or other means.

expatriation *n.* A person's voluntary action of living outside his native country, either permanently or during his employment abroad. *Compare* deportation.

expectant heir A person who has an interest in remainder or in reversion in property or a chance of succeeding to it. An unconscionable contract with an expectant heir (e.g. in which he sells his inheritance at an undervalue in order to raise cash) may be set aside by the court.

expert opinion *See* opinion evidence.

Expiring Laws Continuance Acts Statutes formerly passed annually to continue in force for a further year a number of miscellaneous Acts that were originally stated to remain in force for one year only. The renewal of temporary statutes is now effected individually.

explosive *n.* Any substance made in order to achieve an explosion that causes damage or destruction or is intended to be used in that way by a person who possesses it. If someone committing *burglary has an explosive with him, he is guilty of aggravated burglary, punishable with a maximum of life imprisonment. The Explosive Substances Act 1883 creates special offences of (1) causing an explosion that is likely to endanger life or cause serious damage

to property (even if no harm or damage is actually done); (2) attempting to cause such an explosion; and (3) making or possessing an explosive with the intention of using it to endanger life or to seriously damage property. Under the Offences Against the Person Act 1861, it is an offence to injure anyone by means of an explosion, to send or deliver an explosive to anyone, or to place an explosive near a building, ship, or boat with the intention of causing physical injury. These crimes cover most acts of *terrorism.

ex post facto [Latin: by a subsequent act] Describing any legal act, such as a statute, that has retrospective effect.

expressio unius est exclusio alterius See interpretation of statutes.

express term A provision of a contract agreed to by the parties in words, written or spoken. It may constitute either a *condition of the contract or a warranty. *Compare* implied term.

express trust A trust created expressly by the settlor. There is no need for formal words provided that the intention to create a trust is clear from the documents or from the oral statements of the settlor. *Compare* implied trust.

expropriation *n.* The taking by the state of private property for public purposes, normally without compensation (*compare* compulsory purchase, which carries with it a right to compensation). The right to expropriate is known in some legal systems as the right of *eminent domain*. In the UK, expropriation requires statutory authority except in time of war or apprehended war (*see* royal prerogative).

ex proprio motu (*ex mero motu*) [Latin: of his own motion] Describing acts that a court may perform on its own initiative and without any application by the parties.

extended sentence A sentence longer than the maximum prescribed for a particular offence. It is imposed on persistent offenders when: (1) the defendant has been convicted at least three times since the age of 21 of offences punishable by at least two years' imprisonment; (2) the present offence was committed within three years of the previous conviction or within three years from the end of a prison sentence for the previous conviction; and (3) the total length of sentences imposed for the three convictions is at least five years. In addition to these three conditions, the defendant must either have been (1) sentenced on at least one of the three previous occasions to *preventive detention, or (2) sentenced on at least two of the previous occasions to prison or corrective training, when at least one of the sentences was for three years' imprisonment or more, or two were sentences of at least two years' imprisonment.

extinguishment n. The cessation or cancellation of some right or interest. For example, an *easement is extinguished if the dominant and servient tenements come into the same ownership.

extortion n. A common-law offence committed by a public officer who uses his position to take money or any other benefit that is not due to him. If he obtains the benefit by means of threats, this may also amount to blackmail.

extradition n. The surrender by one state to another of a person accused of committing an offence in the latter. Extradition from the UK relates to surrender to foreign states (*compare* fugitive offender) and is governed by the Extradition Act 1870. There must be an extradition treaty between the UK and the state requiring the surrender. The offence alleged must be a crime in the UK as well as in the requesting state, it must be both covered by the treaty and within the list of extraditable offences contained in the Act itself, and it must not be of a political character.

extrajudicial divorce A divorce granted outside a court of law by a nonjudicial process (such as a *ghet or a *talaq). An extrajudicial divorce will not be recognized in the UK if it takes place in the UK, Channel Islands, or Isle of Man. An extrajudicial divorce that takes place abroad when both parties have been habitually resident in the UK for at least the preceding year will not be recognized in the UK unless it is effective under the law of the country in which it took place and either spouse was a national of that country. If one or both parties were not habitually resident for the preceding year in the UK, an extrajudicial divorce that is effective under the law of the country in which it took place will be recognized in the UK if either spouse was habitually resident or domiciled in that country.

extraordinary general meeting Any meeting of company members other than the *annual general meeting (*see also* general meeting). Except when the meeting is for the passing of a *special resolution, 14 days' written notice must be given (7 days suffices in the case of an unlimited company). Only *special business can be transacted. Such a meeting can be convened by the directors at their discretion or by company members who either hold not less than 10% of the paid-up voting shares (*see* call) or, in companies without a share capital (*see* limited company; unlimited company), represent not less than 10% of the voting rights.

extraordinary resolution A decision reached by a majority of not less than 75% of company members voting in person or by proxy at a general meeting. At least 14 days' notice must be given of the intention to propose an extraordinary resolution; if the resolution is to be proposed at the annual general meeting, 21 days' notice is required.

extraterritoriality n. A theory in international law explaining *diplomatic immunity on the basis that the premises of a foreign mission form a part of the territory of the sending state. This theory is not accepted in English law (thus a divorce granted in a foreign embassy in England is not obtained outside the British Isles for purposes of the Recognition of Divorces Act 1971). Diplomatic immunity is based either on the theory that the diplomatic mission personifies – and is entitled to the immunities of – the sending state or on the practical necessity of such immunity for the functioning of diplomacy.

extrinsic evidence Evidence of matters not referred to in a document offered in evidence to explain, vary, or contradict its meaning. Its admissibility is governed by the *parol evidence rule.

ex turpi causa non oritur actio *See* illegal contract.

F

fact *n.* An event or state of affairs known to have happened or existed. It may be distinguished from law (as in *trier of fact) or, in the law of evidence, from opinion (*see* opinion evidence). The *facts in issue* are the main facts that a party carrying the persuasive *burden of proof must establish in order to succeed; in a wider sense they may include subordinate or collateral facts, such as those affecting the *credit of a witness or the *admissibility of evidence. A distinction is sometimes drawn between *factum probans* (evidentiary fact), a fact offered as proof of another fact; and *factum probandum* (the fact to be proved), of which the *factum probans* is evidence.

factor *n.* An agent entrusted with the possession of goods (or documents of title representing goods) for the purposes of sale. A factor is likely to fall within the definition of a *mercantile

agent in the Factors Act 1889 and to have the powers of a mercantile agent. A factor has a *lien over the goods entrusted to him that covers any claims against the principal arising out of the agency.

factum [Latin] *n.* **1.** A *fact or statement of facts. **2.** An act or deed.

failure to maintain The failure of either spouse to provide reasonable maintenance for the other or to make a proper contribution towards the maintenance of any children of the family during the subsistence of the marriage. Upon proof of such failure, magistrates' courts have jurisdiction to make orders for unsecured periodical payments and for lump-sum orders not exceeding £500. The divorce county courts and High Court have power to make orders for periodical payment (which may also be secured by a charge on the property of the respondent spouse) and for lump-sum orders (of any sum). It is no longer necessary to prove *wilful neglect to maintain* (i.e. deliberate withholding of maintenance).

failure to make discovery Failure of a party to make discovery of documents or to produce them for inspection (*see* discovery and inspection of documents). The court may make any order that it thinks just, which may be an order that the action be dismissed, or (as appropriate) the defence struck out, and that judgment be entered accordingly.

fair comment The defence to an action for *defamation that the statement made was fair comment on a matter of public interest. The facts on which the comment is based must be true and the comment must be fair. Any honest expression of opinion, however exaggerated, can be fair comment, but remarks inspired by personal spite and mere abuse are not. The judge decides whether or not the matter is one of public interest. *See also* rolled-up plea.

fair dismissal *Dismissal of an employee when the employer shows that he acted reasonably in dismissing on the grounds of the employee's capability, qualifications, or conduct; redundancy; the fact that it would be illegal to continue employing the employee; or some other sufficient and substantial reason. *Compare* unfair dismissal.

fair rent Rent fixed by a rent officer or rent assessment committee for the holder of a *protected or *statutory tenancy. The rent is registered in relation to the property. When fixing the rent, no account is taken of the scarcity of rented property and therefore the rent is often lower than a market rent.

fair trading *See* Director General of Fair Trading.

fair wear and tear A phrase often found in repairing covenants in leases. When a tenant is not obliged to repair fair (reasonable) wear and tear occurring during his tenancy, he must nevertheless do any repairs to prevent consequential damage resulting from the original wear and tear. For example, if a slate blows off a roof the tenant is not liable to repair it, but he ought to prevent the rain entering through the hole and doing more damage.

false accounting An offence, punishable by up to seven years' imprisonment, committed by someone who dishonestly falsifies, destroys, or hides any account or document used in accounting or who uses such a document knowing or suspecting it to be false or misleading. The offence must be committed for the purpose of gain or causing loss to another. There is also a special offence (also punishable by up to seven years' imprisonment) committed by a company director who publishes or allows to be published a written statement he knows or suspects is misleading or false in order to deceive members or creditors of the company. *See also* forgery.

false imprisonment Unlawful restriction of a person's freedom of movement, not necessarily in a prison. Any complete deprivation of freedom of movement is sufficient, so false imprisonment includes unlawful arrest and unlawfully preventing a person leaving a room or a shop. The restriction must be total: it is not imprisonment to prevent a person proceeding in one direction if he is free to leave in others. False imprisonment is a form of *trespass to the person, so it is not necessary to prove that it has caused actual damage. It is both a crime and a tort. Damages, which may be *aggravated or *exemplary, can be obtained in tort and the writ of *habeas corpus is available to restore the imprisoned person to liberty.

false plea (sham plea) A pleading that is obviously frivolous or absurd and is made only for the purpose of vexation or delay. A court may order a pleading that would adversely affect the fair trial of a case to be struck out or amended.

false pretence The act of misleading someone by a false representation, either by words or conduct. The former offence of obtaining property by false pretences is now known as obtaining property by *deception. It is, however, a statutory offence punishable by up to two years' imprisonment to persuade a woman by false pretences to have sexual intercourse (the offence is only committed, however, if intercourse actually takes place). It is also an offence under the Official Secrets Act 1926 to practise various false pretences in order to gain entry into a prohibited place.

false statement *See* perjury.

false trade description A description of goods made in the course of a business that is false in respect of certain facts (*see* trade description). Under the Trade Descriptions Acts 1968 and 1972 it is an offence to apply a false trade description to goods either directly, by

falsification of accounts

implication, or indirectly (e.g. by tampering with a car's mileometer or painting over rust on the bodywork). It is also an offence to supply or offer to supply goods to which a false trade description is attached. These offences are triable either summarily or on indictment (in which case they carry a maximum two years' prison sentence). They are offences of *strict liability, although certain specified defences are allowed (e.g. that the defendant relied on information supplied by someone else). The Acts are supplemented by the Fair Trading Act 1973.

falsification of accounts *See* false accounting.

family *n.* A group of people connected by a close relationship. For legal purposes a family is usually limited to relationships by blood, marriage, or adoption, although sometimes (e.g. for social security purposes) statute expressly includes other people, such as common-law wives (*see* common-law marriage). Recently the courts have interpreted the word "family" in the Rent Acts to include unmarried couples living as husband and wife in permanent and stable relationships.

family assets Property acquired by one or both parties to a marriage to be used for the benefit of the family as a whole. Typical examples are the *matrimonial home, furniture, and car. There is no special body of law dealing with family assets as such, but the courts have wide discretion to make orders in relation to such assets upon dissolution of the marriage and have developed flexible guidelines to apply in the case of family assets. Thus, the wife will often acquire a share in the home owned by the husband, by reason of her contributions to the welfare of the family and its finances. The Law Commission has recently proposed a system of *community of assets* (or *property*), under which all family assets would automati-

cally become the property of both the spouses.

Family Division The division of the *High Court concerned with divorce and other matrimonial actions, the custody and guardianship of minors, wardship proceedings, and noncontentious probate matters. Until 1971, it was known as the *Probate, Divorce and Admiralty Division. The chief judge of the Division is called the *President*.

family name *See* surname.

family provision Provision made by the courts out of the estate of a deceased person in favour of his family or *dependants. The court may award a family provision if it is satisfied that the provision made for the applicant either by the deceased person or by the law of intestacy is, in the circumstances, unreasonable.

fatal accidents Formerly, at common law, the death of either party extinguished the right to bring an action in tort. In addition, a person who caused death was not liable to compensate the deceased's relatives and others who suffered loss because of the death. Both rules have now been abolished by statute.

By the Law Reform (Miscellaneous Provisions) Act 1934, a right of action by (or against) a deceased person survives his death and can be brought for the benefit of (or against) his estate. Thus if a person is killed in a motor accident due to the negligence of the driver, an action can be brought against the driver in the name of the deceased; any damages obtained become part of the deceased's estate. Actions for defamation of a deceased person are excluded from the Act and do not survive his death. The Fatal Accidents Act 1976 confers the right to recover damages for loss of support on the dependants of a person who has been killed in an accident, if the deceased would have been able to recover damages for injury but for his death. The class of dependants who may sue includes such persons as spouses, former spouses, parents, children, brothers, and sisters. The main purpose of the action is to compensate dependants for loss of the financial support they could have expected to receive from the deceased, but a spouse, or parents (if the deceased was an unmarried minor), may also recover £3500 as damages for bereavement.

fee *n.* A legal estate (other than leasehold) in land that is capable of being inherited. Since the Law of Property Act 1925 the term's only modern significance is in the phrase *fee simple absolute in possession*. All other such estates that formerly existed in fee are now equitable interests only.

fee farm rent *See* rentcharge.

fee simple absolute in possession One of only two forms of ownership of land that, under the Law of Property Act 1925, can exist as a legal estate (*see also* term of years absolute). All others take effect as equitable interests. *Fee simple* indicates ownership that is not liable to end upon any person's death, with the expiration of time, or on the failure of a particular line of heirs. *Absolute* means that the owner's rights are not conditional or liable to terminate on the occurrence of any event (except the exercise of a right of *re-entry* – Law of Property (Amendment) Act 1926). *In possession* means that the owner's rights are immediate; thus future interests do not qualify.

fee tail A legal estate in land that was abolished by the Law of Property Act 1925. It can now exist only as an equitable *entailed interest*.

felony *n.* Formerly, an offence more serious than a *misdemeanour*. Since 1967 the term has been abolished (although it is retained in pre-1967 statutes that are still in force) and the law formerly relating to misdemeanours

now applies to felonies. *See also* arrestable offence; indictable offence; summary offence.

feme covert [Anglo-French] A married woman, under the *coverture* of her husband.

feme sole [Anglo-French] An unmarried woman. The term includes a widow or divorcée or a woman whose marriage has been annulled.

ferae naturae *See* classification of animals.

feudal system An economic and social system introduced into England as a result of the Norman Conquest (1066). At its centre was the doctrine of *tenures*. All the land in the country was regarded as being owned by William I as the result of his conquest, and thereafter only the Crown could own land. The subject could merely hold it on a tenure, either directly from the Crown or indirectly through an intermediate superior. Such lands as William did not retain in his own possession he parcelled out to his barons. Holding directly from him, they were known as *tenants-in-chief*, and the tenures on which they held were *knight service* (which involved a duty to render military service for a specified number of days in each year), *sergeanty* (the performance of personal services), or *frankalmoign* (services of a religious character). Tenants-in-chief subgranted portions of their lands to lesser men to hold by tenure from them, the lesser men did likewise, and so on. The process of subgranting was called *subinfeudation*, and a man's immediate superior was known as his *mesne lord*. The principal tenures by which land was held through subinfeudation were knight service, frankalmoign, and *socage* (the rendering of agricultural or other services of a fixed nature, including the payment of money). All these tenures were free tenures. Much land was, however, held by unfree tenure, known as *copyhold*: its tenant (a villein) was required to give any type of labour demanded of him.

The system of tenures did not continue as an active force for more than a few centuries. The services to be performed were gradually commuted to money payments (*quit rents*), tenures were virtually reduced to socage and copyhold by the Statute of Military Tenures (or Tenures Abolition Act) 1660, and copyhold was converted into socage by the Law of Property Act 1922. However, the theory that the subject cannot own the land itself remains at the roots of land law; what he can own is an *estate in land, which entitles him to enjoy the land as much as if he did own it.

fiction *n.* An assumption that something is true irrespective of whether it is really true or not. In English legal history fictions were used by the courts during the development of forms of court action. They enabled the courts to avoid cumbersome procedures, to make remedies available when they would not be otherwise, and to extend their jurisdiction. For example, the action of *trover was originally based on the defendant's finding the plaintiff's goods and taking them for himself. In time, it became unnecessary to prove the "finding": a remedy was granted on the basis only of proving that the goods were the plaintiff's and that the defendant had taken them.

fiduciary [from Latin: *fiducia*, trust] **1.** *n.* A person, such as a trustee, who holds a position of trust or confidence with respect to someone else and who is therefore obliged to act solely for that person's benefit. **2.** *adj.* In a position of trust or confidence. Fiduciary relationships include those between trustees and their beneficiaries, company promoters and directors and their shareholders, solicitors and their clients, and guardians and their wards.

fieri facias (*fi. fa.*) [Latin: you should cause to be done] A writ of execution to

enforce the payment of a debt when judgment has been entered against the debtor. The writ can also be used to enforce a judgment for payment of damages. The writ is addressed to the *sheriff requiring him to seize the property of the debtor in order to pay the debt, interest, and costs.

fieri feci [Latin: I have caused to be done] The report of the *sheriff or other appropriate officer saying how much he has recovered by levying execution under a writ of *fieri facias.

fi. fa. See fieri facias.

final judgment The *judgment in civil proceedings that ends the action, usually the judgment of the court at trial. Appeal against a final judgment may be made without leave of the court. *Compare* interlocutory judgment.

final process A *writ of execution on a judgment or decree.

Finance Bill A parliamentary Bill dealing with taxation matters, usually introduced each year to enact the Budget proposals.

financial assistance (in company law) A loan, guarantee, security, indemnity, or gift by a registered company or any of its subsidiaries made for the purpose of assisting someone to acquire its shares. Under the Companies Act 1981 private companies may make such transactions, subject to procedural and financial safeguards for creditors and company members; otherwise, financial assistance is unlawful.

financial provision order An order made by the courts when granting a decree of divorce, nullity, or judicial separation for payments by one spouse in favour of the other or in favour of the children. These payments are meant to provide for income, rather than capital (*see also* property adjustment order); they may take the form of periodical payments (which can be secured on property owned by the payer) or lump-sum orders. The court has wide discretion to make and subsequently to vary such orders as it thinks fit, with the general aim of putting the parties as far as possible in the financial position they would have been in had the marriage continued. The Matrimonial Causes Act 1973 lists seven matters that the court must take into account as part of the circumstances it is to consider, in addition to the parties' conduct (which is, however, usually of very minor relevance), and five matters to be considered when making orders in favour of children. The Law Commission has recently suggested that financial provision orders should be made primarily for the benefit of the children or until the recipient is able to support herself. *See also* clean break.

financial relief Any or all of the following: orders for *maintenance pending suit, *financial provision orders, *property adjustment orders, and orders by the High Court for maintenance during the marriage. The court has powers to set aside transactions made by a husband or wife with the intention of preventing his spouse from making a claim for financial relief, or to prevent such a transaction from taking place (*see* avoidance of disposition order).

financial year For statutes referring to finance, the period fixed by a statute of 1854 as the 12 calendar months ending on 31 March. Annual public accounts are made up for this period. For income-tax purposes, the year runs to 5 April. Companies and other bodies are free to choose their own financial years for accounting purposes. *See also* tax year.

fine *n.* **1.** A sum of money that an offender is ordered to pay on conviction. Most *summary offences are punishable by a fine with a fixed maximum, in accordance with a standard scale of five levels contained in the Criminal Justice Act 1982. The present fines are as fol-

lows: level 1 – £25; level 2 – £50; level 3 – £200; level 4 – £500; level 5 – £1000 (the Act provides for increases in the scales with changes in the value of money). Sometimes provision is made for imprisonment in cases of failure to pay the fine. A fine may also be imposed instead of, or in addition to, any other punishment for someone convicted on indictment (except in cases of murder). This fine is *at large*, i.e. the amount is at the discretion of the judge. Fines are often imposed upon companies for breach of statutory obligations; although the sums may be relatively small, companies will try to avoid being fined because of the bad publicity this may cause.

When imposing a fine on an offender under the age of 17 (*see* juvenile offender), the court is not normally empowered to order the offender to pay the fine himself unless his parent or guardian cannot be found or it would be unreasonable in the circumstances to expect his parent or guardian to pay it. In all other cases, the order must be made against the parent or guardian.

2. A lump-sum payment by a tenant to a landlord for the grant or renewal of a lease. *See also* premium.

firearm *n.* For the purposes of the Firearms Act 1968, any potentially lethal weapon with a barrel that can fire a shot, bullet, or other missile or any weapon classified as a *prohibited weapon (even if it is not lethal). The Act creates various offences in relation to firearms. The main offences include: (1) buying or possessing a firearm without a licence; (2) buying or hiring a firearm under the age of 17 or selling a firearm to someone under 17; (3) possessing a firearm under the age of 14; (4) supplying firearms to someone who is drunk or insane; (5) carrying a firearm and suitable ammunition in a public place without a reasonable excuse; (6) trespassing with a firearm; (7) possessing a firearm with the intention of endangering life; (8) using a firearm with the intention of resisting or preventing a lawful arrest; (9) having a firearm with the intention of committing an indictable offence; (10) possessing a firearm or ammunition after having previously been convicted of a crime; and (11) having a firearm in one's possession at the time of committing or being arrested for such offences as rape, burglary, and certain offences against the person. The Firearms Act 1982 extends the provisions of the 1968 Act to imitation firearms that can be easily converted to firearms.

Under the Theft Act 1968 someone who has with him a firearm or imitation firearm while committing a burglary is guilty of aggravated burglary. For the purposes of this Act, a firearm may include an airgun, air pistol, or anything that looks like a firearm. *See also* offensive weapon.

fire damage An occupier of land or buildings is not liable for a fire that begins there accidentally (Fires Prevention (Metropolis) Act 1774). Liability is imposed if the fire is caused by negligence, nuisance, or a non-natural user of the land or if the fire, having started accidentally, is negligently allowed to spread.

fiscal year *See* tax year.

fishery *n. See* piscary.

fishing interrogatory An *interrogatory that does not relate to any matter in question in the case or matter before the court. Leave to serve such interrogatories will not be granted.

fit for habitation A statutory implied covenant applied to furnished tenancies and certain tenancies at a low rent. Premises are regarded as not reasonably fit for habitation if they are defective in one or more of the following: repair, stability, freedom from damp, natural lighting, ventilation, water supply, drainage and sanitary conveniences, facilities for cooking and for storage and preparation of food, and disposal of waste water. A landlord normally has no obligation to see that premises are fit for habitation when the statutory provisions do not apply.

fitness for purpose A standard that must be met by one who sells goods in the course of a business. When the buyer makes known to the seller any particular purpose for which the goods are being bought, there is an implied condition that the goods are reasonably fit for that purpose, except when the circumstances show that the buyer does not rely on the skill or judgment of the seller.

fixed charge *See* charge.

fixed-date summons A summons in the county courts used to initiate actions in which a claim is made for any relief other than the payment of money. The *return day is the date of the *pretrial review.

fixed-sum credit Any facility (other than *running-account credit) under a *personal-credit agreement by which the debtor is entitled to receive credit, either in one amount or by instalments.

fixed term A tenancy or lease for a fixed period. The date of commencement and the length of a lease must be agreed before there can be a legally binding lease. It may take effect from the date of the grant, an earlier date, or a date up to 21 years ahead. At the end of the fixed term, the lease or tenancy comes to an end automatically: there is no need for a notice to quit. *See also* half a year; long tenancy.

fixture *n.* A chattel that has been annexed to land or a building so as to become a part of it, in accordance with the maxim *quicquid plantatur solo, solo cedit* (whatever is annexed to the soil is given to the soil). Annexation normally involves actual affixation, but a thing resting on its own weight can be regarded as annexed. Fixtures become the property of the freeholder, subject to certain rights of removal (as, for example, in the case of *trade fixtures).

flagrante delicto [Latin] In the commission of an offence. Certain types of arrest can only be made when a person is in the act of committing an offence (*see* arrestable offence; citizen's arrest). Someone who kills his or her spouse in the act of adultery may have a defence of *provocation.

floating charge *See* charge.

flotation *n.* A process by which a public company can, by an issue of securities (shares or debentures), raise capital from the public. It may involve a *prospectus issue*, in which the company itself issues a *prospectus inviting the public to acquire securities; an *offer for sale*, in which the company sells the securities on offer to an *issuing house*, which then issues a prospectus inviting the public to purchase the securities from it; or a *placing*, whereby an issuing house arranges for the securities to be taken up by its clients in the expectation that they will ultimately become available to the public on the open market. *See also* tender offer; underwriter.

f.o.b. (free on board) contract A type of contract for the international sale of goods in which the seller's duty is fulfilled by placing the goods on board a ship. There are different types of f.o.b. contract: the buyer may arrange the shipping space and the procurement of a bill of lading and nominate the ship to the seller; he may nominate a ship and leave it to the seller to place the goods on board and to procure a bill of lading; or the seller may be asked to make all the shipping arrangements for which the buyer will pay. The risk of accidental loss or damage normally passes to the buyer when the goods are loaded onto the ship. Insurance during the sea transit is the responsibility of the buyer.

following trust property *See* tracing trust property.

footpath *n.* Under the Highways Act 1959, any *highway (other than a *footway) over which the public have a right of way on foot only.

footway *n.* Under the Highways Act 1959, any way over which the public have a right of way on foot only and which is part of a highway that also comprises a way for the passage of vehicles. *Compare* footpath.

forbearance *n.* A deliberate failure to exercise a legal right (e.g. to sue for a debt). A forbearance to sue at a debtor's request may be *consideration for some fresh promise by the debtor. A promise not to enforce a claim that is bad in law may still be consideration if the claim is believed to be valid. A requested forbearance, even if it is not binding, may have more limited effects either at common law or in equity (e.g. in certain circumstances it may not be revoked without reasonable notice).

force majeure [French] Irresistible compulsion or coercion. The phrase is used particularly in commercial contracts to describe events that might affect the contract and that are completely outside the parties' control.

forcible entry A common-law offence (as amended by various statutes) that applied under certain circumstances when force was used to gain entry to premises. The common-law offence has now been replaced by a new statutory *arrestable offence of using or threatening violence against people or property in order to secure entry into premises (Criminal Law Act 1977). The offence only applies if there is someone present on the premises who is opposed to the entry and the offender knows of this. The fact that the offender is the legal owner or occupier of the premises is not in itself a defence, although there is a special defence if he can prove that he was at the relevant time a displaced *residential occupier seeking to regain entry or to pass through premises that

foreclose down

form an access to his own place of residential occupation. Thus it will be an offence for a factory owner to use force to eject workmen engaged in a sit-in or for a landlord to use force to expel a tenant at the end of a tenancy, since they are not displaced residential occupiers. It is not an offence, however, for a person unlawfully evicted from his own home to use force to re-enter, subject to the common-law rule that the force must not be excessive. It is also not an offence for the police to use force to gain entry to premises when they have a right of entry.

foreclose down *See* redeem up, foreclose down.

foreclosure *n.* A remedy available to a mortgagee when the mortgagor has failed to pay off a *mortgage by the contractual date for redemption. The mortgagee is entitled to bring an action in the High Court, seeking an order fixing a date to pay off the debt; if the mortgagor does not pay by that date he will be foreclosed, i.e. he will lose the mortgaged property. If, after this order (a foreclosure order *nisi*) is made, the mortgagor does not pay on the date and at the place (usually a room in the Royal Courts of Justice) named, the foreclosure is made *absolute* and the property thereafter belongs to the mortgagee. However, the court has discretion to allow the mortgagor to reopen the foreclosure and thereby regain his property. The remedy is unpopular: the mortgagee's *power of sale is more useful; further, if the mortgaged property is worth less than the loan, the mortgagee cannot sue for the balance.

foreign agreement An agreement or contract the proper law of which is the law of some country other than the UK. *See* proper law of a contract.

foreign bill Any bill of exchange other than an *inland bill. The distinction is relevant to the steps taken when the bill has been dishonoured (*see* dishonour).

foreign company A company incorporated outside Great Britain but having a place of business within Great Britain. Foreign companies are subject to provisions of the Companies Acts relating to registration, accounts, name, etc.

foreign enlistment The offence under the Foreign Enlistment Act 1870 of enlisting oneself or others (except with the licence of the Crown) for armed service with a foreign state that is at war with a state with which the UK is at peace. It is also an offence under the Act (again, except with licence) to build or equip any ship for such service or to fit out any naval or military expedition for use against a state with which the UK is at peace.

foreign judgments The *judgment of a foreign court may be enforced in England provided that the foreign court was competent and that the judgment is for a definite sum and is final and conclusive. At common law a foreign court is regarded as competent if (1) the judgment debtor, being a defendant in the original court, submitted to the jurisdiction of that court by voluntarily appearing in the proceedings otherwise than for the purpose of either protecting or obtaining the release of property seized (or threatened with seizure) in the proceedings or of contesting the jurisdiction of that court; (2) the judgment debtor was plaintiff in or counterclaimed in the proceedings in the original court; (3) the judgment debtor, being a defendant in the original court, had agreed before the proceedings commenced to submit to the jurisdiction of that court or of the courts of that country; or (4) the judgment debtor, being a defendant in the original court, was resident in the country of that court when the proceedings were instituted (or, in the case of a corporation, had its principal place of business in that country).

In addition to the common-law rule, foreign judgments may be registered for enforcement by the English courts under a number of statutory powers, notably those contained in the Foreign Judgments (Reciprocal Enforcement) Act 1933 and the Civil Jurisdiction and Judgments Act 1982.

foreign law For the purposes of *private international law, any legal system other than that of England. A foreign legal system may be the system of a foreign state (one recognized by public *international law) or of a law district. Thus the law of Scotland, Northern Ireland, the Channel Islands, and Isle of Man and the law of each of the American or Australian states or Canadian provinces is a separate foreign law. When an element of foreign law arises in an English court, it is usually treated as a question of fact, which must be proved (usually by expert evidence) in each case. The English courts retain an overriding power to refuse to enforce (or even to recognize) provisions of foreign law that are against English public policy, foreign penal or revenue laws, or laws creating discriminatory disabilities or status. *See also* Community law.

foresight *n.* Awareness at the time of doing an act that a certain consequence may result. In the case of some crimes an *intention by the accused to bring about a certain consequence must be proved before he can be found guilty; foresight is not enough. Conviction for many crimes, however, requires only that the accused foresaw a specified consequence as likely or possible (*see also* recklessness). In all cases where foresight is required, the court may not assume that the defendant had foresight merely because the particular consequence that occurred was the natural and likely consequence of his acts. In crimes for which proof of *negligence is sufficient, however, all that has to be proved is that a reasonable man would have had foresight of the consequences, even if the defendant did not.

forfeiture *n.* Loss of property or a right as a consequence of an offence or of the breach of an undertaking. There are three main situations in which the courts may order forfeiture of property. (1) Property that is illegally possessed is subject to forfeiture. (2) Any property relating to an offence under the Misuse of Drugs Act 1971 may be forfeited and either destroyed or dealt with as the court sees fit (this includes the proceeds of the sale of drugs). (3) Property may be forfeited if it is legally possessed but used (or intended to be used) to commit a crime (e.g. a getaway car) when the owner has previously been convicted of an offence punishable by two years' imprisonment or more. Property confiscated under this heading is held by the police for six months and then disposed of.

Most *leases provide for the landlord to terminate the lease when the tenant is in breach of his covenants. The landlord must follow a particular procedure before effecting forfeiture. In the case of forfeiture for nonpayment of rent, the landlord must make a formal demand for the rent unless the lease exempts him from the need to do this. When other covenants have been breached, the landlord must serve a statutory notice on the tenant specifying the breach, requiring him to put it right where this is possible, and requiring compensation in money if appropriate. If the tenant fails to comply with the notice the landlord may proceed with forfeiture. This may be done through court proceedings for possession or, more rarely, by *re-entry. A landlord loses his right of forfeiture if he treats the lease as continuing when he is entitled to forfeit it. This is known as *waiver of forfeiture. See also* relief from forfeiture.

forgery *n.* The offence of making a "false instrument" in order that it may be accepted as genuine, thereby causing harm to others. Under the Forgery and Counterfeiting Act 1981, an "instrument" may be a document, a stamp issued by the Post Office or the Inland

forum

Revenue, or any device (e.g. magnetic tape) in which information is recorded or stored. An instrument is considered to be "false" if, for example, it purports to have been made or altered (1) by or on the authority of someone who did not in fact do so; (2) on a date or at a place when it was not; or (3) by someone who is nonexistent. In addition to forgery itself, it is a criminal offence under the Act to copy or use a false instrument, knowing or believing it to be false. It is also an offence merely to have in one's possession or control any one of certain specified false instruments with the intention of passing them off as genuine. It is also an offence to make or possess any material that is meant to be used to produce any of the specified false instruments. These specified instruments include money or postal orders, stamps, share certificates, passports, cheques, cheque cards and credit cards, and copies of entries in a register of births, marriages, or deaths. All the above offences are punishable on indictment by up to ten years' imprisonment and upon summary trial to a fine of £1000 and/or six months' imprisonment.

The Act also deals with the offences of *counterfeiting currency* (notes or coin), with or without the intention of passing it off as genuine; possessing counterfeit currency; passing it off; making or possessing anything which can be used for counterfeiting; and importing or exporting counterfeit currency. It is also an offence to reproduce any British currency note (e.g. to photocopy a pound note) and, under certain circumstances, to make an imitation British coin. Some of these offences are subject to the same penalties as forgery.

forum [from Latin: public place] *n.* The place or country in which a case is being heard. If a case involving a foreign element is brought in the English courts, the forum is England. *See lex fori.*

forum rei [Latin: forum of the thing] The court of the country in which the subject of a dispute is situated.

foster child A child who is cared for by someone other than its natural or adopted parents (*see* foster parent). Local authorities are obliged by law to supervise the welfare of foster children within their area and to inspect and control the use of premises as foster homes. Foster children do not include children who are looked after by relatives or guardians or boarded out by a local authority or voluntary organization.

foster parent A person looking after a *foster child. Foster parents have no legal rights over the children they foster, who may be removed from their care by their parents or the person who has legal custody over them. They may, however, apply to have the child made a ward of court and ask for care and control. If the child has been living with them for at least 12 months they may apply to adopt him, and if he has been living with them for at least 3 years (or 12 months if the person who has legal custody over the child consents), they may apply for a *custodianship order.

four-day order A supplemental order of a civil court fixing the time for the performance of an act in cases in which no time has been fixed by the principal order. In the Chancery Division this is known as a four-day order although four days is not invariably the time fixed.

four unities *See* joint tenancy.

franchise *n.* **1.** A special right conferred by the Crown on a subject. Also known as a *liberty*, it is exemplified by the right to hold a market or fair or to run a ferry. **2.** The right to vote at an election. To qualify to vote at a parliamentary or local-government election, a person must be a *commonwealth citizen or a citizen of the Republic of Ireland, must be aged 18 or over, must be shown on the register of electors governing the election (*see* elector) as resident on the qualifying date in the parliamentary constituency or local government area concerned, and must not be subject to any legal incapacity to vote. Those incapacitated are peers and peeresses in their own right (for parliamentary elections only, and not including peers of Ireland), persons serving sentences of imprisonment, persons convicted during the preceding five years of certain offences relating to elections or to the bribery of public officials, and persons who are incapable of understanding the nature of their acts.

franked income Income that a person or a company receives on which *advance corporation tax has been paid. In the case of an individual the tax paid is imputed (*see* imputation system) to the basic income-tax liability of the recipient. In the case of a company, it is imputed to its own liability to corporation tax.

fraud *n.* A false representation by means of a statement or conduct in order to gain a material advantage. If the fraud results in injury to the deceived party, he may claim damages by suing for the tort of *deceit. A contract obtained by fraud is voidable on the grounds of fraudulent *misrepresentation. *See also* concealed fraud; constructive fraud.

Fraud itself is not a crime, but there are certain offences in which fraud is one of the elements. The most important of these are: (1) obtaining property, a pecuniary advantage, or services by *deception; (2) *false accounting and false statements made by company directors; (3) dishonest *suppression of documents and procuring the execution of a valuable security; and (4) cheating at common law (which now only applies in relation to frauds against the public revenue). If a person, by fraud, induces someone to part with money he would not otherwise have parted with,

this may amount to theft. *See also* conspiracy; defrauding; false pretence; forgery.

fraud on a power An exercise of a *power of appointment that, although made to an object within the class chosen by the donor, was made in circumstances that render it void. Examples are when the appointor intended to obtain a benefit for himself or another or when there was deliberate intention to defeat what the donor of the power had wished.

fraud on the minority An improper exercise of voting power by the majority of members of a company. It consists of a failure to cast votes for the benefit of the company as a whole and makes a resolution voidable. Examples are the ratification of an expropriation of company property by the directors (themselves the majority shareholders) and alteration of the articles of association to allow the compulsory purchase of members' shares when this is not in the company's interests. Actual or threatened fraud on the minority may give rise to a *derivative action.

fraudulent conveyance A transfer of land made without valuable *consideration and with the intent of defrauding a subsequent purchaser. An example of fraudulent conveyance is when A, who has contracted to sell to B, conveys the land to his associate C in order to escape the contract with B. Under the Law of Property Act 1925, B is entitled to have the conveyance to C set aside by the court.

fraudulent misrepresentation *See* misrepresentation.

fraudulent preference 1. The favouring by an insolvent debtor of one creditor to the detriment of his other creditors. This constitutes an act of *bankruptcy. If the debtor is made bankrupt within six months of a fraudulent preference, the transaction that constituted the act is void and the creditor can be compelled to return any property that passed to him as a result of it. **2.** A payment, charge, delivery of goods, etc., by a registered company to one creditor with the intention of satisfying that creditor at the expense of any others. If such a transaction is carried out when the company is unable to pay its debts as they fall due and within six months before commencement of *winding-up, it is ineffective. **3.** A floating *charge created by a registered company to secure a debt arising other than as a result of a cash payment (e.g. a loan to the company). This charge is invalid, even without proof of an intention to prefer, if it was created within one year before commencement of winding-up and the company was insolvent immediately before the charge was created.

fraudulent trading Carrying on business with the intention of defrauding creditors or for any other fraudulent purpose, e.g. accepting advance payment for goods with no intention of either supplying them or returning the money. Such conduct may lead to those responsible becoming personally liable for the company's debts on a winding-up. *See also* lifting the veil.

freedom from encumbrance The freedom of property from the binding rights of parties other than the owner. In contracts for the sale of goods, unless the seller makes it clear that he is contracting to transfer only such title as he or a third person may have, there is an implied *warranty that the goods are free from any charge or encumbrance not disclosed or known to the buyer before the contract was made.

freedom of testation A person's right to provide in his will for the distribution of his estate in whatever manner he wishes. The principle is restricted by the powers of the court to set aside a will made by a person of unsound mind (*see* testamentary capacity) and to award *reasonable financial provision

from an estate to certain relatives and dependants of the deceased under the Inheritance (Provision for Family and Dependants) Act 1975.

freehold *n.* The most complete form of ownership of land: a legal estate held in *fee simple absolute in possession.

freeing for adoption Giving consent in general terms to the *adoption of one's child, as opposed to consenting to an adoption by particular prospective adopters. The procedure is used by an *adoption agency in cases in which the parents freely agree that the child may be adopted, or their consent is dispensed with by the court on one of the statutory grounds. Once an order is made, the parental rights and duties are transferred to the adoption agency, who may then proceed to arrange for the child's adoption without asking the parents' consent or notifying them who the adopters are.

free movement The movement of goods, persons, services, and capital within an area without being impeded by legal restrictions. This is a basic principle of the EEC, whose treaty insists on the free movement of goods (involving the elimination of customs duties between member states and the setting up of a common external customs tariff) as well as the free movement of services, capital, and persons (including workers and those wishing to establish themselves in professions or to set up companies).

free on board *See* f.o.b. contract.

frustration of contract The unforeseen termination of a contract as a result of an event that either renders its performance impossible or illegal or prevents its main purpose from being achieved. Frustration would, for example, occur if the goods specified in a sale of goods contract were destroyed (impossibility of performance); if the outbreak of a war caused one party to become an enemy alien (illegality); or if X were to hire a room from Y with the object (known to Y) of viewing a procession and the procession was cancelled (failure of main purpose). Unless specific provision for the frustrating event is made, a frustrated contract is automatically discharged and the position of the parties is, in most cases, governed by the Law Reform (Frustrated Contracts) Act 1943. Money paid before the event can be recovered and money due but not paid ceases to be payable. However, a party who has obtained any valuable benefit under the contract must pay a reasonable sum for it. The Act does not apply to certain contracts for the sale of goods, contracts for the carriage of goods by sea, or contracts of insurance.

fugitive offender A person present in the UK who is accused of committing an offence in a Commonwealth country or a dependent territory of the UK and is liable to be surrendered for trial under the Fugitive Offenders Act 1967. The requirements for surrender are similar to those for *extradition to a foreign state, except that no treaty is involved.

full age *See* majority.

fundamental breach *See* breach of contract.

funeral expenses The reasonable cost of a deceased person's burial, which is the first priority for payment from his estate.

furnished tenancy *See* protected tenancy.

future goods Goods to be manufactured or acquired by a seller after a contract of sale has been made. Future goods must be distinguished as the subject of a contract of sale from existing goods, which are owned or possessed by a seller.

future interest Any right to property that does not take effect immediately. An example is B's interest in property held in trust for A for life and then for B. Under the Law of Property Act 1925 future interests in land (with the exception of *future leases) can exist as equitable interests only and not as legal estates.

future lease A lease that confers on the tenant the right to possession of land only from a specified future time. A lease, or contract to grant a lease, that is made in consideration of a capital payment or a rent and will take effect more than 21 years after its commencement is void under the Law of Property Act 1925. Subject to this, a future lease can qualify as a legal estate in land.

G

game *n.* Wild animals or birds hunted for sport or food. The Game Acts define these as including hares, pheasants, partridges, grouse, heath or moor game, black game, and bustards. The right to game belongs basically to a tenant rather than his landlord, but a lease frequently reserves it to the landlord instead. *See also* poaching.

gaming (gambling) *n.* Playing a game in order to win money or anything else of value, when winning depends on luck. There are various restrictions upon gaming, depending on whether it takes place in controlled (i.e. licensed or registered) or uncontrolled premises. If the premises are uncontrolled, it is illegal to play a game that involves playing against a bank or a game in which each player does not have an equal chance or the chance of winning is weighted in favour of someone other than the players (e.g. a promoter or organizer), unless the game takes place in a private house in the course of ordinary family life. Thus one cannot play roulette with a zero in uncontrolled premises, but one may play such games as bridge, whist, poker, or cribbage. It is also illegal (subject to one or two exceptions) to game when a charge is made for the gaming or a levy is charged on the winnings. Gaming in any street or any place to which the public has access is illegal, except for dominoes, cribbage, or any game specially authorized in a pub (provided the participants are over 18). If the premises are controlled (either by the grant of a licence or by registration as a gaming club), the restrictions applying to uncontrolled premises apply unless they have been permitted by regulation. Thus casino-type games may be played on controlled premises for commercial profit if permission has been obtained, but only by members of licensed or registered clubs and their guests. There are also restrictions relating to playing on Sundays, and no one under 18 may be present when gaming takes place. It is illegal to use, sell, or maintain gaming machines without a certificate or licence.

gaming contract A contract involving the playing of a game of chance by any number of people for money or money's worth. A *wagering contract* is one involving two parties only, each of whom stands to win or lose something of value according to the result of some future event (e.g. a horse race) or to which of them is correct about some past or present fact; neither party can have any interest in the contract except his stake. In general, gaming and wagering contracts are by statute null and void and no action can be brought to recover any money paid or won under them.

garnishee *n.* A person who has been warned by a court to pay a debt to a third party rather than to his creditor. *See* garnishee proceedings.

garnishee proceedings A procedure by which a judgment creditor may obtain a court order against a third party

who owes money to, or holds money on behalf of, the judgment debtor. The order requires the third party to pay the money (or part of it) to the judgment creditor. For example, if the judgment debtor has £1000 in a bank account and judgment has been entered against him for £500, the court may order the bank to pay £500 direct to the judgment creditor.

gazumping *n.* The withdrawal by a vendor from a proposed sale of land in the expectation of receiving a higher price elsewhere after agreeing the price with a purchaser but before a legally binding contract has been made (*see* exchange of contracts). The first prospective purchaser has no legal right either to compel the vendor to sell to him or to recover his wasted expenditure (such as surveyor's and solicitor's charges).

GBH *See* grievous bodily harm.

general agent *See* agent.

general and special damages A classification of *damages awarded for a tort or a breach of contract, the meaning of which varies according to the context. **1.** General damages are given for losses that the law will presume are the natural and probable consequence of a wrong. Thus it is assumed that a libel is likely to injure the reputation of the person libelled, and damages can be recovered without proof that the plaintiff's reputation has in fact suffered. Special damages are given for losses that are not presumed and have been specifically proved. **2.** General damages may also be damages given for a loss that is incapable of precise estimation, such as pain and suffering or loss of reputation. In this context special damages are damages given for losses that can be quantified, such as out-of-pocket expenses or loss of earnings.

general average *See* average.

General Council of the Bar *See* Bar Council.

general equitable charge A class of *land charge, registrable under the Land Charges Act (*see* registration of encumbrances), that affects a *legal estate in land but neither arises under a trust nor is secured by depositing the title deeds.

general improvement area A predominantly residential area in which a housing authority considers that it should improve or help to improve living conditions by improving dwellings or amenities (or both). *See also* housing action area, priority neighbourhood.

general issue A plea in which every allegation in the opposite party's pleading is denied. In civil proceedings it is no longer permitted. Instead, each allegation must be specifically admitted or denied. In criminal cases the defendant pleads the general issue by pleading *not guilty and cannot generally be required to disclose the nature of his defence until his own case is presented (*but see* alibi).

general legacy *See* legacy.

general lien *See* lien.

general meeting A meeting of company members whose decisions can bind the company. Certain *reserved powers*, specified by the Companies Acts, can only be exercised by a general meeting. These include alteration of the memorandum and articles of association, removal of a director before his term of office has expired, *alteration of share capital, the appointing of an auditor other than upon a casual vacancy, and putting the company into voluntary winding-up. Powers may also be reserved by the articles of association of a particular company. Powers other than reserved powers are usually delegated in the articles to the directors. The general meeting cannot overrule the directors' decisions relating to these powers, although it could, while exercising reserved powers, dismiss the directors or alter the articles and thus the

delegation. General meetings are either *annual general meetings or *extraordinary general meetings. Unless the articles of association provide or the court orders otherwise, at least two company members must be present personally.

general power *See* power of appointment.

general verdict 1. (in a civil case) A *verdict that is entirely in favour of one or other party. **2.** (in a criminal case) A verdict either of *guilty or *not guilty. *Compare* special verdict.

general warrant A warrant for arrest that does not name or describe the person to be arrested, or a search warrant that does not specify the premises to be searched or the property sought. Such warrants are usually illegal, although they may sometimes be expressly authorized by statute (*see* power of search). Someone arrested under an illegal general warrant can bring an action for trespass and false imprisonment. Sometimes, however, Parliament grants a general power of arrest while searching premises with a search warrant, e.g. under the Betting, Gaming and Lotteries Act 1963.

general words Words in a *conveyance describing rights and benefits that are incidental to the land (such as easements and profits *à prendre*) and that are conveyed with it. Under the Law of Property Act 1925 such words are no longer necessary, since a conveyance of land is deemed to include all such ancillary rights unless a contrary intention is expressed in the document.

Geneva Conventions A series of international conventions on the laws of war, the first of which was formulated in Geneva in 1864. The 1864 and 1906 Conventions protect sick and wounded soldiers; the Geneva Protocol of 1925 prohibits the use of gas and bacteriological warfare; the three Conventions of 1929 and the four Conventions of 1949 protect sick and wounded soldiers, sailors, and prisoners of war, and the 1949 Conventions protect, in addition, certain groups of civilians. The First Protocol of 1977 supplements the 1949 Conventions, extending protection to wider groups of civilians, regulating the law of bombing, and enlarging the category of wars subject to the 1949 Conventions (to include, for example, civil wars). The 1949 Conventions are accepted by many states and are generally considered to embody customary international law relating to war. *See also* Hague Conventions.

genocide *n.* Conduct aimed at the destruction of a national, ethnic, racial, or religious group. Genocide includes not only killing members of the group, but also causing them serious physical or psychological harm, imposing conditions of life that are intended to destroy them physically or measures intended to prevent childbirth, or forcibly transferring children of the group to another group, if these acts are carried out with the intention of destroying the group as a whole or in part. Destruction of a cultural or political group does not amount to genocide. The Genocide Convention 1948 declares that genocide is an international crime; the parties to the Convention undertake to punish not only acts of genocide committed within their jurisdiction but also complicity in genocide and conspiracy, incitement, and attempts to commit genocide. The Convention has been enacted into English law by the Genocide Act 1969. It is generally considered that the Convention embodies principles of customary international law that bind all nations, including those that are not parties to the Convention.

ghet *n.* A Jewish religious divorce, executed by the husband delivering a bill of divorce (which must be handwritten according to specific detailed rules) to his wife in the presence of two witnesses. In theory a ghet does not require a court procedure, but in practice it is usually executed through a court because of the many complexities of the relevant religious law. *See also* extrajudicial divorce.

gift *n.* A gratuitous transfer or grant of property. A legally valid gift must normally be effected by deed, by physical delivery in the case of chattels, or by *donatio mortis causa*; the donor must intend ownership to pass as a gift. However, an *imperfect gift* (i.e. one for which the legal formalities have not been observed) may be treated as valid in equity in certain circumstances (*see*, for example, (equitable) estoppel).

gift over A provision in a will or other settlement enabling an interest in property to come into existence on the termination of an earlier interest.

gipsy (gypsy) *n.* A person of a nomadic way of life. Local authorities must by statute provide adequate sites for gipsies resorting to their areas and may take steps to remove unlawful gipsy encampments (e.g. encampments within highway boundaries).

going public The process of forming a public company or of reregistering a private company as a public company.

golden rule *See* interpretation of statutes.

good behaviour A term used in an order by a magistrate or by a Crown Court upon sentencing. The person named in the order should "be of good behaviour" towards another person (the complainant). The court may order that the person named enter into a *recognizance, and if he does not comply with the order he may be imprisoned for up to six months. The procedure may be used against anyone who has been brought before the court if there is a fear that he may cause a breach of the peace or if he is the subject of a complaint by someone (which need not be based on the commission of a criminal offence).

good consideration *See* consideration.

good faith Honesty. An act carried out in good faith is one carried out honestly.

good leasehold title A form of title to registered leasehold land (*see* land registration) that is equivalent to *absolute title except that the landlord's right to grant the lease is not guaranteed. Good leasehold title usually occurs when the documents proving the landlord's title have not been registered at the Land Registry.

goods *pl. n.* Personal chattels or items of property. Land is excluded, and the statutory definition in the Sale of Goods Act 1979 also excludes *choses in action and money. It includes *emblements and things attached to or forming part of land that are agreed to be severed before sale or under a contract of sale.

goodwill *n.* The advantage arising from the reputation and trade connections of a business, in particular the likelihood that existing customers will continue to patronize it. Goodwill is a substantial item to be taken into account on the sale of a business; it may need to be protected by requiring the vendor to agree not to set up in the same business for a stated period in competition with the business he has sold.

government circulars Documents circulated by government departments on behalf of ministers, setting out principles and practices for the exercise of ministerial powers delegated to others. These may provide mere administrative guidelines or they may be intended to have legislative effect (i.e. as *delegated legislation), in which case any purported exercise of the delegated powers is invalid unless it complies with them. *See ultra vires.*

government department An organ of central government responsible for a particular sphere of public administra-

tion. It is staffed by permanent civil servants and is normally headed by a minister who is politically responsible for its activities.

Grand Committees, Scottish and Welsh Committees of the House of Commons involved with matters relating to Scotland and Wales, respectively. The former consists of the 72 members representing Scottish constituencies and 10–15 other members. A Bill certified by the Speaker as relating exclusively to Scotland may by standing orders of the House be referred to the Committee for its second reading, and the Committee also debates other purely Scottish matters. The Welsh Grand Committee, which consists of the 38 members representing Welsh constituencies and up to 5 others, is purely deliberative. It considers matters relating exclusively to Wales but is not empowered to undertake second readings.

grant *n.* 1. The creation or transfer of the ownership of property (e.g. an estate or interest in land) by written instrument; for example, the grant of a lease. *See also* lie in grant. 2. A *grant of representation. 3. The allocation of money, powers, etc., by Parliament or the Crown for a specific purpose.

grant of representation Authority granted by the court to named individuals or to a *trust corporation to administer the estate of a deceased person. The grant is of *probate when the will is proved by the executors named in it or of *letters of administration when the deceased died intestate, the deceased's will did not appoint executors, or the executors named do not prove the will.

grants in aid Central government grants towards local authority expenditure, comprising specific grants for particular services (e.g. the police) and rate support grants to augment income generally.

Gray's Inn

Gray's Inn One of the four *Inns of Court, situated in Holborn. The earliest recorded claim for its existence is 1391.

Greater London A local government area consisting of the areas of 32 *London boroughs* (12 inner, and 20 outer), the *City of London, and the Inner and Middle Temples. A Greater London Council and London borough councils are elected every fourth year, counting from 1981 and 1982 respectively (*see also* local authority). The distribution of functions between these councils approximates broadly to that between the *county councils and *district councils of metropolitan counties, but certain matters are the responsibility of specially constituted authorities (e.g. the Inner London Education Authority for the inner boroughs). The City of London is distinct in both constitution and functions. The Temples have limited independent functions (e.g. public health), but are administered in many respects by the City's Common Council.

green form The form upon which an application for legal advice and assistance is made. The form is completed by the client with the assistance of his solicitor, who then decides whether the application (particularly the client's financial resources) is within the limits of the scheme. If so, he may render legal advice and assistance and recover costs not exceeding £40 from the legal aid fund. *See also* legal aid scheme.

green paper *See* Command Papers.

grievous bodily harm (GBH) Very serious physical injury. Under the Offences Against the Person Act 1861 there are two offences involving grievous bodily harm. It is an offence, punishable by up to five years' imprisonment, to inflict (by direct acts) grievous bodily harm upon anyone with the intention of harming them (even only slightly); if the intention was merely to frighten the victim the defendant is guilty of *assault and *battery. It is an offence, punishable by a maximum sentence of life imprisonment, to cause grievous bodily harm to anyone with the intention of seriously injuring them or of resisting arrest. "Causing" in this offence includes indirect acts, such as pulling a chair away from a person so that he falls and dislocates his spine. If a person intends to cause grievous bodily harm but his victim actually dies, he is guilty of murder, even though he did not intend to kill him. Causing grievous bodily harm may also be an element in some other offence, e.g. *burglary. The courts have said that judges should not attempt to define grievous bodily harm for the jury, but should leave it to them, in every case, to decide whether the harm caused was really serious. *See also* wounding with intent.

gross *See* in gross.

gross indecency A sexual act that is more than ordinary *indecency but falls short of actual intercourse. It may include masturbation and indecent physical contact, or even indecent behaviour without any physical contact. It is an offence for a man to commit an act of gross indecency with another man unless both parties are over 21, consent to the act, and it is carried out in private. This is punishable by up to two years' imprisonment or, if one of the parties is under 21, by up to five years' imprisonment. It is also an offence to cause or arrange for a man to commit an act of gross indecency with another man, even if the act is carried out in private and between consenting adults. It is an offence, punishable by up to two years' imprisonment, to commit an act of gross indecency with or towards a child (of either sex) under the age of 14 or to incite a child to commit such an act.

gross negligence A high degree of *negligence, manifested in behaviour substantially worse than that of the average reasonable man. Gross negligence is required before someone can be convicted of manslaughter. In many other crimes, proof of negligence not amounting to gross negligence is sufficient for a conviction.

ground rent A rent reserved by a long lease of land. For example when a house or flat is sold on a lease for 99 years, the lessor may reserve a small annual rent payable throughout the term as well as the capital price payable on the grant of the lease. *Building leases are sometimes granted in return for a ground rent rather than a capital sum.

group accounts *Accounts required by law to be prepared by a registered company that has a subsidiary company. Group accounts deal with the financial position of the company and its subsidiaries collectively.

guarantee *n.* **1.** A secondary agreement in which a person (the *guarantor*) is liable for the debt or default of another (the principal debtor), who is the party primarily liable for the debt. A guarantee requires an independent *consideration and must be evidenced in writing. A guarantor who has paid out on his guarantee has a right to be indemnified by the principal debtor. If the principal debt is void, there can be no valid guarantee. *Compare* indemnity. **2.** *See* warranty.

guarantee company *See* limited company.

guarantee payment Under the Employment Protection (Consolidation) Act 1978, the sum that an employer must pay to an employee for whom he is unable to provide work during the whole of any working day or shift. However, an employee is not entitled to a guarantee payment if he is laid off because of industrial action affecting his own or an associated employer, if he unreasonably refuses other suitable work, or if he fails to comply with the employer's reasonable requirements for ensuring that he is available for work if

and when needed. Generally, employees only become entitled to a guarantee payment after four weeks' *continuous employment in the business; one employed for a specific task that is not expected to last more than 12 weeks and one having a fixed-term employment contract of a year or less do not qualify at all. The payment is limited to the employee's basic wage for the relevant shift, subject to a maximum prescribed by regulations made by the Secretary of State for Employment and reviewed annually. An employee is not entitled to more than five guarantee payments in any period of three months. The statutory payment is offset by any amount payable to the employee under his employment contract while he is laid off. An employee may complain to an industrial tribunal if his employer fails to pay him any sum due as a guarantee payment, and the tribunal can order the employer to pay the sum due.

guard dog A dog kept specifically for the purpose of protecting people, property, or someone who is guarding people or property. Under the Guard Dogs Act 1975 it is a summary offence punishable by fine to use a guard dog, or to allow its use, unless either it is secured and cannot roam the premises freely or a handler is controlling it. The Act does not, however, affect civil liability for injuries or damage caused by the dog, which depends on the law of tort (*see* classification of animals). In some cases the owner may be criminally liable for injury caused by a guard dog; for example, if it kills someone, the owner may be guilty of manslaughter by gross negligence or of constructive *manslaughter.

guardian *n.* One who looks after the interests of a minor and is entitled to exercise parental rights and duties over it. The parents of a child are its natural guardians, and they may appoint guardians, either by deed or by will, to look after the child after they die. The

High Court may also appoint a guardian if a child has no parent or guardian or if either of the parents die without appointing a guardian. The powers of guardians, and provisions for dealing with disputes between joint guardians, are provided for in the Guardianship of Minors Act 1971.

guardian *ad litem* *See* ad litem.

guardianship order An order, made under the Mental Health Act 1959 or by a juvenile court in care proceedings, placing a child suffering from any of certain types of mental illness under the guardianship of a local social services authority or an approved person.

guillotine *n.* A House of Commons procedure for speeding up the passing of legislation. The number of days allowed for a Bill's Committee and Report stages is limited by an allocation-of-time order moved by the government; the total time available is then allotted between particular portions of the Bill. When the time limit for any portion is reached, debate on it ceases and all outstanding votes are taken forthwith. *Compare* closure.

guilty *adj.* **1.** An admission in court by an accused person that he has committed the offence with which he is charged. If there is more than one charge he may plead guilty to some and *not guilty to others. **2.** A *verdict finding that the accused has committed the offence with which he was charged or some other offence of which he can be convicted on the basis of the evidence in the case. *See also* conviction.

guilty knowledge The knowledge of facts or circumstances required for a person to have *mens rea* for a particular crime. Knowledge is usually actual knowledge, but when a person deliberately ignores facts that are obvious, he is sometimes considered to have "constructive" knowledge.

guilty mind *See mens rea.*

gypsy *n.* *See* gipsy.

H

habeas corpus A prerogative writ used to challenge the validity of a person's detention, either in official custody (e.g. when held pending deportation or extradition) or in private hands. Deriving from the royal prerogative and therefore originally obtained by petitioning the sovereign, it is now issued by the Divisional Court of the Queen's Bench Division, or, during vacation, by any High Court judge. If on an application for the writ the Court or judge is satisfied that the detention is prima facie unlawful, the custodian is ordered to appear and justify it, failing which release is ordered.

habitual criminal *See* persistent offender.

habitual residence The place or country in which a person has his home. Habitual residence is necessary in order to establish *domicile.

Hague Conventions The Hague Conventions for the Pacific Settlement of International Disputes: a series of international conventions on the laws of war (3 in 1899 and 13 in 1907). The 1899 Conventions established a Permanent Court of Arbitration, which was active before the Permanent Court of International Justice and the *International Court of Justice functioned. The Hague Conventions are still in force but their provisions are often inapplicable to modern warfare. *See also* Geneva Conventions.

Hague Rules *See* bill of lading; international carriage.

half a year (in a lease) A *fixed term that begins on a quarter day and ends on the next but one quarter day.

half blood *See* consanguinity.

half-secret trust (semisecret trust) A trust whose existence is disclosed by the will or other document creating it but the beneficiaries of which are undisclosed, though known. *See also* secret trust.

handling *n.* Dishonestly receiving goods that one knows or believes to be stolen or undertaking, arranging, or assisting someone to retain, remove, or dispose of stolen goods. Under the Theft Act 1968, this is an offence subject to a maximum of 14 years' imprisonment. "Stolen goods" include not only goods that have been the subject of theft but also anything that has been obtained by *blackmail or *deception. The theft or other crime may have occurred at any time (even before 1968) and anywhere in the world, provided the handling occurs in England or Wales. There is also a provision to extend the concept of stolen goods to the proceeds of their sale. Thus if A steals goods, sells them for £3000, and gives part of the money to B, B is guilty of handling if he knows the money represents the proceeds of the sale of stolen goods. If A then buys a car with the rest of the £3000 and C agrees to dispose of the car for A, knowing or believing that it was bought with the proceeds of sale of stolen goods, C will also be guilty of handling, since he has "undertaken to dispose of stolen goods". The crime is therefore very widely defined; it also covers, for instance, forging or providing new documents and number plates for stolen cars and contacting and negotiating with dealers in stolen property (fences).

Hansard *n.* The name by which the Official Report of Parliamentary Debates is customarily referred to (after the Hansard family, who – as printers to the House of Commons – were concerned with compiling reports in the 19th century). Reporting was taken over by the government in 1908, and separate reports for the House of Commons and the House of Lords are published by HMSO in daily and weekly parts. They contain a verbatim record of debates and all other proceedings (e.g. question time). Members of Parliament have the right to correct anything attributed to them, but may not make any other alterations. *Compare* Journals.

harassment of debtors Behaviour designed to force a debtor or one believed to be a debtor to pay his debt. This is a criminal offence, punishable by fine, if the debt is based on a contract and the nature or frequency of the acts subject the debtor (or members of his household) to alarm, distress, or humiliation. Harassment also includes false statements that the debtor will face criminal proceedings or that the creditor is officially authorized to enforce payment and using a document that the creditor falsely represents as being official. The offence may overlap with the crime of *blackmail, but it will also cover cases in which the creditor believes he is entitled to act as he does (which might not amount to blackmail).

harassment of occupier The offence of using or threatening violence or any other kind of pressure to obtain possession of one's property from a tenant (the residential occupier) without a court order. The offence includes interfering with the tenant's peace or comfort (or that of his household), withdrawing or not providing services normally required by the tenant (e.g. cutting off gas or electricity, even when the bills have not been paid), and preventing the tenant from exercising any of his rights or taking any legal or other action in respect of his tenancy. The Act does not apply, however, to a displaced residential owner, as opposed to a landlord (*see also* forcible entry).

harbouring *n.* Hiding a criminal or suspected criminal. This will normally constitute the offence of *impeding apprehension or prosecution. *See also* escape.

harmonization of laws The process by which member states of the EEC make changes in their national laws, in accordance with *Community legislation, to produce uniformity, particularly relating to commercial matters of common interest. The Council of Ministers of the European Communities has, for example, issued directives on the harmonization of company law and of units of measurement. *Compare* approximation of laws.

hay bote *See* estovers.

headings *pl. n.* Words prefixed to sections of a statute. They are treated in the same way as *preambles and may be used to assist in resolving an ambiguity.

Health and Safety Commission A body responsible for furthering the general purposes of the Health and Safety at Work Act 1974, for example by advising and promoting research and training. It also appoints a Health and Safety Executive, which shares with local authorities responsibility for enforcing the Act and operates for this purpose through such inspectorates as the Factories and Nuclear Installations Inspectorates. *See also* safety at work.

Health Service Commissioners Commissioners (one each for England and Wales) instituted by the National Health Service Reorganization Act 1973. They investigate complaints by members of the public of hardship or injustice suffered through failure in a health authority service and other cases of maladministration by a health authority. Certain matters (e.g. alleged professional negligence) are excluded from investigation. Both offices are in practice held by the *Parliamentary Commissioner for Administration.

hearing *n.* The trial of a case before a court. Hearings are usually in public

but the public may be barred from the court in certain circumstances (*see in camera*).

hearsay evidence (second-hand evidence) Evidence of the oral statements of a person other than the witness who is testifying and statements in documents offered to prove the truth of what was asserted. In general, hearsay evidence is inadmissible (the *rule against hearsay*) but this principle is subject to numerous exceptions. Thus in civil cases, most hearsay statements, whether of fact or opinion, are admissible under the Civil Evidence Acts 1968–72. At common law, there are numerous exceptions applicable to both civil and criminal cases, e.g. *declarations of deceased persons, evidence given in former trials, *depositions, *admissions, and *confessions. Some exceptions apply only to criminal cases, e.g. *dying declarations and statements admitted under the Criminal Evidence Act 1965 (admissibility of certain business records: *see* admissibility of records). *See also* original evidence.

heir *n.* Before 1926, the person entitled under common law and statutory rules to inherit the freehold land of one who died intestate. The Administration of Estates Act 1925 abolished these rules of descent and the concept of heirship, except that *entailed interests and in certain rare cases the property of mental patients devolve according to the old rules. In addition, the Law of Property Act 1925 provides that a conveyance of property in favour of the heir of a deceased person conveys it to the person who would be the heir under the old rules. Where these exceptions apply, an *heir apparent* is the person (e.g. an eldest son) who will inherit provided that he outlives his ancestor; an *heir presumptive* is an heir (e.g. a daughter) whose right to inherit may be lost by the birth of an heir with greater priority (e.g. a son). *See also* heirs of the body.

heir apparent *See* heir.

heirloom *n.* A *chattel that, by custom, passes on the owner's death with his house and does not form part of his residuary estate. When heirlooms are held, together with land, under a settlement, the *tenant for life is entitled under the Settled Land Act 1925 to sell the heirlooms. The price is payable to the trustees as *capital money.

heir presumptive *See* heir.

heirs of the body Lineal descendants who were entitled to inherit freehold land under the rules applying on intestacy before the Administration of Estates Act 1925. A conveyance of land "to A and the heirs of his body" creates an *entailed interest that devolves to descendants only, according to the old rules. Thus (1) males are first in priority and the principle of primogeniture applies, e.g. an older son is preferred to a younger; (2) in the absence of male heirs, females in equal degree share the land equally; and (3) lineal descendants of an heir represent him, thus the son of an older son who dies will inherit to the exclusion of a younger son.

hereditament *n.* **1.** Real property. *Corporeal hereditaments* are tangible items of property, such as land and buildings. *Incorporeal hereditaments* are intangible rights in land, such as easements and profits *à prendre*. **2.** A unit of land that has been separately assessed for rating purposes.

High Court of Justice A court created by the Judicature Acts 1873–75, forming part of the *Supreme Court of Judicature. It is divided into the three Divisions: the *Queen's Bench Division, *Chancery Division, and *Family Division.

high seas The seas beyond *territorial waters. The English courts have jurisdiction to try offences committed by anyone anywhere on the high seas in a British ship. They also have jurisdiction to try offences committed anywhere in the world on board a British-controlled aircraft while it is in flight. Sometimes these offences amount to the special crimes of *hijacking or *piracy. *See also* law of the sea.

highway *n.* A road or other way over which the public may pass and repass as of right. Highways include *footpaths, *bridle ways, and cul-de-sacs. A highway is created either under statutory powers or by dedication (express or implied) by a landowner and acceptance (by use) by the public. Obstructing a highway is a public nuisance (*see also* obstruction), and misuse of the public right to pass and repass over a highway is a trespass against the owner of the subsoil of the highway.

hijacking *n.* Seizing or exercising control of an aircraft in flight by the use or threat of force. Hijacking is prohibited in international law by the Tokyo Convention 1963, which defines the conditions under which jurisdiction may be assumed over hijackers, but does not oblige states to exercise such jurisdiction and does not create an obligation to extradite hijackers. There is also a Hague Convention of 1970 and a Montreal Convention of 1971 creating offences of unlawfully seizing or exercising control of an aircraft by force or threats and of sabotaging aircraft; these conventions provide for compulsory jurisdiction as well as extradition. In English law, hijacking and similar offences are governed by the Hijacking Act 1971, the Protection of Aircraft Act 1973, and the Aviation Security Act 1982.

hire 1. *vb.* To enter into a contract for the temporary use of another's goods, or the temporary provision of his services or labour, in return for payment. In the case of goods, the person hiring them is a bailee (*see* bailment). **2.** *n.* **a.** The act of hiring. **b.** The payment made under a contract of hire.

hire purchase A method of buying goods in which the purchaser takes possession of them as soon as he has paid an initial instalment of the price (a *deposit*) and obtains ownership of the goods when he has paid all the agreed number of subsequent instalments. A *hire-purchase agreement* differs from a *credit-sale agreement and a sale-by-instalments contract because in these transactions ownership passes when the contract is signed. It also differs from a contract of *hire, because in this case ownership never passes. Hire-purchase agreements were formerly controlled by government regulations stipulating the minimum deposit and the length of the repayment period. These controls were removed in July 1982. Hire-purchase agreements were also formerly controlled by the Hire Purchase Act 1965, but most are now regulated by the Consumer Credit Act 1974. In this Act a hire-purchase agreement is regarded as one in which goods are bailed in return for periodical payments by the bailee; ownership passes to the bailee if he complies with the terms of the agreement and exercises his option to purchase.

A hire-purchase agreement often involves a finance company as a third party. The seller of the goods sells them outright to the finance company, which enters into a hire-purchase agreement with the hirer.

HM Procurator General *See* Treasury Solicitor.

holder *n.* The person in possession of a *bill of exchange or promissory note. He may be the payee, the endorsee, or the bearer. A holder may sue on the bill in his own name. When value (which includes a past debt or liability) has at any time been given for a bill, the holder is a *holder for value*, as regards the acceptor and all who were parties to the bill before value was given. A *holder in due course* is one who has taken a bill of exchange in good faith and for value, before it was overdue, and without notice of previous dishonour or of any defect in the title of the person who negotiated or transferred the bill. He holds the bill free from any defect of title of prior parties and may enforce payment against all parties liable on the bill.

holding company *See* subsidiary company.

holding out Conduct by one person that leads another to believe that he has an authority that does not in fact exist. By the doctrine of *estoppel, the first person may be prevented from denying that the authority exists. For example, a person who wrongly represents himself as being a partner in a firm will be as liable as if he were in fact a partner to anyone who gives credit to the firm on the faith of the representation.

holding over The action of a tenant continuing in occupation of premises after his lease has expired. If this is without the landlord's consent, the landlord may claim damages from the tenant. If, however, a landlord accepts rent from a tenant who is holding over, a new tenancy is created.

holograph *n.* A document written completely by the hand of its author; for example, a will in the testator's own handwriting.

homeless person One who either has no living accommodation that he is entitled to occupy or is unlawfully excluded from his own living accommodation. Certain homeless people (e.g. the elderly or infirm or those with dependent children) have a statutory right to permanent local-authority accommodation or, if they became homeless intentionally, to temporary accommodation.

home-loss payment Additional compensation paid under the Land Compensation Act 1973 to a person on the compulsory acquisition of his property if he has occupied it as his principal residence throughout the preceding five years.

Home Secretary The minister in charge of the Home Office, who is responsible throughout England and Wales for law and order generally (including matters concerning the police and the prison, fire, and security services) and for a variety of other domestic matters, such as nationality, immigration, race relations, extradition, and deportation. He also advises the sovereign on the exercise of the prerogative of mercy.

homicide *n.* The act of killing a human being. *Unlawful homicide*, which constitutes the crime of *murder, *manslaughter, or *infanticide, can only be committed if the victim is an independent human being (*see* abortion), the act itself causes the death (*see* causation), and the victim dies within a year and a day after the act alleged to have caused the death. A British citizen may be tried for homicide committed anywhere in the world. *Lawful homicide* occurs when somebody uses reasonable force in preventing crime or arresting an offender, in self-defence or defence of others, or (possibly) in defence of his property, and causes death as a result. *See also* excusable homicide.

homosexual conduct Sexual behaviour between persons of the same sex. The acts of *buggery and *gross indecency are not crimes if the act is committed in private and both parties are over the age of 21 and consent to the act. This does not apply, however, to acts of buggery or gross indecency between members of the UK merchant navy on board a UK merchant ship, which remain criminal under all circumstances. There are also special statutory offences of "disgraceful conduct of an unnatural (or indecent) kind", which apply to members of the armed forces and presumably cover some kinds of homosexual conduct. Lesbianism is not a criminal act.

honorarium *n.* A payment made to a person for services rendered by him voluntarily.

honour clause An express statement in a *contract that an agreement is intended to be binding in honour only. The courts will usually allow it to take effect and so will not enforce the agreement.

hospital order An order of the Crown Court or a magistrates' court authorizing the detention in a specified hospital (for a period of 12 months, renewable by the hospital managers) of a convicted person suffering from *mental disorder. Unless a *restriction order has also been made, discharge while an order is in force may be authorized by the managers or the doctor in charge or directed by a *mental health review tribunal.

hostage *n.* A person who is held as a security. Under the Taking of Hostages Act 1982, it is an offence, punishable in the English courts by a maximum sentence of life imprisonment, to take anyone as a hostage against his will anywhere in the world and to threaten to kill, injure, or continue to hold him hostage in order to force a state, international governmental organization, or person to do or not to do something. This is an extraditable offence, but prosecutions may only be brought with the consent of the Attorney General. *See also* hijacking; terrorism.

hostile witness An *adverse witness who wilfully refuses to testify truthfully on behalf of the party who called him. A hostile witness may, with *leave of the court, be cross-examined by that party, for example by putting to him a *previous statement that is inconsistent with his present testimony.

hotchpot *n.* The bringing into account, on distribution of an intestate's estate, of certain benefits separately conferred on the beneficiaries. In the case of total intestacy, the Administration of Estates

Act 1925 provides that property given by the intestate during his lifetime to any of his children must be brought into account. Thus if A gives £10,000 to his son B, and dies intestate leaving an estate worth £50,000 to which his children B and C are entitled equally, B will in fact receive £20,000 and C £30,000. The rule applies only to lifetime gifts made by way of advancement (i.e. as permanent provision and not for maintenance or temporary purposes). In the case of partial intestacy, benefits conferred by the will on a surviving spouse and on the deceased's issue (i.e. his children, grandchildren, and remoter direct descendants) are also brought into account.

house bote *See* estovers.

housebreaking *n.* Forcing one's way into someone else's house. If this causes damage to the house, or is carried out with the intention of committing certain specified crimes in the house, or if, after breaking into a house, certain crimes then take place, the housebreaking amounts to *burglary. It is also a statutory offence punishable by up to three years' imprisonment if a person has with him any article that he intends to use in connection with burglary, theft, or criminal deception. In addition to the usual housebreaking implements, this includes such things as rubber gloves to conceal fingerprints.

House of Commons The representative chamber of *Parliament (also known as the *Lower House*), composed of 650 members elected for 523 single-member constituencies in England, 72 in Scotland, 38 in Wales, and 17 in Northern Ireland (*see* election; franchise). The total number of members may within certain limits be varied as a result of constituency changes proposed by the *boundary commissions.

A number of people are disqualified from membership. They include those under 21, peers and peeresses in their own right (except Irish peers), civil servants, the police and the regular armed forces, most clergy (but not Nonconformist ministers), aliens, convicted prisoners and people guilty of corrupt or illegal practices, the holders of most judicial offices (but not lay magistrates), and the holders of a large number of public offices listed in the House of Commons Disqualification Act 1975. Public offices that disqualify include the *Chiltern Hundreds and the Manor of Northstead. The number of members who may hold ministerial office is limited to 95.

The House is presided over by the *Speaker*, who is elected by the members at the beginning of each Parliament. He is responsible for the orderly conduct of proceedings, which he must supervise with complete impartiality, and is the person through whom the members may collectively communicate with the sovereign. The *Leader of the House* is a government minister responsible for arranging the business of the House in consultation with the Opposition.

House of Commons Commission A body established in 1978 to supervise the staffing of the House. It consists of the Speaker, the Leader of the House, and four other members, one of whom is appointed by the Leader of the Opposition.

House of Lords The nonrepresentative chamber of *Parliament (also known as the *Upper House*), consisting of the *Lords Spiritual* and *Lords Temporal*. The former comprise the Archbishops of Canterbury and York, the Bishops of London, Durham, and Winchester, and 21 other Anglican bishops selected according to seniority of appointment. The latter consist of hereditary peers and peeresses in their own right, life peers and peeresses, and the *Lords of Appeal in Ordinary. The Peerage Act 1963 allows a hereditary peerage to be disclaimed, thereby making its holder eligible for membership of the House of Commons instead. Disclaimer, which lasts for the holder's life-time, must take place within 12 months of succession to the title or, in the case of a person who is already a member of the Commons at the time of succession, within one month.

The House is presided over by the *Lord Chancellor and its business is arranged, in consultation with the Opposition, by a government minister appointed *Leader of the House*. The Lords has judicial as well as parliamentary functions. It is the final court of appeal in the UK in both civil and criminal cases. In that capacity it formally adopts opinions delivered by an *Appellate Committee* (of which there are two), and it is a constitutional convention that the only peers who participate in the proceedings of the committee are the Lord Chancellor, the Lords of Appeal in Ordinary, and others who have held high judicial office.

housing action area An area declared to be such by a housing authority on the grounds that living conditions in it are unsatisfactory and should be dealt with comprehensively over a five-year period. This is done by special measures to improve the standards and management of accommodation and the well-being of the inhabitants. It may incorporate a *general improvement area. *See also* priority neighbourhood. *Compare* clearance area.

housing association A non-profit-making organization whose main purpose is to provide housing. A tenancy from a housing association registered with the Housing Corporation is excepted from the *protected tenancy provisions. However, the *secure tenancy provisions may apply.

housing association tenancy A tenancy in which the landlord is a housing association, a housing trust, or the Housing Corporation.

Housing Corporation A body with functions under the Housing Acts 1964,

1974, and 1980. These include maintaining a register of *housing associations, promoting and assisting the development of – and making and guaranteeing loans to – registered housing associations and unregistered *self-build societies, and providing dwellings for letting or sale.

housing subsidy An annual contribution from central government funds, payable under the Housing Act 1980, towards the provision of housing by local authorities and new town corporations.

housing trust A trust whose funds are used to provide housing. A tenancy from a housing trust that is registered with the Housing Corporation, or that meets certain statutory requirements, is excepted from the *protected tenancy provisions. However, the *secure tenancy provisions may apply.

human rights Rights and freedom to which every human being is entitled. Protection against breaches of these rights committed by a state (including the state of which the victim is a national) may in some cases be enforced in international law. It is sometimes suggested that human rights (or some of them) are so fundamental that they form part of *natural law, but most of them are best regarded as forming part of treaty law. The United Nations Universal Declaration of Human Rights (1948) spells out most of the main rights that must be protected but it is not binding in international law. There are two international covenants, however, that bind the parties who have ratified them: the 1966 International Covenant on Civil and Political Rights and International Covenant on Economic, Social and Cultural Rights. The United Nations has set up a Commission on Human Rights, which has power to discuss gross violations of human rights but not to investigate individual complaints. The Human Rights Committee, set up in 1977, has power to hear complaints from individuals, under certain circumstances, about alleged breaches of the 1966 Covenant on Civil and Political Rights. There are also various regional conventions on human rights, some of which have established machinery for hearing individual complaints. The best known of these is the *European Convention on Human Rights and the Inter-American Convention on Human Rights (covering South America).

hybrid Bill *See* Bill.

hybrid power *See* power of appointment.

hypothecation *n.* (in maritime law) A mortgage granted by a ship's master to secure the repayment with interest, on the safe arrival of the ship at her destination, of money borrowed during a voyage as a matter of necessity (e.g. to pay for urgent repairs). The hypothecation of a ship itself, with or without cargo, is called *bottomry*; that of its cargo alone is *respondentia*. It is effected by a bond, and the bondholder is entitled to a maritime *lien.

I

identity *n.* (in the law of evidence) *See* evidence of identity.

ignorance of the law *See* mistake.

ignorantia juris non excusat [Latin] Ignorance of the law is no excuse, i.e. no defence against criminal or other proceedings arising from its breach. The Statutory Instruments Act 1946 modifies the rule slightly (*see* statutory instrument). *See also* mistake.

ignoring traffic signals Failing to comply with traffic signs, traffic lights, or road markings. A number of different offences are included in this category, all concerned with breaches of the rules relating to traffic signals as laid down in the Highway Code. All these offences are subject to a fine, *endorsement (carrying 3 points under the *totting-up system), and *disqualification at the discretion of the court. Sometimes charges may also be brought under the head of *careless, *inconsiderate, or *reckless driving, depending on the circumstances. It is also an offence not to comply with road directions given by a uniformed police officer acting in the course of his duties or engaged in a traffic census or survey.

Prosecutions for ignoring traffic signals or police directions are subject to a *notice of intended prosecution.

illegal contract A contract that is prohibited by statute (e.g. one between traders providing for minimum resale prices) or is illegal at common law on the grounds of *public policy. An illegal contract is totally void, but neither party (unless innocent of the illegality) can recover back any money paid or property transferred under it, according to the maxim *ex turpi causa non oritur actio* (a right of action does not arise out of an evil cause). Related transactions may also be affected. A related transaction between the same parties (e.g. if X gives Y a promissory note for money due from him under an illegal contract) is equally tainted with the illegality and is therefore void. The same is true of a related transaction with a third party (e.g. if Z lends X the money to pay Y) if the original illegality is known to him.

illegal practices *See* corrupt and illegal practices.

illegal trust A trust that contravenes statute, morality, or public policy. Such a trust is void and of no effect.

illegitimacy *n.* The status of a child born out of wedlock (a *bastard). Although evidence of illegitimacy is readily available from the entry in the birth register relating to the child's parents, it is usual for a short form of birth certificate to be issued, which makes no mention of the parents. Entry in the register of the name of a man who is not married to the mother (which may only be done with the consent of the mother) is evidence of his paternity.

The main differences between illegitimate and legitimate children are as follows. (1) The mother of an illegitimate child has exclusive rights to its custody, parental rights, and duties (although the father may apply to the courts to obtain custody). (2) The father of an illegitimate child is not obliged at common law to maintain it: the mother (or custodian) must obtain an *affiliation order, usually within a three-year time limit. Affiliation orders may also be sought by local authorities in respect of illegitimate children in their care. (3) Illegitimate children cannot share in the intestate estate of any relative other than their parents. (4) An illegitimate child under the age of 18 must obtain his mother's consent to marry. (5) Illegitimate children cannot succeed to a title of honour or property devolving with such a title.

The Law Commission has recently recommended the complete abolition of the status and disadvantages of illegitimacy.

illusory appointment The giving of property under a *power of appointment that confers little or no benefit to one or more objects of the power. Before 19th-century legislation such appointments were void; they are now valid.

illusory trust A conveyance by a debtor to a trustee on trust for his creditors, which in some cases may be revoked. This is contrary to the normal rule that an *executed trust is irrevocable.

immigration *n.* The act of entering a country other than one's native country with the intention of living there permanently. Immigration into the UK is subject to control under the Immigration Act 1971. This control extends to all potential entrants except those to whom the Act gives the *right of abode* in the UK and except citizens of the Republic of Ireland. As originally enacted, the Act gave the right of abode to all citizens of the UK and Colonies who either owed their status to their own (or a parent's or grandparent's) birth, registration, or naturalization in the UK or were or became at any time settled in the UK and had at that time been ordinarily resident there for at least five years. Commonwealth citizens had the right of abode if one of their parents was a citizen of the UK and Colonies by reason of birth in the UK. A person having the right of abode was termed a *patrial*. As from 1 January 1983 the Act was amended by the British Nationality Act 1981 to confine the right of abode to *British citizens as defined by that Act and to *commonwealth citizens enjoying it before the Act came into force; the term patrial was discarded. With minor exceptions, a person subject to immigration control may not enter or remain in the UK except with leave, which may be granted either indefinitely or for a limited period; if leave is granted for a limited period, an immigrant is subject to further conditions (e.g. conditions restricting employment). The 1971 Act itself gave indefinite leave to stay to those not entitled to the right of abode but who were lawfully settled in the UK when it came into force. Whether or not leave is needed, whether it should be granted, and whether a time limit and any other conditions should be imposed are decided initially by immigration officers acting in accordance with immigration rules made by the Secretary of State. Appeals against the decisions of immigration officers are made to adjudicators at the ports of entry, and thence to the Immigration Appeal Tribunal.

Immigration Appeal Tribunal A tribunal appointed by the Lord Chancellor, under the Immigration Act 1971, to hear appeals against immigration and deportation decisions. It has a legally qualified chairman and is subject to the supervision of the *Council on Tribunals.

immoral contract A contract based on sexual immorality, such as a contract of prostitution. Such contracts are *illegal on the grounds that they contravene *public policy.

immovables *pl. n.* Tangible things that cannot be physically moved, particularly land and buildings.

immunity *n.* Freedom or exemption from legal proceedings. Examples include the immunity of the sovereign personally from all legal proceedings (*see* royal prerogative); the immunity of members of the House of Commons and the House of Lords from proceedings in respect of words spoken in debate (*see* parliamentary privilege); *judicial immunity; and the immunity from the jurisdiction of national courts enjoyed by members of diplomatic missions and by foreign sovereigns (*see* diplomatic immunity; sovereign immunity).

imparlance *n.* Permission given to a defendant to delay his answer to the plaintiff's claim, to enable him to attempt to settle the claim amicably.

impeachable waste *Waste that results in liability on the part of the person who commits it. Thus when a tenant commits impeachable waste his landlord may sue him for damages or obtain an injunction to prevent him committing any further waste.

impeding apprehension or prosecution Giving assistance to a criminal with the intention of preventing or delaying his capture, arrest, or prosecution (*see* assisting an offender). There are also special offences of (1) agreeing not to disclose information that might help to convict or prosecute a criminal

(*see* compounding an offence), (2) refusing to aid a police officer when asked to help stop a breach of the peace, and (3) wasting police time by giving them misleading information. *See also* escape.

imperfect gift *See* gift.

imperfect trust *See* executory trust.

impersonation *n.* Pretending to be another person. It is an offence to use impersonation to persuade a woman to have sexual intercourse, to impersonate the holder of a Crown office in order to gain access to prohibited places, and to impersonate a juror. Obtaining property, services, or certain financial advantages through impersonation may amount to the crime of *deception.

implied condition A term or obligation implied by law in a contract, any breach of which will entitle the innocent party not only to damages but to treat the contract as discharged (*see* condition). In a contract of sale of goods there are implied conditions that the seller has the right to sell the goods, that the goods will correspond with the contract description, and, in the case of sales in the course of business, that the goods are of *merchantable quality and fit for the buyer's declared purpose.

implied contract A contract not created by express words but inferred by the courts either from the conduct of the parties or from some special relationship existing between them.

implied malice *Mens rea* that the law considers sufficient for a crime, although there is no intention to commit that crime. The term is usually now used only in relation to murder, referring to the intention to cause grievous bodily harm (*see* malice aforethought).

implied term A provision of a contract not agreed to by the parties in words but either regarded by the courts as necessary to give effect to their presumed intentions or introduced into the contract by statute (as in the case of contracts for the sale of goods; *see caveat emptor*). An implied term may constitute either a *condition of the contract or a warranty; if it is introduced by statute it often cannot be expressly excluded. *Compare* express term.

implied trust A trust that arises either from the presumed but unexpressed intention of the settlor or by operation of law. Equity imposes an obligation to create such trusts by inference from the facts, including the conduct or situation of the parties. An implied trust may be subdivided into or overlap with *resulting trusts and *constructive trusts.

implied use *See* resulting use.

importune *vb.* To solicit (*see* soliciting). It is a statutory offence for a man to persistently (i.e. more than once) importune for immoral purposes in a public place. There is no fixed definition of "immoral purposes", which is left for the jury to decide; it may include noncriminal conduct, such as permitted *homosexual conduct.

impossibility of performance The impossibility of carrying out a contract, which occurs, for example, when it relates to subject matter that does not exist. The event making fulfilment impossible may arise either before or after the contract is made. In the former case (e.g. if X agrees to sell Y a horse that, unknown to either, is already dead) the contract is void for *mistake. In the latter case (e.g. if the horse dies between contract and performance) the contract will be discharged under the doctrine of *frustration.

impotence *n.* The inability of either partner to have normal sexual intercourse (*see also* consummation of a marriage). In the case of a married couple this is sometimes called *canonical disability* (i.e. a disability recognized by canon law as a ground for annulment of the marriage). If the impotence is permanent and incurable, the marriage is voidable and either party may apply for a nullity decree. Impotence must be distinguished from *wilful refusal to consummate.

imprisonment *n.* *See* sentence; false imprisonment; life imprisonment.

improvement *n.* (of rented premises) An addition or alteration that improves the premises from the tenant's point of view; it does not necessarily have to increase the value of the premises. In the case of a lease that contains an obligation by the tenant to obtain the landlord's consent before making improvements, the landlord cannot withhold his consent unreasonably. He can, however, claim from the tenant any expense or loss he suffers as a result and he can require the tenant, at the end of the tenancy, to put the premises back into the condition they were in before the improvement was carried out. When rented dwellings lack certain basic amenities, such as a bath, the local authority can require the landlord to provide these amenities and carry out other repairs and improvements after service of an *improvement notice. In the case of business tenancies and agricultural holdings, the tenant can claim compensation for improvements.

improvement notice 1. A local-authority notice requiring a person to provide a dwelling under his control with certain standard amenities (e.g. a bath). If he fails to do this the authority may do so at his expense. **2.** A notice requiring any person responsible for a breach of the Health and Safety at Work Act 1974 (or associated legislation) to take steps to remedy the breach or prevent its repetition. *Compare* prohibition notice.

imputation *n.* An allegation of misconduct or bad character made by an accused against the prosecutor or one of his witnesses. When this occurs the accused may (under the Criminal Evidence Act 1898), with *leave of the court, be cross-examined about his own *previous convictions and bad character.

imputation of unchastity A statement imputing unchastity or adultery to a woman or girl, which is defamatory and actionable whether or not it has caused actual financial or material loss. *See* slander; defamation.

imputation of unfitness or incompetence A statement calculated to disparage someone in his office, profession, calling, trade, or business, which is defamatory and actionable whether or not it has caused actual financial or material loss. *See* slander; defamation.

imputation system A system of taxation applying to the payment of *corporation tax on the distributed profits of a company. In this system, which has been in force in the UK since April 1973, that part of the tax paid by the company as *advance corporation tax (ACT) is imputed to the shareholders and their dividends are franked (*see* franked income) accordingly.

If a company has £10,000 of taxable profits (distributed and undistributed) and the current rate of corporation tax is 38%, it would have a corporation-tax liability of £3800. If the company distributed £2100 to its shareholders in a year in which the basic rate of income tax was 30%, the distribution to the shareholders would be treated by the Inland Revenue as a gross dividend of £3000 from which income tax at 30% had been deducted. The company would pay the tax of £900 to the Inland Revenue as ACT. This would be credited against its total corporation tax liability of £3800. Shareholders would have discharged their basic-rate income-tax liability and their dividend slips would be franked to show the amount of tax imputed to them. If the recipient is a company the amount is imputed to its own liability to corporation tax. *See also* qualifying distribution.

inadmissible reason (in employment law) A reason for dismissing an employee that is based on his membership or participation in the activities of an *independent trade union or his refusal to become or remain a member of a union that is not independent. Dismissal for an inadmissible reason is always treated as *unfair dismissal, and the employee may apply to an *industrial tribunal whatever his age and length of continuous employment. *See also* compensation.

inalienability *n.* *See* rule against inalienability.

in camera [Latin: in the chamber] In private. A court hearing must usually be public but the public may be barred from the court or the hearing may continue in the judge's private room in certain circumstances; for example, when it is necessary for public safety or when a child gives evidence in a case involving indecency.

incapacity *n.* A lack of full legal competence in any respect; for example, the incapacity of minors to conclude valid contracts (*see* capacity to contract). A person suffering from incapacity is frequently referred to as a *person under disability*.

incest *n.* Sexual intercourse between a man and his mother, daughter, sister, half-sister, or granddaughter or between a woman over the age of 16 and her father, son, brother, half-brother, or grandfather. Even if both parties consent, incest is a criminal offence if the parties know of their relationship. It is punishable by up to seven years' imprisonment (or, with a girl under the age of 13, by a maximum sentence of life imprisonment), but no prosecution may be brought without the consent of the Director of Public Prosecutions. The relationships listed above include illegitimate relationships. It is a statutory offence for a man to incite a girl under the age of 16 to have incestuous intercourse with him, but being under 16, she would not be guilty of any crime if intercourse took place.

Inchmaree clause A clause frequently inserted in marine insurance policies to provide cover for a variety of risks that are not covered as *perils of the seas. It provides protection against such events as accidents in loading or discharging cargo or taking on fuel, bursting of boilers, breakage of shafts, and explosions on board ship or elsewhere.

inchoate *adj.* Incomplete. Certain acts, although not constituting a complete offence, are nonetheless prohibited by the criminal law because they constitute steps towards the complete offence. These inchoate offences include *incitement, *attempt, and *conspiracy. One may be guilty of inciting someone to commit the crime of incitement or of attempting to incite, but one cannot be guilty of incitement to conspire or of attempting to conspire.

incitement *n.* Persuading or attempting to persuade someone else to commit a crime. If the other person then actually carries out the criminal act, the inciter becomes a participator in the crime and is guilty of aiding or abetting. If the other person does not carry out the crime, the person who attempted to persuade him to do so may nonetheless be guilty of the crime of incitement. Incitement may be by means of suggestion, persuasion, threats, or pressure, by words or by implication; for example, advertising an article for sale to be used to commit an offence may constitute incitement to commit that offence.

incitement to racial hatred Acting in a manner likely to stir up hatred against any racial group in Great Britain. Such behaviour is a crime, punishable with up to two years' imprisonment and/or a fine on indictment, if it consists of publishing or distributing anything in writing (or any visible representation) that is either threatening, abusive, or insulting or of using threatening, abusive, or insulting words in a public place or at a public meeting. There need be no intention to stir up racial hatred nor any awareness that the words are threatening, abusive, or insulting; the offence is committed if the behaviour is likely to stir up hatred. There is a special defence, however, in the case of written material, if the defendant proves that he did not know (and had no reason to suspect) that it was threatening, abusive, or insulting. There are also exceptions for fair and accurate reporting of parliamentary debates or public judicial proceedings. *See also* racial discrimination.

income tax A tax on a person's wages or salary and on most other sources of income, including unearned income and the profits from an unincorporated business. The amount of tax is based on the person's entire income for the year, less certain allowances, on a progressive basis. The effect is that those with higher incomes pay higher rates of tax. The allowances include a personal allowance (under the 1983 Budget proposals, single: £1785, married: £2795, for wife's earned income: £1785), allowances for dependent relatives, mortgage interest, certain life assurance premiums, and pension contributions.

The first £12,800 of taxable income is charged at 30% (this is known as the *basic rate*); any further income is charged at progressively higher rates up to a maximum of 60%. *Investment income is charged at higher rates. Although assessed annually, in many cases tax is deducted at source, in particular by employers (*see* Pay As You Earn). For tax purposes, the income of a married woman living with her husband is treated as belonging to the husband. However, they can choose to be taxed separately. Nonresidents in the UK are subject to income tax if their income originates in the UK, as are UK residents who receive income from abroad.

incompletely constituted trust

However, there are agreements with many countries to give relief against double taxation. Certain income is exempt from tax, including the interest paid by most building societies (this is exempt from the basic rate), interest on national savings certificates, most social security benefits, and redundancy payments up to £25,000.

Income tax was introduced as a temporary measure in 1799. It is renewed annually in a Finance Act, which traditionally enacts the Chancellor of the Exchequer's Budget proposals. The types of taxable income are set out in the Income and Corporation Taxes Act 1970 under six schedules:

A: payments from UK land;

B: occupation of commercial woodlands;

C: public revenue dividends;

D: annual profits or gains of any trade, profession, or vocation; interest, annuities, and annual payments discounts; and income from securities or possessions outside the UK;

E: *emoluments from offices and employments;

F: distributions, etc.

incompletely constituted trust *See* executory trust.

inconsiderate driving Driving a car or other vehicle on a road, without reasonable consideration for other road users. The offence includes, for instance, deliberately driving through a puddle so as to drench pedestrians or driving so as to force pedestrians or other drivers to move out of the way; to constitute an offence, the act must affect some other road user. Such behaviour may also constitute *careless driving. The offence requires *notice of intended prosecution.

incorporation *n.* **1.** The formation of an association that has *corporate personality*, i.e. a personality distinct from those of its members. A corporation (such as a company) has wide legal capacity (subject to the doctrine of *ultra

vires): it can own property and incur debts. Company members have no liability to company creditors for such debts (though they may be under some liability to their company). An incorporated company has its own rights and liabilities and legal proceedings in respect of them should be brought by and against it in its own name (*but see* derivative action). It can be convicted of crimes; when *mens rea is a requirement of the offence, the *mens rea* of the officers responsible may be attributed to the company. A company is usually incorporated by *registration under the Companies Acts 1948–81 but there are other methods (e.g. by royal charter or private Act of Parliament). *See also* certificate of incorporation; lifting the veil. **2.** *See* doctrine of incorporation.

incorporation by reference Reference in a will to another document without which the will cannot be understood (the document then forms part of the will). For example, a will leaving a specified sum "to each of the persons listed in my notebook" incorporates the notebook.

incorporeal hereditament *See* hereditament.

incriminate *vb.* **1.** To charge with a criminal offence. **2.** To indicate involvement in the commission of a criminal offence. A witness in court need not answer a question if, in the judge's opinion, the answer might expose him to the danger of criminal prosecution. A witness does not have this protection when his answer might lead only to civil action against him.

incumbrance *n. See* encumbrance.

indecency *n.* Conduct that the average man would find shocking or revolting. There are common-law offences of outraging public decency and conspiring to outrage public decency (*see* conspiracy); examples might include staging an indecent exhibition, keeping a *brothel, or *indecent exposure. Indecency is a question of fact that is left in each case to the jury to decide. *See also* gross indecency.

indecent assault An *assault or *battery in circumstances of indecency. If committed against a woman (either by a man or by another woman) it is punishable by up to two years' imprisonment; indecent assault against a man (either by a woman or by another man) is punishable by up to ten years' imprisonment. Consent is normally a defence, except when the victim is under the age of 16. Touching or attempting to touch the genitals of another person without their consent would constitute an indecent assault. *See also doli capax*; gross indecency; indecent exposure.

indecent exposure Exposing one's body in public in a way that outrages public decency. When the exposure (by a man or woman) goes far beyond the generally accepted standards of decency and at least two people could have seen it, it amounts to a common-law offence, even if no one was actually disgusted or upset. If a man exposes his genitals to a woman, even in private, with the intention of insulting her, he is guilty of a statutory offence and is liable to imprisonment. Such conduct, if threatening or frightening, may also amount to an *indecent assault.

indefeasible *adj.* Incapable of being made *void.

indemnity *n.* An agreement by one person (X) to pay to another (Y) sums that are owed, or may become owed, to him by a third person (Z). It is not conditional on the third person defaulting on the payment, i.e. Y can sue X without first demanding payment from Z. If it is conditional on the third person's default (i.e. if Z remains the principal debtor and must be sued for the money first) it is not an indemnity but a *guarantee. Unlike a guarantee, an indemnity need not be evidenced in writing. *See also* (indemnity) insurance.

indemnity basis A basis of taxation of *costs under which the receiving party recovers all costs incurred except any that have been unreasonably incurred or are of an unreasonable amount. The receiving party is given the benefit of any doubt on questions of reasonableness.

indenture *n.* A deed, generally one creating or transferring an estate in land (e.g. a conveyance or a lease).

independent contractor A person or firm engaged to do a particular job of work, as opposed to a person under a *contract of employment. An independent contractor is his own master, bound to do the job he has contracted to do but having a discretion as to how to do it. A taxi-driver, for example, is the independent contractor of the passenger who hires him. A person who employs an independent contractor is not generally vicariously liable for torts committed by the contractor; situations in which *vicarious liability is imposed include those in which the contractor is employed in particularly hazardous activities, to perform statutory duties or powers, or to work on or over (but not merely near) the highway.

independent trade union A trade union holding a certificate of independence issued by the *Certification Officer. A certificate will only be issued if the union is not under the domination or control of any employer, group of employers, or employers' association and is not liable to any interference from them tending towards such control. A union that is refused a certificate of independence may appeal to the *Employment Appeal Tribunal. Trade unions that do not hold a certificate of independence cannot conclude a collective agreement restricting employees' rights to strike and have no statutory right to certain information that employers must disclose to recognized independent trade unions (*see* disclosure of information). Only officials of independent trade unions have a statutory right to time off work to pursue union activities and duties. Rules regarding the dismissal of an employee for an *inadmissible reason and rules that prohibit employers from taking other action to deter employees from participating in a union only apply if the union holds a certificate of independence.

indictable offence An offence that may be tried on *indictment, i.e. by jury in the Crown Court. Most serious common-law offences are indictable (e.g. murder, rape) and many are created by statute. When statute creates an offence without specifying how it is to be tried, it is automatically an indictable offence. An attempt to commit an indictable offence is itself an indictable offence; the same is not true for a *summary offence. Some indictable offences, if not very serious, may be tried either by magistrates or on indictment (*see* offences triable either way).

indictment *n.* A formal document accusing one or more persons of committing a specified *indictable offence or offences. It is read out to the accused at the trial. An indictment is in a particular form. It is headed with the name of the case and the place of trial. There is then a statement of offence, stating what crime has allegedly been committed, followed by particulars of offence, i.e. such details as the date and place of the offence, property stolen, etc. If the accused is charged with more than one offence, each allegation and charge appears in a separate paragraph called a *count.* Counts may, however, be *framed in the alternative,* i.e. two or more counts may charge different offences arising out of the same allegation of fact but the defendant may be convicted of only one of them; for example, when a defendant is charged as a principal in one count and as an accessory in another in respect of the same

incident. *See also* bill of indictment; trial on indictment.

indirect evidence *See* circumstantial evidence.

indivisible contract *See* performance of contract.

indorsement *n.* *See* endorsement.

inducement *n.* **1.** The promise of some advantage (e.g. bail) held out by a person in authority in relation to a prosecution to a person suspected of having committed a criminal offence. A *confession made after an inducement has been offered is inadmissible: relatively slight inducements are sufficient for this purpose. **2.** *See* misrepresentation.

industrial death benefit A state pension payable to the widow of a man who has died from injuries sustained in the course of his employment or from a prescribed industrial disease. A widower whose wife has died from such a cause may also claim if he is unable to support himself.

industrial democracy Participation in company management by employees. The *Bullock Report* (1977) recommended that the board of directors of large companies should be reconstituted to include not only directors elected by company members but also an equal number elected by employees. *See also* employees' share scheme.

industrial development certificate A certificate that must be obtained from the Department of the Environment before application may be made for planning permission to develop land for industrial purposes.

industrial disablement benefit A pension or lump sum payable by the state to a person disabled by injury or a prescribed industrial disease sustained or contracted in the course of his employment. A lump sum is paid when the degree of disablement is assessed at less than 20% and a weekly pension when the degree of disablement is greater. In each case the amount of the benefit depends on the degree of disablement, which is assessed by a specialist or a board of two doctors. The benefit is payable from three days after the injury occurs or the disease develops, when this does not prevent the employee from working; otherwise it is paid from the end of the 26-week period during which *industrial injury benefit is payable.

industrial dispute *See* trade dispute.

industrial injury benefit A state benefit payable weekly to an employee who is prevented from working by injuries sustained, or a prescribed industrial disease contracted, in the course of his employment. It must be claimed within 21 days (on the first occasion), or 6 days thereafter, of the employee becoming incapable of work. It is payable only while the employee remains incapable of work and for a maximum of 26 weeks. Thereafter, he may qualify for *industrial disablement benefit.

industrial tribunal Any of the bodies established under the employment protection legislation to hear and rule on certain disputes between employers and employees or trade unions relating to statutory terms and conditions of employment. For example, the tribunals hear complaints concerning *unfair dismissal, *redundancy, *equal pay, and *maternity rights. The tribunal usually consists of a legally qualified chairman and two independent laymen. It differs from a civil court in that it cannot enforce its own awards (this must be done by separate application to a court) and it can conduct its proceedings informally. Strict rules of evidence need not apply and the parties can present their own case or be represented by anyone they wish at their own expense; legal aid is not available. The tribunal has wide powers to declare a party in breach of a *contract of employment, to award *compensation, and to order

the *reinstatement or *re-engagement of a dismissed employee.

Before conducting a full hearing of the case, the tribunal may consider (on either party's application or on its own initiative) what the parties have said in the written complaint to the tribunal (the *originating application*) and the answer to it (the *notice of appearance*). If these suggest that either party is unlikely to succeed, the tribunal may warn him that he may be ordered to pay the other's costs if he insists on pursuing his case to a full hearing. This procedure is called a *prehearing assessment*. When a full hearing takes place, the tribunal will not award costs to the successful party unless the other has been warned of this likelihood at a prehearing assessment or has acted vexatiously, frivolously, or unreasonably in bringing or defending the proceedings.

inevitable accident An accident that could not have been prevented by the exercise of ordinary care and skill.

infant (minor) *n.* Since 1969, a child under the age of 18. Certain rights (such as parents' rights to custody, the right to make a child a ward of court, and the right to withhold consent to marriage) only apply to infants. Other rights (such as the right to marry with consent) are governed by different age limits, often 16. Infants have a limited *capacity to contract.

infanticide *n.* The killing of a child under 12 months old by its mother. If the mother can show that the balance of her mind was disturbed because of the effects of the childbirth or lactation, she will be found guilty of infanticide, rather than murder, and punished as though she was guilty of *manslaughter. Most cases of infanticide are dealt with by probation or discharge. *See also* diminished responsibility.

inferior court Any of the courts that are subordinate to *superior courts, having a jurisdiction limited to a particular geographical area, size of claim, or type of case. Their decisions are normally subject to appeal to a superior court, and the exercise of their jurisdiction may be subject to control by a superior court. In England and Wales, *county courts and *magistrates' courts are inferior courts.

information *n. See* laying an information.

informer *n.* A person who gives information to the police about crimes committed by others. An informer who is himself involved in the crimes may sometimes receive a lighter sentence in return for cooperation with the police that leads to the conviction of other offenders. The police may not employ their own informers, however, to participate in crimes and then arrest the criminals, and a police informer who pretends to join a plot to commit a crime may himself be guilty of *conspiracy. It is generally thought, however, that if a police informer pretends to help in committing a crime with the intention of frustrating it, he will not be considered an *accessory if he fails to prevent the crime taking place.

in gross Absolute, i.e. existing in its own right and not as ancillary to land or any other thing. For example a profit *à prendre* can exist in gross, conferring rights on persons whether or not they own land capable of benefiting. An easement cannot exist in gross since there must be a dominant tenement.

inherent vice An inherent defect in certain goods that makes them liable to damage. Some fibres, for example, are liable to rot during shipment. If a carrier or insurer of such goods has not been warned of the inherent vice, he will not be liable for damage resulting directly from the defect.

inheritance *n.* **1.** The devolution of property on the death of its owner, either according to the provisions of his will or under the rules relating to intes-

tacy contained in the Administration of Estates Act 1925 as amended. **2.** Property that a beneficiary receives from the estate of a deceased person.

inhibition *n.* (in land law) An entry in the proprietorship register relating to registered land (*see* land registration) that prohibits the registration of any dealing with the land (such as a transfer or mortgage) for a specified time or until a specified event occurs. An inhibition may be registered on the application of any person having a sufficient interest; for example, when the owner of land claims that another has become registered as proprietor by fraud. An inhibition must be registered when a receiving order in bankruptcy is made against the proprietor or when registered land is transferred to the incumbent of a benefice.

injunction *n.* A remedy in the form of a court *order addressed to a particular person that either prohibits him from doing or continuing to do a certain act (a *prohibitory injunction*) or orders him to carry out a certain act (a *mandatory injunction*). For example, a prohibitory injunction may be granted to restrain a nuisance or to stop the infringement of a copyright or trademark. A mandatory injunction may be granted to order a person to demolish a wall that he has built in breach of covenant. The remedy is discretionary and will not be granted if damages would be a sufficient remedy.

Injunctions are often needed urgently. A temporary injunction (*interlocutory injunction*) may therefore be granted at a special hearing pending the outcome of the main hearing of the case. If it is granted, the plaintiff must undertake to compensate the defendant for any damage he has suffered by the grant of the injunction if the defendant is successful in the main action. If judgment is given for the plaintiff in the main action, a *perpetual injunction* is granted. A person who fails to abide by the terms of an injunction is guilty of *contempt of court. *See also ex parte*; *quia timet*.

injurious falsehood *See* malicious falsehood.

injury *n.* **1.** Infringement of a right. **2.** Actual harm caused to people or property.

injury benefit *See* industrial injury benefit.

inland bill A *bill of exchange that is (or on the face of it purports to be) both drawn and payable within the British Islands or drawn within the British Islands upon some person resident there. All other bills are foreign bills. Unless the contrary appears on the face of a bill, the holder may treat it as an inland bill. The distinction is relevant to the steps taken when a bill has been dishonoured (*see* dishonour).

Inland Revenue, Board of The body responsible for the care, management, and collection of most taxes within the UK. The officials of which it is made up are the Commissioners. The day-to-day administration is carried out by civil servants. Inspectors of Taxes are responsible for assessing taxes, which are collected by Collectors of Taxes. A taxpayer can appeal against an inspector's assessment either to the General Commissioners for his district (lay persons appointed to hear appeals) or to a Special Commissioner (a full-time official appointed by the Treasury to hear appeals).

in limine [Latin] Preliminary: used, for example, to describe an objection or pleading.

in loco parentis [Latin] In place of a parent: used loosely to describe anyone looking after children on behalf of the parents, e.g. foster parents or relatives. In law, however, only a guardian or custodian stands *in loco parentis*; their rights and duties are determined by statutory provisions.

Inner Temple An *Inn of Court situated in the Temple between the Strand and the Embankment. The earliest recorded claim for its existence is 1440. Its Hall and Library were destroyed by bombing in World War II but have since been rebuilt.

innocent misrepresentation *See* misrepresentation.

Inns of Chancery Formerly, Inns similar but subordinate to the *Inns of Court, to which they were attached (for example, Staple Inn and Barnard's Inn were attached to Gray's Inn). Originally they were societies in which students prepared for admission to the Inns of Court; later they became societies of attorneys. They were dissolved in the late 19th century.

Inns of Court Ancient legal societies situated in central London; every *barrister must belong to one of these societies. The early history of the Inns is disputed, but they probably began as hostels in which those who practised in the common law courts lived. These hostels gradually evolved a corporate life in which *Benchers, barristers, and students lived together as a self-regulating body. From an early date they had an important role in legal education. In modern times four Inns survive: *Gray's Inn, *Inner Temple, *Lincoln's Inn, and *Middle Temple.

innuendo *n.* In an action for *defamation, a statement in which the plaintiff explains the defamatory meaning of apparently innocent words that he alleges are defamatory. The plaintiff must set out in his pleadings the facts or circumstances making the words defamatory.

in personam [Latin: against the person] Describing a court action or a claim made against a specific person or a right affecting a particular person or group of people (*compare in rem*). The *maxim of equity "equity acts *in personam*" refers to the fact that the Court of Chancery issued its decrees against the defendant himself, who was liable to imprisonment if he did not enforce them.

inquest *n.* An inquiry into a death the cause of which is unknown. An inquest is conducted by a *coroner and often requires the decision of a jury of 7–11 jurors. It must be held in the case of a sudden death whose cause is unknown or suspicious, a death occurring in prison, or when the coroner reasonably suspects that the death was caused by violent or unnatural means. Inquests are not, however, criminal proceedings; witnesses are usually cross-examined only by the coroner and the strict laws of evidence do not apply. If unlawful *homicide is suspected, and criminal proceedings are likely, the coroner will usually adjourn the inquest (and must do so if requested to by a chief police officer). If the inquest jury find that a particular person caused the death in circumstances amounting to homicide, that person may stand trial. It is an offence to bury a body with the intention of preventing an inquest being held.

inquisition *n.* A document containing the verdict of a coroner's *inquest. It consists of the *caption* (details of the coroner, jury, and the inquest hearing), the *verdict* (identification of the body and probable cause of death), and the *attestation* (signatures of the coroner and jurors). An *open verdict* may be recorded when there is insufficient evidence of the cause of death.

inquisitorial procedure A system of criminal justice, in force in some European countries but not in England, in which the truth is revealed by an inquiry into the facts conducted by the judge. In this system it is the judge who takes the initiative in conducting the case, rather than the prosecution or defence; his role is to lead the investigations, examine the evidence, and interrogate the witnesses. *Compare* accusatorial procedure.

in re [Latin: in the matter of] A phrase is used in the headings of law reports, together with the name of the person or thing that the case is about (for example, cases in which wills are being interpreted). It is often abbreviated to *re*, in which form it is used in headings to letters, etc.

in rem [Latin: against the thing] **1.** Describing a right that should be respected by other people generally, such as ownership of property, as distinct from a right **in personam.* **2.** Describing a court action that is directed against an item of property, rather than against a person or group of people. Actions *in rem* are a feature of the *Admiralty Court.

insanity *n.* Mental abnormality or disturbance. For the purposes of criminal law, a person accused of a crime is presumed sane and therefore responsible for his acts, but he can rebut this presumption and escape a conviction if he can prove that at the time of committing the crime he was insane. For purposes of this defence, insanity is defined by the *McNaghten Rules. Medical evidence may be brought, but the jury are entitled to form their opinion on the facts. To succeed in a defence of insanity, the defendant must prove his case on a balance of probabilities. If found to be insane within the meaning of the McNaghten Rules, he is given a *special verdict* of "not guilty by reason of insanity" and may be admitted to hospital. He is entitled to appeal against this verdict. In cases of homicide, the accused must be sent to hospital (usually a *special hospital, such as Broadmoor). Magistrates' courts, however, are not empowered to return a special verdict. They will either grant a complete acquittal, if the defendant's evidence of mental abnormality amounts to a denial that he had the necessary *mens rea* for the crime, or they may make a *hospital order, if the crime with which he is charged is one for which they could usually imprison him.

If someone in custody for trial is suffering from mental illness or severe subnormality, he may be detained in hospital and not brought to trial until he is fit. A person who is insane at the time of his trial, in the sense that he does not understand the charge and cannot properly instruct his lawyers, may be found *unfit to plead.

See also automatism; diminished responsibility; irresistible impulse.

insider dealing Dealing in company securities with a view to making a profit or avoiding a loss while in possession of information that, if generally known, would affect thier price. Under the Companies Act 1980 those who are or have been connected with a company (e.g. directors, the company secretary, employees, and professional advisers) are prohibited from such dealing on or, in certain circumstances, off the *Stock Exchange if they acquired the information by virtue of their connection and in confidence. The prohibition extends to certain unconnected persons to whom the information has been conveyed.

inspection and investigation of a company An inquiry into the running of a company made by inspectors appointed by the Department of Trade. Such an inquiry may be held to supply company members with information or to investigate fraud, unfair prejudice, nominee shareholdings, or share dealings by directors. The inspectors' report is usually published.

inspection by judge *See* view.

inspection of documents *See* discovery and inspection of documents.

inspection of property (in court procedure) The High Court or the county courts may order the inspection, photographing, preservation, custody, and detention of any property that is (or may become) the subject matter of

proceedings or in respect of which any questions may arise in proceedings. If the action is one in respect of personal injuries, such an order may be obtained after the commencement of the action against someone who is not a party to it. If the order is sought before proceedings are initiated it is made by *originating summons; if after, it is made by *summons.

instant committal A short committal under section 1 of the Criminal Justice Act 1967. *See* committal for trial.

insufficient evidence A direction by a judge to a jury that, as a matter of law, the evidence does not entitle them to make a certain finding. For example, if there is insufficient evidence for a conviction, the judge may direct the jury to return a verdict of not guilty.

insulting behaviour Conduct or words that offend other people. It is an offence to use insulting words or behaviour in a public place or at a public meeting if this is intended or likely to cause a *breach of the peace. It is also an offence to use threatening or abusive words or behaviour in public or to show or distribute any writing, sign, picture, etc., that is threatening, insulting, or abusive. The penalty is up to six months' imprisonment and/or a fine of up to £1000. *See also* incitement to racial hatred.

insurable interest An interest (financial or otherwise) in the subject matter of a contract of *insurance, which provides the person insured with the right to enforce the contract. An insurable interest (e.g. ownership of goods insured) distinguishes a contract of insurance from a wager or bet: the insured person stands to lose if the eventuality insured against occurs. An interest is required by statute for various types of insurance contract (e.g. life insurance).

insurance *n.* A contract in which one party (the *insurer*) agrees for payment of a consideration (the *premium*) to make monetary provision for the other (the *insured*) upon the occurrence of some event or against some risk. For such contracts to be enforceable, there must be some element of uncertainty about the events insured against and the insured must have an *insurable interest in the subject matter of the contract. (The term *assurance* has the same meaning as insurance but is generally used in relation to events that will definitely happen at some time or another (especially death), whereas insurance refers to events that may or may not happen.) There are two types of insurance: *indemnity insurance*, which provides an indemnity against loss and in which the measure of the loss is the measure of payment (e.g. a fire policy); and *contingency insurance*, which involves payment on a contingent event and in which the sum paid is not measured by the loss but stated in the policy (e.g. a life policy). A contract of insurance is one requiring the utmost good faith (*see uberrimae fidei*) and is voidable if the party seeking insurance fails in preliminary negotiations to disclose a fact material to the risk. It may also be made voidable by innocent or fraudulent *misrepresentation or terminated for breach of an essential term (*see* warranty). Particular types of insurance include *life assurance, fire insurance, liability insurance, motor-vehicle insurance (*see* third-party insurance), *marine insurance, and guarantee insurance. There is considerable statutory regulation of insurance business.

Insurers are either *insurance companies* or *Lloyd's underwriters. Insurance companies are regulated by statute, aimed, among other things, at ensuring the insurance companies have sufficient funds to meet all claims made on them. *Insurance brokers* negotiate insurance contracts with insurance companies or Lloyd's underwriters on a commission basis and usually handle claims on their clients' behalf. In the event of a claim the insured receives either the amount agreed in the policy or an appropriate sum that is calculated by an independent *insurance assessor*.

insurance broker *See* insurance.

insurance company *See* insurance.

insurance policy A formal document issued by an insurer setting out the terms of a contract of *insurance. Insurance contracts are not required by law to be in writing. Before the issue of a policy an insurer may issue a *cover note*, which is itself a temporary contract of insurance.

intangible property *Property that has no physical existence: *choses in action and incorporeal *hereditaments.

intention *n.* The state of mind of one who aims or desires to bring about a particular consequence. Intention is one of the main forms of *mens rea*, and for some crimes the only form (for example, in the crime of threatening to destroy someone's property, with the intention that he should fear that the threat will be carried out). A person is assumed to intend those consequences of his acts that are inevitable but cannot be presumed to intend a consequence merely because it is probable or natural. In the latter case, the jury must decide, on all the available evidence, whether or not in fact the accused did intend the consequences. For purposes of the law of murder, however, a person is presumed to intend to cause death if he foresees that it is a highly likely consequence of his acts. This is sometimes known as *oblique intention*. Intention is often contrasted with *recklessness. For some purposes, offences are divided into crimes of basic intention or specific intention (*see* intoxication).

intention of testator The meaning that a testator intends his will to have. In interpreting a will, the court seeks to give effect to the intention of the testator as expressed in the will and will not generally hear evidence to show that his real intention was different from clear provisions in the document. *See also* armchair principle; interpretation of wills.

interest *n.* (in land law) A right in or over land. It may comprise equitable ownership of the land (such as the interest of the tenant for life under a settlement), where the legal estate is owned by trustees; or the benefit of some other right over the land of another, such as an easement or rent-charge. Interests of the latter type can be legal or equitable, but under the Law of Property Act 1925 only interests owned on terms equivalent to a *fee simple absolute in possession or a *term of years absolute qualify as legal interests. A person interested in land is one who has rights in it. *See also* equitable interests.

interest in expectancy Any future interest in property.

interfering with subsisting contract *See* procuring breach of contract.

interfering with vehicles *See* loitering.

interfering with witnesses Attempting to prevent a witness from giving evidence or to influence the evidence he gives. Making improper threats against witnesses may amount to the common-law offence of *perverting the course of justice; persuading a witness to tell a lie constitutes – in addition to this – the offence of subornation of *perjury. It is also perverting the course of justice to put pressure upon a witness to give evidence or to pay him money to testify in a particular way. Sometimes interfering with witnesses may also amount to *contempt of court. There is also a separate common-law offence of *tampering with witnesses* when one uses threats to persuade them not to give evidence.

interim payment Payment on account by a defendant of any damages, debt, or other sum (excluding costs) that he is

liable to pay to the plaintiff. The High Court (but not the county courts) may order a defendant to make an interim payment. When the plaintiff claims damages it is necessary to show that (1) the defendant has admitted liability; (2) the plaintiff has already obtained judgment for damages to be assessed; or (3) if the action proceeded to trial the plaintiff would obtain judgment for substantial damages. Application is made by *summons. Slightly different rules govern applications in respect of *mesne profits.

interim relief (interlocutory relief) A temporary remedy, such as an interlocutory *injunction or *interim payment, granted to a plaintiff by a court pending the trial. Application is made either by *summons or (in the Chancery Division) by *motion as directed by *rules of court.

interim rent Rent that a landlord can request a court to fix for a *business tenancy when he has given the tenant notice to quit or when the tenant has applied for a new tenancy.

interlineation *n.* Writing between the lines of a document. The effect is the same as that of an *alteration.

interlocutory appeal An appeal against an order made during the interlocutory (i.e. pre-trial) stage of civil litigation. In the High Court, appeal against an order by the master may be made to a judge as a matter of right; appeal from the judge to the *Court of Appeal requires leave of the judge or the Court of Appeal. In the county court, appeal lies from the *registrar to the judge and thence (with leave) to the Court of Appeal.

interlocutory injunction *See* injunction.

interlocutory judgment An interim *judgment in court proceedings: the decision only deals with part of the matter in dispute. *Compare* final judgment.

interlocutory proceedings

interlocutory proceedings The preliminary stages (such as *pleading and *discovery and inspection of documents) in civil proceedings, occurring between the issue of the originating process and the trial. Their principal functions are to define the issues that will have to be decided at the trial and to prevent *surprise.

interlocutory relief *See* interim relief.

international carriage The carriage of persons or goods between two or more nations, which is regulated by various international conventions. The international carriage of goods by sea is governed by the Hague Rules (1924), the Hague–Visby Rules (1968), and the Hamburg Rules (1978); that of goods by road by the Geneva Convention (1956); and that of goods by rail by a convention of 1970. (*See also* carriage of goods by air.) There are also conventions regulating the international carriage of passengers by sea, rail, and road. The UK is a party to various of these conventions and has legislated to give them legal effect; for example, the Carriage of Goods by Sea Act 1971 covers the Hague–Visby Rules.

International Court of Justice A court at The Hague, consisting of 15 judges elected for 9-year terms of office, that has power to determine disputes relating to international law. It was set up by the United Nations in succession to the Permanent Court of International Justice, and all members of the UN are automatically parties to the Statute of the Court. No state may be brought before the Court in contentious proceedings unless it has accepted its jurisdiction, either by agreement in a particular case or by recognition of the authority of the Court in general, in respect of any dispute with another state accepting the general jurisdiction of the Court (the *principle of reciprocity*). The Court may also give advisory opinions, which do not bind the parties but are of great *persuasive authority.

international law (*jus gentium,*** law of nations)** The system of law regulating the interrelationship of sovereign states and their rights and duties with regard to one another. In addition, certain international organizations (such as the *United Nations), companies, and sometimes individuals (e.g. in the sphere of *human rights) may have rights or duties under international law. International law deals with such matters as the formation and recognition of states, acquisition of territory, war, the law of the sea and of space, treaties, treatment of aliens, human rights, international crimes, and international judicial settlement of disputes. The usual sources of international law are (1) *conventions and *treaties; (2) international custom, insofar as this is evidence of a general practice of behaviour accepted as legally binding; (3) general principles of law recognized by civilized nations.

International law is also known as *public international law* to distinguish it from *private international law, which does not deal with relationships between states.

international supply contract A contract for the sale of goods made by parties whose places of business (or habitual residences) are in the territories of different states. The limitations imposed by the Unfair Contract Terms Act 1977 on the extent to which a person may exclude or restrict his liability (e.g. by an *exemption clause) do not apply to such a contract if (1) when it is made, the goods are in carriage (or due to be carried) from one state to another; (2) the offer and its acceptance take place in different states; or (3) the goods are to be delivered in a state other than that in which the offer and acceptance take place.

interpleader summons A procedure used to decide how conflicting claims against the same person should be dealt with. It applies when there are two or

interpretation of statutes

more claims against the applicant (whether or not court proceedings have been issued) that conflict with each other; for example, when two or more people claim the same goods that are being held by the applicant. The court decides how the matter should be dealt with; it may, for example, direct that there should be a court action between the rival claimants.

Interpleader can be of two types. A *stakeholder's interpleader* applies to any person holding any debt, goods, or chattels in respect of which there are rival claims. A *sheriff's interpleader* applies when the applicant is the *sheriff, who has to deal with rival claims after execution of a writ of *fieri facias* when a third party (e.g. a television rental company) claims that the goods seized belong to him.

interpretation (construction) *n.* The process of determining the true meaning of a written document. It is a judicial process, effected in accordance with a number of rules and presumptions. So far as is relevant, the rules and presumptions applicable to Acts of Parliament (*see* interpretation of statutes) apply equally to private documents, such as deeds and wills.

Interpretation Act An Act of 1978 (originally 1889) that defines a number of common words and expressions and provides that the same definitions are to apply in all other Acts except those specifically indicating otherwise. For example, "person" includes (in addition to an individual) any body of persons corporate or unincorporate.

interpretation clause A clause in a written document that defines words and phrases used in the document itself. In an Act of Parliament it is called an *interpretation section. See also* Interpretation Act.

interpretation of statutes The judicial process of determining, in accordance with certain rules and presumptions, the true meaning of Acts of Parliament. The principal rules of statutory interpretation are as follows.

(1) An Act must be construed as a whole, so that internal inconsistencies are avoided.

(2) Words that are reasonably capable of only one meaning must be given that meaning whatever the result. This is called the *literal rule.*

(3) Ordinary words must be given their ordinary meanings and technical words their technical meanings, unless absurdity would result. This is the *golden rule.*

(4) When an Act aims at curing a defect in the law any ambiguity is to be resolved in such a way as to favour that aim (the *mischief rule*).

(5) The *ejusdem generis rule* (of the same kind): when a list of specific items belonging to the same class is followed by general words (as in "cats, dogs, and other animals"), the general words are to be treated as confined to other items of the same class (in this example, to other *domestic* animals).

(6) The rule *expressio unius est exclusio alterius* (the inclusion of the one is the exclusion of the other): when a list of specific items is not followed by general words it is to be taken as exhaustive. For example, "weekends and public holidays" excludes ordinary weekdays.

The House of Lords has ruled against the existence of an alleged *social policy rule*, which would enable an ambiguous Act to be interpreted so as to best give effect to the social policy underlying it, and it is well established that ambiguities may not be resolved by looking at external matters, such as explanations of a proposed Act contained in a White Paper or given by ministers during its passage through Parliament.

There are some general presumptions relating to the interpretation of statutes. They are presumed (1) not to bind the Crown (including the sovereign personally); (2) not to operate retrospectively so far as substantive (but not procedural) law is concerned; (3) not to

189

interfere with vested rights (particularly without compensation); (4) not to oust the jurisdiction of the courts; and (5) not to derogate from constitutional rights or international law. But clear words or necessary implication may override these presumptions. A consolidating statute is presumed not be intended to alter the law, but this does not apply to codifying statutes, which may be concerned with clarifying law that was previously unclear. Penal and taxing statutes are subject to *strict construction*, i.e. if after applying the normal rules of interpretation it is still doubtful whether or not a penalty or tax attaches to a particular person or transaction, the ambiguity must be resolved in favour of the subject.

See also Interpretation Act; interpretation clause.

interpretation of wills The process of determining the true meaning of wills to give effect, as far as possible, to the testator's intention expressed in the will. Generally the words used are given their ordinary meaning except when this produces an ambiguous or unclear result. Evidence of relevant circumstances at the time the will was made may then be used to establish the testator's intention (*see* armchair principle). Such evidence may not be used to contradict a clear expression in the will. There are also many detailed rules relating to the meaning of particular phrases and to imprecise gifts for charitable purposes.

interregnum *n.* **1.** The period between the death of a sovereign and the accession of his or her successor. **2.** Temporary rule exercised during such a period. In the UK a sovereign's death does not result in an interregnum (*see* demise of the Crown).

interrogation *n.* The questioning of suspects by the police. Suspects are not obliged to answer such questions (*see* right of silence), and the right of the police to question suspects is governed by the *Judges' Rules. When children are questioned, Home Office directives require that, so far as possible, they should be questioned in the presence of their parents or (in the absence of parents) by a person who is not a police officer and is of the same sex as the child. In the case of a foreigner making a statement through an interpreter, the Judges' Rules require that the interpreter take the statement down in the suspect's native language and that the suspect should sign it. An official English translation should be made and proved as an *exhibit with the original statement.

interrogatory *n.* A formal written question submitted by one party to civil litigation to another party and required to be answered on oath. In modern practice, *leave of the court is required to administer an interrogatory and may only be given if the court considers it necessary either for disposing fairly of the case or matter or for saving costs. Interrogatories must relate to some matter in question in the case. *See also* fishing interrogatory.

in terrorem [Latin] Intimidating. The doctrine of *in terrorem* applies to conditions attached to gifts of personal property in wills or elsewhere. Such conditions are *in terrorem* if it is apparent that the donor does not really intend the recipient to lose the gift, but is merely making an idle threat; for example, when a donor makes a gift subject to a condition against marriage without another person's consent but does not make provision for the disposal of the gift if the recipient does not comply with the condition. Such conditions are void.

intestacy *n.* The state in which a person dies without having made a will disposing of all his property. A *total intestacy* occurs when the deceased leaves no will at all; a *partial intestacy* arises when a will deals with only part of the testator's estate. The Administration of

Estates Act 1925 as amended governs the manner in which an intestate estate is to be administered, the persons entitled to inherit, and the amounts and proportions of the estate they receive.

intimidation *n.* **1.** The act of frightening someone into doing something. Intimidation is not in itself a crime, but it may constitute part of a crime. For example, it is a crime to have sexual intercourse with a woman if her agreement was obtained by intimidation. It is a crime to intimidate a juror or witness in relation to proceedings with which he is connected (*see* contempt of court). If one intimidates someone into handing over money or property, this may amount to theft, and in some cases to blackmail. There are also special statutory offences of threatening to destroy or damage someone else's property and threatening to kill someone. A person who commits a crime when intimidated by others may sometimes have a defence of *duress. **2.** A tort in which A, with the intention of injuring B, threatens C with some unlawful act in order to make him cause damage to B. Thus if A threatens to do an unlawful act to B's employer (C) unless he dismisses B, and C succumbs to the threat, B has an action for intimidation against A for causing the loss of his job. It is irrelevant if C was entitled to dismiss B and did not act unlawfully: the essence of the tort is A's unlawful threat. The operation of the tort in *trade disputes is limited by statute.

intoxicating liquor For the purposes of the Licensing Act 1964, spirits, wine, beer, cider (including perry), and any other fermented, distilled, or spirituous liquor. *See also* licensing of premises.

intoxication *n.* The condition of someone who is drunk or under the influence of drugs. Although intoxication itself is not an offence (*but see* dangerous intoxication), it is an element in a number of offences. These include *drunken driving, being found drunk in a public place, being drunk and disorderly in a public place, and being drunk in a public place while possessing a loaded firearm. When a person is so intoxicated that he is incapable of forming the *mens rea* required to be guilty of a particular crime, he will usually have a defence of intoxication and is entitled to be acquitted if the crime is one that requires a *specific intention* (but not if it requires a *basic intention*). A crime is one of basic intent if the *mens rea* required does not go beyond the *actus reus* of the crime (for example, rape, in which the *actus reus* is sexual intercourse without the woman's consent and the *mens rea* is intention to have sexual intercourse without her consent, or recklessness whether she consents or not). A crime is one of specific intent if the *mens rea* required goes beyond the *actus reus* (for example, theft, in which the *actus reus* is merely appropriating someone else's property, but the *mens rea* – in addition to the intention of appropriating it – requires an intention to deprive the owner of it for good). Intoxication will not be a defence, however, if the crime is one of specific intent that can be committed by being reckless and the indictment is framed in terms of recklessness. For example, if a drunken person sets fire to a building and endangers the lives of people in it, he may be guilty of destroying property being reckless as to whether life would be endangered, even though he was unaware of the risk. He could not, however, be guilty of damaging property intending to endanger life. Intoxication is not a defence if a person deliberately drinks or takes drugs in order to give himself courage to commit a crime.

intra vires [Latin: within the powers] Describing an act carried out by a body (such as a public authority or a company) that is within the limits of the powers conferred on it by statute or some other constituting document. *Compare ultra vires.*

invalid care allowance A benefit under the Social Security Act 1975, payable in certain circumstances to a person of working age who is not gainfully employed because he (or she) is regularly and substantially engaged in caring for a severely disabled relative.

invalidity benefit A benefit under the Social Security Act 1975 that replaces sickness benefit after 28 consecutive six-day weeks. It consists of an invalidity pension plus an invalidity allowance when incapacity for work began more than five years before pensionable age.

inventory *n.* A detailed list of assets or property. A lease of furnished premises or a contract for the sale of chattels will usually contain an inventory from which the particular items can be identified. Under the Administration of Estates Act 1925, personal representatives must produce on oath an inventory of the deceased's estate when called upon by the court.

investment company A public listed company with a business of investing its funds mainly in securities in order to spread investment risk and give company members the benefit derived from the management of its funds. Investment companies must give notice in prescribed form to the Companies Registry. Under the Companies Act 1980 they are subject to special provisions in relation to dividends.

investment income Any income other than *earned income, derived from interest, dividends, and other unearned sources. Investment income is treated as the top slice of the taxpayer's income and is taxed at the appropriate income-tax rate(s). For investment incomes exceeding (1983 Budget proposals) £7110 there is an additional rate of tax – the *investment income surcharge* – which is at present 15%.

invitation to treat *See* offer.

invitee *n.* A person permitted to enter land or premises for a purpose in which the occupier of the land has a material interest. An example of an invitee is a customer in a shop. *See* occupier's liability.

involuntary conduct Conduct that cannot be controlled because one is suffering from a physical or mental condition. Involuntary conduct will usually give rise to a defence of *automatism, although it may not be a defence if one is aware of one's condition and the crime is one of negligence. Sometimes conduct is regarded as involuntary if one is in control of one's faculties; for example, when the brakes of a car suddenly fail; this will also afford a defence.

irrebuttable presumption *See* presumption.

irresistible impulse An uncontrollable urge to do something. Irresistible impulse is not usually a defence in law and it will not afford a defence of insanity, unless it arises out of a disease of the mind as defined by the *McNaghten Rules. When, however, an impulse is irresistible in that the body reacts in an instinctive way to it, there may be a defence of *involuntary conduct. An irresistible impulse may also constitute *diminished responsibility. *See also* provocation.

irretrievable breakdown *See* breakdown of marriage.

irrevocable *adj.* Incapable of being rescinded. For example, *powers of appointment may be made irrevocable. On the other hand, a testator of sound mind can revoke his will at any time.

issue *n.* **1.** The matter in dispute in a court action. **2.** The children or other descendants of a person.

issued capital *See* authorized capital.

issue estoppel *Estoppel arising in relation to an issue that has previously been litigated and determined between the same parties or their predecessors in title. The issue must be an essential element of the claim or defence in both sets of proceedings. Unlike estoppel *per rem judicatam*, it does not prevent fresh evidence from being introduced in relation to the issue previously determined. This type of estoppel does not arise in criminal cases and its scope in civil cases is uncertain.

itemized pay statement The written statement with which an employer must provide an employee each time his wage or salary is paid to him. Under the Employment Protection (Consolidation) Act 1978, the statement must contain: (1) the employee's gross pay for the period; (2) the amounts and reason for any deductions; (3) the net amount paid; and (4) the method of calculating the net pay when different parts are calculated differently (e.g. if the pay is partly a basic wage and partly a commission or bonus payment). An employee can apply to an *industrial tribunal if his employer fails to provide the statutory statement or reason for deductions. The tribunal can order the employer to provide statements and to refund any unexplained deductions in respect of a period up to 13 weeks before the application.

J

jactitation of marriage A false assertion that one is married to someone to whom one is not in fact married. An injunction may be sought to restrain such claims being made and may be useful in preventing a presumption of marriage from arising.

joinder of causes of action The combination in one action of several causes of action against the same defendant. Although any number of causes of action may be joined in the first instance,

the court may order that they be severed if the joinder would cause procedural difficulties.

joinder of charges The joining of more than one charge of a criminal offence together in the same *indictment. This may be done when the charges are based on the same facts or are part of a series of offences of the same or similar character.

joinder of defendants Mentioning two or more defendants in one count of an *indictment and trying them together. It is possible to join two or more defendants even if one of them is the principal offender and the other an accessory; if they are separately indicted, however, they cannot subsequently be tried together. Sometimes (e.g. in cases of conspiracy) it is usual to join two or more defendants; one may be convicted even if all his co-conspirators named in the count are acquitted and even though conspiracy by definition requires more than one participant. Two or more defendants may also be joined in one indictment if they are charged with different offences, if the interests of justice require this; for example, if two witnesses commit perjury in relation to the same facts in the same proceedings. Defendants who have been jointly indicted will normally only be tried by separate trials if a joint trial might prejudice one or more of them; for example, when evidence against one accused is not admissible against the other or when the prosecution wish to call one of the defendants to give evidence against another.

joinder of documents The connecting together of two or more documents so that, jointly, they fulfil statutory requirements (such as those of the Law of Property Act 1925) when one of the documents alone would be insufficient.

joinder of parties The combination as plaintiffs or defendants of two or more persons in a single action. Joinder may take place with *leave of the court or when separate actions would result in some common question of law or fact arising in all the actions, and all claims in the action are in respect of or arise out of the same transaction or series of transactions. *See also* joinder of defendants.

joint and several Together and in separation. If two or more people enter into an obligation that is said to be joint and several, their liability for its breach can be enforced against them all by a joint action or against any of them by individual action. *See also* joint tortfeasors.

Joint Committee on Statutory Instruments (Joint Scrutiny Committee) A committee of both Houses of Parliament whose function is to examine most delegated legislation (particularly *statutory instruments of a general character) and to draw Parliament's attention to it on a number of specified grounds; for example, if it imposes a tax, has retrospective effect, has been unduly delayed in publication, or is badly drafted. The Committee consists of seven members appointed by each House.

joint industrial council A statutory body, comprising an equal number of representatives of employers and employees in a particular industry, that negotiates common terms and conditions of employment to be applied in all businesses in that industry. Such councils have power to make orders directing minimum terms and conditions of employment. If the two sides cannot agree, either may refer the dispute to *ACAS for conciliation and – if that fails – to the *Central Arbitration Committee, whose award is binding on the council. Under the Employment Protection Act 1975 the Secretary of State may by order convert a wages council into a joint industrial council and may abolish a council if he considers that voluntary collective bargaining

would be more effective in the industry concerned.

Joint Scrutiny Committee *See* Joint Committee on Statutory Instruments.

joint tenancy Ownership of land by two or more persons who have identical interests in the whole of the land (*compare* tenancy in common). A joint tenancy can only arise when four conditions (the *four unities*) are satisfied. (1) Each joint tenant must be entitled to possession at the same time. (2) The estate or interest each has in the land must be identical. (3) Each must have the same *title to the land, i.e. their ownership must be traced from the same instrument, such as a conveyance "to A and B as joint tenants". (4) Each joint tenant's interest must *vest at and subsist for the same time. Under a joint tenancy the *right of survivorship* applies: thus ownership passes automatically on the death of one joint tenant to the survivor(s). The last survivor becomes the sole and absolute owner. Under the Law of Property Act 1925 beneficial joint tenants own land as trustees for themselves upon a statutory trust for sale. As trustees they are bound ultimately to sell the land but may postpone sale as long as they agree. Any joint tenant may apply to the court for an order for sale, which will be made if it is just to do so, but the court can itself postpone sale.

joint tortfeasors Two or more people whose wrongful actions in furthering a common design cause a single injury. For example, if two men searching for a gas leak both applied a naked light to a gas pipe and caused an explosion, they are said to be joint tortfeasors. But if a single injury is caused by several people acting without a common design they are said to be *concurrent tortfeasors*. An example of concurrent tortfeasors would be two motorists in separate cars, both driving negligently and causing a collision in which a pedestrian is injured. In both cases, the injured plaintiff is entitled to sue any or all of the tortfeasors for his whole loss; if he obtains a judgment against one tortfeasor that is not satisfied, he may proceed against the others. A tortfeasor liable for damage may recover contribution from other tortfeasors (whether joint or concurrent) liable for the same damage. *See* civil liability contribution.

joint will A will comprising a single document executed by two or more persons as the will of all of them. It is treated as the separate will of each testator, and probate will be granted separately on the death of each. A joint testator may revoke the will only insofar as it applies to himself. A joint will is a convenient instrument for the exercise of a power conferred on persons jointly to appoint by will (*see* power of appointment) but has no other practical benefit.

Journals *pl. n.* The authentic record of proceedings in Parliament, as opposed to the verbatim record of debates (*see* Hansard). There are two series: *Journals of the House of Lords* (beginning in 1509) and *Journals of the House of Commons* (beginning in 1547).

JP *See* justice of the peace.

judge *n.* A state official with power to adjudicate on disputes and other matters brought before the courts for decision. In English law all judges are appointed by the Crown, on the advice of the Lord Chancellor in the case of *circuit judges and High Court *puisne judges and on the advice of the Prime Minister in the case of judges of the *Court of Appeal and the *Lords of Appeal in Ordinary. All judges are experienced legal practitioners, mostly barristers, but solicitors can be appointed circuit judges after completion of three years' service as recorders. The independence of the higher judiciary is ensured by the principle that they hold office during good behaviour and not at the pleasure of the Crown (with the ex-

ception of the Lord Chancellor). They can only be removed from office by a resolution of both Houses of Parliament assented to by the Queen. Their salaries are a charge on the *Consolidated Fund and are not voted annually. Circuit judges may be removed by the Lord Chancellor for incapacity or misbehaviour. All judicial appointments are pensionable and there is a compulsory retirement age. *See also* judicial immunity. *Compare* magistrate.

judge advocate A barrister who advises a *court martial on questions of law. He is appointed by the Judge Advocate-General's Department or, in the case of naval courts martial, by the Judge Advocate of the Fleet. At the conclusion of the evidence the judge advocate sums up the case to the members of the court.

Judge Advocate-General's Department A department that advises the Secretary of State for Defence and the Defence Council on matters relating to the administration of military law and reviews proceedings of army and air-force courts martial.

judge in his own cause *See* natural justice.

Judges' Rules Rules of practice drawn up by the High Court, governing the questioning and charging of suspects by police. They are designed to ensure that confessions are voluntary and, although they do not have the force of law, a trial judge has discretion to exclude evidence obtained in breach of the Rules.

The Rules provide that the police are entitled to question anyone in relation to any offence he may have been involved in. However, no one is obliged to answer any questions, unless statute expressly obliges him to do so (for example, the Road Traffic Acts oblige the owner of a car to tell the police who was driving it at the time a driving offence was allegedly committed). The police cannot normally compel anyone

judgment

to go with them to a police station unless they arrest him or have the power to search him.

When a police officer reasonably suspects that someone has committed an offence, he may question him, but only after giving a *caution that he does not have to answer the questions but that if he does, his words may be taken down and used in evidence. When he is charged with an offence or told that he may be prosecuted, the suspect must be cautioned again and asked if he wishes to say anything. After the second caution, he may not normally be asked further questions (except, for instance, to clarify his earlier statements).

judgment *n.* **1.** A decision made by a court in respect of the matter before it. Judgments may be *interlocutory*, deciding a particular issue prior to the trial of the case; or *final*, finally disposing of the case. They may be *in personam*, imposing a personal liability on a party (e.g. to pay damages); or *in rem*, determining some issue of right, status, or property binding people generally. **2.** The process of reasoning by which the court's decision was arrived at. In English law it is the normal practice for judgment to be given in open court or, in some appellate tribunals, to be handed down in printed form. If the judgment contains rulings on important questions of law, it may be reported in the *law reports. See also* enforcement of judgment; foreign judgments.

judgment creditor The person in whose favour a court judgment is made against a debtor.

judgment debtor A person against whom a court judgment has been entered, ordering him to pay money that he owes (the *judgment debt*). *See also* enforcement of judgment.

judgment in default *See* default.

judgment summons A summons, issued on the application of a person entitled to enforce a judgment, that requires a judgment debtor to appear and be examined on oath as to his means. If it can be shown that the debtor had the means to pay the debt but has failed to do so the judge may make an order committing him to prison, suspended for as long as specified instalments are paid. Since the virtual abolition of imprisonment for debt, this procedure has been available only in respect of certain *maintenance orders and judgments for payment of certain taxes and state contributions.

judicial cognizance *See* judicial notice.

Judicial Committee of the Privy Council A tribunal, created by the Judicial Committee Act 1833, consisting of the Lord Chancellor, Lord President of the Council and ex-Lords President, Lords of Appeal in Ordinary, and other members of the *Privy Council who have been Lords of Appeal in Ordinary or who have held high judicial office. Certain judges of Commonwealth countries who are Privy Councillors are also members. The Committee's jurisdiction is to hear appeals from courts in dependent territories and those Commonwealth countries that have retained appeals to the Privy Council since attaining independence; it also hears appeals under certain statutes. The Committee's decisions are not technically judgments but merely advice to the Crown: they do not become final until incorporated into an *Order in Council. For this reason also, until 1966 dissenting opinions were not disclosed. The Committee's decisions are not binding as precedents upon English courts but are merely of *persuasive authority.

judicial dictum *See obiter dictum.*

judicial discretion The power of the court to take some step, grant a remedy, or admit evidence or not as it thinks fit. Many rules of procedure and evidence are in discretionary form or provide for some element of discretion. It is sometimes said that in criminal cases the judge can always disallow otherwise admissible evidence if it would operate unfairly against the accused. However, the true principle is probably much narrower and may be limited to evidence of *previous convictions, *evidence obtained illegally, and *similar-fact evidence. The *Court of Appeal is reluctant to review the exercise of discretion by trial judges.

judicial immunity The exemption of a *judge or *magistrate from personal actions for damages arising from the exercise of his judicial office. The immunity is absolute in respect of all words or actions of the judge while acting within his *jurisdiction and extends to acts done without jurisdiction provided that they were done in good faith.

judicial notice (judicial cognizance) The means by which the court may take as proven certain facts without hearing evidence. *Notorious facts* (i.e. matters of common knowledge) may be judicially noticed without inquiry; some other facts (e.g. matters that can easily be checked in a standard work of reference and are reasonably indisputable) may be noticed after inquiry. When judicial notice has been taken, *evidence in rebuttal is not permitted.

judicial precedent *See* precedent.

judicial review The simplified procedure by which, since 1977, prerogative and other remedies have been obtainable in the High Court against inferior courts, tribunals, and administrative authorities. On an application for the judicial review of a decision, the Court may grant *certiorari, *mandamus, *prohibition, a *declaration, or an *injunction; it may also award damages.

judicial separation order An order by the courts that a husband and wife do not have to cohabit. The order does not terminate the marriage but it does free the parties of marital obligations. Judicial (*or* legal) separation is appropriate when there are religious objections to divorce or when the parties have not finally decided upon divorce. The grounds for judicial separation are the same as those for divorce (except that it is not necessary to prove irretrievable breakdown of the marriage). The courts have the same powers in relation to financial orders and children as they do when making a decree of divorce.

judicial trustee A trustee appointed by the court under the Judicial Trustee Act 1906, either as sole trustee or as cotrustee. He is an officer of the court, is subject to the court's control, and is entitled to such remuneration as the court allows. In practice, the *Public Trustee has replaced a trustee appointed under the Act.

junior barrister Any barrister who is not a *Queen's Counsel. The word "junior" does not necessarily imply youth or lack of seniority: many members of the Bar remain juniors throughout their careers.

juridical *adj.* Relating to judicial proceedings or the law. Juridical days were days on which legal business could be transacted.

jurisdiction *n.* **1.** The power of a court to hear and decide a case or make a certain order. (For the limits of jurisdiction of individual courts, see entries for those courts.) **2.** The territorial limits within which the jurisdiction of a court may be exercised. In the case of English courts it comprises England, Wales, Berwick-upon-Tweed, and those parts of the sea claimed as *territorial waters. Everywhere else is said to be *outside the jurisdiction*. **3.** The territorial scope of the legislative competence of Parliament. *See* sovereignty of Parliament.

juris et de jure [Latin] Of law and from law: an irrebuttable *presumption is so described.

juristic person (artificial person) An entity, such as a *corporation, that is recognized as having legal personality, i.e. it is capable of enjoying and being subject to legal rights and duties. It is contrasted with a human being, who is referred to as a *natural person*.

juror *n.* A member of a *jury. Each juror must swear that he will faithfully try the case and give a true verdict according to the evidence. Jurors are chosen from the electoral register; they must be aged between 18 and 65 and must have been resident in the UK for a period of at least five years since the age of 13. The following are ineligible for jury service: (1) past and present holders of any judicial office; (2) solicitors, barristers, members of a court staff, police officers, and others concerned with the administration of justice, if they have held the office within the preceding 10 years; (3) clergymen; and (4) the mentally ill. Members of Parliament, full-time members of the armed forces, and practising doctors, chemists, and vets may claim excusal from jury service and there are also special categories of discretionary excusal. Anyone who has ever been imprisoned for five years or more, or who has been imprisoned for more than three months within the preceding 10 years, is disqualified from jury service.

A defendant is entitled to challenge individual jurors (*see* challenge to jury); if he succeeds in his challenges, another person takes the place of the challenged juror.

jury *n.* A group of *jurors (usually 12) selected at random to decide the facts of a case and give a verdict. Most juries are selected to try crimes but juries are also used in coroner's *inquests and in some civil cases (e.g. defamation actions). The judge directs the jury on matters of law (such as the definition of the crime charged and the nature and scope of possible defences) and sums up the evidence of the prosecution and defence for them, but he must leave the jury to decide all questions of fact themselves. He must also make it clear to them that they are the only *triers of fact and must acquit the defendant unless they feel sure that he is guilty beyond reasonable doubt. The verdict of a jury should, if possible, be unanimous, but when there are at least 10 people on the jury and they cannot reach a unanimous verdict, a *majority verdict is acceptable. Many offences must be tried by a jury; many others may be tried by a jury or by magistrates (*see* indictable offence). *See also* challenge to jury.

It is a criminal offence to attempt to influence a jury's discussions or to question them about their discussions when the case is over. *See also* contempt of court.

jus [Latin] *n.* A law or right.

jus accrescendi [Latin] *See* right of survivorship.

jus accrescendi inter mercatores pro beneficio commercii locum non habet [Latin: for the advancement of commerce there is no place for the right of survivorship between merchants] A maxim stating the principle that equity will treat as tenants in common (*see* tenancy in common) those in partnership whose interest in partnership property is at common law a *joint tenancy. Thus on the death of a partner his interest in the partnership property is part of his estate rather than belonging to the surviving partners.

jus civile [Latin: civil law] 1. *Municipal law. 2. The whole body of Roman law.

jus cogens [Latin: coercive law] A rule or principle in international law that is so fundamental that it binds all states and does not allow any exceptions. Such rules (sometimes called *peremptory norms*) will only amount to *jus cogens* rules if they are recognized as such by the international community as a whole. A treaty that conflicts with an existing *jus cogens* rule is void, and if a new *jus cogens* rule emerges, any existing treaty that conflicts with it automatically becomes void. States cannot create regional customary international law that contradicts *jus cogens* rules. Most authorities agree that the laws prohibiting slavery, genocide, piracy, and acts of aggression or illegal use of force are *jus cogens* laws. Some suggest that certain human rights provisions (e.g. those prohibiting racial discrimination or apartheid) and any acts defined as international crimes also come under the category of *jus cogens*.

jus gentium [Latin: the law of peoples] *See* international law.

jus in re aliena [Latin] A right in the property of another (*see* encumbrance). It is contrasted with *jus in re propria* – a right in one's own property.

jus naturale [Latin: natural law] The fundamental element of all law. *See* natural law.

jus quaesitum tertio *See* privity of contract.

just and equitable winding-up A *compulsory winding-up by the court on grounds of fairness. This may occur, for example, when the purpose of the company cannot be achieved, when the management is deadlocked or has been guilty of serious irregularities, or, in small companies run on the basis of mutual trust between members, when the majority have exercised their legal rights in circumstances not taken into account by the members when the company was formed. No order will be made if another form of *minority protection would be more appropriate.

jus tertii [Latin: right of a third party] A defence raised by a party who is sued in respect of property alleging that some third party has a better claim to the property than the plaintiff. The Torts (Interference with Goods) Act 1977 provides that this is a good defence to an action in *conversion, but a special procedure is laid down for the joinder of the third party in the action.

justice *n.* A moral ideal that the law seeks to uphold in the protection of rights and *punishment of wrongs. Justice is not synonymous with law – it is possible for a law to be called unjust. However, English law closely identifies with justice and the word is frequently used in the legal system; for example, in justice of the peace, Royal Courts of Justice, and administration of justice.

justice of the peace (JP) A person holding a commission from the Crown to exercise certain judicial functions for a particular *commission area*. JPs are appointed on behalf of and in the name of the Queen by the Lord Chancellor and may be removed from office in the same way. On reaching the age of 70 they are placed on a supplemental list and cease to be able to exercise any judicial functions. Their principal function is to sit as *magistrates in the *magistrates' courts but they may also sit in the *Crown Court when it is considering committals for sentence and appeals from magistrates' courts, sign warrants of arrest and search warrants, and take statutory declarations. All High Court judges are *ex officio* justices of the peace for the whole of England and Wales.

justices' clerk *See* clerk to the justices.

justification *n.* **1.** The defence to an action for *defamation that the defamatory statement made was true. Truth is a complete defence to a civil action for defamation, even if the statement was made maliciously. **2.** The defence that interference with the contractual or business relations of another was justified. The scope of the defence is uncertain, but the fact that the wages of chorus girls were so low that they were compelled to resort to prostitution has been held to justify a theatrical performers' protection society inducing theatre owners to break their contracts

justifying bail

with the girls' employer (*Brimelow* v *Casson* 1924). *See* procuring breach of contract.

justifying bail Demonstrating to a court granting bail that one is capable of meeting the surety specified in the bail (for example, disclosing one's financial resources). A person standing surety for bail must be able to provide the bail out of his own resources. It is a criminal offence (*bail-bonding*) for a defendant who is granted bail to agree to indemnify his surety against any loss arising out of standing surety.

juvenile court A *magistrates' court exercising jurisdiction over crimes committed by *juvenile offenders and other matters relating to children under 17. The court consists of three lay *magistrates drawn from a special panel, at least one of whom must be a woman. The proceedings of the court are not open to the public and are generally conducted in a more informal manner than in ordinary magistrates' courts. As far as possible, juvenile courts sit in different locations from other courts; by statute they may not sit in a room in which a sitting of another court has been or will be held within an hour before or after the sitting of the juvenile court. The press may not publish the identity of any child or young person concerned in the court's proceedings unless the court or the Home Secretary so orders.

juvenile offender A person under the age of 17 who has committed a crime. The word "juvenile" normally refers to a child under the age of normal criminal liability (*see doli capax*); between the ages of 14 and 17 a person is known as a *young offender*, and between 17 and 21 as a *young adult offender (or *juvenile adult*). A child under the age of 14 cannot normally be tried on indictment (even for an *indictable offence) except when charged with homicide. A young offender may be tried on indictment when charged with homicide or an of-

fence for which an adult could be sentenced to at least 14 years' imprisonment (e.g. arson or robbery) or if he is jointly charged with someone aged 17 or over and it is felt to be necessary that they be tried together. In all other cases, juvenile offenders must be tried summarily by a magistrates' court or a *juvenile court; they can be "found guilty" of an offence but may not be described as "convicted".

A juvenile offender cannot be sentenced to imprisonment; instead he may be detained under the direction of the Home Office in a *detention centre or a local authority *community home (if found guilty of murder, he must be detained). Nor may a juvenile offender be sentenced to do community service or to probation, but he may be fined (*see* fine), sent to hospital, or discharged (absolutely or conditionally) and may sometimes be sent to *borstal or be subject to a *supervision order or to a *care order.

Important changes in the law relating to the punishment of juvenile and young adult offenders will come into effect when the relevant provisions of the Criminal Justice Act 1982 are brought into force. Borstal orders will be abolished, and juvenile offenders whom the court wishes to keep in custody will be subject to detention centre orders or *youth custody orders*, depending on their age and sex (usually 14 or over for detention centre orders, 15 or over for male offenders and 17 or over for female offenders in the case of youth custody orders). Detention centre orders will normally be for not less than 21 days and not more than 4 months; youth custody orders (to be served in new *youth custody centres) will normally be for not less than 4 months and not more than 12 months (or, in the case of a young adult offender, not more than the maximum term of prison that could be imposed on an adult offender).

K

keeping house A debtor's avoidance of, or refusal to see, his creditors with the intention of delaying or avoiding payment of his debts. This constitutes an act of *bankruptcy.

keeping term *See* term.

keeping the peace Behaving in such a way as not to cause or threaten a breach of the peace, i.e. a disturbance of public order. Magistrates' courts have very wide powers to bind people over to keep the peace or to make them enter into *recognizances (either personally or through a surety) to pay a sum of money into court if they fail to keep the peace. The order may be made against a defendant on a criminal charge or merely upon complaint by a member of the public (if there is some evidence that a *breach of the peace may occur). A person may be bound over for any sum of money or any period of time; if he refuses to be bound over or to enter into the recognizance, he may be sentenced immediately to imprisonment (even if he has committed no criminal offence).

kidnapping *n.* Carrying a person away, without his consent, by means of force, threats, or fraud. Kidnapping is a common-law offence punishable with a maximum sentence of life imprisonment. A man may be guilty of kidnapping his wife. Disputes between parents about the right to their children are dealt with in civil custody proceedings (*see* custody disputes). A parent who has been awarded custody of his child in such proceedings may obtain a warrant for the arrest of the other parent if he or she takes the child away. Failure to comply with an order for the return of the child amounts to contempt of court. *See also* abduction; child stealing.

King's Bench (KB) *See* Court of Queen's Bench.

King's Counsel (KC) *See* Queen's Counsel.

knock-out agreement An agreement by dealers not to bid against each other at an auction. Such an agreement is illegal (although there have never been any prosecutions for this offence) and would require registration under the Restrictive Trade Practices Act 1956, enabling anyone injured by the agreement to sue for damages.

L

laches [from Norman French *lasches*, slackness, negligence] *n.* Neglect and unreasonable delay in enforcing an equitable right. If a plaintiff with full knowledge of the facts takes an unnecessarily long time to bring an action (e.g. to set aside a contract obtained by fraud) the court will not assist him; hence the maxim "the law will not help those who sleep on their rights".

Lady Day *See* quarter days.

land *n.* Those parts of the surface of the earth that are capable in law of being owned and are within the court's jurisdiction. Generally, ownership of land includes the *airspace above it and the subsoil below. For the purposes of land law, the Law of Property Act 1925 defines land as including mines and minerals (whether or not owned separately from the surface), buildings, and most interests in land. Chattels fixed to the land so that they become part of it are also treated in law as land, under the maxim *quicquid plantatur solo, solo cedit* (*see* fixture).

land certificate A document issued by the Land Registry to the proprietor of registered land as proof of his owner-ship of it. *See* land registration.

land charge An interest in land that imposes an obligation on the land-owner in favour of some other person (the *chargee*). If validly created and registered where appropriate (*see* registration of encumbrances), land charges will be binding on all third parties who acquire the land. Examples of land charges created by act of the parties include mortgages, rentcharges, restrictive covenants, and estate contracts. Some land charges arise under statute; for example, a spouse's right to occupy the matrimonial home under the Matrimonial Homes Act 1967 (a Class F land charge), capital transfer tax in certain circumstances (a Class D land charge), and various *local land charges*, arising in favour of local authorities from the exercise of their statutory powers.

Land Charges Department A department of the Land Registry, established under the Land Charges Act 1925 to maintain registers of certain interests affecting the rights of persons owning *unregistered land (called *estate owners*). For the interests capable of being registered, *see* registration of encumbrances. Registration of land charges against the name of the estate owner constitutes notice to everyone of their existence and renders them binding upon third parties who acquire any interest or estate in the land affected. A person contemplating taking such an interest may apply to the Department for an *official search certificate, which will reveal all interests registered against the estate owner's name.

landlord *n.* A person who grants a lease or tenancy. He need not be the outright owner of the tenanted premises (he may, for example, be a lessee himself). A landlord may be an individual, a local authority, a trustee, a personal representative, or a corporation (such as a company). A landlord may provide services to the tenant, such as heating,

lighting, and porterage. There are statutory controls on the amount that a landlord can charge for such services and procedures for consultation with the tenants. When the services are personal to the tenant, his *security of tenure may be affected (*see* attendance). The person who receives the rent is obliged to reveal the landlord's identity on the tenant's request. When there is a change of ownership the new landlord must inform the tenant within two months or when rent is next due, whichever is the later. The kind of security of tenure a tenant has is affected by who his landlord is. *See* assured tenancy; protected tenancy; secure tenancy; restricted contract.

land registration The system of registering, at local branch offices of HM Land Registry, certain legal estates or interests in land. Under the Land Registration Act 1925 compulsory registration may be introduced in a specified area by Order in Council. When registration becomes compulsory there is no obligation on existing owners to register, but the first subsequent purchaser of a freehold estate or of a lease having at least 40 years to run must register his title. If he fails to do so he does not acquire the legal estate and therefore runs the risk that the vendor or landlord may sell to someone else who can acquire a better title by registration. In a compulsory area, an existing owner or the tenant under a lease having at least 21 years to run may register his title if he wishes.

Upon registration of a title the Land Registry issues a *land certificate* to the owner (who is known as the *registered proprietor*) or, if the land is in mortgage, a *charge certificate* to the mortgagee. The certificate represents the title deeds and is in four parts, comprising copies of:

(1) The *property register*. This describes the land and any additional rights incidental to it, such as rights of way over adjoining land.

(2) The *proprietorship register*. This names the registered proprietor(s) of the land and notes any restriction on their powers to dispose of it. It also states the nature of the title, which may be *absolute, *qualified, *possessory, or *good leasehold.

(3) The *charges register*. This details interests adverse to the proprietor, such as mortgages, restrictive covenants, or easements to which the land is subject. (4) The *filed plan*. This shows the location of the land, usually with a general indication of the position of the boundaries. Registration of precise boundaries is possible under a special procedure involving notice to adjoining owners and hearing their objections.

A registered proprietor's title is guaranteed by the state subject to *overriding interests, which are not registrable in the charges register. The extent of the guarantee depends on the nature of the title. The register can be rectified by the court in certain circumstances to correct a mistake; compensation is generally paid by the government to a party who suffers loss as a result.

Land Registry A statutory body established under the Land Registration Act 1925 to maintain registers of certain legal estates in land. *See also* land registration.

Lands Tribunal A tribunal established by the Lands Tribunal Act 1949 to decide disputes concerning compensation for the compulsory acquisition of land and similar questions involving land valuation. Its members, who must be legally qualified or experienced in valuation, are appointed by the Lord Chancellor, and it is subject to the supervision of the *Council on Tribunals.

lapse *n.* The cancellation of a bequest when the beneficiary dies before the testator. Thus, in general, if A's will leaves property to B but B predeceases A, the bequest does not take effect. The property becomes part of A's residuary estate and is distributed to his residuary beneficiaries. This rule is subject to the following exceptions. (1) When property is bequeathed to two or more persons as joint tenants, those who survive the testator take the property. (2) Under the Wills Act 1837, if property is left in tail (*see* entailed interest) to a person who predeceases the testator, the beneficiary is deemed to have died immediately after the testator. Thus the property goes to the next person entitled under the entail. (3) The Wills Act 1837 also provides that when property is bequeathed to a direct descendant of the testator who predeceases him but leaves direct descendants of his own, those descendants take the property.

lapse of offer The termination of an *offer as a result of the passage of time, death, or the nonfulfilment of a condition. An offer made subject to a specified time limit lapses after that time has passed; all other offers lapse after a reasonable time. Death of the offeree causes an offer to lapse, but death of the offeror does not always do so. The offer remains available for acceptance if the death is unknown to the offeree and the resulting contract could be performed by the offeror's personal representatives. An offer lapses if one or more conditions are not fulfilled. An offer to buy goods, for example, is made on the assumption that they will remain in the same condition until acceptance; it lapses if that ceases to be the case. *See also* rejection of offer; revocation of offer.

larceny *n.* Formerly (before 1968), *theft. Larceny was more limited than theft; it required an *asportation* (carrying away of the property) and could only be committed if the victim actually had the property in his possession (as opposed, for example, to owning but not possessing it).

latent ambiguity *See* ambiguity.

latent defect *See* defect.

law *n.* **1.** The enforceable body of rules that govern any society. *See also* common law; natural law. **2.** One of the rules making up the body of law, such as an *Act of Parliament.

Law Commission A body established by the Law Commissions Act 1965 to take and keep the law under review with a view to systematically developing and reforming it. In particular, it considers the codification of the law, the elimination of anomalies, the repeal of obsolete and unnecessary enactments, a reduction in the number of separate enactments, and simplification and modernization generally. The Commission consists of a chairman and four other members, appointed by the Lord Chancellor from among the holders of judicial office, barristers, solicitors, and academic lawyers. There is a separate Commission for Scotland.

Law Lords *See* Lords of Appeal in Ordinary.

law merchant The international practice of merchants relating to commercial and maritime matters. In early times it influenced Admiralty law and the law administered in local courts. Parts of the law merchant were absorbed into the common law of England (e.g. that relating to negotiable instruments and the transfer of bills of lading).

law officers of the Crown The *Attorney General, *Solicitor General, *Lord Advocate, and Solicitor General for Scotland.

law of nations *See* international law.

law of the sea The rules of international law governing rights over the seas. The seas are divided into several different areas. (1) The internal waters of a state (e.g. rivers, lakes, ports, and harbours). A state may usually apply its laws to any merchant ship within its internal waters. It may also apply naviga-

tion or health regulations to foreign warships in such waters and exclude foreign warships from its ports. (2) The *territorial waters. (3) The *high seas, beyond the territorial waters, which are open to all nations for such purposes as navigation, fishing, laying of submarine cables, and over-flying. Ships on the high seas are usually subject only to international law (for example, in relation to acts of piracy) and the law of the flagstate (usually dependent on registration in that state). There is also a limited right of *hot pursuit*, entitling a coastal state to pursue a ship suspected of breach of its laws from its territorial waters into the high seas. (4) The *continental shelf, which – although geographically part of the high seas – is subject to specific rules.

The law of the sea is contained in customary international law and in the four Geneva Conventions of 1958. When the 1982 United Nations Convention on the Law of the Sea comes into force, there will be a comprehensive code governing the whole of this law, which will include some completely new rules. For example, the Convention envisages establishing an International Seabed Authority to control the resources of the deep seabed, based on a General Assembly Resolution (2749) of 1970.

law reports Reports of cases decided by the courts. The earliest reports were contained in the *Year Books*, which were published annually between 1283 and 1535. Their authors were anonymous and may have been student lawyers. The *Year Books* were superseded by personalized reports, i.e. reports written privately by lawyers (e.g. Chief Justice Coke) who appended their names to them. In 1865 was established the Incorporated Council of Law Reporting, a semiofficial body that publishes *The Law Reports*. These are reports of important cases selected by the Council, written by lawyers, and approved by the judges involved. There are in addition still a number of commercially published reports, e.g. the *All England Law Reports.*

law sittings *See* sittings.

Law Society The professional body for solicitors in England and Wales, incorporated by royal charter in 1831. The Society exists both to further the professional interests of solicitors and to discharge important statutory functions in relation to the admission to practice, the conduct, and discipline of solicitors. It issues annual *practising certificates to solicitors, without which they may not practise, and through its disciplinary committee may strike a solicitor's name off the rolls or take other disciplinary action, subject to an appeal to the High Court. The Society is responsible for the examination of intending solicitors and organizes educational and training courses both through the College of Law and recognized polytechnics. It also administers the *legal aid scheme.

lay days The number of days specified in a charterparty to enable the charterer to load or discharge cargo. They begin to run as soon as the ship is an *arrived ship,* i.e. has reached the berth or mooring specified in the charterparty. If only a port is specified, the ship must have reached a position within that port at which it is at the immediate and effective disposition of the charterer (the *Reid test*). Unless the charterparty provides otherwise (e.g. by restricting them to good-weather working days), lay days are *running days,* i.e. they run consecutively, without any break. *See also* demurrage.

laying an information Giving a magistrate a concise statement (an *information*), verbally or in writing, of an alleged offence and the suspected offender, so that he can take steps to obtain the appearance of the suspect in court. Information can be laid by any member of the public, although it is usually done by the police. If an arrest warrant is required, the information must be in writing and on oath. Objections cannot normally be made to information laid, on the grounds of formal defects or discrepancies between it and the prosecution's subsequent evidence. But if the defect is fundamental to the charge the information will be dismissed, and if the defendant was misled by a discrepancy, he may be granted an adjournment of the trial.

LCJ *See* Lord Chief Justice.

leader *n.* A *Queen's Counsel or any barrister who is the senior of two counsel appearing for the same party.

Leader of HM Opposition The leader in the House of Commons of the party in opposition to the government that has the greatest numerical strength in the House. By statute a salary is payable to him (in addition to his salary as an MP); any doubt as to his identity is resolved by the Speaker.

Leader of the House *See* House of Commons; House of Lords.

lead evidence To call or adduce evidence.

leading case A case, the decision in which establishes an important principle of law. *See* precedent.

leading question A question asked of a witness in a manner that suggests the answer sought by the questioner (e.g. "You threw the brick through the window, didn't you?") or that assumes the existence of disputed facts to which the witness is to testify. Leading questions may not be asked during *examination-in-chief (except relating to formal matters, such as the witness's name and address) but may normally be asked in *cross-examination.

leapfrog procedure The procedure for appealing direct to the House of Lords from the High Court or a Divisional Court, bypassing the Court of Appeal.

lease

The procedure is only allowed in exceptional cases. All parties must consent and the case must raise a point of law of public importance, which either relates wholly or partly to the interpretation of a statute or a statutory instrument or is one in respect of which the trial judge is bound by a previous decision of the Court of Appeal or the House of Lords. The trial judge must certify that he is satisfied as to the importance of the case and the House of Lords must grant leave to appeal in this way.

lease *n.* A contract under which an owner of property (the *landlord or *lessor*) grants another person (the *tenant or *lessee*) exclusive possession of the property for an agreed period, usually in return for rent. Unless it satisfies the conditions for a *parol lease, a lease must be made by a formal document (a *deed), which is itself called a lease. If this is not done, however, there may still be an *agreement for a lease. The lessee must have exclusive possession, i.e. the right to control the property and to exclude everyone else from it. If possession is not exclusive, there is no lease but there may be a *licence. A lease must be for a definite period, which may be a *fixed term or by way of a *periodic tenancy. *See also* equitable lease; legal lease.

The deed that creates the lease sets out the terms, which include the parties, the property, the length of the lease, the rent, and obligations to carry out repairs. Certain obligations (known as *covenants*) are implied in all leases (though the lease may vary or exclude them). In the case of the lessor these are: (1) not to derogate from his grant (i.e. he must not do anything that would make the property unfit for the purpose for which it was let); (2) *quiet enjoyment; and, in certain cases, (3) to ensure that the premises are *fit for habitation. In the case of the tenant, the implied covenants are: (1) to pay the rent; (2) to pay all ordinary rates and taxes; (3) not to commit *waste; and (4) to use the property in a tenant-like manner, i.e. to do the sort of small maintenance jobs that any reasonable tenant would be expected to do (he is not, however, responsible for *fair wear and tear or other disrepair that is not his fault). *See also* covenant to repair.

leasehold *adj.* Held under a *lease, i.e. for a period of fixed minimum duration. *See* term of years absolute.

leasehold ownership Ownership of property under a *lease. The period of ownership depends on the terms of the lease: it may vary from a very short time, such as a week, to a very long period, such as 999 years. The tenant's ownership is also restricted by the terms of the lease.

leave *n.* Permission given by the court to take some procedural step in litigation. Situations in which leave is required include *service out of the jurisdiction, service of *subsequent pleadings, and *appeals to the House of Lords.

leave to defend An order of the High Court on a summons for *summary judgment under Order 14, granting the defendant leave to continue with his defence to the action. The leave may be *conditional* (e.g. subject to the defendant paying the whole or part of the plaintiff's claim into court) or *unconditional*.

legacy *n.* A gift of personal property effected by will (*compare* devise). A *general legacy* is a gift of property not identifiable with a specific asset or fund; for example, a simple legacy of "£1000 to A". A *specific legacy* is a particular identifiable object, for example a named painting. It is liable to *ademption but is otherwise payable by the deceased's personal representatives in priority to general legacies. A *demonstrative legacy* is payable from a specified fund; for example, "£500 from the £1000 kept under my bed". Such a legacy is not adeemed if the testator disposes of the fund during his lifetime and is payable in priority to general legacies. *Pecuniary legacies* (i.e. gifts of cash) carry interest from one year after the testator's death. A *residuary legacy* is one that disposes of the whole of the testator's personal property after payment of debts and specific, demonstrative, and general legacies.

legal aid order *See* legal aid scheme.

legal aid scheme A scheme for the payment out of public funds of the legal costs of those unable to meet the costs themselves. There are separate provisions for civil and criminal cases. Civil legal aid has two components: *legal advice and assistance* (sometimes known as the *green form scheme), which is intended to provide payment for legal advice and help preliminary to litigation; and *legal aid*, which covers all stages of litigation, including appeals. In criminal cases the decision whether or not to grant legal aid rests with the court, which will make a *legal aid order* when this is desirable in the interests of justice. A defendant receiving legal aid may, however, be required to pay a contribution towards his legal aid costs.

The scheme is administered by the Law Society through a system of general and area committees covering the whole of England and Wales. The funds are provided by an Exchequer grant, costs recovered from opposing parties, and contributions that may be payable by those who do not qualify for free legal aid.

legal assignment *See* assignment.

legal custody *See* custody of child.

legal easement *See* easement.

legal estate Ownership of land either in *fee simple absolute in possession or for a *term of years absolute. Under the Law of Property Act 1925 these are the only forms of ownership that can exist

as legal estates in land. All other forms, e.g. life interests and entailed interests, are equitable only.

legal fiction *See* fiction.

legal fraud *See* constructive fraud.

legal lease A contract or grant that creates an estate in land for a *term of years absolute. A legal lease must normally be created by deed; however, there are no formal requirements for the creation of a legal lease for a term that takes effect on possession and does not exceed three years at a full market rent without a premium. *Compare* equitable lease.

legal memory The period over which the law's recollection extends. Its commencement was arbitrarily fixed at 1189 by the Statute of Westminster I 1275. Time before legal memory is referred to as *time immemorial*. *Compare* living memory.

legal mortgage *See* mortgage.

legal person A natural person (i.e. a human being) or a *juristic person.

legal rights 1. Rights recognized by the common law courts, as distinct from *equitable rights or interests recognized by the Court of Chancery. In their developed form, legal rights affect everyone whether or not they know (or ought to know) of their existence. **2.** Generally, all rights recognized by the law (both common law and equity) as having legal existence and effect.

legal separation *See* judicial separation order.

legal year The period made up, in any year, of the four court *sittings.

legatee *n.* The person to whom a *legacy is given.

legislation *n.* **1.** The whole or any part of a country's written law. In the UK the term is normally confined to *Acts of Parliament, but in its broadest sense it also includes law made under powers conferred by Act of Parliament (*see* delegated legislation), law made by virtue of the *royal prerogative, and Measures (*see* Church of England). **2.** The process of making written law.

legislature *n.* The body having primary power to make written law. In the UK it consists of Parliament, i.e. the Crown, the House of Commons, and the House of Lords.

legitimacy *n.* The legal status of a child born to parents who were married at the time of his conception or birth (or both). There is a *presumption of legitimacy* in all cases when the mother is married, so that children of the marriage are presumed to be the offspring of the mother's husband. This may be rebutted, however, either by showing that the husband was impotent or absent on the date on which the child must have been conceived or by *blood tests showing that he could not be the father. Children born of a voidable marriage annulled since 1949 are legitimate; those born of such a marriage annulled between 1937 and 1949 are legitimate only if the grounds of nullity were that the other spouse was of unsound mind or epileptic or suffering from a communicable venereal disease. Since 1959, children born of a void marriage are treated as legitimate if at the time of their conception at least one of their parents reasonably thought the marriage was valid and the father was domiciled in England at the time of the child's birth.

Under certain conditions (specified in the Matrimonial Causes Act 1973) a person may seek a court declaration of his legitimacy.

legitimation *n.* The process of replacing the status of illegitimacy by that of legitimacy. A living child may be legitimated if his parents marry one another, provided that the father is domiciled in England or Wales at the date of the marriage. Evidence that the husband recognized the child as his own may be

sufficient to establish his paternity for purposes of legitimation. Legitimation takes effect from the date of the marriage and the child is treated thereafter as if he had been born legitimate.

lessee *n.* The person to whom a *lease is granted. *See also* tenant.

lessor *n.* The person by whom a *lease is granted. *See also* landlord.

letter of attorney *See* power of attorney.

letter of credit A document authorizing a bank, at the request of a customer, to pay money to a third party (the *beneficiary*) on presentation of documents specified in the letter (e.g. bills of lading and policies of insurance). A contract of sale of goods may require the buyer to open an *irrevocable letter of credit* in favour of the seller. This cannot be revoked by the issuing bank or the purchaser of the goods before its expiry date, without the consent of the beneficiary. A *confirmed letter of credit* is one in which the negotiating bank guarantees payment to the beneficiary should it not be honoured by the issuing bank.

letter of request (rogatory letter) A letter issued to a foreign court requesting a judge to take evidence from a specific person within that court's jurisdiction. The resulting *deposition may be read at a subsequent court hearing.

letters of administration Authority granted by the court to a specified person to act as an *administrator of a deceased person's estate when the deceased dies intestate. Letters of administration *cum testamento annexo* (with the will annexed) are granted when the deceased's will did not appoint executors or when the executors named do not prove the will. In certain circumstances, letters of administration may be granted for limited purposes to persons not entitled to deal with the whole estate (*see ad colligenda bona*; *du-*

rante absentia). See also de bonis non administratis.

lex causae [Latin: the law of the case] In *private international law, the system of law (usually foreign) applicable to the case in dispute, as opposed to the *lex fori.

lex domicilii [Latin] The law of *domicile. In *private international law, the law of the country of domicile determines such matters as capacity to make a will in respect of personal property, the validity of such a will, succession to personal property, consent to marriage, and the *proper law of a marriage contract or settlement.

lex fori [Latin] The law of the *forum. In *private international law, the law of the forum governs matters of procedure, the mode of trial, most matters relating to evidence, the nature of the remedy available, and most matters of *limitation of actions based on time bars.

lex loci actus [Latin] The law of the place where a legal act takes place. In *private international law, this law governs such questions as whether or not property in a bill of exchange or promissory note passes to the transferee and the formal validity of an assignment of an intangible movable (e.g. a share in a trust fund). *See also lex loci celebrationis; lex loci contractus.*

lex loci celebrationis [Latin] The law of the place of celebration of a marriage. In *private international law, this law governs such questions as the formalities required for a marriage (subject to four special exceptions), whether or not such a marriage is monogamous or polygamous, and possibly what law governs impotence or wilful refusal to consummate a marriage.

lex loci contractus [Latin] The law of the place where a contract was made. In *private international law, this law governs such matters as the formal require-

ments of a contract and the capacity to incur liability as a party to a bill of exchange. Most other matters relating to contracts are governed by the *proper law of the contract.

lex loci delicti commissi [Latin] The law of the place in which a delict (tort) is committed. In *private international law as applied in most countries in Europe, this law governs liability for torts. In some cases, however, it may be difficult to establish where the tort was committed (for example, when goods negligently manufactured in one country are distributed in another) or the place may be a matter of mere chance (for example, when an aeroplane crashes and lands). For these reasons, England does not accept the theory that liability in tort is governed by the *lex loci delicti.*

lex loci situs [Latin] The law of the place where an object is situated. In *private international law, this law usually governs such matters as succession to, and the right to possession of immovables and the essential validity of trusts of immovables (for example, what estates can be created and whether or not gifts to charities are valid).

lex loci solutionis [Latin] The law of the place where a contract is to be performed or a debt is to be paid. In *private international law as applied in England, the *lex loci solutionis* governs the due date for payment of a *bill of exchange but does not usually govern matters relating to the law of contract.

liability *n. See* business liability; occupier's liability; parents' liability; products liability; strict liability; vicarious liability.

libel *n.* A defamatory statement made in permanent form, such as writing, pictures, or film (*see* defamation). Radio and television broadcasts for general reception and public performance of plays are treated as being made in permanent form for the purposes of the law of defamation. A libel is actionable in tort without proof that its publication has caused special damage (actual financial or material loss) to the person defamed. Libel can also be a crime (*criminal libel*). Proof of publication of the statement to third parties is not necessary in criminal libel and truth is a defence only if the statement was published for the public benefit.

licence *n.* **1.** Formal authority to do something that would otherwise be unlawful. Examples include a *driving licence, a licence for selling intoxicating liquor (*see* licensing of premises), and a licence by the owner of a patent to manufacture the patented goods. **2.** (in land law) Permission to enter or occupy a person's land for an agreed purpose. A licence does not usually confer a right to exclusive possession of the land, nor any estate or interest in it: it is a personal arrangement between the licensor and the licensee. A *contractual licence* cannot be revoked during the period the parties intended it to last. A *bare licence* (i.e. gratuitous permission to enter or occupy the licensor's land) can be revoked at any time and cannot be assigned by the licensee to a third party (*see* bare licensee). Neither type is binding on third parties acquiring the land from the licensor. However if the licence is *coupled with a grant* of property or of an interest in land, the licence may be irrevocable and binding on the licensor's successors in title. For example, if A grants B the right to enter A's land to cut down trees, the licence may be irrevocable if B is also given the right to keep the timber.

licensee *n.* **1.** A person who has been granted a licence, most commonly used of one who has been granted a licence to sell intoxicating liquor (*see* licensing of premises). **2.** A person with permission to do what would otherwise be unlawful. In relation to land, a licensee is one who enters land with the express or implied permission of the occupier. *See* licence; occupier's liability.

licensing of premises The granting of a justices' licence authorizing the sale by retail of *intoxicating liquor either for consumption on or off the premises (an *on-licence*) or for consumption off those premises only (an *off-licence*). Licensing justices deal with the grant, renewal, and transfer of licences at a general annual licensing meeting (the *brewster sessions*) in the first fortnight of every February and at regular licensing sessions thereafter.

lie in grant To be capable of being transferred by deed. Land and interests in it lie in grant; property that can be transferred by physical delivery *lies in livery*.

lie in livery *See* lie in grant.

lien [via Old French from Latin *ligamen*, a binding] *n.* The right of one person to retain possession of goods owned by another until the possessor's claims against the owner have been satisfied. The lien may be *general*, when the goods are held as security for all outstanding debts of the owner, or *particular*, when only the claims of the possessor in respect of the goods held must be satisfied. Thus an unpaid seller may in some contracts be entitled to retain the goods until he receives the price, a carrier may have a lien over goods he is transporting, and a repairer over goods he is repairing. Whether a lien arises or not depends on the terms of the contract and usual trade practice. A lien may be waived and can be lost, for example when an owner in possession sells goods to a buyer ignorant of a third party's lien. This type of lien is a *possessory lien*, but sometimes actual possession of the goods is not necessary. In an *equitable lien*, for example, the claim exists independently of possession. If a purchaser of the property involved is given notice of the lien it binds him; otherwise he will not be bound. Similarly a *maritime lien*, which binds a ship or cargo in connection with some maritime liability, does not depend on possession and can be enforced by arrest and sale (unless security is given). Examples of maritime liens are the lien of a salvor, that of seamen for their wages and of masters for their wages and outgoings, that of a bottomry or *respondentia* bondholder (*see* hypothecation), and that over a ship at fault in a collision in which property has been damaged. *See also* solicitor's lien.

life assurance *Insurance providing for the payment of a sum on the occurrence of an event that is in some way dependent upon a human life. In *endowment assurance* the insurer is liable to pay a fixed sum either at the end of a fixed period or at death if the insured should die in the meantime. *Whole-life assurance* provides for the payment of a fixed sum on the death of the insured. *Term* (or *temporary*) *assurance* provides for a fixed sum to be paid in the event of the death of the insured within a specified period.

life estate *See* life interest.

life imprisonment Punishment of a criminal by imprisonment for the rest of his life. The only crime that always carries a sentence of life imprisonment is murder, but there are many crimes (e.g. arson, manslaughter, wounding with intent, and rape) that carry a maximum penalty of life imprisonment, which is imposed in serious cases. In practice the imprisonment may often not be for life: although there is no remission for life sentences, the Home Secretary may order the release of a prisoner on licence, on the advice of the Parole Board (*see* parole) and after consulting the Lord Chief Justice (and, if possible, the trial judge). When imposing life imprisonment for murder, the judge may make a recommendation that the defendant should serve a *minimum term* (number of years), which is

usually not less than 12 years and up to 35 years. This recommendation is not legally binding on the Home Secretary, but in practice he will almost always follow it. Judges are also empowered to make a private representation to the Home Secretary, when imposing a life sentence, pointing out any special mitigating factors that might induce him to release the prisoner at an early date.

life interest (life estate) An interest in property subsisting only during the lifetime of the person to whom it was granted (e.g. "to A for life") or of some other person (e.g. "to A during the life of B"). The latter type is called an *estate (or interest) *pur autre vie*. Under the Law of Property Act 1925 a life interest in land cannot exist as a legal estate, only as an *equitable interest. The creation of a life interest in land therefore creates a settlement, governed by the Settled Land Act 1925.

life peerage A nonhereditary peerage of the rank of baron or baroness created by the Crown by letters patent under the Life Peerages Act 1958. The purpose of the Act was to strengthen the composition of the House of Lords, and there is no limit to the number of peerages that may be created. The peerage of a Lord of Appeal in Ordinary is also for life but is not customarily included among life peerages.

life policy A policy providing a formal embodiment of a contract of *life assurance. The benefit of a life policy can be assigned to a third party.

life tenant *See* tenant for life.

lifting the veil The act of disregarding the veil of incorporation that separates the personality of a corporation from the personalities of its members. This exceptional course is occasionally sanctioned by statute, for example in relation to fraudulent trading and inaccurate use of company names, when it may result in members of a limited company losing their limited liability. It is also employed by the courts, for example if incorporation has been used to perpetrate fraud or gives rise to unreal distinctions between a company and its subsidiary companies, but never so as to defeat limited liability. Very occasionally the courts openly disregard corporate personality but more often they evade its inconvenient consequences by deciding that the acts were performed by the corporation acting as agent or trustee for the company members, to whom therefore they should be attributed.

limitation of actions Statutory rules limiting the time within which civil actions can be brought. Actions in simple contract and tort must be brought within six years of the accrual of the cause of action. If the claim is for damages in respect of personal injuries or death the limit is three years from the accrual of the cause of action or (if later) the plaintiff's date of knowledge of the relevant circumstances, but the court has discretion to extend this period. In actions in respect of land and of contracts under seal the period is twelve years from the accrual of the cause of action. Time does not run against a party under a disability until the disability ceases. The present law is contained in the Limitation Act 1980.

limited administration (special administration) The administration of a deceased person's estate for restricted purposes specified by the court in the *letters of administration. Examples of such grants include grants *ad colligenda bona* and *durante absentia* and grants for the administration of an estate during the minority of a child appointed as executor by the will.

limited company A type of company incorporated by registration under the Companies Acts 1948–81 whose members have a limited liability towards their company. In a company limited by shares members must pay the nomi-

nal value (*see* authorized capital) of their shares either upon *allotment or subsequently (*see* call). In a company limited by guarantee (a *guarantee company*) members must pay an agreed nominal amount (the guarantee), usually £1–£5, to their company in the event of a winding-up. The guarantee fund is intended to be for the benefit of company creditors when the company is wound up and members' liability to contribute to it cannot be reduced or extinguished by the company. Because payment of the guarantee is postponed guarantee companies often lack a working capital and are therefore more appropriate for charitable or social purposes than for trading. Before 1980, it was possible to overcome this difficulty by forming a guarantee company with an authorized capital.

The name of a limited company must end with the words "Limited" (or "Ltd.") in the case of a private company and "public limited company" (or "p.l.c.") in the case of a public company as a warning to creditors of the limit upon members' liability. *Compare* unlimited company.

limited executor A person appointed by a will to deal only with specified property, not the whole of the deceased's estate. *Compare* limited administration.

limited owner A *tenant for life or a *statutory owner of land comprised in a settlement.

limited owner's charge A charge on land securing repayment to a *limited owner of capital transfer tax paid by him on the acquisition of his interest. The tax is normally payable out of the trust property but if the limited owner pays it personally (e.g. to avoid having to sell land when the trust money is insufficient to cover the tax) the charge arises to secure his reimbursement. The charge is registrable (*see* registration of encumbrances).

limited partnership *See* partnership.

Lincoln's Inn An *Inn of Court situated between Carey Street and Holborn. The records of the Inn, the *Black Books*, survive in a continuous series from 1422 to the present. By tradition, barristers practising in the *Chancery Division of the High Court normally belong to Lincoln's Inn.

linked transaction (under the Consumer Credit Act 1974) A transaction (except one for the provision of security) that is linked to, but not part of, a *regulated agreement (the *principal agreement*) and is entered into by a debtor or hirer with any other person. A linked transaction may comply with a term of the principal agreement (e.g. if the principal agreement requires that the goods be insured with X) or it may be financed by the principal agreement if the latter is a *debtor-creditor-supplier agreement. Alternatively it may be suggested by a creditor or owner to the debtor or hirer. The latter then enters into the linked transaction either to induce the creditor or owner to enter into the principal agreement, or for some other purpose related to the principal agreement, or – when the principal agreement is a *restricted-use credit agreement – for a purpose related to a transaction financed by the principal agreement.

liquidated damages *See* damages.

liquidated demand A demand for a fixed sum, e.g. a debt of £50. Such a demand is distinguished from a claim for unliquidated *damages, which is the subject of a discretionary assessment by the court.

liquidation *n. See* winding-up.

liquidator *n.* A person who conducts the *winding-up of a company. In a *compulsory winding-up by the court, the court can appoint a *provisional liquidator* (who is always the *official receiver) at any time after the petition for

winding-up has been presented. It subsequently appoints the official receiver or someone else as liquidator. Liquidators owe *fiduciary duties to the company and creditors and duties under the Companies Acts 1948–81.

lis alibi pendens [Latin] A suit pending elsewhere. The fact that there is already litigation pending between the same parties in respect of the same subject matter in another jurisdiction may give the defendant a ground on which he can obtain a *stay of proceedings. However, he must show that the continuance of the English action would cause an injustice to him and would not cause injustice to the plaintiff.

lis mota [Latin] A court action that has been set in motion.

lis pendens [Latin] A *pending action.

listed building A building of special architectural or historic interest specified on a list compiled or approved by the Secretary of State. It may be demolished or altered in character only with listed-building consent granted by the local planning authority (*see* town and country planning) or the Secretary of State. *See also* building preservation notice; conservation area.

listed company A company that has entered a *listing agreement* with the *Stock Exchange and whose shares therefore have a *quotation. The listing agreement incorporates the Rules of the Stock Exchange and listed companies are subject to stringent *disclosure requirements and scrutiny by the Council of the Exchange.

lists *pl. n.* Calendars of cases awaiting trial. A court may maintain several lists comprising different types of case. Thus in the High Court there is the Queen's Bench nonjury list, the jury list, the *short cause list, etc. A case enters the list after it has been set down for trial.

literal rule *See* interpretation of statutes.

litigant

litigant *n.* A person who is a party to a court action. A litigant may present his case personally to the court. If he does so, he may be assisted by a friend who can take notes and advise but cannot assist in the actual presentation of the case (a *McKenzie man*). Alternatively, a litigant may be represented by a *barrister or, where appropriate, a *solicitor. A successful litigant can usually claim his legal *costs from his opponent. If the litigant did not have legal representation he may claim costs for the work he has done himself that would otherwise have been carried out by a lawyer.

litigation *n.* **1.** The taking of legal action by a *litigant. **2.** The field of law that is concerned with all contentious matters.

lives in being *See* rule against perpetuities.

livestock *See* classification of animals.

living apart The condition required to establish *desertion or separation for two or five years as a basis for divorce (*see* breakdown of marriage). The courts have held that living apart requires that the spouses should cease to share life together and recognize that the marriage has effectively come to an end. Spouses may thus be "living apart" even though they are still under the same roof. In the case of divorce based on five years' separation, it is sufficient if only one of the parties recognizes this. In such cases there are special statutory provisions to protect the interests of the other spouse.

living memory The period over which the recollection of living people extends. *Compare* legal memory.

living on immoral earnings Using money obtained from prostitution for one's livelihood or upkeep. It is an offence punishable by up to seven years' imprisonment for a man (but not for a woman) to knowingly live on the pro-

ceeds of female prostitution. The offence is normally committed by a man who lives with a prostitute and is wholly or mainly kept by her or by a man who runs a *brothel or in any other way forces or helps a prostitute to commit prostitution. In all these cases he is assumed to be knowingly living on her immoral earnings unless he can prove that he is not. The offence also covers supplying goods or services that relate only to prostitution (e.g. advertising for pay the names and addresses of prostitutes or driving them and their clients to places where they might have intercourse). The offence does not include selling ordinary items to prostitutes or renting them accommodation (unless this is used only for prostitution or a higher rent is charged because they are prostitutes). It is also an offence for either a man or a woman to knowingly live on the proceeds of male prostitution, and it is an offence for one woman to force another into prostitution or to aid her prostitution for financial gain.

living together *See* cohabitation.

LJ *See* Lord Justice of Appeal.

Lloyd's A society of individual *underwriters that was incorporated by Act of Parliament in 1871. Originally Lloyd's only provided marine insurance but they now also provide other kinds. The *insurance is undertaken by syndicates of private underwriters (*names*), each of which is managed by a professional underwriter. Each name underwrites a percentage of the business written by the syndicate and has to deposit a substantial sum with the corporation before being admitted as an underwriter. The public deals with the underwriters only through Lloyd's brokers.

loan capital Money borrowed by a company, corporation, or other organization in the form of *debenture stock, corporation stock, or funded debt. Loan capital does not include bank overdrafts or loans for less than 12 months.

loan creditor A creditor of a company, such as a person who holds redeemable *loan capital issued by the company. Loan creditors (other than banks) are participators in *close companies.

local Act *See* Act of Parliament.

local authority A body of councillors elected by the inhabitants of a local government area (*see* franchise) to exercise local government functions. In England (except *Greater London) and Wales, the local authorities are the *county council, the *district council, and the council of a *parish (England) or *community (Wales).

All councillors are elected for four years. County councillors are elected every fourth year counting from 1981, and parish and community councillors every fourth year from 1979. Metropolitan district councillors are elected by thirds, one in each year other than a county council year, and other district councillors according to whether their council has opted for this method or for simultaneous election in every fourth year from 1979. A candidate for election to any local authority must be over 21 and a commonwealth citizen or citizen of the Republic of Ireland, must have sufficient local connection (e.g. residence), and must not be disqualified (e.g. by reason of being a bankrupt or holding paid employment under the authority).

Local authorities and children. Local authorities have various duties in relation to the welfare of minors. They must give advice, guidance, and assistance to prevent a child from having to be received into care or brought before a juvenile court. They may work with voluntary associations and give assistance in kind or cash. They must also look after children who come into their care, either as a result of *care proceedings, criminal proceedings, or orders made by the courts under the divorce jurisdic-

tion, in custody disputes (either under the Guardianship of Minors Act 1971 or the Domestic Proceedings and Magistrates' Courts Act 1978), or in proceedings for adoption, custodianship, or wardship. A local authority is also obliged (under conditions specified in the Child Care Act 1980) to receive a child under the age of 17 into care of its own accord and may subsequently assume parental rights and duties over it. Local authorities are also obliged to supervise the welfare of foster children and children under a supervision order, to establish and maintain an adoption service, and to report to the court in respect of non-agency adoption applications and applications for custodianship orders.

local government A form of government in which responsibility for the regulation of certain matters within particular localities (*local government areas) is delegated by statute to locally elected councillors (*see* local authority).

local government area An area constituting a unit for local government purposes. The local government areas in England (except *Greater London) and Wales are the *county, the *district, and the *parish (England) or *community (Wales).

local government boundary commissions Two bodies established by the Local Government Act 1972 to undertake regular reviews of local government areas in England and Wales, respectively, and to propose alterations designed to improve the effectiveness and convenience of local government.

local land charge *See* land charge; registration of encumbrances.

local land charges register *See* registration of encumbrances.

locus sigilli [Latin: place of the seal] *See* deed.

locus standi [Latin: a place to stand] The right to bring an action or challenge some decision. Questions of *locus standi* most often arise in proceedings for *judicial review.

lodger *n.* A person who is given occupation of part of a house in return for rent, where the premises remain under the close control of the owner. Although a lodger normally has a mere *licence rather than a tenancy, he may have some protection under the provisions for *restricted contracts.

loitering *n.* Lingering in a public place for some purpose of a criminal nature. Since 27 August 1981 it is no longer an offence for a suspected person or reputed thief to loiter in or frequent a public place with the intention of committing an arrestable offence (the so-called *sus law*), and the police no longer have the power to arrest such people. However, there is now a new offence of *interfering with vehicles*, which is committed by a person who in any way interferes with a vehicle or anything carried in or on it if he intends to steal it (or anything in it) or to take it for a joyride. The offence is punishable by imprisonment for up to three months and/or a fine of up to £500, and the police may arrest anyone they reasonably suspect of this offence. It is also a statutory offence for a prostitute to loiter or solicit in a public place (*see also* soliciting).

London *See* City of London; Greater London.

London borough *See* Greater London.

long tenancy For statutory purposes, a *fixed-term tenancy for a period exceeding 21 years. Where the rent is less than two-thirds of the property's rateable value, the tenancy is excluded from being a *protected tenancy. However, it will qualify for special protection if it would have been a protected tenancy had the rent not been a low one. This allows the tenant to continue the tenancy beyond the fixed term. In such

cases, if the landlord wishes to terminate the tenancy at the end of the fixed term, he must serve a statutory notice at least 6 months, but not more than 12 months, before the end of the tenancy. In this notice he can either propose a *statutory tenancy (the terms of which must be agreed with the tenant or settled by a court) or he can claim the right to resume possession of the premises. In the latter case he must have statutory grounds for possession, which correspond to those required for possession of a protected tenancy. If the tenant contests this notice, the landlord must apply for a court order for possession. If this is refused, the tenant will be entitled to a statutory tenancy. *See also* enfranchisement of tenancy.

long title *See* Act of Parliament.

Long Vacation A *vacation of the Supreme Court lasting from 1 July to 30 September. During the Long Vacation only certain kinds of urgent business (*vacation business*) can be transacted. It was formerly the rule in the High Court that pleadings could not be served during the Long Vacation, but this rule now applies only to the month of August.

Lord Advocate The chief law officer of the Crown in Scotland, corresponding to the *Attorney General in England. He has ultimate responsibility for criminal prosecutions in Scotland, being assisted by a Solicitor General, advocates depute, and procurators fiscal. He is normally a supporter of the ruling party and resigns his office upon a change of government, but he is not always a Member of Parliament.

Lord Chancellor The head of the judiciary, a government minister (normally of Cabinet rank), and Speaker of the House of Lords. He thus combines judicial, executive, and legislative functions. He is entitled to preside over the House when it sits as a final court of appeal; he appoints magistrates, makes recommendations for higher judicial appointments, and oversees such matters as the administration of the courts, legal aid, and law reform. As *Speaker*, he normally presides from the Woolsack over legislative proceedings but is free to vacate his seat and take part in debates and divisions. He is appointed by the Crown on the advice of the Prime Minister and (since 1974) may be a Roman Catholic.

Lord Chief Justice (LCJ) The chief judge of the *Queen's Bench Division of the High Court. He ranks second only to the Lord Chancellor in the judicial hierarchy. It was formerly the practice to appoint the Attorney General when a vacancy in the office occurred but this practice has now been abandoned and recent LCJs have been either *Lords Justices of Appeal or *Lords of Appeal in Ordinary on appointment. The LCJ is *ex officio* a member of the Court of Appeal and is President of its Criminal Division.

Lord Justice of Appeal (LJ) An ordinary judge of the *Court of Appeal. The Lords Justices (LJJ) are normally appointed from among the *puisne judges of the High Court but in principle a barrister of at least 15 years' standing could be appointed. They become members of the Privy Council on appointment.

Lords of Appeal in Ordinary (Law Lords) Up to 11 persons, holders of high judicial office or practising barristers of at least 15 years' standing, who are appointed to life peerages under the Appellate Jurisdiction Act 1876 to carry out the judicial functions of the *House of Lords.

Lords Spiritual and Temporal *See* House of Lords.

loss of amenity Loss or reduction of a plaintiff's mental or physical capacity to do the things he used to do, suffered as a result of personal injuries. In actions for personal injuries the plaintiff may recover damages for loss of amenities, in addition to his financial losses and an award for pain and suffering. Thus loss of the ability to play games or a musical instrument, if these were the plaintiff's hobbies, will be taken into account in fixing damages. The assessment is based on an objective view of the value of the loss of these amenities to the plaintiff.

loss of services An action in tort (*per quod servitium amisit*) could formerly be brought against someone who had caused a parent to be deprived of the services of a child or a master to be deprived of the services of a menial servant. Both forms of action were abolished by the Administration of Justice Act 1982.

lost modern grant A legal fiction by which the court will uphold the right of a claimant showing 20 years' uninterrupted use of a right over another's land, by presuming that the *easement was created by a formal deed of grant that has been lost. The claim can be defeated only by proof that the grant could not have been made at any time during the period of use; for example, if the *servient tenement was at all relevant times owned by someone with no power to grant easements.

lottery *n.* A game of chance in which the participants buy numbered tickets and the prizes are distributed by drawing lots. Lotteries are usually illegal (*see also* gaming) unless they are: (1) on behalf of registered charities or sports, (2) restricted to members of a private club, (3) run by a local authority and registered with the Gaming Board, or (4) small lotteries that take place as part of an entertainment (e.g. in a bazaar or at a dance). Premium Bonds are also expressly permitted.

lump-sum award The form in which damages in tort are given. It covers both past losses (up to the time of judgment) and losses likely to be suffered in the future as a result of the tort. The general rule is that only one award of damages may be made, unless the tort is a continuing one (such as continuing trespass or nuisance). However, in actions for personal injuries *interim payments can be ordered pending the final estimation of damages, and in cases in which the plaintiff may develop some serious disease or suffer some serious deterioration in his condition, a *provisional award* may be given. This enables the plaintiff to come back for further damages at a future date if the disease or deterioration occurs.

M

machinery and plant The machines, parts of machines, and all other apparatus used for carrying on a business, but excluding stock in trade. Capital expenditure on machinery and plant is eligible for *capital allowances.

magistrate *n.* A *justice of the peace sitting in a *magistrates' court. Most magistrates are lay persons and have no formal legal qualifications: they receive no payment for their services but give their time voluntarily. There are also, however, *stipendiary magistrates in London and other major cities.

magistrates' clerk *See* clerk to the justices.

magistrates' court A court consisting of between two and seven *magistrates or a single *stipendiary magistrate exercising the jurisdiction conferred by the Magistrates' Courts Act 1980 and other statutes. The principal function of magistrates' courts is to provide the forum in which all criminal prosecutions are initiated. In the case of an *indictable offence or an *offence triable either way for which the defendant elects *trial on indictment, the court sits as *examining

justices to consider whether or not there is sufficient evidence to justify committing the defendant to the *Crown Court. For a *summary offence or an offence triable either way in which the defendant elects *summary trial, the court sits as a *court of summary jurisdiction*, i.e. as a criminal court of trial without a jury in which justices, assisted by the *clerk to the justices, decide all questions of law and fact.

Magistrates' courts also have a limited jurisdiction in civil matters relating to debt and affiliation and matrimonial proceedings. Each magistrates' court sits for a *petty-sessions area* and its jurisdiction is generally confined to that area, although it may in some cases extend beyond. A magistrates' court may sit on any day of the year, including (if the court thinks fit) Christmas Day, Good Friday, or any Sunday, but in practice it is unusual for magistrates' courts to sit on public holidays or at weekends.

Magna Carta The Great Charter of Runnymede, acceded to by King John in 1215 after armed rebellion by his barons. It guaranteed the freedom of the church, restricted taxes and fines, and promised justice to all. Confirmed frequently by subsequent feudal kings, it has since been largely repealed as having only symbolic significance.

main purpose rule *See* repugnancy.

main residence For the purposes of *enfranchisement of a tenancy, a dwelling in which the tenant has lived for at least the last three years or for periods amounting to three years in the last ten years. Whether or not the dwelling has in fact been his main residence is also considered in each case. For the purposes of *capital gains tax there is an exemption for gains on the disposal of owner-occupied homes. If an individual has more than one residence he may nominate the one that he wishes to qualify for exemption. There is also *income-tax relief on mortgage interest on an individual's main residence, on mortgages up to £30,000 (1983 Budget proposals).

maintenance *n.* The provision of food, clothing, and other basic necessities of life. At common law a husband is liable to provide his wife with reasonable maintenance, but the courts will not decide how much is reasonable as long as the spouses are living together and the wife has not applied for a court order on the grounds of *failure to maintain. Since 1978 wives may also be obliged to maintain their husbands. Parents are bound at common law to maintain their minor children, but the father of an illegitimate child has no such obligation unless an *affiliation order is made against him (*see also* putative father). For the purposes of the Supplementary Benefits Act 1976, however, the father of an illegitimate child is deemed to be liable to maintain him in that any money paid by the Supplementary Benefits Commission for the child to the mother can be claimed back by them from the father.

Before 1881 it was common for settlements to include a power for the trustees to maintain and educate minors. Since then, a statutory power has existed enabling trustees to pay money for the maintenance, education, or benefit of a minor; this power is subject to any contrary provision in the settlement.

The obligation after a divorce of one spouse to support another or of a parent to support a child of the family is often referred to as maintenance; this is more correctly known as financial provision or *financial relief.

maintenance agreement An agreement between spouses concerning their financial obligations to one another or a separation agreement containing no financial provisions. Such agreements are enforceable as contracts if they are under seal or there is valid consideration. If they are in writing, they are governed by the provisions of the Matrimonial Causes Act 1973. Any clause that attempts to deny the right of either spouse to apply to a court for financial relief will be void, and the county courts and High Court (and, to a more limited extent, the magistrates' courts) have wide powers to vary the terms of maintenance agreements. When one party has died the other spouse may apply to the court, under the special provisions for *dependants, to have the terms of the agreement altered, but only if it was in writing.

Parties to a divorce may submit the terms of a maintenance agreement to the court for approval (in which case it may be embodied in a court order), though the court is not bound to approve it. They are encouraged to do so, in order to achieve a final *clean break.

maintenance order A court order providing for payment of sums for the maintenance of a spouse or child. Strictly speaking the term now applies only to *maintenance agreements incorporated into a court order; orders in the magistrates' courts or High Court on the ground of *failure to maintain and orders in the divorce courts for maintenance are now called *financial provision orders.

Spouses may try to evade their financial obligations to each other or their children by emigrating. In such cases the Domestic Proceedings and Magistrates' Courts Act 1978 grants powers to obtain maintenance from emigrant spouses in certain designated ("convention") countries. For these purposes maintenance orders include any order providing for periodical payments to a person whom the payer is liable to maintain, including *affiliation orders.

maintenance pending suit A court order for temporary periodical payments during the hearing of a petition for divorce, nullity, or judicial separation.

majority (full age) *n.* The age of 18 years. The state of being below that age is a state of *minority* (*see* infant). The age of majority was originally 21 years, but was reduced to 18 by the Family Law Reform Act 1969. This majority applies for the purposes of any relevant legal rule and for the interpretation of any relevant statute, whenever it was made. It does not apply, however, to deeds, wills, and other private documents made before 1969, in which reference is made to majority or minority.

majority rule The principle by which the majority of company members has the power to control the company through voting at a company meeting. There are various ways to safeguard the minority (*see* minority protection).

majority verdict The verdict of a *jury reached by a majority. The verdict need not be unanimous if there are not less than 11 jurors and 10 of them agree on the verdict or if there are 10 jurors and 9 of them agree on the verdict. The jury must be given at least two hours in which to reach a unanimous verdict and the foreman of the jury must state in open court the number of jurors who respectively agreed to and dissented from the majority verdict. Majority verdicts can be taken in both criminal and civil cases.

making off without payment Leaving premises without paying for goods or services received and with the intention of avoiding payment, when payment on the spot is expected. This is now an offence punishable by up to two years' imprisonment, but it must be proved that the person who made off knew that payment on the spot was expected. It will usually cover such behaviour as walking out of a restaurant after having had a meal, without paying (even if there was originally no intention not to pay for the meal, and therefore no theft, and no *deception when the meal was ordered); taking a taxi and disappearing without paying; and collecting any items from a shop that has repaired or cleaned them, without paying. *See also* shoplifting.

male issue Direct descendants through the male line, e.g. sons and sons of sons (but not sons of daughters).

malfeasance *n.* An unlawful act. *Compare* misfeasance.

malice *n.* **1.** (in criminal law) A state of mind (*see* mens rea) usually taken to be equivalent to *intention or *recklessness: it does not require any hostile attitude. Malice is said to be *transferred* when someone intends to commit a crime against one person but in fact commits the same crime against someone else (for example, if he intends to shoot X but misses, and instead kills Y). Malice is *universal* (or *general*) when the accused has no particular victim in mind (for example, if he shoots into a crowd intending to kill anyone). In both cases this constitutes *mens rea*. *See also* constructive malice. **2.** (in tort) A constituent of certain torts. In the English law of tort, the general rule is that a malicious motive cannot make conduct unlawful if it would otherwise be lawful. For example, a right to take water from under one's own land can lawfully be exercised solely in order to cause damage to a neighbour. However, in some cases malice can be relevant. An action for *malicious prosecution requires proof that the prosecution was instigated maliciously, i.e. without reasonable and probable cause. In *defamation, a malicious motive invalidates the defences of fair comment and qualified privilege. Malice is also an element in *conspiracy to injure someone.

malice aforethought The *mens rea* (state of mind) required for a person to be guilty of murder. It is not necessary, however, for there to be any element of hostility (*see* malice) or for the intention to kill to be "forethought" (i.e. premeditated). The term covers (1) intention to kill (*direct express malice* *aforethought*), (2) intention to cause *grievous bodily harm (*direct implied malice aforethought*), (3) realizing while doing a particular act that death would almost certainly or very probably result (*indirect express malice*), and (4) realizing that grievous bodily harm would very probably result from the act, e.g. shooting at someone without intending to kill him, but realizing that he may at least suffer a serious injury (*indirect implied malice*). The prosecution must prove one of these four types of malice aforethought to secure a conviction of murder.

malicious damage Formerly (before 1971), *criminal damage.

malicious falsehood (injurious falsehood) A false statement, made maliciously, that is calculated to injure the property or business of another. The oldest forms of this tort are *slander of title and *slander of goods, but other false and malicious statements (e.g. that a businessman has ceased to trade) can also give rise to an action in tort.

malicious prosecution The malicious institution of legal proceedings against a person. Malicious prosecution is only actionable in tort if the proceedings were initiated both maliciously and without reasonable and probable cause and they were unsuccessful. No one who has been convicted of a criminal charge can sue for malicious prosecution.

malicious wounding *See* wounding.

managing director A *director to whom management powers have been delegated, either absolutely or subject to supervision, by the other directors of the company under the terms of the articles of association. Managing directors are agents of the company and have wide authority to act on its behalf.

managing trustee *See* custodian trustee.

mandamus [from Latin: we command]

n. A *prerogative order from the High Court instructing a tribunal, public official, corporation, etc., to perform a specified public duty (*see also* judicial review); for example, an instruction to a statutory tribunal to hear a particular dispute.

mandate *n.* **1.** (in private law) An authority given by one person (the *mandator*) to another to take some course of action. A mandate is commonly revocable until acted upon and is terminated by the death of the mandator. A cheque is a mandate from the customer to his bank to pay the sum in question and to debit his account. **2.** (in international law) The system by which dependent territories (such as the former German colonies in Africa) were placed under the supervision (but not the sovereignty) of mandatory powers by the League of Nations after World War I. After World War II, all remaining mandated territories became *trust territories under the United Nations with the exception of South-West Africa (now Namibia) and a strategic trust area consisting of a number of Pacific Islands north of the equator. The mandate over Namibia was terminated by the General Assembly of the UN in 1966, which placed the territory under the direct responsibility of the United Nations. The Pacific Islands territories are still administered by the USA.

mandatory injunction *See* injunction.

Manor of Northstead *See* Chiltern Hundreds, stewardship of the.

mansion house *See* principal mansion house.

manslaughter *n.* Homicide that does not amount to the crime of murder but is nevertheless neither lawful nor accidental. Manslaughter may be committed in several ways. It may arise if the accused had the *mens rea* required for murder (*see* malice aforethought), but mitigating circumstances (either *diminished responsibility or *provocation) reduce the offence to manslaughter; this is known as *voluntary manslaughter*. It may also be committed when there was no *mens rea* for murder in one of two situations: (1) if the accused committed an act of *gross negligence or (2) if the act, although not negligent, was criminally illegal and also involved an element of danger to the victim. For example, it would be manslaughter to knock some bricks off a bridge into the path of a train (*criminal damage), killing the driver, even if one had no idea that there was a train in the area. Such cases are known as *involuntary manslaughter*. A person may also be guilty of manslaughter if he kills someone when drunk (*see* intoxication). The maximum punishment for manslaughter is life imprisonment, although this is rarely imposed. Most cases of *causing death by reckless driving are usually not charged as manslaughter but as a special statutory offence under the Road Traffic Act 1972.

mansuetae naturae *See* classification of animals.

Mareva injunction [from the case *Mareva Compania Naviera S.A.* v *International Bulkcarriers S.A.* (1975)] An injunction, now consolidated in statute, that enables the court to freeze the assets of a defendant (whether resident within the jurisdiction of the English court or not). This prevents the defendant from removing his assets abroad and thus makes it worthwhile to sue such a defendant.

marine insurance A form of *insurance in which the insurer undertakes to indemnify the insured against loss of the ship (*hull insurance*), the cargo, or any sums paid in freight (*freight insurance*) occurring during a sea voyage. A marine insurance contract may be extended to losses on inland waters or to risks on land that may be incidental to a sea voyage. The risks listed in marine insurance policies include *perils of the seas, fire, war perils, jettisons, and *barratry, and the cover may be for a particular voyage, or for a specified time, or both (*see* time policy). In marine insurance a distinction is made between an *actual total loss and a *constructive total loss; partial loss is subject to *average. The law relating to marine insurance is codified by the Marine Insurance Act 1906.

mariner's will *See* privileged will.

marital privileges Privileges protecting information given by one spouse to the other from disclosure in court. In criminal proceedings, a person to whom a statement was made in confidence by his (or her) spouse cannot be compelled to disclose it and cannot be called as a witness except by the accused spouse. However, in certain crimes (mainly of a sexual nature or against children) the accused's consent is not required, and there is no marital privilege when one spouse is instituting proceedings against the other.

In civil proceedings marital privilege has now been abolished, but a person may still not be compelled to disclose a statement made by his (or her) spouse with a view to effecting a reconciliation between them. Nor may someone be compelled to give evidence that could criminally incriminate his (or her) spouse.

maritime lien *See* lien.

market *n.* A facility for the sale and purchase of goods. The concept of an *available market* is important in deciding the amount of damages for breach of contracts of sale of goods: it assumes that goods of the contract description can be sold at a market price fixed by supply and demand. The disappointed buyer or seller will usually, upon breach, make a substitute purchase or sale on the market and his damages will be the difference between the contract price and the market price.

market overt An open, public, and legally constituted market or fair. When goods are sold in market overt according to the usage of the market, the buyer acquires a good title to the goods, provided he buys them in good faith and without notice of any defect in the seller's title. This is one of the exceptions to the general principle of *nemo dat quod non habet*.

marriage *n.* **1.** The relationship between husband and wife. **2.** A ceremony, civil or religious, that creates the legal status of husband and wife and the legal obligations arising from that status (*see* marriage ceremony). All marriages must be registered by an authorized marriage registrar. The minimum age for marriage is 16, and capacity to marry in general is governed by the law of *domicile of both parties before the marriage. Relationships within which marriage is prohibited are specified in the Marriage Act 1949 (*see* prohibited degrees of relationships). Parties to a marriage must be respectively male and female as determined at birth (sex-change operations have no legal effect), must not be already married to someone else (*see* bigamy; polygamy), and must enter into the marriage freely. *See also* marriage by certificate.

marriage articles The clauses setting out the terms of a *marriage settlement.

marriage brokage contract A contract in which one person undertakes, for financial gain, to arrange a marriage for another. Such contracts are void because they contravene *public policy.

marriage by certificate Marriage authorized by a certificate issued by the Superintendent Registrar of Births, Deaths, and Marriages. All marriages other than those solemnized in the Church of England must be authorized by a certificate (or certificate and licence – *see* marriage by certificate and licence); marriages solemnized in the Church of England may be authorized either by a certificate or by a religious procedure (e.g. *banns, common li-

cence, or special licence – *see* marriage by religious licence). Notice must be given of the intended marriage to the Superintendent Registrar of the district(s) in which the parties have lived for seven days previously, together with a declaration that there are no lawful obstacles to the marriage and that all necessary consents have been obtained. This notice is made public for 21 days, to give members of the public the opportunity to point out the existence of a lawful obstacle, after which the Registrar must issue a certificate. The marriage must take place within three months from the day the notice was entered in the notice book.

marriage by certificate and licence Marriage authorized by a certificate and licence issued by the Superintendent Registrar. The main difference between this procedure and that of *marriage by certificate alone is its speed – the marriage may take place any time after 24 hours have elapsed from the day of giving notice. This procedure may also be used when only one party has been resident in the district (although the minimum period of residence is 15 days), and the notice of intended marriage need not be publicly displayed. The procedure costs more than marriage by certificate.

marriage by Registrar-General's licence Marriage authorized by a licence issued by the Registrar-General of Births, Deaths, and Marriages. This exceptional procedure is designed to authorize a non-Anglican marriage outside a register office or registered building; it is used when one of the parties to the marriage is seriously ill and cannot be moved ("deathbed marriage"). The marriage must be celebrated at the place specified by the parties in giving notice within one month from the date on which the notice was entered in the notice book.

marriage by religious licence A marriage in the Church of England based on the grant of an ecclesiastical licence, rather than on publication of *banns. A *common licence* may be granted if one of the parties swears an affidavit that he believes there is no lawful impediment, that at least one of the parties has been resident in the parish for at least 15 days previously (or usually worships at the church), and that (in the case of a minor) parental consent has been obtained. If no caveat is issued against the grant of a licence, the ecclesiastical judge will grant a licence and the marriage may take place immediately. The Archbishop of Canterbury may also grant a *special licence* authorizing a marriage at any time of the day or night in any church, chapel, or other convenient place (even if unconsecrated).

marriage ceremony The ceremony creating the status of marriage. There are four main types of marriage ceremony (excluding marriage in military chapels). In a civil marriage, the ceremony takes place in a register office, with open doors, in the presence of the Superintendent Registrar (who conducts the ceremony), a registrar (who supervises registration formalities), and at least two witnesses. In a Church of England marriage, the ceremony usually takes place in church and is celebrated by a clergyman in the presence of at least two witnesses according to the rite of the Book of Common Prayer (or any alternative authorized form of service). A clergyman may refuse to marry anyone whose former marriage has been dissolved if the former spouse is still living. The marriage ceremony in Quaker and Jewish marriages is governed by the rules of those religions and need not be celebrated in a registered building, or by an authorized person, or in public. All other religious marriage ceremonies must be celebrated in a registered building designated as a place of meeting for religious worship, with open doors, and in the presence of at least two witnesses and a registrar or previously notified authorized person.

marriage settlement A *settlement made between the parties to a marriage. A settlement made before the marriage ceremony is called an *antenuptial settlement*; that made after the marriage is a *postnuptial settlement*. The purpose of a marriage settlement is to provide an income for one spouse or the children, while securing the capital for the other spouse. The courts have power when giving decrees of divorce, nullity, or judicial separation either to order property owned by one spouse to be settled for the benefit of the other spouse and children or to vary the terms of any existing ante- or postnuptial settlement. This power is often used to retain the use of the matrimonial home until the children are independent, as well as to retain the parents' financial investment.

marshalling of assets A process in which the claims of different creditors are directed towards different funds of the same debtor in an attempt to reach a fair result. When there are two creditors and two funds, and one has a claim exclusively on one fund but the other can claim against either fund, the rule of marshalling requires the latter to claim against the fund from which the former is excluded. The aim is, so far as possible, to allocate the assets so as to satisfy all the creditors.

marshalling of securities An application of *marshalling of assets. If A mortgages two properties to B and then mortgages one of the properties in addition to C (who may or may not know of B's mortgage) B, as first mortgagee, may obtain his money from whichever mortgaged property he chooses. However, if he chooses to obtain his money from the property mortgaged to C, C may if necessary obtain his money from the other property. This right cannot be exercised when a purchaser has obtained the property without knowing of the facts giving rise to the right to marshal.

martial law Government by the military authorities when the normal machinery of government has broken down as a result of invasion, civil war, or large-scale insurrection. The constitution of the UK does not provide for a declaration (with specified consequences) of martial law: it is no more than a situation capable of arising. While the military authorities are restoring order, their conduct could not be called into question by the ordinary courts of law. After the restoration of order, the legality of their actions would be theoretically capable of examination, but the standards that would be applied by the courts are unknown. Martial law should not be confused with military law (*see* service law); any courts held by the military authorities to try civilians during a state of martial law would not enjoy the status of courts martial.

master *n.* **1.** One of the *Masters of the Supreme Court or the Masters of the Bench (*see* Benchers). **2.** Formerly, an *employer. *See also* employer and employee.

Master of the Rolls (MR) The judge who is president of the Civil Division of the *Court of Appeal. The office is an ancient one and was originally held by the keeper of the public records. Later the holder was a judge of the Court of Chancery and assistant to the Lord Chancellor, with his own court, the *Rolls Court*. Since 1881 he has been a judge of the Court of Appeal only, but retains important duties in relation to public records. He also admits solicitors to practice.

Masters of the Bench *See* Benchers.

Masters of the Supreme Court Inferior judicial officers of the *Queen's Bench and *Chancery Divisions of the High Court. Their principal function is to supervise *interlocutory proceedings in litigation and (especially in the Chancery Division) to take accounts.

By convention, Chancery Masters are solicitors and Queen's Bench Masters are barristers. In the provinces a comparable jurisdiction is exercised by *district registrars* of the High Court (*see* district registry).

material facts (in pleadings) *See* pleading.

maternity rights The rights a woman has against her employer when she is absent from work wholly or partly because of her pregnancy or confinement. Provided she remains at work until the end of the 12th week before the expected date of her confinement and notifies her employer at least three weeks before she leaves of the reason for her absence, she is entitled under the Employment Protection (Consolidation) Act 1978 to maternity pay. The employer may demand a doctor's certificate of the expected date of confinement. Maternity pay is nine-tenths of a week's pay, less the amount of the National Insurance maternity allowance, payable for a maximum of six weeks' absence from work. The employer can pay it as a lump sum in advance or by instalments over the six weeks, but he may not defer it. He should obtain a receipt from the employee in the prescribed form, which entitles him to a full rebate from the Maternity Pay Fund administered by the Department of Employment.

The employee is also entitled to return to her former job at any time within 29 weeks after the beginning of the week of the baby's birth provided she notifies her employer in writing three weeks before she leaves work (or if that is not reasonably practicable, as soon as possible) of the reason for her absence, her intention to return, and the expected date of her confinement. The employer may demand the appropriate doctor's certificate. He may also, within 49 days after the actual or expected week of confinement, seek the employee's written confirmation of her intention to return. Provided he clearly advises her in writing of the consequences of her failure to reply, the employee's right to return is lost if she does not give written confirmation within 14 days after the employer's written request.

The employee must give her employer three weeks' notice of the date on which she intends to resume work; the employer can defer that date by up to four weeks. The employee may also defer her return once by up to four weeks if she provides a doctor's certificate saying that she is not yet fit to resume work. If the employer refuses to allow her to return, the employee is treated as having been continuously employed up to the intended date of return notified to her employer and as having been dismissed on that date for the reason for which she was not allowed to return. If she complains to an industrial tribunal that she has been unfairly dismissed (*see* unfair dismissal), the dismissal will be treated as fair under the Employment Act 1980 if the employer shows that it was not reasonably practicable to allow her to return, that the dismissal would have been reasonable if she had not been absent, or that in any event she would properly have been made redundant during her absence.

matrimonial causes *See* matrimonial proceedings.

matrimonial home The home in which a husband and wife have lived together. A husband is under a duty to provide his wife and children with a roof over their heads, and the wife is obliged to cohabit with him in that home. Failure by either party to cohabit may amount to *desertion.

When only one of the spouses owns the matrimonial home statute gives the nonowner certain *rights of occupation*, which may be enforced by court order. These rights will bind third parties (such as banks and building societies) if they are registered as a Class F land charge (in the case of previously unregistered land) or if they are protected by a notice or caution (in the case of registered land) – *see* registration of encumbrances. In Scotland similar rights have now been granted (for a limited period only) to unmarried cohabitees, under the Matrimonial Homes (Financial Provision) (Scotland) Act 1981. When the legal estate is registered under the Land Registration Act and the wife is in actual occupation, she may also be protected against eviction by a third party if she has an interest in the land, even though she has not registered a notice or caution. Such an interest may be acquired by virtue of her contributions to the mortgage payments or, sometimes, to household expenses, as well as by making improvements in the matrimonial home.

Upon divorce, nullity, or judicial separation the court has wide powers to make orders transferring the matrimonial home from one party to the other or altering their rights in it, in particular to provide for dependent children. County courts and magistrates' courts have powers to grant matrimonial injunctions excluding a spouse from the matrimonial home (*see* battered wife).

matrimonial injunctions *See* battered wife.

matrimonial offence Misbehaviour, such as adultery, desertion, or cruelty, by a party to a marriage. Formerly, proof of matrimonial offences provided grounds for divorce and was important in applications in magistrates' courts for financial relief during the marriage. Such conduct now only affects the courts' orders for financial provision upon divorce if it is unusually serious; it does not affect orders for custody unless the conduct is considered to be detrimental to the child's welfare.

matrimonial order An order made by magistrates under the 1960 Matrimonial Proceedings and Magistrates'

Courts Act for periodical payments, custody of children, or noncohabitation clauses. However, both the grounds on which magistrates may exercise jurisdiction and the type of orders they may make are now governed by the 1978 Domestic Proceedings and Magistrates' Courts Act.

matrimonial proceedings (matrimonial causes) Proceedings for *divorce, *nullity, or *judicial separation and applications for leave to petition for divorce within three years of marriage. The term does not include applications for declaration of matrimonial status. All matrimonial proceedings must be heard in a divorce county court or the Divorce Registry in London; if subsequently defended, they must be transferred to the High Court.

maturity *n.* The time at which a *bill of exchange becomes due for payment. When a bill is payable at a fixed period after date, after sight, or after the happening of a specified event, the date of payment is determined by excluding the day from which the time is to begin to run and including the day of payment. When a bill is payable at a fixed period after sight, the time begins to run from the date of *acceptance if the bill is accepted and from the date of noting or *protest if the bill is noted or protested for nonacceptance.

maxims of equity Short pithy statements used to denote general principles that are supposed to run through *equity. Although often inaccurate and subject to exceptions, they are commonly used to justify particular decisions and express some of the basic principles that have guided the development of equity. The main maxims are as follows:

equity acts *in personam*;
equity acts on the conscience;
equity will not suffer a wrong without a remedy (i.e. equity will not allow a person whom it considers as having a good claim to be denied the right to sue);

equity follows the law (i.e. equity follows the rules of common law unless there is a good reason to the contrary);
equity looks at the intent not at the form (i.e. equity looks to the reality of what was intended rather than the way in which it is expressed);
where the equities are equal, the earlier in time prevails (i.e. where rights are equal in content, the earlier right created takes precedence over the later);
he who seeks equity must do equity;
he who comes to equity must come with *clean hands (*see* equitable remedies);
*equality is equity;
equity looks on that as done which ought to be done (*see* conversion);
equity imputes an intent to fulfil an obligation (*see* satisfaction);
equity will not assist a volunteer (*see* voluntary settlement).

mayhem *n.* Serious injury to a part of the body, such as a leg, arm, or eye, that is essential for self-defence. Such an act will amount to a *battery or to *grievous bodily harm. The consent of the victim is no defence.

Mayor's and City of London Court A court formed in 1922 by the amalgamation of the Mayor's Court and the City of London Court. It had an unlimited civil jurisdiction over matters arising within the City. The Court was abolished by the Courts Act 1971, but the name is retained by the *county court for the City of London, which has normal county court jurisdiction.

McKenzie man [from the case *McKenzie* v *McKenzie* (1971)] A person who sits beside an unrepresented *litigant in court and assists him by prompting, taking notes, and quietly giving advice.

McNaghten Rules (M'Naghten Rules) Rules setting out the conditions under which a defendant may successfully escape conviction on the grounds of *insanity. They were formulated by judges after the trial of Daniel

Measure

McNaghten (1843), who killed the Prime Minister's secretary by mistake for the Prime Minister, under the delusion that the government was persecuting him, and was acquitted on the grounds of insanity. According to these rules, the defendant must show that he is suffering from a defect of reason arising out of "a disease of the mind". This would usually include most psychoses, paranoia, and schizophrenic diseases, but psychopaths and those suffering from neuroses or subnormality would not normally fall within the terms of the Rules. The defendant must also show that, as a result of the defect of reason, he did not know the "nature and quality" of his acts, i.e. he did not know what he was doing (for example, if he put a child on a fire, thinking it was a log of wood). Alternatively, he may prove that he did not know that his acts were wrong, even if he knew their nature and quality (for example, if he knew he was murdering, but did not know that this was wrong). If the defendant is suffering from an insane delusion, he is treated as though the delusion was true and will have a defence if there would normally be one on those facts (for example, if he kills someone under the insane delusion that he is acting in self-defence, since self-defence is a defence). *See also* automatism; irresistible impulse; diminished responsibility.

Measure *n. See* Church of England.

Members' interests Interests of members of the House of Commons that might affect their conduct as MPs; for example, employments, company directorships, shareholdings, substantial property holdings, and financial sponsorships. By a 1975 resolution of the House, these must be registered for public information.

memorandum in writing Written evidence of a contract for the sale or other disposition of land or of any interest in it. Under the Law of Property Act 1925 such a contract cannot be enforced by court action unless a memorandum in writing, signed by the party to be held liable and identifying the parties, the land, and other essentials, is produced as evidence of the contract. Usually the contract itself is in writing but a signed memorandum showing that the parties have been bound from the time of an earlier oral agreement is equally valid.

memorandum of association A document that must be drawn up when a *registered company is formed and signed by two or more founder members. It states the company's name and registered office, the purposes for which it was formed (the *objects clause*), the amount of its *authorized capital (if any), and, if applicable, that it is a *limited company. *See also* articles of association; registration of a company; Tables B, C, D, and E.

mensa et thoro See a mensa et thoro.

mens rea [Latin: a guilty mind] The state of mind that the prosecution must prove a defendant to have had at the time of committing a crime in order to secure a conviction. *Mens rea* varies from crime to crime; it is either defined in the statute creating the crime or established by *precedent. Common examples of *mens rea* are *intention to bring about a particular consequence, *recklessness as to whether such consequences may come about, and (possibly) *negligence. Some crimes require knowledge of certain circumstances as part of the *mens rea* (for example, the crime of receiving stolen goods requires the knowledge that they were stolen). Some crimes require no *mens rea*; these are known as crimes of *strict liability. Whenever *mens rea* is required, the prosecution must prove that it existed at the same time as the *actus reus* of the crime (co-incidence of *actus reus* and *mens rea*). A defendant cannot plead ignorance of the law, nor is a good motive a defence. He may, however, bring evidence to show that he had no *mens rea* for the crime he is charged with; alternatively, he may admit that he had *mens rea*, but raise a general defence (e.g. duress) or a particular defence allowed in relation to the crime.

mental disorder For the purposes of the Mental Health Act 1959, mental illness, *arrested development of mind (comprising subnormality and severe subnormality), *psychopathic disorder, and any other disorder or disability of mind. A person suffering (or appearing to be suffering) from mental disorder can be detained in hospital either for observation or for treatment. Detention for observation normally takes place on an application for his admission made by his nearest relative or a mental welfare officer. This is supported in either case by the recommendation of two doctors that it is desirable in the interests of the patient's own health and safety or for the protection of others. The application authorizes detention for up to 28 days. In a case of emergency, however, detention may be for up to 72 hours on an application supported by one doctor only and made by any relative. The procedure for detention for treatment is the same as the normal procedure for detention for observation. The application authorizes detention for up to one year, renewable for a further year and then for periods of two years on a report to the hospital managers by the doctor in charge. Discharge of a person detained may be effected by the managers or the doctor in charge and, within certain limits, the nearest relative; in the case of detention for treatment, discharge may also be directed by a *mental health review tribunal. *See also* hospital order; special hospital.

mental health review tribunal A tribunal to which applications may be made for the discharge from hospital of a person detained there for treatment of *mental disorder or, unless a *restric-

tion order has also been made, under a *hospital order. Such tribunals include legally and medically qualified members appointed by the Lord Chancellor and are under the supervision of the *Council on Tribunals.

mercantile agent A commercial *agent who has authority either to sell goods, to consign goods for the purpose of sale, to buy goods, or to raise money on the security of goods on behalf of his principal.

mercenary *n.* A person who is paid to serve with armed forces other than those of the state of which he is a national. *See also* foreign enlistment.

merchantable quality An *implied condition respecting the state of goods sold in the course of business. Such goods should be as fit for their ordinary purpose as it is reasonable to expect, taking into account any description applied to them, the price (if relevant), and all the other relevant circumstances. Goods are considered to be of merchantable quality if the buyer is satisfied with them, even after specific defects are drawn to his attention before the contract is made, or if he is given the opportunity to examine the goods for such defects.

mercy *n.* *See* prerogative of mercy.

mere equity A right affecting property that is less significant than an *equitable right or a *legal right; it does not affect anyone except the parties to the transaction in which it is contained. An example is the right to rectify a document.

merger *n.* **1.** An amalgamation between companies of similar size in which either the members of the merging companies exchange their shares for shares in a new company or the members of some of the merging companies exchange their shares for shares in another merging company. It is usually effected by a *takeover bid. *Compare* takeover. **2.** The extinguishing of a lesser interest in land when it comes into the same ownership as a greater one. For example, if a freehold owner acquires the unexpired leasehold estate, the latter may merge into the freehold. Whether or not merger occurs depends on the circumstances of the transaction (thus a leasehold that is subject to a subsisting mortgage will not normally merge with the freehold) and the intention of the parties.

mesne profits Money that a landlord can claim from a tenant who continues to occupy property after his tenancy ends, the amount being equivalent to the current market rent of the property. This may be more than the rent that the tenant was paying before the tenancy ended. If the landlord continues to accept the original rent from the tenant at the end of the tenancy, a new tenancy may be created.

messuage *n.* A house and its associated garden, outbuildings, and orchard.

metropolitan stipendiary magistrate *See* stipendiary magistrate.

Michaelmas Day *See* quarter days.

Middle Temple One of the four *Inns of Court, situated in the Temple between the Strand and the Embankment. The earliest recorded claim for its existence is 1404.

Midsummer Day *See* quarter days.

military court A *court martial or the *Court of Chivalry.

military law *See* service law. *Compare* martial law.

military testament *See* privileged will.

minerals *pl. n. See* mining lease.

minimum subscription The amount that the directors of a company decide must be raised by a first offer of shares to the public in order to provide for the purchase of property, preliminary expenses, and working capital. This

amount must be stated in the *prospectus. When the company has received applications for shares (specifying cash payment) to the value of the minimum subscription, together with the amount payable upon application, it can proceed to allot the shares (*see* allotment).

minimum term *See* life imprisonment.

minimum wage The lowest rate of remuneration that an employer may pay. There is no general statutory minimum wage, but in certain industries *wages councils may prescribe minimum rates of pay and other terms and conditions of employment.

mining lease A lease granting a tenant the right to extract minerals from the land for a specified period in return for a rent. The Settled Land Act 1925 allows the tenant for life of settled land to grant mining leases for up to 100 years if he is not liable for any *waste he commits, but three-quarters of the rent must be paid to the trustees as *capital money. The Act defines minerals for these purposes as all substances in or under the land that can be extracted by underground or surface working.

minister *n.* A person (by constitutional convention a member of either House of Parliament) appointed to government office by the Crown on the advice of the Prime Minister. He may be a senior minister in charge of a department (normally styled Secretary of State but sometimes Minister) or without specific departmental responsibilities (e.g. the Lord Privy Seal or a Minister without Portfolio) or a junior minister assisting in departmental business (a Minister of State or a Parliamentary Secretary or Under-Secretary). In the Treasury the ministerial ranks are Chancellor of the Exchequer, Chief Secretary, Financial Secretary, and Ministers of State.

ministerial responsibility The responsibility to Parliament of the Cabinet collectively and of individual ministers for their own decisions and the conduct of their departments. A minister must defend his decisions without sheltering behind his civil servants; if he cannot, political pressure may force his resignation.

minor *n. See* infant.

minor interests Interests in *registered land that cannot be created or transferred by registered disposition, are not *overriding interests, and could be overridden by a registered proprietor unless protected by registration. Such interests include the equitable interests of beneficiaries under a settlement and all charges registrable at the Land Charges Department in the case of unregistered land (*see* registration of encumbrances). Minor interests are protected by registration of a notice, caution, inhibition, or restriction as appropriate.

minority *n.* The state of being an *infant (*or* minor). *Compare* majority.

minority protection Remedies evolved to safeguard a minority of company members from abuse by the *majority rule. They include *just and equitable winding-up, applying for relief on the basis of *unfair prejudice, bringing a *derivative or *representative action, and seeking an *inspection and investigation of the company.

minutes *pl. n.* Records of company business transacted at general meetings, board meetings, and meetings of managers. Registered companies are required to keep such records. Minutes of general meetings can be inspected by company members at the registered office.

miscarriage *n.* **1.** A failure of justice. **2.** A spontaneous *abortion, i.e. one that is not induced.

mischief rule *See* interpretation of statutes.

misconduct *n. See* wilful misconduct.

misdemeanour *n.* Formerly (i.e. before 1967), any of the less serious offences, as opposed to *felony.

misdirection *n.* An incorrect direction by a judge to a *jury on a matter of law. In such cases the Court of Appeal may quash the conviction.

misfeasance *n.* The negligent or otherwise improper performance of a lawful act. *Compare* malfeasance; nonfeasance.

misfeasance summons An application to the court by a creditor, contributory, liquidator, or the official receiver during the course of winding up a company. The court is asked to examine the conduct of a director or promoter who is suspected of a breach of *fiduciary duty and it can order him to make restitution to the company.

misjoinder of parties An incorrect *joinder of parties in an action. In modern practice this does not cause the action to abate but it can be rectified by *amendment.

mispleading *n.* The omission in a *pleading of an essential allegation. In modern practice, it can usually be rectified by *amendment.

misprision *n.* Failure to report an offence. The former crime of misprision of felony has now been replaced by the crime of *compounding an offence. However, the common-law offence of misprision of treason still exists; this occurs if a person knows or reasonably suspects that someone has committed treason but does not inform the proper authorities within a reasonable time. The punishment for this offence is forfeiture by the offender of all his property during his lifetime.

misrepresentation *n.* An untrue statement of fact, made by one party to the other in the course of negotiating a contract, that induces the other party to enter into the contract. The person making the misrepresentation is called the *representor*, and the person to whom it is made is the *representee*. A false statement of law, opinion, or intention does not constitute a misrepresentation; nor does a statement of fact known by the representee to be untrue. Moreover, unless the representee relies on the statement so that it becomes an *inducement* (though not necessarily the only inducement) to enter into the contract, it is not a misrepresentation. The remedies for misrepresentation vary according to the degree of culpability of the representor. If he is guilty of *fraudulent misrepresentation* (i.e. if he did not honestly believe in the truth of his statement, which is not the same as saying that he knew it to be false) the representee may, subject to certain limitations, set the contract aside by *rescission and may also sue for damages. If he is guilty of *negligent misrepresentation* (i.e. if he believed in his statement but had no reasonable grounds for doing so) the representee was formerly entitled only to rescission but may now (under the Misrepresentation Act 1967) also obtain *damages. If the representor has committed merely an *innocent misrepresentation* (one he reasonably believed to be true) the representee is restricted to rescission, subject to the discretion of the court under the 1967 Act to award him damages in lieu. A representee entitled to rescind a contract for misrepresentation may decide instead to *affirm it. *See also* nondisclosure.

mistake *n.* A misunderstanding or erroneous belief about a matter of fact (*mistake of fact*) or a matter of law (*mistake of law*). In civil cases, mistake is particularly important in the law of contract. Mistakes of law have no effect on the validity of agreements, and neither do many mistakes of fact. When a mistake of fact does do so, it may render the agreement void under common-law rules (in which case it is referred to as an *operative mistake*) or it may make it voidable, i.e. liable, subject to certain limitations, to be set aside by

*rescission under more lenient rules of equity.

When both parties to an agreement are under a misunderstanding, the mistake may be classified as either a *common mistake* (i.e. a single mistake shared by both) or a *mutual mistake* (i.e. each misunderstanding the other). In the case of common mistake, there is full *consensus ad idem* and the mistake renders the contract void only if it robs it of all substance. The principal (and almost the only) example is when the subject matter of the contract has, unknown to both parties, ceased to exist (*res extincta*). A common mistake about some particular attribute of the subject matter (e.g. that it is an original, not a copy) is not an operative mistake. However, a common mistake relating to any really fundamental matter will render a contract voidable. In the case of mutual mistake there is no real *consensus*, but the contract is nevertheless valid if only one interpretation of what was agreed can be deduced from the parties' words and conduct. Otherwise, the mistake is operative and the contract void. When only one party to a contract is under a misunderstanding, his mistake may be called a *unilateral mistake* and it makes the contract void if it relates to the fundamental nature of the offer and the other party knew or ought to have known of it. Otherwise, the contract is valid so far as the law of mistake is concerned, though the circumstances may be such as to make it voidable for *misrepresentation.

A deed or other signed document (whether or not constituting a contract) that does not correctly record what both parties intended may be rectified by the courts. When one signatory to a document was fundamentally mistaken as to the character or effect of the transaction it embodies, he may (unless he was careless) plead his mistake as a defence to any action based on the document (*see non est factum*).

In criminal cases, if someone makes a

mistake of law and commits a crime because he does not know that the law forbids it, he is usually guilty (*ignorantia juris neminem excusat*: ignorance of the law is no excuse). However, if that person is unable to find out that a new law has been promulgated (for example because he was on a voyage or because the *statutory instrument bringing an enactment into force has not yet been published) he will have a defence of ignorance of the law.

If a defendant makes a mistake of law that prevents him having the *mens rea* required to be guilty of the crime, he will normally be acquitted of the crime, even if his mistake is unreasonable (for example, if he damages someone else's property in the belief that it is his own, and this belief is caused by a mistake as to the law of property). He will not be acquitted, however, if the crime is one of negligence, because an unreasonable mistake is by definition evidence of negligence. If a defendant makes a mistake of law that does not prevent him having the *mens rea* of the crime, he will only be acquitted if his mistake was reasonable. For example, if someone who is already married goes through a second marriage ceremony, mistakenly believing that English law permits polygamy, he will be guilty of bigamy if (as in most cases) the jury thinks that the mistake was an unreasonable one for him to make. The same rule applies to mistakes of fact.

mistakes in judgment *See* slip rule.

mistrial *n.* A trial that is vitiated by some fundamental defect.

mitigation *n.* **1.** Reduction in the severity of some penalty. Before *sentence is passed on someone convicted of a crime, the defence may make a plea in mitigation, putting forward reasons for making the sentence less severe than it might otherwise be. These might include personal or family circumstances of the offender, and the defence may also dispute facts raised by the prosecu-

tion to indicate aggravating circumstances. In raising mitigating factors, *hearsay evidence or documentary evidence of *character are accepted. **2.** Reduction in the loss or injury resulting from a tort or a breach of contract. The injured party is under a duty to take all reasonable steps to mitigate his loss when claiming *damages.

mixed action A form of court action combining a claim relating to real property with a claim for damages.

mixed fund A fund of money derived from the sale of both real and personal property.

mixed property *Property that has some of the attributes of both real and personal property. *Emblements are an example.

M'Naghten Rules *See* McNaghten Rules.

mock auction An auction during which (1) any lot is sold to someone at a price lower than his highest bid for it; (2) part of the price is repaid or credited to the bidder; (3) the right to bid is restricted to those who have bought or agreed to buy one or more articles; or (4) articles are given away or offered as gifts. Under the Mock Auction Act 1961 it is an offence to promote or conduct a mock auction of plate, plated articles, linen, china, glass, books, pictures, prints, furniture, jewellery, articles of household or personal use, ornaments, or any musical or scientific instrument.

molestation *n.* Behaviour that has the effect or intention of annoying or pestering one's spouse or children. Such an act need not involve violence or physical assault; harassment (by threatening letters or telephone calls) may constitute molestation. Under the 1976 Domestic Violence and Matrimonial Proceedings Act, spouses (and in some cases unmarried cohabitees) can apply for a court injunction to prevent molestation. Magistrates' courts now have similar powers under the 1978 Domestic Proceedings and Magistrates' Courts Act, but only if there is violence and only in relation to married couples. *See also* battered child; battered wife.

money Bill A Bill that, in the opinion of the Speaker of the House of Commons, contains only provisions dealing with taxation, the Consolidated Fund, public money, the raising or replacement of loans by the state, and matters incidental to these subjects. Such a Bill can become an Act without the House of Lords' consent (*see* Act of Parliament).

money had and received A former ground for court action that occurred when the defendant was in possession of money that should have belonged to the plaintiff (for example, when money had been paid to an agent who then failed to pass it on to his principal).

moneylender *n*. A person whose business it is to lend money. The Moneylenders Acts 1900–27 contain provisions for the control of moneylenders, including the form of their contracts. Under the Acts, the term "moneylender" does not include pawnbrokers, friendly or building societies, corporate bodies with special powers to lend money, those carrying on a banking or insurance business, or businesses whose primary object is not the lending of money. When the more extensive provisions of the Consumer Credit Act 1974 are fully in force they will replace the provisions of the Moneylenders Acts.

monism *n*. The theory that national and international law form part of one legal structure, in which international law is supreme. It is opposed to *dualism*, which holds that they are separate systems operating in different fields.

monopoly *n*. A situation in which a substantial proportion of a particular type of business is transacted by a single enterprise or trader. The Fair Trad-

ing Act 1973 contains provisions assigning functions in respect of monopolies to the *Director General of Fair Trading and the Monopolies and Mergers Commission. It defines a monopoly situation, in relation to the supply of goods and services and the export of goods, as one in which a single enterprise, connected group of companies, or trade association has one-quarter of the relevant business. When the Monopolies and Mergers Commission finds that a monopoly situation exists and operates against the public interest, the Minister has powers to remedy or prevent the adverse effects.

month *n*. A calendar month or a lunar month (28 days). The common law adopted the lunar month, but the Interpretation Act provides that the word is to be presumed to mean calendar month in Acts of Parliament and the Law of Property Act 1925 provides similarly for deeds and other written documents.

mortgage *n*. An interest in property created as a form of security for a loan or payment of a debt and terminated on payment of the loan or debt. The borrower, who offers the security, is the *mortgagor*; the lender, who provides the money, is the *mortgagee*. Virtually any property may be mortgaged (though land is the most common); exceptions include the salaries of public officials. The name is derived from Old French (literally: dead pledge), since at common law failure to repay on the due date of redemption (which in most mortgages is set very early) formerly resulted in the mortgagor losing all his rights over the property. By the rules of equity the mortgagor is now allowed to redeem his property at any time on payment of the loan together with interest and costs (*see* equity of redemption). In face of continued nonpayment of the loan, however, the mortgagee may seek possession of the mortgaged property, sell it under a *power of sale, appoint a *receiver, or obtain a decree of *foreclosure.

Under the Law of Property Act 1925 the only valid *legal mortgages* are (1) a lease subject to *cesser on redemption and (2) a deed expressed to be a charge by way of legal mortgage (*see* charge). All other mortgages are equitable interests only (*see* equitable mortgage). All mortgages of registered land are noted in the charges register on application by the mortgagee (*see* land registration), and a *charge certificate is issued to him. When mortgaged land is unregistered, a first legal mortgagee keeps the title deeds. A subsequent legal mortgagee and any equitable mortgagee who does not have the title deeds should protect his interests by registration (*see* registration of encumbrances). *See also* priority of mortgages.

mortgage action A court action brought by a mortgagee for possession of the mortgaged property or payment of all money due to him, when the mortgagor has failed to pay the amounts due under the mortgage.

mortgagee *n. See* mortgage.

mortgagor *n. See* mortgage.

motion *n.* An application made orally and in open court to a judge for an order, most commonly an interlocutory *injunction. Motions may be *interlocutory* (i.e. relating to some pre-trial matter in proceedings begun by some other form of originating *process) or *originating*. In both cases the applicant must normally serve a *notice of motion* on his opponent, warning him of his intention to move the court, but some motions can be brought *ex parte*.

motive *n.* The purpose behind a course of action. Motive is not normally relevant in deciding guilt or innocence (for example, killing to save someone from suffering is still murder), although it may be of some relevance in the crime of *libel. Nor is a bad motive relevant in deciding legal guilt. However, a good motive may be invoked as a reason for mitigating a punishment upon conviction, and a bad motive may provide circumstantial evidence that the defendant committed the crime he is charged with.

motor car *See* motor vehicle.

motor cycle *See* motor vehicle.

motoring offences *See* offences relating to road traffic.

motor insurance *See* third-party insurance.

Motor Insurers' Bureau A body set up by the insurance industry, by agreement with the Department of the Environment. It provides cover if someone has been injured or killed in a motor accident when either (1) a judgment against the party liable is unsatisfied, for example because the party is (in breach of the Road Traffic Act) uninsured, or (2) the wrongdoer cannot be identified.

motor vehicle For the purposes of the Road Traffic Acts, any mechanically propelled vehicle intended or adapted for use on the roads. This includes *motor cars* (vehicles of not more than 3 tonnes in unladen weight, designed to carry loads or up to seven passengers) and *motor cycles* (vehicles of not more than 8 cwt in unladen weight and having less than four wheels). A car from which the engine has been removed may still be considered to be mechanically propelled if the removal is temporary, but if so many parts have been removed that it cannot be restored to use at a reasonable expense, it ceases to be mechanically propelled. A dumper used for carrying materials at a building site is not intended for use on roads, even if it is in fact used on a road near the building site; and a go-kart is not intended nor adapted for use on the roads (even though it is capable of being used on the roads). *See also* conveyance.

motorway driving Contravention of the regulations relating to driving on a motorway, as outlined in the Highway Code, is an offence punishable by *endorsement (which carries 3 points under the *totting-up system) and discretionary *disqualification.

MOT test An annual test originally ordered by the Ministry of Transport (now the Department of the Environment) to be carried out on all motor vehicles over a certain age to ensure that they comply with certain legal requirements relating to vehicle maintenance. The test covers brakes, steering, lights and indicators, windscreen wipers and washers, the exhaust system, horn, tyres (and to some extent, the wheels), bodywork and suspension (insofar as they affect the brakes and steering), and seat belts. It is an offence to put on the road a motor vehicle that has been registered for over three years without a valid test certificate. A certificate is issued for 12 months and must be renewed annually; a vehicle that is subject to a test cannot be licensed without a test certificate (*see* road tax). It is not an endorsable offence not to have an MOT certificate, but this may invalidate the motorist's insurance and result in a charge of *driving without insurance. An MOT certificate does not indicate that the vehicle is roadworthy in all respects and is not a defence to charges brought under the *vehicle construction and maintenance regulations.

movables *pl. n.* Tangible items of property other than land and goods fixed to the land (i.e. immovables).

MR *See* Master of the Rolls.

multiple admissibility The principle of the law of evidence that if evidence is admissible for one purpose it may not be rejected solely because it is inadmissible for some other purpose. However, the *trier of fact may have to be directed not to consider the evidence when deciding those issues in respect of which it is inadmissible.

multiple agreement (under the Con-

sumer Credit Act 1974) An agreement the terms of which are such that (1) part of it falls within one category of agreement mentioned in the Act and another part within a different category of agreement, which may or may not be mentioned in the Act; or (2) a part or the whole of it is placed within two or more categories of agreement mentioned in the Act. When part of an agreement falls within a category mentioned in the Act, that part is treated for the purposes of the Act as a separate agreement. When an agreement falls within two or more categories, it is treated as an agreement in each of the categories in question.

municipal law The national, or internal, law of a state, as opposed to international law. *See also* doctrine of incorporation; private law; public law.

muniments *pl. n.* Documents that prove a person's title to land. They include the relevant *title deeds, certificates of *official search, and other documents tracing ownership of the land through to the present owner.

murder *n.* Homicide that is neither accidental nor lawful and does not fall into the categories of *manslaughter or *infanticide. The *mens rea* for murder is traditionally known as *malice aforethought and the punishment (since 1965) is *life imprisonment. Murder is subject to the two special defences of *diminished responsibility and *provocation.

mute *adj. See* standing mute.

mutiny *n.* An offence against service law committed by any member of HM forces who combines with one or more other members (whether or not civilians are also involved) to overthrow or resist lawful authority in those forces or any forces cooperating with them. If a civilian is involved, his conduct will be a matter for the ordinary criminal law. The offence is also committed if the aim of the combination is to disobey lawful authority in a manner subversive of discipline, or for the purpose of avoiding any duty connected with operations against the enemy, or generally to impede the performance of any duty in HM forces or any cooperating forces.

mutual mistake *See* mistake.

mutual wills Wills conferring reciprocal benefits, made by two or more persons who have agreed that the wills are not to be revoked. The court will enforce the agreement by declaring that the survivor holds the relevant property on an implied trust to give effect to the mutual will. For example, H and W by agreement make wills leaving property to each other absolutely, each providing that if the other dies first the property goes instead to X. If after H's death W makes a fresh will in favour of Y, the court will on W's death nonetheless give effect to the interest left to X under the original mutual will.

N

naked agreement *See* consideration.

naked trust *See* bare trust.

name *n. See* business name; change of name; company name; surname.

name and arms clause A clause in a settlement providing that the beneficiary forfeits his entitlement unless he uses a specified surname and, if appropriate, coat of arms at all times. The clause is valid only if it is sufficiently precise.

National Health Service A service established for England and Wales in 1946, reorganized in 1974, and now governed by the National Health Service Act 1977. It is concerned with the provision of hospital, specialist, general practitioner (medical, dental, ophthalmic, and pharmaceutical), nurs-

ing, ambulance, and related services, under the ultimate responsibility of the Secretary of State for Social Services. In England and Wales it is administered operationally by *district health authorities*, which are grouped under *regional health authorities* with overall planning responsibility. In Scotland the regional tier is omitted and overall responsibility lies with *area health authorities*. There are also family practitioner committees, concerned with the administration of the general practitioner services, and community health councils to represent the public interest.

national insurance A scheme of state-administered social security benefits (e.g. unemployment and sickness benefit and old age pensions). These were inaugurated by the National Insurance Act 1946 and are now given effect by the Social Security Act 1975. A separate industrial injuries insurance scheme was established by the National Insurance (Industrial Injuries) Act 1946, but the 1975 Act now governs the payment of *industrial injuries benefits also. *Compare* supplementary benefit.

national insurance tribunal A tribunal that hears appeals from adjudications by local insurance officers (who are government employees) on claims for social security or industrial injuries benefit (*see* national insurance). Such tribunals are subject to the supervision of the *Council on Tribunals; appeal against their decisions can be made to a National Insurance Commissioner.

nationality *n.* The state of being a citizen or subject of a particular country. *See* British citizenship; British Dependent Territories citizenship; British Overseas citizenship; British subject.

nationalized industries Industries such as coal, gas, electricity, and rail that have by statute been taken into public ownership. They are administered by ministerially appointed boards (rather than by government departments). The minister controls and is accountable to Parliament for matters of general policy, but the day-to-day affairs of the industries are managed by the boards alone and are not subject to detailed parliamentary scrutiny.

natural child 1. An illegitimate child (*see* illegitimacy). Until 1969 a gift by will to one's "children" was presumed to exclude natural (illegitimate) children, but there is now a presumption that it does include them. **2.** A child of one's body, as opposed to an adopted child.

naturalization *n.* The acquisition of *British citizenship or *British Dependent Territories citizenship by means of a certificate of naturalization. This is granted by the Secretary of State to an applicant who has satisfied statutory requirements as to residence and other matters and taken an *oath of allegiance.

natural justice Rules of fair play, originally developed by the courts of common law to control the decisions of inferior courts and then gradually extended (particularly in the 20th century) to apply equally to the decisions of administrative and domestic tribunals and of any authority exercising an *administrative power that affects a person's status, rights, or liabilities. Any decision reached in contravention of natural justice is void as *ultra vires*. There are two principal rules. The first is the *rule against bias – nemo judex in causa sua* (or *in propria causa*) (no man may be a judge in his own cause). This means that any decision, however fair it may seem, is invalid if made by a person with any financial or other interest in the outcome or any known bias that might have affected his impartiality. The second rule is known as *audi alteram partem* (hear the other side). It states that a decision cannot stand unless the person directly affected by it was given a fair opportunity both to state his case and to know and answer the other side's case.

natural law The permanent underlying basis of all law. The philosophers of ancient Greece, where the idea of natural law originated, considered that there was a kind of perfect justice given to man by nature and that man's laws should conform to this as closely as possible. Theories of natural law have been an important part of jurisprudence throughout legal history. Natural law is distinguished from *positive law*, which is the body of law imposed by the state.

natural person A human being. *Compare* juristic person.

natural rights The fundamental rights to which all men are entitled without interference by the state. This is a concept of *natural law that was particularly popular in the 18th century. It has had great influence in the legal history of the USA, as seen, for example, in the Virginian Declaration of Rights: "All men are by nature equally free and independent and have certain inherent natural rights of which when they enter a society they cannot by any compact deprive or divest their posterity". *See also* human rights.

naval court A court convened under the Merchant Shipping Act 1894 either by the captain of one of HM ships on foreign station or by a consular officer. Its purpose is to inquire into the abandonment or loss of any British ship, any complaint by an officer or seaman of such a ship, or any other matter requiring investigation in the interests of the owners of the ship or its cargo. It reports to the Department of Trade and has limited disciplinary powers. A naval court has from three to five members, each of whom must be either a naval officer, the master of a British merchant ship, a consular officer, or a British merchant (each of the first three of these categories must if possible be represented).

naval law *See* service law.

necessaries *pl. n.* Goods or services suitable to the condition in life and actual requirements of a minor or a person subject to incapacity, e.g. essential clothing. Although such a person's legal *capacity to contract is limited, he must pay a reasonable price for necessaries sold and delivered to him.

necessity *n.* Pressure of circumstances compelling one to commit an illegal act. It is not altogether clear whether English law accepts a defence of necessity to a criminal charge (*compare* duress). There have, however, been acquittals on this basis when (1) a prisoner escaped from a burning gaol; (2) the crew of a ship jettisoned the cargo (not belonging to them) to save the ship from sinking; and (3) a woman took an infected child through the streets (a common-law misdemeanour amounting to a nuisance) to seek medical advice. It has also been suggested that a driver of a fire engine may have a defence of necessity if he crossed red lights to save someone trapped by fire, and it may be a defence to charges brought against a surgeon who has to operate without the patient's consent. Necessity is not, however, a defence to charges of theft or murder (e.g. when ship-wrecked victims kill and eat one of their number) and it is not usually a defence to driving offences.

Necessity is in some circumstances a defence to an action in tort, but it is probably limited to action taken in an emergency to protect life or property. The steps taken in the emergency must be reasonable.

negative pregnant An evasive reply to an allegation in a court pleading, which – while being a literal response – in fact evades the true matter at issue. For example, if A denies that he received £1000 from B, this is a negative pregnant if he in fact received a lesser amount and the matter at issue was that he received money from B. *Compare* affirmative pregnant.

negative resolution *See* delegated legislation.

neglect *n.* It is a criminal offence for a parent or guardian to neglect their child in a way that is likely to cause unnecessary suffering or injury to health, when the parent is aware of (or reckless as to) the likely consequences of the neglect. Neglect may also be evidence of *negligence and may give rise to a charge of manslaughter if the neglected person dies.

negligence *n.* **1.** Carelessness: failure to do something that a reasonable man (i.e. an average responsible citizen) would do, or doing something that a reasonable man would not do. In cases of professional negligence, involving someone with a special skill, that person is expected to show the skill of an average member of his profession. Negligence may be an element in a number of crimes, e.g. negligent driving (*see* careless driving) and various regulatory offences, which are usually punished by fine. The main example of a serious crime that may be committed by negligence is *manslaughter (in one of its forms). When negligence is a basis of criminal liability, it is no defence to show that one was doing one's best if one's conduct still falls below that of the reasonable man in the circumstances. *See also* gross negligence. **2.** A tort consisting of the breach of a *duty of care resulting in damage to the plaintiff. Negligence in the sense of carelessness does not give rise to civil liability unless the defendant's failure to conform to the standards of the reasonable man was a breach of a duty of care owed to the plaintiff, which has caused damage to him (*see res ipsa loquitur*). *See also* contributory negligence.

negligent misstatement (negligent

misrepresentation, careless statement) A false statement of fact made honestly but carelessly. A statement of opinion may be treated as a statement of fact if it carries the implication that the person making it has reasonable grounds for his opinion. A negligent misstatement is only actionable in tort if there has been breach of a duty to take care in making the statement that has caused damage to the plaintiff. There is no general *duty of care in making statements, particularly in relation to statements on financial matters. Responsibility for negligent misstatements is imposed only if they were made in circumstances that made it reasonable to rely on them. If a negligent misstatement induces the person to whom it was made to enter into a contract with the maker of the statement, the statement may be actionable as a term of the contract if the parties intended it to be a term or it may give rise to damages or *rescission under the Misrepresentation Act 1967 (*see also* misrepresentation).

negotiable instrument A document that constitutes an obligation to pay a sum of money and is transferable by delivery. The transferee can enforce the obligation even if the transferor's title is defective, provided that he accepted the document in good faith and for value and had no notice of the defect. The most important classes of negotiable instruments are *bills of exchange (including cheques) and *promissory notes.

negotiation of a bill The transfer of a *bill of exchange from one person to another so that the transferee becomes the holder. A bill payable to bearer is negotiated by *delivery; a bill payable to order is negotiated by the *endorsement of the holder completed by delivery. The issue of a bill to the payee is not a negotiation.

nemo dat quod non habet [Latin: no one can give what he has not got] The basic rule that a person who does not own property (e.g. a thief) cannot confer it on another except with the true owner's authority (i.e. as his agent). Exceptions to this rule include the sale of goods in *market overt, sales under statutory powers, and cases in which the doctrine of *estoppel prevents the true owner from denying the authority of the seller to sell.

nemo debet bis vexari [Latin: no man ought to be twice vexed] No person should be twice sued or prosecuted upon the same set of facts if there has been a final decision of a competent court. The maxim reflects the policy underlying the doctrine of *estoppel *per rem judicatam* and *issue estoppel.

nemo est heres viventis [Latin: no one is the heir of a living person] A maxim stating that a person's *heir can be ascertained only at the time of his death, since until then his heir apparent may die or be disinherited. Thus an heir apparent has no legal or equitable interest in property he expects to inherit until it actually devolves upon him.

nemo judex in causa sua (nemo judex in propria causa) See natural justice.

nemo tenetur seipsum accusare [Latin: no one is bound to incriminate himself] A maxim reflecting the policy underlying the *privilege against self-incrimination.

nervous shock A recognizable psychiatric illness caused by shock, as distinct from normal grief, sorrow, or anxiety. Damages cannot be obtained for grief, sorrow, or anxiety alone, but shock that produces an illness is an actionable injury. The test of liability for shock is whether or not the injury produced by the shock was reasonably foreseeable.

new trial (retrial) A second trial of a case ordered by an appellate court. In civil cases the Court of Appeal may order a new trial on grounds including misconduct by the judge (such as a serious misdirection), serious procedural irregularity, or (in rare cases) because fresh evidence has come to light. In criminal cases new trials are rarely ordered and then only if the appeal has been based upon the admission of fresh evidence. *See also venire de novo.*

next friend An adult responsible for the conduct and costs of legal proceedings instituted on behalf of an infant or mentally disordered person. Proceedings against an infant or mentally disordered person are defended by a guardian *ad litem. See also* Official Solicitor.

next of kin A person's closest blood relations. Parents and children are treated as being closer than grandparents, grandchildren, or siblings.

nisi [Latin] *adj.* Not final. *See also* decree nisi.

no case to answer A submission by the defending party in a court action that the plaintiff's or prosecution's case is not sufficient for the defendant to need to make any reply, either because of insufficient legal grounds or because of insufficient factual evidence. If the submission succeeds, judgment is entered for the defence.

no-fault liability The principle that injured persons should receive compensation for their injuries without having to prove fault against any individual. The term is American in origin, and in the USA and Canada it usually refers to compensation schemes for injuries in highway accidents. New Zealand has a comprehensive no-fault compensation scheme for personal injuries caused by accident, which has completely replaced actions in tort for personal injuries. In the UK, industrial injuries compensation is a form of no-fault liability.

nolle prosequi [Latin: to be unwilling to prosecute] A procedure by which the *Attorney General may terminate criminal proceedings. The entry of a *nolle prosequi* automatically terminates crim-

inal proceedings on *indictment, but the leave of the court is required in the case of a *summary trial. The procedure is most commonly employed when the accused cannot be produced in court to plead or stand his trial owing to physical or mental incapacity that is expected to be permanent. It is also sometimes used when the Attorney General considers that a prosecution is not in the public interest. His decision is not subject to any control by the courts. Unlike an acquittal, a *nolle prosequi* does not bar a further prosecution.

nominal capital *See* authorized capital.

nominal damages A token sum of *damages awarded when a legal right has been infringed but no substantial loss has been caused.

nomination *n.* **1.** The naming of a person for a vacant post or office or as a candidate in a parliamentary or local-government election. **2.** The naming by a member of a friendly society of a person to take his interest in the society on his death, without the need for a formal will. The member must be 16 or over and the nomination must be made in writing; it may be revoked at any time by the member himself and is, in any event, revoked on his marriage.

nominee shareholder A company member who holds the shares registered in his name for the benefit of another. The identity of the person with the true interest may be subject to disclosure under the Companies Acts.

nonage *n.* The period during which someone is under the age of majority (18 years). *See* infant.

noncohabitation order An order made by magistrates relieving a wife of the duty of living with her husband. Since 1978 noncohabitation orders have been abolished, but orders made before 1978 may still be of relevance as evidence in divorce proceedings. As long as a noncohabitation order is in force a wife cannot be guilty of desertion.

noncommercial agreement A *consumer-credit agreement or a *consumer-hire agreement made by a creditor or owner but not in the course of a business carried on by him. Such an agreement is outside certain of the provisions of the Consumer Credit Act 1974.

noncontentious business Any business of a solicitor that is not *contentious business. In practice, it is business of a nonlitigious character.

nondisclosure *n.* **1.** (*or* **concealment**) (in contract law) The failure by one party, during negotiations for a contract, to disclose to the other a fact known to him that would influence the other in deciding whether or not to enter into the contract. A full duty of disclosure exists only in the case of contracts *uberrimae fidei*, which are usually contracts of insurance. If the person to be insured tells an untruth, the contract will (like any other) be voidable for *misrepresentation; if he also suppresses a material fact, it will be voidable for nondisclosure. In the case of other contracts, there is no general duty to volunteer information and mere silence cannot constitute misrepresentation. There is, however, a very limited duty of disclosure. A person who does volunteer information must not tell only a partial truth and must correct any statement that subsequently becomes to his knowledge untrue; breach of this duty will render the contract voidable for misrepresentation. **2.** (in court procedure) Failure of a party to include a document that should have been disclosed in his list of documents for *discovery and inspection. The other party may seek an order for *specific discovery* of the document or an order requiring the party making discovery to verify his list of documents by *affidavit.

nondiscrimination notice Notice served by the Commission for Racial Equality or by the Equal Opportunities Commission requiring an offender who has practised illegal *racial or *sex discrimination not to commit such acts.

non est factum [Latin, from *non est factum suum*, it is not his deed] A plea that an agreement (originally a deed) mentioned in the pleading was not the act of the defendant. It can be used as a defence to actions based on *mistakes in documents when the defendant was fundamentally mistaken as to the character or effect of the transaction embodied in the document.

nonfeasance *n.* Failure to perform an act required by law. Until 1961, a highway authority guilty of nonfeasance by failing to carry out repair and maintenance was not liable for injuries caused because of this. It was, however, liable for *misfeasance. The defence of nonfeasance was then abolished by statute, but an authority can plead instead that it took all reasonable care to secure that the highway was not dangerous.

nonjoinder *n.* A plea in *abatement alleging that the plaintiff had failed to join all necessary parties in the action. In modern practice this does not cause the action to abate but it can be rectified by *amendment.

nonjury list A list of cases for trial by judge alone in the High Court. *See also* lists.

nonmolestation order *See* battered wife; molestation.

nonprovable debt A debt that cannot be claimed in the course of *bankruptcy proceedings. Examples are maintenance payments to a wife, *statute-barred debts, and debts that cannot be fixed or estimated. *Compare* provable debt.

nonsuit *n.* **1.** The withdrawal by a judge of a case from a jury with a verdict being entered in favour of the accused. **2.** Formerly, a plaintiff's withdrawal from a civil court action.

non-user *n.* The failure to exercise a right over land, which may be extinguished if the non-user continues for a sufficient period.

Northern Ireland Assembly A body established under the Northern Ireland Act 1982. It consists of 78 members elected by proportional representation, and its initial function is to scrutinize and report on the policies and activities of the Northern Ireland department. It may opt for the devolution of power, but any proposals for this must have the support of 70% of its members and must, in the view of the Secretary of State, command widespread acceptance throughout the community.

notary (notary public) *n.* A legal practitioner, usually a solicitor, who attests or certifies deeds and other documents and notes or *protests dishonoured bills of exchange. *Ecclesiastical notaries* are usually diocesan registrars and the legal secretaries of bishops; *general notaries* may practise anywhere in England and Wales; and *district notaries* practise in a limited area. Diplomatic and consular officials may exercise notarial functions outside the UK.

not guilty 1. A denial of the charges by an accused person in court. If there is more than one charge, the accused may plead guilty to some and not guilty to others. **2.** A *verdict finding that an accused person has not committed the offence with which he was charged. However, he may, at the same time, be found guilty of other offences. *See also* acquittal; insanity.

notice *n.* **1.** Knowledge of a fact. A person is said to have *actual notice* of anything that he actually knows; *constructive notice* of anything that he ought reasonably to know (for example, any fact that he would have discovered if he had made any inquiry that a reasonable

man would have made); and *imputed notice* of anything of which any agent of his has actual or constructive notice. **2.** (in employment law) Formal notification, given by either party to a contract of employment, that the contract is to be terminated after a specified period. The period of notice to which each party is entitled is governed by the contract, subject to statutory minimum periods if the employee has been continuously employed in the business (*see* continuous employment) for more than four weeks. An employee who has been so employed for up to two years is entitled to a week's notice; one employed for a longer period is entitled to one week's notice for each year's continuous employment up to 12 years. Thus an employee who has been employed for 20 years must be given a statutory minimum of 12 weeks' notice, although his employment contract may entitle him to a longer period. An employee with four weeks' continuous employment must give at least one week's notice of his resignation. An employee whose conduct justifies immediate dismissal is treated as waiving his right to notice, as is an employer whose conduct amounts to *constructive dismissal. A fixed-term contract cannot be terminated by notice unless the contract expressly provides for this.

notice of abandonment *See* abandonment; constructive total loss.

notice of discontinuance Notice served by a plaintiff (or by a defendant in respect of a *counterclaim) voluntarily terminating an action. If the notice is served within 14 days of the service of the defence no *leave of the court is necessary, unless there has been an order for an *interim payment. After this, leave of the court or the written consent of all other parties is required.

notice of dishonour A notice that must be given by the holder of a *bill of exchange to the drawer and each endorser when a bill has been

notice of intended prosecution

dishonoured; any drawer or endorser to whom notice is not given is discharged. The notice must identify the bill and state that it has been dishonoured by nonacceptance or nonpayment. The notice must be given within a reasonable time of the *dishonour (to which strict rules apply). Certain excuses are recognized for failure to give notice or delay.

notice of intended prosecution A written notice issued to someone charged with any of certain specified driving offences stating that he will be prosecuted. These offences are: *speeding, *reckless driving, *careless or *inconsiderate driving, *ignoring traffic signals, and leaving a car in a dangerous position (*see* obstruction). If the offender was not warned when he committed the offence that he might be prosecuted for it, he cannot normally be subsequently prosecuted unless he is served with either a summons or a notice of intended prosecution within 14 days of committing the offence. If he is prosecuted nonetheless, he may appeal against his conviction. If the notice was posted by registered or recorded mail so that it would normally have arrived within the 14 days, the motorist cannot plead that he did not receive it within that time. It is not necessary to serve a notice of intended prosecution when: (1) an accident happened at the time of the alleged offence owing to the presence on the road of the car involved in the alleged offence; (2) it was not possible to find out the name and address of the accused (or registered owner) in time; or (3) the motorist is charged with *causing death by reckless driving or *drunken driving.

notice of intention to defend An *acknowledgment of service containing a statement to the effect that the person by whom or on whose behalf it is signed intends to contest the proceedings to which the acknowledgment relates. If the defendant fails to give notice of intention to defend within the time prescribed by the Rules of the Supreme Court, the plaintiff may obtain judgment in default.

notice to produce Notice by one party to a civil action requiring another to produce documents in his possession at the trial. If he fails to do so, *secondary evidence of the documents may be given. If there has been *discovery and inspection of documents, in the High Court the person making discovery is deemed to be on notice to produce the documents that he stated were in his possession, custody, or power.

notice to quit The formal notification from a landlord to a tenant (or vice versa) terminating the tenancy on a specified date. The notice must be clear and unambiguous and it must terminate the tenancy in relation to the whole of the rented property: a notice to quit part of the property can be valid only if specifically allowed by the tenancy. When the tenant lives in the rented property, the notice to quit must be in a statutory form that tells the tenant his legal rights. Otherwise no particular form is required for a notice to quit.

The period of notice varies according to the kind of tenancy and any agreement between the parties. In the case of periodic tenancies for which no period has been agreed the following periods apply: a yearly or longer tenancy – six months; a monthly tenancy – one month; a quarterly tenancy – one quarter; a weekly tenancy – one week. The notice must be given so that it expires at the end of one of the periods of the tenancy, for example in a yearly tenancy beginning on 1 January, the notice must expire on 31 December. If tenants have statutory protection this can affect the length of the notice to quit. Thus residential tenants must be given at least four weeks' notice, tenants of *agricultural holdings must be given a year's notice, and tenants of *business tenancies are entitled to at least six months' notice. In these cases a tenant may be entitled to continue in occupation of the rented property even after the notice to quit has expired. If the landlord treats the tenancy as continuing after the notice to quit has expired, a new tenancy may be created.

noting a bill *See* protest.

not negotiable Words marked on a crossed cheque indicating that a transferee for value of the cheque gets no better title to it than his transferor had.

not proven A *verdict used in Scottish courts when the prosecution's case has not reached a sufficient standard of proof to establish the accused person's guilt, but there is some doubt about his innocence. The effect is the same as a not guilty verdict: the accused is released and cannot be tried again for the same offence.

nova causa interveniens *See novus actus interveniens.*

novation *n.* The substitution of a new contract for one already existing. The new contract may be between the same parties or it may involve the introduction of a new party, as in the case of the substitution of debtors. If A owes B £100 and B owes C £100, novation would occur if all three agreed that the existing debts were to be extinguished and that A is to pay C a new debt of £100.

novus actus interveniens (nova causa interveniens) [Latin: a new intervening act (or cause)] An act or event that breaks the causal connection between a wrong or crime committed by the defendant and subsequent happenings and therefore relieves the defendant from responsibility for these happenings. *See* causation.

nudum pactum [Latin: naked agreement] *See* consideration.

nuisance *n.* An activity or state of affairs that interferes with the use or en-

joyment of land or rights over land (*private nuisance*) or with the health, safety, comfort, or property of the public at large (*public nuisance*). Private nuisance is a tort, protecting the occupier of land from damage to his land, buildings, or vegetation or unreasonable interference with his comfort or convenience by excessive noise, dust, fumes, smells, etc. The occupier's main remedies are damages and an injunction. Alternatively he has a limited right to abate (i.e. remove) the nuisance himself.

Public nuisance is a crime. At common law it includes such activities as obstructing the highway, carrying on an offensive trade, and selling food unfit for human consumption. Statutory nuisances are created by provisions dealing with noise, public health, and the control of pollution. The Attorney-General may bring a civil action for an injunction on behalf of the public but a private citizen may obtain damages in tort only if he can prove some special damage over and above that suffered by the public at large.

nulla poena sine lege [Latin: no punishment without a law] The principle that a person can only be punished for a crime if the *punishment is prescribed by law. The punishment may be specified by a statute as a term of imprisonment or fine or it may be based on common-law principles. With the exception of treason and murder, for which the punishment is fixed, all statutory punishments are expressed in terms of the maximum possible punishment; judges have discretion to impose a lesser punishment according to the circumstances. At common law punishment is said to be *at large*, i.e. the amount of the fine or length of the prison sentence is entirely at the judge's discretion. In many cases, however, there are now statutes specifying the punishment for common-law offences; these too are maximum punishments. Magistrates' courts are subject to shorter maxima than Crown courts; they are also usually subject to a minimum sentence of five days in cases of imprisonment.

nullity of marriage The invalidity of a marriage due to some defect existing at the time the marriage was celebrated (or, sometimes, arising afterwards). A marriage may be null in the sense that it is *void*, i.e. it was never in the eyes of the law a valid marriage (and the "spouses" are legally merely cohabitees). It may alternatively be *voidable*, i.e. valid until made void by a court decree of *annulment, which (since 1971) acts like a decree of divorce and does not end the marriage retrospectively. The form of decree, however, always states that the marriage "is and has been null and void". The grounds for nullity are: close relationship, lack of age, lack of consent, and nonconsummation (*see* consummation of a marriage). When granting a decree of nullity the court has wide discretionary powers to make orders for *financial provision or *property adjustment. *See also* legitimacy.

nullum crimen sine lege [Latin: no crime without a law] The principle that conduct does not constitute crime unless it has previously been declared to be so by the law. Most serious offences are well-defined common-law offences (although the details relating to their definition may often be unclear until ruled upon by the judges); many regulatory offences (e.g. those involving road traffic and the manufacture of products) are constantly being created by statute. The principle invalidates the power occasionally attributed to judges to create new offences in order to punish morally harmful conduct (such as conspiracy to corrupt public morals).

nunc pro tunc [Latin: now instead of then] A phrase used of a judgment that is entered in such a way as to have legal effect from an earlier date.

O

oath *n.* A pronouncement swearing the truth of a statement or promise, usually by an appeal to God to witness its truth. An oath is required by law for various purposes, in particular for *affidavits and giving evidence in court. The usual *witness's oath* is: "I swear by Almighty God that the evidence which I shall give shall be the truth, the whole truth and nothing but the truth". Those who object to swearing an oath, on the grounds that to do so is contrary to their religious beliefs or that they have no religious beliefs, may instead *affirm.

oath of allegiance An oath to be faithful and bear true allegiance to the Crown. It is taken by members of both Houses at the opening of every new Parliament, by certain officers of the Crown on their appointment, and by those who become British citizens, British Dependent Territories citizens, British Overseas citizens or British subjects by registration, or British citizens or British Dependent Territories citizens by naturalization.

obiter dictum [Latin: a remark in passing] Something said by a judge while giving judgment that was not essential to the decision in the case. It does not form part of the *ratio decidendi* of the case and therefore creates no binding precedent, but may be cited as *persuasive authority in later cases.

objection in point of law A form of pleading by a defendant in his defence that raises an issue of law. When such an objection is raised the court may order the issue to be tried as a *preliminary point of law.

objection to indictment A procedure in which the accused in a *trial on indictment attempts to prove some objection to the indictment on legal grounds (e.g. that it contravenes, or fails to comply with, an enactment). The objection is raised by *motion to quash the indictment.

objects clause *See* memorandum of association.

objects of a power Persons in whose favour a *power of appointment may be exercised, i.e. potential appointees.

obligation *n.* **1.** A legal duty. **2.** A *bond by deed.

obliteration *n.* The deletion of words in a will. An obliteration is valid if the words deleted are indecipherable or if the alteration is properly signed and witnessed. Otherwise *probate is granted on the basis that the deleted words remain part of the will.

obscene publications Material that tends to deprave or corrupt. Under the Obscene Publications Acts 1959 and 1964 it is an offence to publish an obscene article or to have an obscene article for publication for gain. For the purposes of the Acts, obscenity is not limited to pornographic or sexually corrupting material: a book advocating drug taking or violence, for instance, may be obscene. Whether or not particular material is obscene is a question of fact in each case, to be decided by the jury, and expert evidence is not usually permitted. Material that merely tends to shock or disgust is not obscene. The intention or motive of the author in writing or depicting the material is irrelevant.

"Publishing" an obscene article includes distributing, circulating, giving, hiring, or lending the article or offering it for sale or hire (the latter does not include displaying such material in a shop, which is merely an invitation to treat and not an offer). An "article" may be material that is to be looked at or played over, rather than read, and can also include, for instance, a negative of a film or any article used to reproduce material to be read or looked at. This offence is one of *strict liabil-

ity, but there is a defence of *lack of knowledge*, if the defendant can show he had not examined the article he published and that he had no good reason to suspect that publishing it would constitute an offence. There is also a special defence of *public good*, which applies when the defendant shows that publication of the article was justified as being in the interests of science, literature, art, learning, or similar matters. Expert evidence as to the merits of the material is admitted in relation to this defence. The offence of possessing an obscene article in the expectation that it will be published for financial gain is also subject to the defences of lack of knowledge and public good. If a magistrate reasonably suspects that obscene articles are kept in any premises in order to be published for gain, he may issue a warrant authorizing the police to search for and seize the articles. If the articles prove to be obscene, the magistrate may order them to be forfeited.

The Acts do not apply to material published by means of television or broadcasting, but they do apply to cinema screening and theatre performances, subject to the rule that prosecutions in such cases require the consent of the Director of Public Prosecutions or the Attorney General, respectively. These offences, too, are subject to the public good defence, defined in terms of the interests of drama, opera, ballet, or other art.

There are also various special offences relating to obscenity, e.g. publishing obscene advertisements, sending unasked for material describing sexual techniques, or sending through the post any "indecent or obscene article" (the latter offence is limited to sexual obscenity, but also includes material that is merely indecent).

obstructing a police officer The offence of hindering a police officer who is in the course of doing his duty, which is punishable with up to one month's imprisonment and/or a fine of up to

obstruction

£200. "Obstruction" includes any intentional interference, e.g. by physical force, threats, telling lies or giving misleading information, refusing to cooperate in removing an obstruction, or warning a person who has committed a crime so that he can escape detection (e.g. warning a speeding driver that there is a police trap ahead). It is not, however, an offence merely to advise someone not to answer police questions that he does not have to answer. A police officer is acting in the course of his duty if he is preventing or detecting crime (in particular, breaches of the peace) or obeying the orders of his superiors. He is not acting in the course of his duty, however, when he is merely assisting the public in some way not connected with crime. When the obstruction amounts to an *assault, the offence is punishable by up to six month's imprisonment and/or a fine of up to £1000. One may be guilty of this offence even if the police officer was in plain clothes and there was no way of knowing that he was a police officer.

obstruction *n.* The offence of causing or allowing a motor vehicle or trailer to stand on a road in such a way that it is likely to impede other road users or to use a vehicle on the road in a similar way (e.g. by driving unreasonably slowly). It is not necessary to show that any other vehicle or person has in fact been obstructed. This offence is punishable by a fine. It is also an offence to leave a motor vehicle on a road in such a position or in such circumstances that it is likely to cause danger to other road users. This offence requires a *notice of intended prosecution and is punishable by a fine, *endorsement (which carries 3 points under the *totting-up system), and discretionary *disqualification.

obstruction of recovery of premises *See* recovery of premises.

occupation *n.* **1.** (in land law) The physical possession and control of land. Under the Land Registration Act 1925

the rights of a person in actual occupation may be an *overriding interest binding a purchaser of registered land, unless the rights are disclosed on inquiry. **2.** (in international law) The act of taking control of territory belonging either to no one (*peaceful occupation*) or to a foreign state in the course of a war (*belligerent occupation*). Peaceful occupation is one of the methods of legally acquiring territory, provided the occupier can show a standard of control superior to that of any other claimant. Denmark acquired Greenland in this way. A belligerent occupant cannot acquire or annex the occupied territory during the course of the war. Certain provisions for the protection of enemy civilians in the Hague and Geneva Conventions are applied to those parts of the enemy territory that have been effectively occupied. A belligerent occupier must retain in force the ordinary penal laws and tribunals of the occupied power, but may alter them or impose new laws to ensure the security and orderly government of the occupying forces and administration.

occupier *n.* A person in possession of land or buildings as owner, tenant, or trespasser. If he is a trespasser he may obtain a right to lawful occupation if the owner accepts money from him as rent, in which case a tenancy may be created, or through *adverse possession for a sufficient period.

occupier's liability The liability of an occupier of land or premises to persons on the land. At common law the extent of an occupier's liability varied according to whether the visitor entered under a contract, as an *invitee, as a *licensee, or as a trespasser. In England, the Occupiers' Liability Act 1957 replaced the common-law rules by a *common duty of care, owed to all persons who enter by the occupier's invitation or permission. The English Act does not cover trespassers. An occupier need only show "common humanity" to trespassers, but this requires more consideration for trespassing children than for adult trespassers. In Scotland, the Occupiers' Liability (Scotland) Act 1960 requires an occupier to show to *all* persons entering the premises such care as is reasonable in all the circumstances of the case.

occupying tenant A person in possession of premises in accordance with his rights under a lease or tenancy agreement, or as a *statutory tenant or a *protected occupier, or under his rights as a tenant with a *restricted contract.

offence *n.* A *crime. The modern tendency is to refer to crimes as offences. Offences may be classified as *indictable or *summary and as *arrestable or nonarrestable.

offences against international law and order Crimes that affect the proper functioning of international society. Some authorities regard so-called international crimes as crimes of individuals that all or most states are bound by treaty to punish in accordance with national laws passed for that purpose. Examples of this type of crime are *piracy, *hijacking, and *war crimes. The International Law Commission has formulated Draft Articles on State Responsibility, which attempt to define international crimes for which individual states are liable. It gives as examples: (1) a serious breach of an international obligation essential to safeguard international peace (e.g. aggression) or peoples' rights to self-determination (e.g. colonial domination by force); (2) a widespread and serious breach of obligations essential to safeguard individuals (e.g. slavery, *genocide, or apartheid) or the environment (e.g. massive pollution).

offences against property Crimes that affect another person's rights of ownership (or in some cases possession or control). The main offences against property are *theft, *burglary, offences of *deception and *making off without payment, *criminal damage, *arson, *forgery, and *forcible entry. Some offences against property, such as *robbery and *blackmail, also contain elements of *offences against the person.

offences against public order Crimes that affect the smooth running of orderly society. The main offences against public order are *riot, *rout, *affray, *unlawful assembly, using *insulting behaviour in public, *incitement to racial hatred, public *nuisance, and *obstruction of highways. There are also a number of other offences in this category contained in the Public Order Act 1936.

offences against the person Crimes that involve the use or threat of physical force against another person. The main offences against the person are *homicide, *infanticide, illegal *abortion, and *causing death by reckless driving (fatal offences against the person) and *rape, *wounding, causing or inflicting *grievous bodily harm, *assault, aggravated assault, *battery, *kidnapping, and offences involving *indecency (nonfatal offences against the person).

offences against the state Crimes that affect the security of the state as a whole. The main offences against the state are *treason and *misprision of treason, *sedition (and incitement to *mutiny), offences involving *official secrets, and acts of *terrorism.

offences relating to road traffic Crimes that are associated with driving vehicles on public roads and related acts. The main offences in this category are *careless driving, *inconsiderate driving, *reckless driving, *causing death by reckless driving, *drunken driving, *driving while disqualified, *driving without insurance, *driving without a licence, *speeding, *ignoring traffic signals, *parking offences, *obstruction, and *reckless cycling. Some road traffic offences require *notice of intended prosecution. Road traffic offences carry various penalties or combinations of penalties, such as fines, *endorsement of driving licence, *disqualification from driving, and in some circumstances imprisonment. The court may also make a *driving-test order. Many road traffic offences (especially the minor ones) are offences of *strict liability. *See also* driving licence; MOT test; road accidents; road tax; seat belt; vehicle construction and maintenance.

offences triable either way Crimes that may be tried either as an *indictable offence or a *summary offence. These crimes are listed in the Criminal Law Act 1977 and include offences of deception, assault, bigamy, and sexual intercourse with a girl under the age of 16. Certain other offences are triable either way under various other statutes.

When an offence is triable either way, the magistrates' court must decide, on hearing the initial facts of the case, if it should be tried on indictment rather than summarily (for example, because it appears to be a serious case). Even if they decide that they can deal with the matter adequately themselves, they must give the defendant the choice of opting for trial upon indictment before a jury. There are three exceptional cases, however. (1) If the prosecution is being conducted by or on behalf of the Attorney General, Solicitor General, or Director of Public Prosecutions, and they apply for trial on indictment, the case must be tried on indictment. (2) If the case concerns criminal damage or any offences connected with criminal damage (except arson), and the damage appears to be less than £200, the case must be tried summarily. (3) If the defendant is a child or young person, he must be tried summarily unless: (a) he is charged with homicide; (b) he is charged jointly with someone over 17, and it would be better if they were tried together; or (c) he is aged between 14 and 17 and charged with an offence punishable by 14 years' imprisonment or more, and the court thinks that he should be sentenced to a long period of detention.

offender *n.* One who has committed a *crime. *See also* fugitive offender; persistent offender.

offensive weapon Any object that is made, adapted, or intended to be used to cause physical injury to a person. Examples of objects made to cause injury are revolvers, coshes, and daggers; objects adapted to cause injury include bottles deliberately broken to attack someone with and razor blades inserted in a potato. In theory any object may be intended to be used to cause injury, but articles commonly intended for such use include sheath knives (or any household knife), pieces of wood, and stones.

Under the Public Order Act 1936, it is an offence, punishable by up to three months' imprisonment and/or a fine of £500, to have an offensive weapon in one's possession at a public meeting or at a public procession. There are special exceptions for police officers, fire officers, Crown servants, and other limited categories. It is also an offence, under the Prevention of Crime Act 1953, to have an offensive weapon in one's possession in a public place. This offence is punishable summarily by up to three months' imprisonment and/or a fine of up to £200 or on indictment with up to two years' imprisonment and/or a fine, and the court may order the weapon to be forfeited. There are special exceptions for those (such as soldiers or police officers) who carry offensive weapons in the course of duty and in cases of "reasonable excuse", but the defendant must prove that he comes within these categories. Self-defence is not usually a reasonable excuse unless there is an imminent and particular threat.

See also firearm; weapon of offence; prohibited weapon.

offer *n.* An indication of willingness to do or refrain from doing something that is capable of being converted by *acceptance into a legally binding *contract. It is made by an *offeror* to an *offeree* and is capable of acceptance only by an offeree who knows of its existence. Thus, a person giving information cannot claim a reward if he did not know that a reward was being offered. An offer must be distinguished from an *invitation to treat*, which is an invitation to others to make offers, as by displaying goods in a shop window; and a *declaration of intention*, which is a mere statement of intent to invite offers in the future, as by advertising an auction. *See also* lapse of offer; rejection of offer; revocation of offer.

office copy An exact copy of an official document, supplied and marked as such by the office that holds or issues the original. Office copies are generally admissible in evidence to the same extent as the original. Thus office copies of entries recorded at HM Land Registry are used in *conveyancing as an *abstract of title to registered land, and an office copy grant of probate may be used to prove an executor's right to receive or deal with the deceased's assets.

Office of Fair Trading *See* Director General of Fair Trading.

Official Custodian for Charities A corporation sole created by the Charities Act 1960 for the purpose of acting as a custodian trustee of property held for charitable purposes.

Official Journal *The Official Journal of the European Communities*: the official organ of the EEC, usually published every day and in each of the official languages of the communities. It is currently divided into two parts. One part contains *Community legislation. The other contains proposals of the Commission of the European Communities, reports of proceedings in the European Parliament, notices concerning matters in the Court of Justice of the European Communities, and other matters of general information.

Official Petitioner The *Director of Public Prosecutions when acting in respect of an application for a *criminal bankruptcy order under the Powers of Criminal Courts Act 1973. He must consider whether or not it is in the public interest to present a petition and, if it is, decides when to present it.

official receiver The person appointed by the Department of Trade who acts in *bankruptcy matters as interim receiver and manager of the estate of the debtor, presides at the first meeting of creditors, and takes part in the debtor's public examination. In the *compulsory winding-up of a company, he becomes provisional *liquidator when a winding-up order is made.

official referee Until 1972, a judicial officer of the *Supreme Court to whom certain matters could be referred, usually cases involving prolonged examination of accounts or large numbers of small items (such as building claims). The office was abolished by the Courts Act 1971 but the functions previously discharged by official referees can now be discharged by *circuit judges nominated by the Lord Chancellor to take *official referees' business*.

official search A search, in response to an applicant's *requisition, into the registers of local land charges, the Land Charges Department, or HM Land Registry (as appropriate) in order to disclose any registered matter relevant to the requisition. A certificate is issued by the registrar giving details of encumbrances that the search has revealed. In the case of Land Charges Department and HM Land Registry searches, a purchaser is not bound by any encumbrance that this search fails to reveal provided his purchase is completed within 15 days after the certificate is issued. A local land charge search certificate is valid only at the time it is issued and a purchaser is bound by any local charge registered subsequently. A search at HM Land Registry may only be made by or on the written authority of the registered proprietor of the title; the registers of local land charges and the Land Charges Department are open to public inspection.

official secrets For the purpose of the Official Secrets Acts 1911–36, information that is categorized as a secret code or password or is intended to be (or might be) useful to an enemy. It is an offence to make a sketch, plan, model, or note that might be useful to an enemy. It is also an offence to obtain, record, or communicate to anyone else a secret official code or password or any information or document that is intended to be useful to an enemy. It is also an offence to enter, approach, inspect, or pass over (e.g. in an aircraft) any prohibited place. Such places include naval, military, or air-force establishments, national munitions factories or depots, and any places belonging to or used by the Crown that an enemy would want to know about. For all three offences the prosecution must prove that the act was done for a purpose that prejudices the safety or interests of the state. Even if no particular prejudicial act can be proved, someone may be convicted if it appears from the circumstances of the case, his conduct, or his known and proven character that his purpose was prejudicial to the interests of the state. There is also a presumption (which may be disproved by the defendant) that any act done within the scope of the three offences without lawful authority is prejudicial to the state's interests. All three offences are punishable by up to 14 years' imprisonment.

It is also an offence under the Official Secrets Acts for the holder of a Crown office who has any document or information as a result of his position to pass it on to an unauthorized person, keep it, or use it in any other way that prejudices the state's interests. The information need not be secret or confidential and the defendant need not have realized that harm might result from his act. The offence is punishable by up to two years' imprisonment, and anyone who receives the information knowing or suspecting that it was given in breach of the Acts is liable to the same punishment. It is also an offence to attempt to commit, or incite, or aid and abet any of the above offences and to do any act of preparation for any of these offences. All such acts are subject to the same penalties as the offence they relate to. Thus, for example, buying paper in order to sketch a military installation is a preparatory act carrying a sentence of up to 14 years' imprisonment.

See also sabotage; spying; treason.

Official Solicitor An officer of the Supreme Court who, when directed by the court, acts as *next friend or guardian *ad litem* for those under a disability who have no one else to act for them; he may also be called upon to intervene and protect the interests of children under the Matrimonial Causes Act 1973. He can be appointed *judicial trustee in proceedings relating to disputed trusts under the Judicial Trustee Act 1896.

Old Bailey *See* Central Criminal Court.

Ombudsman *n. See* Parliamentary Commissioner for Administration.

omission *n.* A failure to act. It is not usually a crime to fail to act; for example, it is not usually a crime to stand by and watch a child who has fallen into a river drown. Sometimes, however, there is a duty on a person to act, either because of the terms of his job, or because he is a parent or guardian of a minor, or because he has voluntarily assumed a duty (e.g. looking after a disabled relative). In such cases, omission may constitute a crime. Usually this will be a crime of *negligence (e.g. manslaughter, if the victim dies because of the defendant's omission); if it is a deliberate omission with a particular intention (e.g. the intention of starving someone to death) it will amount to murder. *See also* neglect.

omnia praesumuntur rite et solemniter esse acta *See* presumption.

onus of proof *See* burden of proof.

open contract A contract for the sale of land in which the only express terms are the identity of the parties, the property, and the price. Under the Law of Property Act 1925 an open contract is valid if it is in writing or evidenced by writing (*see* memorandum in writing) or *part performance. Other necessary terms are implied, including: (1) a condition that the vendor must convey an unencumbered freehold title, although the purchaser is bound by any defect of which he knew and which cannot be removed; (2) the vendor must within a reasonable time produce at his own expense an abstract of title beginning with a *root of title at least 15 years old or, in the case of registered land, the documents specified by the Land Registration Act 1925; (3) a condition that the vendor will convey as *beneficial owner; (4) the purchaser must deliver any requisitions on or objections to the title within a reasonable time after receiving the abstract; (5) the conveyance must be prepared by the purchaser at his own expense; (6) the vendor must give vacant possession on completion; (7) the transaction must be completed within a reasonable time: if it is not, the vendor is entitled to interest on the unpaid price and the purchaser to the income of the property from the time when completion should have occurred.

In the case of contracts made by correspondence, statutory conditions set out in regulations made under the Law of Property Act 1925 apply. A vendor cannot insist on preparing the conveyance himself (a contractual term to this effect is void), but apart from this the implied and statutory conditions may be dispensed with, varied, or supplemented by agreement between the parties. In practice, the forms of contract generally used specify the parties' rights and obligations much more precisely.

opening speech A speech made by the prosecution counsel at the beginning of a criminal trial, briefly outlining the case against the accused and summarizing the evidence that the prosecution intends to call to prove its case.

operative mistake *See* mistake.

operative part *See* deed.

operative words The part of a conveyance that effects the essence of the transaction; for example, the words "the Vendor hereby conveys Blackacre to the Purchaser in fee simple". No specific form of words is necessary provided that the intention is clear.

opinion *n.* **1.** A judgment by the House of Lords. **2. (counsel's opinion)** A barrister's advice on a particular question.

opinion evidence Evidence of the opinions or beliefs of a witness, as opposed to evidence of facts about which he can give admissible evidence. At common law, opinion evidence is in general inadmissible but this rule is subject to many exceptions. Thus a nonexpert witness may testify as to age, speed of vehicles, handwriting, or identity. Expert witnesses (e.g. doctors) may give their opinions on any matter falling within their expertise. At common law, a witness could not give his opinion on an ultimate issue (i.e. the question that the court had to decide) but this rule, which was not very strictly applied in practice, was relaxed in respect of civil cases by the Civil Evidence Act 1972. *See also* hearsay evidence.

option

option *n.* A right to do or not to do something, usually within a specified time. An enforceable option may be acquired by contract (i.e. for consideration) or by deed to accept or reject an *offer within a specified period. An option to acquire land or an interest in it on specified terms will only bind third parties if it is registered (*see* registration of encumbrances). If an option to buy does not specify the price it will only be valid if it specifies a means for determining the price, e.g. by a valuation to be made by a specified third party who is or will be under a duty to act. Thus an option to buy at a price to be agreed is void for uncertainty.

On the London *Stock Exchange, options to sell or to buy quoted securities are purchased for a certain sum of money, which is forfeited if they are not taken up. An option to sell is known as a *put option*, that to buy is a *call option*, and an option to either sell or buy is a *double option*. Under the Companies Act 1967, directors, shadow directors, and the spouses or children of either are prohibited from buying or selling options in the shares of their own company.

oral agreement A contract made by word of mouth, as opposed to one made in writing. *See also* implied contract.

oral evidence Spoken evidence given by a witness in court, usually on *oath. A witness's evidence must usually relate what he knows through the use of his own senses. However, in certain circumstances *hearsay evidence may be permitted.

orality *n.* The principle that evidence must be given orally and subject to *cross-examination unless *affidavit evidence is admissible.

order *n.* **1.** A direction or command of a court. In this sense it is often used synonymously with *judgment. **2.** The document bearing the seal of the court

recording its judgment in a case. **3.** A subdivision of the *Rules of the Supreme Court and the County Court Rules.

order for account An order in civil cases that the amount of money due from one party to another may be investigated. The order may be made before trial. Accounts are usually taken by a master or a referee and are most frequently ordered in partnership and trust matters.

order of discharge A court order resulting in the *discharge of a bankrupt.

Orders in Council Government orders of a legislative character made by the Crown and members of the Privy Council either under statutory powers conferred on Her Majesty in Council (*see* delegated legislation; statutory instrument) or in exercise of the *royal prerogative. *Compare* Orders of Council.

Orders of Council Orders of a legislative nature made by the Privy Council under statutory powers conferred on the Council alone. They relate mainly to the regulation of certain professions and professional bodies. *See* delegated legislation. *Compare* Orders in Council.

ordinance *n.* One of the forms taken by legislation under the *royal prerogative, normally legislation relating to UK dependencies.

ordinary resolution A decision reached by a simple majority (i.e. of more than 50%) of company members voting in person or by proxy. *Compare* extraordinary resolution; special resolution.

ordinary share *See* share.

original evidence **1.** Evidence of a statement made by a person other than the testifying witness, which is offered to prove that the statement was actually made rather than to prove its truth. Thus, if in an action for slander a witness testifies that he heard the defendant defame the plaintiff, his testimony is original evidence and not *hearsay. **2.** *See* direct evidence.

originating process *See* process.

originating summons A form of originating *process in the High Court, used in cases in which the issues are likely to be ones of law or the interpretation of documents. It should not be used when disputed questions of fact are involved, for which proceedings begun by *writ are more appropriate. The summons must include a statement of the questions on which the plaintiff seeks the determination or direction of the court or the relief that he claims and sufficient *particulars to identify the cause of action. Evidence at the hearing of originating summonses is usually by *affidavit.

ouster *n.* The act of wrongfully dispossessing someone of any kind of *hereditament, such as freehold property.

ouster of jurisdiction The exclusion of judicial proceedings in respect of any dispute. There is a presumption that statutes and other documents (e.g. contracts) do not oust the jurisdiction of the courts. *See* interpretation of statutes.

outer Bar (utter Bar) Junior barristers, collectively, who sit outside the bar of the court, as opposed to *Queen's Counsel, who sit within it.

outstanding term *See* satisfied term.

overcrowding *n.* For statutory purposes a dwelling is overcrowded when two or more people of opposite sexes over the age of ten, and not married to one another or cohabiting, are obliged because of lack of space to sleep in the same room. There is also a test for overcrowding based on the number of people living in the dwelling compared with the number of rooms and the floor area of those rooms. Local authorities have a duty to prevent overcrowding

and can take action against an owner-occupier, a landlord, or a tenant.

overreaching *n.* The process by which the interests in *remainder and in *reversion under a settlement of land are converted on sale of the land by the tenant for life into corresponding interests in the *capital money arising from the sale. Under the Settled Land Act 1925 the tenant for life always has the right to sell the settled land and overreach other interests, with certain statutory exceptions (*see*, for example, principal mansion house).

overriding interests Certain rights and interests in registered land, listed in the Land Registration Act 1925, that cannot be protected by registration but do bind the registered proprietor and any third party acquiring the land or any interest in it.

overrule *vb.* To set aside the decision of a court in an earlier case. Because of the doctrine of *precedent, a court can generally only overrule decisions of courts lower than itself. The setting aside of the judgment of a lower court on appeal is called a *reversal*.

owner-occupier *n.* A person who has legal ownership of a dwelling in which he lives or in which he lived before letting it on a regulated tenancy. For statutory purposes, the term includes a tenant under a *long tenancy.

ownership *n.* The exclusive rights to use, possess, and dispose of property, subject only to the rights of persons having a superior interest and to any restrictions on the owner's rights imposed by any act of the parties or by operation of law. Ownership may be *corporeal*, i.e. of a material thing, which may itself be a *movable or an *immovable; or it may be *incorporeal*, i.e. of something intangible, such as of a copyright or patent. Ownership involves enjoyment of a number of rights over the property. The owner can sell or give away some of these rights while still re-

P

taining others; for example, an owner of land may grant a right of way or a patent owner may grant a licence to manufacture the patented goods. Ownership may be held by different persons for different interests, for example when a freehold owner grants a lease or when land is settled on persons with interests in succession to one another (*see* settled land). More than one person can own the same property at the same time. They may be either joint owners with a single title to the property (*see* joint tenancy); or owners in common, each having a distinct title in the property that he can dispose of independently (*see* tenancy in common).

A person may be both the legal and beneficial owner, or the legal ownership of property may be separate from the beneficial (equitable) ownership (i.e. the right to enjoy the property), as when a trustee owns the legal estate in land for the benefit of another.

A legally valid transaction may confer specific rights to use, possess, or deal with property without conferring ownership of it; for example, a contract may appoint a person as the owner's agent for the sale of specified land. *See also* estate.

P

P. *n.* President (of the *Family Division of the High Court).

pacta sunt servanda [Latin] Agreements are to be kept.

paid-up capital *See* authorized capital.

palatine courts Originally, courts of the counties palatine of Durham, Lancaster, and Chester. In modern times, only the Chancery courts of Durham and Lancaster survived, but their jurisdiction was transferred to the High Court by the Courts Act 1971. *See also* Vice Chancellor.

paramount *adj.* (in land law) Superior; having or denoting a better right or title.

paramount clause *See* bill of lading.

parcels *pl. n.* **1.** Plots of land. **2.** *See* deed.

pardon *n.* The withdrawal of a sentence or punishment by the sovereign under the *prerogative of mercy. Once a pardon is granted, the accused cannot be tried and if he has already been convicted, he cannot be punished. The responsibility is upon him, however, to plead the pardon as a bar to prosecution or punishment; if he does not do so as soon as possible, he may be held to have waived it. A person may also be granted a *reprieve*, i.e. the temporary suspension of a punishment (for example, if he becomes insane after sentence is passed).

parent *n.* The mother or father of a child. The term also includes adoptive parents (*see* adoption) but does not usually include step-parents. Parents have *parental rights* over their children while they are minors, which include the right to physical custody of the child, to control their education and determine their religion, to consent to medical treatment, to administer their property, to represent them in legal proceedings, and to discipline them reasonably. They also have *parental duties*, notably to maintain and educate their children, which can be legally enforced. Both parents exercise parental rights jointly, except in the case of illegitimate children, over whom the mother has exclusive parental rights. Parental rights decline as the child grows older; in any dispute over their enforcement the welfare of the child is the first and paramount consideration. *See also* custody disputes; custody of child; guardian; parents' liability.

parent company *See* subsidiary company.

parents' liability Parents are not liable for their children's torts, but they may be liable for their own negligence in failing to supervise or train young children, where the absence of supervision or training has led a child to cause damage to others. In the case of older children, a parent can be vicariously liable for the torts of a child employed as a servant or agent on ordinary principles of *vicarious liability. There is no fixed age determining a child's liability for its own torts. A child may, however, be too young to form the intention necessary for a particular tort. In cases in which the negligence or contributory negligence of a child is in question, the test applied is whether the child's conduct measured up to the standard of care to be expected from an average child of that age.

parish *n.* A *local government area in England (outside Greater London) consisting of a division of a *district (though not all districts are so divided). All parishes have meetings and many have an elected parish council, which is a *local authority with a number of minor local governmental functions (e.g. the provision of allotments, bus shelters, and recreation grounds). A parish council may by resolution call its area a town, itself a town council, and its chairman the town mayor.

parking offences Offences relating to parking a motor vehicle. These include parking a vehicle within the limits of a pedestrian crossing or wherever signs or kerb markings indicate that parking is prohibited or restricted and failing to comply with the regulations associated with the use of parking meters. If the accused can show that road markings or signs indicating parking restrictions were absent or deficient, he may be acquitted. Parking offences are punishable by fine only; they are not subject to endorsement. *See also* obstruction.

Parliament *n.* The legislature of the UK, consisting of the sovereign, the House of Lords, and the House of Commons. Under the Parliament Act 1911, the maximum duration of any particular Parliament is five years, after which its functions expire. In practice, a Parliament's life always ends by its earlier *dissolution* by the sovereign under the royal prerogative, in a proclamation that also summons its successor. The date of dissolution is chosen by the Prime Minister. The life of a Parliament is divided into sessions, normally of one year each, which are ended when Parliament is prorogued (also under the prerogative) by a royal commission. Each House divides a session into sittings, normally of a day's duration, which end when a motion for adjournment is passed. The functions of Parliament are the enactment of legislation (*see* Act of Parliament), the sanctioning of taxation and public expenditure, and the scrutiny and criticism of government policy and administration. *See also* sovereignty of Parliament.

Parliamentary Commissioner for Administration (Ombudsman) An independent official appointed under the Parliamentary Commissioner Act 1967 to investigate complaints by individuals or corporate bodies of injustice arising from maladministration by a government department. Appointment is by the Crown on the Prime Minister's advice. The Commissioner may investigate complaints only if they are submitted to him in writing through a member of Parliament; certain matters are outside his jurisdiction (e.g. action taken by health authorities; *see* Health Service Commissioners). Apart from these restrictions, investigation is entirely at his discretion. If he upholds a complaint and it is not remedied, he reports this to Parliament.

parliamentary committees *See* Committee of the whole House; Grand Committees; Joint Committee on Statutory Instruments; standing committee; select committee.

parliamentary counsel Civil servants (barristers or solicitors) who draft government Bills, government amendments to Bills, and any procedural motions required in connection with the passing of Bills.

parliamentary papers Papers published on the authority of either House of Parliament. They include Bills, the Official Reports of Parliamentary Debates (*see* Hansard), and reports of parliamentary committees.

parliamentary privilege Special rights and immunities enjoyed by the Houses of Parliament and their members to enable them to carry out their functions effectively and without external interference. They are conferred mainly by the common law but partly by statute; they can be extended by statute but not by the resolution of either House.

The Commons have five main privileges. (1) The right of collective access to the sovereign through the Speaker. (2) The right of individual members to be free from civil (but not criminal) arrest. Since the abolition of imprisonment for debt, this privilege has been of only minor significance, but it would still shield a member against (for example) imprisonment for disobeying a court order in civil proceedings. (3) The individual right to freedom of speech. This substantial privilege means that a member cannot be made liable either civilly (e.g. for defamation) or criminally (e.g. for breach of the Official Secrets Acts) for anything said by him in the course of debates or other parliamentary proceedings. Under the Parliamentary Papers Act 1840 members are also not liable for statements repeated in reports published on the authority of the House. (4) The collective right to exclusive control of its own proceedings, so that it can (for example) exclude the public, prohibit reporting, and expel any member whom it may

consider unfit to sit. (5) The collective right to punish for any *breach of privilege* or other *contempt*. Examples of breaches of privilege are initiating defamation proceedings in respect of privileged words and the reporting of secret proceedings. Other contempts include any conduct prejudicial to the proper functioning or dignity of the House, e.g. by refusing to give evidence to a committee, bribing members, or insulting the House. Members may be punished for contempt by expulsion, suspension, or imprisonment; others by reprimand or imprisonment. Imprisonment is terminated by prorogation. Whether or not particular conduct amounts to a contempt, and if so what punishment (if any) is appropriate, is considered by the Committee of Privileges, whose report the House is free to accept or reject after debate.

The privileges of the Lords are similar, except that members have an individual right of access to the sovereign and the House can fine for contempt and imprison for a fixed term, which is not affected by prorogation.

parol contract *See* simple contract.

parole (release on licence) *n.* The conditional release of a prisoner from prison. Anyone sentenced to more than three years' imprisonment may be considered for parole after he has served one year in prison (including time spent in custody) or one-third of his sentence (whichever is later). Local review committees in each area consider all cases and advise the Home Secretary, who may either release the prisoner himself or refer his case to the Parole Board. This Board includes a past or present judge, a psychiatrist, a person experienced in caring for discharged prisoners, and a person trained in the treatment of offenders. The Board considers reports and evidence relating to the prisoner (whom it may interview) and defines the conditions under which he may be released.

Parole remains in force until the prisoner would have been released had he been granted *remission of his sentence. The Home Secretary may recall him to prison at any time, either on the recommendation of the Parole Board or whenever he thinks it necessary to do so without consulting the Board (but the prisoner has the right to appeal to the Parole Board).

If a prisoner on parole commits an offence punishable on indictment with imprisonment, the court trying him may revoke his parole, so that he returns to prison for the original offence. In such cases limitations are imposed on his right to be considered again for parole.

parol evidence Evidence given orally, as opposed to *documentary evidence.

parol evidence rule The rule that parol evidence (i.e. oral evidence) cannot be given to contradict, alter, or vary a written document (such as a judicial record or a contract) unless there are allegations of fraud or mistake.

parol lease A lease that is made either orally or in writing, but not by deed, and fulfils certain conditions. These are that it takes effect immediately it is made; it is for a period less than three years; and it is at the full market rent. *Periodic tenancies usually fulfil these conditions. Parol leases are the exception to the general rule that leases are not legally enforceable unless they are made by deed.

partial loss (in marine insurance) Any loss of the subject matter of an insurance policy other than an *actual total loss or a *constructive total loss. In the case of a partial loss there is a lesser measure of indemnity than in the case of a total loss. *See also* average.

partibility *n.* (of chattels) *See* partition of chattels.

participator *n. See* close company.

particular average *See* average.

particular lien *See* lien.

particulars *pl. n.* Details of an allegation of fact made in a *pleading. When an allegation is ambiguous or pleaded in insufficient detail, the opposing party may make a request for further and better particulars in writing; if these are not provided voluntarily, the party may seek an order of the court that they be provided. The principal function of particulars is to prevent *surprise.

parties *pl. n.* **1.** Persons who are involved together in some transaction, e.g. the parties to a deed or a contract. **2.** Persons who are involved together in litigation, either civil or criminal. *See also* joinder of parties.

partition *n.* **1.** The division of a territory into two or more units, each under a different government. **2.** The division of supreme power over a territory between different governments (e.g. federal and state). **3.** The formal separation, effected by deed, of land held in common ownership into parts, so that each co-owner takes his part solely, beneficially, and free from any rights of the others. Partition of land cannot be enforced without the consent of all the co-owners. *Compare* partition of chattels.

partition of chattels The division between co-owners of chattels held in undivided shares, so that each takes his part of the goods solely and absolutely. If chattels are *partible* (i.e. capable of being divided), the court may order partition under the Law of Property Act 1925 on the application of a co-owner.

partnership *n.* An association of two or more people formed for the purpose of carrying on a business. Partnerships are governed by the Partnership Act 1890. Unlike an incorporated *company, a partnership does not have a legal personality of its own and therefore partners are liable for the debts of the firm. *General partners* are fully liable for these debts, *limited partners* only to the extent of their investment. A *limited partnership* is one consisting of both general and limited partners, and is governed by the Limited Partnership Act 1907. A *partnership at will* is one for which no fixed term has been agreed. Any partner may end the partnership at any time provided that he gives notice of his intention to do so to all the other partners.

part performance A doctrine of equity that a contract required to be evidenced in writing will still be enforceable even if it is not so evidenced provided that one of the parties does certain acts by which the contract is partly performed. This doctrine applies primarily to contracts for the sale of land. For an act to bring the doctrine into play (i.e. a sufficient act of part performance) it must be performed by the person alleging the contract to exist and must relate unequivocally to the contract; an example would be taking possession of property alleged to have been sold to the person who takes possession.

party and party costs *See* costs.

passing off Conducting one's business in such a way as to mislead the public into thinking that one's goods or services are those of another business. The commonest form of passing off is marketing goods with a design, packaging, or trade name that is very similar to that of someone else's goods. It is not necessary to prove an intention to deceive: innocent passing off is actionable.

passport *n.* A document, issued by the Foreign and Commonwealth Office under the royal prerogative, that provides prima facie evidence of the holder's nationality. It is not required by law for leaving the UK, but it is required for entry into most other countries. Its issue is purely discretionary and the government may withdraw or revoke a passport at will.

past consideration *See* consideration.

patent *n.* The grant of an exclusive right to exploit an invention. In the UK patents are granted by the Crown through the Patent Office, which is part of the Department of Trade. An applicant for a patent (usually the inventor or his employer) must show that the invention is new, is not obvious, and is capable of industrial application. An expert known as a *patent agent* often prepares the application, which must describe the invention in considerable detail. The Patent Office publishes these details if it grants a patent. A patent remains valid for 20 years from the date of application (the *priority date*) provided that the person to whom it has been granted (the *patentee*) continues to pay the appropriate fees. During this time, the patentee may assign his patent or grant licences to use it. Such transactions are registered in a public register at the Patent Office. If anyone infringes his monopoly, the patentee may sue for an *injunction and *damages or an *account of profits. However, a patent from the Patent Office gives exclusive rights in the UK only: the inventor must obtain a patent from the European Patent Office in Munich and patents in other foreign countries if he wishes to protect the invention elsewhere.

patent agent *See* patent.

patent ambiguity *See* ambiguity.

patent defect *See* defect.

patentee *n.* A person who has been granted a *patent.

Patents Court A court forming part of the *Chancery Division of the High Court, having jurisdiction over matters arising under the Patents Acts 1949–77, the Registered Designs Acts 1949–61, and the Defence Contracts Act 1958. Two *puisne judges of the Chancery Division with special experience of patent law are assigned to hear its cases.

patrial *n. See* immigration.

pawn (pledge) *n.* An item of goods transferred by the owner (the *pawnor*) to another (the *pawnee*) as security for a debt. (The word is also used for the transfer itself.) A pawn involves a *bailment and the pawnor remains owner of the goods; the pawnee is liable for failure to take reasonable care of them. If the pawnor fails to repay the loan at the agreed time, the pawnee has the right at common law to sell the pawn; he must account to the pawnor for any surplus after discharging his debt. *Pawnbrokers* are dealers licensed to lend money at a specified rate of interest on the security of a pawn. Pawnbroking is regulated by provisions of the Consumer Credit Act 1974 (replacing the Pawnbrokers Acts 1872 and 1960) with regard to such matters as pawn receipts, rates of interest, redemption period and procedure, consequences of failure to redeem, and realization of the pawn. Under the Act, a pawn can be redeemed at any time within six months, or longer if agreed by both parties. At the end of this period ownership of the pawn passes to the pawnbroker if the value of the debt is £15 or less. If it is more than £15 the pawnbroker may sell the pawn after giving the pawnor notice, but the pawnor may still redeem the pawn at any time until it is sold. The pawnbroker must account to the pawnor for any surplus from the proceeds of sale after discharging his debt but he may claim any balance of the debt if the proceeds are insufficient.

Pay As You Earn (PAYE) A system for collecting *income tax in which the employer deducts tax direct from the employee's pay. The Inland Revenue gives every employee a code number, which the employer uses, together with tax tables, to work out how much tax to deduct (*see* PAYE week number). The employer is then responsible for paying the tax to the Inland Revenue by the 19th day of each month.

PAYE *See* Pay As You Earn.

PAYE week number One of a series of consecutive numbers given to successive seven-day periods within the tax year, used by employers in the calculation of tax due under *Pay As You Earn. Thus, Week 1 is the period 6–12 April inclusive, Week 2 is 13–19 April, and so on. The employer uses the week number in conjunction with the employee's tax code to determine his tax-free pay for the current tax year to date. This in turn is used to calculate the tax due. The week number relates to the period in which the pay day occurs, not necessarily the period in which the pay was earned.

payment by post The payment of a debt by the posting of notes, a cheque, or some other negotiable instrument. If the letter is lost in the post, the debt is not discharged unless the creditor has expressly or by implication requested payment by post and the debtor has sent a properly addressed letter.

payment in due course Payment made at or after the *maturity of a *bill of exchange to the holder of the bill by a payer in good faith and without notice that the holder's title to the bill is defective. A bill is discharged by payment in due course by or on behalf of the drawee or acceptor. When a bill is paid by the drawer or endorser it is not discharged and the party paying may have rights on it.

payment into court The payment by a defendant, into an account maintained by the court, of a sum in satisfaction of any or all of the plaintiff's claims. The plaintiff must acknowledge receipt of the notice of payment within 3 days and has 21 days thereafter in which to decide whether or not to accept the sum paid into court. If he does so, the action is terminated and the plaintiff receives the sum in court plus his *costs. If he decides not to accept the sum and fails to *beat the payment in* at trial (i.e. he fails to recover more than the amount paid in) he is usually ordered to pay the defendant's costs from the date of the payment in. For this reason, a payment in must not be disclosed to the trial judge, unless there is a defence of *tender before action. Payment in may also be ordered by the court in some circumstances, but the plaintiff may then only take the sum out with leave of the court.

pay statement *See* itemized pay statement.

PC *See* Privy Council.

pecuniary legacy *See* legacy.

penal statute A statute that creates a criminal offence or provides for any penalty (e.g. a forfeiture) enforceable in civil proceedings. It is subject to strict construction (*see* interpretation of statutes).

penalty *n.* **1.** A *punishment for a crime. A penalty must be clearly stated before it can be enforced. When statute creates an offence and specifies a penalty without saying how the offence is to be tried, there may be an implication that it is to be imposed by a magistrates' court. **2.** A sum specified in a contract as payable on its breach but not constituting a genuine estimate of the likely loss. *See* damages.

pendente lite [Latin] Until trial. When a will or the right to administer an estate is being disputed, the court may if necessary appoint an administrator *pendente lite* to deal with the estate until the proceedings have been resolved.

pending action Proceedings in court that relate to land or to some interest in it. The claimant should register the pending action as a land charge (*see* registration of encumbrances) as soon as the proceedings begin. If he fails to do this a purchaser acquiring the land

without knowing of the action will not be bound by the outcome.

peppercorn rent An insignificant rent reserved for the purpose of showing that a lease or tenancy is granted for valuable *consideration.

per autre vie *See* estate *pur autre vie*.

per capita [Latin: by heads] For each person. Distribution of an estate or fund *per capita* is an equal distribution in the specified shares among all those entitled to it. *Compare per stirpes*.

per curiam [Latin] By the court. A proposition *per curiam* is one made by the judge (or, if there is more than one judge, assented to by all).

peremptory challenge *See* challenge to jury.

peremptory pleas *See* pleas in bar.

perfect and imperfect rights Legally recognized rights. Perfect rights are enforceable through court action but imperfect rights are not.

perfect trust *See* executed trust.

performance bond *See* bond.

performance of contract The carrying out of obligations under a contract. Performance by both parties discharges the contract completely; performance by one party discharges him alone. The rules relating to performance distinguish between a *divisible contract* and an *indivisible* (or *entire*) *contract*. In a divisible contract the obligations of the parties are independent of each other, so that one party can demand performance by the other without rendering performance himself. Thus a landlord, though liable to be sued by his tenant for not carrying out a repairing covenant, is not prevented by his own default from enforcing the tenant's covenant to pay rent. Most contracts, however, are indivisible, i.e. the obligations are interdependent. Neither party can demand performance unless he himself either has performed or is ready and willing to do so. At common law, complete and precise performance was originally required, so that a party who rendered anything short of this (for example, a builder who carried out the contract work, but defectively in some respects) could recover nothing for his efforts. This extreme position was subsequently modified by the doctrine of *substantial performance*. A party who has substantially performed his obligations can now recover the contract price, reduced by damages awarded to the other party in respect of the defects.

A *tender of performance* is the equivalent of performance, so that a seller who tenders the correct goods is discharged from the contract (and entitled to damages for breach) if the buyer rejects them. *Vicarious performance* (e.g. by a subcontractor) is good performance, except when personal performance is demanded by the contract. *See also* part performance; specific performance.

perils of the seas One of the heads of risk included in a marine insurance policy. It covers the insured against loss caused by such events as unusual violence of wind or waves, striking submerged rocks, and collisions with other ships. The ordinary action of wind and waves in causing wear and tear is not, however, regarded as a peril of the seas.

per incuriam [Latin] Through lack of care. A decision of a court is made *per incuriam* if it fails to apply a relevant statutory provision or ignores a binding precedent.

periodic tenancy A tenancy in which rent is payable at fixed intervals, usually weekly, monthly, quarterly, or yearly. The tenancy continues automatically from one period to another until terminated by *notice to quit. Periodic tenancies can be created by express agreement, orally or in writing. Alternatively they can be created by implication when rent is accepted by the owner

of the land from the person who occupies it. This may arise, for example, when a tenant under a *fixed-term tenancy remains in possession at the end of his tenancy and the landlord continues to accept rent from him. The length of notice required to terminate the tenancy is usually the same as one of the periods of the tenancy.

perished goods Under the Sale of Goods Act 1979, goods under a contract of sale that have been either totally destroyed or so damaged that they no longer fit the contract description. The Act provides that a contract is void if it relates to specific goods that, unknown to the seller, have perished before it is made. If the goods perish after the contract is made, this event will make the contract void unless the risk has by then passed to the buyer (*see* transfer of risk). These two propositions give statutory recognition to common-law rules relating to *mistake and *frustration of contract, respectively.

perjury *n.* The offence of giving false evidence or evidence that one does not believe to be true (even if it is in fact the truth). It is punishable by up to seven years' imprisonment and/or a fine. The offence may be committed by any witness who has taken the oath or affirmed, by the defendant at any stage of the trial, and by an interpreter. Perjury is only committed, however, in judicial proceedings, which include any proceedings before a court, tribunal, or someone with the power to hear evidence on oath (e.g. Commissioners of Income Tax hearing appeals against tax assessments). The evidence given must be relevant to the proceedings and must be given with knowledge that it is false or recklessly.

The Perjury Act 1911 also creates various offences related to perjury. These include making a *false statement* on oath in nonjudicial proceedings and making a false statement or declaration relating to marriage (e.g. to obtain a licence to marry or make an entry in a register of marriage) or to the registration of a birth or death. These offences are punishable by up to seven years' imprisonment on indictment. The offences of making a false statement in a statutory declaration or in any account, balance sheet, or document required to be made by Act of Parliament are punishable by up to two years' imprisonment.

See also subornation.

permissive waste A kind of *waste that occurs when a tenant fails to maintain the property he leases and allows it to deteriorate.

per my et per tout [Norman French: by the half(?) and by all (the meaning of *my* is uncertain)] Denoting the unity of possession that is an essential characteristic of joint ownership of land. *See also* joint tenancy.

perpetual injunction *See* injunction.

perpetual trusts *See* rule against perpetual trusts.

perpetuating testimony A procedure for the recording of evidence in civil cases in which there is a danger that it might be lost (e.g. because of the death of a witness) before it can be used in a future action. It is rarely ordered.

perpetuity *n*. *See* rule against perpetuities.

per quod consortium amisit [Latin: by which he lost the benefit of her society] *See* consortium.

per quod servitium amisit [Latin: by which he lost services] *See* loss of services.

persistent offender A person whose previous criminal record makes him liable to be given an *extended sentence of imprisonment. Before 1948 persistent offenders were known as *habitual criminals*.

personal Act *See* Act of Parliament.

personal chattel *See* chattel.

personal-credit agreement An agreement between an individual (the debtor) and any other person (the creditor) by which the creditor provides the debtor with credit of any amount. Personal-credit agreements exclude loans, etc., to companies. *See also* consumer-credit agreement.

personal property (personalty) All *property that does not comprise land or incorporeal *hereditaments.

personal protection order An order under the Domestic Proceedings and Magistrates' Courts Act 1978 for the protection against violence of a spouse or child. *See* battered wife.

personal representative A person entitled to deal with a deceased person's estate in accordance with his will or under the rules relating to intestacy. Personal representatives include *executors and *administrators of all descriptions.

personal service The *service of a document in litigation (e.g. a writ) effected by leaving a copy of the document with the person to be served. It is often wrongly supposed that it is necessary to touch the person to be served with the document, but it is in fact sufficient to leave it in his presence having informed him of its nature.

personalty *n*. *See* personal property.

per stirpes [Latin: by the roots] According to descent. When property in an estate or fund is distributed *per stirpes*, beneficiaries a generation removed from the primary class of beneficiaries receive between them the share attributable to their ancestor. For example, a will may leave property to A and B in equal shares with provision that if either predeceases the testator, the deceased beneficiary's children take his share in equal shares *per stirpes*. If, on the testator's death, both A and B have already died, A leaving two children and B three, A's children will each receive a quarter of the property, and B's children one-sixth each. *Compare per capita.*

persuading to murder The statutory offence, punishable by a maximum sentence of life imprisonment, of persuading or encouraging any person to murder anyone else. This offence is committed even by a foreigner temporarily in England who persuades someone to commit a murder abroad (such a person would not normally be guilty of *incitement), and thus applies to the activities of international terrorist organizations (*see* terrorism).

persuasive authority A decision or other pronouncement of law that, under the doctrine of *precedent, a court may but need not apply when deciding the case before it. Persuasive authorities include decisions of courts of equal or lesser standing, decisions of courts outside the English legal system (particularly, courts of Commonwealth countries having systems based on the common law), *obiter dicta*, and the opinions of eminent textbook writers.

perverse verdict A *verdict of a jury that is either entirely against the weight of the evidence or contrary to the judge's direction on a question of law.

perverting the course of justice Carrying out an act that tends or is intended to obstruct or defeat the administration of public justice. Common examples are inventing false evidence to mislead a court (in either civil or criminal proceedings) or an arbitration tribunal, making false statements to the police, stealing or destroying evidence, threatening witnesses, and attempting to influence jurors. The common-law offence of perverting the course of justice overlaps with certain forms of *contempt of court and with the separate offence of tampering with witnesses. It is not an offence, however, to offer money to someone to persuade

him not to proceed with an action in the civil courts; nor is it an offence to offer to pay reasonable compensation to the victim of a crime, if he will agree not to take criminal proceedings. However, once he has made a statement to the police in connection with possible proceedings, it is an offence to attempt to induce him to withdraw or alter his statement.

petition *n.* An application for a legal remedy, e.g. a petition for *divorce, a *bankruptcy petition, an *election petition, or a petition for winding up a company (*see* compulsory winding-up by the court).

petition of right *See* Crown proceedings.

petroleum revenue tax A tax levied on the profits from sales of oil and gas extracted in the UK or on the continental shelf. The rate of tax (in 1983) is 75%.

petty sessions A court of summary jurisdiction now known as a *magistrates' court. The term was formerly used to denote a meeting of two or more *justices of the peace other than a general or *quarter sessions. A *petty-sessions area* is a geographical area for certain purposes of magistrates' court administration.

phasing of rent The process of increasing the rent for *protected tenancies by stages up to the full *fair rent registered by a rent officer.

philanthropic purposes Purposes that are narrower than *benevolent purposes but wider than charitable purposes. *See* charitable trust.

picketing *n.* Attendance by employees and their trade union representatives at or near a place of work for the purpose of persuading others to work or not to work, or to exchange information, in contemplation or furtherance of a *trade dispute. There is no specific legal right to picket, nor any prohibition on picketing. Pickets have no immunity from prosecution for committing criminal offences and they have no right to compel others to stop or to listen to the pickets' views. However, employees and their trade union representatives picketing their own place of work are immune from civil legal action for inducing others to break commercial or employment contracts with the employer involved in the dispute. Such immunity extends to persons engaged in secondary picketing in certain circumstances. *Secondary picketing* occurs when the premises of an employer who is not an immediate party to the dispute are picketed. Persons picketing customers or suppliers of the employer in dispute have immunity, provided they are likely to achieve their principal purpose of disrupting their own employer's trade with the employer in dispute. Thus in a dispute between an employer (A) and his workers, A's own employees may picket A's premises and employees of A's supplier (B) may picket B's premises (to prevent supplies reaching A), with the benefit of immunity from certain types of civil legal action.

When an employer tries to avoid the impact of the dispute by transferring business to his associated employer, the latter and his customers and suppliers may be picketed. Again, the pickets will have immunity if they are likely to achieve their principal purpose of disrupting the supply of goods or services transferred.

"Flying pickets", who are neither employees nor trade union representatives of employees at the workplace picketed, have no immunity. The courts will grant injunctions to stop or prevent unlawful picketing. A *code of practice on picketing is published by the Department of Employment.

piracy *n.* **1. (piracy *jure gentium*)** Any illegal act of violence, detention, or robbery committed on a private ship for personal gain, against another ship, people, or property on the high seas. Piracy may also be committed on or against an aircraft. Piracy also includes operating a pirate ship or aircraft and inciting or assisting any other act of piracy. However, acts committed for political purposes are not piracy; nor are any acts committed by a warship or government ship or aircraft. Piracy is an international crime and all nations may exercise jurisdiction over pirates, regardless of the nationality of the ship or the pirates. British courts have traditionally exercised such jurisdiction, and the power to do so is confirmed in the Tokyo Convention Act 1967.

English municipal law has created certain offences of. piracy that are not covered by international law, but they are not subject to the jurisdiction of the English courts unless committed on board a British ship or within British territorial waters. Examples of such offences are revolt by the crew of a ship against their master and hijacking of the ship by the crew. These offences, if tried as piracy, are subject to life imprisonment (and if accompanied by acts endangering life, or by an assault with intent to murder, by the death penalty).
2. (in marine insurance) One of the risks covered by a marine insurance policy, extending beyond the criminal offence to include plundering generally.
3. Infringement of *copyright. The copyright owner's usual remedy is to obtain an injunction to end the infringement.

piscary (fishery) *n.* A *profit *à prendre* or *common conferring the right to take fish from water on another's land.

plaint *n.* A statement in writing of a cause of action, used to initiate actions in the county courts. The plaint is entered by an officer of the court in the records of the court, based upon information provided by the plaintiff in his request. It is followed by the issue of a *summons.

plaintiff *n.* A person applying for relief against another person in an action, suit, petition, motion, summons, or any other form of court proceeding. *Compare* defendant.

plaint note A document sent by a county court to the plaintiff in an action. It is a receipt for court fees and gives the *plaint number*, a reference that must be quoted in all correspondence and court documents concerning the action.

planning permission *See* town and country planning.

plant *n.* *See* machinery and plant.

p.l.c. (public limited company) *See* limited company; public company.

plea *n.* **1.** A formal statement in court by or on behalf of an accused person as a response to the charge made against him. *See also* guilty; not guilty; pleas in bar. **2.** A defendant's answer to a plaintiff's declaration in an action at common law.

plea bargaining An agreement between the prosecution and the defence by which the accused changes his plea from not guilty to guilty in return for an offer by the prosecution (for example, to drop a more serious charge against the accused) or when the judge has informally let it be known that he will minimize the sentence if the accused pleads guilty. Any negotiations taking place between the judge and defence counsel must be in the presence of the prosecuting counsel: the accused is not a party to the negotiations. The accused must be allowed to make up his own mind freely about the proposals.

plead *vb.* To make a *plea.

pleading *n.* A formal written statement in a civil action served by each party on the other, containing the *allegations of fact that the party proposes to prove at trial (but not the evidence by which they are to be proved) and stating the remedy (if any) that the party claims in the action. Pleadings are usually *settled* by counsel, whose signature must appear on the pleading. In modern practice pleadings must contain only *material facts*, i.e. those facts essential to the party's claim or defence, and not the subordinate facts that are the means of proving them. It is customary to include the inferences of law that the party claims are to be drawn from the facts pleaded, although this is not essential. Allegations of law as such (legal arguments) are not permitted in pleadings. Since the purpose of pleadings is to define clearly the issues in the action and to give the parties notice of the other side's case, sufficient *particulars must be given of each allegation. *See also* defence; reply; statement of claim; subsequent pleadings.

pleading guilty by post A procedure that allows a person to plead guilty to certain minor offences by letter without appearing at the court. The procedure applies only to *summary offences punishable with a maximum of three months' imprisonment. The accused may send details of any mitigating circumstances and these are read out to the court. A person who has pleaded guilty by post may appear at the court if he subsequently wishes to. The court cannot, in any event, sentence him to imprisonment in his absence or disqualify him from driving without warning him of the possibility and giving him the opportunity to appear.

pleading in the alternative In civil cases, the process of including in a *pleading two or more inconsistent allegations and inviting the court to grant relief in respect of whichever allegation it finds to be well-founded.

pleas in bar (peremptory pleas) Pleas in *trials on indictment setting out some special ground for not proceeding with the indictment. There are four such pleas: *autrefois acquit*, *au-*

trefois convict, pardon, and special liability to repair a road or bridge.

pledge *n. See* pawn.

plene administravit [Latin: he has fully administered] The defence of a personal representative who has completed administration of a deceased's estate to a creditor's action to recover a debt of which he had no knowledge. Unless the creditor can prove that the personal representative still holds assets of the estate, he will obtain a judgment enforceable only against any such assets coming into the personal representative's hands in the future.

plough bote *See* estovers.

poaching *n.* Taking game without permission from private land or from land on which the killing of game is restricted. This normally amounts to theft; there are, however, various statutory offences to cover poaching that do not amount to theft. For example, the Deer Act 1980 creates offences relating to taking, killing, or injuring deer or trespassing on land with the intention of committing any of these acts. There are also special offences relating to taking or destroying fish in private waters or in waters with a private right of fishery. In addition, there is special legislation dealing with the poaching of endangered species.

poison *n.* A substance that, if ingested, is capable of endangering life or injuring health. It is an offence (punishable by up to five years' imprisonment) to cause someone to consume a poison or similar substance (which can include drugs or alcohol) with the intention of injuring or annoying them, even if no injury results. It is also an offence (punishable by up to ten years' imprisonment) to cause someone to consume such substances so that their life is endangered or they suffer grievous bodily harm as a result, even if this was not intended. There is also a special offence of causing a woman to take any drug or

other substance to stupefy or overpower her so that someone can have sexual intercourse with her, even if intercourse does not take place. Administering poison with the intention of killing someone or causing them serious harm may amount to an attempt to murder or to inflict grievous bodily harm. In both cases the attempt will be punishable with a maximum sentence of life imprisonment.

The sale of poisons is controlled by various statutes, principally the Medicines Act 1968 and Poisons Act 1972.

police authorities *See* police force.

Police Complaints Board An independent body appointed by the Prime Minister under the Police Act 1976 to supervise the investigation of complaints against the police. It considers reports by chief constables on the results of such investigations and has power to direct that disciplinary charges be preferred. It may also direct that the charges be heard by a disciplinary tribunal consisting of the chief constable and two members of the Board.

police court A *magistrates' court.

police force A body of police officers maintained for a police area by a police authority. In England and Wales the police areas are the individual counties (or two or more counties combined), the metropolitan police district, and the City of London; the *police authorities* are police committees in the case of county forces, the Home Secretary in the case of the Metropolitan Police Force, and the Court of Common Council in the case of the City of London police. A police committee (sometimes referred to as a *watch committee*, a term more correctly restricted to borough police forces, now extinct) consists of two-thirds county councillors and one-third magistrates. Police authorities are responsible for maintaining adequate and efficient forces and in county forces, subject to the Home Secretary's approval, for appointing chief constables. (The London forces have Commissioners, and the appointment of the Commissioner of Police of the Metropolis is technically by the Crown.) Police authorities do not, however, exercise operational or managerial control. Appointments to a force, and the direction of its operations, are matters for the chief constable or Commissioner, and its detailed management is largely determined by regulations made by the Home Secretary.

police officer A person who, whatever his rank within a police force, holds the ancient office of *constable*, i.e. one who has undertaken to serve the Crown as an officer of the peace. His office is, in law, independent. He is not technically a Crown servant, since the Crown neither appoints him nor pays him, nor is he a local authority employee. *See* police force.

political asylum Refuge granted to a person on political grounds. A person subject to UK immigration control (*see* immigration) is allowed to enter and remain in the UK if he would be liable to persecution for reasons of race, religion, nationality, or political opinion if he was returned to the country from which he came.

political offence An offence that is of a political character, so that the alleged offender cannot be extradited or surrendered as a *fugitive offender.

pollution *n.* Any action rendering the environment impure. Statutes relating wholly or partly to *air pollution* include the Clean Air Acts 1956 and 1968, the Health and Safety at Work Act 1974, and the Control of Pollution Act 1974, which control respectively the emission of smoke into the atmosphere, the emission of noxious or offensive substances, and the composition of petrol and other fuels. *Water pollution* generally is gov-erned by the Control of Pollution Act 1974, under which it is an offence (among other things) to allow polluting matter to enter rivers or other inland waters or to impede their flow so as to aggravate pollution due to other causes. Control of pollution by oil is covered by the Prevention of Oil Pollution Act 1971. Pollution by the deposit of waste on land is governed primarily by the Control of Pollution Act 1974, which permits household, commercial, and industrial waste to be deposited only on licensed sites. Local authorities are required by the Act to collect and dispose of household waste free of charge; for the purposes of *refuse disposal* by their residents, they are also, by the Refuse Disposal (Amenity) Act 1978, obliged to provide free refuse dumps.

polygamy *n.* The practice of having more than one spouse. English law considers a marriage *actually polygamous* if there is in fact more than one spouse, and *potentially polygamous* if there is only one spouse but the marriage was contracted under a system of law that permits polygamy. No polygamous marriage may be validly contracted in England. If it is celebrated abroad, however, it will be recognized if at the time it was celebrated neither spouse was domiciled in England; if either spouse was at that time domiciled in England the marriage will be void.

portion *n.* Funds or other property given or left to a child by his parent or someone standing *in loco parentis* and intended to make permanent provision for him or to establish him in life (e.g. a sum provided to set the child up in business). Sums provided for the child's maintenance or education or to supplement his income do not qualify. A portion may be brought into *hotchpot and may be presumed to adeem a legacy (*see* ademption) unless there is evidence that the testator intended the portion to be disregarded on his death.

positive law *See* natural law.

possession *n.* Actual control of property combined with the intention to use it, rightly or wrongly, as one's own. In the case of land, possession may be actual, when the owner has entered onto the land, or possession in law, when he has the right to enter but has not yet done so. *See also* quiet possession.

possessory lien *See* lien.

possessory title Ownership of land that can only be proved by evidence of the requisite period of *adverse possession or possession coupled with a defective documentary title. A proprietor of registered land having only possessory title is not protected against any adverse estate interest or right subsisting or capable of arising up to the time when the title was first registered.

possibility *n.* (in land law) An interest in land that depends on the occurrence of an uncertain future event. A *bare possibility*, such as a person's expectation of inheriting land under the will of a testator who is still alive (i.e. depending on the testator dying without having revoked the will), confers no legal or equitable interest. A *possibility coupled with an interest* (e.g. B's rights under a conveyance "to A for life, and if C is living at A's death then to B") can be transferred by will or by deed. *See also* possibility of a reverter; tenant in tail after possibility of issue extinct.

possibility of a reverter The interest of a person who has conveyed freehold land to another subject to a condition. Thus when A conveys land "to B on condition he never marries X", A has the possibility of a reverter if B should marry X.

post-mortem (autopsy) The examination of a body after death in order to establish the cause of death. Post-mortems are frequently requested by coroners (*see* inquest).

postnuptial settlement *See* marriage settlement.

power *n.* A legal discretion (as opposed to a *duty) to carry out or refrain from carrying out any act. When powers affect the rights of others (e.g. the powers of *trustees and *administrative powers), their exercise can be challenged in the courts. An act that goes beyond the scope of a power as specified in the instrument creating it (e.g. a trust deed or statute) is invalid; so, too, is any act carried out in abuse of a power (e.g. when it is exercised after taking irrelevant considerations into account, for improper motives, or capriciously). *See also* ultra vires.

power of appointment A right given to someone to dispose of property that is not his to a third party, within bounds established by the owner of the property (it is sometimes called a *mere* or *bare power*; *compare* trust power). The owner of the property (the *donor* of the power) gives a power to another (the *donee* of the power, or *appointor*) to appoint (give) the property to a person (the *appointee*) chosen by the appointor. The power may be *general* (under which an appointment may be made to anyone), *special* (an appointment may be made only within a class chosen by the donor), or *hybrid* (an appointment may be made to virtually anyone except a small class). The appointees have fewer rights than the beneficiaries under a trust. An appointment is void if it is made to someone not within the class chosen or if it is a *fraud on a power.

power of attorney (letter of attorney) An authority given by one person to another to act on his behalf. A power to execute a *deed must itself be given by a deed.

power of sale 1. The right of a mortgagee to sell mortgaged property if the mortgagor has not repaid his loan by the contractual date of redemption. This power arises when the contractual

270

date (stated in the mortgage document and usually very early in the period of the mortgage) has passed, but may only be exercised if interest due under the mortgage is two months in arrears, if there has been a breach of certain terms in the mortgage, or if notice has been served on the mortgagor to repay the loan and the loan has not been repaid within three months of the notice. If the mortgagee sells the property under the power of sale, he must act with reasonable care and hold any money surplus to that needed to pay his mortgage debt for the mortgagor's benefit. **2.** The right of a *tenant for life under the Settled Land Act 1925 to sell the settled land for the best price in money that can be obtained. Such a sale *overreaches the interests of the subsequent beneficiaries.

power of search The legal right to search people or property. Private people have no powers of search, but various statutes confer such powers on police or other officials on the authority of a *search warrant* issued by a magistrate or a High Court judge. Under the Theft Act 1968, for example, police may obtain a warrant to search for stolen goods when there are reasonable grounds for believing that they are in someone's possession or on his premises. In some cases the police may carry out a search on the written authorization of any officer above the rank of police superintendent, without obtaining a magistrates' warrant. For example, such authorization may be given under the Theft Act to search for stolen goods on premises occupied by someone with a previous conviction for any offence involving dishonesty and subject to imprisonment. Under certain circumstances the police are given powers of search without requiring either a warrant or superior authorization; for example, under the Misuse of Drugs Act 1971 (*see* controlled drugs) or the Prevention of Terrorism Act 1976 (*see* proscribed organization). The police also

have a general power, when arresting someone for an *arrestable offence, to enter and search any place in which the suspect is believed to be. Statutes sometimes give powers of search to public officials, e.g. customs officers, Board of Trade officials, or Inland Revenue officers. In the case of a suspected tax fraud, for example, a judge will issue a warrant to Revenue officers if he reasonably suspects that there is evidence relating to the fraud on the premises to be searched.

When police or other officials have powers of search, they are sometimes also given the power to seize property they find. For example, police officers searching for stolen goods may seize any goods they reasonably believe to be stolen or to relate to criminal charges against a defendant. They may keep any goods seized for as long as they need to complete their investigations. The police also have the power to obtain an injunction to "freeze" any money in a bank or deposit account that they believe to be stolen or the proceeds of stolen goods. Inland Revenue officials conducting a search may seize material they reasonably believe might be required as evidence of tax frauds. The courts have recently held that they are not obliged to give reasons for seizing items before criminal proceedings have taken place. Seizure can only be challenged, therefore, if it can be shown that the official did not believe (or had no reasonable grounds for believing) that the material seized might be required as evidence.

The police also have various powers of search at common law. Once they have made an arrest, they may take and keep any property found in the arrested person's possession that may provide evidence of the offence for which he is charged. They may also, after entering premises with a search warrant or in order to make an arrest, take any property that will provide evidence of the offence for which they entered. When a search or seizure has been carried out unlawfully, the evidence obtained is still admissible (although the trial judge has discretion to exclude it). Civil proceedings can be brought for wrongful detention.

practice *n.* **1.** The mode of proceeding to enforce a legal right. It is virtually synonymous with *procedure, but is sometimes used to denote informal rules of procedure as distinct from those derived from rules of court. **2.** A book on practice and procedure, such as the *Supreme Court Practice or the County Court Practice.

Practice Directions Published statements, usually issued by the head of the court or division to which they relate, indicating the procedure to be followed in particular matters or the court's intended policy in certain cases. Unlike *rules of court, they have no statutory authority. They are normally published in the law reports. Masters' Practice Directions are issued by the Queen's Bench Masters and concern the administration of the *Queen's Bench Division.

practice master *See* Central Office.

practising certificate An annual certificate issued by the *Law Society to a solicitor entitling him to practise. The fee chargeable for the certificate includes the premium of an insurance policy indemnifying the solicitor against the consequences of professional negligence.

praecipe [Latin: command] *n.* **1.** A court document on which a party writes the particulars of a document (e.g. a summons) that he wishes to have prepared or issued. **2.** Formerly, a writ requiring the sheriff to command the defendant either to do a certain thing or to show cause why he had not done it. In county court procedure, this document is now called a *request*.

preamble *n.* The part of a statute that sets out its purposes and effects. It follows immediately after the long title and date of royal assent. Preambles are now virtually confined to statutes originating in private Bills.

precarious possession Possession of property at the will of another person.

precatory trust *See* precatory words.

precatory words Words that accompany a gift of property in a document, hoping, desiring, or requesting that the donee will dispose of the property in a particular way. It is often difficult to decide whether there is sufficient certainty of intention to create a trust (*precatory trust*) or whether the property is an absolute gift to the recipient. The courts have tended to construe gifts so as not to create a trust, unless there is no doubt that a trust was intended, although a few very recent cases may have reversed this trend.

precedent *n.* A judgment or decision of a court, normally recorded in a *law report, used as an authority for reaching the same decision in subsequent cases. In English law, decisions of the *House of Lords are binding upon the *Court of Appeal and all lower courts and are normally followed by the House of Lords itself. Decisions of the Court of Appeal are binding on all lower courts and, subject to some exceptions, on the Court of Appeal itself. Decisions of the High Court are binding on inferior courts, but decisions of inferior courts do not create any binding precedent. A lower court is not bound by all aspects of a previous decision but only by those parts of the judgment that constitute the principles of the decision (*see* ratio decidendi) and are not merely passing comments (*obiter dicta*) of the judge.

precept *n.* A lawful demand or direction, particularly a demand from a rating authority to another authority to levy rates for the benefit of the former. For example, a district council's rates include an amount that it collects as a result of a precept from its county council.

predecessor *n.* (in land law) A person through whom an owner's title to land is traced. Examples are a previous owner who sold, bequeathed, or settled the land and a mortgagee who exercised his power of sale.

pre-emption *n.* The right to an opportunity of purchasing land in priority to other people. For example, if A makes a covenant that for five years he will not sell his land other than to B at £5000, A cannot be forced to sell (*compare* option) but B's right of pre-emption prevents him from selling other than on the stated terms for five years. A right of pre-emption is valid only if it is sufficiently precise; it will bind third parties only if registered as an *estate contract (*see* registration of encumbrances).

pre-emptive right 1. The right of some shareholders under the Companies Act 1980 to be offered a proportion of certain classes of newly issued securities before they are offered to anyone else and upon terms at least as favourable. (*See also* rights issue.) **2.** The right conferred by the articles of association upon shareholders in some private companies to be offered, on specified terms, first refusal of the shares of any shareholder wishing to transfer his holding.

preference share *See* share.

preferential debts The debts of a bankrupt that have priority of payment over his other debts. These are rates and taxes and the wages, salaries, and holiday pay of the bankrupt's employees.

preferment *n.* **1.** The submission of a statement or information. **2.** The act of bringing a *bill of indictment before an appropriate court.

pregnancy *n.* (in employment law) *See* dismissal; maternity rights.

pregnancy *per alium* [Latin: by another] Pregnancy of a woman at the time of her marriage by someone other than her husband. If the husband was unaware of the true facts of the pregnancy, the marriage is voidable.

prehearing assessment *See* industrial tribunal.

pre-incorporation contract A contract purporting to be made by a person acting as agent for a company not yet formed. Under the European Communities Act 1972, that person is personally liable on the contract.

prejudice *n.* *See* unfair prejudice; without prejudice.

preliminary investigation (preliminary inquiry) The procedure in a magistrates' court to decide whether or not there is a sufficient case to commit an accused person for trial by the Crown Court. *See* committal for trial.

preliminary point of law A question of law ordered to be tried before the facts of the case are determined. Orders of this kind are normally made if the point of law will be decisive in the litigation or will result in a substantial saving of *costs.

premises *pl. n.* **1.** Land or buildings; a parcel of land. **2.** *See* deed.

premium *n.* **1.** The sum payable (usually annually) by the insured to the insurer under a contract of *insurance. **2.** A lump sum sometimes paid by a tenant at the time of the grant, assignment, or renewal of his lease or tenancy. It is illegal to demand a premium in respect of a *protected tenancy. This includes demanding an excessive payment for furniture as a condition of the grant of the tenancy. However, a landlord is entitled to ask for a deposit of up to one-sixth of the annual rent.

prerogative of mercy The power of the Crown, on the Home Secretary's advice, to pardon a criminal offence absolutely (thereby relieving the defendant of all the consequences of conviction), to commute a sentence to a milder form, or to remit a sentence in part.

prerogative orders Orders issued by the High Court for the supervision of inferior courts, tribunals, and other bodies exercising judicial or quasi-judicial functions. The orders are *certiorari*, *mandamus*, and *prohibition*. Until 1938 they were *prerogative writs*, but since the Administration of Justice Act 1938 the only remaining prerogative writ is *habeas corpus.

prescribed limit The maximum amount of alcohol a person is legally allowed to have in his blood if he is driving or in charge of a motor vehicle on a road or public place (*see* drunken driving). The level is currently fixed at 80 milligrams of alcohol per 100 millilitres of blood.

prescription *n.* The acquisition for the benefit of one's own land (the dominant tenement) of an *easement or *profit *à prendre* over another's land (the servient tenement) by uninterrupted use over a long period (*acquisitive prescription*). *Negative prescription* is the extinguishing of rights as a result of the dominant owner failing to exercise them over a similar long period. A person claiming a right by prescription must show that his use did not have the servient owner's permission and was not kept secret or exercised by force. Under the Prescription Act 1832 most easements may be acquired by prescription over 20 years, the period being extended when the servient owner is under a disability (e.g. a child or person of unsound mind), although 40 years' use establishes an absolute right. The periods are 30 and 60 years in the case of profits. An absolute easement of light is acquired after 20 years' use. Rights can also be acquired at common law under the doctrine of *lost modern

grant, or by proof of continuous use since time immemorial, i.e. since 1189.

presentment *n.* The act of presenting a *bill of exchange to the person upon whom it is drawn for his *acceptance or for payment. When a bill is payable after sight, presentment for acceptance is necessary in order to fix its *maturity. Bills must normally be presented for payment; otherwise the drawer and endorsers are discharged. There are rules as to the time and place of presentment.

presents *pl. n. See* deed.

presiding judge A *puisne judge appointed by the Lord Chancellor to supervise the work of a circuit (*see* circuit system). Each circuit has two presiding judges with the exception of the South-Eastern circuit, which has the Lord Chief Justice and two puisne judges.

presumption *n.* A supposition that the law allows or requires to be made. Some presumptions relate to people, e.g. the presumptions of innocence and of sanity (see entries below). Others concern events, e.g. the presumption of legality (*omnia praesumuntur rite et solemniter esse acta*: all things are presumed to have been done correctly and solemnly). Most relate to the interpretation of written documents, particularly statutes (*see* interpretation of statutes). Almost every presumption is a *rebuttable presumption*, i.e. it holds good only in the absence of contrary evidence. Thus, the presumption of innocence is destroyed by positive proof of guilt. An *irrebuttable presumption* is one that the law does not allow to be contradicted by evidence, as, for example, the presumption that a child below the age of 10 is incapable of committing a crime (*see doli capax*). *See also* equitable presumptions.

presumption of advancement *See* advancement.

presumption of death A common-law presumption that someone has died.

The presumption will be made if a spouse has been missing for at least seven years (with nothing to indicate that he or she is still alive) or by proof of other reasonable grounds (e.g. that the spouse was on a ship that sank). The courts are empowered to grant a decree of *presumption of death and dissolution of marriage*, enabling the other spouse to remarry; the remarriage will be valid even if the first spouse later reappears.

presumption of innocence The legal presumption that every person charged with a criminal offence is innocent until proved guilty. *See* burden of proof.

presumption of legality *See* presumption.

presumption of legitimacy *See* legitimacy.

presumption of negligence *See res ipsa loquitur.*

presumption of sanity The legal presumption that every person charged with a criminal offence was sane (and therefore responsible in law) at the time he is alleged to have committed the crime. *See* insanity; McNaghten Rules.

presumption of survivorship *See* commorientes.

presumptive evidence *See* prima facie evidence.

pre-trial review A hearing in a county court for the preliminary consideration of an action or matter. The hearing is before the *registrar, who is required to consider the course of the proceedings and give all necessary directions for their future conduct. The registrar also has power to enter judgment at the pre-trial review in some circumstances, e.g. if the defendant does not file a defence or appear at the hearing.

preventive detention Imprisonment for longer than the normal prescribed maximum term, formerly imposed to protect society from habitual criminals. Preventive detention was abolished in 1969 and replaced by the *extended sentence.

previous convictions (in the law of evidence) In general, evidence that a party or witness has been convicted of a criminal offence on some previous occasion is inadmissible in both civil and criminal cases as part of the opposing party's own case, unless it is admissible *similar-fact evidence or, in civil cases (under the Criminal Evidence Act 1968), unless it is relevant to any issue in the proceedings. However, a witness (other than an accused person) may be cross-examined about his previous convictions in order to impeach (discredit) him. Under the terms of the Criminal Evidence Act 1898, the accused may only be cross-examined about his previous convictions if (1) they are relevant to show that he is guilty of the offence with which he is charged (i.e. they would be admissible similar-fact evidence if tendered as part of the prosecution's own case); (2) the accused has attempted to establish his own good character or has cast imputations upon the character of the prosecutor or his witnesses; or (3) he has given evidence against any other person charged in the same proceedings. If a witness is asked about a previous conviction and denies the conviction, *evidence in rebuttal may be given. *See also* credit.

previous statements (in the law of evidence) If a witness has on some previous occasion made a statement that is inconsistent with his present testimony, this may be put to him in *cross-examination in order to impeach (discredit) him; if he denies having made the statement, it may be proved by *secondary evidence. Evidence of the previous consistent statements of a witness is not in general admissible. It may, however, be given in order to rebut the suggestion that his present testimony is a recent fabrication or when it concerns the *complaint of the victim of a sexual offence. *See also* credit.

price *n.* In a contract of sale, the money *consideration given in exchange for the transfer of ownership. In a contract of *sale of goods the price may be fixed by the contract, it may be left to be fixed in a manner agreed by the contract, or it may be determined by the course of dealing between the parties. If the price is not determined in any of the above ways, the buyer must pay a reasonable price.

prima facie [from Latin *prima facies*, first appearance] At first appearance; on the face of things.

prima facie case A case that has been supported by sufficient evidence for it to be taken as proved in the absence of adequate evidence to the contrary.

prima facie evidence 1. (*or* **presumptive evidence**) Evidence that is sufficient to discharge any evidential *burden of proof borne by a party and that may be sufficient to discharge the persuasive burden of proof if no evidence in rebuttal is tendered. **2.** Evidence of a fact that is of sufficient weight to justify a reasonable inference of its existence but does not amount to conclusive evidence of that fact.

primary evidence Evidence, such as the original of a document, that by its nature does not suggest that better evidence is available. Even if an item of primary evidence is inadmissible (e.g. because it is the subject of a private *privilege), the same fact may, in most cases, be proved by *secondary evidence.

primary facts Facts found by the trial court to be established on the basis of the testimony of witnesses and the production of real or documentary evidence. Appellate courts are generally unwilling to change the trial court's findings concerning primary facts, but may reverse its decisions concerning the inferences to be drawn from them.

Prime Minister The head of the UK government, who is appointed by the Crown to select and preside over the *Cabinet and bears ultimate responsibility for the policy and machinery of government. The Prime Minister also advises the Crown on such matters as the dissolution of Parliament, the creation of peerages, and the making of senior appointments (e.g. the Ombudsman). Like the Cabinet, the office derives from *constitutional convention, which requires that the person appointed is the party leader able to command sufficient support in the House of Commons.

principal *n.* **1.** (in criminal law) The person who actually carries out a crime (the *principal in the first degree*) or who aids and abets when it is being carried out by someone else (the *principal in the second degree*). A person can be a principal in the first degree even if he does not carry out the act himself; for example, if he acts through an innocent agent, such as a child, or if he is legally responsible for the acts of another (e.g. because of *vicarious liability). Before 1967 someone who merely incites or procures a crime but is not present when it is carried out was called an *accessory before the fact*, but this term is now abolished and such a person is now also a principal. The Law Commission has recommended that the actual perpetrator of the crime be called the principal and all other accomplices be called *accessories. **2.** (in the law of agency) The person on whose behalf an *agent acts. **3.** (in finance) The sum of money lent or invested, as distinguished from the interest.

principal clerks in Chancery chambers Officials of the *Chancery Division of the High Court who, if of the grade of Principal or Senior Executive Officer, may assist the Masters in making certain orders on *ex parte* application relating to (for example) the examination of judgment debtors. They may also sign certificates of attendance in chambers for the purpose of *taxation of costs without reference to the Master.

principal mansion house The main house (other than a farmhouse or a house whose accompanying garden, park, and grounds occupy less than 25 acres) comprised in a settlement of land. Under the Settled Land Act 1925, if the terms of the settlement so provide, the tenant for life cannot sell the principal mansion house without the consent of the trustees or the court. Consent is necessary under a settlement made before 1926 unless its terms dispense with the requirement.

principle of legality *See nullum crimen sine lege.*

priority *n. See* priority of assignment; priority of mortgages; priority of time.

priority caution An entry at HM Land Registry recording the equitable *assignment or mortgage of a *minor interest in registered land (*compare* priority inhibition). The priority of such dealings is governed by the order in which the respective priority cautions or inhibitions are registered on the application of the assignee or mortgagee.

priority inhibition An entry at HM Land Registry recording the absolute *assignment of a minor interest in registered land. *See also* priority caution.

priority neighbourhood An area declared such by a housing authority, being broadly similar to a *housing action area. A priority neighbourhood is declared when it is not practicable either to constitute the area itself a housing action area or a general improvement area or to include it in one. Priority neighbourhoods are typically areas surrounding or adjoining housing action areas or general improvement areas.

priority notice 1. A notice lodged at

HM Land Registry that prevents, for 14 days, anyone other than the person lodging the notice from registering title to the land concerned or any dealing in it. Provided that he lodges his application for registration of his own title or dealing within the period of protection, he will not be bound by any other encumbrances lodged for registration before his own. In practice, dealings (i.e. transfers, mortgages, etc.) in land that is already registered are usually protected by the applicant's certificate of *official search rather than by separate registration of a priority notice. **2.** In the case of unregistered land, a notice lodged at the Land Charges Department of the intended registration of a charge. The priority notice is lodged at least 14 days before the intended charge is to take effect, and the subsequent registration of the charge will be effective from the time the charge was created, provided the application for registration is presented within 28 days after the priority notice. Thus when A is about to convey land to B, who is to give a restrictive covenant in A's favour, A may lodge a priority notice before completing the transaction and register the covenant afterwards. This will ensure that the covenant will bind any purchaser or mortgagee from B whose interest may arise before A can register the covenant as a charge.

priority of assignment The order in which two or more assignments of a chose in action takes effect. This order is determined according to the date of receipt of the notice of assignment by the legal owner of the property assigned.

priority of mortgages The order in which two or more mortgages of the same property take effect. If there are several mortgages of the same property, and its value is less than the amount due on the mortgages, the respective claims of the mortgagees must be determined. Before 1926, priority often de-pended on the order in which the mortgages were created. Since 1925 the order of priority in the case of registered land is according to the order in which the respective mortgages are registered. A first mortgagee of unregistered land usually retains the title deeds and has priority over others except prior mortgages that are registered. Otherwise the order is governed by the order of registration. Priority of equitable interests is determined by the date at which notice is received by the trustees. *See also* consolidation of mortgages; tacking.

priority of time When there are two or more competing interests, the equitable maxim *qui prior est tempore potior est jure* (he who is earlier in time is stronger in law) applies. This means that the first in time prevails over the others. For example, where a property is subject to two mortgages, the one granted first has priority (*see* priority of mortgages). However, the priority can be affected by the existence of a purchaser for value without notice, fraud, estoppel, gross negligence, registration, and overreaching.

privacy *n.* The right to be left alone. English law does not give a legal right to privacy as such, although some protection is given indirectly, for example by the laws relating to *defamation, *trespass, and *copyright.

private Act *See* Act of Parliament.

private arrest *See* citizen's arrest.

private Bill *See* Bill.

private carrier *See* carrier.

private company A type of registered company that cannot offer its securities to the public. The *transfer of shares and number of company members may be restricted by the articles of association. Restrictions applicable to *public companies (e.g. relating to the number and age of directors) may not apply. *See also* financial assistance.

private defence Action taken in reasonable defence of one's person or property. It can be pleaded as a defence to an action in tort. The right of private defence includes the defence of one's family and, probably, of any other person from unlawful force.

private international law (conflict of laws) The part of the national law of a country that establishes rules for dealing with cases involving a foreign element (i.e. contact with some system of foreign law). For example, if a contract is made in England but is to be fulfilled abroad, it will be necessary to decide which law governs the validity of the contract. This is known as the question of *choice of law*. Sometimes the courts must also decide whether or not they have jurisdiction to hear the case and whether or not to recognize a *foreign judgment (e.g. a divorce obtained abroad).

Private international law must not be confused with public *international law.

private law The part of the law that deals with such aspects of relationships between individuals that are of no direct concern to the state. It includes the law of property and of trusts, family law, the law of contract, mercantile law, and the law of tort. *Compare* public law.

private member's Bill *See* Bill.

private nuisance *See* nuisance.

privilege *n.* **1.** A special right or immunity in connection with legal proceedings conferred upon a person by virtue of his rank or office. For example, Members of Parliament enjoy certain privileges in relation to arrest, which, however, do not extend to arrest in connection with indictable offences (*see* parliamentary privilege). *See also* absolute privilege; qualified privilege. **2.** (in the law of evidence) The right of a witness when testifying to refuse to answer certain types of question or of a party when making discovery (*see* discovery and inspection of documents) to refuse to produce certain types of document on the ground of some special interest recognized by law. Privileges are divided into two groups: *public-interest privilege* and *private privilege*. The Crown has always been able to claim public-interest privilege in relation to secrets of the state and other matters whose confidentiality is essential to the functioning of the public service (*see* Crown privilege). It is now recognized that a similar privilege may be claimed by private parties when some overriding public interest is involved. Private privileges include the *privilege against self-incrimination*, according to which a witness may not be asked a question the answer to which might tend to incriminate him; *legal professional privilege*, which protects confidential communications between lawyers and their clients and between lawyers and third parties with a view to advising their clients; and a privilege attaching to *without prejudice communications in the course of litigation. *See also* marital privileges.

privileged communication 1. A confidential official communication that may be withheld from production in court proceedings because disclosure of its contents would be against the public interest. 2. A communication between parties in a confidential relationship, such as husband and wife or solicitor and client, evidence of which may not be given without the consent of the party to whom the privilege belongs. Communications between patient and doctor are not privileged. 3. (in the tort of *defamation) A communication that is protected by absolute or qualified privilege. No action for defamation may be brought for a communication protected by *absolute privilege. A communication covered by *qualified privilege is protected unless it was made maliciously.

privileged will A will that is valid even though it does not comply with the formal requirements of the Wills Act 1837 (e.g. in being written but not witnessed or in being oral) or is made by a minor. The right to make a privileged will is conferred by the 1837 Act (as extended by the Wills (Soldiers and Sailors) Act 1918) on any soldier in actual military service (a *soldiers's will* or *military testament*) and any mariner or seaman at sea (a *mariner's will*). It also applies to airmen on actual military service and, on normal principles of statutory interpretation, to females as well as to males (for example, a female secretary aboard an ocean liner has been held to be a mariner at sea). *Actual military service* has been very widely interpreted. It is not confined to service as a combatant during time of war, but extends to service in any other capacity (e.g. as an auxiliary or a trainee) and to service when war is merely imminent. Service with an occupying force after a war is also included. *At sea* has received a similarly wide interpretation. A member of the naval forces is treated as being at sea if he is in an equivalent position to a soldier or airman on actual military service (e.g. if he is on shore leave during wartime).

privilege of witness *See* privilege.

privity *n.* The relationship that exists between people as a result of their participation in some transaction or event; for example, *privity of contract and *privity of estate.

privity of contract The relationship that exists between the parties to a contract. The common-law doctrine of privity of contract establishes that only the parties to a contract can sue and be sued on it: it can neither confer rights nor impose liabilities on others. If, for example, X and Y agree that X will paint Y's house, in return for which Y will pay £1000 to Z, Z cannot sue Y for the money. If he could, the contract would be creating a *jus quaesitum tertio*

privity of estate

(Latin: right acquired for a third party), and English law does not recognize such a right.

privity of estate The relationship between landlord and tenant under the same lease; as long as the relationship subsists, the landlord and tenant may enforce their respective obligations against one another even though they were not original parties to the lease. Thus when A grants a lease to B who subsequently assigns his interest to C, while A conveys his reversion to D, D may enforce against C the tenant's covenants given by A although there is no contract between D and C. There is no privity between different leasehold estates. For example if A grants a lease to B who sublets to C, A cannot sue C to enforce obligations in either the lease or the sublease.

Privy Council (PC) A body, headed by the Lord President of the Council, that formerly advised the Crown on government policy but has been superseded in that role by the *Cabinet. Its functions are now mainly formal (e.g. a few members are summoned to make *Orders in Council), but it has limited statutory powers of legislation (*see* Orders of Council) and it also advises the sovereign, through committees, on certain judicial matters (*see* Judicial Committee of the Privy Council) and other matters of a nonpolitical nature (e.g. the grant of university charters). There are about 350 Privy Councillors, who include members of the royal family, all Cabinet ministers, the Speaker and other holders of high nonpolitical office, and persons honoured for public services. A Privy Councillor is addressed as "Right Honourable".

prize court A court that, in accordance with *international law, deals with questions relating to ships or goods captured during wartime at sea or in port by the naval or air forces of a belligerent power. The Supreme Court of Judicature (Consolidation) Act 1925 constituted the High Court a prize court; jurisdiction in prize was vested in the Probate, Divorce and Admiralty Division until its transfer in 1970 to the Admiralty Court. Prize appeals go to the Judicial Committee of the Privy Council.

probate *n.* A certificate issued by the Family Division of the High Court, on the application of *executors appointed by a will, to the effect that the will is valid and that the executors are authorized to administer the deceased's estate. When there is no apparent doubt about the will's validity, probate is granted in *common form* on the executors filing an *affidavit. Probate granted in common form can be revoked by the court at any time on the application of an interested party who proves that the will is invalid. When the will is disputed, probate in *solemn form* is granted, but only if the court decides that the will is valid after hearing the evidence on the disputed issues in a *probate action. All parties who knew of the probate action and of their interest in the estate are bound by the court's order, whether or not they were parties to the action.

probate action Proceedings in court to determine whether or not a disputed will is valid. Contentious probate business is dealt with by the Chancery Division of the High Court. A will may be challenged on the grounds that it was not properly executed (*see* execution of will), that the testator lacked testamentary capacity, or that it has been revoked.

Probate, Divorce and Admiralty Division A division of the *High Court created by the Judicature Acts 1873–75 to take over the jurisdiction formerly exercised by the Court of Probate, the Court for Divorce and Matrimonial Causes, and the High Court of Admiralty. The Division was renamed the *Family Division by the Administration of Justice Act 1970: the Admiralty jurisdiction was transferred to the

*Queen's Bench Division and the contentious probate jurisdiction to the *Chancery Division.

probation hostel Premises for the accommodation of persons who may be required to reside there by *probation orders.

probation officer An officer whose duties include supervising persons bound by (for example) *probation orders, *supervision orders, or *community service orders. A probation officer advises, assists, and befriends these and others (e.g. persons who have been released from prison or are on bail) and inquires into the circumstances of offenders in order to assist the court to determine how best to deal with them.

probation order A court order placing an offender under the supervision of a *probation officer for a period of between one and three years, imposed (with the consent of the offender) instead of a sentence of imprisonment. Probation orders may be imposed on any offenders over the age of 17; they are most commonly imposed on first offenders, young offenders, elderly offenders in need of support, and offenders whose crimes are not serious. The order contains conditions for the supervision and behaviour of the offender during the probation period, including where he should live, when and how often he should report to his local probation officer, and a requirement that he should notify the probation officer of any change of address. The order may also require him to live in an approved probation hostel (for probationers employed outside the hostel) or an approved probation home (for probationers not employed outside). An order may also be made that the offender should attend a specified *day-training centre*, designed to train him to cope with the strains of modern life, for a period of up to 60 days.

A probation order has the same legal effect as a *discharge. If the proba-

tioner is convicted of a further offence while on probation, he may be punished in the normal way for the original offence (for which the probation order was made) as though he had just been convicted of that offence. If he does not comply with the conditions specified in the probation order, he may be fined up to £50 or the court may make a *community service order or order for attendance at a day centre or it may punish him for the original offence as though he had just been convicted of it.

Probation orders may also be imposed on offenders who, though not insane, are suffering from some mental problem. Such orders usually specify conditions relating to medical treatment.

procedure *n.* (in court proceedings) The formal manner in which legal proceedings are conducted. *See also* practice; rules of court. *Compare* substantive law.

process *n.* **1.** (in court procedure) A document issued by a court to require the attendance of the parties or the performance of some initial step in the proceedings by a defendant. When it is used to initiate the proceedings it may be called the *originating process*. In the High Court this may be a *writ of summons, an *originating summons, originating petition, or originating notice of *motion; in the county court and magistrates' court it is a *summons. **2.** *See* abuse of process.

Procurator General *See* Treasury Solicitor.

procurement *n.* Persuading or inviting a woman to have sexual intercourse. The following are offences of procurement. (1) Procuring a woman to have sexual intercourse with oneself or anyone else, anywhere in the world, by means of threats or false pretences. (2) Procuring a girl under the age of 21 to have sexual intercourse with a third person anywhere in the world. (3) Procuring a severely subnormal woman (who is incapable of guarding herself against exploitation) to have sexual intercourse anywhere in the world. These three offences are committed only if sexual intercourse takes place. (4) Procuring a woman to become a prostitute or to leave the UK with the intention that she should join or frequent a brothel. All these offences are punishable by up to two years' imprisonment.

procuring breach of contract (inducing breach of contract) The tort of intentionally persuading or inducing someone to break a contract made by him with a third party. It is actionable by the party who suffers loss from the breach. Thus a theatre manager may sue the person who induces a singer to break her contract to perform at his theatre. In some circumstances a defence of *justification is available. The tort also covers indirect procurement of breach of contract (i.e. by inducing persons not parties to the contract to procure the breach) and interference with the performance of a subsisting contract without actually causing a breach. These forms of the tort, however, are only actionable if unlawful means are used to procure the breach or interference. The operation of the tort in *trade disputes is limited by statute.

production of documents The act of a party in making available documents in his possession, custody, or power either for inspection by the other party (*see* discovery and inspection of documents) or for use as evidence at trial in accordance with a *notice to produce.

products liability The liability of a manufacturer or distributor of defective products. In the USA a manufacturer is strictly liable for defective products and the term products liability derives from American law. In England, liability depends on whether the action is brought in contract or tort. The purchaser of a defective product may sue the seller for *breach of contract in failing to supply a product that conforms to the contract (including its *implied conditions). If a defective product causes damage to anyone (either the purchaser or someone else) that person may have an action in tort but must usually prove that the defect was the result of *negligence. The action is brought against the person whose negligence caused the damage, who may be the manufacturer or someone else, such as a distributor or a repairer.

profit-and-loss account A document presenting in summary form a true and fair view of the company's profit or loss as at the end of its financial year. It must show the items listed in one of the four formats set out in the Companies Act 1981. Its function is to show as profit or loss the difference between revenue generated and the expenditure incurred in the period covered by the account. *See also* accounts.

profit *à prendre* The right to take produce (such as wood, turf, or fish) from another's land (the servient tenement) or to graze animals on it. It may exist as a legal or equitable interest. A profit *in gross* (i.e. which exists independently of any ownership of land by the person entitled) may be exercisable without any limit on the amount of produce taken and may be sold, bequeathed, or otherwise dealt with. Profits existing for the benefit of the owner's land (the dominant tenement) are generally exercisable only to the extent to which the dominant tenement can benefit. They may be *appurtenant, when the nature of the right depends on the terms of the grant; or *pur cause de vicinage* (Norman French: because of vicinity), in respect of cattle grazing the dominant tenement and straying onto the unfenced adjacent servient tenement. Profits may be created by express or implied grant or by statute; profits appurtenant may also arise by *prescription. They are extinguished by express release, by the owner acquiring the servient tenement, by an irrevocable alteration of the servient tenement (e.g. from pasture to industrial estate), by *approvement, or by long *non-user.

prohibited degrees of relationships Family relationships within which marriage is prohibited (and, if celebrated, void) although sexual intercourse within the relationship may not amount to *incest. A man, for example, may not marry his grandmother, aunt, niece, or mother-in-law; a woman may not marry her grandfather, uncle, nephew, or father-in-law.

prohibited weapon A weapon suitable only for use by the armed forces and having no normal function in civilian life. Prohibited weapons include automatic firearms, weapons designed or adapted to discharge a poisonous liquid or gas, and ammunition containing poisonous substances. It is an offence (punishable with up to two years' imprisonment) to produce, sell, buy, or possess any prohibited weapon without the permission of the Defence Council. *See also* firearm; offensive weapon.

prohibition *n.* A remedy in which the High Court orders an inferior court, tribunal, or administrative authority not to carry out an *ultra vires* act (for example, hearing a case that is outside its jurisdiction). It is available in cases in which, had the act been carried out, the remedy would have been *certiorari* and it is governed by broadly similar rules.

prohibition notice A notice under the Health and Safety at Work Act 1974 specifying activities that, in the opinion of an inspector, involve a risk of serious personal injury and prohibiting them until specified safeguards have been adopted. *Compare* improvement notice.

prohibitory injunction *See* injunction.

prolixity *n.* Excessive length or repetitiveness in *pleadings, *affidavits, or other documents. Modern rules of procedure discourage prolixity: prolix doc-

uments may be struck out or the costs of them disallowed.

promise *n.* An undertaking given by one person (the *promisor*) to another (the *promisee*) to do or refrain from doing something. It is legally binding only if contained in a *contract or made by *deed.

promissory estoppel *See* estoppel.

promissory note An unconditional promise in writing, made by one person to another and signed by the maker, engaging to pay a specified sum of money to (or to the order of) a specified person or to the bearer, either on demand or at a future time. Promissory notes are *negotiable instruments and many of the provisions in the Bills of Exchange Act 1882 apply with necessary modifications to promissory notes. Promissory notes are not presented for acceptance and the party primarily liable is the maker of a note. A bank note is a promissory note issued by a bank; the sum of money mentioned on the note is payable to the bearer on demand.

promoter *n.* **1.** A person engaged in the formation or flotation of a company. A promoter stands in a *fiduciary relationship to the company and his duties may include drafting a *prospectus, negotiating preliminary agreements, instructing solicitors, and obtaining directors. Solicitors, bankers, and other professionals involved in the company are not regarded as promoters. **2.** One who introduces a private *Bill.

proof *n.* **1.** The means by which the existence or nonexistence of a fact is established to the satisfaction of the court, including testimony, documentary evidence, presumptions, and judicial notice. Since most facts with which a court is concerned are not capable of being tested empirically, proof in the legal sense is quite different from its use in mathematics or science. The uncorroborated evidence of one credible witness is sufficient proof for most pur-

proof beyond reasonable doubt

poses in the law. *See* standard of proof.
2. (*Informal*) The written statement of a
prospective witness obtained by a solicitor. A witness is said not to have *come
up to proof* if he fails to testify in accordance with his proof.

proof beyond reasonable doubt The
*standard of proof required in criminal
proceedings. If the jury has any reasonable (even if unlikely) doubts about the
guilt of the accused, it may not convict
him. It is often paraphrased by the
judge instructing the jury that they
must be "satisfied so that they are sure"
of the guilt of the accused. It is disputed
whether this standard is ever applicable
in civil proceedings (e.g. when there is
an allegation of fraud): it is generally
held that it is not. *See also* burden of
proof.

proof of age The age of a person may
be proved by *direct evidence, such as
the testimony of someone present at the
person's birth, and in some cases from
his appearance. It is usually proved by
producing a birth certificate, under the
exception to the hearsay rule relating to
statements in *public documents, and
evidence that the person in question is
the one referred to in the birth certificate.

proof of birth Birth is usually proved
by the production of a birth certificate,
which is admissible under the exception
to the hearsay rule relating to statements in *public documents, coupled
with evidence identifying the person in
question with the person referred to in
the birth certificate.

proof of handwriting Handwriting
may be proved by the testimony of the
person whose handwriting it is or by
that of someone who saw him execute
the document in question. It may also
be proved by the opinion of someone
familiar with the handwriting of the alleged writer or by comparison with a
proved example of the writer's hand-

writing. Expert testimony is also admissible.

proof of marriage Legally valid evidence that a *marriage was celebrated.
This will usually be shown by possession of a marriage certificate and proof
of identity, but may also be shown by
other forms of evidence.

proper law of a contract The system
of law that is applied in *private international law to a contract with foreign
elements. Which system governs the
contract will depend on the intention of
the parties to the contract, to be determined in each case by considering the
terms of the contract, and all the surrounding facts. If the parties have expressly agreed which law should govern
the contract, that law will normally be
applied. If, as is usual, they have not expressly agreed, the courts try to infer
their intention from all the circumstances; if it cannot be inferred, they
will apply the system of law with which
the contract has "its closest and most
real connection".

property *n.* Anything that can be
owned. A distinction is made between
real property (land and incorporeal
*hereditaments) and *personal property*
(all other kinds of property) and between *tangible property* (that which has
a physical existence, e.g. chattels and
land) and *intangible property* (*choses
in action and incorporeal hereditffa-
ments). For purposes of the law of
*theft, property includes all real, per-
sonal, and intangible property, although land can only be stolen under
certain specified conditions. For purposes of the law of *criminal damage,
property does not include intangible
property.

property adjustment order An order
made by the court on or after granting
a decree of divorce, nullity, or judicial
separation that affects rights of ownership of property belonging to either
spouse. Such orders include the transfer

of property from one spouse to another, settling property for the benefit of the other spouse or children, varying marriage settlements, or extinguishing rights under such settlements. The courts have exceptionally wide discretion in making property adjustment orders, and each case will depend on its own facts. The general aim of the discretion, and factors to be considered, are identical with those listed in relation to *financial provision orders; two other factors to be considered are the need to provide adequate housing for both spouses, and especially for minor children, and the need to allow each spouse a share in the capital value of the family assets, especially the *matrimonial home. The courts have often said that a wife is entitled to one-third of the joint assets as a "starting point", which may be altered subject to particular circumstances. The courts have power to make the home subject to a deferred trust for sale, e.g. until the children grow up, but recently have tended to favour a *clean break wherever possible. Property adjustment orders are often awarded in addition to financial provision orders.

property in goods A right of *ownership.

property register See land registration.

proponent n. The party who bears the evidential, and in some cases the persuasive, *burden of proof in relation to an issue in litigation.

propositus [Latin] n. **1.** The person immediately concerned. **2.** An ancestor through whom descent is traced. **3.** A testator when making his will.

propounder n. A person in a *probate action who claims that a disputed will is valid.

proprietary estoppel See estoppel.

proprietor n. One who owns land. In the case of registered land, the regis-

tered proprietor is the person entitled to the *legal estate and is recorded as such in the proprietorship register (see land registration). The owners of equitable interests are protected by registration of their *minor interests in the appropriate manner.

proprietorship register See land registration.

prorogation n. See Parliament.

proscribed organization An organization or association declared to be forbidden by the Home Secretary under the Prevention of Terrorism (Temporary Provisions) Act 1976, because it appears to be concerned with *terrorism in the UK connected with Northern Irish affairs (for example, the IRA). It is an offence (punishable on indictment by up to five years' imprisonment and/or a fine) to belong to a proscribed organization, to attempt to obtain financial support or services for it, to make or receive any contribution for it in money or property, or to speak at or assist in arranging a meeting of three or more people intended to support such an organization. It is not, however, an offence merely to express support for a proscribed organization or even to arrange a broadcast expressing support if there are less than three people present in the studio. It is also an offence (punishable summarily by up to six months' imprisonment and/or a fine of up to £400) for someone to wear an item of dress or display an article in a public place if this creates a reasonable suspicion that he is a member or supporter of a proscribed organization, even if he neither intended nor foresaw that such a suspicion would be aroused.

A police officer may arrest without warrant anyone whom he reasonably suspects to be guilty of any of these indictable offences and may detain him initially for up to 48 hours or for a further five days by order of the Home Secretary. He may also stop and search any person whom he reasonably suspects of having any object on him that could provide evidence that he is guilty of one of the specified offences, and hence subject to arrest. There are also offences under the Public Order Act 1936 of: (1) controlling, managing, organizing, or training any quasi-military organizations (e.g. organizations intended to usurp the functions of the police or armed forces or to use physical force to promote a political aim) and (2) wearing a uniform in a public place or at a public meeting indicating membership of a political organization or the promotion of any political object.

prosecution *n.* The pursuit of legal proceedings, particularly criminal proceedings. (The term is also used for the party instituting the proceedings.) Criminal prosecutions on indictment are in the name of the Crown and summary prosecutions are in the name of an individual, usually a police officer, although a private individual may bring a prosecution (most private prosecutions are for assault). The *Attorney General can intervene in a private prosecution and either take it over or abandon it. Many government departments and other authorities have power to prosecute; for example, the Inland Revenue, the Department of Health and Social Security, and local authorities. Some cases (such as certain sexual offences) must be referred to the *Director of Public Prosecutions (DPP) before prosecution. The DPP's office undertakes the prosecution of many serious or sensitive cases (such as those involving corruption). In some cases the Attorney General's consent is required before prosecution; for example, in cases involving official secrets.

prosecutor *n.* The person who institutes criminal proceedings on behalf of the Crown. *See* prosecution.

prospectus *n.* A document inviting the public to invest in shares or debentures of a public company (*see* flotation). It is unlawful to issue a prospectus unless it contains the information specified in the Companies Act 1948, which includes details of the company's financial affairs, the names and addresses of its directors, and the amount payable on application and allotment of shares.

prostitution *n.* The offering of her body by a woman for sexual intercourse or other sexual activities in return for payment. Prostitution itself is not a crime, but various activities related to it are (*see* brothel; living on immoral earnings; loitering; procurement; soliciting). Advertising details of prostitutes may amount to a *conspiracy at common law or an *obscene publication. Certain offences concerned with brothels and living on immoral earnings also apply to male prostitution.

protected child A child whom someone wishes to adopt and over whom a local authority must exercise supervision. Under the 1976 Adoption Act, such supervision will only be required when the child was not placed for adoption by an adoption agency; in agency cases, the agency itself will be responsible for supervision.

protected goods (under the Consumer Credit Act 1974) Goods that are the subject matter of a regulated *hire purchase or *conditional sale agreement of which the debtor is in breach, but under which he has already paid to the creditor one-third or more of the total price of the goods. The creditor may not recover possession of the goods except on an order of the court, which may allow the debtor further time to pay. The restriction does not apply if the debtor has terminated the agreement.

protected occupier An agricultural worker who occupies a *tied cottage and who has statutory protection similar to that of a *protected tenancy. In certain circumstances a local authority can be required to rehouse a protected occupier. *See* agricultural dwelling-house advisory committee.

protected person A head of state (or a member of a corporate head of state), head of government, or minister for foreign affairs, or any member of his family accompanying him; or a representative or official of a state or intergovernmental international organization who is entitled under international law to special protection from personal injury or any member of his family who is also a member of his household. The Internationally Protected Persons Act 1978 incorporates into English law the provisions of the 1974 New York Convention on Crimes against Internationally Protected Persons. The Act gives jurisdiction to English courts to try those charged with committing certain serious acts against protected persons (e.g. rape, assault, causing actual bodily harm, wounding or inflicting grievous bodily harm, kidnapping, and certain attacks on premises), even if the alleged acts were committed outside the UK. It also creates offences of threatening to commit any of the above acts anywhere in the world, and extends jurisdiction to various types of attempts and assistance. It is no defence to any of these offences that the defendant did not know that the victim was a protected person.

protected shorthold tenancy A special kind of *protected tenancy for a fixed term at the end of which the landlord is entitled to recover possession. A protected shorthold tenancy must satisfy the following conditions: (1) the fixed term must be for not less than one or more than five years; (2) it must have been granted after 28 November 1980; (3) the only method of termination by the landlord before the end of the term must be by *re-entry for nonpayment of rent or breach of some other obligation; (4) the landlord must give the tenant notice before the grant of the tenancy that it is a protected shorthold

tenancy; (5) the tenancy must be at a *fair rent; and (6) the tenant must not have been a protected or *statutory tenant of that property immediately before the grant of the shorthold tenancy. The tenant can terminate the tenancy by giving the landlord notice, which must be at least one month for tenancies up to two years or three months for longer tenancies. This kind of tenancy cannot be assigned.

protected state A state that, although nominally sovereign, is under the protection of another state. Usually the protected state allows the protector full control over its external affairs but retains control over its internal affairs. Examples are the Kingdom of Bhutan under the protection of India and the State of Brunei under British protection.

protected tenancy A contractual residential tenancy in which the tenant has the right to a *fair rent and *security of tenure. To qualify, the premises must be let as a separate dwelling that is within certain rateable value limits. There are some exceptions, including lettings to students, holiday lettings, local authority housing, and lettings in which the rent includes payment for board or *attendance. If a landlord wishes to terminate a protected tenancy he must first terminate the contractual tenancy in the usual way (*see* notice to quit). A *statutory tenancy then comes into existence and the landlord can obtain possession only by a court order. To do this he must have suitable grounds, such as nonpayment of rent, provision of suitable alternative accommodation for the tenant, or if the landlord needs the property for himself or one of his family to live in.

There were formerly two kinds of protected tenancy: controlled and regulated. All controlled tenancies have now been converted into *regulated tenancies. (*See* converted tenancy.) *Furnished tenancies* now have the same protection as unfurnished tenancies, though they are more likely to fall within one of the exceptions to protection. *See also* assured tenancy; protected shorthold tenancy; secure tenancy; restricted contract.

protection and indemnity association An association of shipowners formed to meet, out of funds contributed by its members, liabilities that arise from maritime activities and are not covered by insurance.

protective award *See* redundancy.

protective trust (alimentary trust) A trust for a period no longer than the beneficiary's life, the period ending if certain events (for example, the bankruptcy of the beneficiary) take place. At the end of the period the income of the property is applied at the absolute discretion of the trustees for the beneficiary or his family, the beneficiary no longer having any right to receive the income himself.

protector of settlement The first person entitled, under a *strict settlement of land, to a life interest preceding the ,*entailed interest or (if there is no prior life interest) the settlor. Under the Fines and Recoveries Act 1833, a person entitled in *remainder to an entailed interest can only bar the entail completely, so as to create a fee simple in remainder, if the protector's consent is given by deed on or before execution of the disentailing deed. Without the protector's consent only the tenant in tail and his issue are barred; when they die out the land passes to the person next entitled in remainder or in reversion.

protest *n.* **1.** An express indication that an act is not to carry an implication that might otherwise attach to it. For example, when a payment is made *under protest*, the payer does not agree that he is liable for the payment. **2.** A procedure by which a *notary provides formal evidence of the *dishonour of a

bill of exchange. When a bill has been dishonoured by nonacceptance or non-payment it is handed to the notary, who usually presents it again. If it is still dishonoured, the notary attaches a slip showing the answer received and other particulars – a process called *noting*. The protest, in the form of a formal document, may then be drawn up at a later time.

protocol *n.* The original draft of a document, particularly of a diplomatic document showing the agreed terms of a treaty.

provable debt A debt in respect of which a creditor can claim a share of a bankrupt's assets. A provable debt must either be incurred by the bankrupt before a *receiving order is made against him or arise after the order is made as a result of an obligation that existed beforehand. *Compare* nonprovable debt.

proving a will Obtaining *probate of a will or *letters of administration *cum testamento annexo.*

provisional liquidator *See* liquidator.

provisional orders Orders made by government ministers but requiring confirmation by Act of Parliament (a Provisional Order Confirmation Act) before becoming law. They do not, therefore, constitute *delegated legislation. Provisional orders were formerly used extensively, primarily to confer powers on local authorities, but have been largely superseded by *special procedure orders.

proviso *n.* A clause in a statute, deed, or other legal document introducing a qualification or condition to some other provision, frequently the one immediately preceding the proviso itself.

In criminal appellate procedure, *applying the proviso* occurs when the Court of Appeal uses the power conferred by the proviso to s. 2 of the Criminal Appeal Act 1968. This empowers the court to dismiss an appeal if it considers that no miscarriage of justice has occurred, even though it believes that the point raised in the appeal might be decided in favour of the appellant.

provocation *n.* Conduct or words causing someone to lose his self-control. Provocation is not recognized as a defence to a criminal charge in English law, with the single exception of a charge of murder, which may be reduced to manslaughter if provocation is shown (it is not, however, a defence to a charge of attempted murder).

The test for provocation is whether the acts or words involved did in fact make the defendant lose his self-control, and if so, whether they would also have made a reasonable man in the defendant's position do the same. This is a question of fact for the jury to decide in each case: there are no longer any rules of law defining what can or cannot amount to provocation. A reasonable man for these purposes must be a person of the same sex and age as the defendant and sharing any characteristics of the defendant that might affect the seriousness of the provocation. For example, a sexually impotent defendant might be more easily provoked by taunts about his impotence than an ordinary man. The jury would therefore have to consider how a reasonable impotent man would have reacted. Such characteristics as intoxication from alcohol or drugs, however, cannot be attributed to the reasonable man.

proxy *n.* A person (not necessarily a company member) appointed by a company member to attend and vote instead of him at a company meeting. Directors often offer themselves as proxies by sending out proxy forms with the notice of the meeting. When this is done at company expense, forms must be sent to all company members alike. Such forms may specify either the way in which the proxy is to vote or that he is to vote as he thinks fit. Usu-

ally a proxy can vote only upon a poll (*see* voting). In private companies the proxy can speak at the meeting.

psychopathic disorder For the purposes of the Mental Health Act 1959, a form of *mental disorder consisting of a persistent disorder or disability of mind (which may or may not include subnormality of intelligence) that results in abnormally aggressive or seriously irresponsible conduct and requires, or is susceptible to, medical treatment.

Public Accounts Committee A select committee of the House of Commons, established in 1861 to examine government expenditure and report on any irregularity or other matter to which it considers that attention should be drawn. It has 15 members and its chairman is customarily a member of the Opposition.

public Act *See* Act of Parliament.

publication *n.* **1.** (in the law of *defamation) The communication of defamatory words to a person or persons other than the one defamed. In the English law of tort, publication to at least one other person must be proved. Communication between husband and wife does not amount to publication, but communication by the defendant to the spouse of the plaintiff is sufficient. Dictation of a defamatory statement to a secretary or typist is publication. Publication to persons other than the one defamed is not required in Scottish law or in criminal libel. **2.** (in copyright law) The issuing of reproductions of a work or edition to the public. Protection under the Copyright Act 1956 may depend on whether the work has been published. **3.** For the purposes of the Obscene Publications Acts, *see* obscene publications.

public Bill *See* Bill.

public body Any body, corporate or otherwise, that performs its duties and exercises its powers for the public benefit, as opposed to private gain.

public company A type of registered company that can offer its shares to the public (*compare* private company). Its memorandum of association must state that it is a public company, that its name ends with the words "public limited company" (*or* p.l.c.), and that its *authorized capital is at least the authorized minimum (£50,000). It cannot do business until it has allotted shares with a nominal value corresponding with the authorized minimum. It cannot allot shares except upon payment of one-quarter of their nominal value plus any *share premium. Under the Companies Act 1980 an undertaking to do work or perform services is not an acceptable *consideration for shares in a public company, and other non-cash considerations are subject to independent valuation and must be transferred to the company within five years of *allotment. *See also* flotation; Stock Exchange.

public corporation A corporation established to perform a public function, frequently commercial but not necessarily so (it may be social, advisory, or of any other character). Thus the British Gas Council and other bodies established to manage nationalized industries are public corporations, as are such bodies as the Manpower Services Commission and the Nature Conservancy Council. A public corporation is normally a *statutory corporation*, i.e. established by Act of Parliament; exceptions include the British Broadcasting Corporation, which was established by royal charter.

public decency The normal standards of decency of the general public. There is a common-law offence of outraging public decency, which might include *indecent exposure, keeping a *disorderly house, or mounting an indecent exhibition. There is also an offence of *conspiracy to outrage public decency.

public document A document concerned with a public matter, made under a public duty to inquire into all the circumstances recorded and meant for public inspection. Statements in public documents are admissible as an exception to the rule against *hearsay.

public duties Certain public officers, including magistrates, councillors, school and college governors, and members of health and water authorities, are entitled under the Employment Protection (Consolidation) Act 1978 to time off work to fulfil their official duties. Part-time employees (i.e. those whose normal working week is between 8 and 16 hours) have this right only after five years' *continuous employment. An employee entitled to time off work for public duties does not have a statutory right to be paid for his periods of absence.

public examination In bankruptcy proceedings, an investigation into the conduct, dealings, and property of a debtor. It takes place in a court after the debtor has delivered, or failed to deliver, his *statement of affairs. The debtor is compelled to attend and answer questions on oath. A court may make an order dispensing with a public examination if the debtor is mentally or physically unfit to attend or if it considers the examination unnecessary.

public general Act *See* Act of Parliament.

public good A special defence to some charges under the Obscene Publications Act. *See* obscene publications.

public house Under the Local Government Act 1966, any premises licensed for the sale of intoxicating liquor for consumption on the premises, this (apart from any ancillary or incidental trade or business) being the only trade carried on there.

public law The part of the law that deals with the constitution and functions of the organs of central and local government, the relationship between individuals and the state, and relationships between individuals that are of direct concern to the state. It includes constitutional law, administrative law, tax law, and criminal law. *Compare* private law.

public limited company (p.l.c.) *See* limited company; public company.

public mischief Conduct damaging the interests of the community; for example, making bogus telephone calls to the police. Until 1975 this was regarded as a crime but it is now no longer so regarded, nor is conspiracy to effect a public mischief. There is, however, now a special statutory offence of *wasting police time (but not, for example, the time of ambulancemen or firemen).

public morals The basic moral structure of society. Judges have occasionally said that they retain a general overriding discretion to punish as crimes behaviour that is destructive of public morals but it is not at all clear to what extent they should do so, although some crimes, such as incest, are presumably based on moral factors. The abolition of the crimes of homosexual conduct and suicide was based on the assumption that matters of morals that do not directly affect other people should not be the subject of criminal legislation. *See also* corruption of public morals.

public nuisance *See* nuisance.

public or general rights *See* declaration concerning public or general rights.

public place A place to which the public has access. The main offences relating to public places are: (1) being found drunk or being drunk and disorderly in a public place; (2) driving in a public place with an excessive blood-alcohol level (*see* drunken driving); (3) carrying a *firearm or an *offensive weapon in a public place; (4) *loitering or *soliciting in a public place; (5) using threatening, abusive, or insulting words or behaviour in a public place with the intention of provoking a *breach of the peace or in a manner likely to arouse racial hatred; and (5) displaying support for a *proscribed organization in a public place.

public policy The interests of the community. If a contract is (on common-law principles) contrary to public policy, this will normally make it an *illegal contract. In a few cases, however, such a contract is void but not illegal, and is treated slightly more leniently (for example, by *severance). Contracts that are illegal because they contravene public policy include any contract to commit a crime or a tort or to defraud the revenue, any contract that prejudices national safety or the administration of justice, and any *immoral contract. Contracts that are merely void include contracts in *restraint of trade and in *restraint of marriage and *marriage brokerage contracts.

public prosecutor *See* Director of Public Prosecutions.

public trust A trust for the benefit of the public, which may or may not be a *charitable trust.

Public Trustee A public officer, appointed under the Public Trustee Act 1906, who is a *corporation sole and who may act as a *custodian trustee, a *judicial trustee, or an ordinary trustee. He cannot accept certain trusts, e.g. those exclusively for charitable or religious purposes, those governed by foreign law, or those involving the management of a business. He has a duty to administer small estates unless there is some good reason for his refusal.

puisne [from Old French *puisne*, later born] *adj.* Inferior; of lesser rank.

puisne judge Any ordinary judge of the High Court. Puisne judges are referred to as (for example) "Mr Justice Smith", even though they are knighted upon appointment. They must be barristers of at least ten years' standing.

puisne mortgage A legal mortgage of unregistered land in which the mortgagee does not keep the title deeds of the land as security. Usually a first mortgagee retains the deeds; thus subsequent mortgages will be puisne and should be protected by registration (*see* registration of encumbrances).

punishment *n.* A penalty imposed on a defendant duly convicted of a crime by an authorized court. The punishment is declared in the *sentence of the court. The two basic principles governing punishment are *nullum crimen sine lege* and *nulla poena sine lege*. The powers of the court to punish also depend on whether the crime is an *indictable offence or a *summary offence.

There are a number of different theories of punishment, and different aims and purposes underly the legal provisions of the English criminal system. The concept of *retribution* implies that a criminal merits his just punishment because he has done something morally or socially evil. Another aspect of retribution implies that the punishment should be related to the harm done by the crime, rather than to the moral guilt of the criminal. The utilitarian school, by contrast, believes that all punishment is evil, insofar as it adversely affects human happiness. It can only be justified, therefore, if it prevents greater unhappiness or harm. This is the basis of the theory of *deterrence*, in which the punishment is aimed at deterring the criminal from repeating his offences or deterring others from committing similar acts. Custodial sentences may be required to protect the public from further harm, particularly when the crimes involve violence. Sometimes these sentences are also justified as an expression of public condemnation and outrage. Recent thinking replaces the concept of retribution by the belief that sentences should be designed to assist in the rehabilitation of the criminal. To some extent these concepts are accepted in relation to young offenders, and are also reflected in the system of *remission and *parole (*see also* spent conviction). Legislators and judges have to bear in mind these concepts in laying down and applying sentences. They must also be aware of society's need for a humane system of criminal justice.

Clearly the extent to which crimes should be punished without proof of *intention or *recklessness (e.g. crimes of *negligence and *strict liability) depends on which theory of punishment one adopts. Parliament has created a large number of so-called *regulatory offences* (e.g. road traffic offences and offences relating to production of food), which usually do not involve moral guilt and are often punished despite the absence of *mens rea*. It is also a matter of considerable controversy whether or not the criminal law should punish morally objectionable conduct that does not obviously harm anyone (e.g. obscene publications and various sex-related offences). The European Convention on Human Rights forbids the use of "inhuman or degrading" punishment; it has been held that the practice of birching comes under this category.

punitive damages *See* exemplary damages.

pur autre vie *See* estate *pur autre vie*.

purchaser *n.* **1.** (in land law) Any person who acquires land otherwise than by mere operation of law. Thus a purchaser may be a mortgagee or one to whom land is given or bequeathed as well as one who buys land for money or other consideration. A tenant in tail (whose interest devolves upon him automatically on his ancestor's death) is not a purchaser, nor is one who acquires title by *adverse possession. **2.** A *buyer.

purchaser for value without notice One who acquires land either in return for money or other consideration having monetary value or under a marriage settlement and who does not know and has no reason to know of an encumbrance that adversely affects the land. Such a purchaser is not bound by equitable encumbrances, such as restrictive covenants or the rights of beneficiaries under a trust. However, relevant equitable encumbrances are generally registrable (*see* registration of encumbrances) and a purchaser is deemed to know of any interest that is registered. Legal encumbrances (such as legal easements) always bind a purchaser of the land whether or not he knows of their existence.

purpose trust A trust that is not for the benefit of a human beneficiary and is not a *charitable trust. Such trusts are normally invalid as there is no one to enforce them; exceptions that are valid include trusts for the benefit of individual animals, for the maintenance of individual graves, and for the saying of masses.

putative father A man alleged to be the father of an illegitimate child. If the court accepts the mother's allegations (in affiliation proceedings), the man is declared the putative father and may be ordered to make periodical payments or a lump sum for the maintenance and education of the child (*see* affiliation order). The putative father's name may also be entered on the child's birth certificate.

Q

QBD *See* Queen's Bench Division.

QC *See* Queen's Counsel.

qualified acceptance An *acceptance of a bill of exchange that varies the ef-

fect of the bill as drawn; for example, either by making payment by the acceptor dependent on fulfilling a condition or by accepting to pay part only of the amount for which the bill is drawn (a *partial acceptance*). A qualified acceptance is distinguished from a *general acceptance*, which assents without qualification to the order of the drawer. The holder of a bill may refuse to take a qualified acceptance; if he does not obtain an unqualified acceptance he may treat the bill as dishonoured by nonacceptance. If a qualified acceptance is taken (subject to an exception as to partial acceptances) and the drawer or an endorser has not authorized the holder to take a qualified acceptance or does not subsequently assent to it, such drawer or endorser is discharged from his liability on the bill.

qualified privilege The defence that a statement cannot be made the subject of an action for *defamation because it was made on a privileged occasion and was not made maliciously, for an improper motive. Qualified privilege covers statements made fairly in situations in which there is a legal or moral obligation to give the information and the person to whom it is given has a corresponding duty or interest to receive it and when someone is acting in defence of his own property or reputation. Qualified privilege also covers fair and accurate reports of public meetings and various other public proceedings. The privilege attaching to professional communications between solicitor and client is probably qualified, rather than absolute. *Compare* absolute privilege.

qualified title Ownership of a legal estate in registered land subject to some exception or qualification specified in the register. If, for example, X applies to register his title to land and there is some possibility that part of it may already have been sold to another person, X's title may be registered subject to the rights of anyone having a better title to that part. The state's guarantee of good title does not protect the proprietor in respect of the specified qualification. *Compare* absolute title.

qualifying distribution A distribution of profits by a company on which *advance corporation tax has to be paid (*see also* imputation system). Redeemable securities issued as a bonus are not treated as qualifying distribution.

quango [*q*uasi-*a*utonomous *n*on-governmental *o*rganization] *n.* A body appointed wholly or partly by the government (but not constituting a department of government) to perform some public function, normally administrative or advisory and frequently involving the distribution of public moneys. Examples are the University Grants Committee and the Sports Council.

quantum meruit See quasi-contract.

quantum valebat [Latin: as much as it was worth] An action to claim the value of goods that were sold without any price having been fixed, when there was an implied promise to pay as much as they were worth.

quarantine *n.* A period of isolation of people or animals that have been in contact with a communicable disease. The period was originally 40 days (hence the name, which is derived from the Italian *quarantina*), but is now approximately the incubation period of the suspected disease. Quarantine is imposed, for example, by public health regulations relating to ships and aircraft or by orders made under the Rabies Act 1974.

quarter days 25 March (*Lady Day*), 24 June (*Midsummer Day*), 29 September (*Michaelmas Day*), and 25 December (*Christmas Day*). Rents are sometimes made payable on these days.

quarter sessions Originally, quarterly meetings of the *justices of the peace for a county. City and borough quarter

sessions were presided over by the recorder sitting alone. In modern times quarter sessions became a court for the trial of offences triable on indictment, other than those that had to be tried at *assizes. Quarter sessions were abolished by the Courts Act 1971 and their jurisdiction is now exercised by the *Crown Court.

quasi-contract *n.* A field of law covering cases in which one person has been unduly enriched at the expense of another and is under an obligation *quasi ex contractu* (as if from a contract) to make restitution to him. In many cases of quasi-contract, the defendant has received the benefit from the plaintiff himself. The plaintiff may have paid money to him under a mistake of fact, or under a void contract, or may have supplied services under the mistaken belief that he was contractually bound to do so. In that case, he is entitled to be paid a reasonable sum and is said to sue on a *quantum meruit* (as much as he deserved). Alternatively, the plaintiff may have been required to pay to a third party money for which the defendant was primarily liable. The defendant's receipt of the benefit need not necessarily, however, have been from the plaintiff. It is enough that it was at the latter's expense, and he may therefore be liable in quasi-contract for money paid to him by a third party on account of the plaintiff.

quasi-easement *n.* A right in the nature of an *easement enjoyed over a plot of land for the benefit of another plot owned by the same person. If the second plot (the quasi-dominant tenement) is sold, the purchaser will acquire a full easement under the Law of Property Act 1925 provided the two parcels were occupied by different persons immediately before the sale. For example A, the owner of Blackacre and Whiteacre, lets Whiteacre to B, who uses a track across Blackacre. If A then sells the freehold estate in Whiteacre to B, B acquires an easement of way over the track. If the plots are not separately occupied an easement may still arise in favour of the purchaser of the quasi-dominant tenement under the doctrine of *implied grant* if the easement claimed is permanent in nature and identifiable from inspection of the land.

quasi-entail *n.* An equitable interest in land that is in the nature of an *entailed interest but subsists only during the life of a specified person. For example, if a life tenant A settles his life interest on B and the heirs of his body with remainder to C, B acquires a quasi-entail. The interests of B, his issue, and C all cease on A's death.

quasi-judicial *adj.* Describing a function that resembles the judicial function in that it involves deciding a dispute and ascertaining the facts and any relevant law, but differs in that it depends ultimately on the exercise of an executive discretion rather than the application of law.

queen *n.* **1.** The sovereign if female (*see* Crown). **2.** The wife of the sovereign (*queen consort*). **3.** The widow of a sovereign (*queen dowager*).

Queen *n.* By the Royal Titles Act 1953, "Elizabeth II by the Grace of God of the United Kingdom of Great Britain and Northern Ireland and of Her other Realms and Territories Queen, Head of the Commonwealth, Defender of the Faith". The Act empowers Her Majesty to adopt by proclamation such other style and titles as she may think fit. *See also* Crown.

Queen's Bench Division (QBD) The division of the *High Court whose principal business is the trial of civil actions based upon contract or tort. It also has important appellate functions in relation to appeals from *magistrates' courts and certain tribunals and exercises supervisory jurisdiction over all inferior courts. The *Admiralty Court

and *Commercial Court are part of the QBD.

Queen's Bench Masters *See* Masters of the Supreme Court.

Queen's Counsel (QC) A senior *barrister who has received a patent as "one of Her Majesty's counsel learned in the law". QCs are appointed on the recommendation of the Lord Chancellor and a list of new appointees is published annually on Maundy Thursday. In court they sit within the bar and wear silk gowns (hence they are also known informally as *silks*). If the monarch is a king these barristers are known as *King's Counsel* (*KC*).

Queen's evidence Evidence given on behalf of the prosecution by an accused person who has confessed his own guilt and who then acts as a witness against his accomplices. Such evidence is generally considered less reliable than other evidence because the witness is likely to minimize his own role and exaggerate that of his accomplices. If it is not corroborated, the judge must warn the jury of the danger of convicting on the basis of this evidence alone. *See also* corroboration.

Queen's Proctor A solicitor who, under the direction of the Attorney General, gives legal advice to the courts on difficult or disputed legal problems involving divorce and who intervenes, generally to prevent a divorce from being made absolute, in cases in which not all the material facts were before the court when the *decree nisi was granted. The office of Queen's Proctor is held by the *Treasury Solicitor.

Queen's Regulations *See* service law.

Queen's Speech (Speech from the Throne) A speech prepared by the government and read by the Queen to Parliament (assembled in the House of Lords) at the beginning of a parliamentary session. It outlines the government's principal legislative and policy proposals for the session.

que estate [Norman French: whose estate] A claim to have acquired by *prescription an easement or profit *à prendre* by virtue of the continuous use of the right both by the claimant and by those whose estate he has, i.e. those who owned the dominant tenement before him.

questioning of suspects *See* interrogation.

quia timet [Latin: because he fears] A type of *injunction that is sought in order to restrain an anticipated wrong. The court will only grant such a remedy if the applicant can show that there is imminent danger of a substantial kind or that the injury, if it occurs, will be irreparable.

quicquid plantatur solo, solo cedit *See* fixture.

quiet enjoyment One of the obligations of a landlord, which is implied in every *lease unless specifically excluded. It entitles the tenant to possess and enjoy the land he leases without interference from the landlord or anyone claiming rights through the landlord.

quiet possession Freedom from disturbance in the enjoyment of property. In contracts for the sale of goods, unless the seller makes it clear that he is contracting to transfer only the title that he or a third person has, there is an implied *warranty that the buyer will enjoy quiet possession of the goods. This warranty is broken not only if the seller and those claiming through him interfere with the buyer's quiet possession but also if the interference is by a third party lawfully claiming by virtue of a better title to the goods. The corresponding covenant upon the sale of land extends only to interferences by the seller and those claiming through him.

quit rent *See* rentcharge.

quittance *n.* A document that acknowledges payment of a debt.

quorum *n.* **1.** The minimum number of people who must be present at a meeting in order for business to be transacted. The required number is usually laid down in the *articles of association, constitution, or rules of the company or other body concerned. **2.** Formerly, an indication in a Commission of the Peace of the particular justices (called *justices of the quorum*) required, at least one of whom had to be present in order for business to be done.

quotation *n.* A listing of a share price on the *Stock Exchange, which indicates that the share can be dealt in on the Exchange. A quotation can be cancelled or suspended if the company does not comply with the Rules of the Stock Exchange or if it becomes impossible to rely on market forces to arrive at a price for the securities (e.g. because of inaccurate accounts or manipulation of the market).

R

R. *n.* *Rex* or *Regina* [Latin: King or Queen] Criminal prosecutions on indictment are brought in the name of the Crown, since a crime is viewed as a wrong against the public at large, or the state, represented by the monarch. Hence the formula *R.* v *Defendant* (the Crown versus the defendant).

Race Relations Board A body constituted to enforce the Race Relations Acts 1965 and 1968. These Acts have been replaced by the Race Relations Act 1976 and the Board by the *Commission for Racial Equality.

racial discrimination Discrimination on the grounds of colour, race, nationality, or ethnic origins. It is dealt with by the Race Relations Acts of 1965,

1968, and 1976. The 1965 Act created an offence of *incitement to racial hatred and made racial discrimination illegal in public places. The 1968 Act prohibits discrimination in respect of goods, services, facilities, employment, accommodation, and advertisements. The 1976 Act prohibits indirect racial discrimination, as well as discrimination in clubs with more than 25 members. It also prohibits the types of discrimination dealt with by the 1975 Sex Discrimination Act (*see* sex discrimination). The *Commission for Racial Equality has the power to conduct formal investigations into complaints. Individual complaints in the field of employment are dealt with by *industrial tribunals; other complaints are dealt with in specified county courts.

rack rent The yearly amount of rent that a tenant could reasonably expect to pay on the open market.

rape *n.* Sexual intercourse with a woman without her consent, as a result of physical force or threats, or because she was unconscious or asleep, or because consent was obtained through fraud. It is also rape if the woman is mentally incapable of understanding what she is consenting to. The defendant must know that the woman does not consent or be reckless as to whether or not she consents. In 1982 the Court of Appeal held that indifference by the defendant to the question of her consent would constitute recklessness. If, however, he honestly believed that the woman was consenting he will be entitled to be acquitted, even if his belief was unreasonable. The maximum penalty for rape is life imprisonment (and for attempted rape, seven years) but this is rarely imposed. Public outcry against the leniency of recent sentences resulted in a directive (1982) that all rape cases should be tried by judges who are empowered to try murder cases.

A husband cannot be guilty of raping his wife unless she has obtained a decree of judicial separation or injunction against molestation, but he can be guilty of inciting or aiding and abetting others to rape her. A boy under the age of 14 is not guilty of rape even if he had intercourse with the woman, since he is presumed to be incapable of intercourse. A "rape" by a husband or a boy, however, and an unsuccessful rape, can be treated as an *indecent assault or an assault occasioning bodily harm or causing grievous bodily harm, depending on the circumstances.

rape offence Any one of the offences of rape, attempted rape, aiding, abetting, counselling, or procuring rape or attempted rape, and incitement to rape. In cases where the defendant to a rape offence pleads not guilty, the Sexual Offences (Amendment) Act 1976 limits the right to ask questions about the alleged victim's sexual experiences. It also prohibits (subject to special leave of the court) the reporting of details about the case that might enable members of the public to identify either the woman or the defendant. If such details are published, the publishers may be fined up to £500.

rate rebate scheme A scheme, administered by local authorities, for subsidizing the rates of needy residential occupiers.

rates *pl. n.* Local taxes charged on property by local authorities to pay for the services they provide. (Some property is exempt from payment of rates, including Crown property, places of religious worship, and agricultural land and buildings.) All rateable land and buildings in the local authority's area are given a rateable value assessed by the Inland Revenue (*see* annual value of land). The occupier can appeal to a local valuation court against the valuation of his property. Each year, the local authority fixes its rate, as an amount per pound of rateable value. For example, if the rate is 75p in the pound, the rates payable for the year on a property with a rateable value of £100 will be £75. The person who occupies the property is liable for the rates whether he is an owner-occupier, a tenant, or is using it for business purposes. A local authority can obtain a distress warrant from a magistrates' court against anyone who fails to pay his rates. This entitles the local authority to seize goods on the ratepayer's property and sell them to pay the rates.

ratification *n.* **1.** Confirmation of an act. If, for example, X contracts with Y as agent for Z, but has in fact no authority to do so, Z may nevertheless adopt the contract by subsequent ratification. **2.** (in international law) The approval of a *treaty, usually by the head of state (or by the head of state and legislature or part of the legislature). This takes place when documents of ratification are either exchanged or deposited with a named depositary. Normally a treaty states expressly whether it will bind a party as soon as it is signed by that party's representative or whether it requires ratification. The Vienna Convention on Treaties (1969) provides that when a treaty does not specify whether or not ratification is required, reference will be made to the party's intention. Performance of a treaty may amount to implicit ratification. **3.** (in company law) A resolution of a general meeting sanctioning some irregularity in the running of a company. Some irregularities cannot be sanctioned, such as acts that are *ultra vires* or a *fraud on the minority.

ratio decidendi [Latin: the reason for deciding] The principle or principles of law on which the court reaches its decision. The *ratio* of the case has to be deduced from its facts, the reasons the court gave for reaching its decision, and the decision itself. Only the *ratio* of a case is binding on inferior courts, by reason of the doctrine of *precedent.

re *prep. See in re.*

real *adj.* **1.** Relating to land. *See also* real estate; real property. **2.** Relating to a thing, rather than to a person. *See also* real evidence.

real estate Under the Administration of Estates Act 1925, all interests in land held by the deceased at his death but excluding interests in money arising under a trust for sale of or charged on land.

real evidence Evidence in the form of material objects (e.g. weapons). When an object is admitted in evidence, it is usually marked as an *exhibit. Documents are not usually classified as real evidence, but may be treated as such if the physical characteristics of the document (rather than its content) are of significance. Some authorities include evidence of identification and the demeanour of witnesses within the classification of real evidence, but this usage has not gained wide acceptance.

realized development value The value of the net proceeds obtained on disposal of land less the base value of that land. There are different ways of calculating the base value; one way is by taking 115% of the cost of acquisition of land. The calculation that produces the highest figure is used in computing the realized development value. *Development land tax is calculated on the basis of realized development value.

real property (realty) Land and incorporeal *hereditaments. *See* property.

real security 1. A mortgage. **2.** A *rentcharge secured on freehold land.

realty *n. See* real property.

reasonable contemplation *See* remoteness of damage.

reasonable doubt *See* proof beyond reasonable doubt.

reasonable financial provision The financial provision that the *dependants of a deceased person can reasonably expect to receive from his estate. If the deceased's will does not make such provision, or he dies intestate and the intestacy laws do not make such provision, the dependants may apply to the court to make provision for them. A spouse is entitled to reasonable financial provision even if he or she already has enough resources for maintenance; in all other cases, reasonable financial provision comprises what is required for maintenance.

reasonable force At common law one may use reasonable force in *self-defence and, in extreme circumstances, may be justified in killing an attacker. Reasonable force may be used in defending one's property, and if someone intrudes on one's property at night, one might be justified in treating this as a threat not merely to property, but to personal safety. An occupier of premises (even if he is not the owner) and possibly even a licensee (such as a lodger) may use reasonable force against a trespasser. The Criminal Law Act 1967 permits the use of reasonable force in order to prevent crime, to lawfully arrest a criminal or suspected criminal (or to help in arresting him), or to capture someone who has escaped from lawful detention. The Act extends to both police and private citizens. It is not altogether certain whether the statutory right includes the right to kill.

It is a statutory offence to set spring guns or mantraps, except in a private house between sunset and sunrise. One may use a dog in self-defence if this use is reasonable (*see* guard dog).

If a person mistakenly thinks that he is entitled to use reasonable force when he is not, he will nonetheless be treated as if he was entitled to use such force, provided that the mistake he made was a reasonable one. It seems, however, that this does not apply if he made a mistake of law, rather than fact.

See also forcible entry.

reasonable man The ordinary man, sometimes referred to as the "man on the Clapham omnibus". The standard of care in actions for *negligence is based on what a reasonable man might be expected to do considering the circumstances and the foreseeable consequences. The standard is not entirely uniform: a lower standard is expected of a child, but a higher standard is expected of someone, such as a doctor, who purports to possess a special skill.

rebuttable presumption *See* presumption.

rebutter *n.* A pleading served by a defendant in reply to the plaintiff's *surrejoinder. Such a pleading is very rare in modern practice and can only be served with *leave of the court.

recall of witness The further examination of a witness after his evidence has been completed. The judge may permit the recall of a witness even after the close of a party's case to allow *evidence in rebuttal.

recaption *n.* The retaking of goods that have been wrongfully taken or are being wrongfully withheld. It is a form of *self-help.

receiver *n.* **1.** A person appointed by the court to preserve and protect property that is at risk, to enable another person to obtain the benefit of rights over the property or to obtain payment of a debt if the common-law remedy is inadequate. *See also* equitable execution. **2.** A person appointed under the terms of a *debenture or by the court to realize assets charged and apply the proceeds for the benefit of those entitled. Notice of appointment must be given to the Companies Registry and must appear upon business documents. The receiver may have power to manage the company. *Compare* official receiver.

receiving *n.* Acquiring exclusive control of stolen property or joint possession of it with the thief or another receiver. Thus if someone merely examines stolen goods in the presence of the thief, he is not guilty of receiving. Before 1968 this was an offence in itself, but it is now one form of the wider offence of *handling.

receiving order A court order made during the course of *bankruptcy proceedings that places the debtor's property under the control of the *official receiver or of a *trustee in bankruptcy. Once a receiving order has been made against a debtor, his creditors cannot take legal proceedings to recover their debts. They can, however, claim *provable debts in the course of bankruptcy proceedings.

recitals *pl. n. See* deed.

reckless cycling Riding a bicycle, tricycle, or any other unmotorized cycle recklessly on a road (which includes any way over which the public have a right of way on foot or on horseback). The offence is punishable summarily by fine and, on subsequent convictions, by a fine or up to three months' imprisonment. *See also* recklessness.

reckless driving The offence of driving a motor vehicle on a road in such a way as to create a real risk of causing physical injury to other road users or fairly substantial damage to property (*see* recklessness). It is punishable summarily with up to six months' imprisonment and/or a fine of up to £1000 and on indictment with up to two years' imprisonment and/or a fine. Reckless driving requires a *notice of intended prosecution. It is normally subject to *endorsement and under the *totting-up system carries 10 points; it is also subject to discretionary *disqualification. *See also* causing death by reckless driving.

recklessness *n.* A form of *mens rea that amounts to less than *intention but more than *negligence. Many common-law offences can be committed either intentionally or recklessly, and it is now common for statutes to create offences of recklessness. Recklessness has normally been held to have a subjective meaning of being aware of the risk of a particular consequence arising from one's actions but deciding nonetheless to continue with one's actions and take the risk. However, the House of Lords has recently held that, in the context of *reckless driving and *criminal damage, recklessness also has an objective meaning of giving no thought or being indifferent to an obvious risk. This definition makes the concept of recklessness far stricter and brings it very close to the traditional definition of negligence. In most cases the subjective definition applies to common-law offences and the objective definition to statutory offences. There are, however, recent dicta in the Court of Appeal in which the objective definition of recklessness is applied to some common-law offences (e.g. rape).

recognition *n.* (in international law) **1.** The process by which one state declares that another political entity fulfils the conditions of statehood (*see* state) and that it is willing to deal with it as a member of the international community. Recognition usually takes place when a new state comes into being. Some authorities believe that recognition is constitutive, i.e. it is one of the conditions that create a state in international law. Most, however, regard it as being merely declaratory, i.e. an acceptance of a fact that already exists. **2.** Acceptance of a government as the legal representative of the state. This may be *de facto* or *de jure*. The distinction is a fluid one, often involving a political element, since international law allows states discretion as to whether or not to accord recognition and of which kind. The according of recognition of either kind is usually an acknowledgment that the government recognized has effective control, but the decision to give merely *de facto* recognition may reflect a wish not to show approval of the nature of the government concerned (and at the same time to be able to continue to give *de jure* recognition to the ousted government). The significance of the distinction (which is of little legal consequence) therefore depends on the intention of the recognizing government. Recognition may be express or implied (for example, by entering into diplomatic relations with a new government).

For purposes of English municipal law, the question of whether or not a state is recognized is sometimes relevant. Thus: (1) only a recognized state is entitled to *sovereign immunity from jurisdiction; (2) an unrecognized state cannot sue in English courts; and (3) when a foreign law is to be applied under the principles of *private international law, this can only be the law of a recognized state or subsidiary body set up by it. A Foreign Office certificate stating that an entity is or is not recognized by the British government is usually taken as conclusive evidence in the courts. Since 1980 Britain has abandoned the practice of recognizing governments – only states are now the subject of express recognition.

recognition issue A trade dispute as to whether a particular trade union should be recognized by an employer as having the right to negotiate terms and conditions of employment on behalf of its members among the employer's workforce.

recognizance *n.* An undertaking by an offender (or by sureties on his behalf) to forfeit a sum of money under certain conditions. Recognizances may be entered into to answer to judgment, i.e. to appear before the court for pronouncement of judgment on a specified date. This procedure may be appropriate if the accused wishes to appeal against conviction. Alternatively, recognizances may be used in addition to or in place of any other sentence or judgment, the offender being obligated to keep the peace and be of good behaviour. Magistrates have wide powers of binding over upon recognizances under the Justices of the Peace Act 1361 and the Magistrates' Courts Act 1952; they may punish failure to comply with the order with six months' imprisonment. *See* keeping the peace.

reconciliation *n.* The coming together of estranged spouses. It is the general policy of the law to encourage reconciliation, and there are special organizations to help with this. Solicitors in divorce cases must certify whether or not they have discussed the possibility of reconciliation with their clients, and proceedings may be adjourned if the court feels there is a chance of reconciliation. If spouses have lived together for more than six months after separation in cases of divorce applications based on adultery, unreasonable behaviour, desertion, or separation, there is a presumption of law that they have become reconciled and a divorce is refused.

reconstruction of a company The transfer or sale of the property of a registered company in voluntary liquidation to another company in exchange for shares in that company to be distributed among members of the company in liquidation. The liquidator effects the reconstruction, and he can only be authorized to do so by *special resolution. A member who does not agree to the arrangement can require the liquidator to buy his shares.

reconversion *n.* The imaginary process by which a fictional *conversion is considered not to have taken place: the property is reconverted in law to the state that, in fact, it has always held.

record *n.* The documents constituting an authentic account of the proceedings before a court, including the originating *process, the *pleadings, and the *judgment or order, but usually not the evidence tendered. The record of an inferior court is the only part of the proceedings that can be considered by the High Court when deciding whether to grant an order of *certiorari.

recorder *n.* **1.** A barrister or solicitor appointed as a part-time judge. Recorders agree to make themselves available regularly (unlike deputy judges, who are appointed *ad hoc*) and for at least four weeks a year. Recorders usually sit in the Crown Court but may sit in the county courts or the High Court. **2.** Formerly, a member of the Bar appointed to preside at City or borough *quarter sessions.

recovery *n.* Regaining possession of land from an unlawful occupier by proceedings in the High Court or a county court. *See* recovery of premises.

recovery of costs *See* bill of costs.

recovery of premises The right to regain possession of property from which one has been unlawfully dispossessed (*see* forcible entry) or the right of a court officer to enforce a judgment for this. It is a summary offence, punishable by up to six months' imprisonment and/or a fine of up to £1000, to resist or intentionally obstruct a court officer in the process of enforcing such a judgment, whether or not one knows that he is a court officer. There is, however, a specific defence if one can show that one believed that he was not a court officer. This offence covers most action taken by squatters to resist eviction, such as physical assaults, boarding up doors, or merely refusing to leave.

recreational charity A charity that provides facilities for leisure-time occupation in the interests of social welfare. After doubts expressed in the courts, Parliament confirmed in 1958 that these trusts were valid, as long as the facilities were provided with the aim of improving the conditions of life for those for whom they were primarily intended and were available to the public.

rectification *n.* The correction of a document if it does not correctly express the common intention of the parties to it. Conveyances, leases, contracts, and certain registers of companies may be rectified on application to the court; the court exercises the jurisdiction to rectify with very great caution and only on the most cogent evidence. Parties to a document may, by agreement, rectify it without the court's consent, provided that the rights of third parties are not affected.

reddendum *n.* The clause in a *lease that specifies the amount of the rent and when it should be paid.

redeemable share *See* share.

redeem up, foreclose down A maxim applied in the context of *priority of mortgages. When there are successive mortgages of the same property, a mortgagee who is second or below in the order of priority may buy out (redeem) an earlier mortgagee. Any mortgagee may be redeemed by a mortgagee with a lower priority. If the matter is complicated and a court action is necessary, any person who might suffer in such an action must be made a party to it, i.e. the mortgagor and any mortgagees of lower priority to the mortgage being redeemed. Any person seeking to redeem by action must not only redeem any mortgages standing between him and the prior mortgage; he must also foreclose all subsequent mortgagees and the mortgagor. The principle does not apply to redemptions out of court.

redemption *n.* The return or repossession of property offered as security upon payment of a mortgage debt or a charge. The property may alternatively be conveyed by the mortgagee to a third party nominated by the mortgagor. *See* equity of redemption.

redress *n.* *See* remedy.

reduction of capital The reduction by a limited company of its share *capital.

Under the Companies Act 1948 there are two principal methods by which this may be achieved. When the company has capital in excess of its needs it can extinguish or reduce the liability of its members on any uncalled capital or it can repay to them the nominal value of their shares. When the company has suffered losses it can cancel paid-up shares because they are unrepresented by available assets. The reduction, which requires a *special resolution, must be authorized by the articles of association and confirmed by the court. If a variation of *class rights is involved, the consent of the shareholders is usually necessary. *See also* alteration of share capital.

redundancy *n.* **1.** (in employment law) The position of an employee whose services are no longer needed by his employer. Under the Employment Protection (Consolidation) Act 1978, dismissal for redundancy occurs when the reason is wholly or mainly that the employer has ceased or intends to cease carrying on the business in which the employee was employed, that he is transferring the business in which the employee works to another location, or that he needs fewer employees to carry out the work in the place in which the employee is employed. An employee dismissed in such circumstances is entitled to a statutory *redundancy payment if he has been continuously employed in the business (*see* continuous employment) for 104 weeks prior to the *effective date of termination of his employment, ignoring any period during which the employee was under the age of 18, and provided he is not over the age of 65. He may also be disqualified from receiving payment if the employer has offered him suitable alternative employment, starting within four weeks after his old employment ends, and the employee unreasonably refuses it. He may however try out alternative employment for up to four weeks without forfeiting his redundancy payment, if he decides not to continue thereafter.

An employee who is laid off (i.e. not provided with work) or kept on short-time working, otherwise than as a result of industrial action, for four or more weeks continuously, or for six or more weeks (not more than three consecutively) in any thirteen-week period, may claim a redundancy payment in certain circumstances. He must give his employer at least the minimum required period of *notice terminating his employment, stating his intention to claim a redundancy payment. This notice must be given within four weeks after the end of the relevant period of lay-off or short-time working. However, the employer is not liable to give him a redundancy payment if he honours a written undertaking, given within seven days after receiving the employee's notice, to restore full-time working within four weeks after the employee's notice, for at least 13 weeks without interruption.

An employee who is made redundant must be given reasonable time off during the notice period to seek other employment. If he is offered a new job starting before his notice expires, he may bring forward the termination of his old employment. However, the employer can challenge his right to a redundancy payment if he justifiably requires the employee to work for the full notice period. An employee forfeits his redundancy payment if, during the notice period, his employer justifiably dismisses him for misconduct other than strike action.

Disputes concerning redundancy and redundancy payments are determined by application to an industrial tribunal. The tribunal can also make a *protective award* to employees on the application of an *independent trade union when the employer has failed to give sufficient notice of his intention to declare redundancies (*see* disclosure of information).

redundancy payment

2. (in pleadings) The inclusion of unnecessary or irrelevant material. The court may order redundant material in a pleading to be struck out.

redundancy payment The sum that an employee dismissed because of *redundancy is entitled to receive from his employer under the Employment Protection (Consolidation) Act 1978. The sum is the total of: (1) one and a half weeks' pay for each year of the employee's *continuous employment in which he was aged 41 or more; (2) one week's pay for each year's service between the ages of 22 and 41; and (3) half a week's pay for each year between the ages of 18 and 22. Continuous employment exceeding 20 years is ignored, and a maximum amount of weekly pay to be used in the calculation is prescribed by regulations made by the Secretary of State for Employment and reviewed annually. Employees under 18 or over normal retiring age (65 for men, 60 for women) have no statutory right to a redundancy payment. The sum payable to men over 64 and women over 59 is reduced by one twelfth for each complete month by which their age exceeds 64 or 59, respectively.

The employer should obtain a receipt in the prescribed form from the employee; this entitles him to a rebate (currently 41% of the redundancy payment) from the Department of Employment's Redundancy Payments Fund. The employer may lose up to 10% of this rebate if he has failed to notify the Department of his intention to make employees redundant (*see* disclosure of information). No rebate is given on any sum paid in excess of the statutory payment, although the employer may be obliged under a collective agreement or individual employees' contracts of employment to pay larger sums.

re-engagement order An order made by an *industrial tribunal directing an employer who has unfairly dismissed an employee (*see* unfair dismissal) to provide him with comparable or other suitable employment in a post different from that from which he was dismissed (*compare* reinstatement order). A re-engagement order might be made, for example, when the employee's former job no longer exists following a reorganization, but he could be similarly employed in a different post. The order is accompanied by the tribunal's directions specifying the nature and remuneration for the new employment, benefits that must be restored to the employee, and the date by which he is to be re-engaged. An employer cannot be forced to comply with the order; if he fails to do so the tribunal will award *compensation on the usual principles together with an additional sum.

re-entry Repossession by a landlord of land held under a lease when he effects *forfeiture. There are restrictions on re-entry without a court order. The normal method of enforcing a right of re-entry is therefore by issuing court proceedings for possession. *See also* eviction.

re-examination *n.* The questioning of a witness by the party who originally called him to testify, following the *cross-examination of the witness by the opposite party. *Leading questions may not be asked in re-examination. Re-examination must be confined to matters arising out of the cross-examination; new matter may only be introduced with *leave of the judge.

referee *n.* A person to whom a dispute is referred for an opinion. *See also* official referee; reference.

reference *n.* **1.** The referral by a court of a case (or an issue arising in a case) to another court or an arbitrator (*referee*) for a decision or opinion. In the High Court any action or any question or issue of fact arising from it may be referred to an *official referee for trial. In the county courts, a case may be referred to the registrar for an opinion and report. Under the EEC Treaty, a court may refer to the *Court of Justice of the European Communities a question of Community law for a preliminary ruling and must do so if it is a court from which there is no appeal within the national system. **2.** (in succession) *See* incorporation by reference.

referential settlement A settlement incorporating by reference terms of an earlier settlement, either with or without variations. If the two settlements are inconsistent, a referential settlement may give rise to difficult questions as to what precisely is meant.

reform *n. See* punishment.

refreshing memory A procedure in which a witness may, while testifying, remind himself of events that he has forgotten by referring to a document that was made at the same time as the occurrence of the events in question and was accepted as accurate by the witness while the facts were fresh in his memory. At common law the document itself did not become evidence in the case, but it is now admissible in civil cases under the Civil Evidence Act 1968.

refuse disposal *See* pollution.

regent *n.* A person exercising all the royal functions while the sovereign is under 18 or totally incapacitated. Under the Regency Acts 1937 and 1953, the regent is the person next in line to the throne who is of age and is a commonwealth citizen domiciled in the UK. *Compare* Counsellors of State.

Regional Health Authorities *See* National Health Service.

registered company A company incorporated by *registration under the Companies Acts 1948–81. There are several types of registered company (*see* limited company; private company; public company; unlimited company).

registered design A design registered at the Designs Registry, which is part of the Patent Office (*see* patent). Registration gives monopoly rights over the outward appearance of an article, including its shape, configuration, pattern, or ornament, but not over the underlying idea. Works of sculpture, wall plaques, medals, and printed matter primarily of a literary or artistic character cannot be registered. A design may remain on the register for up to 15 years.

registered land Land to which the title in question is registered (*see* land registration). Land in an area of compulsory registration may be both registered and unregistered; for example, the freehold owner's title need not be registered if he acquired the land before compulsory registration was introduced in the area, but if he grants a lease for 40 years or more the tenant's leasehold title must be registered. Strictly, it is the legal estate or title that is registered, not the land itself.

registered office The official address of a registered company. It must be notified to the Companies Registry before *registration of the company and it must appear on company letter-heads and order forms. Documents may be served to a company's registered office and various registers and records may be inspected there.

register of members A record of the names, addresses, and shareholdings of members of a registered company, which is kept at the registered office or wherever it is compiled. The register must be kept open for public inspection (members free, others 5p) for at least two hours daily; it may not be closed for longer than 30 days in any year.

registrar *n.* **1.** An official responsible for compiling and keeping a register, e.g. the Registrar of Companies. The office of Registrar of the Chancery Division of the High Court has now been abolished. **2.** In the county courts, a judicial officer appointed by the Lord

Chancellor from solicitors of not less than seven years' standing. The registrar supervises the interlocutory and post-judgment stages of the case, but can also try cases within a financial limit defined by statute.

registration as citizen or subject A method by which certain persons can, either by right or at the Secretary of State's discretion, acquire *British citizenship, *British Dependent Territories citizenship, or *British Overseas citizenship. Some people can also become *British subjects by registration. An *oath of allegiance must be taken by most adult applicants. *Compare* naturalization.

registration of a company The most usual method of forming an incorporated company (*see* incorporation). Under the Companies Acts 1948–81 the following documents must be delivered with the appropriate fee to the *Companies Registry: the *memorandum of association signed by at least two company members, *articles of association (if any), statements relating to the directors, secretary, and the *registered office, and a statutory declaration that the Companies Acts have been complied with. The Registrar will then enter the company's name in the *companies register and issue a *certificate of incorporation.

registration of birth The recording of a birth by a Registrar of Births and Deaths under the Births and Deaths Registration Act 1953. Information for this purpose must be supplied to him within 42 days of the birth by a parent of the child, the occupier of the premises in which the birth takes place, a person present at the birth, or a person having charge of the child. The informant must supply details of the date and place of birth, the name and sex of the child, and its parentage. A *birth certificate* may be obtained from the Registrar, the Superintendent Registrar, or the General Register Office; a short

form of the certificate, relating to the child's name, sex, and date of birth but not parentage, may also be obtained (*see* illegitimacy).

registration of commons *See* common land.

registration of death The recording of a death by the Registrar of Births and Deaths under the Births and Deaths Registration Act 1953. This must take place within five days of the death or, if written notice of the death is given to the Registrar within that period, within 14 days. It may be effected by any relative of the deceased present at the death or during the last illness, by any other relative, by any person present at the death, or by the occupier or any inmate of the premises on which the death occurred. The informant must supply details of the date and place of death, the name, sex, address, and occupation of the deceased, and the cause of death. A *death certificate* may be obtained from the Registrar, the Superintendent Registrar, or the General Register Office.

registration of encumbrances Registration of *land charges affecting the rights of landowners. If registered, these charges are binding on third parties who acquire the land affected or any interest in it. If not registered, however, they will not bind most third parties and thus lose their effectiveness as interests in the land itself. A person contemplating buying or taking an interest (e.g. a mortgage) in land should therefore search the relevant registers to ensure that there are no charges registered that would influence him against proceeding. The registers are therefore always searched in any *conveyancing transaction by the purchaser or his solicitor. There are four relevant registers. (1) *Local land charges*, arising in favour of a local authority from the exercise of its statutory powers, are recorded in a *local land charges register* maintained by the authority concerned. Examples include rights to the repayment of improvement grants, compulsory purchase and smoke control orders, and planning decisions affecting the development or use of premises. Local land charges do not appear in any national register.

(2) In the case of *unregistered land, a register is maintained by the *Land Charges Department of the following types of interest recorded against the names of persons owning land.

(a) Land charges, comprising *Class A*: certain statutory charges registered on the application of the chargee; *Class B*: similar charges registered automatically; *Class C*: (i) *puisne mortgages, (ii) *limited owners' charges, (iii) *general equitable charges, and (iv) *estate contracts; *Class D*: (i) Inland Revenue charges for *capital transfer tax, (ii) *restrictive covenants created after 1925 and affecting freehold land, and (iii) *equitable interests created after 1925; *Class E*: annuities created before 1926 and registered after 1925; and *Class F*: spouses' rights of occupation under the Matrimonial Homes Act 1967.

(b) *Pending actions relating to land or any interest in it, and petitions for *bankruptcy.

(c) Writs or orders of the court imposing a charge on, or the appointment of, a receiver or sequestrator of land, and all *receiving orders in bankruptcy.

(d) *Deeds of arrangement affecting land.

Land charges remain registered until discharged by the chargee or the court. Registration of pending actions, writs and orders, and deeds of arrangement must be renewed every five years.

(3) When the title to land is registered (*see* land registration), encumbrances other than local land charges can be protected by registration of the appropriate entry in the charges register of the title at the Land Registry.

(4) A floating charge on the assets (including land) of a limited company and any other charge on a company's land created before 1970 for securing money need only be registered in the companies register, under the Companies Act 1948. A fixed charge on a company's land created after 1969 should be registered both in the companies register and the Land Charges Department (or charges register of the registered title as appropriate).

Although a chargee is protected by registration against all persons acquiring any interest in the land affected, the Law of Property Act 1969 provides that a purchaser is bound only by registered charges of which he knew or ought to have known when the contract was made. Thus if he discovers an undisclosed registered charge before completing the contract, he may rescind or pursue other contractual remedies against his vendor as the circumstances allow. If he completes the transaction, however, he will be bound by the charge.

registration of marriage The official recording of details relating to a marriage after it has been solemnized. (It is not to be confused with registration of notice of an intended marriage.) The details usually registered include the names, ages, occupations, and addresses of the parties, names and occupations of their fathers, and place of solemnization of the marriage. Certified copies of the details may be issued on request.

registration of title *See* land registration.

regulated agreement (under the Consumer Credit Act 1974) Any *consumer-credit agreement or *consumer-hire agreement other than one specifically exempted by the Act. Exempted agreements include debtor-creditor-supplier agreements secured by a land mortgage, in which the creditor is a local authority or building society who finances the purchase of that land or the provision of dwellings on the land, and *debtor-creditor agreements secured by a land mortgage. The Act also enables the Secretary of State to exempt other consumer-credit agreements in which the number of payments to be made by the debtor does not exceed a specified number, the rate of the total charge for credit does not exceed a specified rate, or the agreement has a connection with a country outside the UK.

regulated tenancy A *protected tenancy or a *statutory tenancy. It is a protected tenancy until the contractual element is terminated, when it becomes a statutory tenancy. *See also* converted tenancy.

regulations of European Communities *See* Community legislation.

rehabilitation *n. See* punishment; spent conviction.

rehabilitation order An order relating to a building in a *clearance area that is, in the housing authority's opinion, capable of being improved so as to be available for use as a dwelling for 15 years. Under a rehabilitation order, the authority's duty to demolish the building is replaced by one to improve it or ensure that it is improved.

rehearing *n.* **1.** A second hearing of a case already adjudicated upon, e.g. an *appeal to the Crown Court from conviction by a magistrates' court. All the evidence is heard again and either side may introduce fresh evidence without leave. **2.** The hearing of an appeal by the *Court of Appeal, in which the Court will consider all the evidence presented to the trial court (if it is relevant to the appeal) by reading the verbatim transcript of the trial; it will not usually permit fresh evidence to be given. The Court will usually not disturb the trial judge's findings on *primary facts, as opposed to the inferences to be drawn from those facts.

Reid test *See* lay days.

reinstatement order An order made

by an *industrial tribunal directing an employer who has unfairly dismissed an employee (*see* unfair dismissal) to restore him to his former job (*compare* re-engagement order). The employee is to be treated as if he had not been dismissed and is therefore entitled to recover any benefits (such as arrears of pay) that he has lost during his period of unemployment. However, pay in lieu of notice, *ex gratia* payments by the employer, state unemployment or supplementary benefits, and other sums he has received because of his unemployment will be taken into account. An employer cannot be forced to comply with an order for reinstatement; if he fails to do so, *compensation will be awarded to the employee on the usual principles together with an additional sum.

reinsurance The procedure in which an insurer insures himself with another insurer against some or all of his liability for a risk that he has himself underwritten in an earlier *insurance contract. Reinsurance is undertaken when the potential loss attached to the risk is too great for the insurer to bear alone. A valid contract of insurance gives the insurer an *insurable interest to support a reinsurance.

rejection of offer The refusal of an *offer by the offeree. Once an offer has been rejected, it cannot subsequently be accepted by the offeree. A counter-offer ranks as a rejection, but a mere inquiry as to the possibility of varying some term does not. *See also* lapse of offer; revocation of offer.

rejoinder *n.* A pleading served by a defendant in answer to the plaintiff's *reply. Such a pleading can only be served with *leave of the court.

relation back The treating of an act or event as having legal effect from a date earlier than that on which it actually takes place. Thus a grant of *probate relates back to the date of the testator's death, and an adjudication in *bankruptcy to the date of the act of bankruptcy.

relator *n.* A person at whose request an action is brought by the *Attorney General to enforce some public right. Although the relator is not the plaintiff, he is liable for the *costs of the proceedings. The Attorney General must consent to the issue of the writ and his discretion in deciding whether or not to sue on behalf of the relator is absolute and cannot be reviewed by the court.

release *n.* **1.** The renunciation of a right of legal action against another. The fact that a release has been granted should be specifically pleaded as a defence if the person who granted it subsequently initiates court proceedings. **2.** Any document by which one person discharges another from any claim with respect to a particular matter. **3.** The freeing of a person formerly detained, either upon *discharge when sentencing him or at the end of a prison sentence. The release of prisoners is also subject to *parole and *remission. In addition, the Secretary of State may, at his discretion (subject to prior approval of Parliament), order the release of a specified class of prisoners at any time up to six months earlier than they would normally be released. This power does not apply, however, in the case of prisoners serving a life sentence or convicted of specified excluded offences listed in the Criminal Justice Act 1982. The Secretary of State also has a special emergency power to release prisoners at any time up to one month before they would normally be released, without obtaining the prior consent of Parliament. When a person is serving an *extended sentence, the order for early release takes effect as an order for release on parole.

release on licence *See* parole.

relevance (relevancy) *n.* (in the law of evidence) The relationship between two

facts that renders one probable from the existence of the other, either taken by itself or in connection with other facts. Although most relevant facts are admissible in evidence, relevance is not the same as *admissibility, since even relevant evidence must be excluded if it falls within one of the *exclusionary rules. If no exclusionary rule is involved, all facts that have logical relevance to a fact in issue may be proved even though they are not in issue themselves.

relevant evidence *See* relevance.

relevant facts *See* relevance.

relief *n.* **1.** *See* remedy. **2.** A tax concession; for example, a personal allowance (*see* income tax), roll-over relief (*see* capital gains tax), or *stock relief.

relief from forfeiture A discretionary power of the courts to restore a lease to a tenant when the landlord claims or has exercised his right of *forfeiture.

remainder *n.* An interest in land that comes into effect in possession only when a prior interest ends. For example if A settles land on B for life then on C in fee simple, C's interest is in remainder until B dies. All interests in remainder are necessarily equitable (*see* fee simple absolute in possession). A settlement may create several successive remainders, e.g. a settlement on A for life, remainder to B for life, remainder to C in tail, remainder to D in fee simple. B, C, and D are called *remaindermen*. There can be no remainder after a fee simple. *See also* reversion.

remainderman *n.* *See* remainder.

remand *vb.* To commit an accused person to custody or release him on *bail during an adjournment. After arrest a suspect is normally kept at the police station until he is brought before the magistrates. If the offence with which he is charged is triable summarily or is an indictable offence that is being tried summarily (*see* offences triable either way), the court may adjourn the case and remand the accused. If the offence is being tried on indictment, the court may likewise adjourn the case and remand the accused before inquiring into the offence as examining justices. Remand in custody is normally made for no more than eight clear days (excluding the day on which the accused was remanded and the day on which he is to appear again before the court). If the accused is to be remanded for more than eight days, he must normally be released on bail unless there is some special reason why bail should be refused. However, the court may remand a suspect for a further period (or any number of further periods) of eight days after the end of the original remand order. If the period of time spent on remand becomes excessive, the accused may apply for bail. A remand order may also be made upon adjournment of a trial at any stage, at the request of either the prosecution or the defence, or after conviction, if the court wishes to obtain a report before sentencing. Bail must normally be granted, however, when remanding for reports.

Upon remand the suspect is sent to the local prison. *Juvenile offenders may be remanded instead in a special remand centre.

remand home An institution formerly provided by a local authority for the detention of children and young persons convicted of offences or awaiting trial. By the Children and Young Persons Act 1969, remand homes have been replaced by *community homes.

remedy (redress, relief) *n.* Any of the methods available at law for the enforcement, protection, or recovery of rights or for obtaining redress for their infringement. A *civil remedy* may be granted by a court to a party to a civil action. It may include *damages, an *injunction, a decree of *specific performance, or a *declaration (*see also* equitable remedies). In the High Court,

the nature of the remedy claimed by a plaintiff must be endorsed upon the *writ by which the action is begun and repeated in the prayer of the *statement of claim.

remission *n.* Cancellation of part of a prison sentence. A prisoner can earn remission of one-third of his sentence by good behaviour in prison and will be released upon remission without any conditions. If he is serving an *extended sentence, however, or is serving more than 18 months' imprisonment and was under the age of 21 when sentenced, he can only be released on licence (*see* parole). There is no remission of sentence for *life imprisonment.

remoteness of damage The extent to which a defendant is liable for the consequences of his wrongful act or omission. In contract, the defendant compensates for damage only if it was within his *reasonable contemplation*. He is presumed to have contemplated (and is therefore liable for) damage likely to result from the breach according to the usual course of events. Unusual damage resulting from special circumstances is regarded as within his contemplation only if a reasonable man, knowing what he knew or ought to have known, would have thought it liable to result.

In tort there is no single test to determine whether or not damage is too remote. In actions for *negligence and other forms of liability based on fault, the defendant is responsible only for damage of the type he should have foreseen, but if damage of that type is foreseeable, it is no defence that the extent of the resulting damage is greater than could have been expected. In torts of *strict liability, the defendant may be liable even for unforeseeable damage. Thus the keeper of an animal belonging to a dangerous species is liable for any damage it causes, whether foreseeable or not.

removal of action The transfer of a High Court action from a district registry to London (or vice versa) or of a county court action to the High Court (or vice versa).

renewal of lease The grant of a fresh *lease on similar terms to those of a pre-existing lease between the same parties. A lease sometimes contains a clause that gives the lessee an option to renew the lease when it expires. If the renewal is to be on the same terms, including the option to renew, the lease is known as a *perpetually renewable lease*; by statute, however, it is instead deemed to be a lease for 2000 years.

renewal of writ An order extending the validity of a writ for service beyond the usual 12 months. The extension may be for any period up to a further 12 months. It will not be ordered if its effect is to deprive the defendant of an accrued defence of *limitation of actions.

renouncing probate An executor's refusal, after the testator's death, to accept the office of executor. In such circumstances the person who would be entitled on intestacy to apply for letters of administration may apply for a grant of *letters of administration *cum testamento annexo*.

rent *n.* Payment by a tenant to his landlord under the terms of a *lease or *tenancy agreement. The obligation to pay rent is implied in all leases. If the tenant fails to pay his rent, the landlord can levy *distress for rent, take action for *forfeiture of the lease, or bring a court action against the tenant to claim the rent due. The manner and time of payment is as specified in the lease or tenancy agreement. If there is no express provision, rent should be paid to the landlord or his agent at the end of each *rental period or, in the case of a *fixed term, at the end of each year. The tenant can only deduct from the rent amounts that the lease or tenancy agreement allows. If the parties wish, the rent need not be paid in money: it

may be in the form of service to the landlord or payment in kind. However, the amount of rent must be certain or capable of being ascertained. *See also* fair rent.

rental period A period in a lease or tenancy for which the tenant must make a payment of rent. In the absence of agreement, this is yearly in the case of a *fixed term. For other periods, *see* periodic tenancy.

rent assessment committee A committee that decides any dispute concerning the amount of a *fair rent determined by a rent officer for a tenancy of a dwelling-house. Committees' members are drawn from panels appointed by the Secretary of State and the Lord Chancellor, and they are under the supervision of the Council on Tribunals. *See also* rent tribunal.

rent book A book or other document used to record rent paid and other tenancy details. A landlord must give his tenant a rent book when there is a weekly tenancy of residential property. This must show the name and address of the landlord, the amount of the rent and rates, an explanation of the tenant's statutory rights in relation to *security of tenure and rent, and an explanation of any rent-allowance schemes.

rentcharge *n.* A periodic payment of money charged on land, but excluding rent payable under a lease or tenancy and sums payable as interest. Depending on the manner in which the rentcharge arose it may be called a *chief rent*, *fee farm rent*, or *quit rent* but the effect is similar. A rentcharge owned on terms equivalent to a fee simple absolute in possession or term of years absolute can be a legal interest in land, but one subsisting on other terms (e.g. for life) is an equitable interest, registrable as a *general equitable charge. If the rent falls into arrears, the owner of the rentcharge may (on 40 days' arrears) enter the land and take its income until the debt is paid or lease the land to trustees who have powers to realize the money. On 21 days' arrears, he may enter the land and seize the debtor's goods as security for the rent. In general, a deed creating a rentcharge also reserves to its owner the right to forfeit the debtor's interest in the land if the rent is not paid. The Law of Property (Amendment) Act 1926 provides that freehold land subject to a rentcharge owner's right of forfeiture can still qualify as a fee simple absolute in possession. A rentcharge may also be secured on another rentcharge, rather than directly on land. For example, A grants a rentcharge (R1) over his land of £50 a year to B, who grants a rentcharge (R2) secured on R1 of £25 a year to C. If B defaults, C may appoint a receiver to collect the £50 from A and to pay C his £25 plus the expenses of the recovery, and account to B for any surplus.

The Rentcharges Act 1977 prohibits the creation of new rentcharges, except for (1) certain charges, usually in favour of the landowner's family, the effect of which is to make the land settled under the Settled Land Act 1925; and (2) *estate rentcharges*. The latter are usually reserved by a developer selling plots on an estate subject to covenants given by the purchasers to protect the character of the estate; they entitle the owner of the rentcharge to enforce the purchasers' covenants even after all the plots have been sold off.

rent officer A local official who determines *fair rents and keeps a register of all fair rents in his area.

rent rebate A rent subsidy paid by local authorities to needy tenants. The conditions vary from one local authority to another.

rent registration 1. The registration by a rent officer of a *fair rent determined by himself or a rent assessment committee. **2.** The registration by a local authority of a *restricted contract rent determined by a rent tribunal.

rent restriction A statutory limit on rent. The statutory rent freeze that was introduced in 1974 is no longer in operation. *See also* fair rent.

rent service 1. Any rent payable where a landlord and tenant relationship exists. **2.** Originally, a rent payable to a feudal lord.

rent tribunal A tribunal to whom the determination of the rent properly payable under a *restricted contract may be referred. Rent tribunals also have power to grant limited security of tenure, but only if the contract was made before the commencement of the Housing Act 1980. Until that Act they were distinctly constituted bodies, but their functions are now carried out by *rent assessment committees sitting as rent tribunals.

renvoi [French: sending back] *n.* The problem arising in private international law when one country's rule as to conflict of law refers a case to the law of a foreign country, and the law of that country refers the case either back to the law of the first country (*remission*) or to the law of a third country (*transmission*). For example, under English conflict rules, if a person dies intestate, the succession to his personal property is governed by the law of the country in which he is domiciled. Under Italian conflict rules, however, succession to personal property in such cases is governed by the law of the intestator's nationality. Thus if an English national dies intestate while domiciled in Italy, a *renvoi* problem will arise – English law will refer the matter to the law of his domicile (i.e. Italian law) and Italian law would refer the matter to the law of his nationality (i.e. English law).

repairs *pl. n.* (in landlord and tenant law) *See* covenant to repair.

reparations *pl. n.* (in international law) **1.** Compensation for injuries or international torts (breaches of international obligations). Whenever possible, international courts or arbitration tribunals will rule that reparations be made by means of restitution in kind; if this is not possible, compensation is by payment of a sum equivalent to the value of restitution in kind. The aim of reparations is to eradicate the consequences of the illegal act. It is not clear, however, whether there is an obligation to make reparations for all breaches of international law. **2.** Payments made by a defeated state to the conquering state to compensate for damage suffered by the victor.

repatriation *n.* A person's voluntary return from a foreign country to that of which he is a national. *Compare* deportation.

repeal *n.* The total or partial revocation of a statute by one passed subsequently. A statute is normally repealed by express words, but if provisions of a later statute are inconsistent with those of an earlier one this will imply that Parliament intended a repeal. Repeal does not affect any transaction that has been completed under the repealed statute.

replevin *n.* A procedure to recover goods that have been taken out of the plaintiff's possession (usually by way of distress for unpaid rent), the effect of which is to restore them to the plaintiff provisionally, pending the outcome of an action to determine the rights of the parties.

reply *n.* A pleading served by the plaintiff in a civil action in answer to the *defence. It is often contained in the same document as a defence to a *counterclaim.

representation *n.* **1.** The state of being represented, e.g. by an elected representative in the House of Commons (*see also* Parliament), by a defending counsel in court, or by an agent acting on behalf of his principal. **2.** (in succession) Taking the place of another. The court grants to executors or administra-

tors the right to represent the deceased, i.e. to collect, sell, and transfer the deceased's assets (in accordance with the will or intestacy rules) as if they were the owners. Under the Administration of Estates Act 1925, a legacy to a child of the testator who predeceases him leaving descendants of his own does not lapse but is inherited by those surviving descendants, who therefore represent their deceased ancestor. **3.** (in contract law) A statement. A person who has been induced to enter into a contract on the basis of a statement that is untrue or misrepresents a material fact may sue for damages or rescission of the contract (*see* misrepresentation). Under the Consumer Credit Act 1974 a representation includes a *condition, *warranty, or any other statement or undertaking, either oral or in writing.

representative action An action brought by or against one or more persons as representative(s) of a larger group. All the persons represented must have the same interest in the proceedings, and therefore a representative action cannot generally be brought if each member of the group has a separate claim for damages. Judgment in a representative action is binding upon all the persons represented. An example of a representative action is one brought by company members on behalf of themselves and other members against the company in respect of a wrong done to them by it (e.g. a denial of their voting or class rights embodied in the articles of association or an *ultra vires* act). *Compare* derivative action.

republication of will The re-execution of a will that has been revoked, or the execution of a *codicil to it, showing the testator's intention that the will should be effective notwithstanding the earlier revocation. Under the Wills Act 1837 these are the only ways in which a will that has been revoked can be revived. When republished, the will takes

effect as if made at the date of republication.

repudiation *n.* (in contract law) **1.** An
anticipatory *breach of contract. **2.** A
minor's disclaimer of a contract that is
voidable because of his minority (*see*
capacity to contract; rescission).

repugnancy *n.* Contradiction or inconsistency in the terms of a document.
Generally the court construes documents to give effect to the parties' primary intention (the *main purpose rule*).
If this cannot be established and the
document's provisions are directly contradictory, the court treats the later
provision as effective in the case of a
will and the earlier one in the case of a
deed. Thus a transfer of property to A
and B "as beneficial joint tenants in
equal shares" confers a *joint tenancy
unless it was effected by will, when it
will be treated as conferring a *tenancy
in common in equal shares.

reputation *n.* *See* character; defamation.

reputed ownership Goods that at the
beginning of the bankruptcy of a trader
are in his possession with the consent of
the true owner and in circumstances
suggesting that the bankrupt is the
owner are said to be in the bankrupt's
reputed ownership. Such goods are
treated as his own goods and are therefore available for distribution to his
creditors.

requisition *n.* **1.** (in land law) An application to HM Land Registry, the
Land Charges Department, or a local
authority for a certificate of *official
search to reveal whether or not land is
affected by encumbrances. **2.** (in *conveyancing) A request by an intending
purchaser or mortgagee arising from
the *abstract of title supplied by the
owner. For example if an abstracted
deed shows that the land is affected by
encumbrances contained in an earlier
deed that has not been abstracted, the
purchaser will raise a requisition de-

manding proper evidence of the encumbrances. **3.** (in military law) The compulsory acquisition of property for use
by the armed forces. The Army Act
1955 and the Air Force Act 1955, for
example, contain provisions that, if
brought into force by a government order made in the public interest, enable
commanding officers to issue requisi-
tioning orders authorizing the acquisition (in return for payment and compensation for damage) of vehicles,
horses' food, and stores.

reregistration *n.* The procedure enabling a registered company to change
its status, e.g. from limited to unlimited
or from public to private (or, in either
case, vice versa).

resale *n.* *See* right of resale.

resale price maintenance The fixing
by a supplier of the price at which his
goods may be sold by others. This may
be attempted by contractual arrangements or by nonlegal means, such as
blacklisting by trade associations. Resale price maintenance is now regulated
by the Resale Prices Act 1976, under
which the collective enforcement of
price maintenance agreements is illegal.
Provisions in contracts of sale between
suppliers and dealers fixing minimum
prices are void except when an exemption has been granted by the *Restrictive Practices Court. Contractual provisions fixing maximum prices may,
under certain circumstances, be enforced against a third party who
purchases the goods with notice of the
provision.

rescission *n.* The setting aside of a
*voidable contract, which is thereby
treated as if it had never existed. Rescission is an irrevocable step and can
be effected by any clear indication of
intention to be no longer bound by the
contract; this intention must be either
communicated to the other party or
publicly evidenced in some way. Rescission can also be effected by a formal ac-

tion (a remedy developed by the courts of equity). There are limits on the right of rescission. It cannot be exercised unless *restitutio in integrum* is possible, i.e. unless it is possible to restore both parties to their original positions, and it cannot be exercised if this would involve upsetting rights acquired by third parties. Thus, a buyer of goods cannot rescind if he cannot return the goods, and a seller of goods cannot rescind if they have been resold to a third party.

The setting aside of a proprietary contract by a minor is normally called *repudiation* rather than rescission, but there is no distinction in substance. The treating of a contract as discharged by breach (*see* breach of contract) is frequently, but misleadingly, called rescission. It does not operate retrospectively and is permissible whether or not *restitutio* is possible.

rescue *n.* **1.** Action to save people or property from danger. There is no general duty to rescue people or property from danger, though a master of a ship is bound by statute to render assistance to people in danger at sea. Voluntary acts of rescue are encouraged by the law. Someone injured in a rescue attempt may recover damages from the person whose negligence created the danger. The rescuer is not regarded as having assumed the risk of being injured and courts are reluctant to find that his injuries were due to *contributory negligence. **2.** The forcible removal of a person in the custody of the law, which is a criminal offence. **3.** The recovery of property that has been taken by way of *distress. If the distress was unlawful, the owner is entitled to recover it.

resealed probate A grant of *probate issued in one country and approved (and sealed again) by the court of another, giving the executor authority to deal with the testator's property in that second country.

reservation *n.* The creation of an ease-

ment or other right in a conveyance of land that is for the benefit of land retained by the vendor or transferor. For example, if A is selling Blackacre but requires a right of way over it for access to land he is retaining, the conveyance of Blackacre to the purchaser will reserve the right of way for the benefit of A's retained land.

reserve capital *See* authorized capital.

res extincta [Latin] Matter that has ceased to exist. *See* mistake.

res gestae [Latin: things done] The events with which the court is concerned or others contemporaneous with them. In the law of evidence, *res gestae* denotes: (1) a rule of relevance according to which events forming part of the *res gestae* are admissible; (2) an exception to the *hearsay rule under which statements forming part of the *res gestae* are admissible, for example if they accompany and explain some relevant act or relate to the declarant's contemporaneous state of mind or his contemporaneous physical sensations.

residence *n.* **1.** The place in which a person has his home. The term has been defined in various ways for different purposes in Acts of Parliament. For example, the Income and Corporation Taxes Act 1970 provides that, for the purposes of tax, a person is resident in the UK if: (1) he has an established home in the UK; (2) he stays in the UK for over six months of the year; or (3) he makes regular visits to the UK over a number of years. It is possible to be a resident of more than one country at the same time. *See also* domicile; habitual residence; main residence. **2.** The country from which control of a company is exercised; this depends upon the facts not upon where the company has its *registered office. Residence determines the company's liability to *corporation tax.

residential occupier A person who is living in a property as a result of his contractual rights, his statutory rights, his rights under a rule of law, or because other people are restricted by law from removing him. It is an offence to force a residential occupier to leave the property without complying with the proper procedure. *See* adverse occupation; eviction; forcible entry; harassment of occupier.

residuary devise *See* devise.

residuary estate (residue) The property comprising a deceased person's estate after payment of his debts, funeral expenses, costs of administration of the estate, and all specific and demonstrative bequests. If a will does not dispose of the whole of a testator's property, the residue passes to those entitled under the rules applying on *intestacy.

residuary legacy *See* legacy.

residue *n.* *See* residuary estate.

res ipsa loquitur [Latin: the thing speaks for itself] A principle often applied in the law of tort of *negligence. If an accident has occurred of a kind that usually only happens if someone has been negligent, and the state of affairs that produced the accident was under the control of the defendant, it may be presumed in the absence of evidence that the accident was caused by the defendant's negligence.

resisting arrest Taking any action to prevent one's arrest. A person may use *reasonable force to resist an illegal arrest. If he resists a legal arrest, however, he lays himself open to a charge of assaulting or *obstructing a police officer in the course of his duty. The fact that the police officer was in plain clothes is no defence to such a charge. The House of Lords has ruled that it is the right and duty of every citizen to take reasonable steps to prevent a breach of the peace by detaining the offender. The offender therefore has no right to resist such an arrest on the grounds of *self-

defence; if he uses force to do so, he may be guilty of an assault.

res judicata [Latin: a matter that has been decided] The principle that when a matter has been finally adjudicated upon by a court of competent jurisdiction it may not be reopened or challenged by the original parties or their successors in interest. It does not preclude an appeal or a challenge to the jurisdiction of the court. Its justification is the need for finality in litigation. *See also* estoppel.

resolution *n.* A decision reached by a majority of the members at a company meeting. *See* extraordinary resolution; ordinary resolution; special resolution.

respondeat superior [Latin: let the principal answer] The doctrine by which an employer is responsible for certain wrongs committed by his employee in the course of his employment. *See* vicarious liability.

respondent *n.* The defending party in an appeal or petition to the courts. *See also* co-respondent. *Compare* defendant.

respondentia *n.* *See* hypothecation.

restitutio in integrum [Latin] Restoration to the original position. *See* damages; rescission.

restitution *n.* The return of property to the owner or person entitled to possession. If one person has unjustifiably received property or money from another, he has an obligation to restore it to the rightful owner in order that he should not be unjustly enriched or retain an unjustified advantage. This obligation exists when, for example, goods or money have been transferred under compulsion (duress), under mistake, or under a transaction that fails because of illegality, lack of formality, or for any other reason or when the person who has taken the property has acquired a benefit through his actions without justification.

In certain circumstances the courts may make a *restitution order* in respect of property. Under the Theft Act 1968, if someone is convicted of any offence relating to stolen goods the court may order that the stolen goods or their proceeds should be restored to the person entitled to recover them. The court will only exercise this power, however, in clear cases that do not involve disputed questions of fact or law. Under the Police (Property) Act 1897, magistrates' courts are empowered to make a restitution order in favour of a person who is apparently the owner of property that has been obtained by the police in connection with any crime, even when no charge can be brought or the goods are seized under a search warrant. If the owner cannot be found, the court may make any order it thinks fit (usually an order for sale by auction). The police have no power to retain property lawfully seized merely because they think the court will probably make a restitution order.

restitution of conjugal rights *See* conjugal rights.

restraint of marriage A condition in a contract or other disposition intended to prevent someone from marrying. Such conditions are usually (unless they are very limited) void, as they are considered to be against *public policy.

restraint of trade A contractual term that limits a person's right to exercise his trade or carry on his business. An example is a term in an employment contract or partnership agreement prohibiting a party from engaging in a similar business for a specified period after the relationship ends. Such a term is void unless the party relying on it shows that it does not offend *public policy; it must also be reasonable as between the parties.

restraint on alienation Provisions in a grant or conveyance of land that purport to prevent the owner from disposing of it. Such provisions are generally void.

restraints of princes (in marine insurance) Political or executive acts causing loss or damage, as distinct from such acts as riots or ordinary judicial processes.

restricted contract For the purposes of the Rent Act 1977, a contract granting someone the right to occupy a dwelling for a rent that includes payment for the use of furniture or for services. A contract creating a *regulated tenancy is not, however, a restricted contract. *See also* rent tribunal.

restricted-use credit agreement (under the Consumer Credit Act 1974) A regulated *consumer-credit agreement that either (1) finances a transaction (which may or may not form part of the agreement) between the debtor and the creditor, e.g. a purchase of goods; (2) finances a transaction between the debtor and a person (the supplier) other than the creditor; or (3) refinances any existing indebtedness of the debtor's, to either the creditor or another person.

restriction order An order placing special restrictions (for a specified period or without limit of time) on the discharge from hospital of a person detained there by a *hospital order. It may be made by the Crown Court (but not a magistrates' court) when this appears necessary for the public protection, and its principal effects are that discharge may be authorized only by the Home Secretary and may be subject to conditions (e.g. subsequent supervision by a mental welfare officer).

restrictive covenant An obligation created by *deed that curtails the rights of an owner of land; for example, a covenant not to use the land for the purposes of any business. A covenant imposing a positive obligation on the landowner (the covenantor), for example to repair fences, is not a restrictive covenant. Third parties who acquire freehold land affected by a restrictive covenant will be bound by it if it is registered (*see* registration of encumbrances) or, in the case of covenants created before 1926, if they have notice of it. The covenant may also be enforceable by successors of the original beneficiary (the covenantee) if it was annexed to (i.e. expressly taken for the benefit of) the covenantee's land. The covenant will not be annexed, however, if the covenantee's land is not actually capable of benefiting from the covenant; for example, if it is too far away to be affected. Restrictive covenants contained in leases are not registrable but are nevertheless generally enforceable between third parties (*see* covenant running with the land). *See also* building scheme.

restrictive endorsement An *endorsement that prohibits the further negotiation (transfer) of a *bill of exchange (for example, "Pay X only") or states that it is a mere authority to deal with the bill as thereby directed and not a transfer of ownership of the bill (for example, "Pay X or order for collection"). A restrictive endorsement gives the endorsee the right to receive payment of the bill and to sue any party to it that his endorser could have sued, but gives him no power to transfer his rights as endorsee unless it expressly authorizes him to do so.

Restrictive Practices Court A superior *court of record created by the Restrictive Trade Practices Act 1956. Its jurisdiction is to determine matters arising under the legislation controlling *restrictive trade practices and *resale price maintenance, principally determining whether or not restrictive agreements registered with the *Director General of Fair Trading are contrary to the public interest. There is one court for the whole of the UK, comprising three puisne judges of the High Court nominated by the Lord Chancellor, one judge of the Court of Session nominated by the Lord President, one judge of the Supreme Court of Northern Ireland nominated by the Lord Chief Justice of Northern Ireland, and not more than ten lay members qualified by their knowledge or experience of industry, commerce, or public affairs. The court may sit in more than one division and in any country of the UK.

restrictive trade practices Arrangements in industry designed to maintain high prices or earnings or to exclude outsiders from a trade or profession. Examples include *resale price maintenance contracts, agreements between manufacturers to restrict output so that demand remains unsatisfied and a high price is maintained, similar agreements concerning the provision of services, and rules restricting entry to a trade or profession. Under the Restrictive Trade Practices Act 1976, certain types of restrictive agreement are presumed to be against the public interest (and therefore void) unless they are first registered with the *Director General of Fair Trading and then justified to the *Restrictive Practices Court. The Court can declare whether or not an agreement is contrary to the public interest and make orders restraining the parties from giving effect to it and from making a new similar agreement. It can also decide whether or not goods of any particular class should be exempt from the statutory prohibition on resale price maintenance.

Agreements that are important to the national economy or hold down prices may be exempted by the Secretary of State. The provision of certain services (including legal, dental, educational, surveying, and medical and related services) are exempt under the Act, as are ministers of religion and certain exclusive dealings and "know-how" agreements.

resulting trust A trust created by operation of law and in some cases based on the unexpressed but presumed intention of the settlor. When the beneficial interest of a trust is not completely disposed of, the undisposed interest results (i.e. goes back) to the settlor or to his estate. A resulting trust is also created when purchased property is transferred to someone other than the person who provides the price (*compare* advancement); it may also arise when property is transferred voluntarily. Resulting trusts may be regarded either as similar to *implied trusts or as a category of them.

resulting use (implied use) A *use that arose when legal ownership (seisin) was transferred, but the transferor did not state for whose use (benefit) the property was to be: the benefit of the property therefore still belonged to the transferor.

retirement of jury The withdrawal of the *jury from the court at the end of the trial so that they may decide on their verdict in private. The jury members are not allowed contact with the public until they reach (or fail to reach) a verdict. They may not afterwards disclose the content of their discussions in reaching a verdict.

retirement of trustees A right of trustees to be released from their trusteeship. Originally trustees were not allowed to retire, but retirement is now possible subject to certain safeguards.

retour sans protêt [French: return without protest] A direction on a *bill of exchange to the effect that the bill should be returned without *protest if it is dishonoured.

retrial *n. See* new trial.

retribution *n. See* punishment.

retrospective legislation (retroactive legislation) Legislation that operates on matters taking place before its enactment, e.g. by penalizing conduct that was lawful when it occurred. There is a presumption that statutes are not intended to have retroactive effect unless they merely change legal procedure (*see* interpretation of statutes).

return *n.* **1.** A formal document, such as an *annual return or the document giving particulars of shares allotted and to whom (*return of the allotment*), which must be delivered to the Companies Registry within one month of *allotment. **2.** The official result of the votes cast in an election.

return day The day specified in a *summons for the hearing of the summons.

revenue statute An Act of Parliament concerning taxation.

reversal of judgment The alteration of a *judgment on appeal, either wholly or in part.

reversion (reverter) *n.* The interest in land of a person (called the *reversioner*) who has granted some lesser interest than his own to another but has not disposed of the whole of his own interest. For example, if A grants land to B for life, A has an interest in reversion, since the land reverts to him on B's death. Similarly, a person who lets or sublets land to another retains an interest in reversion. The reversionary interest of a lessor can subsist as a legal estate, but the reversion after any other interest than a lease is necessarily an equitable interest.

reversionary lease Any lease for a term beginning at a future date. However, under the Law of Property Act 1925 a lease granted at a rent or for a capital sum is void if it is to take effect more than 21 years after it is executed.

reverter *n. See* reversion.

revival of will *See* republication of will.

revocation of offer The withdrawal of an *offer by the offeror so that it can no longer be accepted. Revocation takes effect as soon as it is known to the offeree (from whatever source); offers can be revoked at any time before acceptance unless they are coupled with an *option. *See also* lapse of offer; rejection of offer.

revocation of probate The cancellation by the court of a grant of probate that was obtained by fraud or mistake. The revocation does not affect those who have purchased assets of the estate from the executors before the revocation.

revocation of will The cancellation of a will. The testator may revoke his will by destroying it with that intention or by making a new will inconsistent with the original. A will is automatically revoked by the testator's marriage, unless made expressly in contemplation of marriage to the particular spouse.

right *n.* **1.** Title to or an interest in any property. **2.** Any other interest or privilege recognized and protected by law. **3.** Freedom to exercise any power conferred by law. *See also* human rights; natural rights.

right of abode *See* immigration.

right of action 1. The right to take a particular case to court. **2.** A chose in action (*see* chose).

right of audience The right of an *advocate to be heard in legal proceedings. Barristers have the right of audience in the Crown Court, High Court, Court of Appeal, and House of Lords. Solicitors have a limited right of audience in some Crown Court centres specified by the Lord Chancellor. In the county courts and magistrates' courts both barristers and solicitors can appear. Many administrative tribunals have no rules concerning rights of audience and a party may be represented by any person he chooses.

right of common *See* common.

right of establishment The right under the Treaty of Rome of a national of a member state of the European Economic Communities to engage in and manage businesses in any other member state.

right of re-entry *See* re-entry.

right of resale The right that the seller in a contract of sale has to resell if the buyer does not pay the price as agreed. When the goods are perishable or the *unpaid seller gives notice to the buyer of his intention to resell, and the buyer does not pay the price within a reasonable time, if the seller is in possession of the goods he may resell them and recover from the first buyer damages for any loss.

right of silence The right of someone charged with an offence or being tried on a criminal charge not to make any statement or give any evidence. When being questioned by police, the suspect normally has the right to keep quiet (*see* Judges' Rules), and his failure to answer cannot amount to obstructing the police. Sometimes, however, statute obliges him to answer. The owner of a vehicle, for example, must give information about who was driving it at the time of an alleged driving offence, and the suspect has a duty to answer a chief police officer's questions relating to *official secrets. At his trial, the accused has an absolute right not to give or call evidence or to submit to cross-examination (which might incriminate him). If he is then convicted, however, he cannot give evidence on appeal that he could have given at the trial. The prosecution is not allowed to comment on the silence of the accused (or his spouse), but the judge may comment on it in his summing-up to the jury providing that he does not suggest that the silence amounts to an admission of guilt.

The right to silence is often cited as a prime example of the fairness of the English criminal system, but it has also often been criticized as unduly hampering the conviction of criminals.

right of support An *easement conferring on the owner of the dominant tenement the right to have buildings on his land supported by those on the servient tenement. For example, houses forming a semidetached pair are likely to have mutual rights of support.

right of survivorship (*jus accrescendi*) The right of a joint owner of property to acquire absolute ownership of the property on the death of the other owner(s). *See* joint tenancy.

right of way The right to pass over another's land. It may exist as a public right exercisable by anyone; as an *easement for the benefit of a particular piece of land; or as a *licence, purely personal to the person to whom it is granted.

rights issue A method of raising share *capital for a company from existing members rather than from the public at large. Members are given a right to acquire further shares, usually in proportion to their existing holding and at a price below the market value of existing shares. This right may be sold (*renounced*) to a third party. *See also* preemptive right.

right to air The right to a flow of air over land or buildings from neighbouring premises. It may be enjoyed on any terms agreed by personal arrangement between neighbouring landowners, but can only exist as an *easement if the right can be sufficiently defined. Thus an easement for the flow of air through a specific ventilation passage may exist, but a right to a general flow of air over the chimneys of a house does not qualify as an easement so is not an interest in the land itself.

right to begin The right of a party at trial to present his case to the court first (i.e. to *open the case*) by making the opening speech and presenting his evidence. The right to begin usually belongs to the party who carries the persuasive *burden of proof. Thus, in a criminal case the prosecution always has the right to begin; in civil cases the plaintiff normally begins, but the defendant may do so when he has the burden of proving all issues.

riot *n.* A common-law offence committed when at least three people use force or violence in carrying out or initiating together some purpose, with the intention of using force if necessary against anyone attempting to stop them, and alarming at least one person of average courage by their actions. The purpose must be an illegal one or the force used must be unnecessary and without any reasonable justification. Robbery involving more than three robbers may amount to a riot. Riot is a form of *breach of the peace. Under the Riot (Damages) Act 1886, when property has been destroyed, damaged, or stolen in the course of a tumultuous riot (i.e. a riot by a large number of people in a state of agitated commotion), the owner is entitled to compensation out of public funds.

road *n.* For purposes of offences relating to road traffic, any *highway or other route to which the general public has access. A road must be a route leading from one place to another, and this is always a question of fact. It may include a hotel forecourt, a road privately owned but to which the public has access, or a bridge over which a road passes, but a car park is usually not regarded as a road. Some traffic offences are defined to cover roads and "other public places".

road accidents If an accident has been caused by the presence of a motor vehicle on a road and results in injury to anyone or damage to anyone else's vehicle or to property on the road or neighbouring land (e.g. someone's garden wall), it is an offence for the driver of the vehicle not to stop, unless he can show that he did not know that the accident happened. It is also an offence to refuse to give one's name and address to anyone who reasonably requires it (e.g. a police officer or another driver or pedestrian involved in the accident), unless one reports the accident to the police as soon as possible (not later than 24 hours after it occurred). If a person has been injured in a road accident, it is an offence not to produce one's certificate of insurance (*see* third-party insurance) for a police officer or anyone else with reasonable grounds for asking for it, unless one reports the accident to the police not later than 24 hours after it occurred and, at the same time or within five days, produces the certificate of insurance at any police station one specifies.

Failure to stop after an accident or give particulars is an endorsable offence (carrying 5–9 points under the *totting-up system) and is subject to a fine of up to £1000 under the Transport Act 1981 and to discretionary *disqualification.

road tax A tax that must be paid in respect of any mechanically propelled vehicle used, parked, or kept on a public road. It is an offence to fail to pay it. Electrically propelled vehicles and invalid vehicles do not have to be taxed, and no tax is required when a motorist is driving to and from a prearranged *MOT test. It is also an offence to fail to display a tax disc showing that the vehicle has been taxed, unless one has applied for a new disc before the old one expired and it is within 14 days from the date of expiry. The tax disc must be displayed on the nearside lower corner of the windscreen. Failure to pay road tax or display the tax disc is punishable by fine, but is not subject to endorsement.

robbery *n.* The offence of using force against any person, or putting them in fear of being subjected to force, in order to commit a theft, either before the theft or during the course of it. It is also robbery to threaten to use physical force in these circumstances, even if the

person threatened is not frightened by the threats. The degree of force required is a question of fact in each case to be decided by the jury; nudging someone so that he loses his balance may constitute sufficient force. The force must, however, be directed against the person, rather than his property. Robbery and assaults with intent to rob are punishable by a maximum sentence of life imprisonment.

rogatory letter *See* letter of request.

rolled-up plea A form of the defence of *fair comment in an action for defamation. If the words complained of contain a mixture of statements of fact and comment, the defendant may plead that "the said words in so far as they consist of allegations of fact are true in substance and in fact, and in so far as they consist of expressions of opinion they are fair comments made in good faith and without malice upon the said facts, which are a matter of public interest". The defendant must give particulars of which words he alleges are statements of fact and of the circumstances he relies on to show that the words are true.

root of title The document from which an owner of unregistered land traces his ownership. A good root must be at least 15 years old, deal with the whole legal and beneficial ownership of the land, describe it sufficiently to identify it, and cast no doubt on the title. A vendor must supply and the purchaser must accept such a root unless their contract provides otherwise.

rout *n.* An offence intermediate between *unlawful assembly and *riot, committed when an unlawful assembly begins to move towards fulfilling its common purpose, even though it has not yet carried out or begun the purpose.

royal assent The agreement of the Crown, given under the royal prerogative and signified either by the sover-

rule against double portions

eign in person or by royal commissioners, that converts a Bill into an *Act of Parliament or gives a Measure the force of an Act. It is the duty of the Clerk of the Parliaments to endorse the date on which it was given immediately after the long title.

royal prerogative The special rights, powers, and immunities to which the Crown alone is entitled under the common law. Most prerogative acts are now performed by the government on behalf of the Crown. Some, however, are performed by the sovereign in person on the advice of the government (e.g. the dissolution of Parliament) or as required by constitutional convention (e.g. the appointment of a Prime Minister). A few prerogative acts (e.g. the granting of certain honours, such as the Order of the Garter) are performed in accordance with the sovereign's personal wishes.

The Crown has limited powers of legislating under the prerogative, principally as respects the civil service and UK dependent territories. It does so by Order in Council, ordinance, letters patent, or royal warrant. The dissolution and prorogation of Parliament and the granting of the royal assent to Bills take place under the prerogative. Originally the fountain of justice from which the first courts of law sprang, the Crown still exercises (through the Home Secretary) the *prerogative of mercy and retains the right (through the Attorney General) to stop a prosecution by entering a *nolle prosequi. In foreign affairs, the sovereign declares war, makes peace and international treaties, and issues passports under the prerogative. Many appointments (e.g. the higher judiciary, archbishops, and diocesan bishops) are made under the prerogative, and a variety of honours, including new hereditary peerages, are conferred by the Crown as the fountain of honour. The sovereign is head of the armed forces, and, although much of the law governing these is now statu-

tory, their disposition generally remains a matter for the prerogative. There is a prerogative power, subject to the payment of compensation, to expropriate or requisition private property in times of war or apprehended war. Miscellaneous prerogative rights include the rights to *treasure trove and to *bona vacantia. An important immunity of the sovereign is the prerogative of perfection. The common-law maxim that *the King can do no wrong* resulted in the complete immunity of the sovereign personally from all civil and criminal proceedings for anything that he or she might do. This personal immunity remains, but actions may now be brought against the Crown under the Crown Proceedings Act 1947 (*see* Crown proceedings).

If a statute confers on the Crown powers that duplicate prerogative powers, the latter are suspended during the existence of the statute unless it either abolishes them or preserves them as alternative powers.

royal proclamation A document by which the sovereign exercises certain prerogative powers (e.g. the summoning and dissolution of Parliament) and certain legislative powers conferred on her by statute (e.g. the declaration of a state of emergency; *see* emergency powers).

royal title *See* Queen.

royalty *n.* A sum payable for the right to use someone else's property for the purpose of gain. Royalties are paid on *wasting assets, which have a limited lifespan. For example, the royalty paid by a licensee to mine someone's land is a fixed sum per tonne of the mineral he extracts, and an author's royalty is similarly determined by the total number of his books the publisher sells.

RSC *See* Rules of the Supreme Court.

rule against bias *See* natural justice.

rule against double portions A rule designed to ensure, as far as possible, equality between children entitled under a settlement and under a will, both made by the same person. Thus if a father promises to pay substantial sums of money to certain of his children to advance them and at his death the money has not been paid, but the children (together with others) are entitled to legacies under his will, the payment of the legacies and the moneys due under the settlement will be considered together. Thus if an advancement of £10,000 and a legacy of £5000 are due to one son and a legacy of £10,000 is due to another son, the first son will not receive his legacy, to ensure equality between the children.

rule against inalienability A rule that prevents property from being incapable of being transferred within the perpetuity period, i.e. a life presently existing plus a period of 21 years. A gift that prevents transfer within this period is void. The rule is similar to the *rule against perpetual trusts.

rule against perpetual trusts The rule that prohibits noncharitable trusts from lasting beyond the perpetuity period, i.e. a lifetime presently existing plus a period of 21 years. A trust that may last beyond that period is void. *Compare* rule against inalienability; rule against perpetuities.

rule against perpetuities (rule against remoteness of vesting) A rule designed to ensure that a *contingent interest in land vests absolutely (if it is to vest at all) within the *perpetuity period*. This is defined as the period of the lives of those mentioned in the disposition (the *lives in being*) plus 21 years plus any actual period of gestation (in the case of a posthumous beneficiary). The period is taken from the date of the gift. The purpose of the rule is to prevent land being tied up for an indefinite period, which would hinder its ultimate disposal. The Settled Land Act 1882 provided that the ownership of settled land (in which contingent in-

terests were most commonly found) could be disposed of by the *tenant for life, thus achieving the original purpose behind the imposition of the rule. The rule against perpetuities continued, however, to be applied to interests in funds, as distinct from individual pieces of land. The law relating to perpetuities is now contained in the Perpetuities and Accumulations Act 1964, which allows, in particular, the question of whether the interest will vest within the perpetuity period to be decided during the currency of a contingent interest rather than at the inception of the gift. The Act also provided a new list of lives (the *statutory lives in being*) to be used in making this decision. This amendment (known as the *wait and see principle*) is likely to save many gifts from breaking the rule.

rule against remoteness of vesting *See* rule against perpetuities.

rule of law 1. The supremacy of law. **2.** A feature attributed to the UK constitution by Professor Dicey (*Law of the Constitution*, 1885). It embodied three concepts: the absolute predominance of regular law, so that the government has no arbitrary authority over the citizen; the equal subjection of all (including officials) to the ordinary law administered by the ordinary courts; and the fact that the citizen's personal freedoms are formulated and protected by the ordinary law rather than by abstract constitutional declarations.

rules of court Rules regulating the practice and procedure of a court, usually made by a rule committee acting under a statutory power. *See also* Crown Court rules; Rules of the Supreme Court.

Rules of the Supreme Court (RSC) Rules governing the practice and procedure of the *Supreme Court of Judicature. The rules are made under a statutory power by the *Supreme Court Rule Committee*, a body appointed by the

*Lord Chancellor and comprising himself, the *Master of the Rolls, the heads of the Divisions of the High Court, and four practitioners. The Rules are divided into 114 Orders and cover all aspects of procedure in the High Court and the *Court of Appeal. *See also* Supreme Court Practice, The.

running-account credit (under the Consumer Credit Act 1974) A facility under a *personal-credit agreement that enables a debtor to receive periodically from the creditor or a third party cash, goods or services to an amount or value that does not exceed the *credit limit (if any), taking into account payments made by or to the credit of the debtor. Examples are bank overdrafts and credit cards. The credit provided will be taken not to exceed £5000 and the agreement will be a consumer-credit agreement if the credit limit does not exceed £5000. The Act specifies three situations in which running-account credit will not exceed £5000 in cases in which there is no credit limit or, if there is, it exceeds £5000.

running days *See* lay days.

running with the land *See* covenant running with the land.

Rylands v *Fletcher*, **rule in** A principle of strict liability for dangerous things accumulated on land that escape and cause damage. It was first stated in the case *Rylands* v *Fletcher* (1868), in which the defendant had a reservoir built on his land that caused flooding of the plaintiff's mine. The accumulation of dangerous things must constitute a non-natural use of the land. In modern law a use is non-natural if it is a special use creating an abnormal risk of damage. The occupier of the land is liable for damage caused by an escape, subject to the defences of common benefit, act of a stranger, statutory authority, consent of the plaintiff, default of the plaintiff, or act of God.

S

s. (*pl.* **ss.**) The recognized abbreviation used in citing a particular section of a statute, as in "s. 4", "ss. 70–73".

sabotage *n.* Damage to or destruction of property, especially the property of an employer during a strike or of the state for political reasons. Sabotage as such is not an offence, although it may be treated as *criminal damage. The courts have, however, interpreted the phrase "prohibited place" in the Official Secrets Act 1911 to bring sabotage against the state within the scope of that Act, even though it is clear that Parliament's intention was only to prohibit spying. *See* official secrets.

safety at work Every employer has a common-law duty to take reasonable care for his employees' health, safety, and welfare at work: he may be sued in the courts for damages if an employee is injured through the employer's negligence or failure to observe safety regulations. The employer cannot contract out of this liability and, under the Employers' Liability (Compulsory Insurance) Act 1969, must insure against his liability for employees' injuries and diseases sustained or contracted at work. The Health and Safety at Work Act 1974 further requires employers to ensure, as far as is reasonably practicable, that their working methods, equipment, premises, and environment are safe and to give such training, information, and supervision as will ensure their employees' health and safety (*see* Health and Safety Commission). Anyone employing more than five persons must maintain a written statement of his general policy concerning his employees' health and safety (dealing, for example, with safety rules and protective clothing) and must keep them informed of it. He must also give relevant information to the *safety representatives of his employees' trade unions and establish a *safety committee where appropriate.

Employees also have a duty to take reasonable care for their own health and safety, for example by complying with safety regulations and using protective equipment supplied to them. Employers and employees who fail to comply with the requirements of the Health and Safety at Work Act 1974 face prosecution in the criminal courts.

safety committee A committee that, under the Health and Safety at Work Act 1974, an employer must establish within three months after a written request from at least two employees' *safety representatives. The employer must consult with the representatives as to the composition of the committee and must display a notice in his premises telling his employees its composition and the workplaces it covers. The *code of practice published by the Health and Safety Commission suggests that safety committees' responsibilities should include monitoring accidents and disease and developing improved safety rules and systems of work and training of employees with regard to safety.

safety representatives Employees appointed by trade unions to represent the interests of their colleagues regarding their health, safety, and welfare at work. Regulations made under the Health and Safety at Work Act 1974 give a trade union recognized as having negotiating rights on behalf of a group or class of employees the right to appoint at least one of those employees as a safety representative. The representatives' statutory powers include the investigation of accidents and industrial diseases occurring at the workplace and inspection of the premises to determine their causes. The employer must allow them time off work with pay to train for and perform their duties and to attend meetings of *safety committees. *See also* disclosure of information.

sale *n.* A contract involving the *sale of goods or a similar contract involving the transfer of land.

sale by description A contract of sale of goods containing words identifying its subject matter, e.g. 1000 tonnes of Western White Wheat. Even when the subject matter of the contract is physically ascertained at the time of contracting, e.g. a particular motor car, the contract may contain words of description or identification. The goods delivered must match the contract description; otherwise the seller is in breach of contract and the buyer, if he acts promptly, may reject the goods.

sale by sample A contract of sale of goods made on the basis that the bulk of goods to be delivered to the buyer will match a sample submitted by the seller. If the bulk does not match the sample the seller is in breach of contract and the buyer may reject the goods. The seller must give the buyer a reasonable opportunity of comparing the bulk with the sample and the goods must be free from any defect making them unmerchantable that would not be apparent on reasonable examination of the sample.

sale of goods A contract by which a seller transfers or agrees to transfer the ownership of goods to a buyer in exchange for a money price. If ownership is to pass at a future time the contract is called an *agreement to sell.* The contract, which need not be in writing, may contain *express terms. Terms may also be implied by law (*see also* implied condition); for example, that the seller has a right to sell, the goods correspond with the description under which they are sold, and that the goods are of *merchantable quality and are reasonably fit for the buyer's purpose. Unless the parties agree otherwise the seller must hand over the goods in exchange for the price and the buyer must pay the price in exchange for the goods. Much of the law governing the sale of satisfaction

goods is codified in the Sale of Goods Act 1979.

sale on approval *See* sale or return.

sale or return (sale on approval) The delivery of goods to a person on terms that allow him to keep the goods for a time before he decides whether or not to buy them. Unless otherwise agreed, such a person becomes the owner if he signifies his approval of the goods or carries out any other act adopting the transaction. He will also become the owner if he retains the goods beyond a reasonable time or the time fixed for their return.

salvage *n.* The service rendered by a person who saves or helps to save maritime property. Salvage may be the subject of an express agreement. In the absence of any agreement, a salvor is entitled by law to an award (also known as salvage), which is assessed by the court and payable out of the salvaged property, if he shows that the property was in real danger and that he acted with some skill and in a purely voluntary capacity. The award can also take account of the saving of life, but this alone gives no claim to an award as there is no property saved out of which payment can be ordered.

salvage of trust property A power that existed before 1926 for the court to authorize a payment for preserving (or salvaging) trust property (e.g. repairing buildings) even though the document creating the trust did not permit such payment. A wider power was given by statute in 1925, under which the court can authorize any transaction that is expedient.

sanction *n.* **1.** A *punishment for a crime. *See* nulla poena sine lege. **2.** A measure taken against a state to compel it to obey international law or to punish it for a breach of international law. It is often said that international law is deficient because it lacks the power to impose sanctions or even to compel states

to accept the jurisdiction of courts (*see* International Court of Justice). There are, however, certain sanctions that can be applied. A state may, in certain cases, use force in self-defence, or as a sanction against an act of aggression, or as a reprisal (for example, by expropriating property belonging to citizens of a country that had previously carried out unlawful acts of expropriation). It may also act by way of *retorsion* (a lawful act employed as a sanction, such as cutting off economic aid). There are also certain powers of sanction available under the United Nations system, such as economic (and, at least in theory, military) sanctions, although the powers of the Security Council to impose sanctions are subject to veto.

Sanderson order *See* Bullock order.

sanity *n. See* presumption of sanity.

sans recours **(without recourse to me)** A stipulation that the drawer or an endorser of a *bill of exchange may add to his signature, thus repudiating his liability to the holder. If the bill is dishonoured, the holder has no recourse to the drawer or endorser who has made such a stipulation.

satisfaction *n.* **1.** The fulfilment of a claim. *See also* accord and satisfaction. **2.** A doctrine of equity under which an obligation is discharged by payment, performance, or some similar act. The doctrine applies when the acts of a settlor are unclear. If the settlor discharges his obligation by an act different from that required, the obligation is said to be satisfied provided that the act he does is a sufficient substitute for the act he is charged to do. Thus if he owes a debt and leaves a legacy of the same or a greater amount to the creditor, the creditor is satisfied. Closely analogous to satisfaction are cases in which payment of a legacy is satisfied by payment of a *portion and one legacy is satisfied by payment of another (*see* ademption); in these cases, however, there is no prior obligation owed by the settlor.

satisfied term The expired period of an interest in land for a term of years created for a specific purpose that has been fulfilled. For example, when land under a *strict settlement is assigned to trustees for a term of years on trust to raise capital sums for members of the settlor's family, the term is satisfied when the sums have been raised. Under the Law of Property Act 1925, the estate or interest in the land ceases when the purpose is fulfilled. A term of years that has not expired although the purpose for which it was created has been fulfilled is called an *outstanding term.*

scandalous statement A statement that is irrelevant and abusive. When such a statement appears in *pleadings or in an *affidavit the court or a judge may order it to be struck out.

schedule *n.* An appendix to an Act of Parliament or other legislation that deals with points of detail supplementary to the main part.

scheme *n.* A document, normally approved by the court, containing provisions for the management or distribution of property or for resolving a dispute concerning allegedly conflicting rights. For example, the court or the *Charity Commissioners may approve a scheme for the management of a charitable trust.

scheme of arrangement 1. An agreement between a debtor and his creditors to arrange the debtor's affairs to satisfy the creditors. The debtor usually agrees to such an arrangement in order to avoid *bankruptcy. If the arrangement is agreed when no *receiving order has been made, it is governed primarily by the ordinary law of contract. However, if it is for the benefit of the debtor's creditors generally, or if the debtor is insolvent and it is for the benefit of at least three of his creditors, it is a *deed of arrangement and subject to statutory control. An arrangement agreed after a receiving order has been made is governed by the statutory provisions relating to bankruptcy. The parties must obtain the court's approval of the scheme. If approval is obtained, the arrangement is binding on all the debtor's creditors even if they did not assent to it, and they cannot continue to pursue the debtor's bankruptcy. If an *adjudication order has already been made when an arrangement is agreed, the court may make an order annulling the bankruptcy. **2.** An agreement between a company and its creditors or members when the company is in financial difficulties or to effect a *takeover. It must be approved by at least 50% (representing 75% in value) of those creditors or members at separate meetings and sanctioned by the court. All creditors or members involved in the scheme are bound by it, although the court can make special provision for those who dissent.

scienter rule *See* classification of animals.

Scott Schedule A document used in *official referee's business for giving *particulars when the claim is in respect of a large number of individual items (e.g. a landlord's claim for dilapidations). The Scott Schedule is divided into columns providing for (1) the consecutive numbering of the items; (2) the full description of each item; (3) the contention of each party against each item as to liability or amount; and (4) a column for the use of the court. It is named after a former official referee.

scuttling *n.* Sinking a ship (particularly with a view to making a fraudulent insurance claim) by making or opening holes in its hull to allow the entry of water.

seal *n.* **1.** Wax impressed with a design and attached to any document as a sign of its authenticity. **2.** In the case of a *deed, an impressed wax, an adhesive wafer, or anything else intended to serve the purpose of a seal.

search 1. *vb.* To examine the registers maintained by HM Land Registry, the Land Charges Department, or the registers of local land charges during an *official search. **2.** *n.* *See* power of search.

search before Crown Court The searching of a person on the order of the Crown Court when that person has been ordered by the court to pay a fine or to pay money for some other reason (e.g. forfeiture of a *recognizance). Any money found on the person can be used towards payment of the sum due, any excess being returned.

search of ship The right that a belligerent power has during wartime, under public international law, to search any ship of a neutral power on the high seas in order to discover whether it is carrying *contraband.

search warrant *See* power of search.

seat belt A belt fitted in a motor vehicle, designed to restrict the forward movement of a driver or front-seat passenger in the event of an accident. All passenger vehicles with seating for less than ⁄13 passengers and most four-wheeled goods vehicles registered after 1 January 1965 must comply with statutory regulations governing seat belts, although the details of these regulations vary according to the date the vehicle was first registered. It is compulsory for all drivers and front-seat passengers in cars registered after 1964, light vans registered after 1966, and three-wheeler vehicles registered after 1969 to wear seat belts at all times when the vehicle is moving, subject to certain exceptions. These exceptions are: (1) drivers carrying out any manoeuvre that includes reversing (passengers must still wear their seat belts during such manoeuvres); (2) drivers making local delivery or collection rounds in specially adapted vehicles (e.g. milkmen in milk vans); (3) anyone whose seat belt has become

faulty during the drive or who has already arranged to have a faulty belt repaired; (4) anyone whose belt has locked on a steep hill; (5) anyone supervising a learner who is reversing; (6) certain categories of people with a special exemption certificate on medical grounds.

Any front-seat passenger over the age of 14 is responsible for wearing his own seat belt, but the driver of the car is responsible for ensuring that front-seat passengers under the age of 14 wear a seat belt. Children under the age of one must wear an approved child restraint. Over the age of one they can wear an adult seat belt, preferably with an approved booster cushion to raise them to a suitable height. Alternatively they can sit in the back seat fitted with an approved restraint. Failure to wear a seat belt carries a fine of up to £50.

seaworthy *adj.* Having at the start of a voyage the degree of fitness for that particular voyage that a careful owner might be expected to require of his ship. Obligations as to seaworthiness are implied by law in charterparties and imposed by the Hague Rules in bills of lading. A marine insurance policy incorporates by statute a warranty that the insured ship is seaworthy.

secondary evidence Evidence that by its nature suggests the existence of better evidence and might be rejected if that better evidence is available (e.g. a copy of a document). Secondary evidence is generally admissible if the absence of the *primary evidence is explained.

secondary party An *accessory to a crime.

secondary use *See* shifting use.

second-hand evidence *See* hearsay evidence.

Secretary of State *See* minister.

secret profits Profits made by an *agent during the course of his agency without the knowledge or authorization of his principal. The principal may require the agent to account for secret profits.

secret trust A trust whose existence is not revealed in the document transferring the property to the person who is to be the trustee. It arises when a testator (or more rarely a settlor) gives property to someone on that person's express or implied promise to hold the property on trust for a third party. Such trusts are sometimes called *fully secret trusts*, to distinguish them from *half-secret trusts, but the term secret trust is sometimes used for both. Doctrinal difficulties have arisen with secret trusts because they appear to allow a will to be altered indirectly without the need to comply with the formalities of the Wills Act, and their theoretical basis is unclear.

section 1 committal *See* committal for trial.

secured creditor A person who holds some security, such as a mortgage, for money he has lent. If the debtor becomes bankrupt the creditor has a choice. He may surrender his security and claim the amount of the debt from the bankrupt's assets, like any other creditor; he may realize or evaluate the security and claim any balance of the debt in excess of the value of the security; or he may rely on the security and not make any claim in the bankruptcy proceedings. *Compare* unsecured creditor.

secure tenancy A residential tenancy in which the tenant has statutory protection if he occupies the rented property as his home. It applies only if the landlords are district councils or certain other local authorities, charitable housing trusts, housing associations, or certain public bodies, such as the Housing Corporation. Certain tenants are excluded from protection; these include students, the occupants of almshouses and accommodation for the homeless, and those renting accommodation on long leases.

If a secure tenancy is for a fixed term, the tenancy continues at the end of the term as a *periodic tenancy. A landlord can only terminate a secure tenancy by serving a notice on the tenant in a special statutory form and can only obtain possession with the tenant's consent or, if this is refused, by a court order. An order is granted only if the landlord has statutory grounds similar to those required in the case of a *protected tenancy. When the holder of a secure tenancy dies, his spouse or a member of his family who has lived with him for the past 12 months can succeed him as tenant.

securities *pl. n.* Loosely, *stocks, *shares, *debentures, *bonds, or any other rights to receive dividends or interest. Strictly, the term should only be used for rights that are backed by some sort of security, as in the case of debentures.

security for costs A sum payable by a plaintiff to a civil action as a condition of being permitted to continue with the action. The court has discretion whether or not to order security for costs and may exercise it only in four circumstances: (1) when the plaintiff is ordinarily resident out of the area of the jurisdiction; (2) when the plaintiff is suing on behalf of someone who will be unable to pay the defendant's costs if ordered to do so; (3) when the plaintiff's address is dishonestly not stated or incorrectly stated on the writ or originating process; or (4) the plaintiff has changed his address during the course of the proceedings in order to evade the consequences of the litigation. A defendant may not be ordered to give security for costs. When security is ordered the plaintiff is usually ordered to pay a sum into court.

security of tenure Statutory protection given to tenants that restricts landlords' rights to obtain possession. The conditions for obtaining possession vary according to the kind of tenancy, but a court order is usually required. *See* agricultural holding; business tenancy; long tenancy; protected tenancy; protected shorthold tenancy; protected occupier; secure tenancy; statutory tenancy.

sedition *n.* The speaking or writing of words that are likely to incite ordinary people to public disorder or insurrection. Sedition is a common-law offence (known as *seditious libel* if the words are written) if it is committed with the intention of (1) arousing hatred, contempt, or disaffection against the sovereign or her successors (but not the monarchy as such), the government of the UK, or either House of Parliament or the administration of justice; (2) encouraging any change of the law by unlawful means; or (3) raising discontent among Her Majesty's subjects or promoting ill-will and hostility between different classes of subjects. There must be an intention to achieve these consequences by violence and disorder. An agreement to carry out an act to further any of these intentions is a criminal *conspiracy.

seduction *n.* **1.** Enticement to have sexual intercourse. Until 1971 parents could sue a seducer for loss of services of their child, but this has now been abolished. It is an offence for a parent to cause or encourage the seduction of a daughter under the age of 16. **2.** The offence under the Incitement to Disaffection Act 1934 of maliciously and advisedly endeavouring to persuade any member of HM forces to abandon his duty or allegiance to the Crown.

seisin *n.* Possession of a freehold estate in land. *See also* unity of seisin.

select committee A committee appointed by either House of Parliament or both Houses jointly to investigate and report on a matter of interest to them in the performance of their functions. Examples are the committees of the Commons that examine government expenditure or the activities of government departments and the nationalized industries, and the *Joint Committee on Statutory Instruments.

self-build society A *housing association whose object is to provide, for sale to or occupation by its members, dwellings built or improved principally by their own labour.

self-defence *n.* A defence at common law to charges of *offences against the person (including homicide) when *reasonable force is used to defend oneself, or one's family, or anyone else against attack or threatened attack. The scope of the defence often overlaps with the statutory right to use reasonable force to prevent a crime, but also extends to cases in which the statutory right is inapplicable (for example, when the attacker is for some reason not guilty of a crime). There is no rule of law that a person must retreat before acting in self-defence. If a person acting in self-defence mistakenly uses more force than was necessary in the circumstances and kills his attacker, he has no defence of self-defence (since the force was not reasonable) and the killing will therefore amount to murder, unless he can show that there was also *provocation. However, in deciding whether the force used was justified or reasonably thought to be justified, the jury must bear in mind the difficulty of quickly assessing the correct amount of force to be used.

self-determination *n.* (in international law) The right of a people living within a non-self-governing territory to choose for themselves the political and legal status of that territory. They may choose independence and the formation of a separate state, integration into another state, or association with an independent state, with autonomy in internal affairs. The systems of *mandates and trusteeship marked a step towards recognizing a legal right of self-determination, but it is not yet completely recognized as a legal norm. It is probably illegal for another state to intervene against a liberation movement and it may be legal to give assistance to such a movement.

self-employed *adj.* In business on one's own account, i.e. not engaged as an employee under a *contract of employment. A self-employed person may nevertheless be the employer of others.

self-help *n.* Action taken by a person to whom a wrong has been done to protect his rights without recourse to the courts. Self-help is permitted in certain torts, such as *trespass and *nuisance. A trespasser may be evicted provided only reasonable force is used. A nuisance may be abated (*see* abatement). *See also* recaption.

seller *n.* The party to a contract of *sale of goods who transfers or agrees to transfer ownership of the goods to the buyer. The term may also be used in the context of the transfer of the ownership of land, but a seller of land is more usually called a *vendor*.

semisecret trust *See* half-secret trust.

Senate of the Inns of Court and the Bar The governing body of the barristers' branch of the legal profession, established in 1974 by a merger of the Senate of the Four Inns of Court and the General Council of the Bar.

sentence *n.* The judgment of a court stating the *punishment to be imposed on a defendant who has pleaded guilty to a crime or been found guilty by the jury. Before the sentence is imposed, the prosecution must present the judge with the accused's *antecedents and the defence may then make a plea in *mitigation of the sentence. If the probation officer wishes to make a report, this should be done before the defence makes its plea in mitigation (*see* social

inquiry report). The judge may also obtain reports from nonlegal specialists (medical experts or social workers) on the mental, physical, social, or personal circumstances of the accused; if such reports are not immediately available, he may adjourn the case (and remand the accused) until they are obtained. Reports are desirable when the sentence may involve a *probation order or when the defendant is facing his first prison sentence. The court must have reports before making a *community service order, when the offender is under 21 years old, or before attaching conditions for medical treatment to a probation order.

Sentence must be pronounced in open court by the presiding judge and is almost always pronounced in the presence of the accused. The sentence may be altered (or rescinded) within 28 days by the trial court, and the Crown Court also has a further (common-law) power to postpone sentence for more than 28 days when circumstances require this (e.g. when disqualifying from driving under the *totting-up provisions, if the driving licence is not available). There is also a power to postpone sentence for up to six months (*see* deferred sentence).

Courts have very wide discretionary powers of sentencing in all crimes (except murder and treason). The penalties prescribed by law are maximum penalties, to be imposed in the most serious cases, and the judge must decide what is the appropriate sentence in each case. Apart from imprisonment (which may be a *concurrent sentence, an *extended sentence, or a *suspended sentence) and *fines, the courts can impose probation orders, community service orders, and *hospital orders, as well as an absolute or conditional *discharge. (For the sentencing of young offenders, *see* juvenile offender.) Magistrates' courts have less extensive powers of sentencing, but may sometimes, upon convicting an offender, remit him to the

Crown Court for sentence (e.g. when he has been tried summarily for an offence triable either way). There is usually a right of appeal against sentence to the *Court of Appeal. *See also nulla poena sine lege.*

separate trials *See* joinder of defendants.

separation *n. See* judicial separation order; living apart.

separation agreement An agreement between husband and wife releasing each other from the duty to cohabit. Such an agreement will only be valid (subject to the ordinary rules of the law of contract) if the marriage has already broken down; it will be void (contrary to public policy) if they enter into it to provide for the contingency that the marriage may break down at some future date. Separation agreements often contain further clauses (e.g. nonmolestation clauses, maintenance clauses, *dum casta* clauses) or an agreement not to bring other matrimonial proceedings based on past conduct ("*Rose* v *Rose* clauses"). A spouse may also relinquish his rights or powers in relation to his children, but the court has an overriding discretion not to enforce such provisions if they are not for the children's benefit. A separation agreement in writing may be a *maintenance agreement and governed by the Matrimonial Causes Act 1973.

separation of powers The doctrine that the liberty of the individual is secure only if the three primary functions of the state (legislative, executive, and judicial) are exercised by distinct and independent organs. It was propounded by Montesquieu (*De l'Esprit des Lois*, 1748), who regarded it as a feature of the UK constitution. In fact, however, while the judiciary is largely independent, the legislature and the executive depend on one another and their members overlap. The doctrine had a great influence over the form adopted for the constitution of the USA and many other countries.

sequestration *n.* A court order in the form of a writ to (usually four) commissioners (*sequestrators*), ordering them to seize control of a person's property. The order may be made against someone who is in *contempt of court because he has not complied with a court order (such as an injunction). The property is detained until he complies with the order.

servant *n.* An *employee.

service *n.* **1.** The delivery of a *writ, *summons, or other document relating to court proceedings. Service may be made by physically handing the document to the person concerned (*see* personal service) or it may be delivered to the *address for service supplied by that person (*see also* substituted service). Once the document has been formally issued by the court, it must be served within 12 months unless the court allows this period to be extended. In the case of certain motoring offences, such as speeding and careless driving, the police must serve a summons within 14 days unless the accused was warned at the time of the offence that he might be prosecuted or unless they serve a *notice of intended prosecution within 14 days. **2.** *See* contract of service.

service law The law that regulates the conduct of members of the armed forces. It consists of *naval law, military law,* and *air-force law* (military law is the branch relating to the army, but the expression is frequently used to describe all three branches). Its primary sources are the Naval Discipline Act 1957, the Army Act 1955, and the Air Force Act 1955; supplementary sources are Admiralty Instructions and the *Queen's Regulations* both for the Army and for the Royal Air Force. The three Acts concerned require annual renewal. Every fifth year an Armed Forces Act enables them to continue in force for one year and provides that for each of the following four years they may be continued in force by an Order in Council that has been approved by resolution of each House of Parliament. The purpose of this procedure (which did not apply to the Naval Discipline Act 1957 until this was provided by the Armed Forces Act 1971) is to ensure that Parliament has an annual opportunity of debating matters relating to the armed forces.

Service law is a specialized code of criminal law. Its essential concern is the maintenance of discipline and it embodies a variety of offences (e.g. *desertion, malingering, and insubordination) that have no counterpart in the ordinary criminal law. Commanding officers have powers of dealing with minor offences summarily, but the tribunals primarily responsible for the trial and punishment of offences are the *courts martial. Service law applies to a member of the armed forces wherever he may be. In the UK he is subject both to service law and to the ordinary criminal law. When he is not in the UK, the ordinary criminal law does not in general apply to him; the relevant Acts therefore provide that it is an offence under service law for any serviceman to do anything that constitutes an offence under the ordinary criminal law. The effect of this general provision is to create, in the case of a member of the armed forces who is in the UK, a duality of offences. If, for example, a soldier in the UK steals, he commits an offence against both the ordinary criminal law and service law. He cannot, however, be punished under both.

Although service law applies primarily to members of the armed forces, certain classes of civilians are also subject to it. These include civilians employed outside the UK within the limits of the command of any officer commanding a body of the regular forces and the families of members of the armed forces residing with them outside the UK. The inclusion of the latter has had the effect of extending the jurisdiction of courts martial to cases with which they are manifestly not equipped to deal. This has led to the establishment of *standing civilian courts.

service out of the jurisdiction *Service of the originating *process outside England and Wales. *Leave of the court is required, which will only be granted in a limited number of situations specified by *rules of court. In general, some particular connection must be shown between the defendant or the subject matter of the proceedings and the jurisdiction of the English courts.

service tenancy A tenancy in which the landlord is also the tenant's employer and the premises were let as a condition of that employment. Although such a tenancy is a *protected tenancy, the landlord can obtain possession by applying to the county court when he ceases to employ the tenant and needs the accommodation for another employee.

servient tenement Land that is subject to an encumbrance, such as an easement, profit *à prendre*, or restrictive covenant, created for the benefit of other land, called the *dominant tenement*.

set-off *n.* A monetary cross-claim that is also a defence to the claim made in the action by the plaintiff. In modern practice, any claim by a defendant to a sum of money (whether of an ascertained amount or not) that is also used as a defence may be set off against the plaintiff's claim. The importance of the distinction between a set-off and a *counterclaim arises principally in relation to *costs when both parties are successful. If the defendant's plea is a set-off, the plaintiff will recover the amount of his claim less the amount set off, and in the county courts, the costs will normally be calculated in relation to the net sum recovered. If the defendant's plea is a counterclaim, the plaintiff will recover the costs of the claim and the defendant the costs of the counterclaim,. subject to the court's overriding discretion as to costs.

setting aside An order of a court cancelling or making void some other order or *judgment or some step taken by a party in the action.

setting down for trial The final stage of the *interlocutory proceedings in an action begun by writ in the High Court. The plaintiff is required to file with the court two sets of documents, including the *writ, *pleadings, all orders made on the summons for directions, and certain legal-aid documents (if any). The case is then entered in the appropriate list of cases awaiting trial.

settled *adj.* Ordinarily resident in the UK and not subject under immigration law to any restriction on length of stay there. *See* British citizenship; immigration.

settled land Land that is the subject of a *settlement under the Settled Land Act 1925, i.e. land in which two or more beneficial interests exist in succession to one another or land that is subject to certain other fetters on the owner's powers. The categories are as follows. (1) Land held in trust for any persons by way of succession; for example, in trust for A for life then B for life then C in fee simple. (2) *Entailed interests. (3) Land owned subject to a *gift over on a specified event. (4) Land owned for a *determinable interest. (5) Land conveyed to a person under 18 years (a minor cannot own or convey a legal estate in land). (6) Land in which a future interest may come into possession on a specified event. For example, when land is left to A and B provided they respectively attain the age of 18, the elder is absolutely entitled to a half share on reaching 18 but may become entitled to the whole of the land absolutely if the younger dies during minority. (7) Land charged voluntarily (i.e. without *consideration) or in consideration of marriage or by way of family arrangement with payment of any rentcharge or capital sum; for example, when the owner charges his land with payment of income to his wife during her life or widowhood.

A settlement made during the life of the settlor is effected by a *trust instrument* and a *vesting deed*. The trust instrument declares the beneficial interests in the land and appoints two or more individuals, or a trust corporation (e.g. a bank), as *trustees of the settlement* (*see* Settled Land Act trustees). The vesting deed transfers the legal estate in the settled land to the immediate beneficiary; it must also identify the trustees of the settlement. A will that effects a settlement constitutes the trust instrument; the legal estate devolves upon the testator's personal representatives on trust to vest it, by deed or *assent, in the immediate beneficiary. When the legal estate cannot be transferred to the immediate beneficiary (e.g. because he is under 18), it must be vested in a *statutory owner.

The purpose of the Act is to balance the protection of beneficiaries with future interests against the principle that the person immediately entitled in possession should not be prevented by the existence of future interests from prudently managing and dealing with the land. Thus the Act confers on the immediate beneficiary powers to sell the land at the best price reasonably obtainable, to exchange it for other land, and to grant certain leases (up to 50 years, or 100 years for mining, or 999 years for building or forestry). These transactions *overreach the interests of the subsequent beneficiaries, who acquire corresponding interests in the capital money or income arising from them. The immediate beneficiary may also mortgage the land to raise money to pay off other encumbrances, to give equality of value on an exchange, and to pay for certain improvements. He can insist that the cost of certain improvements (such as rebuilding the *principal mansion house and installation of drainage and electricity) be paid out of capital. His statutory powers may be extended by the terms of the settlement but cannot be excluded or restricted. The Act imposes on the immediate beneficiary, in exercising these powers, the duties of a trustee for all parties having a beneficial interest in the land. When the immediate beneficiary sells or otherwise disposes of settled land, the vesting deed forms the basis of his title. The purchaser is not concerned with the interests of beneficiaries whose rights are overreached (*see* curtain provisions) but must pay the price to the trustees of the settlement or, at the direction of the tenant for life, into court.

Settled Land Act trustees (trustees of the settlement) Two or more individuals or a trust corporation (such as a bank) who are trustees of *settled land. Their primary function is to receive *capital money arising on a sale or other disposition of the land by the immediate beneficiary and to hold it in trust for those entitled under the settlement. Their consent is also necessary before the immediate beneficiary can validly exercise certain of his statutory powers; for example, to sell the *principal mansion house or timber cut from the land if the settlement so requires or to vary rights (such as easements) over other land that benefit the settled land.

The trustees are generally appointed by the trust instrument but must be named in the vesting deed. If no trustees are appointed, the Settled Land Act 1925 provides that they will be either (1) trustees having a power of sale of other land comprised in the settlement and held on similar trusts; (2) trustees having a future power of sale of the settled land; (3) persons appointed by the beneficiaries if they are of full age and

entitled to dispose of the whole settled estate; or (4) the settlor's personal representatives, when the settlement is effected by will. Trustees can also be appointed by the court.

settlement *n.* A disposition of land or other property, made by deed, will, or very rarely by statute (as in the Duke of Marlborough Annuity Act 1706), under which trusts are created by the *settlor designating the beneficiaries and the terms on which they are to take the property. Settlements are of many different kinds; for example, *marriage settlements, *strict settlements, *voluntary settlements, and, particularly, settlements under the Settled Land Act 1925 (*see* settled land).

settlement of action The voluntary conclusion of civil litigation by agreement of the parties. Settlement may be made at any time and is usually followed by the plaintiff filing a *notice of discontinuance. No particular formality must be followed, but if money is claimed by a party under a disability (e.g. a minor or a mental patient), a settlement is not valid (in so far as it relates to his claim) without the approval of the court. *See also* Tomlin order.

settlor *n.* One who creates a *settlement. In a broad sense the term includes testators, but in a more restricted sense it signifies one who settles property during his life.

several *adj.* In separation, as in *joint and several, *several tenancy.

several tenancy Ownership of land by one person absolutely, not jointly or in common with another. *Compare* joint tenancy; tenancy in common.

severance *n.* **1.** The conversion of an equitable *joint tenancy in land into a *tenancy in common. It may be effected by mutual agreement of the joint tenants, the bankruptcy of one of them, or by sale of the land or of one joint tenant's interest. It is not possible to sever a legal joint tenancy, since a tenancy in common cannot exist as a legal estate. Any words in a conveyance of land to two or more people that show an intention that they take separate shares will be construed as *words of severance* creating an equitable tenancy in common, rather than a joint tenancy. **2.** The separation of the good parts of a contract from the bad, which are rejected. The doctrine of severance applies to any contract that is void by statute or common law but not illegal (*see* void contract). The courts will, if possible, save the contract from total invalidity by severing the offending part.

severance pay Money to which an employee is entitled at common law upon the termination of his contract of employment; for example, pay in lieu of notice, when he is dismissed with inadequate notice or none. An employee dismissed before the expiry of a fixed-term contract can claim damages in the courts to compensate him for the loss of pay he would have earned during the rest of the term, unless he was dismissed for a breach of contract entitling the employer to dismiss him. *See also* unfair dismissal; wrongful dismissal.

sex change A change in a person's sexual characteristics, usually by means of surgical operation and hormone treatment. The law does not recognize the validity of such changes. Sex is determined at birth and cannot be legally changed, for example, to enable marriage to take place with a person of the opposite sex to that assumed after the sex change. It may be, however, that this rule contravenes the provisions of the European Convention on Human Rights.

sex discrimination Discrimination on the grounds of sex, which is an offence under two statutes. The Equal Pay Act 1970 forbids having different terms for men and women in their contracts of employment (*see also* equal pay). The Sex Discrimination Act 1975 goes further, prohibiting discrimination when offering a contract of employment and before entering into such a contract. It also prohibits discrimination in employment on the grounds of marital status and discrimination in partnerships with six or more partners, trade unions, qualifying or authorizing bodies, vocational training, and education. The Act provides for special exceptions; for example, when male or female characteristics are a genuine requirement of the job. It is also unlawful to victimize someone who has complained of illegal discrimination. The Act covers both direct and indirect discrimination. The latter includes making conditions that apply to both sexes but in such a way that, for instance, the proportion of women who can fulfil the conditions is considerably less than men. An example would be insisting on a record of continuous service for promotion, which is far more difficult for women to satisfy because of pregnancy and motherhood. The Acts are reviewed by the *Equal Opportunities Commission and enforced by *industrial tribunals.

sexual intercourse The penetration of the vagina by the penis. For the purposes of sexual offences involving intercourse, penetration need only be slight and rupture of the hymen or ejaculation are not required. *See also* unlawful sexual intercourse.

sexual offence Any crime that involves sexual intercourse or any other sexual act. The main crimes in this category are *rape, *buggery, *incest, *indecent assault, *indecent exposure, *gross indecency, *abduction, and *child abuse.

shadow director A person who is not a director of a company but who gives instructions (rather than professional advice) according to which the directors are accustomed to act. Certain statutory provisions (for example, those relating to put and call *options) apply to both shadow directors and directors proper.

sham marriage A marriage entered into for some ulterior motive, without the intention of cohabiting with the other party. Such marriages will usually nonetheless be deemed valid, unless one of the parties (e.g. a person trying to escape extradition) deceives the other party as to his identity or the marriage is entered into to escape a threat to life, limb, or liberty (e.g. to enable a person imprisoned under harsh conditions to leave his or her country) or to escape imprisonment.

sham plea *See* false plea.

share One of a large number of titles of ownership of an incorporated company but not of its property (i.e. it is a chose in action). A *shareholder* is a member of the company and his name is recorded on the *register of members. Shares provide the means by which the members of a company can share in the profits of the company, vote at general meetings, and share in the distribution of the assets on a member's *voluntary winding-up while at the same time limiting their liability in the case of any other kind of winding-up. If a *limited company is forced into liquidation fully paid-up shareholders are not liable for any company debts, although their shareholding itself may become valueless.

Preference shares are usually fixed-interest securities, the holders of which have a prior claim to dividends and return of capital. *Participating preference shares* carry the right to share in any surplus profits or capital. Preference shares are usually cumulative in that if no dividend is declared in one year, holders are entitled to arrears when eventually one is paid. Preference shareholders usually have voting rights restricted to matters concerning their *class rights.

Ordinary shares constitute the risk capital of a company as they carry no prior rights over dividends and returned capital. The ordinary shareholders, however, have other advantages not shared by preference shareholders: if the company is successful and is able to pay high dividends, the bulk of this (after paying the fixed interest preference shareholders) will be shared by the ordinary shareholders. Again, if the company is successful, the value of the ordinary shares will rise while the preference shares will be pegged to a value determined by current interest rates. Ordinary shareholders, except those holding nonvoting "A" shares, will have full voting rights at company meetings. "A" shares rank equally with voting shares in respect of dividends and other rights and are sometimes issued by companies wishing to raise further capital without diluting the control of the company.

Redeemable shares are issued subject to the proviso that they will or may be bought back (at the option of the company or the company member) by the company. They cannot be bought back unless fully paid-up and then only out of profits (*see* capital redemption reserve) or the proceeds of a fresh issue of shares made for the purpose.

share capital *See* capital.

share certificate A document issued by a company certifying that a named person is a company member and stating the number of shares registered in his name and the extent to which they are paid up (*see* call). A company can be precluded by *estoppel from denying its accuracy. The certificate must normally be produced on a *transfer of shares. *Compare* share warrant.

share premium The amount by which the price at which a share was issued exceeds its nominal value (*see* authorized capital). Share premiums must be credited by the company to a *share premium account*, which is subject to the rules relating to *reduction of capital and can only be used for certain purposes, e.g. paying up bonus shares (*see* bonus issue).

share transfer A document transferring registered shares, i.e. shares for which a *share certificate has been issued. A share transfer in proper form must be delivered to the company before it places the transferee's name on the register of members (Stock Transfer Act 1963). *See also* transfer of shares.

share warrant A document issued by a company certifying that the bearer is entitled to the shares specified in it. The name of the bearer will not appear on the register of members until he surrenders the warrant to the company in return for *transfer of the shares, but he may be regarded as a company member under the provisions of the articles of association. The company is contractually bound to recognize the bearer as shareholder. *Compare* share certificate.

sheriff *n.* The principal officer of the Crown in a county. In relation to the administration of justice, his (or her) functions (in practice discharged by the under-sheriff) include the execution of *process issuing from criminal courts, levying forfeiture of *recognizances, and the *enforcement of judgments of the High Court by writs of *fieri facias*, possession, and delivery.

sheriff's interpleader *See* interpleader summons.

shifting use (secondary use) Formerly, a *use that operated to terminate a preceding use. For example, if property was given to X to the use of A, but then to the use of B when C paid £100 to D, B had a shifting use, which arose when C made the specified payment.

ship *n.* For the purposes of the Merchant Shipping Act 1894 (which provides among other things for the registration of British ships), any vessel used in navigation and not propelled by oars. For the purposes of ownership, a British ship is notionally divided into 64 shares. Each share may be in different ownership, but no share may be in the ownership of an alien or a foreign company.

shipwreck *n. See* wreck.

shock *n. See* nervous shock.

shoplifting *n.* Dishonestly removing goods from a shop without paying for them. A shoplifter could be charged with *making off without payment under the Theft Act 1978, but it is more usual to charge them with *theft under the Theft Act 1968. It is not legally necessary to remove the goods from the shop precincts in order to be guilty of shoplifting, but in practice it is advisable to wait until the accused has left the shop before stopping him, as it is then easier to prove the intention to steal (*see also* citizen's arrest). A cashier in the shop who deliberately rings up a lower price than the true price may be guilty of aiding and abetting shoplifting.

short cause list A list of cases for trial in the High Court for which the trial is expected to last less than four hours. Short cause lists are maintained in the Queen's Bench and Chancery Divisions and the Admiralty Court.

short committal *See* committal for trial.

short title *See* Act of Parliament.

sic utere tuo ut alienum non laedas [Latin] Use your own property in such a way that you do not injure other people's: a maxim often used in cases of nuisance. It is misleading, since only an unreasonable interference with a neighbour's property is actionable as a nuisance.

signature of will *See* execution of will.

silence *n. See* right of silence.

silk *n. See* Queen's Counsel.

similar-fact evidence Evidence that a party, especially the accused, has on previous occasions misconducted himself in a way similar to the conduct being alleged against him in the proceedings before the court. The evidence frequently takes the form of a *previous conviction. In general, the prosecution may not offer similar-fact evidence as part of its case unless it can be shown to be relevant to an issue before the jury, for example by rebutting some defence advanced by the accused. Thus, if a person charged with fraud contends that he was honestly mistaken, the fact that he has committed similar frauds on previous occasions may be admissible. The judge may in his discretion exclude otherwise admissible similar-fact evidence if he considers that its prejudicial effect is likely to outweigh its probative value.

simple contract (parol contract) Any *contract other than one made by *deed (a *contract under seal*).

simple trust *See* bare trust.

sittings *pl. n.* (in the *Supreme Court) The four periods of the legal year during which the full range of judicial business is transacted. They are Michaelmas, Hilary, Easter, and Trinity. Sittings were substituted for *terms by the Judicature Act 1873. *See also* vacations.

slander *n.* A defamatory statement made by such means as spoken words or gestures, i.e. not in permanent form. Generally slander is only actionable on proof that its publication has caused special damage (actual financial or material loss), not merely loss of reputation. Proof of special damage is not necessary when the slander implies the commission of a criminal offence punishable by imprisonment, infection with a contagious disease, or unchastity in a woman or is calculated to disparage a person in his office, business, trade, or profession. *See* defamation.

slander of goods (disparagement of goods) A false statement, made maliciously, that disparages the quality of goods manufactured and sold by the plaintiff. It is a form of the tort of *malicious falsehood. In order to be actionable, the statement must allege some specific defect in the plaintiff's goods. A mere assertion by a rival trader that his goods are better is not sufficient, even if the claim was false and malicious.

slander of title A false statement, made maliciously, that impugns a vendor's title to sell property. It is a form of the tort of *malicious falsehood.

slip rule The rule permitting the correction of clerical mistakes arising from any accidental slip or omission in judgments or orders. Such errors can be corrected at any time by the court on *motion or *summons without an appeal.

small agreement (under the Consumer Credit Act 1974) A regulated *consumer-credit agreement for credit not exceeding £30, other than a hire-purchase or conditional-sale agreement, or a regulated *consumer-hire agreement that does not require the hirer to make payments exceeding £30. In both cases the agreement is either unsecured or secured by a guarantee or indemnity only. Some small agreements are outside certain provisions of the Act.

small claims Civil actions in which a small sum is claimed by the plaintiff. The term has come to be applied almost exclusively to actions in which a consumer is suing a commercial concern, e.g. in respect of shoddy goods. In the county courts special provision is made for cases in which a claim not exceeding £500 is defended: such cases are referred to *arbitration before the registrar. A simplified informal procedure is then followed. There were formerly private arbitration schemes for such disputes in London and Manchester calling themselves *Small Claims Courts*, but these have now ceased.

social inquiry report A report prepared by a probation officer and made to a criminal court to assist it in deciding what *sentence to impose on a convicted person. The report gives details of the person's background, family, home circumstances, relationships, attitudes, job situation, and prospects. It is based on interviews with the accused person and his family and friends. The report gives the probation officer's opinion on the suitability of particular kinds of sentence; for example, how well the accused would be likely to respond to an order for community service.

social policy rule See interpretation of statutes.

sodomy n. See buggery.

soldier's will See privileged will.

solemn form See probate.

sole solicitor A solicitor who is the sole principal of a practice, rather than one who practises in partnership with others.

soliciting n. The offence by a prostitute of attempting to obtain prospective clients in a street or public place. It is punishable by a *fine not greater than level 2 of the standard scale (as defined by the Criminal Justice Act 1982) on a first conviction and by a fine not greater than level 3 on a subsequent conviction, even if the offence was committed before the Act came into force. Any act committed by the prostitute (even smiling provocatively) may constitute soliciting, but an advertisement inviting men to visit her is not soliciting. "Street" is widely defined to include roads, lanes, bridges, courtyards, alleyways, passages, etc., open to the public, as well as doorways and entrances of houses on the street, and ground adjoining and open to the street. If a prostitute in a private house attracts the attention of men in the street (for example by tapping on the window and inviting them in, or even merely by sitting at the window illuminated by a red light), this may be considered soliciting "in a street".

It is also an offence for a man to solicit persistently in a public place for immoral purposes. This includes both heterosexual and homosexual conduct (even if this is not in itself not illegal), but its exact scope is unclear. "Persistently" requires either a number of single invitations to different people or more than one invitation to one person.

solicitor n. A legal practitioner admitted to practice under the provisions of the Solicitors Act 1974. Practising solicitors must possess a *practising certificate. Solicitors form much the larger part of the English legal profession (compare barrister), undertaking the general aspects of giving legal advice and conducting legal proceedings. They have *rights of audience in the lower courts but may not act as advocates in the Supreme Court (except in chambers) or the House of Lords. A solicitor may be sued for professional negligence and owes the duties of a *fiduciary to his client, including the duty to preserve the confidentiality of the client's affairs.

solicitor and own client basis of costs A basis of taxation of *costs on which is calculated the sum that a privately represented client must pay his own solicitor. On this basis, all costs are allowed provided that they are of a reasonable amount and have not been unreasonably incurred.

Solicitor General A law officer of the Crown immediately subordinate to the *Attorney General. The Solicitor General is usually a Member of Parliament of the ruling party. He acts as deputy to the Attorney General and may exercise any power vested by statute in the latter (unless the statute otherwise provides) if the office of Attorney General is vacant or the Attorney General is unable to act through illness or has authorized him to act.

Solicitors Disciplinary Tribunal A tribunal established under the Solicitors Act 1974 for hearing applications and complaints against solicitors. It has the power to strike the name of a solicitor off the roll and to restore the name of a solicitor previously struck off, suspend a solicitor from practice, and order the payment of a penalty. The members of the tribunal are practising solicitors of not less than ten years' standing and some lay members. They are appointed by the *Master of the Rolls.

solicitor's lien The right of a solicitor to retain papers or property of his client as security for the payment of his costs. There are two types of lien: a retaining lien, i.e. a right to retain property already in his possession until he has been paid costs due to him; and a lien on property recovered or preserved, i.e. a right to ask the court to direct that personal property recovered under a judgment obtained by his exertions stand as security for his costs of the recovery. By statute the second type has been extended to confer upon the court the power to make a *charging order over real and personal property recovered or preserved in proceedings by the solicitor.

Solicitors Practice Rules Rules, made by the Council of the *Law Society with the agreement of the *Master of the Rolls, for regulating the professional practice, conduct, and discipline of solicitors. The power to make the rules is conferred by the Solicitors Act 1974.

sovereign *n. See* Crown.

sovereign immunity The exemption of the sovereign or other head of a foreign state and foreign governmental departments from the jurisdiction of the English courts. The principles governing this exemption are now contained in the State Immunity Act 1978.

The immunity granted is no longer absolute; it is subject to numerous exceptions outlined in the Act.

sovereignty *n.* Supreme authority in a state. In any state sovereignty is vested in the institution, person, or body having the ultimate authority to impose law on everyone else in the state and the power to alter any pre-existing law. How and by whom the authority is exercised varies according to the political nature of the state. In many countries the executive, legislative, and judicial powers of sovereignty are exercised by different bodies. One of these bodies may in fact retain sovereignty by having ultimate control over the others. But in some countries, such as the USA, the powers are carefully balanced by a constitution. In the UK sovereignty is vested in Parliament (*see* sovereignty of Parliament).

In international law, it is an essential aspect of sovereignty that all states should have supreme control over their internal affairs, subject to the recognized limitations imposed by international law. These limitations include, in particular, the international law of *human rights and the rules forbidding the use of force. However, no state or international organization may intervene in matters that fall within the domestic jurisdiction of another state. The concept of state sovereignty was outlined, among other things, in a declaration on Principles of International Law (Resolution 2625), proclaimed by the General Assembly of the United Nations in 1970.

sovereignty of Parliament The constitutional principle that the legislative competence of Parliament is unlimited. No court in the UK can question its power to enact any law that it pleases. In practice, however, Parliament does not assume unlimited authority; it can legislate only for territories that are recognized by international law to be within its competence, i.e. the UK, the

Channel Islands and the Isle of Man, and UK dependencies.

Speaker *n. See* House of Commons; Lord Chancellor.

special administration *See* limited administration.

special agent *See* agent.

special business Business that can only be transacted at a general meeting if its general nature has been specified in the notice convening the meeting. *See* annual general meeting; extraordinary general meeting.

special case 1. A statement of facts agreed by the parties to a civil action and directed by the court to be tried at a different time from that of the trial of the action. It may raise issues of fact or law and should be signed by counsel if settled by him. **2.** Formerly, a statement of the findings of an arbitrator, submitted for the opinion of the High Court. This procedure has now been replaced by a form of *appeal on a question of law only.

special damages *See* general and special damages.

special endorsement *See* endorsement.

special hospital A hospital (e.g. Broadmoor or Rampton) controlled and managed by the Home Secretary for persons suffering from *mental disorder who require detention under special security conditions, because of their dangerous, violent, or criminal propensities.

special notice The 28 days' notice that is required to be given to a registered company of an intention to propose certain resolutions at a *general meeting. These resolutions are: (1) appointing a new auditor or providing expressly that the retiring auditor shall not be reappointed; (2) removing a director before his term of office expires or appointing a new director to replace

him at the same meeting; and (3) appointing or approving the appointment of a director over the age limit.

special parliamentary procedure *See* special procedure orders.

special plea A *plea in bar of arraignment, e.g. *autrefois acquit* or *autrefois convict*.

special power *See* power of appointment.

special procedure (in divorce proceedings) *See* divorce.

special procedure orders A form of *delegated legislation consisting of orders made by government ministers under powers that are expressed in the enabling statute to be exercisable by order subject to *special parliamentary procedure*. The Statutory Orders (Special Procedure) Act 1945 then applies, and, after a local inquiry is held, the order must be laid before Parliament and petitions for its annulment or amendment may be presented. Special procedure orders, which have largely replaced provisional orders, are used primarily to confer powers on local authorities. The *compulsory purchase of land must also in certain cases (e.g. land owned by local authorities or the National Trust) be effected by a special procedure order.

special resolution A decision reached by a majority of not less than 75% of company members voting in person or by proxy at a general meeting. At least 21 days' notice must be given of the intention to propose a special resolution.

special trust *See* active trust.

specialty *n. See* deed.

special verdict 1. A verdict of not guilty by reason of *insanity. **2.** A verdict on particular questions of fact, without a general conclusion (in criminal cases) as to guilt or (in civil cases) in favour of the plaintiff or the defendant. The judge asks the jury their opinion on the facts, but decides the general question himself. Such verdicts in criminal cases are very rare. *Compare* general verdict.

specification *n.* (in *patent law) A document that must be lodged with an application for a patent for an invention. It must contain a description of the invention, a claim defining the matter for which the applicant seeks protection, and any drawing referred to in the description or claim.

specific delivery *See* writ of delivery.

specific devise *See* devise.

specific goods Goods specifically identified at the time a contract of sale is made, e.g. a named car with a specified registration number. If the subject matter is not so identified, the contract is for the sale of *unascertained goods. In a contract for the sale of specific goods the seller is bound to deliver the identified goods and no others.

specific legacy *See* legacy.

specific performance A court order to a person to fulfil his obligations under a contract. For example, when contracts have been exchanged for the sale of a house, the court may order a reluctant seller to complete the sale. The remedy is a discretionary one and is not available in certain cases; for example, for the enforcement of a contract of employment or when the payment of damages would be a sufficient remedy.

specimen of blood A specimen of blood for analysis, used as an alternative to a *specimen of breath in cases involving *drunken driving. A police officer may require a specimen of blood if he reasonably believes that he cannot demand a breath specimen for medical reasons, if an approved and reliable device for taking a breath specimen is unavailable or cannot be used, or if the defendant is suspected of being unfit to drive and a doctor believes that his condition is due to a drug. A police officer

may also ask for a blood specimen if the suspect is in hospital (subject to the consent of the doctor treating him). A suspect may be asked to give a blood specimen under these conditions even if he has already given a breath specimen.

A blood specimen may only be taken with the defendant's consent and by a medical practitioner, otherwise it cannot be used as evidence in any proceedings. It must be analysed by a qualified analyst, who must sign a certificate stating how much alcohol he found. The suspect may ask to be given half the specimen for his own analysis, which may be used to contradict the prosecution's evidence; if he has asked for but was not given half of the sample, the other half may not be used in evidence against him. A *specimen of urine may sometimes be taken as an alternative to a blood specimen.

In all other respects the law relating to blood specimens is the same as that relating to breath specimens.

specimen of breath A specimen of breath for analysis taken from a person suspected of *drunken driving. It is this specimen that usually forms the evidence for a prosecution and conviction for offences of drunken driving and should not be confused with the preliminary *breath test. It may be required whenever the police are investigating any of these offences, but only if the suspect is at the police station. Usually he will have been brought to the station under arrest as a result of a positive breath test or refusal to undergo such a test. It is an offence not to provide a specimen without a reasonable excuse, and the police officer should warn a suspect of this when asking for the specimen. This offence is punishable by fine or imprisonment, endorsement (carrying 10 points under the *totting-up system), and discretionary disqualification (in cases of being in charge of a vehicle) or compulsory disqualification (in cases of driving or attempting to drive).

The suspect must give two breath specimens, which should be measured by means of an approved electronic device (not the *breathalyser used for the preliminary breath test) that automatically prints out the level of alcohol in the breath. A print-out of the lower of the two readings is used as evidence in a subsequent trial, together with a signed certificate by a police officer that it refers to the defendant's specimen given at the stated time. The defendant must be given a copy of these documents at least seven days before his trial, and he may serve notice not later than three days before the trial that he requires the police officer who signed it to attend the hearing. At his trial, a defendant may bring evidence to show that he drank more alcohol between the time of the alleged offence and giving the specimen and that this accounted for his exceeding the prescribed limit. It is an offence, however, to deliberately drink more alcohol in order to make it difficult to prove his guilt.

Once a suspect has given a specimen he is free to leave the police station, but the police may detain him if they reasonably suspect that he is likely to continue driving with an excess alcohol level or while unfit to drive. Under certain circumstances the suspect can provide a *specimen of blood or a *specimen of urine instead of a breath specimen. If the breath specimen records a reading of more than 35 but less than 50 micrograms of alcohol per 100 ml of breath, the suspect is entitled to ask that it should be replaced by a blood or urine specimen.

specimen of urine A specimen of urine for analysis, used as an alternative to a *specimen of breath in cases involving *drunken driving. A specimen of urine may be required when there are objections to taking a breath specimen and when a medical practitioner thinks that a *specimen of blood should not be taken for medical reasons. A urine specimen must be provided within one hour after it has been asked for; two specimens are asked for, and it is the second specimen that is used as evidence in a subsequent trial. In all other respects the law relating to urine specimens is the same as the law relating to blood and breath specimens.

speeding *n*. Driving a motor vehicle at a speed in excess of that permitted. All vehicles adapted to carry more than seven passengers (apart from the driver) and all goods vehicles are restricted at all times to a maximum speed of 40 mph (unless they weigh less than 30 cwt unladen, in which case the maximum speed is 50 mph). Invalid carriages are restricted to 20 mph. Goods vehicles exceeding 3 tons unladen are restricted on motorways to 60 mph. Other vehicles are subject to speed limits determined by the class of road, unless road signs specifically indicate otherwise (i.e. 30 mph for restricted roads; 60 mph for single carriageways; 70 mph for dual carriageways and motorways).

The penalty for speeding is a fine, *endorsement (carrying 3 points under the *totting-up system), and discretionary *disqualification. A person cannot be convicted of a speeding offence on the evidence of one witness alone, but the evidence of a single police officer reading his speedometer may be enough to secure a conviction. Speeding may itself be evidence of *careless or *reckless driving, but it is an offence in its own right even if it caused no danger and the driver was not in any way at fault. Speeding offences are subject to the requirement of a *notice of intended prosecution.

spent conviction A conviction that, after a specified number of years known as the *rehabilitation period*, may in all subsequent civil proceedings be treated as if it had never existed. The length of the rehabilitation period depends on the gravity of the offence, and some convictions are not subject to rehabilitation (e.g. when the sentence was life imprisonment or imprisonment or corrective training for 30 months or more). Dismissal from a job on the grounds of an undisclosed spent conviction may amount to *unfair dismissal. Similarly, to deny that one has been convicted if the conviction is spent does not amount to *perjury or *deception. The provisions relating to spent convictions do not apply in criminal proceedings, but counsel and the court should, as far as possible, avoid referring to a spent conviction and references to it in open court may only be made with express leave of the judge in the interests of justice. A spent conviction in a record should be marked as such.

split order An order for *custody of a child made by divorce courts, granting legal custody to one parent and *care and control to the other. The purpose of a split order is usually to enable both parents to have some control over the child's upbringing (especially the father, in cases in which the mother has to have day-to-day control of the child but the father is the "innocent" spouse). In recent years the courts have tended to disapprove of split orders, favouring wherever possible an order for joint custody. There are also powers under the Guardianship of Minors Act 1971 and under the Domestic Proceedings and Magistrates' Courts Act 1978 for the court or magistrates to give legal custody to one parent and certain specified parental rights and duties to the other (although they cannot grant legal custody to both parents). *See also* custody disputes.

springing use Formerly, a *use that arose on the occurrence of a future event. If property was given to X to the use of A when A married, A had a springing use that arose on his marriage.

spying (espionage) *n.* Obtaining or passing on to an enemy information that might prejudice the safety or interests of the state or be useful to an enemy. *See* official secrets.

squatter *n.* A person unlawfully occupying land. *See* adverse occupation; adverse possession; trespass.

squatter's title *See* adverse possession.

stag *n.* A speculator who applies for a new issue of securities in a public company with the intention of making a quick profit by reselling them if they increase in value within a few days of issue. This will only occur if the issue is oversubscribed, i.e. if there are more applicants for shares than there are shares available.

stakeholder's interpleader *See* interpleader summons.

stamp duty A tax payable on certain legal documents specified by statute. It can take the form either of a fixed duty, in which the same amount is payable on all documents of the same kind, or an *ad valorem* duty, when the amount of duty varies according to the value of the transaction effected by the document. Documents that are insufficiently or improperly stamped cannot be admitted as evidence in civil proceedings and they are therefore legally unenforceable. Documents must be sent for stamping within certain time limits to avoid incurring penalties. Stamp duty is controlled by the Inland Revenue.

standard-form contract A commercial contract (e.g. a routine contract of carriage or insurance) that is concluded on terms issued by the offeror in standard form and allows for no effective negotiation. In French law such a contract is known as a *contrat d'adhésion*.

standard of proof The degree of proof required for any fact in issue in litigation, which is established by assessing the evidence relevant to it. In criminal cases the standard is *proof beyond reasonable doubt (see also* burden of proof); in civil cases (including divorce petitions) the standard is proof on a balance of probabilities.

standing civilian court A court, provided for by the Armed Forces Act 1976, for the trial outside the UK of lesser offences committed by certain civilians, e.g. the families of servicemen (*see* service law). The Secretary of State for Defence (with the approval of the Lord Chancellor) specifies which areas such courts serve and draws up panels of serving officers and civilians to sit as assessors. The Lord Chancellor appoints legally qualified persons to act as magistrates in the courts.

standing committee A committee of the House of Commons appointed to take the committee stage of public Bills allotted to it by the government. There are about 8 such committees, each consisting of between 16 and 50 members who are nominated by a Committee of Selection to reflect the political composition of the House as a whole. *Compare* Committee of the whole House.

standing mute The refusal of the defendant in a trial on indictment to plead to the indictment. A jury, drawn from any 12 people who happen to be present, must be empanelled to say whether the defendant is *mute of malice* (i.e. is wilfully refusing to plead) or is *mute by visitation of God* (i.e. is suffering from some physical or mental impairment that is preventing him from pleading). None of the jurors may be challenged by the defendant. If the verdict of the jury is mute of malice, a plea of *not guilty is entered; if mute by visitation of God, the jury must consider whether the defendant is *unfit to plead.

A person who is merely deaf and dumb may plead to an indictment through an interpreter.

stare decisis [Latin: to stand by things decided] A maxim expressing the underlying basis of the doctrine of *precedent, i.e. that it is necessary to abide by former precedents when the same points arise again in litigation.

state *n.* A sovereign and independent entity capable of entering into relations with other states (*compare* protected state) and enjoying international legal personality. To qualify as a state, the entity must have: (1) a permanent population (although, as in the case of the Vatican or Nauru, this may be very small); (2) a defined territory over which it exercises authority (although its borders, as in the case of Israel, need not be defined or undisputed); (3) an effective government. There are currently over 150 states. When a new state comes into existence, it is automatically bound by the principles of international law.

For some purposes, entities that do not normally qualify as fully fledged states may nonetheless be treated as such. Liechtenstein, for example, was refused admission as a state to the League of Nations (and is not a member of the United Nations), but is a party to the Statute of the International Court of Justice, which is only open to states. Namibia (*see* mandate) is a member of the International Labour Organisation, which is only open to states.

statement of affairs A document that must be prepared by a debtor after a *receiving order has been made against him. It gives details of his assets, debts and liabilities, the names and addresses of his creditors, and what securities they hold. The debtor must send the statement to the official receiver, and the creditors are entitled to inspect it. *See also* bankruptcy.

statement of claim A *pleading served by the plaintiff in an action begun by *writ of summons in the High Court. According to the *Rules of the Supreme Court, the plaintiff must serve a statement of claim upon the defendant within 14 days after the defendant gives *notice of intention to defend, unless the court gives leave to the contrary or a statement of claim is endorsed on the writ. The statement of claim contains the allegations that the plaintiff is making against the defendant in the action and states the relief that the plaintiff seeks.

statement of reasons for dismissal A written note of the reasons for an employee's dismissal. Under the Employment Protection (Consolidation) Act 1978, a dismissed employee having 26 weeks' *continuous employment in the business may demand such a statement from his employer and may complain to an industrial tribunal if the statement is refused or untrue.

state of emergency *See* emergency powers.

status *n.* A person's legal standing or capacity. The term derives from Roman law, in which it referred to a person's freedom, citizenship, and family rights.

statute *n.* *See* Act of Parliament.

statute-barred debt A debt that has not been recovered within the period allowed by the legislation relating to *limitation of actions. Such a debt can no longer be recovered by action. The limitation period for debts due on promises under seal is 12 years from the date the debt became due. For other debts the limitation period is six years from the date the debt became due. However, in certain contracts of loan that do not provide for repayment of the debt by a fixed date and in which repayment is not conditional on a demand by the creditor, the six-year period will not start to run until the creditor makes a demand in writing for repayment of the debt.

statute book The entire body of existing statutes.

statute law The body of law contained in Acts of Parliament. *Compare* case law.

statutorily protected tenancy A tenancy that has *security of tenure and, in most cases, statutory control of rent.

statutory assignment *See* assignment.

statutory company A *company incorporated by private Act of Parliament. Such companies were commonly formed in the 19th century for the development of railways, canals, gas and water supplies, etc., by private enterprise. Few statutory companies remain, most having been nationalized.

statutory corporation *See* public corporation.

statutory declaration A *declaration made in a prescribed form before a justice of the peace, notary public, or other person authorized to administer an oath. Statutory declarations are used in extrajudicial proceedings and not in court, but have similar effects to declarations made on oath.

Statutory Form of Conditions of Sale Standard terms of contract for the sale and purchase of land, published by the Lord Chancellor under the Law of Property Act 1925. They cover, for example, the vendor's obligations in proving his title to the land, the completion of the transaction, and the payment of interest by the purchaser if he fails to complete on the due date. The Statutory Form applies automatically to contracts made by correspondence subject to any express agreement between the parties, and any valid contract for the sale and purchase of land may be expressed to incorporate the Statutory Form.

statutory instrument Any *delegated legislation (not including subdelegated legislation) to which the Statutory Instruments Act 1946 applies. This includes (1) delegation made under powers conferred by an Act passed after 1947, either on the Crown or on a government minister, and expressed by that Act to be exercisable by Order in

Council in the former case or by statutory instrument in the latter; or (2) delegation made after 1947 under powers conferred by an earlier Act and formerly governed by the Rules Publication Act 1893 (which was replaced by the 1946 Act and provided for the publication of delegated legislation to which it applied in an official series known as *statutory rules and orders*).

The 1946 Act relates in part to the publicity to be given to statutory instruments, requiring them to be numbered, printed, and published by the Queen's printer. They are numbered consecutively for each calendar year in the order in which the printer receives them; for example, the first statutory instrument to be received in 1983 would be cited as "S.I. 1983 No. 1". Moreover, as a modification of the rule *ignorantia juris non excusat*, (ignorance of the law is no excuse), the Act makes nonpublication a defence to proceedings for contravening a statutory instrument unless other adequate steps had been taken to bring it to the public notice. The Act is also concerned with certain aspects of parliamentary control. It standardizes negative resolution procedure for statutory instruments by providing that, if the enabling statute simply makes them subject to annulment by resolution of either House of Parliament, they are to be laid before Parliament for 40 days and liable to annulment during that period. It further provides that any statutory instrument required to be laid (either because of that rule or because the enabling statute expressly says so) must be laid before becoming operative unless there is good reason to the contrary (in which case, an explanation must be given to the Lord Chancellor and the Speaker). *See also* Joint Committee on Statutory Instruments.

statutory interpretation *See* interpretation of statutes.

statutory lives in being *See* rule against perpetuities.

statutory owner A person having the powers of an immediate beneficiary of *settled land, where the beneficiary himself is under 18 or there is no immediate beneficiary (for example, in a discretionary settlement in which no beneficiary has been appointed). The statutory owner is either the person of full age on whom the powers are conferred by the settlement; the trustees of the settlement (*see* Settled Land Act trustees); or, in a settlement made by will on a beneficiary under 18, the testator's personal representatives until a vesting instrument has been effected.

statutory rules and orders *See* statutory instrument.

statutory tenancy A tenancy that comes into existence when the contractual element of a *protected tenancy is terminated and the former protected tenant continues to live in the property (a company cannot be a statutory tenant). A statutory tenancy continues only for as long as the tenant lives in the property (thus it will end if the tenant attempts to sublet). When the tenant dies, however, the statutory tenancy can be transmitted to his spouse or any other member of his family who has lived with him for the last six months. This is known as a *statutory tenancy by succession*. The terms of a statutory tenancy are, in general, the same as those of the original contractual tenancy. If there is no provision for notice in the original tenancy, the tenant must give three months notice to terminate his tenancy. A landlord can terminate a statutory tenancy only by obtaining a court order for possession.

statutory trust A trust created by statute when land is held by trustees on trust pending its sale. Any income from the land prior to its sale and the proceeds of sale itself are held in trust by the trustees. Unless there is a contrary intention, the trustees have the right, at their discretion, to postpone sale.

stay of execution An order suspending the *execution of the order of a court. In the High Court a stay of execution by writ of *fieri facias* may be granted subject to the condition that the debtor pays the judgment debt by specified instalments (unlike the county courts, the High Court has no other power to order the payment of judgment debts by instalments).

stay of proceedings An order by the court suspending proceedings, usually because of some misconduct by the plaintiff (e.g. in a claim for damages for personal injury, unreasonably refusing to attend for medical examination by a doctor nominated by the defendant).

stipendiary magistrate A barrister or solicitor of not less than seven years' standing, appointed by the Lord Chancellor to sit in a magistrates' court on a full-time salaried basis. *Metropolitan stipendiary magistrates* sit in magistrates' courts for Inner London; other stipendiary magistrates sit in large provincial centres. They have power to perform any act and to exercise alone any jurisdiction that can be performed or exercised by two justices of the peace, except the grant or transfer of any licence. In other respects their powers are the same as other justices.

stock *n*. **1.** A fixed-interest loan raised by the government or a local authority. **2.** Shares in a registered company that have been converted into a single holding with a nominal value equal to that of the total of the shares. For example, a holder of 100 shares of £1 each will have £100 stock after conversion.

Stock Exchange A market in London in which securities in public companies are bought and sold. Only securities that have been granted a *quotation can be dealt in on the Exchange. The Stock Exchange consists of an association of *stockbrokers* and *stockjobbers*. Typically, a prospective buyer or seller approaches a broker, who will negotiate a deal with a jobber. Jobbers maintain holdings of quoted securities and will price them according to demand and available information bearing on the company's prospects. The Council of the Exchange regulates proceedings in order to safeguard both members and the investing public; it has the power to discipline both brokers and jobbers for misconduct.

stock relief A tax allowance on the value of a business's stock (or work in progress). The amount of the allowance is a proportion of the value of the stock at the beginning of the accounting period. The allowance is calculated by deducting £2000 from the opening stock and multiplying the balance by appropriate percentages from the All Stocks Index. The resulting figure is deducted from the business's profits for tax purposes.

stop notice 1. A court procedure available to protect those who have an interest in shares but have not been registered as company members. The notice prevents the company from registering a transfer of the shares or paying a dividend upon them without informing the server of the notice. **2.** A notice served by a local planning authority when they consider that any activity specified in an *enforcement notice should be prevented before the time for compliance given by that notice. It takes effect on a date specified therein, which is 3 to 28 days after service, and a site notice may be posted, drawing attention to its provisions.

stoppage *in transitu* A remedy available to an *unpaid seller of goods when the buyer has become insolvent and the goods are still in course of transit. If the seller gives notice of stoppage to the carrier or other bailee of the goods, he is entitled to have them redelivered to him and may then retain possession of them until the price is paid or tendered. If the right is not exercised, the goods will fall into the insolvent buyer's estate and go towards satisfying his creditors generally.

street offence Any offence relating to the use of public streets. Examples are *obstruction, failing to obey police regulations about movement of traffic or pedestrians, *loitering, and *soliciting.

strict construction *See* interpretation of statutes.

strict liability 1. (in criminal law) Liability for a crime that is imposed without the necessity of proving *mens rea*. (It is also known as *absolute liability*.) There are no crimes of strict liability at common law but such crimes are often created by statute, particularly to control or regulate daily activities; examples include offences relating to the production and marketing of food and drugs and *parking offences. The usual penalty for crimes of strict liability is a fine. Most crimes of strict liability do, however, require *mens rea* in respect of at least some of the elements of the crime. In some cases statute provides for strict liability, but then allows a defence if the accused can show that he had no reason to know of or suspect certain facts, so that, in effect, the crime becomes one of *negligence. *Automatism is a defence to all crimes, including crimes of strict liability. **2.** (in tort) Liability for a wrong that is imposed without the necessity of proving intention or negligence on the part of the defendant. Strict liability is exceptional in the law of tort, but is imposed for torts involving dangerous animals (*see* classification of animals) and dangerous things (the rule in **Rylands** v *Fletcher*), *conversion, *defamation, and some cases of *breach of statutory duty. It is no defence in these torts that the defendant took reasonable care to prevent damage, but various other defences are admitted.

strict settlement A trust conferring beneficial interests in land that render it *settled land, governed by the Settled Land Act 1925. Generally the purpose of a strict settlement is to create successive interests that will keep the land in the settlor's family. The usual form of marriage settlement gave a life interest to the husband with remainder (after provisions for the wife during widowhood and for younger children of the marriage) to the first and other sons in *tail, a further remainder to any daughters as tenants in common in tail, and a final remainder to the husband in fee simple. The beneficiaries under a strict settlement have equitable interests in the land. *Compare* trust for sale.

strike *n.* A cessation of work or refusal to work by employees acting together in connection with a *trade dispute to secure better terms and conditions of employment for themselves and/or other workers. Under the Employment Act 1980, dismissal of an employee for taking part in a strike or other industrial action is only *unfair dismissal if the employer does not dismiss all those taking part or if he offers to re-engage some but not all of them after the industrial action ends.

striking off 1. The removal of a solicitor's name from the roll of solicitors of the Supreme Court, either at his request or for misconduct. **2.** A similar procedure in other professions (e.g. the erasure of a doctor's name from the register of general medical practitioners).

subdelegated legislation Legislation made under powers conferred by *delegated legislation or by subdelegated legislation itself (in which case it is technically sub-subdelegated legislation). Subdelegated legislation is quite common (as when the parent Act authorizes a minister to make regulations and these in turn authorize others to make orders), but sub-subdelegated legislation is rare (though examples have existed in wartime); the chain has not in practice been further extended. Subdelegated legislation is not subject to any form of parliamentary control but it is subject to judicial control by means of the doctrine of *ultra vires*.

subject to contract *See* acceptance.

sub judice **rule 1.** A rule limiting comment and disclosure relating to judicial proceedings, in order not to prejudge the issue or influence the jury. *See* contempt of court. **2.** A parliamentary practice in which the Speaker prevents any reference in questions or debates to matters pending decision in court proceedings (civil or criminal). In the case of civil proceedings, he has power to waive the rule if a matter of national interest is involved.

sublease (subtenancy, underlease) *n.* A *lease granted by a person who is himself a lessee of the same property. The sublease must be shorter than the main lease. Thus a lessee with a lease for 10 years can grant a sublease for a period up to 10 years less one day. The formalities for creating and terminating a sublease are the same as those for a lease. There is often a covenant in a lease prohibiting subletting. If a lessee sublets in breach of the covenant the sublease will be valid, but the landlord may have a right of *forfeiture of the lease. In some cases the lease specifies that the lessee may only sublet with the landlord's consent. In this case, the landlord may not withhold his consent unreasonably and he cannot charge a fee for giving his consent unless there is express provision for this in the lease. If the main lease is forfeited, any sublease automatically comes to an end. However, the surrender of a lease does not affect any sublease.

subletting *n.* The granting of a *sublease.

submortgage *n.* A mortgage of a mortgage. A *submortgagor* is a person who holds a mortgage over another's land and charges that mortgage as security for a debt he owes to a third party (the *submortgagee*). If the submortgagor defaults, the submortgagee may sell the mortgage (but not the land) and recover the debt from the proceeds.

subnormality *n.* *See* arrested development.

subordinate legislation *See* delegated legislation.

subornation *n.* Procuring another to commit an offence. Normally subornation is included in the offence of aiding, abetting, or procuring (*see* accessory), but there is a special statutory offence of *subornation of perjury*.

subpoena *n.* An order to a person to appear in court on a certain day to give evidence. The party calling the witness must pay his reasonable expenses. A witness who fails to comply with a subpoena is in *contempt of court. The order is made under penalty (*sub poena*) of fine or imprisonment for default. There are two kinds of subpoena: a subpoena *ad testificandum*, requiring a person to give evidence; and a subpoena *duces tecum*, requiring him to produce particular documents that are required as evidence.

subrogation *n.* The substitution of one person for another so that the person substituted succeeds to the rights of the other. Thus an insurer who indemnifies his insured against the loss of goods may be subrogated to the insured person's rights against a third party whose negligence caused the loss.

subscribing witness A person who signs a written document as witness to the signature of another.

subsequent pleadings Pleadings in a civil action after the *reply of the plaintiff. The subsequent pleadings are *rejoinder, *surrejoinder, *rebutter, and *surrebutter. They can only be served with *leave of the court.

subsidiary company A company controlled by another company, its *holding* (or *parent*) *company*, either through shareholding alone or through shareholding coupled with control of the composition of the subsidiary's board of directors, as defined in the Companies Act 1948. For example, a company is a subsidiary of another if more than half of its ordinary *shares are held by the parent company, which thus has voting control of the general meeting of the subsidiary, or if the parent company holds less than half the ordinary shares but has an unfettered power to appoint or remove all or the majority of the subsidiary. If company A controls company B, which itself controls company C, then company C is the subsidiary of both company B and company A. *See also* group accounts.

substantial damages *See* damages.

substantial performance *See* performance of contract.

substantive law The part of the law that deals with rights, duties, and all other matters that are not matters purely of practice and procedure. *Compare* adjective law.

substituted service The service of documents in civil litigation other than by *personal service or (when postal service is permitted) by post. An order of the court is required for substituted service, and the application for it must be supported by an *affidavit. It may take the form of service by letter, advertisement, or any other method likely to bring the proceedings to the attention of the defendant. Substituted service has all the effects of personal service. It is often sought against defendants who are deliberately evading personal service.

substitutional legacy A legacy that passes to descendants of the beneficiary named in the will if he has predeceased the testator. *See also* representation.

subtenancy *n. See* sublease.

subtenant *n.* A tenant who holds a *sublease.

subtrust (derivative trust) *n.* A trust created out of a trust. If A has an interest under a trust and declares himself trustee of the interest for B and C, B and C have interests under a subtrust as far as the original settlor is concerned.

succession *n.* The law and procedures under which beneficiaries become entitled to property under a testator's will or on intestacy.

sue *vb.* To make a claim for a remedy in the civil courts by issuing court proceedings.

sufferance *n. See* tenancy at sufferance.

suicide *n.* The act of killing oneself intentionally. Since 1961 suicide itself is not a crime, but there is a special statutory crime (punishable by up to 14 years' imprisonment) of aiding, abetting, counselling, or procuring a suicide. In practice very few prosecutions are brought for this offence. Doing nothing to stop someone else from committing suicide is not abetting it, but euthanasia (mercy killing) in the form of giving assistance to the sufferer (rather than actually killing him) may amount to aiding. When two people agree that one of them shall kill the other and then commit suicide (a suicide pact), the one who does the killing is guilty, if he survives, not of murder but of manslaughter.

sui juris [Latin: of his own right] Describing the status of a person who is of full age and capacity. *Compare alieni juris.*

suit *n.* A court claim. The term is commonly used for any court proceedings although originally it denoted a suit in equity as opposed to an action at law. When a case is referred to as (for example) "Jones at the suit of Smith" (*or* "Jones a.t.s. Smith") Jones is the defendant in an action brought by Smith.

summary conviction A *conviction in a magistrates' court. The magistrates are the judges of both fact and law and must either convict the accused or dismiss the case. The usual form of words for a conviction is "We find the case proved", and a conviction may be returned on a simple majority verdict. Under the Magistrates' Courts Act 1952, the magistrates may remand the accused for a medical examination if they are satisfied that he has committed the act he is charged with, but are in doubt as to his mental condition and whether or not to make a hospital order. Such a finding has the force of a conviction for purposes of the accused's right to be granted bail.

summary judgment under Order 14
A procedure enabling a plaintiff in an action for debt or damages in the High Court to obtain judgment without the defendant being permitted to defend the action. It can be used in any action begun by writ except when this includes a claim for *libel, *slander, *malicious prosecution, or *false imprisonment or an allegation of *fraud. The plaintiff takes out an *Order 14 summons* supported by an *affidavit, in which he must swear that he believes there is no defence to the action. The defendant may file affidavits in reply. At the hearing the master may give judgment for the plaintiff, unless the defendant shows that there is an issue or question in dispute that ought to be tried or that there ought, for some other reason, to be a trial. The defendant may then be given *leave to defend.

summary offence An offence that can only be tried summarily, i.e. before magistrates. Most minor offences are summary. Prosecutions for all summary offences must be started within six months of the commission of the offence, unless statute expressly provides to the contrary. *Compare* indictable offence; offences triable either way.

summary trial Trial by magistrates without a jury. All summary offences are tried in this way, as well as some

*offences triable either way. The main procedural principles followed in *trial on indictment also apply to summary trial, but there are some differences of which the most important are as follows. (1) The accused does not usually have to be present at the hearing. (2) Objections cannot usually be made either to information laid before the magistrates or to a summons or warrant served on the defendant on the grounds of "defects of substance or form" (unless they are fundamental defects). (3) In the case of summary offences, the accused may send in a written plea of guilty, together with a statement of mitigation, and the case may then be tried without the prosecution or defence appearing.

summing up A judge's speech at the end of a trial by *jury, in which he explains to the jury what its functions are, directs the members of the jury on any relevant points of law, and summarizes all the evidence that has been given in the trial.

summons *n.* A court order to an individual to appear in court at a specified place and time. The term is used both in criminal cases (for appearance at a magistrates' court) and in civil cases (for hearings in the county court and applications to a judge, registrar, or master sitting in chambers about procedural matters prior to the court hearing). *See also* service; default summons; originating summons. *Compare* writ.

summons for directions A summons that must be taken out by the plaintiff in an action begun by writ in the High Court for the court to consider the preparations for the trial of the action. The summons must be taken out within one month after *close of pleadings. At the hearing of the summons the court will give directions for the trial of the action (including the time for *setting down) and consider any outstanding matters relating to the interlocutory procedure, e.g. whether or not a party should deliver further and better *particulars of his pleadings. *See also* automatic directions.

superior court Any of the higher courts of the legal system, whose decisions have weight as *precedents. In English law, the superior courts are the *House of Lords, the *Court of Appeal, the *High Court, and the *Crown Court, together with the *Judicial Committee of the Privy Council and certain courts of special jurisdiction, such as the *Restrictive Practices Court. Decisions of superior courts are not subject to judicial review by the High Court. *Compare* inferior court.

superior orders A plea that certain conduct does not constitute a crime because it was committed in obedience to the orders of a superior (usually a superior officer in the armed forces). It could arise, for example, on the unjustified shooting of a rioter when the military are restoring order. UK law does not recognize the plea as a defence in itself. If an order is unlawful, a soldier's duty is to disobey it. If, however, an unlawful order is not manifestly so, the plea could be raised as establishing that the soldier did not have the necessary *mens rea.*

supervision order 1. An order entrusting a minor to the supervision of a local authority or a welfare or probation officer. Supervision orders may be made, for example, by the divorce courts, when awarding the *custody of children; by the High Court, in *wardship proceedings; and by the High Court, county courts, or magistrates' courts in *custody disputes between parents or when refusing to make an adoption order. In each of these cases the granting of an order depends upon the existence of exceptional circumstances. These may include poor housing conditions, physical or psychological problems suffered by the child, inadequacy of one or both parents, or quarrels between them (for example, over access rights over the

child), and orders are usually made upon the recommendation of a welfare officer. The supervisor has no compulsory powers and his duties, which are not defined by statute, may consist merely of informal visits.

A supervision order may also be made by a juvenile court in *care proceedings in respect of a child under the age of 17 or upon trial of a *juvenile offender. The order usually contains conditions relating to where the child should live, his activities, and (if appropriate) psychiatric supervision and treatment (if the child is over 14, the latter condition can only be enforced with his consent).

Supervision orders cease when the child reaches the age of 18 (or, in the case of orders made in care proceedings, three years after the order is made, whichever is earlier). They may be varied or discharged by the court. Various changes in the law relating to supervision orders will come into effect when the relevant provisions of the Criminal Justice Act 1982 are brought into force. **2.** *See* suspended sentence.

supplementary benefit A noncontributory benefit (formerly known as *national assistance*) payable under the Supplementary Benefits Act 1976 to persons over 16 whose income is below a certain minimum. It is administered by the *Supplementary Benefits Commission* (part of the Department of Health and Social Security), in accordance with departmental regulations and rules of practice, and takes the form of either a supplementary allowance or a supplementary pension. Appeals from decisions of the Commission are heard by *supplementary benefit appeal tribunals*. These consist of a chairman and two other members and sit in private, except that members of the Council on Tribunals are entitled to attend.

suppression of documents The dishonest destruction, hiding, or defacing of any valuable security (i.e. almost any document creating, extinguishing, or transferring a right in money or property), will or similar document, or any original document (but not a copy) belonging to or filed in any court or governmental department. If done with the purpose of gaining as a result, or causing loss to someone else, it is an offence punishable by up to seven years' imprisonment. *See also* forgery.

supra protest *See* acceptance *supra protest*.

Supreme Court of Judicature A court created by the Judicature Acts 1873–75 to take over the jurisdiction of all the higher courts, other than the House of Lords, existing at that time. It does not sit as a single court but comprises the *High Court of Justice, the *Court of Appeal, and the *Crown Court. Its practice and procedure are regulated by the *Rules of the Supreme Court.

Supreme Court Practice, The A large-scale work of reference on the practice and procedure of the *Supreme Court of Judicature. The work consists of the *Rules of the Supreme Court and all relevant legislation with immensely detailed annotations. Formerly published annually and known as *The Annual Practice*, it is now published every three years. It is known colloquially, from the colour of its binding, as the *White Book*.

Supreme Court Rule Committee *See* Rules of the Supreme Court.

surety *n.* **1.** Security in the form of money to be forfeited upon nonappearance in court, offered either by the defendant himself or by other people of suitable financial resources, character, and relationship to the defendant. **2.** Any person who offers security for another. *See* bail; recognizance.

surname *n.* A family name. Upon marriage a wife is entitled to take her husband's surname (and title or rank) and

to continue using it after his death or divorce (unless she uses it for fraudulent purposes). A legitimate child, by custom, takes the name of his father and an illegitimate child that of his mother (although the father's name may be entered on the birth registration if both parents agree or an affiliation order names the man as the putative father). Upon adoption a child automatically takes the name of his adoptive parents. *See also* change of name.

surprise *n.* (in court procedure) An unexpected event that causes a party to be put at some disadvantage in litigation. Many rules of pre-trial procedure are designed to prevent surprise; for example, any matter that might otherwise take the opposite party by surprise must be specifically pleaded, and there are rules concerning the exchange of the reports of expert witnesses. Surprise is an argument often put forward by parties seeking to resist amendments of pleadings and other documents; if justifiably raised at trial, it may result in an adjournment being offered to the disadvantaged party.

surrebutter *n.* A pleading served by a plaintiff in reply to the defendant's *rebutter. Such a pleading is very rare in modern practice and can only be served with *leave of the court.

surrejoinder *n.* A pleading served by a plaintiff in answer to the defendant's *rejoinder. Such a pleading is very rare in modern practice and can only be served with *leave of the court.

surrender of tenancy The termination of a *lease, which occurs when a tenant gives up his interest to his landlord. Surrender can be express or implied. Express surrender is usually in the form of a deed. When the lease is for less than three years, no deed is needed provided that the tenant signs a written agreement to surrender. Implied surrender occurs when the actions of both parties show that they consider the

Table C

lease to be at an end; for example, when the tenant gives up possession and the landlord reoccupies the property.

surrender to custody To give oneself into the custody of the court or police at an appointed time and place. It is the primary condition of all releases on *bail to surrender to custody; to achieve this, the court may attach conditions to the bail, such as the provision of a *surety or restrictions on movement. Failure to surrender to custody is an offence (*see* absconding). The police may arrest without warrant anyone whom they reasonably believe is not going to surrender to custody or anyone whom they have been informed by a surety (who wishes to be relieved of his undertaking) is not going to surrender.

survival of cause of action on death At common law all causes of action in personal actions (i.e. contract and tort) died with the person in whom they were vested (*actio personalis moritur cum persona*). By statute, however, all such causes of actions, except for defamation, survive against or for the benefit of the deceased.

survivorship *n. See* commorientes; right of survivorship.

sus law The law empowering the police to arrest any reputed thief or suspected person found loitering with intent to commit an arrestable offence. This law caused much public concern and was abolished by the Criminal Attempts Act 1981. *See* loitering.

suspended sentence A prison sentence that does not take effect immediately. When a person is sentenced to imprisonment for less than two years, the court may order that he should not actually be imprisoned unless he commits another offence within a specified operational period of between one and two years. If the suspended sentence is for a prison term of more than six months, the court may also make a *sus-*

pended sentence supervision order, placing the offender under the care of a probation officer. If the offender fails to comply with the terms of such an order he is liable to a fine.

When an offender has been sentenced to a term of imprisonment of more than three months but less than two years, and the court feels that it would not be right to suspend the whole of the sentence, it may instead make an order for a *partially suspended sentence*, under which the offender serves part of the sentence. The part of the sentence actually served must be at least 28 days, and the part suspended must be at least one quarter of the total sentence (the Secretary of State has power to alter these periods).

symbolic delivery *See* delivery.

synallagamatic contract A contract creating mutual obligations, i.e. one in which each party undertakes to do or refrain from doing something. *See also* unilateral contract.

synod *n.* A deliberative assembly of the clergy. *See* Church of England.

T

Table A Model *articles of association set out in the Companies Act 1948. They apply to all companies limited by shares unless other articles excluding or modifying them are delivered to the Companies Registry when the company is registered.

Table B The form of *memorandum of association specified by the Companies Act 1948 for a company limited by shares.

Table C The form of *memorandum and *articles of association specified by the Companies Act 1948 for a company limited by guarantee and not having a share capital (*see* limited company).

Table D The form of *memorandum and *articles of association specified in the Companies Act 1948 for a company limited by guarantee and having a share capital (*see* limited company).

Table E The form of *memorandum and *articles of association specified by the Companies Act 1948 for an *unlimited company having a share capital.

tacking *n.* Before 1926, the right of a mortgagee who made a second advance to the mortgagor to attach his second advance to the first one so that it had priority over the claims of any intervening mortgagee, provided that he has received no notice of any intervening mortgage. This exception to the rules relating to *priority of mortgages was abolished in 1925.

tail *n.* An *entailed interest.

tail general An *entailed interest under which the class of descendants who can succeed to the land is not limited to the issue of a specified spouse of the first tenant in tail. *Compare* tail special.

tail male An *entailed interest under which only male descendants of the original tenant in tail can succeed to the land. If the male line dies out, the land goes to the person next entitled in *remainder or in *reversion. The interest may be general or special: *see* tail general; tail special.

tail special An *entailed interest under which only the descendants of the first tenant in tail and a specified spouse can succeed to the land; for example, when land is settled on "John and the heirs of his body begotten on Mary". *Compare* tail general.

takeover *n.* The acquisition of control by one company over another, usually smaller, company (the *target company*). This is usually achieved (1) by buying shares in the target company with the agreement of all its members (if they are few) or of only its *controllers; (2) by purchases on the *Stock Exchange; or (3) by means of a *takeover bid. *Compare* merger. *See also* concert party; dawn raid.

takeover bid A technique for effecting a *takeover or a *merger. The bidder makes an offer to the members of the target company to acquire their shares (either for cash or in exchange for shares in the bidding company) in the hope of receiving sufficient acceptances to obtain voting control of the target company. Unless there is a *scheme of arrangement – and providing that the court does not order otherwise – if members holding not less than 90% in value of the shares involved in the bid accept the offer, the bidding company can compulsorily acquire the shares of the remaining members.

talaq *n.* An Islamic divorce, usually effected by a triple declaration ("I divorce you") by the husband to the wife. In some Moslem countries this may be done informally; in other countries it must be pronounced before an authorized officer of the court. It may also be effected by a written *talaqnama*. *See also* extrajudicial divorce.

tangible property *Property that has a physical existence, e.g. chattels and land but not *choses in action nor incorporeal *hereditaments (which are *intangible property*).

tax *n.* A compulsory contribution to the state's funds. It is levied either directly on the taxpayer by means of *income tax, *capital gains tax, *capital transfer tax, and *corporation tax; or indirectly through tax on purchases of goods and services (*see* value-added tax) and through various kinds of duty, e.g. *road tax, *stamp duty, and duties on betting and gaming.

taxable person *See* value-added tax.

taxable supply *See* value-added tax.

taxation of costs The method by which the amount of costs payable by one party to another, or payable by a client to his solicitor, is determined by an officer of the court. In the *Supreme Court in London taxations are conducted by *taxing masters; outside London by *district registrars. The process consists of scrutinizing the *bill of costs and applying to it the basis of taxation (*see* costs) ordered by the court. A dissatisfied party may apply for a review of the taxation by a judge who is assisted by assessors (a taxing master and a practising solicitor). In the county court taxations are conducted by the *registrar with appeal to the judge.

tax avoidance The lawful arrangement or planning of one's affairs so as to reduce liability to tax. *Compare* tax evasion.

tax evasion Any illegal action taken to avoid the lawful assessment of taxes; for example, by concealing or failing to declare income. *Compare* tax avoidance.

taxing master An official of the *Supreme Court of Judicature who conducts *taxations of costs. Taxing masters are usually solicitors and are appointed by the Lord Chancellor with the consent of the Treasury.

taxing statute An Act of Parliament that imposes tax. Any ambiguity is construed in favour of the taxpayer (*see* interpretation of statutes).

tax point The date on which a taxable supply becomes liable for *value-added tax. The rate of tax chargeable on the supply is the rate in force at the tax point, and the supply must be accounted for in the tax period in which the tax point occurs. If the supply is a straightforward sale of goods, the tax point is normally the date on which the customer takes possession of the goods.

For the supply of services, the tax point is normally the date on which the service is completed. In the case of hirings, rentals, continuous or metered supplies (e.g. electricity), and supplies that are subject to progress payments, the tax point is either the date on which an invoice is issued or the date on which payment is received, whichever is earlier. If the supplier issues a tax invoice, this must show the tax point.

tax year (fiscal year) The year of assessment for *income tax, *capital gains tax, and *capital transfer tax purposes. It runs from 6 April to 5 April in the following year. *See also* financial year.

telephone tapping Secretly listening to telephone conversations by interfering with the line. It is illegal except when authorized by the Home Secretary. *See also* electronic surveillance.

tenancy *n.* Broadly, the interest of one who holds land by any right or title. The term is often used in a more restricted sense, however, for the arrangement in which the owner (the *landlord) allows another person (the tenant) to take possession of the land for an agreed period, usually in return for rent. There are many ways of establishing a tenancy, from a formal *lease by deed to an informal verbal arrangement. The latter is legally binding on the parties if it satisfies the requirements for an *agreement for a lease (for example, by the tenant taking possession). A tenancy can also come into existence through statute law (*see* statutory tenancy).

The different kinds of tenancy are: tenancy for a *fixed term, *joint tenancy, *periodic tenancy, *tenancy at sufferance, *tenancy at will, *tenancy by estoppel, and *tenancy in common. The terms and conditions of tenancies vary considerably according to the kind of tenancy and the wishes of the parties. There are many statutory controls which affect tenancies, particularly in relation to *security of tenure and rent. *See also* protected tenancy.

tenancy at sufferance A tenancy that arises when a tenant *holds over and the landlord has not indicated whether or not he agrees to the tenant's continued occupation. If the landlord gives his express agreement, the tenancy becomes a *tenancy at will.

tenancy at will A tenancy that can be terminated by the landlord or the tenant at any time. A tenancy at will usually arises by implication, when the owner of land allows a person to occupy it although he has no *fixed term, *periodic tenancy, or *licence (for example, when a landlord agrees that the tenant may *hold over). More rarely, a tenancy at will may be created by express agreement. If the landlord starts to accept rent on a regular basis, an ordinary *periodic tenancy is created. A tenancy at will of business premises does not have the statutory protection given to a *business tenancy. In the case of residential premises, however, the usual statutory protection will apply (*see* protected tenancy). A tenancy at will can be terminated by the landlord demanding possession or if either he or the tenant dies or parts with his interest in the land.

tenancy by estoppel A tenancy that exists despite the fact that the person who granted it had no legal right to do so. Such a tenancy is binding on the landlord and tenant but not on anyone else. If the landlord subsequently acquires the right to grant the tenancy, it automatically becomes a full legal tenancy.

tenancy for years A tenancy for a *fixed term.

tenancy from year to year A yearly *periodic tenancy.

tenancy in common Equitable ownership of land by two or more persons in equal or unequal *undivided shares.

Each co-owner may sell or dispose of his share by will, and a share does not pass automatically by the right of survivorship on the death of a co-owner but forms part of his estate (*compare* joint tenancy). Under the Law of Property Act 1925 the legal estate is held by the co-owners as joint tenants on trust for themselves as equitable tenants in common, and a *trust for sale is implied.

tenant *n.* A person who is granted a *lease or a *tenancy. A tenant need not be an individual; for example, a company can be a tenant.

tenantable repair The maintenance of a property in a condition fit for letting to a tenant. The phrase is sometimes used in a *covenant to repair. The use of the word "tenantable" has no significant effect on the parties' usual obligations under the covenant.

tenant for life (life tenant) A person owning land for an equitable interest that subsists for the whole of his life but terminates on his death (*see also* life interest). The statutory powers of a tenant for life are laid down by the Settled Land Act 1925 (*see* settled land).

tenant in tail A person entitled in possession or on the death of his ancestor to an *entailed interest.

tenant in tail after possibility of issue extinct The interest of an original tenant in *tail special when the specified spouse has died and there are no heirs entitled to succeed to the entailed interest. The tenant in tail retains his powers under the Settled Land Act 1925 (*see* settled land) but cannot bar the entail (*see* entailed interest). This position cannot arise when the land is held in tail general, since while the tenant in tail lives there is always a possibility he may have children by another wife.

tenant *pur autre vie* *See* estate *pur autre vie*.

tenant's fixtures Fixtures attached to rented property by a tenant that the tenant is entitled to remove at the end of the tenancy. These are: *trade fixtures, ornamental and domestic fixtures (such as blinds and mirrors) whose removal does no serious damage, and (subject to certain statutory rules) agricultural fixtures. Tenants are not entitled to remove any other fixtures.

tender *n.* **1.** An offer to supply (or to purchase) goods or services. Normally a tender must be accepted to create a contract, except when the invitation to tender states unequivocally that the lowest (or highest) tender will be accepted. If the tender is to supply goods as required by the other party, it may be a standing offer and creates contracts as and when particular orders are placed. Whether or not the tenderer can withdraw from supplying future orders depends upon the terms of the tender, in particular whether the tenderer binds himself (for consideration) to execute all orders. **2.** An offer of performance, acceptance of which requires the agreement of the other party, e.g. the tender of the price of goods by a buyer to a seller.

tender before action A *defence to a claim for a debt or liquidated demand alleging that the defendant offered to pay the sum claimed before the plaintiff began his action. In order to rely upon this defence the defendant must pay the sum tendered into court and give notice of the payment to the plaintiff. *See also* payment into court.

tender offer An offer of a company's securities to the public (*see* flotation) at a uniform price (above a specified minimum) that is determined by bids received and ensures that all the securities are taken up.

tenure *n.* Under the *feudal system, the relationship between lord and tenant, which determined the conditions under which the land was held. Today the term is used for the nature of a legal estate in land, i.e. freehold or leasehold. *See also* security of tenure.

term *n.* **1.** Originally, any of four periods of the year during which judicial business had to be transacted. For this purpose terms were abolished by the Judicature Acts 1873–75, and the legal year is now divided into *sittings and *vacations. In the *Inns of Court the year is still divided into terms that have the same names as the court sittings but are shorter. A student *keeps term* as part of the qualification for call to the Bar by dining in his Inn on a specified number of occasions during the term. **2.** Any provision forming part of a contract. A term may be either a *condition or a warranty, depending on its importance, and either an *express term or an *implied term, depending on its form. **3.** The duration of a leasehold interest in land. *See* term of years.

term for years *See* term of years.

term of years (term for years) An interest in land that subsists for or by reference to some specific period of time. It includes interests subsisting for less than a year (e.g. a lease for six months) and periodic tenancies (e.g. a weekly, monthly, or yearly tenancy determinable by notice to quit). *See also* term of years absolute.

term of years absolute A leasehold estate in land: a *term of years that may or may not be brought to an end by notice, forfeiture, or any other event except the death of any person. Thus a lease "to X for 25 years if Y shall so long live" is not a valid term of years absolute. Under the Law of Property Act 1925 a term of years absolute can exist as a *legal estate provided it is created in the required manner, i.e. by deed in the case of a term of three years or more.

territoriality *n.* (in international law) The principle that states should not exercise their jurisdiction outside the area of their territory. They are entitled, however, to exercise jurisdiction within their territory over acts committed by their citizens outside their territory, and all states have jurisdiction over *offences against international law and order. The territory of a state for purposes of jurisdiction includes its ships and aeroplanes. A state may exercise jurisdiction over crimes that are either originated within its territory but completed outside or originated outside its territory and completed inside.

territorial limits The geographical limits within which an Act of Parliament operates, which include, in the UK, the territorial sea up to the three-mile limit. The limits are restricted by international law (*see* sovereignty of Parliament).

territorial waters The band of sea between the coastline of a state and the high seas, over which the state has certain specified rights. These rights are governed by a 1958 Geneva Convention, which is taken to represent the position under customary international law. New rules are proposed in a 1982 United Nations Convention on the Law of the Sea, which is not yet in force. A coastal state exercises sovereignty over its territorial waters, which includes, in particular, the following. (1) An exclusive right to fish and to exploit the resources of the seabed and subsoil of the seabed and exclusive use of the airspace above the territorial sea. (2) The exclusive right to use the territorial waters to transport people and goods from one part of the state to another. (3) The right to enact laws concerning navigation, immigration, customs dues, and health, which bind all foreign ships. (4) The right to ask a warship that ignores navigation regulations to leave the territorial waters. (5) Certain powers of arrest over merchant ships and people on board and jurisdiction to try crimes committed on board such ships within the territorial waters. (6) The right to

exclude fighting in the territorial waters during a war in which the coastal state is neutral. All foreign ships, however, have a right of *innocent passage* through the territorial sea, i.e. the right to pass through, provided they do not prejudice the peace, security, or good order of the coastal state (submarines must navigate on the surface).

The extent of the territorial sea is usually measured from the low-tide mark on the shore. The width of the territorial sea is a matter of dispute in international law. Traditionally it has been fixed at 3 nautical miles, but many states have claimed 12 miles or more, and this will probably become the normal width. Beyond the territorial sea, states have a *contiguous zone* (at present 12 miles from the low-tide mark, to be replaced by a 24-mile limit), in which they may exercise jurisdiction over certain infringements of their customs, fiscal, immigration, or sanitary regulations. In recent years many states (including the UK) have also claimed *exclusive fishery zones* extending 200 miles beyond the low-tide mark. The United Nations Convention proposes a new 200-mile *exclusive economic zone*, which would give the coastal state sovereign rights over all the resources of the sea, seabed, and subsoil within the economic zone.

See also law of the sea.

terrorism *n.* The use of violence, or putting the public or any section of it in fear, for political purposes. The Northern Ireland (Emergency Provisions) Act 1978, which applies only to Northern Ireland, contains detailed provisions for questioning, searching, arresting, and trying suspected terrorists; it also creates special offences relating to terrorism. The Act defines a terrorist as a person who is or has been concerned with committing or attempting to commit any act of terrorism or directing, organizing, or training people for the purpose of terrorism.

The 1978 Suppression of Terrorism

Act brings into force in English law the provisions of the 1977 European Convention on the Suppression of Terrorism. It provides that a large number of offences often committed by terrorists are not to be treated as offences of a political nature, so that persons suspected of having committed them are liable to extradition under the relevant Acts. Offences under the Explosive Substances Act 1883 and indictable offences under the Firearms Act 1968 are also made extraditable offences. The Act also gives jurisdiction to the English courts to try specified terrorist offences committed abroad in a Convention country and also provides safeguards for wanted criminals who, if extradited, might suffer on account of their race, religion, nationality, or political opinions.

See also hijacking; hostage; proscribed organization.

testament *n.* A *will. Strictly speaking, a testament is a will dealing only with the testator's personal property, not his land.

testamentary capacity The ability to make a legally valid will. Persons under 18 years (apart from members of the armed forces on active service – *see* privileged will) and mental patients do not have testamentary capacity. The testator must, at the time he makes his will, understand the nature of the document, the property of which he is disposing, the persons who have a natural claim to provision from his estate, and the manner in which he provides for his estate to be distributed.

testamentary expenses Costs incurred by a deceased's personal representatives in administering his estate.

testamentary freedom The principle that a person is free to dispose of his property by will in whatever manner he chooses. This freedom is restricted by the Inheritance (Provision for Family and Dependants) Act 1975, which allows a deceased person's dependants to apply to the court for provision from his estate if his will does not adequately provide for them.

testamentary guardian A person appointed by will to be the *guardian of a child under 18.

testamentary intention The principle that a person's will must reflect his true wishes. Thus a will executed as a result of coercion, fraud, or undue influence will be set aside by the court.

testamentary trust A trust contained in a will.

testate *adj.* Having left, at one's death, a legally valid will.

testator *n.* A person who makes a will.

testatum *n. See* deed.

test case A case brought to test a principle of law that, once established, can be applied in other cases. Thus when there are a number of claimants with similar claims, a test case may be brought by one of them, after which the remainder of the claims can be settled out of court on the same basis. *Compare* representative action.

testimonium *n. See* deed.

testimony (testimonial evidence) *n.* A statement of a witness in court, usually on oath, offered as evidence of the truth of what is stated.

textbooks *pl. n.* Textbooks are sometimes cited in court to assist in the interpretation of the law. They have no authority as a source of law but merely provide an expert opinion as to the current state of the law. There was formerly a convention that only the works of dead authors could be cited, but modern practice also allows citation of living authors. The *Books of Authority*, i.e. the works of Glanvil, Bracton, Littleton, Coke, and Blackstone, are treated as having the same authority as cases of the same period.

theft *n*. The dishonest appropriation of property belonging to someone else with the intention of keeping it permanently. It includes any act showing that one is treating the article as one's own and need not necessarily involve taking it away (for example, purporting to sell someone else's property could amount to an appropriation). "Property" includes all tangible and intangible objects and choses in action (e.g. bank balances) but there are special rules in the Theft Act 1968 governing land and wild plants and animals (*see* poaching). Property belongs to anyone who either owns it or has physical possession or control of it. The dishonesty of the accused is a question of fact to be decided in each case by the jury, on the basis of the standard of honesty of the reasonable man at the time. The Act, however, expressly states that a person is not dishonest if he believes (even if unreasonably) that he is legally entitled to appropriate the property or that the owner would agree. The punishment for theft is up to ten years' imprisonment.

Obtaining goods or services without paying for them is now covered by the offence of *making off without payment (see also* shoplifting). Cases in which property is obtained by deception are usually dealt with as *deception offences. Theft involving the use of force may amount to *robbery (*see also* burglary).

thing *n*. *See* chose.

third-party directions Directions given by the court for the conduct of *third-party proceedings. When a third party has acknowledged service of the third-party notice the defendant who issued it must take out a summons for third-party directions. At the hearing of the summons the matters to be considered will include *pleading and *discovery in the third-party proceedings and the possible joinder of the third party as an additional defendant to the action between the plaintiff and the defendant.

third-party insurance Insurance against risks to people other than those that are parties to the policy. It is illegal to use, or allow anyone else to use, a motor vehicle on a road unless there is a valid insurance policy covering death, physical injury, or damage caused by the use of the vehicle in Great Britain. It also covers any liability resulting from the use of a vehicle (or a trailer) that is compulsorily insurable in EEC countries. The policy is only considered valid when a certificate of insurance has been issued.

There is a duty upon anyone driving a motor vehicle to give his name and address and that of the car owner and to produce the certificate of insurance whenever asked to do so by a police officer. He may, however, produce it within five days at any police station he specifies at the time he was asked to produce it. There is also a duty to give details of one's insurance to any person making a claim against it or to any chief police officer who is checking whether the legal requirements of insurance are complied with. Breach of any of these duties is punishable by fine. *See also* driving without insurance.

third-party proceedings Proceedings brought by a defendant to a civil action against a person not already a party to the action. The most common claim brought in third-party proceedings is one for *contribution or *indemnity, but other claims connected with the subject matter of the action between the plaintiff and the defendant may be brought. The proceedings are begun by a *third-party notice*, which may be issued without leave of the court before service of the defence; thereafter, leave is required. *See also* third-party directions.

three certainties *See* trust.

three-tier system A system for allocating cases between *Crown Court centres. First-tier centres deal with both criminal and High Court civil cases and are served by High Court *puisne judges, *circuit judges, and *recorders. Second-tier centres deal only with criminal cases, but are served by the same kinds of judge as first-tier centres. Third-tier centres deal only with criminal cases and are served by circuit judges and recorders only.

tied cottage A dwelling provided for the tenant of a *service tenancy. The term is usually used in relation to agricultural workers' accommodation. *See also* agricultural dwelling-house advisory committee; protected occupier.

time charter *See* charterparty.

time immemorial *See* legal memory.

time policy A marine insurance policy that covers a ship against risks arising in the course of any voyage during a specified period. It differs from a *voyage policy*, which covers against risks arising in the course of a specified voyage of any duration. A policy may, however, be *mixed*, i.e. restricted in cover as to both time and voyage. *See also* deviation.

time provisions in contracts Provisions in contracts that relate to the time within which acts are to be performed. The question often arises whether or not a time provision constitutes a *condition of the contract. If it does, it is said that time is *of the essence*. In general, time is of the essence only if the contract says so or if an intention that it should be so is to be inferred from the nature of the transaction or the circumstances surrounding it.

title *n.* **1.** A person's right of *ownership of property. Someone with a *good title* has adequate evidence to establish his right. *See* absolute title; qualified title; title deeds. **2.** The heading of an *Act of Parliament, which may be a *long title* or a *short title*. **3.** The name of

a particular court action, which is derived from the heading of the writ or summons that initiated it.

title deeds The documents that prove a person's ownership of land and the terms on which he owns it. In the case of unregistered land they consist of all *conveyances, *mortgages, and other documents tracing ownership of the land back to a good *root of title at least 15 years old. The title deeds to registered land are the land certificate or charge certificate (*see* land registration).

Tolzey Court *See* Bristol Tolzey Court.

Tomlin order A form of order used to give effect to a compromise of litigation in the High Court. It is based on a *Practice Direction issued by Mr Justice Tomlin in 1927. The order is made by consent of the parties and states that on terms agreed between them (which are scheduled to the order) all further proceedings are to be stayed except for the purpose of putting the agreed terms into effect.

tools of trade A workman's tools, which he is entitled to keep if he is made bankrupt. However, the total value of all the goods that a bankrupt may keep (which may include other items, such as bedding) must not exceed £250.

tort [Old French: harm; wrong, from Latin *tortus*, twisted or crooked] *n.* A wrongful act or omission for which *damages can be obtained in a civil court by the person wronged, other than a wrong that is only a *breach of contract. The law of tort is mainly concerned with providing compensation for personal injury and property damage caused by *negligence. It also protects other interests, however, such as reputation (*see* defamation), personal freedom (*see* assault; false imprisonment), title to property (*see* conversion; trespass), enjoyment of property (*see* nuisance), and commercial interests (*see*, for example, intimidation; conspiracy; passing off). It must usually be shown that the wrong was done intentionally or negligently, but there are some torts of *strict liability. Most torts are actionable only if they have caused damage, but torts whose main function is to protect rights rather than to compensate for damage (such as trespass) are actionable without proof of damage. The person principally liable is the one who committed the tort (the *tortfeasor*) but under the rules of *vicarious liability one may be liable for a tort committed by another person. The main remedy for a tort is an action for damages, but in some cases an *injunction can be obtained to prevent repetition of the injury. Other remedies are *self-help and orders for specific restitution of property.

Some torts are also breaches of contract. Negligent driving by a taxi-driver that causes injury to his passenger is both the tort of negligence and breach of the contract to carry the passenger safely to his destination. The passenger may sue either in tort or for breach of contract, or both. Many torts are also crimes. Assault is both a crime and a tort. *Dangerous driving is a crime and may give rise to an action in tort if it causes injury to another person. The crime is prosecuted by agents of the state in the name of the Crown. It is left to the injured person to seek compensation from the wrongdoer by means of an action in tort.

tortfeasor *n.* One who commits a *tort. *See also* joint tortfeasors.

tortious *adj.* Having the nature of a *tort; wrongful.

total loss (in marine insurance) *See* actual total loss; constructive total loss. *Compare* partial loss.

totting up The system under which offences endorsed on a driving licence are added up to empower the courts to or-

der *disqualification from driving. Until 1 November 1982, certain road offences (listed in a Schedule to the Road Traffic Act 1972) were totted up if, within three years before committing the latest offence, the accused had been convicted and had his licence endorsed on two occasions. Since that date the system has been altered. All traffic offences subject to compulsory or discretionary disqualification are now assigned a number of points (reflecting the gravity of the offence). When a person is convicted of any of these offences, and his licence is endorsed but he is not disqualified, the endorsement states the number of points for that offence. If he is disqualified for the offence, the penalty points that would normally apply to that offence are not endorsed. When the penalty points endorsed within the past three years – together with the points acquired on the latest offence – amount to 12 or more, the court must order disqualification for a minimum of six months, but the points applying to the latest offence are not endorsed. If the accused has already been disqualified within the three years before the latest endorsable conviction, the minimum disqualification is for one year; if he has been disqualified more than once, the minimum is two years. Mitigating circumstances are still permitted (to prevent disqualification or shorten the period), but only upon proof of exceptional hardship. When several offences are committed together, the licence is only endorsed with the points relating to the gravest offence. If a person is disqualified under this system, all previous points are eliminated, and he gets back a clean licence after disqualification. Penalty points for the most important offences are as follows.

10 points – *reckless driving; being in charge when unfit or with excess alcohol in the body (*see* drunken driving); failing to provide a *specimen of breath.

5–9 points – failing to stop after a *road accident.

4–9 points – failing to report an accident.

8 points – taking a *conveyance.

4–8 points – *driving without insurance.

6 points – *driving while disqualified.

2–5 points – *careless or *inconsiderate driving.

4 points – any offence involving obligatory disqualification for which disqualification was not ordered because of special reasons or mitigating circumstances; failing to provide a specimen for a preliminary *breath test.

3 points – *speeding; leaving a car in a dangerous position (*see* obstruction).

2 points – *driving without a licence; driving under age.

The Act also provides that (1) all endorsements on the licence before 1 November 1982 are to count as 3 points; and (2) the relevant date for calculating the 3-year period is to be the date such offences were committed (not the date of conviction).

town and country planning A system of controlling the use of land administered by *local planning authorities* under the Town and Country Planning Act 1971, which is subject to supervisory powers of the Secretary of State. These authorities include both county and district councils and also, in Greater London, the Greater London Council, the London borough councils, and the Court of Common Council. The background to control is the *development plan*. County councils and the Greater London Council formulate and keep under review structure plans for their areas, and the other authorities maintain local plans for theirs. Structure plans indicate general policy as to land use and local plans detailed policy; the structure plan and local plan relating to an area together constitute its development plan. The machinery of control is *planning permission*, without which no *development of land may take place. The Secretary of State has granted permission for certain classes of development ("permitted development") by a general development order applicable throughout England and Wales; permission may be granted for particular cases by special development orders. In all other cases permission is a matter for local planning authorities (normally at district or borough level), with a right of appeal to the Secretary of State against its refusal or against conditions attached to it. The implementation of control is by local planning authorities at the same level, primarily by serving an *enforcement notice.

town clerk The office held by the head of the permanent staff (normally a qualified solicitor) of some local authorities. Under the Local Government Act 1972, the office ceased to be obligatory and many authorities now appoint a chief executive instead.

tracing (*or* following) trust property The right of a beneficiary under a *fiduciary relationship to recover trust property or its value if it is wrongfully disposed of by the fiduciary. The right exists against anyone except a person who has purchased the trust property without notice of the fiduciary obligation; a beneficiary may, for example, recover the property from a trustee who has mixed trust property with his own funds, or from a person to whom the property has wrongly been given.

trade description Any direct or indirect indication of certain characteristics of goods or of any part of them, such as their quantity, size, fitness for their purpose, time or place of origin, method of manufacture or processing, and price. Under the Trade Descriptions Act 1968, it is a criminal offence to apply a trade description to goods that is false or to supply or offer to supply any goods to which such a description is applied (*see* false trade description).

trade dispute Any dispute between workers and their own employer relating to one or more of the following: (1) terms and conditions of employment; (2) the engagement or nonengagement, suspension, or dismissal of any employee; (3) allocation of duties between employees; (4) disciplinary matters; (5) trade union membership or nonmembership; (6) facilities for trade union officials; and (7) negotiating machinery and the recognition of trade unions' negotiating rights on behalf of employees. Under the Trade Union and Labour Relations Act 1974, a person cannot be sued in *tort for an act that is committed in contemplation or furtherance of a trade dispute on the grounds that it induces or threatens any breach or interference with the performance of a contract. Generally such immunity extends only to the acts of employees against their own employer. Secondary industrial action may be unlawful when it is directed against an employer who is neither a party to the dispute nor the customer or supplier of the employer in dispute (*see also* picketing).

The 1974 Act, as amended by the Employment Act 1982, gives similar immunity to trade unions for their acts committed in contemplation or furtherance of a trade dispute provided the act concerned is authorized or endorsed by a responsible person (which includes the principal executive committee, general secretary, president, paid officials, or committees to whom they report). The president, general secretary, or principal executive committee may repudiate such authorization or endorsement provided they act promptly and notify the person giving the authorization or endorsement in writing and without delay.

Under the 1982 Act, when a trade union's immunity does not apply and it is ordered to pay damages (other than for causing personal injury or for breach of duty concerning the ownership control or use of property), the amount awarded may not exceed specified limits. These range from £10,000 for a union with under 5000 members to £250,000 for a union with 100 000 or more members, and the limits may be varied by statutory instrument. Payment of damages awarded against a trade union or employers' association may not be enforced against certain protected property, including its political and pension funds and the personal assets of its trustees, members, or paid officials, as distinct from assets they hold for the union's or association's purposes.

trade fixture A fixture attached to rented premises by a tenant for the purpose of his trade or business. A tenant can remove trade fixtures at any time during his tenancy, as well as at the end of it. *See also* tenant's fixtures.

trade mark A distinctive symbol that identifies particular products of a trader to the general public. The symbol may consist of a device, words, or a combination of these. A trader may register his trade mark at the Register of Trade Marks, which is at the Patent Office (*see* patent). He then enjoys the exclusive right to use the trade mark in connection with the goods for which it was registered. Any person or firm that has a trade connection with the goods may register a trade mark. For example, he may be the manufacturer, a dealer, importer, or retailer. Registration is initially for seven years and is then renewable. The right to remain on the register may be lost if the trade mark is not used or is misused. The owner of a trade mark may assign it or, subject to the Registrar's approval, allow others to use it. If anyone uses a registered trade mark without the owner's permission, or uses a mark that is likely to be confused with a registered trade mark, the owner can sue for an *injunction and *damages or an *account of profits.

trade mark at common law A *trade mark that is not registered in the Register of Trade Marks but is identified with particular goods through established use. The trade mark's owner may bring an action for *passing off in the case of infringement.

trade secret Knowledge of some process or product belonging to a business, disclosure of which would harm the business's interests. The courts will generally grant injunctions to prohibit any threatened disclosure of trade secrets by employees, former employees, and others to whom the secrets have been disclosed in confidence.

trade union An organization whose members are wholly or mainly workers and whose principal purposes include the regulation of relations between workers and employers or employers' associations. *See also* independent trade union.

trade union official An officer of a trade union (or of a branch or section of it) or a person elected or appointed in accordance with the union's rules to represent a group of its members. An employee who is a trade-union official and whose normal working week in his employment is of 16 hours or more is entitled to time off work, paid at his normal rate, for certain purposes. These must be official union duties concerning industrial relations between his employer and any associated employer and their employees or training approved by the Trades Union Congress and relevant to his union duties.

trading stamps Stamps bought from a trading-stamp company by a retailer and given to his customers when they purchase goods. The customer obtains stamps in proportion to the goods purchased, and when he has collected enough stamps he can exchange them for goods from the trading-stamp company. The issue of trading stamps is regulated by the Trading Stamp Act 1964. Each stamp must be clearly marked with a monetary value and the

name of the issuing company. The retailer aims to cover the cost of stamps by profits from the increased custom he hopes they will attract.

traffic offences *See* offences relating to road traffic.

transfer *n.* (in land law) A deed by which ownership of registered land is conveyed. *See also* conveyancing.

transfer of action *See* removal of action.

transfer of risk The passing from the seller of property to the buyer of the incidence of the loss if the property is damaged or destroyed. The Sale of Goods Act 1979 provides that, unless it is otherwise agreed, goods remain at the seller's risk until ownership passes to the buyer. After that they are at the buyer's risk, whether or not delivery has been made.

transfer of shares A transaction resulting in a change of share ownership. It usually involves (1) a contract to sell the shares; (2) their transfer by delivery of a *share warrant or execution of a *share transfer; and (3) entry of the transferee's name on the register of members of the company. Shares in private companies and partly paid shares may be subject to restrictions on transfer. *See also* transmission of shares.

transferred malice *See* malice.

transformation *n.* (in international law) *See* doctrine of incorporation.

transmission of shares A *transfer of shares that occurs automatically by operation of law upon bankruptcy (from the bankrupt to his trustee in bankruptcy) or upon death (to the personal representatives of the deceased). The transferees do not become company members until the company enters their names upon the register of members.

travaux préparatoires [French] Preparatory works that form a background to the enactment of legislation; for example, recommendations of Royal Commissions and consultative documents published by the government. They may not be used by the courts as an aid to interpreting the legislation. *See* interpretation of statutes.

traverse 1. *vb.* To deny an allegation of fact made in the pleading of the opposite party. **2.** *n.* The denial itself.

treachery *n.* Conduct that assists an enemy. This was defined under the Treachery Act 1940 as an offence relating to World War II, which was punishable by death. There is now, however, no specific crime of treachery: acts of this sort are usually dealt with under the Official Secrets Acts (*see* official secrets) or, in some cases, as *treason.

treason *n.* Conduct comprising a breach of allegiance owed to the sovereign or the state. Under the Treason Act 1351, high treason included violating the king's wife, eldest unmarried daughter, or wife of the king's eldest son; openly attempting to prevent the heir to the throne from succeeding; and killing the chancellor or any judge while performing their duties. Treason was redefined by the Treason Act 1795 and the principal forms now include: (1) compassing the death or serious injury of the sovereign or his (or her) spouse or eldest son; (2) levying war against the sovereign in his (or her) realm, which includes any insurrection against the authority of the sovereign or of the government that goes beyond *riot or *unlawful assembly; (3) giving aid or comfort to the sovereign's enemies in wartime. The penalty for treason (fixed by law) is death, but the monarch may exercise the prerogative of mercy.

treasure trove Items of gold and silver that have been found in a concealed place, having been hidden by an owner who is untraceable. They belong to the Crown by virtue of the royal prerogative.

Treasury Counsel Treasury Counsel to the Crown at the Central Criminal Court: a group of barristers, nominated by the Attorney General, who receive briefs from the *Director of Public Prosecutions to appear for the prosecution in trials at the *Old Bailey. There are six Senior Counsel (who, despite the name, are not Queen's Counsel) and ten Junior Counsel.

Treasury Solicitor (HM Procurator General and Treasury Solicitor) A solicitor who advises the Treasury on legal matters, instructs parliamentary counsel on Bills, instructs counsel to appear on behalf of the Crown in civil cases involving Treasury issues, and acts as *Queen's Proctor. Between 1883 and 1908 the office was combined with that of *Director of Public Prosecutions.

treaty *n.* An international agreement in writing between two states (a *bilateral treaty*) or a number of states (a *multilateral treaty*). Treaties are binding in international law and constitute the equivalent of the municipal-law contract, conveyance, or legislation. Some treaties create law only for those states that are parties to them, some codify pre-existing customary international law, and some propound rules that eventually develop into customary international law, binding upon all states (e.g. the Genocide Convention). Federal states, colonial states, and public international organizations are sometimes also able to enter into treaty obligations. The Vienna Convention on the Law of Treaties (1969) defines in detail the rules relating to inter-state treaties and is itself generally considered to declare or develop customary international law in this area. Treaties are normally concluded by the process of *ratification.

In England the power to make or enter into treaties belongs to the monarch, acting on the advice of government ministers, but a treaty does not become part of English municipal law until brought into force by an Act of Parliament.

tree preservation order An order made by a local planning authority (*see* town and country planning) prohibiting, in the interests of amenities, the felling of trees without its consent. *See also* conservation area.

trespass *n.* A wrongful direct interference with another person or with his possession of land or goods. In medieval law, any wrongful act was called a trespass, but trespass by force and arms (*vi et armis*) was a breach of the peace and therefore dealt with in the King's Courts. The distinguishing feature of trespass in modern law is that it is a direct and immediate interference with person or property, such as striking a person, entering his land, or taking away his goods without his consent. Indirect or consequential injury, such as leaving an unlit hole into which someone falls, is not trespass. Trespass is actionable *per se*, i.e. the act of trespass is itself a *tort and it is not necessary to prove that it has caused actual damage.

There are three kinds of trespass: to the person, to goods, and to land. *Trespass to the person* may be intentional or negligent, but since negligent physical injuries are remedied by an action for *negligence, the action for trespass to the person is only brought for intentional acts, in the form of actions for *assault, *battery, and *false imprisonment. *Trespass to goods* includes touching, moving, or carrying them away (*de bonis asportatis*). It may be intentional or negligent, but *inevitable accident is a defence. *Trespass to land* usually takes the form of entering it without permission. It is no defence to show that the trespass was innocent (e.g. that the trespasser honestly believed that the land belonged to him). Trespass to land is a tort but not normally a crime: the notice "Trespassers will be prosecuted" therefore carries no actual threat. However, trespass may sometimes constitute

a crime. Thus squatters may be guilty of a crime (*see* adverse occupation); it is a crime to trespass on diplomatic or consular premises or premises similarly protected by immunity; and it is a crime to enter and remain on any premises as a trespasser with a *weapon of offence for which one has no authority or reasonable excuse, or to be on any premises, land, or water as a trespasser with a *firearm for which one has no reasonable excuse. Trespass may also be an element in *burglary. It is, however, a crime to use force against a trespasser, unless one is a displaced residential occupier.

Trespass to land or goods is a wrong to possession rather than to ownership. Thus a tenant of rented property, for example, has the right to sue for trespass to that property. *See also* airspace; trespass by relation.

trespass *ab initio* [Latin: trespass from the beginning] A form of trespass that occurs when a person enters land with authority given by law, e.g. to arrest a criminal or search for stolen goods, and subsequently commits an act that is an abuse of that authority. The authority is cancelled retrospectively and the entry is deemed to have been a trespass from the beginning.

trespass by relation A form of trespass based on the legal fiction that a person's actual possession of land dates from the moment he became entitled to possession. It arose from the rule that only the possessor of land can sue for trespass to it. When someone entitled to immediate possession of land enters into possession of it at some later date, his possession is deemed to relate back to the moment he became entitled to it to enable him to sue for acts of trespass committed in the intervening period.

trial *n.* The hearing of a civil or criminal case before a court of competent jurisdiction. Trials must, with rare exceptions (*see in camera*), be held in public. At the trial all issues of law and fact arising in the case will be determined. *See also* summary trial; trial on indictment.

trial at bar *Trial on indictment before three or more judges of the *Queen's Bench Division and a jury: formerly used for the trial of criminal cases of exceptional public importance. The last such trial was that of Sir Roger Casement for treason in 1916 and the procedure was abolished by the Courts Act 1971.

trial on indictment The trial of a person charged with an *indictable offence, which is by jury in the *Crown Court. The *indictment is read out to the accused at the start of the trial. There are a number of differences between trial on indictment and *summary trial (i.e. by magistrates). The courts have power to impose greater penalties on indictment and there is no time limit before which indictable offences must be tried (most summary offences must be tried within six months).

trial without pleadings A procedure in the High Court that may be ordered for any action in which the defendant has given *notice of intention to defend other than one in which there is a claim for libel, slander, malicious prosecution, false imprisonment, or an allegation by the plaintiff of fraud. The court must be satisfied that the issues can be defined without pleadings or that the case is otherwise suitable and it may order the parties to prepare a statement of the issues in dispute. Such orders are rarely made.

tribunal *n. See* administrative tribunal; domestic tribunal; tribunal of inquiry.

tribunal of inquiry A tribunal appointed under the Tribunals of Inquiry (Evidence) Act 1921 to investigate a matter of public importance. The Act provides machinery for the thorough examination of any matter (e.g. a national disaster or alleged corruption in government) that is a source of public disquiet but is not the subject of ordinary proceedings in the ordinary courts. A tribunal is appointed on resolutions of both Houses of Parliament, its chairman is normally a senior judge, and it has all the powers of the High Court concerning the summoning and examination of witnesses and the production of documents.

trier of fact A member of a court who has the duty to decide questions of fact. In criminal trials on indictment and civil trials with a jury, the jury is the trier of fact; in civil trials by judge alone and in summary trials, the judge and magistrates, respectively, decide all issues both of law and fact.

trover *n.* The original form of the modern action in tort for *conversion of goods. Trover was based on a fictitious allegation that the plaintiff had lost the goods and the defendant found them and converted them to his own use. The old form of action has disappeared, but its name is still sometimes used as a synonym for conversion.

trust *n.* An arrangement in which a *settlor transfers property to one or more *trustees, who will hold it for the benefit of one or more persons (the *beneficiaries* or *cestuis que trust*, who may include the trustee(s) or the settlor) who are entitled to enforce the trust, if necessary by action in court. The trust, recognized originally in Chancery, is based on confidence and developed from the *use; it has been described as the most important contribution of English *equity to jurisprudence. The beneficiary has rights against the trustee and may also have rights over the property in the hands of others (*see* tracing trust property). For a trust to exist, the *three certainties* must be present: certainty of intention (i.e. to create a trust), certainty of subject matter (the property in the trust), and certainty of objects (those who will or may benefit under the trust). There are few formal technical requirements necessary for the creation of a trust, except where land is concerned. *See* active trust; charitable trust; discretionary trust; executed trust; express trust; implied trust; protective trust; secret trust; statutory trust.

trust corporation The *Public Trustee or a corporation either appointed by the court to act as trustee or automatically entitled to do so because it has issued capital of at least £250,000 of which at least £100,000 has been paid up in cash. A trust corporation may exercise all the powers that would otherwise require two trustees (e.g. selling land). The clearing banks and others have subsidiary companies that are trust corporations.

trustee *n.* **1.** A person having a nominal title to property that he holds for the benefit of one or more others, the beneficiaries (*see* trust). Trustees may be individuals or corporate bodies (*see* trust corporation) and can include such specialists as *judicial trustees, *custodian trustees, and the *Public Trustee. A trustee must show a high standard of care towards his beneficiaries, must not allow his interests to conflict with those of his beneficiaries, and must not profit from his trust. He is not usually entitled to remuneration although he may recover expenses necessarily incurred (*see* charging clause). Trustees may refuse their office, retire, or resign, but they remain liable for acts carried out during their trusteeship. The power to appoint replacement trustees is usually given either to the beneficiaries or to the remaining trustees; in default the court will appoint replacement trustees. Trustees have a wide range of powers and duties, including a duty to act equally between the beneficiaries and a power to advance money to them (*see* advancement). In the exercise of their duties they are answerable to the court.

trustee *de son tort* [from Latin: of his own wrongdoing] A person unconnected with a trust who takes upon

himself to act as a trustee. He is thereafter liable, as if he had been appointed a trustee.

trustee in bankruptcy A person in whom the property of a bankrupt is vested for the benefit of the bankrupt's creditors. The trustee in bankruptcy must collect the bankrupt's assets, sell them, and distribute the proceeds among those with valid claims against the bankrupt. Some claims (e.g. by the Inland Revenue) take preference over others.

trustee investments *See* authorized investments.

Trustee Savings Bank Central Board A body established by the Trustee Savings Bank Act 1976 to direct the way in which trustee savings banks carry out their activities, particularly in such matters as conditions of service of employees. The Board also provides banking and other common services (e.g. data processing).

trusteeship *n. See* trust territory.

trustees of the settlement *See* Settled Land Act trustees.

trust for sale A trust under which the trustees have an obligation to sell the trust property and hold the proceeds of sale in trust for the beneficiaries. A trust for sale may be imposed by statute; for example, under the Law of Property Act 1925, when land is owned by two or more persons jointly or as tenants in common, and under the Administration of Estates Act 1925, which provides that an intestate's estate is held on trust for sale by his administrators. It may also be created by will or deed and is used as a method of settling land on beneficiaries in succession to one another. Although the trust imposes an obligation on the trustees to sell the land, the Law of Property Act 1925 gives them power to postpone the sale for as long as they think fit; while the land remains unsold, the trustees have all the powers that the immediate beneficiary and the trustees of the settlement would have in the case of *settled land. Under a trust for sale, however, the beneficiaries are treated for most purposes as having interests in the proceeds of sale, not in the land itself.

trust instrument A deed under which property is vested in trustees upon trust to apply it for the benefit of the beneficiaries specified in the deed. In the case of *settled land, the trust instrument appoints the trustees of the settlement, sets out the interests to which the beneficiaries are entitled and any powers conferred in extension of those contained in the Settled Land Act 1925, and bears any *ad valorem* stamp duty payable in respect of the settlement.

trust power (power in the nature of a trust) A *power of appointment held by trustees. The trustees are bound to consider whether or not to exercise the power, which donees of a mere power are not obliged to do, and to that extent objects of a trust power have rights similar to those of beneficiaries under a trust.

trust property Property subject to a *trust, normally held by trustees (it may include trust documents, which affect the trust). If trust property is wrongfully disposed of, it may be recovered by the beneficiaries (*see* tracing trust property).

trust territory Any of the territories formerly under a League of Nations *mandate, which after 1945 were placed under the *trusteeship* of the United Nations until ready for independence. The only remaining trust territory is the Pacific strategic trust area.

turbary *n.* A *profit *à prendre* or *common conferring the right to take peat or turf from another's land, for use as fuel.

turning Queen's evidence *See* Queen's evidence.

turpis causa [Latin] An evil cause. *See* illegal contract.

two-counsel rule A rule of etiquette of the Bar that required junior counsel to be instructed to assist Queen's Counsel when the latter appeared in court or in chambers. This rule has now been abolished, but two counsel are often instructed when the weight of the case justifies it.

U

uberrimae fidei [Latin: of the utmost good faith] Describing a class of contracts in which one party has a preliminary duty to disclose material facts relevant to the subject matter to the other. *Nondisclosure makes the contract voidable. Examples of this class are *insurance contracts, in which knowledge of many material facts is confined to the party seeking insurance.

ultra vires [Latin: beyond the powers] Describing an act by a public authority, company, or other body that goes beyond the limits of the powers conferred on it. *Ultra vires* acts are invalid (*compare intra vires*). The *ultra vires* doctrine applies to all powers, whether created by statute or by a private document or agreement (such as a trust deed or contract of agency). In the field of public (especially administrative) law it governs the validity of all *delegated (including subdelegated) legislation. This is *ultra vires* not only if it contains provisions not authorized by the enabling power but also if it does not comply with any procedural requirements regulating the exercise of the power. Subdelegated legislation that is within the terms of the delegated legislation authorizing it may still be invalid if the power to make that legislation did not include power to subdelegate (*see delegatus non potest delegare*). The individual can normally establish the invalidity of delegated or subdelegated legislation by raising the point as a defence in proceedings against him for contravening it. The doctrine also governs the validity of decisions made by inferior courts or administrative or domestic tribunals and the validity of the exercise of any *administrative power. The decision of a court or tribunal is *ultra vires* if, for example, it exceeds jurisdiction, contravenes procedural requirements, or disregards the rules of natural justice (the power conferring jurisdiction being construed as requiring the observance of these). Similarly, the exercise of an administrative power is *ultra vires* not only if unauthorized in substance, but equally if (for example) it is procedurally irregular, improperly motivated, or in breach of the rules of natural justice (where applicable). The remedies available for this second aspect of the doctrine are *certiorari*, *prohibition, *declaration, and *injunction (the first two of these are, however, public remedies and are not therefore available against decisions of domestic tribunals whose jurisdiction is based solely on contract).

Acts by a registered company are *ultra vires* if they exceed the purposes specified in the objects clause of the *memorandum of association. An act within or reasonably incidental to these purposes is *intra vires* and valid. However, an individual dealing with a company in good faith may be able to enforce certain *ultra vires* transactions under the European Communities Act 1972. Good faith is presumed unless, for example, the company can show that the person knew the act was *ultra vires*. Under the Act *constructive notice of the memorandum and articles of association cannot be used to establish such knowledge.

umpire *n. See* arbitration.

UN *See* United Nations.

unascertained goods Goods that are not specifically identified at the time a contract of sale is made. For example, in a contract for the sale of 1000 tonnes of soya bean meal, the seller may deliver any 1000 tonnes that answer the contract description. When the correct quantity has been set aside for delivery to the buyer, the goods are described as *ascertained*. Ownership does not pass to the buyer until the goods have been ascertained. *Compare* specific goods.

unchastity *n. See* imputation of unchastity.

uncollected goods *See* disposal of uncollected goods.

unconscionable bargain *See* catching bargain.

uncontrollable impulse *See* irresistable impulse.

undefended cause 1. A court action in which the defendant: (1) fails to acknowledge service of the writ; (2) fails to enter a statement of defence; or (3) fails to appear, or be represented, at the hearing of the case despite the fact that he has received notice of it. In such actions, judgment may be entered in favour of the plaintiff; in special circumstances, however, the defendant may apply for the judgment to be cancelled (*see* setting aside). **2.** A petition for divorce, nullity, or judicial separation not contested by the respondent. This may be because: (1) the respondent declares in his acknowledgment of service that he does not intend to contest the petition; (2) he gives notice of his intention to defend but fails to file an answer to the petition within the time allowed (usually 29 days from the day he received the petition); (3) he files no answer at all; or (4) the answer filed has been struck out. County courts only have jurisdiction to hear undefended causes; if they become defended, they must be transferred to the High Court. Undefended causes for divorce or judicial separation may be dealt with under the special procedure (*see* divorce).

underlease *n.* *See* sublease.

underwriter *n.* **1.** A member of an insurance company or a *Lloyd's syndicate who decides whether or not to accept a particular risk for a specified premium. In general, the public only deal with underwriters through a broker. **2.** An individual, finance company, or issuing house who undertakes for an agreed remuneration to acquire, at their issue price less a discount, those securities of a company that are not taken up by the public during a *flotation.

In both cases the underwriter may relieve himself of part of his liability by effecting similar arrangements with *subunderwriters*.

undischarged bankrupt A person who has been made bankrupt and who has not yet received an order of discharge from the court. Such a person is disqualified from holding certain offices, which include justice of the peace, councillor, and Member of Parliament. He must not obtain credit for more than £50 without informing the creditor that he is an undischarged bankrupt, and he must not carry on a business without disclosing the name under which he was made bankrupt to those who deal with him. *See also* bankruptcy.

undisclosed principal *See* agent.

undivided shares The equitable interests in land owned by tenants in common. Each co-owner has a specified (but not necessarily equal) share in the property, which he may dispose of separately from the others. He may be entitled to enjoy with the other co-owners possession of the whole of the land until it is sold under the statutory *trust for sale or to receive his share of its income. *See also* tenancy in common.

undue influence Influence that prevents someone from exercising an independent judgment with respect to any transaction. A contract or gift procured by the exercise of undue influence is liable to be set aside by the courts. The exercise of undue influence must normally be proved affirmatively. However, in the case of certain relationships (for example, between parent and child, doctor and patient, solicitor and client) undue influence is presumed to be exercised in the absence of evidence to the contrary.

unemployment benefit A benefit payable under the Social Security Act 1975 to an unemployed person satisfying certain conditions (e.g. a qualifying contribution record and willingness to undertake any suitable work). It is paid (with increases for dependants) for a maximum of 312 days of unemployment beginning with the fourth day, Sundays being disregarded for these purposes.

unenforceable contract A contract that, although valid, cannot be enforced by action because it is neither *evidenced in writing* nor (when this is a permissible alternative) supported by a sufficient act of *part performance. Two classes of contracts are involved – guarantees and contracts for the sale of land. By the Statute of Frauds 1677 (in the case of guarantees) and the Law of Property Act 1925 (for land contracts), no contract of either class is enforceable unless its existence and its terms are evidenced by some written note or memorandum signed by the defendant or his agent. By the equitable doctrine of part performance, a land contract (but not a guarantee) can be enforced if, alternatively, the plaintiff has carried out some act that can be taken as evidencing the existence of the contract.

unenforceable trust A trust that is valid but cannot be directly enforced by a beneficiary. *See* purpose trust.

unfair consumer practices *See* consumer protection.

unfair contract terms Contractual terms relating to the exclusion or restriction of a person's liability that, under the Unfair Contract Terms Act

1977, are either ineffective or effective only so far as is reasonable. *See* exclusion and restriction of negligence liability; exemption clause; international supply contract.

unfair dismissal The dismissal of an employee that the employer cannot show to be fair. Under the Employment Protection (Consolidation) Act 1978 employees have the right not to be unfairly dismissed, provided they have served the required period of *continuous employment and are not over normal retirement age (65 for men, 60 for women). However, employees dismissed for an *inadmissible reason have this right whatever their age or length of service. An employee who considers he has been unfairly dismissed can apply within three months after the *effective date of termination of his employment contract to an industrial tribunal for *reinstatement, *re-engagement, or *compensation. The tribunal will make an award unless the employer shows that the principal reason for the dismissal was the employee's incapability, lack of qualifications, or conduct; redundancy; the fact that it would be illegal to continue employing him; or some other substantial reason. The employer must also show that he acted reasonably in dismissing the employee.

The statutory protection does not apply to the following: (1) employees ordinarily working outside Great Britain; (2) an employee under a fixed term of one year or more dismissed only by the expiry of the contract if he has agreed before the expiry not to claim; (3) a person employed by his spouse; (4) members of the police and armed forces; (5) registered dock workers; and (6) the crews of fishing vessels in certain circumstances.

unfair prejudice Failure of those conducting a company's affairs to treat all members alike. Under the Companies Act 1980 the court can grant such relief as it thinks fit to those members who suffer harm because of this. *See also* minority protection.

unfavourable witness An *adverse witness who is not *hostile towards the party who called him to testify. An unfavourable witness may not be cross-examined by that party.

unfitness or incompetence *See* imputation of unfitness or incompetence.

unfit to plead Describing an accused person who is under a disability (e.g. mental incapacity) that would constitute a bar to his being tried. When the question of fitness to plead arises (e.g. when the defendant *stands mute by visitation of God), a jury is empanelled to determine the question of the accused's fitness; if they find him under disability the court must order that the accused be admitted to a hospital specified by the Secretary of State. The court may postpone consideration of the question of the accused's fitness to plead until the defence case is opened so that (for example) the strength of the prosecution case may be tested. The procedure is governed by the Criminal Procedure (Insanity) Act 1964.

unilateral contract A contract in which one party (the promisor) undertakes to do or refrain from doing something if the other party (the promisee) does or refrains from doing something, but the promisee does not undertake to do or refrain from doing that thing. An example of a unilateral contract is one in which the promisor offers a reward for the giving of information. *See also* synallagmatic contract.

unilateral discharge *See* accord and satisfaction.

unilateral mistake *See* mistake.

unincorporated body An association that has no legal personality distinct from those of its members (*compare* corporation). Examples of unincorporated bodies are *partnerships and *clubs.

union membership agreement *See* closed-shop agreement.

United Nations (UN) An international organization, based in New York and Geneva, set up by the United Nations Charter in 1945 to replace the League of Nations. The main aims of the UN are: (1) to maintain international peace and security and to bring about settlement of international disputes by peaceful means; (2) to develop friendly relations among nations; and (3) to achieve international cooperation in solving international problems of an economic or cultural nature and in promoting respect for human rights. The Charter sets out certain fundamental principles, which include the undertaking to refrain from using or threatening force against the territory or political independence of any state.

The Charter established six principal organs, of which the most important are the General Assembly, the Security Council, the Economic and Social Council, and the *International Court of Justice. The General Assembly is the debating forum of the UN, consisting of all the member states; it can pass resolutions, but these are not legally binding upon member states. The Security Council has five permanent members (China, France, the USSR, the UK, and the USA), and ten temporary members elected for two-year periods. Its resolutions are binding on member states. It is empowered, under certain conditions, to make recommendations and take measures to maintain the peace, although the provisions for a UN military force envisaged in the Charter have not been implemented.

The United Nations has lost credibility as an international legal organization because it has often been divided upon issues on the basis of political (rather than legal) factors or has passed resolutions of a political nature. Nevertheless it remains important as the only world organization (almost all independent states are members of the UN) and as a forum for discussion and development of international law.

unit trust A *trust enabling small investors to buy interests in a diversity of companies and other investments. These investments are held by trustees (responsible for holding the investments and collecting and distributing income), who enter into a trust deed with the managers of the fund (who select, buy, and sell the investments). The managers sell units to investors, who thus acquire an interest in the fund proportionate to their investment. There is a service charge that provides the remuneration of the managers. Unit trusts are subject to regulation and supervision by the Department of Trade.

unity of personality Formerly, the common-law doctrine that husband and wife were one person in the eyes of the law. This doctrine has now been almost entirely abolished. However, the court still has jurisdiction to stay proceedings in tort brought by one spouse against another if there will be no substantial benefit from it; a husband and wife may not be convicted of criminal conspiracy together with each other (unless a third person is involved); and there are certain limitations on criminal proceedings in relation to theft of property belonging to one's spouse.

unity of seisin The ownership of two plots of land by the same person. Easements and other rights over a *servient tenement for the benefit of a *dominant tenement are extinguished if both tenements come into the same ownership.

universal malice *See* malice.

unjust enrichment *See* quasi-contract.

unlawful assembly A common-law crime committed when three or more people come together with the common intention of committing a crime of violence or of achieving any purpose in such a way as to cause reasonable people to fear a breach of the peace. The assembly may be unlawful even if it is in a private place, provided that at least one innocent third party is present. If the purpose of the assembly is to carry out an unlawful act that is not likely to cause a breach of the peace (for example, to plan a fraud) this will not be an unlawful assembly, although it may be a *conspiracy. The police may call upon a lawful assembly to disperse, in order to preserve the peace; if it does not disperse, it then becomes an unlawful assembly. *See also* riot; rout.

unlawful possession of drugs *See* controlled drugs.

unlawful sexual intercourse Sexual intercourse that occurs in any of the *sexual offences involving intercourse, including intercourse with a girl under the age of 16 or a mentally defective woman. In this context it implies extramarital intercourse: these offences cannot normally be committed by a husband against his wife.

unlawful trust *See* void trust.

unlawful wounding *Wounding or *wounding with intent that is not justified by, for example, self-defence or by statutory powers given to the police to arrest criminals.

unlimited company A type of *registered company whose members have an unlimited liability. Thus on winding-up, the company can make demands upon its members until it has sufficient funds to meet the creditors' claims. The risk that members of unlimited companies assume is balanced by certain advantages: unlimited companies do not have to deliver their *accounts to the Companies Registry and they have more freedom to deal with their capital than limited companies. Unlimited companies may be formed with an *authorized capital, thus enabling them to issue shares and raise working capital,

but members' liability is not limited to the nominal value of these shares.

unliquidated damages *See* damages.

unnatural offence *Buggery. Other "unnatural" forms of intercourse, however, are not included in the term.

unopposed proceedings Proceedings in which any person entitled to oppose fails to take any step (or any further step) in the proceedings, having been given an opportunity to do so. Unopposed proceedings often end in a judgment in *default but may not do so in proceedings in which the remedy claimed by the plaintiff can only be obtained by some judicial determination, e.g. in *undefended causes in divorce proceedings.

unpaid seller A seller of goods who has not been paid in full for them or who has received a cheque or other *negotiable instrument that has not been honoured. Although ownership of the goods may have passed to the buyer, an unpaid seller has certain rights against the goods themselves, in addition to his right of action for damages. Under the Sale of Goods Act 1979, these rights are: (1) a possessory *lien (particular, not general); (2) a right of *stoppage *in transitu*; and (3) a *right of resale.

unreasonable conduct Conduct of a respondent that may be evidence that a marriage has broken down irretrievably, entitling the petitioner to a divorce. Such conduct need not be unreasonable in itself – the real test is whether it is reasonable to expect the petitioner to continue living with the respondent, taking into account the behaviour of both spouses and their particular personalities and characteristics. For example, the behaviour may be morally blameless (as in the case of an insane spouse) or it may be "positive" (active) or "negative" (passive); each case will depend upon its own specific facts. *See also* breakdown of marriage.

unregistered company A *company incorporated otherwise than by registration under the Companies Acts. Unregistered companies, which include *statutory companies and *foreign companies, are subject to some provisions of the Companies Acts 1948–81.

unregistered land Land to which the title in question is not registered at HM Land Registry. *Compare* registered land. *See also* registration of encumbrances.

unruly character The character of a child over the age of 14 when it is such that he cannot be committed to the care of a local authority. If, when making an interim care order in respect of the child, the court certifies that the child is of an unruly character, it must commit him to a remand centre for up to 28 days. A child can only be certified in this way if: (1) he is charged either with an offence for which an adult could receive a sentence of 14 years' imprisonment or more or with a crime of violence, or he has previously been found guilty of a crime of violence, and he cannot be accommodated in a community home; or (2) he has persistently run away from or disrupted a community home and the court feels this behaviour would be likely to be repeated.

unsecured creditor A person who has lent money without obtaining any security. *Compare* secured creditor.

unsolicited goods Goods sent to someone (other than a trader) who has not asked for them to be sent. It is not in itself an offence to send unsolicited goods (except for matter describing human sexual techniques or advertisements for such matter), but it is a criminal offence to demand payment for them. A person who receives unsolicited goods is an involuntary bailee of them (*see* bailment) and may not destroy or damage them. If he disposes of them, he might be guilty of theft. Statute, however, permits him to treat them as his own property after six months (or 30 days if he has asked the sender to take them back).

unsworn evidence Evidence given by a child in a criminal case in accordance with the provisions of the Children and Young Persons Act 1933. The child must be sufficiently intelligent to justify the reception of his evidence and understand the duty of speaking the truth. The child's evidence must be supported by some *corroboration.

unsworn statement A statement made from the dock by an accused person while not on oath. The evidentiary effect of such a statement was much disputed, but the right to make one, which had been preserved when the accused was made a competent witness by the Criminal Evidence Act 1898, was abolished by the Criminal Justice Act 1982.

urine specimen *See* specimen of urine.

usage *n.* A long-established and well-known practice in a particular market or trade. It may affect the interpretation of, and the nature of implied terms in, a contract made in that market or trade.

use [possibly from Latin: *opus*, benefit] *n.* Formerly, a right, recognized only in Chancery, of a beneficiary (the *cestui que use*) against the legal owner of land. The medieval common law recognized only legal rights, which were often restricted in nature, but the Chancery protected those to whose use or benefit land was given, although they were not the legal owners. If A held property to the use of B, A was the legal owner (*feoffee to uses*) and B was the beneficiary (*cestui que use*). Uses gave flexibility and helped the evasion of feudal incidents (the medieval equivalent of tax liability). In 1535 the Statute of Uses executed the use, i.e. converted the rights of a *cestui que use* to legal rights, but the statute proved ineffective (*see* use upon a use); it was repealed and uses were abolished in 1925.

use and occupation Possession and/or use of land by a person in unlawful occupation of it. A person claiming to recover possession of the land by proceedings in court can also claim a money sum to compensate him for the defendant's unlawful use and occupation.

use classes *See* development.

user *n.* The use or enjoyment of property.

use upon a use Formerly, a right recognized by the Chancery after the Statute of Uses 1535 (*see* use). In a situation in which A held property to the use of (i.e. for the benefit of) B, who held to the use of C, the Statute made B the legal owner but did not affect the second use to C (the use upon a use), who remained entitled to the benefit. The second use eventually became the *trust.

usual covenants The covenants that a good conveyancing practitioner would insert in a *lease. When an *agreement for a lease does not specify the terms of the lease, there is a term implied in the agreement that the lease will contain the usual covenants. The following are generally accepted as usual: by the landlord, a covenant for *quiet enjoyment; by the tenant, to pay rent, to pay tenants' rates and taxes, to keep the premises in repair, and to allow the landlord to enter to see the state of repair. There is also a condition for *re-entry for nonpayment of rent. Whether or not any other covenant is usual is a matter of evidence.

utter Bar *See* outer Bar.

uttering *n.* Using or attempting to pass off forged documents or coins. The offences relating to uttering contained in the Forgery Act 1913 have now been replaced by new offences in the Forgery and Counterfeiting Act 1981. *See* forgery.

V

vacantia bona *See bona vacantia.*

vacant possession The exclusive use of land, to which a purchaser is entitled on completion of the transaction unless he has contracted to buy subject to another's right of occupation.

vacations *pl. n.* The periods between the end of any of the *sittings of the Supreme Court and the beginning of the next sitting, i.e. the *Long Vacation, Christmas Vacation, Easter Vacation, and Whitsun Vacation.

vagrant *n.* A person classified under the Vagrancy Act 1824 as an "idle and disorderly person", a "rogue and vagabond", or an "incorrigible rogue". The first of these groups includes pedlars who trade without a licence, prostitutes who behave indecently in a public place, and those who beg in a public place. Rogues and vagabonds include those with a second conviction for being idle and disorderly, those who collect charity under false pretences, those armed with offensive weapons with the intention of committing an arrestable offence, and tramps who do not make use of available places of shelter. Incorrigible rogues include those with a second conviction for being rogues and vagabonds. Vagrants are usually liable to imprisonment for between one month and one year, depending on which class they fall under, although beggars and tramps sleeping rough are liable only to fines. The Act also provides for various powers to search them or their property. *See also* loitering.

valuable consideration *See* consideration.

value *n.* Valuable *consideration.

value-added tax (VAT) A tax payable on a wide range of supplies of goods and services by way of business. As well as straightforward sales, *taxable sup-*

plies include hirings, rentals, the granting of rights, and the distribution of promotional gifts. VAT is also payable on imports. The amount of tax payable is a percentage of the value of the supply (at present 15%) and the liability for the tax arises at the time of the supply (*see* tax point). Any person, firm, or organization that makes regular taxable supplies above a certain annual value (£18,000, 1983 Budget proposal) must register with the Customs and Excise, who administer the tax. A registered person (known as a *taxable person*) must collect from his customers the tax due on the supplies that he makes. This is known as his *output tax*. He pays the tax to the Customs and Excise on a periodic basis (usually quarterly), but in doing so he may reclaim any VAT that he has himself paid in the course of his business (his *input tax*). The entire tax is therefore borne by the ultimate consumer. VAT came into force on 1 April 1973, replacing purchase tax and selective employment tax. *See also* exempt supply; zero-rated supply.

valued policy An insurance policy that specifies the value of the property insured as agreed between the parties. A policy is not valued merely because it specifies an amount as the sum insured, for that is no more than an estimate of value by the person insured. The essence of a valued policy is that it is based on an agreed valuation, which is conclusive; the insured will recover its full amount even if this exceeds the actual value of the property at the time of loss.

value received Words that may appear on a *bill of exchange indicating either that value has been received by the drawer from the payee or by the acceptor from the drawer. Such words are not necessary; every party whose signature appears on a bill is presumed, unless the contrary is proved, to have become a party for value.

vandalism *n.* Defacing or damaging property. There is no offence of vandalism as such, but it will usually constitute an offence of *criminal damage (it is not clear, however, whether or not daubing graffiti constitutes criminal damage).

variance *n.* A discrepancy between a statement in the writ and the pleadings or between a statement in pleadings and the evidence adduced in support of it at trial. In modern practice, it can be rectified by *amendment.

VAT *See* value-added tax.

VC *See* Vice Chancellor.

vehicle *n. See* motor vehicle.

vehicle construction and maintenance There are detailed rules governing the manufacture and subsequent maintenance of motor vehicles, failure to comply with which may constitute a criminal offence. The main rules deal with such matters as the brakes and steering system, mirrors, windscreen wipers and washers, petrol tanks, door hinges and latches, silencers, pollution prevention, indicators, speedometers, lights, and tyres. There are also regulations governing the use of a motor vehicle. Breach of the regulations relating to brakes, steering system, or tyres or breach of any of the regulations relating to construction, maintenance, or use in a manner that causes or is likely to cause danger is an offence punishable by *endorsement (carrying 3 points under the *totting-up system) and discretionary disqualification. Other breaches are subject to fines but not to endorsement. There are also special offences relating to the sale or attempted sale of vehicles whose use on the roads would be a breach of the regulations, to the fitting of parts to a vehicle in such a way that its subsequent use would be in breach of the regulations, and to selling or supplying parts whose fitting would cause the vehicle's subsequent use to be in breach of the regulations. These offences do not apply, however, if the defendant proves that the vehicle was sold for export or that he reasonably believed that it would not be used in Britain in an unlawful condition.

See also MOT test.

vehicle insurance *See* third-party insurance; driving without insurance.

vehicle interference *See* loitering.

vendor *n.* A seller, particularly one who sells land.

vendor and purchaser summons A procedure enabling parties to a contract for the sale of land, who disagree on a matter that prevents completion of the contract, to apply to a judge in chambers for a ruling. It is often employed to resolve questions of interpretation of terms of the contract.

venereal disease Any infectious disease transmitted through sexual contact (such as syphilis or gonorrhoea). If a spouse at the time of marriage was, unknown to his (or her) partner, suffering from a venereal disease this constitutes a ground for annulment of the marriage. Evidence of a venereal disease contracted since the marriage, when neither partner was previously suffering from it, may be prima facie evidence of adultery. A husband suffering from a venereal disease is not entitled to insist on sexual intercourse with his wife. If he does so he is probably not guilty of a criminal offence, but this may constitute unreasonable behaviour and entitle his wife to a divorce on an order in the magistrates' courts.

venire de novo [Latin: to come anew] An order made by the Court of Appeal (Criminal Division) annulling a trial on indictment and ordering a *new trial on the ground of some fundamental flaw in the proceedings (e.g. failure to obtain a necessary consent to the institution of proceedings). Originally, it was a writ (*venire facias de novo juratores*) addressed to the sheriff, ordering him to cause new jurors to try the case afresh.

verbals *pl. n.* Any remarks that an accused person has made in the presence of the police. These are written down by the police and may be read out as evidence at the trial. *See also* caution.

verdict *n.* **1.** A *jury's finding on the matters referred to it in a criminal or civil trial. The jury is asked to give its decision to the court separately for each of the questions it was asked to consider (for example, when there are several charges on the *indictment). The reply is usually given by the foreman. A jury reaches its verdict in secret and no subsequent inquiry can be made as to how it was reached. The jury must try to reach a unanimous verdict but a *majority verdict is accepted in certain circumstances. If the jury cannot agree a verdict at all they are discharged and there is a new trial. Verdicts are either *general or *special. The usual form of verdict is general (such as a finding of *guilty or *not guilty); special verdicts are exceptional. A jury may decide that the accused is not guilty of the offence charged but guilty of some lesser offence (*see* alternative verdict). *See also* perverse verdict. **2.** The finding of a coroner's inquest. *See* inquisition.

vest *vb.* **1.** To confer legal ownership of land on someone. **2.** To confer legal rights on someone.

vested in interest Indicating a present right to a future interest in property. For example, if property is left by will "to A for life, remainder to A's first son", A being childless at the testator's death, A's first son's right to the property is vested in interest as soon as he is born and his interest is a *vested remainder*. *Compare* vested in possession.

vested in possession Indicating an immediate right to the enjoyment of an interest in property. *Compare* vested in interest.

vested remainder *See* vested in interest.

vested rights Rights that have accrued to a person, as opposed to rights that he may or may not acquire. There is a presumption that Acts of Parliament are not intended to interfere with vested rights, particularly without payment of compensation. *See* interpretation of statutes.

vesting assent A document that transfers ownership of land from a deceased's personal representatives to the beneficiary entitled to it. The assent must be signed by the personal representatives but need not be executed as a deed.

vesting declaration A statement in a deed appointing new trustees that the trust property is to vest in them, i.e. be in their possession.

vesting deed *See* settled land.

vesting order An order of the High Court creating or transferring a legal estate in land. Such an order may be made, for example, when an equitable mortgagee exercises his power of sale: the court may make an order vesting the land in the purchaser.

veto *n.* (in international law) The power given to any permanent member of the Security Council of the *United Nations to refuse to agree to any nonprocedural proposal (there is no such power in relation to procedural matters) and thereby defeat it. An abstention is not equivalent to a veto. The President of the Security Council has power to determine which questions are nonprocedural. The General Assembly of the UN passed a Uniting for Peace resolution in 1950, providing for the Assembly to take over some of the functions of the Security Council when the Council's work has been paralysed by use of the veto.

vexatious action An action brought for the purpose of annoying the opponent and with no reasonable prospect of success. A *vexatious litigant* is a person who regularly brings such actions. The actions may be struck out and the court may order, on an application made by the Attorney General, that no legal proceedings may be begun or continued by the vexatious litigant without the leave of the court.

vicarious liability (vicarious responsibility) Legal liability imposed on one person for torts or crimes committed by another (usually an employee but sometimes an independent contractor or agent), although the person made vicariously liable is not personally at fault. An employer is vicariously liable for torts committed by his employees when he has authorized or ratified them or when the tort was committed in the course of the employees' work. Thus negligent driving by someone employed as a driver is a tort committed in the course of his employment, but if the driver were to assault a passing pedestrian for motives of private revenge, the assault would not be connected with his job and his employer would not be liable. The purpose of the doctrine of vicarious liability is to ensure that an employer pays the costs of damage caused by his business operations. His vicarious liability, however, is in addition to the liability of the employee, who remains personally liable for his own torts. The person injured by the tort may sue either or both of them, but will generally prefer to sue the employer.

Vicarious criminal liability may be imposed on an employer for offences committed by an employee in relation to his employment. Thus it has been held that an employer is guilty of selling improper food under the Food and Drugs Acts when his employee does the physical act of selling. Likewise, an employer may be guilty of supplying goods under a false trade description when it is his employee who actually delivers them. For an offence that normally requires *mens rea*, an employer will only be vicariously liable if the offence relates to licensing laws. For example, if a licensee has delegated the entire management of his licensed premises to another person, and that person has committed the offence with the necessary *mens rea*, the licensee will be vicariously liable.

Vicarious liability for crimes may be imposed in certain other circumstances. The registered owner of a vehicle, for example, is expressly made liable by statute for fixed-penalty and excess parking charges, even if the fault for the offence was not his. If the offence is a regulatory offence of *strict liability, the courts often also impose vicarious liability if the offence is defined in the statute in a way that makes this possible (for example, certain offences are defined passively).

vicarious performance *See* performance of contract.

vicarious responsibility *See* vicarious liability.

Vice Chancellor (VC) 1. A judge who is vice president of the *Chancery Division of the High Court (the *Lord Chancellor is the president but in practice rarely, if ever, sits in the Division). The Vice Chancellor is by statute responsible to the Lord Chancellor for the organization and management of the business of the Division and is *ex officio* a member of the *Court of Appeal. **2.** Formerly, a judge of the *Palatine Courts. The title is still held by the circuit judge assigned to exercise Chancery jurisdiction in Lancashire.

vi et armis [Latin: by force and arms] The allegation in medieval pleading that a trespass had been committed with force and therefore was a matter for the King's Courts because it involved a breach of the peace. The term survived as a formal requirement of pleading until 1852. *See* trespass.

view *n.* (in court proceedings) The inspection by a judge, or judge and jury, of any place or thing with respect to which any question arises in the course of litigation, including if necessary places or things outside the jurisdiction of the court. A view is part of the evidence in the case and the judge should not hold a private view of a public place in the absence of the parties. The judge has discretion to decide whether or not to hold a view; he may decide to do so even if the parties are opposed.

vinculo matrimonii *See* a vinculo matrimonii.

vindictive damages *See* exemplary damages.

violence *n.* **1.** *See* criminal violence. **2.** For domestic violence, *see* battered wife.

violence for securing entry *See* forcible entry.

visiting forces Commonwealth forces stationed in the UK and any other forces from abroad designated by Order in Council, including their civilian components. The Visiting Forces Act 1952 empowers the service courts of such forces to exercise jurisdiction over their members according to their national law (but not to carry out the death penalty). It exempts their members from trial by UK criminal courts in the case of offences committed on duty, against other members, or against the property of the force or other members.

visitor *n.* A person appointed to visit and inspect an institution and, in particular, to inquire into internal irregularities. Many universities have a visitor (frequently the Crown), and judges are visitors of the Inns of Court. Boards of Visitors, appointed for prisons by the Home Secretary, act as disciplinary tribunals for breaches of the Prison Rules. A Lord Chancellor's Visitor is appointed under the Mental Health Act 1959 to visit patients and inquire into their ability to manage their affairs.

void *adj.* Having no legal effect.

voidable *adj.* Capable of being set aside.

voidable contract A contract that, though valid when made, is liable to be subsequently set aside (*compare* void contract). Voidable contracts may arise through *misrepresentation, some instances of *mistake, *nondisclosure, and *undue influence. Certain proprietary contracts entered into by minors are also voidable (*see* capacity to contract). The setting aside of a voidable contract is effected by *rescission.

voidable marriage *See* nullity of marriage.

voidable trust A trust that can be set aside, e.g. a trust created by an *infant. It may be repudiated by the infant on his attaining majority (18) or shortly thereafter; if the trust is not repudiated, it becomes valid and binding.

void contract A contract that has no legal force from the moment of its making (*compare* voidable contract). Void contracts occur when there is lack of *capacity to contract and by the operation in some instances of the doctrine of *mistake. An *illegal contract is void. In addition, certain contracts (e.g. *gaming and wagering contracts) are declared void but not illegal by statute, and certain contracts that are at common law contrary to *public policy are merely void but not illegal. Contracts that are void but not illegal may be saved by *severance.

void marriage *See* nullity of marriage.

void trust (unlawful trust) A trust that it is against the policy of the law to enforce. Such trusts include those that offend the *rule against perpetuities and the *rule against inalienability. If a trust is void, the property in the trust will normally be held on *resulting trust for the settlor or his estate.

voir dire (voire dire) [Norman French: to speak the truth] **1.** The preliminary examination by a judge of a witness to determine his competence or of a juror to determine his qualification for jury service. **2.** An inquiry conducted by the judge in the absence of the jury into the admissibility of an item of evidence (e.g. a *confession). It is sometimes called a *trial within a trial*.

A special oath is taken by witnesses called to testify on the *voir dire*.

volenti non fit injuria [Latin: no wrong is done to one who consents] The defence that the plaintiff consented to the injury or (more usually) to the risk of being injured. Knowledge of the risk of injury is not sufficient; there must also be (even if only by implication) full and free consent to bear the risk. A plaintiff who has assumed the risk of injury has no action if the injury occurs. The scope of the defence is limited by statute in cases involving business liability and public and private transport.

voluntary *adj.* Without valuable *consideration.

voluntary bill procedure A procedure enabling the prosecution to apply to a judge of the High Court to obtain consent for preferring a *bill of indictment against a defendant. This procedure is usually used when a magistrates' court has held committal proceedings but has refused to commit the defendant for trial on indictment.

voluntary confession *See* confession.

voluntary conveyance *See* voluntary disposition.

voluntary disposition A conveyance or other transfer of ownership of land, made otherwise than for valuable *consideration. Under the Law of Property Act 1925, a voluntary disposition made with intent to defraud a purchaser can be set aside at the instigation of the purchaser.

voluntary liquidation *See* voluntary winding-up.

voluntary settlement A *settlement made without valuable *consideration. For any voluntary settlement to be enforced, a trust must be executed, i.e. completed; hence the maxim "equity will not assist a volunteer".

voluntary waste A kind of *waste that occurs when a tenant takes positive action that damages the land he leases.

voluntary winding-up (voluntary liquidation) A *winding-up procedure initiated by a special or extraordinary resolution of the company. In a *members' voluntary winding-up*, the directors must make a statutory *declaration of solvency* within the five weeks preceding the resolution. This declaration states that the directors have investigated the affairs of the company and are of the opinion that the company will be able to pay its debts in full within a specified period, not exceeding 12 months from the date of the·resolution. The liquidator is appointed by the company members. In a *creditors' voluntary winding-up*, the creditors can appoint the liquidator and, if they choose, a *committee of inspection.

volunteer *n.* A person who, in relation to any transaction, has not given valuable *consideration.

voting *n.* (in a registered company) The process of casting a vote on a motion proposed at a company meeting. Initially the vote is taken upon a show of hands, i.e. each company member present in person has one vote. Once the result has been declared, any member present in person or by *proxy may demand a *poll*, in which votes are cast (in person or by proxy) in accordance with the number and class of *shares held. Particulars of these voting rights are usually stated in the memorandum or articles of association. The chairman usually has a casting vote in the event of an equality of votes.

voyage charter *See* charterparty.

voyage policy *See* time policy.

W

wagering contract *See* gaming contract.

wages council A body established under the Wages Councils Act 1959 and empowered to prescribe minimum rates of pay and other terms and conditions of employment in a particular industry. Each council consists of representatives of employers and employees in the industry concerned and independent members. Usually the councils are established for industries in which employees' collective bargaining power is comparatively weak.

wait and see principle *See* rule against perpetuities.

waiver *n.* The act of abandoning or refraining from asserting a legal right.

war *n.* The legal state of affairs that exists when states use force to vindicate rights or settle disputes between themselves. States can engage in hostilities (e.g. reprisals) without being in a technical state of war, and they can be in a state of war without much fighting taking place. The legal condition of war automatically terminates diplomatic relations and certain types of treaties between the participants.

In the Kellogg–Briand Pact (also known as the Pact of Paris) of 1928, the contracting parties renounced war as an instrument of national policy and undertook to settle their disputes by peaceful means. The United Nations Charter declares that all parties to it "shall refrain ... from the threat or use of force against the territorial integrity or political independence of any state" or in a manner inconsistent with the Charter, and this is commonly accepted as an accurate statement of customary international law. Nonetheless it appears that states still retain a right of self-defence, at least if they have been the victims of armed attack and until the Security Council can act. The Security Council is also authorized to use force (or to call upon states to do so) under certain circumstances in order to protect the peace, although in practice this power has not been invoked. The right of self-defence includes a collective right to assist other states acting in self-defence.

The Hague Conventions and Geneva Conventions provide rules governing the conduct of wars and stating the rights and duties of both combatants and noncombatants during war. However, they do not deal with all aspects of warfare or all types of war. There have also been various specific conventions governing particular issues, including a 1972 convention on the use or possession of bacteriological and toxic weapons, a 1976 convention on the military use of environmental modification techniques, and a 1981 convention and three protocols on cruel or indiscriminate non-nuclear weapons. Civil wars are not usually illegal from the point of view of international law, but it is uncertain whether or not other states may legally help either the insurgents or the established authorities. The 1977 First and Second Protocols to the Geneva Conventions of 1949, respectively, extend some of the laws of war to civil wars and wars of national liberation (*see* self-determination).

See also aggression; occupation; offences against international law and order; war crimes.

war crimes Any violation of the laws or customs of war amounting to a criminal act. According to the Charter of the Nuremberg International Military Tribunal of 1946, war crimes include murder, ill-treatment, or deportation of civilian populations, murder or ill-treatment of prisoners of war, killing hostages, plundering property, and wanton destruction of population centres or devastation not justified by military necessity. The Nuremberg Tribunal also defined a new category of *crimes against humanity*, consisting essentially of murder, extermination, enslavement, deportation, and other inhumane acts committed against civilians and persecution on political, racial, or religious grounds (but only if the persecution is connected with war crimes or crimes against peace). Crimes against humanity need not have been committed during the war, however. The Tribunal also created a third category of *crimes against peace*, i.e. planning, preparing, or waging a war of aggression or a war in violation of international treaties. It is generally considered that these definitions now form part of customary international law.

ward of court 1. A minor under the care of a *guardian (appointed by the parents or the court), who exercises rights of custody over the child subject to the general control and discretion of the court. **2.** A minor in respect of whom a *wardship order has been made and over whom the court exercises parental rights and duties. A child becomes a ward of court when a wardship order is made and remains a ward until he reaches the age of 18 or the court orders that he should cease to be a ward. Any child who is actually in England (or ordinarily resident in England) may be made a ward of court, even though he is neither domiciled there nor a British subject. Marriage of a ward does not terminate the wardship.

wardship *n.* The jurisdiction of the High Court to make a child a *ward of court and assume responsibility for its welfare. The jurisdiction is almost unlimited, although subject to consideration of the child's welfare and, to some extent, the rights of other persons and the public interest. The court exercises detailed control of the ward and may appoint the Official Solicitor to act as his guardian *ad litem*. It may order either parent to make periodical payments for his maintenance, commit the ward to the care of a local authority, or make a *supervision order in respect of him. Wardship proceedings are heard in private and the usual rules of evidence may be relaxed (e.g. in respect of hearsay evidence). The court may enforce its orders by injunction; breach of this or tampering with the ward may constitute contempt of court.

Wardship proceedings are usually used (1) when there is a dispute between estranged parents but no divorce proceedings have been started; (2) when a foster parent or potential adopter wishes to prevent relatives interfering with the child or when a third party wishes to remove the child from parents who are unfit to have custody; (3) when a child has been "kidnapped" by a parent who has lost custody to the other parent; and (4) to exercise control over a wayward child or to question decisions of local authorities and juvenile courts.

warned list *See* Cause List.

warning of caveat A notice given to a person who has entered a *caveat warning him to appear and state what his interest is.

warrant *n.* **1.** A document authorizing some action, especially the payment of money. A *warehouse* (or *wharfinger's*) *warrant* is issued when goods are taken into a public warehouse and must be produced when they are removed. This document is negotiable and transferable by endorsement. *See also* enforcement of judgment; share warrant. **2.** A written document issued by a magistrate for the *arrest of a person or the search of his property (*see* power of search). When a suspect has fled abroad and there is an extradition treaty covering the offence he is suspected of, the magistrate who has jurisdiction over the place in which the offence was allegedly

committed may issue an arrest warrant to enable the Director of Public Prosecutions and the Home Secretary to extradite the suspect. *See also* general warrant; witness warrant.

warrant backed for bail *See* backed for bail.

warranty *n.* **1.** (in contract law) A term or promise in a contract, breach of which will entitle the innocent party to damages but not to treat the contract as discharged by breach. *Compare* condition. **2.** (in insurance law) A promise by the insured, breach of which will entitle the insurer to treat the contract as discharged by breach. The word thus has the same meaning as condition in the general law of contract. **3.** Loosely, a manufacturer's written promise as to the extent he will repair, replace, or otherwise compensate for defective goods; a *guarantee.

waste *n.* **1.** Any alteration of tenanted property caused by the tenant's action or neglect. It includes damage, deterioration, and improvement (*see* ameliorating waste; equitable waste; permissive waste; voluntary waste). Landlords can take action against tenants who cause waste (*see* impeachable waste). The extent of a tenant's liability varies according to the kind of tenancy. Most tenants are liable for equitable and voluntary waste. *Fixed-term tenants are also liable for permissive waste, as are yearly *periodic tenants (but only to the extent that they must keep the premises wind- and water-tight). **2.** *See* pollution.

wasting assets Property forming part of a deceased's estate and having a reducing value (e.g. a leasehold interest in land). Unless the will directs otherwise, the personal representatives have a duty to sell such assets.

wasting police time An offence committed by someone who causes wasteful employment of the police by making a false report about an offence or by implying that a person or property is in danger or that he has information relevant to a police inquiry. The consent of the Director of Public Prosecutions is required for prosecutions for this offence, which is punishable by a fine and/or imprisonment.

watch committee *See* police force.

water pollution *See* pollution.

weapon of offence Any *offensive weapon or any article made, adapted, or intended for incapacitating someone (e.g. a rope to tie someone with or pepper to make him sneeze). There are special offences of aggravated *burglary and of *trespass with a weapon of offence.

wear and tear *See* fair wear and tear.

weekly tenancy A weekly *periodic tenancy.

welfare law Law enacted to give effect to society's responsibility for the well-being of individuals. It relates to such matters as social security (*see* national insurance) and supplementary benefit, employment protection, health and safety at work, housing, and legal aid.

Welsh company A registered company whose memorandum of association states that its registered office is situated in Wales. Welsh companies may lodge documents at the Companies Registry in Welsh and may adopt in their name the Welsh equivalents for "limited" (cyfyngedig) and "public limited company" (cwmni cyfyngedig cyhoeddus). An English translation must be provided.

White Book *See* Supreme Court Practice, The.

white paper *See* Command Papers.

whole blood *See* consanguinity.

widow's benefit A benefit payable, subject to certain conditions, under the Social Security Act 1975. It comprises a widow's allowance, payable for 26 weeks after the death of the husband; a widowed mother's allowance (when applicable); and a widow's pension.

wife's services *See* consortium.

wild animals *See* classification of animals; dangerous animals.

wilful *adj.* Deliberate: usually used of wrongful actions.

wilful default The failure of a person to do what he should do, either intentionally or through recklessness; for example, nonappearance at court.

wilful misconduct Intentionally doing something that is wrong.

wilful neglect Deliberate failure to perform a duty.

wilful neglect to maintain *See* failure to maintain.

wilful refusal to consummate The unjustified decision not to consummate a marriage, which may be grounds for annulment of the marriage. There will be no wilful refusal if the unwillingness to consummate is temporary, due to shyness, or due to some physical abnormality that cannot be safely corrected by surgical means. *See also* consummation of a marriage.

will *n.* A document by which a person (called the *testator*) appoints *executors to administer his estate after his death, and directs the manner in which it is to be distributed to the beneficiaries he specifies. To be valid, the will must comply with the formal requirements of the Wills Act 1837 (*see* execution of will) and the testator must have *testamentary capacity when the will is made. A will can be amended by the execution of a *codicil. It can be revoked by the testator destroying it with that intention, or making another will. It is automatically revoked if the testator marries, unless it was made in contemplation of that marriage. *See also* interpretation of wills; joint will; mutual wills; privileged will.

winding-up (liquidation) A procedure by which a company can be dissolved. It may be instigated by members or creditors of the company (*see* voluntary winding-up) or by order of the court (*see* compulsory winding-up by the court). In both cases the process involves the appointment of a *liquidator to assume control of the company from its directors. He collects the assets, pays debts, and distributes any surplus to company members in accordance with their rights.

with costs A phrase appended to the order of a court that has the effect of awarding the *costs of the proceedings to the successful party.

withdrawal of defence A procedure enabling a defendant in an action in the High Court to serve a notice on the plaintiff indicating that he is not proceeding with his defence or with part of it. The defendant is then in *default of defence and the plaintiff may proceed to judgment by *summons or *motion.

withdrawal of issue from jury A procedure enabling a judge, who is not satisfied that there is sufficient evidence to discharge the evidential *burden of proof borne by a party, to discharge the jury and enter judgment for the opponent if the issue is decisive of the litigation. If the issue is not decisive of the litigation as a whole, he may direct the jury to find against that party in respect of that issue.

without prejudice A phrase used to enable parties to negotiate settlement of a claim without implying any admission of liability. Letters and other documents headed "without prejudice" cannot be adduced as evidence in any court action without the consent of both parties.

without recourse to me *See sans recours.*

witness *n.* **1.** A person who observes the signing of a legal document in case it is subsequently necessary to verify the authenticity of the signature. He adds his own signature to the document as a witness. Many legal documents are only valid if properly witnessed (*see* deed; will). **2.** A person who gives *evidence. In court, witnesses are required either to give evidence on *oath or to *affirm that their evidence is true. Most people are qualified to give evidence in any case (*see* competence) but there are certain exceptions; for example, when the judge considers the witness mentally unfit to give evidence. In civil cases a child who is too young to understand the nature of an oath is not a competent witness, although in criminal cases a young child may be allowed to give *unsworn evidence. Most competent witnesses can be compelled to give evidence (a witness who refuses to answer is in *contempt of court) but again there are exceptions. For example, a witness cannot be compelled to answer a question that may *incriminate him. A witness's evidence is usually given orally in open court. However in certain circumstances evidence is allowed by *affidavit (*see* commission). The evidence of certain witnesses is considered to be unreliable and requires *corroboration. *See also* adverse witness; hostile witness; zealous witness; interfering with witnesses; perjury; Queen's evidence.

witnessing part *See* deed.

witness order An order to a person to appear at a particular court on a certain day to give evidence in a criminal trial. There are two kinds of order: a *full order*, which requires the witness to attend the court; and a *conditional order*, which warns the person that he may be required to attend if his evidence is found to be necessary. A person who fails to comply with a witness order is in *contempt of court. *See also* witness warrant.

witness's oath *See* oath.

witness warrant An order by the Crown Court for a witness to be arrested and brought before the court. The court may issue a warrant when sworn evidence is given showing that the witness is unlikely to comply with a *witness order served on him.

When a witness has failed to attend the court in accordance with a witness order, the court may order a notice to be served on him requiring his attendance immediately or at a specified time in the future. If he fails to comply with this notice without a reasonable excuse, the court may issue a warrant for his arrest. A witness who has been arrested may be remanded in custody until his evidence is required.

words of art Words whose legal interpretation has been fixed so that the legal effect of their use is known.

words of limitation Words in a conveyance of land that define the interest transferred; for example, "in fee simple".

words of procreation The words in a settlement of land that create an *entailed interest. Unless the land is expressly settled on the beneficiary "and the heirs of his body" or "in tail", an entailed interest will not result.

words of purchase The words in a conveyance of land that identify the person to whom the property is transferred.

words of severance *See* severance.

work done and materials supplied, contract for A contract the substance of which is that skill and labour must be exercised in carrying out the contract, in addition to supplying the materials used in the work. Examples are contracts by an artist to paint a portrait and by a builder to fit double glazing. Such a contract is distinct from a contract of sale of goods, in which the subject of the contract is the finished product.

worker *n.* An *employee.

work-in *n.* Industrial action in which employees occupy their workplace against the will of their employer and continue working. Generally such action constitutes *trespass, and the employer can apply to the court for an order that the employees restore possession of the premises to him.

working day 1. For banking and financial purposes, any day other than Saturday, Sunday, and *bank holidays. **2.** (of a court) Any day other than Sunday or holidays, called a *dies juridicus*. A day on which no legal business can be carried on is called a *dies non*.

wounding *n.* Breaking the continuity of the skin or of a membrane (such as that lining the cheeks or lips). Scratching, bruising, burning, or breaking a bone without tearing the skin do not constitute wounding. *Malicious wounding* is an offence punishable by up to five years' imprisonment. It requires an intention to cause some physical harm (not necessarily a wound) or foresight of the risk of causing physical harm. A person is not guilty of this offence if he intended only to frighten his victim but in fact accidentally wounded him, although he would be guilty of *assault or *battery.

wounding with intent *Wounding someone with the intention of causing *grievous bodily harm (even if grievous harm does not in fact result) or wounding with the intention of resisting a lawful arrest. Wounding with intent carries a maximum sentence of life imprisonment.

wreck *n.* **1. (shipwreck)** The destruction of a ship at sea, as by foundering in a storm or being driven onto rocks. **2.** The remains of a wrecked ship. **3.** Goods cast up by the sea from a wrecked ship.

writ *n.* An order issued by a court in the sovereign's name directing some act or forebearance, especially a *writ of summons. Originally, a writ was an instrument under seal bearing some command of the sovereign.

writ of delivery A *writ of execution to enforce a judgment for delivery of goods. It directs the *sheriff to seize the goods and deliver them to the plaintiff or to recover their assessed value. If the writ does not offer the defendant the option of retaining the goods by paying their assessed value, it is known as a *writ of specific delivery*.

writ of execution A writ used in the *enforcement of a judgment. It may be a writ of *fieri facias*, a *writ of possession, a *writ of delivery, a writ of *sequestration, or any further writ in aid of any of these writs.

writ of possession A writ directing the *sheriff to enter upon land to give vacant possession to the plaintiff. It is used to enforce judgments for the possession of land.

writ of summons A writ by which an action is commenced in the High Court. Proceedings are initiated by writ whenever there are likely to be contentious issues of fact in the case; a writ must be used when the action is one in tort (other than trespass to land) in which a claim made by the plaintiff is based upon an allegation of fraud, or one in which damages are claimed in respect of personal injuries, death, or the infringement of a patent. The present form of writ instructs the defendant to return the *acknowledgment of service.

In modern legal terminology, a writ of summons is usually referred to as a *writ simpliciter*.

wrong *n.* An illegal or immoral act. A distinction must be drawn between moral wrongs and legal wrongs. Some moral wrongs, such as murder or theft, are also crimes punishable by law. But many moral offences are not legal wrongs and some technical legal offences, such as parking offences, are not generally regarded as morally blameworthy. Legal wrongs may be criminal or civil. *Crimes are offences against society as a whole, not merely against the victim of the crime. Civil wrongs, such as *torts, *breaches of contract, and interferences with property rights, are wrongs to the individuals affected.

wrongful dismissal The termination of an employee's contract of employment in a manner that is not in accordance with that contract. Thus when an employee is dismissed without the notice to which he is entitled (in circumstances that do not justify summary dismissal) or when the employer prematurely terminates the employee's fixed-term contract, the employee is entitled to claim damages in the courts for wrongful dismissal. The court's jurisdiction concerns only the parties' contractual rights and not their statutory rights under the employment protection legislation (*compare* unfair dismissal). The Employment Protection (Consolidation) Act 1978 empowers the Secretary of State for Employment to give industrial tribunals jurisdiction to hear claims of wrongful dismissal but he has not yet done so.

wrongful interference with goods Under the Torts (Interference with Goods) Act 1977, any of various torts to goods. It includes *conversion, *trespass to goods, negligence so far as it results in damage to goods or to an interest in goods, and any other tort (except *detinue, which is abolished by the Act) that results in damage to goods or an interest in goods.

Y

year and thereafter from year to year Words sometimes used in a tenancy agreement, the effect of which is that the tenant has a *fixed-term tenancy for the first year, followed by a yearly *periodic tenancy.

Year Books *See* law reports.

yearly tenancy A yearly *periodic tenancy.

yielding and paying Words that usually introduce the clause in a *lease that specifies the rent. *See also* reddendum.

York–Antwerp rules *See* average.

young adult offender (juvenile adult) A person aged between 17 and 21 who has committed an offence. In general such offenders are subject to the same procedures and penalties as adults, subject to the following provisions. (1) If an offender is remanded in custody, he is sent to a special remand centre (if one is available), rather than to prison. (2) He can only be imprisoned if the court feels that there is no other way of dealing with him; in such cases the court must obtain information about the circumstances of the offence and the offender's character and physical or mental condition. (3) He cannot be sentenced to an *extended sentence. (4) He can be ordered to attend an *attendance centre.

Various changes in the law relating to the punishment of young adult offenders will come into effect when the relevant provisions of the Criminal Justice Act 1982 are brought into force. *See also* juvenile offender.

young offender An offender between the ages of 14 and 17. *See* juvenile offender.

youth custody centre A place to which an offender aged over 14 and under 21, whom the court wishes to keep in custody, may be sent (*see* juvenile offender). Under the Criminal Justice Act 1982, provision will also be made for detaining women over 21 (but not men) in youth custody centres instead of prison.

Z

zealous witness A *witness who displays undue favouritism towards one party in the case.

zebra crossing A road crossing for pedestrians, identified by studs and alternating black and white stripes on the carriageway and lighted yellow globes (normally flashing) at each end. Pedestrians take precedence over vehicles on crossings uncontrolled by police or traffic wardens, and it is an offence for vehicles to wait or overtake within their limits.

zero-rated supply A supply within the scope of *value-added tax but charged at a nil rate. Examples are food (including restaurant meals), books and journals, and children's clothes; all exports are also zero-rated. Unlike *exempt supplies, zero-rated supplies count towards the turnover limit above which registration for VAT is compulsory, and any input tax relating to them may be reclaimed by the registered trader.